May of 1936 to take a position with the President's Committee on Administrative Management, Robert Frase took over the study of the Social Security Administration and remained until the end of March 1937. During November and December of 1936 and January of 1937, the two worked together on the project. Their assignment was to "capture and record" the process of organization; both men had access to confidential documents of the Social Security Board, and to board members and others responsible for setting up the program. The two reports, taking on the quality of a special kind of memoir, were combined in 1941, but lest the criticism, explicit and implicit, of the administration should jeopardize the social security program itself, their publication was postponed.

McKinley and Frase weave an unusual inside story of the formation of a government agency. *Launching Social Security: A Capture-and-Record Account, 1935-1937* will be of great value to students of public administration, political science, and history, and will interest anyone curious about how a political philosophy is transformed into an effective program of action.

Professor Emeritus of Political Science at Reed College at the time of his death in March 1970, McKinley had had extensive experience in public affairs, governmental agencies in particular. He had been President of the American Political Science Association and the author of a number of books on the role of the federal government in resource management. Robert W. Frase, who has also devoted his life to public affairs, is Vice President and Director of the Washington Office of the Association of American Publishers

LAUNCHING SOCIAL SECURITY

LAUNCHING SOCIAL SECURITY

A CAPTURE-AND-RECORD ACCOUNT

1935-1937

Charles McKinley

Robert W. Frase

THE UNIVERSITY OF WISCONSIN PRESS

Madison, Milwaukee, and London

Published 1970
The University of Wisconsin Press
Box 1379, Madison, Wisconsin 53701

The University of Wisconsin Press, Ltd.
27-29 Whitfield Street, London, W.1

First printing

Printed in the United States of America
Pantagraph Printing, Bloomington, Illinois

ISBN 0-299-05800-X; LC 70-121771

CONTENTS

FOREWORD, By Wilbur J. Cohen   ix

PREFACE

    The Study from November 1935 to Mid-May 1936   xiii
    The Study from Mid-May 1936 to the End of March
    1937   xxii

1 INTRODUCTION TO THE ACT, THE BOARD, AND
  MAJOR TRENDS, OCTOBER 1935 TO MARCH 1937

    The Genesis and Nature of the Social Security Act
    of 1935   3
    The Social Security Act   12
    Outline of Major Trends, October 1935 to March
    1937   17

2 PROBLEMS OF BUDGET AND ORGANIZATIONAL
  STRUCTURE

    Preparing the First Estimates and Crystallizing the
    Organization   37
    Revising and Defending the 1937 Budget Estimates   52
    Preparing the Estimates for Fiscal 1938   64
    Congress and the Board's 1938 Estimates   77
    Use of the Budget for Administrative Control   94

3 THE FIELD ORGANIZATION

    Preliminary Studies and Plans   96
    Launching the Regional Organization   105

OPERATION OF THE REGIONAL ESTABLISHMENT BEFORE
REGISTRATION   113
THE FIELD ESTABLISHMENT AT THE CLOSE OF REGISTRA-
TION   129

4 THE ADMINISTRATION OF GRANTS-IN-AID FOR
   THE AGED, DEPENDENT CHILDREN, AND THE
   BLIND

THE FIRST GRANTS AND THE ESTABLISHMENT OF THE
BUREAU OF PUBLIC ASSISTANCE   138
SPECIAL LEGAL PROBLEMS ENCOUNTERED IN APPROVING
STATE LAWS   149
A FIELD STAFF GOES TO THE STATES, BUREAU ORGANIZA-
TION LAGS   155
POLITICAL "HOT SPOTS": KANSAS, OHIO, COLORADO, AND
KENTUCKY   165
THE IMPROVEMENT OF STATE ADMINISTRATIVE STANDARDS   180
THE BUREAU OF ACCOUNTS AND AUDITS AND THE COMP-
TROLLER GENERAL   197

5 UNEMPLOYMENT COMPENSATION

LEGAL PROBLEMS RAISED BY THE FIRST STATE LAWS   218
EARLY INABILITY TO HELP NEW STATE ADMINISTRATIVE
AGENCIES   231
ADVISING THE STATES ON UNEMPLOYMENT COMPENSATION
LEGISLATION   243
THE PROCESS OF MAKING ADMINISTRATIVE GRANTS TO
THE STATES   253
THE DEVELOPMENT OF ADMINISTRATIVE ASSISTANCE FOR
THE STATES   284
RELATIONS WITH THE UNITED STATES EMPLOYMENT
SERVICE   295

6 OLD AGE BENEFITS

PLANNING THE BUREAU AND ITS RELATIONSHIPS WITH
THE TREASURY   308
EMPLOYEE ACCOUNT NUMBERS AND IDENTIFICATION
TOKENS   320
BUREAU DEVELOPMENT AND PLANS FOR REGISTERING EL-
IGIBLE EMPLOYEES   329
HOW THE REGISTRATION WAS CARRIED THROUGH   364
OTHER ADMINISTRATIVE DEVELOPMENTS IN THE BUREAU
OF OLD AGE BENEFITS   374

7 GENERAL MANAGEMENT

    The Board and the Executive Director   382
    The Coordinator   391
    Gravitation of Powers to the Executive Director's Office   400
    Personnel Management, The Expert Clause   407
    Personnel Management, Political Pressures and Patronage Appointments   424
    Other Personnel Management Problems   432
    Publicity Activities, The Bureau of Informational Service   447
    The Planning Function, The Bureau of Research and Statistics   459

8 A FEW CONCLUSIONS   473

    LIST OF NAMES   495

    INDEX   507

TABLES

1 ESTIMATES AND APPROPRIATIONS FOR THE SOCIAL SECURITY BOARD, FISCAL 1936   47

2 SUMMARY FINANCIAL HISTORY OF THE SOCIAL SECURITY BOARD'S BUDGET FOR FISCAL 1938   89

   ORGANIZATION CHART OF THE SOCIAL SECURITY BOARD AS ADOPTED DECEMBER 4, 1936.
From the *United States Government Manual, 1936,* issued by the National Emergency Council   505

FOREWORD

BY WILBUR J. COHEN
Secretary of Health, Education, and Welfare, 1968-69

The administration of the federal social security program in the United States has been one of the great accomplishments of government. Its operation has demonstrated the invalidity of every cliché about the inefficiency of government which newspapers, politicians, and businessmen may have circulated either in ignorance or by design. The program has been administered efficiently and economically during the past thirty-five years, in a nonpolitical manner and with due regard for individualized service. As a result, the Congress and six Presidents have endorsed its general principles and have recommended its expansion and improvement.

Over the same period of time state unemployment insurance, employment service, and welfare programs have been the object of much criticism for their performance, their limitations, and their lack of effectiveness. It comes as no surprise therefore that a Republican President recommended in 1969 that the state welfare program for dependent children should be taken over by the federal government.

There are now several books which tell the story of the early years of social security. Edwin E. Witte's *The Development of the Social Security Act,* and a selection of his speeches and articles, *Social Security Perspectives,* were both published in 1962. Arthur J. Altmeyer, a central figure in this book by McKinley and Frase, has given his own account of the development of the social security program in *The Formative Years of Social Security,* published in 1966. Quite typical of Altmeyer, he wrote in terms of issues and problems, making a special effort to avoid personalities. His book is almost devoid of the names and personalities of the persons who participated in the whole process.

The McKinley-Frase volume deals with personalities as well as problems. It gives insight into how a small number of men and women went about organizing themselves in this new and daring adventure in a relatively short period from 1935 to 1937. It describes the growing pains of a new agency; it clearly illuminates the interaction of policies, politics, and personalities in a gigantic effort. There are some of its observations and conclusions with which I disagree, but I have strongly urged its publication for a number of years because I believe it is a unique and useful document. (Some of my own recollections of the early social security days have been recounted in an article, "Random Memories and Opinions of an Oldtimer," in the U.S. Department of Labor *Unemployment Insurance Review* for August–September, 1968.)

The problems and difficulties which McKinley and Frase recount in this book seem relatively simple today. They seem simple because they were resolved. The fact that they were resolved and that social security was well and efficiently administered set the stage for the repeated improvements which Congress has added to the program: survivors' insurance in 1939, disability insurance in 1965, and medicare in 1965.

We speak about political science and public administration many times as if they were a science, but anyone who has participated in the creation of a new institution knows that any human organization has human failings. How to minimize human frailty in the administration of a large enterprise is the important problem put before us.

When I look back on the work of the Committee on Economic Security and the Social Security Board, I think that the driving force that made possible the whole initial effort and its successful send-off was the forceful personality of Roosevelt, Perkins, Hopkins, Witte, Altmeyer, Winant, and Corson. They all instilled a great enthusiasm in their subordinates—an enthusiasm and willingness to work hard, despite overwhelming difficulties, that the country saw again with John F. Kennedy and Sargent Shriver in the Peace Corps and the antipoverty programs of 1961 and 1964, respectively.

I was privileged to know these men and women, as well as the other persons in this book. They were all able and intelligent people, but more than that, they were dedicated and wonderful men and women with a vision of a better and fairer society. What I learned from them I tried to carry out during the eight years, 1961–69, during which I was in a position to influence policy, legislation, administration, and the selection of personnel.

The impact of Witte, Altmeyer, and Corson on the administration of the social security program has continued and can still be felt now, thirty-five years later. The institution is but the lengthened shadow of a man, or men, and their ideas. Theirs was an idea of a nonpolitical, public-service career, of performance of the highest quality.

I hope the McKinley-Frase volume will be read by younger men and women coming up the line, and will instill in them an interest in administering and improving the social security system.

I regret that my friend Professor McKinley died before this book was published, but the knowledge that it was going to be published was in his mind long before his death. I am glad he knew that younger people would be able to read about how a new institution was created and how human effort made a difference that affected millions upon millions of people.

PREFACE

THE STUDY FROM NOVEMBER 1935
TO MID-MAY 1936

When I was invited to undertake the "capture and record" study of the administration of the 1935 national Social Security Act, the Committee on Public Administration of the Social Science Research Council hoped that it might not only throw light on the special problems encountered in a new field of public activity in the United States but also help to determine whether there are discernible principles of public administration. Arthur Macmahon, John Millett, and Gladys Ogden were already on a comparable quest following the work relief programs of the early New Deal. My willingness to participate in this activity came in part from my interest in these new and exceedingly important public programs, but I was also stimulated by E. C. Lindeman's analysis some years earlier of the potential role of the outside observer of group activity, when integrated with participating observers, in developing a social science.[1]

In the effort to observe what was taking place, and why, in this administrative organization, the great size and nationwide coverage for which it was destined and the multitude of federal and state partners sharing in the operation of its programs argued the necessity of adopting a selective principle in recording. This was made less difficult than it might have been by the failure of the Seventy-fourth Congress to provide appropriations, before it adjourned in the late summer of 1935, for launching the Social Security Administration. Senator Huey Long's filibuster had resulted in the dependence of the Social Security Board on relief funds for getting the job under way. This fiscal

[1] *Social Discovery: An Approach to the Study of Functional Groups* (New York: Republic Publishing, 1924), pp. 193–200.

xiii

malnutrition compelled a relatively slow tempo of organization and staffing during the first three months (from mid-November to mid-February 1936) of observation.

Even so, not all of the administrative experience could be "captured and recorded." My criteria of selection were probably not fully consistent, but I quickly decided to disregard such matters as procedural details, filing systems, mails, purchases, details of accounting and audit, and most of the routinized activities. With a few exceptions, my major interest came to center in matters of social policy expressed or implied in administrative decisions, structural arrangements, personnel policies, budgetary programs, interdepartmental and intradepartmental conflicts, integrations, centralization and decentralization, field services, and the influence of politics in both the narrow and the broad sense of that word. I also found myself watching for indications of the influence of legal phraseology embedded in the Social Security Act on problems of program, on federal-state relations, and on the prospects of validation of programs by the courts. The last of these became of great importance to the board and all other participating agencies all through 1936 right up to the Supreme Court's decision of early 1937, when a new balance of constitutional philosophies within that body affirmed the constitutionality of the several programs authorized in the Social Security Act.

It must be confessed that my approach was dictated in large measure by my lack of specialized knowledge of federal administrative procedures and practices and of the European administration of comparable programs. Had I been an administrative technician, it is very probable that I would have made a different selection of events and decisions from the stream flowing through the experience of the first six months after mid-November 1935.

In beginning my work, at first concerned exclusively with the Social Security Board, I had the great advantage of Professor Joseph P. Harris's introductions to members of the board, and to many of their principal staff who had been Harris's colleagues on the research staff which had prepared the studies on which the Committee on Economic Security had based its recommendations and drafts of proposed legislation for the social security programs. A former Wisconsinite, Harris was well acquainted with board member Arthur Altmeyer. He also had a close friendship with Frank Bane, who had been chosen as the board's executive director. Thus my way was greatly smoothed for learning not only about the board's initial operative activities but also—and this was of prime importance at the time—about the thinking and planning underway during November and December 1935 and early 1936, before the board had received congressional appropriations for full-fledged operations. I was also favored in making initial contacts within the board's organization, as well as within the agencies of the Department of Labor, the Treasury, and the United States Public Health Service, by the high regard entertained by key officers there for Chairman Louis Brownlow. He gave fatherly guidance and advice to all research staff members conducting studies then and later under the auspices of the Committee on Public Administration. The universal regard for "Brownie" readily unlocked doors which might otherwise have opened a mere crack or not at all.

Another initial asset for my study was the fact that Wilbur Cohen, a very able young man whom Professor Witte had brought from Madison to help with the work of the Committee on Economic Security, had followed the congressional legislative process during 1935 relating to the drafting and enactment of the social security law and had prepared an extensive memorandum covering that history. This was made available and together with many conversations with Cohen and Thomas Eliot, the principal draftsman used during the legislative gestation period, helped to provide a good understanding of important features of the act.

But there was one source of difficulty which occasionally hampered access to the full "truth" during my period of observation. Unfortunately there had been no written statement between Messrs. Brownlow and Harris, speaking for the committee, and the Social Security Board members describing the extent of confidence which would be permitted in building the observational history. It came as a surprise, therefore, when I was told early by Executive Director Bane that the board had decided that I could not have copies of its official minutes, though I might read them and take notes. My surprise turned to dismay when I discovered that the minutes were so abbreviated, recording only motions made and actions taken, as to throw little light upon the reasons for board decisions (or indecisions), or upon the discussions which had transpired. There was the additional impediment that the minutes were not available to me until after their approval, which was often long delayed. Thus, to keep track of board actions it was necessary to depend upon interviews with either members or the top staff. Altmeyer was very reticent and my interviews with him rarely produced grist for my mill. I came therefore to rely on the infrequent but very fruitful interviews with Chairman Winant, who once I had been able to break into his exceedingly heavy schedule of visitors was generous to a fault with his time and willingness to talk candidly and at length about gestating policy, personnel, and organization plans. Miles, the third board member, was also accessible and generous with comment.

In addition to the limitation placed upon the use of board minutes, the order was given Bane that all interoffice memoranda should be regarded as confidential. Actually this edict was not fully enforced, which made the laborious task of note-taking easier. Since so much of the story told herein is based on such memoranda, the decision placing them in a confidential category would make it impossible to publish without board consent.

At the outset of my study, Director Bane gave me a desk in an office adjacent to his own. This I shared with his administrative assistant, who generously aided me in obtaining initial interviews with other members of the board's staff and with people in the Children's Bureau, the United States Public Health Service, the United States Employment Service, the Treasury, and the Office of Education, all of which agencies were participants in one or more phases of social security administration. It was a great boon to my study that James Bennett, the able career civil servant (then associated with the federal Bureau of Prisons) moved into the same room to act as the board's business manager. Conversations with him greatly contributed to a more speedy and intimate grasp of board thinking and activity than would otherwise have been likely.

During the early weeks of the study, the executive director and the board members were so fully occupied with important questions of program and policy, and with meeting state and other officials involved that I pursued a policy of spiralling up to them after conversations with many lesser members of the staff and the perusal of documents and memoranda which they provided. In this way my own education was accelerated, and I felt that I could conserve Bane's time and that of the board members by confining my questions to matters of board policy or action not clarified by lower-ranking informants, and to their plans for future action.

I would have liked to attend board meetings so that I might listen to the discussion, but I felt certain, particularly because of Altmeyer's uncommunicativeness, that this would be denied even if requested. It was therefore a godsend to me that Miss Maurine Mulliner, who was made secretary to the board, offered early in January 1936 to make her notes of board discussions and action available to me. These notes were the basis for many of my accounts of the thought behind the decisions taken by the board, but they were not completely satisfactory for that purpose. Miss Mulliner did not pretend to take down a full verbatim report of what was said. Her notes were rather a summary of the remarks made, and an accurate report of actions taken. Sometimes her summary was so abbreviated that it was difficult to be certain of the precise nature of the views expressed. In such instances it was often possible to check them later by personal interviews. In doing this I was quite circumspect; I did not know then that Miss Mulliner had screened from the notes she turned over to me those items she felt might be too sensitive for inclusion. I feared lest Altmeyer, particularly, might object to my seeing the notes, as he had objected to allowing me to see the budget materials after Chairman Winant had promised them to me.

When, in January, the executive director invited me to attend the weekly top-staff meetings, I had high hopes that these would prove a source of great value in keeping up with the most significant events; as it turned out they were not. Bane did not use his staff meetings to discuss important problems.

They were, instead, opportunities to thresh over routine matters and to announce decisions of the board. Moreover, Bane's frequent absence from Washington and the constant meetings of the board during these early months meant that I missed many staff meetings. Only occasionally did they yield for my study pay dirt of marked value, but they did assist me in maintaining a footing of friendly intimacy with the staff. This was important.

There were many other meetings held by staff committees created by the board, the executive director, or the bureau heads to which I, and later my successor, were generously admitted. These proved of considerable value in obtaining an understanding of special problems with which the staff was confronted and which would ultimately come to the board. They often made the gestation process visible as no documentary instrumentality could do.

It was only after I had been around the board offices for some days that I first talked with Chairman Winant and his associates. I then found that the chairman was a little anxious lest I had obtained the wrong impressions about the slowness with which the board's organization was getting under way. That anxiety may have been an advantage to me, because he took a great deal of time, including an hour at lunch, to go back to the beginning and give me a full account as he saw it of what had happened, and a review of the major problems confronting the board.

I knew that it was basic to the success of my enterprise that I secure a sense of rapport between myself and the public officials with whom I would be talking, and that this should be established as quickly and fully as possible. For I was trying to find out not only what was taking place but why. I also knew that most of the people in positions of considerable administrative responsibility would soon be more concerned with safeguarding their administrative situations than with giving me the real explanations of what was transpiring. The best way, therefore, to preserve the opportunity of confidence with which I started was to come to be regarded as one of the group. This was my objective, and I think that it was in considerable measure realized.

There were a few important persons, however, with whom I did not have much success, and most important of these was Altmeyer. His technical competence and my early ignorance may have made for this lack of success. At any rate, he rarely volunteered information that would help me. His apparent concern to forfend against administrative embarrassment which might come fom possible leakage through me created the impression, when I saw him, of daring me to get information out of him if I could. Consequently I soon ceased trying to pump from what seemed to be a blocked well. Wagenet, chief of the Bureau of Unemployment Compensation, was the only bureau head from whom it was difficult to obtain reasonably cooperative response. One board official who in the early weeks was very generous with his time and

explosive comment was Henry Seidemann, the coordinator. His later reluctance to see me or to comment on the operations of the board may have
been generated by the fact that I shared an office with James Bennett, the
business manager, from early December until the middle of April 1936, when
Bennett moved to the Old Labor Building. Bennett was a Bane-sponsored
appointee, and the struggle of Seidemann to create for himself a position independent of Bane (which our story discloses and which caused increasing
friction) may have cooled his cordiality toward me as I was thrown into
daily friendly contact with Bennett. At any rate, he grew reluctant to see me
and his early communicativeness was replaced by circumspection.

One special difficulty in relying heavily upon interviews for building a
history of a rapidly evolving administrative organization and process was encountered in the early months of the board's history. Save for the small staff
cadre that had been taken over from the research group assembled by the
Committee on Economic Security, the people being recruited by the board
were in large part new to Washington and to each other. Their first need
was to learn their particular jobs and to become acquainted with the staff in
their particular units. They had little time to "go across lots" or to develop
any intimacy with officials in other activities in the larger organization. The
fact that my assignment compelled me to move horizontally as well as verti-
cally within the board's structure led in those early weeks to rather frequent
requests by people with whom I talked for information of what officers elsewhere in the organization were thinking or doing. I also received a considerable number of requests for information or for my own opinion about policies
or decisions under consideration. To have refused to respond to these requests
for information or comment would have broken the favorable emotional current developing during the interview, yet to have made critical comment or disclosed information not yet common knowledge would have run the risk of
backfiring. Whether or not my responses were sufficiently useful to the interviewee or adequately safeguarded the interests of the parties not present I was
never quite certain. I hoped that heaven, where concern with order is presumed to prevail, would care enough about public administration to guide my
words and conduct on these occasions.[2]

My interviewing did not stop with Social Security Board people. The programs supervised by the Social Security Board under grant-in-aid relationships, particularly the Children's Bureau and the U.S. Employment Service of
the Department of Labor, the Surgeon General for the U.S. Public Health

---

[2] I encountered this kind of curiosity particularly during my visit to the state
agencies in New England in February 1936, when I was trying to discover how the
state organizations were getting into their participating programs. To a lesser extent
the experience was repeated during early 1937 when I stopped at the regional offices
of the board en route to the Pacific Coast.

Service in the Treasury, and the Vocational Rehabilitation Service in the Office of Education. These agencies were also making preparations to undertake enlarged services simultaneously with those being planned for by the Social Security Board. There would also be need for close articulation of the Treasury Department's revenue-collecting units with the Social Security Board, because these Treasury services would collect both the taxes on which the solvency of the social security programs rested, and certain information essential to the board's operations. Therefore I undertook to follow the beginning of plans and prospective operations in these other agencies.[3]

As may be surmised from what has been said above, interviewing was my principal activity during these first months of the board's administrative history. This involved a good many difficulties and some dangers. One difficulty was that of proof. Evidence adduced by an interview is easily challenged; to substantiate it, when documents are lacking, the testimony of other witnesses may be required. The credibility of interview information would depend, in case of publication, on willingness of the witness to corroborate, and a good memory of what may have transpired long ago. The fact that I attempted to faithfully reduce to writing the substance of each conversation immediately or shortly after it occurred may not always have provided an accurate statement of what was said. I was not a shorthand expert. Even had I been, I would not have used this skill during the interview except for quantitative or similar data, because of the inhibiting effect which the appearance of pencil and paper would have had upon the person being interviewed, reminding him that he was being quoted.

By scheduling appointments with intervals between them to allow time for hasty notes from memory or for stenographic dictation, it was possible to record a good many interviews while the material was fresh. In many cases I had the advantage of going from an interview in the Labor Building, where in the early months most of the board's people were housed, to my typewriter in Bennett's office in the same building, and recording at once what had been said. In other cases a period of three or four hours might have elapsed before an interview could be either dictated or written out. That was true when the interview ran over the time scheduled and necessitated the keeping of another appointment (or occasionally two or three appointments) before the first interview could be reduced to writing. It seemed possible, however, to train myself as a listener so as to improve the accuracy of what was remembered. Many

[3] Because of the great increase in the volume of documents which accompanied the completion of the board's organization, and the rapid expansion in its organization and activities during the late summer of 1936 and first quarter of 1937, Robert Frase found it impossible to follow developments in these other federal agency social security programs, except for those Treasury functions relating to the collection of social security taxes and information. Therefore this volume omits the story of these other programs.

statements from interviews were also cross-checked with other informants, and both errors of memory and of statement were caught.

In the process of recording an interview I at times became aware of a desire to have the interviewee express ideas which harmonized with my own prepossessions about particular situations. I did develop hypotheses about a number of administrative episodes. I also had a personal desire to see the program of social insurances get a favorable start. I may therefore have introduced slanting words or phrases in the record, even though I tried to guard against this.

Another problem arose during interviews as my relationships with some members of staff and board became more firm. I was fairly often told of events with the injunction "This is off the record; it isn't to go to your committee." How to handle these interview materials? I pursued the policy of writing them out, just as I did the other interviews, but kept them in a separate, personal, file. In presenting the narrative of this study I have at times generalized from such confidential statements but have kept the sources of the information anonymous. There remain a few episodes in the administrative history which are not as fully explained as would be possible had there been no restrictions of this kind.

The story told herein is often a personal one. It must be remembered that the basic unit in the administrative process studied was the human being. It was not a position, section, division, bureau, or board, however convenient and essential are these organizational concepts for thinking about the relationships planned for individual activities. To describe what went on meant that one had often to tell what individuals thought or did. Had I consistently depersonalized the record it would have been robbed of significant meaning for anyone desiring to understand administration. Difficulties were often the result of the behavior of particular persons, either within or without the organization. Consequently it has been necessary in describing some events to reflect criticism of certain people, despite a desire to refrain from ladling out blame. Successes, too, can often be personalized. But an account describing the launching of a great and (in the United States) virtually unprecedented set of programs is bound to highlight the difficulties. An effective administrative organization is not born from the brow of an administrative Zeus. However able and sincere the individuals participating, until mutual acquaintance and trust have developed the tissue of habitual cooperative effort, administrative operations cannot be fully effective or smooth-working. At first, all of the important tasks stand in a sea of unknowns which shroud in whole or in part many of the answers to be expressed in administrative policy, structure, and specific ways of performance.

Whether or not the story told in this study contains much significance for those questing for a science or art of public administration depends in large part, I believe, on the subsequent history of the agencies that will inherit the tasks begun by the Social Security Board of 1935–36.

There were a few decisions that as early as the close of the study in March 1937 seemed clearly to have been mistakes in judgment. One of these, both Frase and I believe, was the special reliance on the "expert" category for staffing the higher positions, instead of an earlier resort to examination processes. The effort to discover a coordinator role, independent of the executive director, was also misconceived. The three-membered board at the top of the structure was in many respects a marked handicap to prompt and effective decision-making, but this was something for which the board members cannot be held responsible. The major difficulties of getting a system of state unemployment compensation administration under way and of articulating it with the placement services were also matters of congressional determination, and not of the board's making. The problems of spoils and incompetent administration of public assistance grants for the aged, which quickly emerged in certain states during 1936 and 1937, were not of the board's doing. In fact, its decisions in this area blazed trials which ultimately erased much of the early inadequacy of state administration of these programs.

Yet a major test of the wisdom or unwisdom of decisions made by the board and its top administrators during the first months of this New Deal agency waits upon a careful review of subsequent administrative history. Only by that kind of inquiry will it be possible to evaluate how great were the consequences, for good or ill, of decisions taken during the first sixteen months of the life of the board.

CHARLES McKINLEY

THE STUDY FROM MID-MAY 1936
TO THE END OF MARCH 1937

McKinley's observations about his point of view and methodology in conducting this study would to a considerable extent be my own about the conduct of the subsequent study. One major difference between our situations was that I had been a member of the board's staff from October 1, 1935 to May 1936. It was not easy to shift from the administrative position of one carrying out and trying to influence the formation of policy to that of a completely disinterested observer. Particularly during the summer of 1936 I found it difficult to confine interviews to the gathering of information: not only did a number of interviewees ask my advice on many matters, but I undoubtedly steered the conversation toward problems which were of particular interest to me. Many of these were technical problems of unemployment compensation or old age benefits.

While my interests corresponded fairly closely to those of McKinley, I had a particularly sharp interest in the unemployment compensation program because of its close relationship to industrial regulation by government. This was increased by my participation as an assistant to Walter Matscheck during a two-week study, in June and July of 1936, of the operations of the New Hampshire Division of Unemployment Compensation, and later in that summer in an investigation of the English, German, French, and Austrian systems of old age and unemployment insurance and public employment offices.[4] I found the American program of special interest because of the novel principle incorporated in the Social Security Act by which the national government made 100 percent grants-in-aid to state administrations, and because of the necessity for close cooperation with the United States Employment Service, also administering a state grant-in-aid program. Thus my contacts with the board's unemployment compensation activities were more extensive than were those with its public assistance or old age benefits operations.

There were also a number of other matters that interested me, including:

Editor's note. Robert W. Frase, on a Harvard University fellowship from October 1935 to May 1936, served first as an assistant to Chairman Winant, then as an assistant to the director of the Bureau of Informational Service, and lastly with the Bureau of Research and Statistics. He also joined those members of the board's staff who spent some weeks in Europe during the fall of 1936 studying the problems of administration in certain European nations where social insurance programs had long been established.

[4] In 1938 the Social Security Board published two studies resulting from this investigation: Walter Matscheck, *The Administration of Unemployment Insurance in Great Britain,* and Robert W. Frase, *The Administration of Unemployment Insurance in Germany.*

1. The range of discretion left by statute to the administrative agency and the impact of this on problems of administrative law.
2. The influence of pressure groups, particularly labor organizations, on board decisions.
3. The influence of overhead federal control agencies: the Civil Service Commission, the General Accounting Office, the Bureau of the Budget, and the Treasury.
4. Cooperation between the board and other federal agencies, especially the Treasury, the Post Office, and the U.S. Employment Service.
5. The board's publicity and informational activities.

I shared McKinley's lack of interest in details of procedure, files, forms, accounting, and other office management activities, business office equipment, etc., though some acquaintance with these matters was necessary to understand important happenings. It was also essential to understand (and occasionally to use) the technical "lingo" in the fields of unemployment compensation, old age insurance, and public welfare and in the many professions represented on the board's staff, in order to carry on interviews with understanding and rapport.

While interviewing and recording consumed the largest portion of my time, it did not bulk so large as it had with McKinley, because when I took up the study where he had left off, the board was moving rapidly from a primarily planning function into program operations. Thus the secretion of reports, instructions, and decision documents increased rapidly. These had to be read, evaluated, and recorded. From October 1935 to May 1936 the board's secretary had accumulated only two hundred documents on which the board had acted. During the following eleven months these mounted to a total of over fourteen hundred. Note-taking became a heavy burden after December 1936, when the board terminated the informal arrangement between its secretary and McKinley which had provided him with copies of her notes on board discussions, minutes, and related documents. I was compelled by this change to take extensive notes of the secretary's minutes and of memoranda and official documents.

The expansion of staff also greatly accelerated, so that it was impossible to develop the acquaintance with new people that I had had with the key officials of the early months. This was particularly true with the people in the field offices, who came only occasionally to Washington and whom I could interview in their field stations only rarely. I was also handicapped in interviewing because I was regarded by many in the organization as a "Winant" man, which, while an advantage in establishing full confidence with some, produced distrust and reluctance to communicate on the part of others. Perhaps my youth was also a handicap. There may have been factors of personality hampering the establishment of quick rapport. At any rate, I did not see Bane, Altmeyer, and Miles very often, though in each case I did have good contact with an assistant.

I did have two decided assets for interviewing: (1) My digestion could stand the wear and tear of interviews during luncheon, a time and situation in which it is much easier to elicit friendly responses than during work hours in a man's office; for months on end I popped questions between swallows every day in the week; (2) The absence of family obligations at that time made it possible for me to associate with younger unmarried staff members after hours, and thus to pick up many a bit of gossip or interesting tip which might otherwise have escaped "uncaptured" and "unrecorded."

As time passed, increasing doubts assailed me about this kind of study, perhaps because I was playing the role of a mere historian when so much needed to be done and so many problems to be solved. More fundamental were other uncertainties: Was I getting close to the real story? What would be the value of it when completed? If the study should not be published for many years, perhaps I was getting enough detail, but if it was to be used by the board later or by some other federal agency it might not be adequate. The committee had given me no guidance as to what to include or exclude or what use would be made of the finished product. I had McKinley's account of the first seven months, but the increasing volume of board business made it impossible to follow developments as closely as he did. Thus I was compelled to use a shotgun attempt to cover everything and envisage all purposes for which the study might be used. This courted the danger that important developments would be treated too superficially for one purpose and too carefully for another.

The role of a pioneer in this type of research has been a trying one, even though there is fascination in the idea of getting the inside story of an important government agency in operation. As I close my account my remarks may strike too pessimistic a note. Others will be able to judge the value of the finished product more objectively—and a year later I may revise my present opinion very considerably.

ROBERT W. FRASE

LAUNCHING SOCIAL SECURITY

.1.

INTRODUCTION TO THE ACT, THE BOARD, AND MAJOR TRENDS, OCTOBER 1935 TO MARCH 1937

THE GENESIS AND NATURE OF THE SOCIAL SECURITY ACT OF 1935

The enactment of the Social Security Act of 1935, like so many legislative innovations, was the culmination of a series of social experiences, in this case climaxed by the eruption of the most serious national economic crisis the United States had ever experienced. When Franklin D. Roosevelt passed through New York City on his way to Washington to take up his duties as President, the newspapers were saying that the greatest city in the nation was then discharging thousands of relief workers because money for their wages had been exhausted. Its sister city of Newark had already ceased to meet its regular payroll. Beginning late in October 1932 a creeping banking paralysis had started to spread across the nation. At that time the governor of Nevada closed all the banks in that state for a twelve-day holiday in order to save a chain of banks. Though bank failure there was averted, depositors everywhere became increasingly anxious about the safety of their money. Late in January 1933 the United States Comptroller of the Currency published a report which showed that during the preceding year, bank deposits had declined by twelve billion dollars, and that a somewhat larger shrinkage of bank resources had occurred.

A year earlier President Hoover had persuaded Congress to create the Reconstruction Finance Corporation. By early 1933 that new agency had already loaned nearly a billion dollars to shore up some six thousand banks and trust companies. It had also rushed to the rescue of many major railroads then on the verge of bankruptcy. In Republican Iowa, the legislature during January 1933 gave Iowa's superintendent of banking the authority to take over the operation of any bank for a year, without the stigma of a formal receivership. The next month the danger signals moved to Louisiana, whose governor announced a general banking holiday to ease the strain on some New Orleans banks. Less than two weeks later Michigan followed suit, with a gubernatorial proclamation for a week's bank holiday. Thereafter the speed of bank closures accelerated. By March 4, 1933, as Mr. Hoover and Mr. Roosevelt rode together to the inauguration ceremonies, the banks of thirty-eight states had been closed, and those in all of the other ten states were operating under restrictions. Early on inauguration morning the governors of the two greatest financial states, Illinois and New York, suspended all banking operations. On that morning, also, the New York Stock Exchange, the Kansas City Board of Trade, and the Chicago Board of Trade shut their doors.

Roosevelt's inaugural speech called for an end to the panic fear that seemed to have gripped the nation. He asked the people to act "as a trained and loyal army willing to sacrifice for the good of a common discipline." The country, he said, had not been stricken by a plague of locusts, for there were plenty of material things at its doorstep "the use of which languished within sight of generous supply." This evil was caused by the "rulers of the exchange of mankind's goods who have failed through their own stubborness and their own incompetence, have admitted their failure and have abdicated." He promised to present Congress with a plan of action, but if Congress did not respond and the emergency continued, he said,

I shall not evade the clear course of duty that will then confront me. I shall ask the Congress for the one remaining instrument to meet the crisis—the broad Executive power to wage a war against the emergency, as great as the power that would be given me if we were in fact invaded by a foreign foe.[1]

Roosevelt was giving notice that if Congress failed to provide the specific legislation required he would follow Lincoln's precedent—namely, to proceed on his own to master the crisis.

On the evening of March 4 the President ordered his new Secretary of the Treasury to draft an emergency banking bill and gave him five days to complete the job. The next day he issued a call for a special session of Congress on March 9. He also proclaimed a national bank holiday pending new bank legislation and regulations.

When Congress assembled on the afternoon of March 9, the Speaker of the House read from the text of the single copy of the bill. The bill would validate

[1] Inaugural Address, March 4, 1933. Printed in *Public Papers and Addresses of Franklin D. Roosevelt*, vol. 2, *The Year of Crisis, 1933* (New York: Random House, 1938), p. 15.

actions of the President already taken, give him complete control over gold movements, penalize hoarding, authorize the issue of new Federal Reserve Bank notes, and arrange for the reopening of banks with liquid assets and for the reorganization of the rest.[2] After less than forty minutes of debate the House shouted unanimous approval. The Senate approved by a vote of seventy-three to seven, without amendment, and by 8:36 that evening the President had signed the bill into law. Over five thousand banks opened within eleven days of the inauguration; hoarded money returned to their vaults despite the need for cash resulting from the holidays. The President, in his first famous fireside chat, assured the people that the banks which had opened were now safe, and the people took him at his word.[3]

The mood of this crisis period, when the people accepted without much protest the leadership of the new Democratic president, was not limited to the farmers and city workers whose situations were so desperate. Charles and Mary Beard well described it as follows:

Despite minor dissents and controversies over details, the country as a whole rallied enthusiastically to the support of President Roosevelt during the spring and summer of 1933. Companionship in misery and fear almost turned politics into a love feast. Powerful business leaders cooperated with the administration in a spirit of cheerful compliance contrasting sharply with the hostility which they had displayed toward Bryanism, Progressivism and the New Freedom. It seemed that the concussions of the crisis had shaken their assurance in themselves and their system. The old program of "letting nature take its course" had lost its glitter. They themselves had always made use of government whenever advantages could be obtained by that method; the Coolidge and Hoover administrations had favored them by special policies and had let them alone in most of their major operations. Yet catastrophe had come upon them, under the most beneficent auspices. In the spring and summer of 1933 the Lords of Creation were distraught and for the moment had no rallying point save the Chief Executive of the nation.[4]

On March 6, 1933, while the state governors were assembled in conference in Washington, a number of the outstanding national group leaders sent them an open letter calling for national unity in support of this Democratic President. It said in part:

We are convinced that there is throughout the nation a spontaneous spiritual

---

[2] A lot of "funny money" expedients had been used in various communities as substitutes for legal money during the closure.

[3] William E. Leuchtenburg, *Franklin Roosevelt and the New Deal, 1932–1940* (New York: Harper-Row, 1963), pp. 39–43, briefly summarizes the sequence of actions by FDR and the first New Deal Congress.

[4] Charles and Mary Beard, *The Rise of American Civilization*, vol. 3, *America in Midpassage* (New York: The Macmillan Co., 1939), pp. 244–45.

uprising of confidence and hope in our chosen leader. The nature of our national crisis calls for an expression of this confidence in the combined voice of the people to show that they are behind him, alert and vocal and united in heart. Prompt and decisive action of a national scope, and in several directions, is necessary to prevent economic collapse throughout the land. The ordinary operations of government that prevail and are suitable in time of prosperity with normal conditions may be too slow to meet adequately this emergency and avoid the danger of this economic avalanche carrying all before it.[5]

The letter not only asked the governors to support the President but to appeal to the patriotism of the Congress to do likewise. The signers included the head of the American Federation of Labor, the president of the American Chamber of Commerce, the heads of the National Grange and the National Farm Bureau Federation, Cardinal Mundelein, Rabbi Stephen Wise, Dr. Harry Emerson Fosdick, ex-governor Alfred E. Smith, Newton D. Baker, President Nicholas Murray Butler of Columbia University, Daniel Willard, president of the Baltimore and Ohio Railway, and Walter Lippmann.[6]

This is not the place to describe all the legislative projects sent to Congress in rapid succession during the hundred days after inauguration, or to inquire into their economic consistency as real contributions to recovery of the national economy. While the change of the Volstead Act to permit 3.2 percent beer could hardly be regarded as an important contribution to the relief of the fifteen million unemployed, it probably boosted morale as it wetted the whistles of those citizens possessing some extra "jingly" money. But the economic distresses of the day were confronted by a new series of measures which appealed to various groups to whom the Hoover regime had been unresponsive. Particularly important politically, and of some economic importance, were the following:

1. The Agricultural Adjustment Act, a measure intended to increase farm income, and framed by the leaders of the chief farm organizations. It set forth alternative methods of subsidizing major staple farm crops to provide price supports.

2. A farm credit act which merged all the government farm loan agencies under the "new management" of Henry Morgenthau, Jr. The new agency ultimately refinanced 20 percent of all outstanding farm mortgages, many after scaling down the principal owed the creditors.

3. Roosevelt, by "decree," took the nation off the gold standard and yielded to the silver-mining interests of the Rocky Mountain states, who demanded a guaranteed price for silver higher than its price on the international market. This also pleased the farm groups, who wanted inflationary measures. Per-

[5] Ibid., pp. 253-54.
[6] Ibid., p. 254.

haps these moves played some part in checking the deflationary spiral of the economy.

4. For unemployed city boys FDR dreamed up the Civilian Conservation Corps. Its goals involved a combination of aims: to provide youth with an experience of social service in the healthy rural environment of state and national forests and parks and on farm lands plagued with erosion, poor drainage, and other serious problems; and to provide them with educational opportunities which they had missed or neglected.[7]

5. To ease the tragedy of urban dwellers who could not pay home mortgage obligations because of lost income and who, in massive numbers, were losing their homes through foreclosure, Congress in June 1933 adopted a Home Owners Loan Act. Ultimately the Home Owners Loan Corporation re-financed the debts on one out of every five urban private homes.[8]

But the need for immediate funds to relieve hunger and other basic depriva-tion in clothing and housing, etc., could not wait for the impact of these and other official measures. Though the President had also pushed contradicting deflationary programs of budget curtailment through Congress, depriving even veterans of some of their pension funds, he was compelled by the situa-tion to ask Congress for unprecedented new funds with which to increase relief money for the states (grants, this time, rather than Hoover's program of loans with interest) to care for those too old and ill, or otherwise disquali-fied, to work. He also wanted still more money to put millions of the able or partly able unemployed to work at jobs of greater or less utility. A half billion dollars was granted by Congress on May 12, 1933, half to be given to the states on a matching grant basis to shore up and improve existing relief activities, and the other half to the new Federal Emergency Relief Administration (authorized by the same statute) to be used for buying huge quantities of food and clothing then glutting the market, for distribution by state and local governments.

The President's broad construction of the Constitution was expressed in this statement: "While it isn't written in the Constitution, nevertheless it is the inherent duty of the Federal Government to keep its citizens from starvation." This view also justified the establishment in November 1933 of the Civil Works Administration—later metamorphosed into the Works Prog-ress Administration—primarily to provide public jobs for the unemployed. These two new agencies were the first general emergency means established

---

[7] Congress was so enthusiastic about the CCC program that it pushed the measure through in ten days, with a voice vote. James McGregor Burns, *Roosevelt: The Lion and the Fox* (New York: Harcourt Brace, 1956), p. 169.

[8] In 1932 a quarter of a million families lost their homes. During 1933 this tragic trend accelerated, with more than a thousand homes a day facing foreclosure. Leuchten-burg, *Roosevelt and the New Deal*, p. 53.

by the federal government for saving the lives, health, and in part the skills and self-respect, of millions of citizens deeply damaged by the economic disintegration during the long three and one-half years which followed upon the heels of the 1929 stock market crash.

While Harry Hopkins and his dedicated crew who managed these new federal relief agencies were concerned first with putting money where it would keep people fed, clothed, and housed, they placed increasing emphasis upon finding useful jobs for the able-bodied on relief and for those who had been barely able to get along without public relief. This emphasis was felt increasingly in the existing state relief policies, where more and better work projects were organized; and particularly in the new programs developed in the federally administered relief activities under FERA and more completely in CWA and its successors, the Works Progress Administration and the Works Projects Administration. It was also the emphasis of the programs later developed by the National Youth Administration.[9]

The relief function which Hopkins inherited from the Hoover administration was not entirely a dole system, but its work activities were variable in quality and were minimal in many parts of the country. Moreover, store orders were given the recipients, rather than cash. Hopkins's programs not only greatly increased the work aspect of relief but also provided for money payments. Nor were the states burdened with the prospect of repaying the grants. Until the Works Projects Administration got under way in the spring of 1934, the FERA and the CWA were responsible directly and indirectly for most of the general relief activities. The number of cases fell from a high of slightly over 3,250,000 in April of that year to 2,635,000 in Novem-

[9] For a brief but vivid account of Hopkins, as administrator, meeting with imagination and ceaseless energy (ably supported by assistant administrators Frank Bane and Aubrey Williams) the immense task set before him, see Robert Sherwood, *Roosevelt and Hopkins* (New York: Harper-Row, Bantam, 1950), pp. 53ff. Hopkin's speed in getting relief money allocated to the states where funds provided under the Hoover regime had already run out was remarkable. He also showed great ingenuity in discovering worthwhile work projects for an infinite variety of unemployed people possessing an infinite variety of skills that were being allowed to deteriorate. He and his associates deeply sensed the trauma that had overtaken these people, denied the opportunity to work at tasks in which they were trained and experienced, and whose loss of occupation meant loss of self-esteem and sense of social status. There can be no doubt also that this emphasis of Hopkins and his associates influenced many of the other segmental programs of federal agencies directed toward assistance to both rural and urban population groups. For a balanced but appreciative account of the entire federal work-relief effort in the New Deal period down to approximately 1941, see the masterly study by Arthur W. MacMahon, John D. Millett, and Gladys Ogden entitled *The Administration of Federal Work Relief* (Chicago: Public Administration Service, 1941). Chapter 1, "Planning the Works Program," is especially valuable for sensing the evolution of the works program.

ber. But there were other special programs in which the case number climbed to nearly 200,000 by November; these provided rural rehabilitation, emergency education efforts, and special student aid. It was estimated by the Committee on Economic Security that by the fall of 1934 nearly 18,500,000 persons were receiving emergency relief during September and October.[10] Whereas the Hoover regime had stressed the use of private relief agencies, Hopkins, urged by Frank Bane and Aubrey Williams, accepted the necessity of using state and local public agencies for distributing public relief moneys. Hopkins also adopted the policy that in addition to food, those on relief who needed clothing, shelter, and medical care should be allowed money for these purposes.[11]

Some of the foregoing measures had elements of longtime commitment. With a few exceptions, however, they were conceived as temporary efforts to deal with a crisis, but the President came to realize that in many aspects this crisis indicated long run continuing need for permanent solutions to widespread social distress. He stressed this attitude in his congressional message of June 8, 1934. He aimed at reconstruction measures for the security of the nation's men, women, and children. He translated this to include the provision of decent housing, productive work, and "some safeguards against the misfortunes which cannot be wholly eliminated in this man-made world of ours."

To explore this goal he issued an executive order creating a Committee on Economic Security to make recommendations to him, a top-level group consisting of Frances Perkins of the Department of Labor, chairman, Morgenthau of the Treasury, Henry A. Wallace of the Department of Agriculture, Homer E. Cummings of the Department of Justice, and Harry Hopkins, Federal Emergency Relief Administrator. This committee selected an advisory council of distinguished private citizens (some who had served in government) drawn from labor, agricultural, and civic organizations, business, universities, and religious and charitable agencies and associations. A technical board chaired by Arthur Altmeyer, then Second Assistant Secretary of Labor, guided the committee in designing a program of studies to be undertaken and in the review of alternative proposals for attaining the security goals. This board included the top professionals in the many related fields of knowledge

[10] *Supplement to the Report to the President of the Committee on Economic Security* (Washington: U.S. Government Printing Office, 1935), p. 2, table 3.

[11] New Deal agencies and programs intended to improve the employment situation but not discussed here included the Tennessee Valley Authority programs, the Resettlement Administration and its successor, the Farm Security Administration, the Public Works Administration, and the National Recovery Administration. Limited public-housing programs were authorized to three of these agencies. Considerable housing construction was completed in both rural and urban areas.

within the federal career service, many of whom were recent recruits to the public service. Professor Edwin E. Witte, chairman of the economics department of the University of Wisconsin, was appointed director, heading a full-time research staff to make studies relevant to this board assignment. Flanking these professional workers was a group of technical advisory committees for consulting purposes, made up of actuarial consultants, medical doctors, public health, hospital, dental, public employment, public assistance, and child welfare professionals. Top people throughout the country accepted service on these bodies.

From the combined effort and discussion of these people and their committee superiors came the report of the top committee to the President, dated January 15, 1935. It contained the recommendations for action that led to the Social Security Act of 1935.

It was clear that these recommendations did not cover the health hazard problems, though they did propose expansions and improvements in traditional public health activities. They also indicated the importance of further early study of this segment of human need and of its ultimate recognition in a national security program. The act as finally drafted ignored one other field of permanent activity recommended by the committee as an obligation of government: the maintenance of public works programs, not only to be ready for great expansions in time of economic depression but also to deal with pockets of unemployment developing in stranded communities where industries were declining, to help impoverished farm families, and to care for the needs of the large numbers of people not covered by its proposed unemployment compensation program. This general function it called "employment assurance." [12] This portion of the recommendations suggests the influence of Hopkins and the other members of his top staff on the technical committees of the Economic Security Committee—people who reflected the attitude of his organizations, in which work relief seemed highly preferable to dole oriented programs. Not only was Hopkins a member of the top committee of five, but his assistant administrators, Williams, Corrington Gill, and Howard Meyers, director of FERA's Division of Research and Statistics, were members of the Technical Advisory Committee. Williams was also chairman of the subcommittee of the board dealing with public employment and public assistance. [13]

We omit an account of the legislative history of the bill and its competitors during its journey through Congress. But it is important to call attention to major alternatives simultaneously proposed in Congress, since they affected

[12] See pp. 8–9 of the committee's report, under the heading "Public Employment."
[13] See MacMahon, Millett, and Ogden, *Administration of Federal Work Relief*, pp. 25–27.

the psychological atmosphere that influenced administrative attitudes and decisions in the early months of the Social Security Board's work. As the early fear of catastrophic crisis wore off throughout the nation, discontent with Roosevelt's accomplishments began to gather. There were four principal leaders of that discontent: Huey Long of Louisiana (elected to the Senate in 1932), Father Coughlin of Michigan, Francis Townsend of California, and Milo Reno of Iowa. Only two proposals were importantly involved in the legislative history of the Social Security Act. They were Long's plan to "share the wealth," and the Townsend Plan for a pyramided transaction tax with which to pay $200 a month to everyone over sixty-five. Both were introduced in the House as substitutes for the Social Security Bill. The Townsend Plan was still attracting new converts when the bill was passed, and it continued to gain momentum politically across the country.[14] As prestigious a senator as Borah of Idaho found it prudent, in his reelection campaign in 1936, to endorse the Townsend Plan in order to assure his return to the Senate. This was a year after the Social Security Act had been adopted and some months after it began to operate.

[14] Even as late as December 1935 Chairman Buchanan of the House Appropriations Committee was flirting with a sales tax for financing the social security program, as a partial concession to the Townsend movement. Joseph Robinson, Senate Democratic leader, was also facing, at that time, the opposition candidacy in Arkansas of an ex-preacher who had espoused the Townsend Plan. Professor Edwin Witte wrote Merrill Murray, one of the top members of the board's staff, on December 11, 1935, a very pessimistic view of the inroads being made in public opinion against the Social Security Act because of the growing Townsend movement. He said, in part: "In the last three months I have become more concerned than ever with the Townsend Plan. There is no doubt that this movement has made tremendous headway. The battle against the Townsend Plan has been lost, I think, in pretty nearly every state west of the Mississippi, and the entire Middle Western area is likewise badly infected. At this time the Republican party organization is at least flirting with the Townsendites, and I think it is mighty significant that not one of the major business organizations of the country has attacked the plan. . . . I think these groups are playing with dynamite, as I do not think they can doublecross the Townsendites should their political maneuvering prove unsuccessful. Be that as it may, I think that the Townsend movement has become a terrific menace which is likely to engulf our entire economic system. Do not think that because fewer letters are now coming to Washington that the Townsend movement has subsided. It is much stronger than ever before, only it is now primarily directed to the next presidential election. One factor which the Townsendites were helped by was Senator Huey Long's filibuster. Since September 1 I have made eighteen speeches on social security, most of them in this state [Wisconsin] but also in Missouri, Illinois and Iowa. Everywhere there is skepticism that there ever will be federal aid for old age assistance. Should there be a long delay in Congress in the passage of the appropriation bill or if the Social Security Board should take a very technical attitude on the state old age assistance laws, I think our last hope of stopping the Townsend movement will be gone."

THE SOCIAL SECURITY ACT

We turn our attention now to the basic features of the Social Security Act as approved on August 14, 1935.[15] The act determined not only what the fundamental programs should be but also where they would be located within the federal administrative system, what agencies would be in charge of them, broadly how the state and local governments should fit into the administrative picture, how and by whom the taxes for their support would be collected, where the reserved funds would be held and managed, and many other details relating to the job to be done. It was a multiple-purpose direction in which this security effort would move. Briefly summarized, the act authorized a national system of contributory old age annuities, a state administered, federally supervised unemployment insurance system, and a program of large federal subsidies to induce nationwide financial aid to the needy aged, the blind, and children deprived of parental support. It also amplified national financial encouragement of improved public health services by expanding research, by helping the states to improve their health staffs, by giving special aid for crippled and disadvantaged children, and by renewing promotional health work for mothers and infants.

When the Committee on Economic Security made its report in January 1935, it expected that the administration of grants-in-aid to the states for the aged, the blind, and dependent children would be assigned to the Federal Emergency Relief Administration and not to the "Social Insurance Board" (a title which Congress changed to Social Security Board). The committee proposed that the board be located within the Department of Labor, where it would be a new member of a family of agencies already embracing the United States Employment Service and the National Reemployment Service, two units separated at the local level but under a single federal supervising agency directed by a single official of the Department of Labor. The former was a system of employment exchanges for private placement, administered by the states under grants-in-aid provided by the Wagner-Peyser Act; the latter was a series of directly administered employment agencies, chiefly for hiring workers for work projects financed or subsidized by federal funds.

But Congress changed the proposed overhead structure. It made the Social Security Board an independent agency, reporting directly to the President and itself, and gave it not only the two social insurance tasks (contributory old age annuities and unemployment compensation) but three public assistance supervisory tasks as well. Increased provision for various health needs

[15] 49 Stat. 620 (1935). All references to the Social Security Act in this study are to the original act and do not relate to any subsequent amendments, since there were no changes made until after the study was concluded.

and the special requirements of childen were split between the United States Public Health Service and the Children's Bureau.[16]

The original Social Security Act was broken into eleven titles. The board was directly concerned with Titles I, II, III, IV, VII, IX, and X, while the Treasury found its new tax duties under Titles VIII and IX and other provisions scattered throughout the act.

The Social Security Board of three members was created by Title VII. Its members, not more than two of them to be from the same political party, were to be selected by the President with the consent of the Senate. Their terms were for six years, on a staggered, two-year pattern. The President was to name the chairman. In addition to its specified administrative duties the board was directed to continuously study and recommend "methods of providing economic security through social insurance. . . ." It was authorized to appoint such employees, fix their compensation, and make such expenditures as its duties required. Appointments of attorneys and experts, however, might be made without regard to the civil service laws.

Undoubtedly the program of grants to the states for aid to the needy aged was the focus of the most public interest. For this purpose Congress not only authorized a specific sum for the first fiscal year but also pledged itself thereafter to a sum "sufficient to carry out the purposes of this title" (Title I). Such funds were to go to states whose plans the board had approved. That approval was contingent upon the fulfillment of conditions that can be briefly summarized as follows: the plan must be in effect in all political subdivisions of the state, and if administered by the subdivisions must be mandatory on them; the state must pay a part of the costs of the program; a single state agency must administer or supervise the plan; a fair hearing before the state agency must be given to any oldster whose application has been denied; the plan must provide "such methods of administration (other than those relating to selection, tenure of office, and compensation of personnel) as are found by the Board to be necessary for the efficient operation of the plan"; states must provide reports and information to the board; half the net amount collected from the estate of any recipient relating to aid furnished should be paid to the United States.

The Secretary of the Treasury was to make quarterly payments equal to half the amount spent by the state for every person sixty-five or over (exclud-

---

[16] Because this study is centered upon the experiences of the Social Security Board, reference to the provisions of the Social Security Act authorizing new duties for the Children's Bureau and the Public Health Service will be omitted. The work of the Treasury's fiscal units was so closely intertwined with certain functions and administrative experiences of the Social Security Board that considerable material relating to those Treasury units has been included.

ing inmates of public institutions) of up to $30 a month for each recipient. He would add 5 percent either for administrative costs of the state or for old age assistance, or for both. A skeleton procedure to aid the Treasury, plus specified information, was to be certified by the board to the Treasury before the beginning of each quarter. If the board should find through notice and hearing that any state had failed to "comply substantially" with the approved plan or had violated the act's prohibitions about age, residence, or citizenship, it was to stop payments until satisfied that noncompliance had ceased.

The legal foundations for aid to the blind and to dependent children closely resembled those just sketched. They included approved plans, quarterly estimates, certifications to the Treasury, statewide application of the program, and so forth. Certain differences applied to grants for dependent children: no plan could be approved if it excluded a child living in the state for a year immediately before application for aid, or whose mother was a state resident for a year prior to the birth of the child; and the federal proportion of the children's aid funds was limited to one-third, with maximum total payment of $18 for the first child and $12 each for subsequent children. No aid should be given a blind person who also received aid under the aged grant program. Federal funds for individual blind grants could provide 50 percent, up to an individual total maximum of $30 a month. Again 5 percent would be added for either administrative costs or further aid. Sanctions for these grants were identical to those for old age assistance.

Unemployment compensation administration grants, for which a global limit was fixed at $49,000,000 after 1936, also required approved state laws and were subject to certain minimum requirements to be met by the states. These included (1) benefits to be paid through public employment offices or other agencies chosen by the Social Security Board; (2) no benefits to be paid until two years after the first contributions due; (3) state unemployment fund moneys to be sent immediately after collection to the U.S. Treasury for an "Unemployment Trust Fund," this fund to be used solely for paying benefits. Three limits on denial of compensation to otherwise eligible persons refusing to accept work were stipulated:

(a) If the position offered is vacant due directly to a strike, lockout, or other labor dispute; (b) if the wages, hours, or other conditions of work offered are substantially less favorable to the individual than those prevailing for similar work in the locality; (c) if as a condition of being employed the individual would be required to join a company union or to resign from or refrain from joining any bona fide labor organization.

The board was authorized to withhold the annual certification to the Treasury if either the state law or its administrative regulations "failed to comply substantially" with these stipulations of the act.

The financial basis for state unemployment compensation programs was a payroll tax, levied by the U.S. Treasury upon all "employers of eight or more," starting in 1936 at 1 percent and rising ultimately to 3 percent of total wages paid during the year. The taxpayer, under an approved state law, would receive a credit against the federal tax of up to 90 percent. This tax provision was the propulsive force that pushed the states, in many cases very reluctantly, into the unemployment compensation system. These 90 percent moneys would be sent to the Treasury for deposit in the national Unemployment Trust Fund. The Treasury would invest them when not needed for current withdrawals by the states for paying claimants for unemployment compensation.

The states would provide an administrative agency whose costs would be budgeted in an administrative plan and reviewed by the Social Security Board. It would allocate precise amounts for administrative expenditures. While it had wide discretion in fixing these sums it was enjoined to consider the state's population and the coverage of the state law. But before the board should certify to the Treasury the payments to which the state was entitled, the state must meet the following requirements:

1. Methods of administration ("other than those relating to selection, tenure of office, and compensation of personnel") must be calculated to "insure full payment of unemployment compensation when due."
2. Chance for "fair hearing" before an impartial tribunal must be provided for persons whose claims have been rejected.
3. Reports must be submitted as required by the board.
4. Any federal agency "charged with the administration of public works or assistance through public employment" must be furnished occupational information about each recipient of unemployment benefits.

For failure to substantially comply with these requirements, or denial of unemployment benefits to a substantial number of persons entitled thereto, the board, after notification to the state, might withhold further certification to the Treasury.

The sole federally administered service under the board's jurisdiction was authorized by Title II, "Federal Old Age Benefits." This was to be a system of contributory retirement annuities (called benefit payments) to which persons over age sixty-five would be entitled. It is unnecessary to recite the formula upon which payments were to be based, but it is important to note that pensions (benefits) would roughly vary with wages accumulated, up to a maximum monthly payment of $85. Seven kinds of employment, involving agricultural workers, domestic servants, casual labor, maritime workers, governmental employees, and the employees of philanthropical, educational, and similar institutions, were excluded from the system. The initial number of workers whose wage accounts would have to be kept by the board was estimated at upwards of twenty-two millions, and the number was expected ultimately to swell to perhaps fifty millions. While the payment of benefits to those reaching sixty-five was postponed until January 1, 1942, the board, beginning January 1, 1937, would face the task of paying to persons reaching sixty-five years, lump sums equal to 3.5 percent of wages earned after December 31, 1936, and before their sixty-fifth birthdays. It would also have to begin paying death benefits of like amounts to the estates of wage earners.

Actual benefit payments would be handled by the Treasury through its Division of Disbursement, after certification by the board.

In addition to the close connection between the board and the Secretary of the Treasury suggested by provisions reviewed above, other Treasury activities were authorized which would be of vital concern to the board's work. Thus under Title VIII the Treasury not only was enjoined to collect a tax from the wage earner and the employer at rates calculated to yield revenue sufficient to pay for the system of old age benefits, but was also to furnish stamps, stamp books, and so on to the Postmaster General, for sale to employers, to be used in collecting the tax and in recording individual benefit accounts.[17] The Treasury was also to set up an "Old Age Reserve Account," to which should be appropriated each year an amount sufficient to provide for the payment of old age benefits. The actuarial calculations upon which this annual premium would be based were likewise the duty of the Treasury, as was the management of the investments of the account. The sweeping power to issue rules and regulations in connection with collection of taxes, and the penal sanctions given the Treasury, were also bound to be of interest to the Social Security Board in the performance of its duties.

The Social Security Act marked a belated acceptance of the general principles of social insurance which western European nations had developed at least a generation earlier. This was a great achievement. But the legislation omitted provisions for general health insurance even though it expanded, in important ways, special public health programs for certain disadvantaged groups. Moreover, unemployment compensation coverage was so restricted that some of the most weakly placed industrial and agricultural workers were left totally without federal protection against the hazards of unemployment. Some critics, particularly those in academic institutions, objected to state management of unemployment compensation, fearing that given the interstate character of the labor market only direct administration by a national agency could achieve proper placement and prompt, full benefit payments. In addition, the state-local sharing of cost under the grant system for old age assistance left the needy aged without any assurance of a decent minimum income.

---

[17] The stamp method of tax payment and information was not used; the inclusion of elaborate reference to it in the Social Security Act was the result of the experts' recommendations to the Committee on Economic Security.

Aid to dependent children was similarly jeopardized, though an early amendment permitted an increase in the percentage of federal contribution for this group, so vulnerable in any contest of political strength either at the state or the national capitols. It must be noted too that the acceptance of the goal of "work assurance" for which Hopkins and his group had been plugging so hard was not included in the statute, nor did the national government offer to share any part of the general relief needed by the large number of unemployables, save those sixty-five and over who might find some more-or-less modest alms from the needy grants. Future oldsters under sixty-five at the time who could live long enough and who worked for sufficiently high pay to accumulate a decent retirement old age benefit income were protected.

A final comment: the payroll tax methods of financing both unemployment compensation and old age annuities and survivors insurance were regressive and deflationary. The grant programs also quickly stimulated the states, hard-pressed by the failure of the general property tax as a source of assured income during the depression, to turn to regressive general sales taxes for financing their part in the security programs, and many other state and local functions. Payroll taxes had been adopted despite their regressive tendencies. The issue was, in the President's words, "politics all the way through." "We put the payroll contributions there," he said, "so as to give the contributors a legal, moral and political right to collect their pensions and their unemployment benefits. With those taxes in there, no damn politician can ever scrap my social security program." [18]

OUTLINE OF MAJOR TRENDS
OCTOBER 1935 TO MARCH 1937

It can be said with assurance that in the collection of information and the drafting of suggested legislation, the Committee on Economic Security had been much less concerned with foreseeing administrative problems and devices than with the substantive content of the law. Moreover, certain congressional changes before the legislation was completed set the stage for additional administrative complications, some of which were to show themselves clearly soon after the administrative organization was constituted. There is always a gap between the social intent and the administrative fact, because human beings are human beings. But if their quality is high and their purpose in harmony with their function the gap will tend to close, unless the legal

[18] Quoted by Leuchtenburg, *Roosevelt and the New Deal,* p. 133.

framework by which administration is released or constricted thwarts their energy. The intensive study of the experience of the Social Security Board during its first eighteen months of life throws some light upon the typical, as well as the peculiar, administrative problems encountered by a new federal administrative agency rendering vital services to large numbers of people.

Before we tell that story in detail let us first note in broad outline the principal administrative developments which influenced the evolution of the board's work during this time.

The Social Security Board was in a double sense a continuation of the Committee on Economic Security: not only were its activities an application of the new functions envisaged by that investigating committee, but the staff nucleus with which the board began was carried over from the committee. Board member Arthur Altmeyer had been chairman of the committee's Technical Board, Chairman Winant had been a member of its Advisory Council. The inherited staff of about twenty people included one of the leading American students of unemployment compensation, who was later to become a high officer in the bureau supervising that activity. Another able young man was used in a number of vital tasks and ended up on the personal staff of Altmeyer. Thomas Eliot, the young Labor Department attorney who while detailed to the Committee on Economic Security had drafted the original Social Security Bill, remained with the board as its general counsel. The first director of the Bureau of Research and Statistics and the first head of the Bureau of Old Age Benefits had been members of the Technical Board. The executive director and the head of the Bureau of Public Assistance had served on special advisory subcommittees. Thus, the new administrative organ which was to undertake the grave responsibility of translating the terms of the statute into the blood and tissue of American life had access, at the beginning of its career, to the accumulated information and thought of the group responsible for its conception.

But these advantages had one immediate counterpoise: the lack of a congressional appropriation during the three and one-half months after the board members arrived in Washington in the summer of 1935. Huey Long's last filibuster had killed the deficiency bill containing funds for the board and the other agencies sharing the responsibilities of the Social Security Act. It was only by the use of a WPA allotment of $112,610, made through the Department of Labor to the Social Security Board (officially available on October 19, 1935), and by borrowing staff from the demobilizing NRA and other sympathetic agencies (FERA and NYA) that the board could begin its job.

All three members of the board—Chairman John G. Winant, Republican, Arthur Altmeyer and Vincent Miles, Democrats—were in Washington ready for work by the middle of September. Much of their time during the next six weeks was spent in canvassing for top members of a staff, and in particular deciding whom to select as chief executive, the board being divided in its judgment between two names—Henry Seidemann of the Brookings Institution staff and Frank Bane, director of the American Public Welfare Association. Toward the end of October the matter was concluded by employing both men, Bane as executive director and Seidemann as an administrative consultant with the title of coordinator, the latter to be employed for a temporary period of six to nine months to help set up the organization. Both men began work on November 1, 1935. During this same period the board had used Meredith Givens on a part-time basis as a personnel officer to help find other key members for the staff.

Like so many typical efforts to break history into neat periods characterized by nicely divided trend distinctions, the use of time divisions in this first eighteen months of board history does some violence to processes that did not stop. Yet for convenience in summarizing a series of simultaneous developments within manageable units, the whole period will be broken into three time divisions marked to some extent by a change of pace at which events were moving. Within each period an attempt will be made to summarize the more important growth tendencies for all phases of the organization and program.

PERIOD 1: NOVEMBER 1935 INTO LATE JANUARY 1936

By the middle of November, when this study was launched, the board had more than doubled the staff on its WPA payroll and had borrowed from NRA, FERA, and other federal agencies until it had a total of 101 persons in its organization. William Sorrells, loaned by the Civil Service Commission on the first of November, was at work on classifying staff positions, interviewing applicants for jobs, giving the soft answer to congressmen, and advising the board generally about the employment of staff.

The executive director divided his time between meeting with the board, working on organization plans, canvassing personnel possibilities, and carrying on public relations work with the states, particularly with reference to the state laws and proposals for public assistance to the aged, whose cause Dr. Francis Townsend had brought to intense national consciousness. Three borrowed social workers, with Helen V. Bary in charge, were busily functioning as a public assistance section under the Federal-State Relations Division, to answer the many inquiries pouring in from the states concerning the provisions of law and state administrative arrangements necessary to qualify for federal grants for the aged, the blind, and dependent children. These questions led to the need for legal construction of many statutory provisions, a need which required the transfer of the queries to the small but exceedingly busy legal staff of the board's general counsel. There was some friction between the two groups because of the slowness with which the legal questions were being answered. Two technically competent men were likewise trying to review legislation and proposed legislation for unemployment compensation, one of them spending a good deal of his time sitting with committees of state legislators for this purpose. The coordinator was hovering over a number of diverse developments: the establishment of an accounting system with the aid of staff loaned by the General Accounting Office; the preparation of budget requests for the balance of the current 1936 fiscal year for early action by the Congress when it should assemble in January; the drafting of information forms to be used by the states applying for grants-in-aid; the perfection of a system of identification numbers to be given the millions of workers whose old age insurance accounts must be kept; and the drafting of plans looking toward the early registration of these clients of the new system. Already an interdepartmental committee representing other agencies, and particularly the United States Employment Service, had been set to work to assist the board in perfecting its decisions concerning individual account numbers and registration.

The board members were busy with a great variety of matters: holding long meetings to determine initial policies relating to the interpretation of their duties under the act, discussing personnel, talking to politicians, engaging in a multitude of small administrative tasks, and listening to the advice of experts. Among the members of this rather limited group were three European specialists who spent considerable time with the board and its initial staff. Pierre Tixier, a French member of the International Labor Office, was persuaded by Chairman Winant, whose membership on the Geneva agency had brought him in touch with European leaders in social insurance administration, to spend about three weeks during November and December in Washington advising the board on how to meet its administrative problems. He prepared memoranda dealing with the registration of employees for old age benefits, the collection of taxes, and the handling of the individual accounts. He also advised on the problems of definition, and the task of coordinating the various forms of social insurance into one harmonious administrative organization.

On the whole, Tixier was very skeptical about the successful administration of the Social Security Act unless it were to be drastically amended. He felt that the reports required of employers would be so difficult for them to make that the resulting irritation was likely to lead to the repeal of the act. He believed the differences in tax coverage between Titles IX and VIII (unemployment compensation and old age benefits) and between the state laws for unemployment compensation and the federal act would present almost insuperable administrative difficulties. He was concerned about the split of the tax-collecting and the information-collecting functions between the Treasury and the board. He privately expressed himself as appalled at the lack of thinking about administrative procedures and details in connection with the work of the Committee on Economic Security. Tixier nevertheless conceded that his knowledge of American business practices was too slight for him to render adequate advisory service to the board without more time in which to familiarize himself with the American scene.

Ronald Davidson, retired official of the British Ministry of Labour, followed Tixier. He had the advantage of having spent some months in this country so that he was more familiar with the American situation. He sat in with the board and its bureau staff in the discussion of many of their problems, but prepared no written memoranda. While less dogmatic than Tixier about the prospects of successful administration, he was exceedingly skeptical of the future of unemployment compensation. Davidson's views on this subject are more fully recounted on pp. 237–38.

Miss Ethel Foster, retired staff member of the British Labour Ministry, also advised the board on the legal interpretation of coverage questions.

The attitude of the board members and Seidemann to these foreign visitors, while not the same in each case, was that on the whole they were not very useful. They ranked Davidson at the head of the list in helpfulness. Both Altmeyer and Seidemann felt that Tixier was too ignorant of American constitutional requirements, public sentiment, and business practice to see the administrative problems here in correct perspective.

During November, December, and January, while the rate of organizational development was slow, a number of important events occurred.

General Organization

Early in December James V. Bennett, assistant director and business manager, for the Bureau of Prisons, was selected as the board's business manager, but his obligations to the Department of Justice required that he carry on his old work along with this new job. Notwithstanding this part-time arrangement, he greatly accelerated the appointment of clerical and stenographic help and set up improved routines for handling correspondence, maintaining the records of the board, making purchases, facilitating appointments, and so forth.

A chief of the Bureau of Unemployment Compensation, R. Gordon Wagenet, was chosen and arrived for duty at the end of December. At about the same time the director (Louis Resnick) and associate director (Robert Huse) of the Bureau of Informational Service reported for duty. Early in January 1936 the board announced the selection of a director for the Bureau of Public Assistance (Jane Hoey) to arrive on January 15. Shortly afterwards it named the chairman of the Railroad Retirement Board, Murray Latimer, as head of the Bureau of Old Age Benefits, and he, with an associate, took over from Coordinator Henry Seidemann and the board the direction of plans for the organization of that bureau. At the very end of January the board announced the selection of the chief (Walton H. Hamilton) and the assistant chief (Ewan Clague) of the Bureau of Research and Statistics. It was still negotiating for a chief personnel officer with a hope, destined to disappointment, that its first choice would accept.

In addition to its dependence upon a WPA allotment and gratuitous assignments from other agencies, which greatly restricted the rate of expansion of its organization, the board had problems of personnel which exercised a constricting influence at this time. These centered in the use of the expert- and attorney-exemption clause (though attorneys quickly dropped out of the issue) and the problem of salaries under the classification act. The board's desire to pick the best men for its key places led to reliance upon the use of experts and to an attempt to boost salaries to a point where it could detach its choices from good positions. The Civil Service Commission proposed an agreement under which it would determine whether a position was one calling for an expert, and whether a candidate was in fact an expert. That proposed agreement at first seemed likely to be accepted by the board, but toward the end of January, as efforts to obtain high classification for staff were questioned and sometimes denied, irritation was growing. Moreover, the commission pressed for some disposition of the personnel inherited from the Committee on Economic Security, NRA, and other emergency agencies not possessed of civil service status. Toward the end of January an agreement was reached under which all the nonstatus employees would be replaced gradually by permanent people, with no member of the former group remaining later than June 30, 1936. While pressure for political appointments to the staff began with the creation of the board, it increased markedly after Congress returned early in January. A few compromises with merit were made, chiefly by way of the expert and lawyer clause.

Early in December a staff committee set to work upon plans for a regional and field organization. It drew upon the aid of other federal agencies, particularly the Employment Service, and by the end of January its report was ready for discussion.

At the very time when the permanent bureau heads were arriving and the prospects for rapid development of the organization seemed particularly bright, the Supreme Court invalidated the Agricultural Adjustment Act. The net psychological effect of this decision upon the board was probably not very great, although at first it appeared to stun the chief members of the staff. It pointed towards the possible invalidation of major provisions of the Social Security Act, although everyone discounted the danger to grants-in-aid for public assistance.

The board decided to go ahead as if the Court had not spoken and to let the constitutional issue take its usual course, expecting that resistance to tax collection in 1937 would furnish an occasion for a court test. The chief effect of the decision on board behavior related to its publicity policy, which as will be shown below was thereafter carefully guided by the general counsel's office on all points that might complicate the constitutionality problem. It is probable also that the Supreme Court's invalidation of the Agricultural Adjustment Act influenced a few prospective staff appointees to withdraw their candidacies.[19]

Public Assistance

December was a month of feverish activity to secure the approval of the state laws and administrative plans, particularly for the aged, before the quarter beginning January 1, 1936, should start. To speed the process of submission, review, and approval as well as to establish friendly personal relations with the states, a conference of all state administrative agencies concerned with the three grants under the board's jurisdiction (as well as with grants administered by the Children's Bureau) met in Washington on December 14–15 with the board and the Children's Bureau. By the end of December there were ready for certification to the Treasury for grants state plans as follows: sixteen for aid to the aged, eleven for aid to the blind, ten for aid to dependent children, for a total of thirty-seven.

Only two more plans for the aged and one for children were added to the list during January. But the staff was absorbed in advising the states, chiefly by correspondence.

Unemployment Compensation

By early December, eight states and the District of Columbia had submitted unemployment compensation laws to the board for approval. Only one was rejected as not fulfilling the requirements of the Social Security Act. Scarcely was the ink dry on some of these state measures before the administrative officers charged with this new function were inquiring in person and by mail for advice about administrative organization, employer-report forms, procedure, and interpretation of their statutes. But the slight staff of the board's bureau was unable to give this kind of aid, because its time was absorbed in giving legislative advice and redrafting the model state bill which had originally been drawn and circulated by the Committee on Economic Security. Toward the end of January the board called a conference of dele-

---

[19] Later in the spring of 1936 a good deal of time was consumed in the general counsel's office and at board meetings in the discussion of suggested amendments to the Social Security Act which might make it less vulnerable to constitutional attack. At that time the entire statute was reviewed with the assistance of Professor Edwin E. Witte, former director of the Committee on Economic Security, and members of the legal staff. A series of modifications was agreed upon which attempted to strip from the act all ties between Titles II and VIII, and III and IX, but these were not introduced at that session of Congress.

gates from New York, Wisconsin, and the New England states to discuss certain problems of legislation and administration. This was the beginning of a practice that was continued and broadened, ultimately giving rise to an association of all state administrators of unemployment compensation.

Old Age Benefits

The early November decision to institute a new special number system for assigning accounts to employees was held up as a result of protests from other federal agencies. Discussion of the kind of system that should be used continued throughout the period, as did other plans (such as time and method) for this registration. While the Bureau of Old Age Benefits was particularly interested in the plans for a field organization being made by the board's committee, the director was also concerned with developing a scheme for organizing his headquarters units. Actual organization did not advance beyond studies and discussion.

PERIOD 2: FEBRUARY INTO JUNE 1936

General Organization

While the board had added only about 20 people to its payroll during January, toward the end of that month it had accepted for appointment 25 others who would be sworn in as soon as Congress should pass the board's administrative appropriation. By February 16, when its WPA payroll list was transferred to its regular appropriation, the total staff numbered 148. With the permanent bureau heads selected by that time (except for Accounts and Audits) and with its own chief personnel officer chosen, the board seemed ready for a rapid expansion. The actual growth was as follows:

	Washington	*Field*
March 31	342	7
April 30	486	12
May 31	582	32
June 30	677	71

This increase fell far short of expectations when the budget was prepared (it had been expected that the board would have 1,360 full-time employees on June 30, 1936). Its curtailment may be partly explained by the depressing effects of the Supreme Court's AAA decision early in January upon state legislation relating to unemployment compensation. The belief of businessmen and labor leaders that such laws would also be declared unconstitutional reduced pressure for enlargement of the board's staff to supervise that function. Reconsideration and postponement of the decisions precedent to registration meant that staff organization hardly got under way in the Bureau of Old Age

Benefits. Reliance upon the expert clause and friction with the Civil Service Commission over appointments and classification also acted as brakes on growth.

Nevertheless, the increase in personnel produced serious problems of office space. Originally housed in the new Labor Department Building, on Constitution Avenue, the board was compelled early in January to find additional quarters for one bureau in the neighboring Commerce Building and for others in the old Farm Credit Building some blocks away. During April, all but the legal staff were moved into the Old Labor Building, despite the confusion all through that month of a general structural renovation which proceeded simultaneously with occupation. These physical facility facts had important administrative consequences. The work of the administrative staff was rather seriously impeded, first, by the frequent moving, and second, by separation between the bureaus. It was particularly important at this stage of development when the staff members were new to one another and needed every encouragment to become quickly and intimately acquainted. The administrative inconvenience of this experience is epitomized by a remark of Frank Bane's to the effect that he would be quite willing to set up his establishment in a barn, if he could have everyone under the same roof.

During the second half of February the board reviewed its committee's report on regional and field organization and decided to set up twelve regional centers. For that purpose it first recruited a corps of executive assistants, organized a special in-service training course for them, and then lodged them in the various bureaus doing special tasks and learning more intimately the nature of the board's work until the regional directors were also chosen, and, after a very brief training, were ready for their regional assignments. On the first of May, seven regional directors were sent out to open up their offices. The other five were soon thereafter selected, so that by the middle of June all twelve were on the job with their executive assistants and waiting for the bureaus to assign special representatives to their establishments.

Irritation with the Civil Service Commission convinced the board that it would have to take into its own hands the application of the expert clause. But it was defeated in this purpose by its fear of criticism from congressional appropriation committees and by the commission's refusal to play a purely advisory role in this matter. Despite its capitulation in March to the commission, the problems of definitions and classification remained, leading to plenty of opportunity for recrimination even though a large proportion of the professional staffs of the technical bureaus were successfully qualified as experts.

Although the board's budget estimates for fiscal 1937, and supplemental estimates for the balance of the current 1936 fiscal year, had been transmitted to the Budget Bureau on March 17, 1936, it was nearly a month later before that agency was ready to hear the board. By the time Congress had held its hearings and was ready to adopt the appropriation bill it was past the middle of June. This delay in appropriation also contributed to retardation in the rate of staff growth, because the resources of the first appropriation were insufficient for the large organization which the board had projected for the last part of the fiscal year 1936.

Public Assistance

Public assistance laws and plans continued to arrive for approval, with a high point reached in March when twenty such plans (nine for aged, six for blind, and five for dependent children) were processed and certified for grants. Just as in the consideration of earlier applications, the board was disposed to accept makeshift devices for establishing legal conformity, and to fall back upon the persuasive powers of its executive director and its professional bureau staff to obtain proper personnel and standards of administration. When the first field staff for this bureau was sent to the states in March, it found many situations calling for drastic modification of personnel and practice. Even before the recruitment of such a staff special difficulties had erupted in some of the states, notably Ohio. There, under Governor Davey, the Eagles had assumed an important role in state and local welfare agencies and the bureau received complaints and charges of favoritism, inefficiency, and corruption.[20] When demand was made early in February that the state's plan be accepted, the board countered with a proposal for an administrative audit of the system. This was carried out by a team recruited partly from the staff and partly from outside professional people. The bureau was discovering in state after state during this period that the center of the administrative difficulties was in state and local personnel—the aspect of administration which Congress had attempted to insulate from board control.

During all this period the bureau continued to be shorthanded. The result was delayed field investigation, excessive hours for the staff, and congestion in the Washington office which caused irritation on the part of board, field staff, and state officials.

Some friction developed during the spring between the Bureau of Public Assistance and the Bureau of Accounts and Audits over the legal construction given by the recently appointed head of the latter bureau to the financial provisions controlling grants to the states. This discord was destined to increase when the first field auditors for public assistance expenditures got busy in the states. The first group of field auditors was sent out late in the spring, but the huge task of a detailed audit by the board, allegedly required by the

---

[20] The Eagles lodges in Ohio had been particularly active in supporting proposals to relieve the distress of the aged. They had backed Governor Davey, and after his election they took a major part in manning public assistance agencies.

Comptroller General, was hardly started by early summer because of the delay in securing a large and qualified auditing staff.

Unemployment Compensation

While some assistance to the state agencies in setting up an organization and in designing accounts, forms, and procedures was given by the technical staff of the bureau, the staff competent to aid in these administrative matters remained very small.

Some administrative advice was secreted in the process of reviewing and and approving the applications of the states for grants to defray administrative expenses. This job began shortly after the February appropriations became available. Special emphasis was placed on the review of grants, because in this program federal funds were defraying all the state administrative costs. Many of the requests for the two quarters in the period were drastically pruned. A policy of hunch, suspicion, and "horse sense" guided the activity, since there were no cost norms and very slight administrative knowledge to go by. Only one state had ever performed this function before, Wisconsin, and it had a law so different from the rest, and a state tradition of effective service so superior to most states, that its administrative needs could be only very rough guides for other states just beginning their organization. The first grants were made on March 4 and were for the District of Columbia, New Hampshire, and New York.

One unit in the bureau was created for the express purpose of coordination with the Employment Service. Crucial questions of articulation of state organization and grant funds were inescapable for the board and the United States Employment Service. But the small staff which studied these questions was unable to make headway, and late in the spring turned its attention to other matters.

Advice on legislation continued as a major activity of the bureau, which with its new model bills gave guidance to Mississippi, Indiana, Colorado, Ohio, and the few other states whose legislatures were in session during the spring. Already the experience of some of the states, particularly New Hampshire, had revealed the administrative complications implicit in the January and earlier drafts. Thus a new design for measuring benefit payments which would simplify the record collecting and bookkeeping process was under way as summer opened.

The board encouraged the administrators of the state unemployment insurance agencies to form a permanent organization with which it might hold periodical conferences. Since all were starting from scratch, these meetings (held about once a quarter) permitted the board and its staff to explain its own policies, talk over uncertainties, and feel the pulses of the states; and allowed the state people to exchange experiences, explore their interstate interests, and even upon occasion to unite more easily in criticism of the board's proposals.

During late spring, requests from some of the states for money to expand the placement staffs, in anticipation of the ultimate payment of benefits through employment offices, raised basic issues of the ultimate relation of the social security grants and the Wagner-Peyser grants. Raised also was the question of how the two federal agencies respectively concerned could work out an integrated and efficient program. Disavowing the creation of precedents, the board made grants and left the solution of these issues to the future.

Old Age Benefits

The expansion of the Bureau of Old Age Benefits proceeded at snail's pace. As late as March 15 there were only five employees, including the director and his associate. A man was borrowed from the Veterans' Administration (he ultimately joined the staff) to help plan the procedure for the claims unit. While the organization chart and outlines prepared during March for the submission of the budget estimates projected a staff, as of January 1, 1937, which would number some 4,300 permanent people and over 9,000 temporary additions for registration, this was avowed by the director to be a highly tentative plan. (Nothing approaching this size developed by that time.) It proposed for permanent organization four divisions—records, actuarial valuation, field service, and claims. As a matter of fact the board, in anticipating the fulfillment of these paper plans for this unit, requested nearly $15,-000,000 for its administrative expenses in fiscal 1937 (exclusive of a large fund for registration) which was more than half the total administrative request for the entire board job.

The absorption of Director Latimer in his railroad retirement obligations from April on not only led to a dispersion of control over the bureau but probably accounted for the slight staff development and, more important still, the difficulty of getting ready for the assignment of account numbers. Some preliminary decisions had been taken. There was a definite written agreement with the Treasury, perfected in April, by which the two agencies divided their responsibilities in registration, and in collecting and recording the information obtained from the taxpayers under Title VIII. By the middle of June it was also agreed that stamps would not be used and that the Treasury would assume full responsibility for complete tax collection.

The account number question, after much backing and filling, the board thought it had settled on February 14, only to find it necessary to make a further revision early in the summer. By June it had also decided (after much perturbation over possible political effects) what kind of identification token should be given each registered worker, and what information to request when the account number was assigned.

The job of preparing detailed plans for registration was turned over in March to the committee which had worked out the regional and field organization report. It enlisted the aid of representatives of other federal agencies, but found itself unable to go ahead until the board could make up its mind when to hold the registration. The board delayed, fearful of the reciprocal effects of registration and the 1936 election campaign. It finally decided in early June to hold the registration immediately after the November election. At the same time it determined to accelerate the recruitment of the bureau's permanent staff (including its field personnel) and get ready to conduct the registration with its own force, under a special coordinating officer appointed for this particular job. This decision came after months of fruitless talk and negotiation with the United States Employment Service, which the board and its committee hoped would consent to take over the registration job. But the director of that agency finally refused, and Chairman Winant spent the days immediately preceding his departure to Geneva, late in May, trying to employ a high officer in one of the big life insurance companies to supervise this important task for which the board itself would have to organize. That effort also failed.

PERIOD 3: EARLY SUMMER 1936 TO MARCH 1937

General Organization

By the end of June the board was amply financed (despite a 20 percent cut in its requests) for all its administrative tasks in the fiscal year ending June 30, 1937. But the rate of growth was still not very rapid during the summer, partly because of the continued influence of factors present in the preceding periods. Even though the regional offices had been opened, they had little to do pending the registration job after the elections. The three line bureaus were very reluctant to place field representatives in the regions, so that the accumulation of a full regional staff (aside from the Informational Service and lawyers assigned by the general counsel) was very slow until Christmas. Even as late as March 1937 permanent assignments by the Bureau of Unemployment Compensation were incomplete. Nevertheless it was clear by that time that the regional offices were going to play a very important part in the ultimate administration of the board's work.

In September the presidential election campaign burst in upon the board's organization with great force, when Governor Alf M. Landon, of Kansas, Republican candidate, opened up with a broadside attack upon the Social Security Act. Chairman Winant replied with a dramatic resignation that permitted him to rush to the open political defense of the system. When to Landon's barrage was added a payroll propaganda-stuffing campaign by employers, abetted by the Republican party chiefs, the board broke loose from the inhibitions that had largely paralyzed the work of its Informational Service since the AAA court decision. Leaflets and moving picture films intended to educate the people for the postelection registration effort were brought out of hiding and given to the public with a free hand. The board and its staff, in the last weeks before the election, vigorously cooperated with the Democratic party and the labor unions in getting out publicity in defense of the social security plan.

When the storm was over, the public was prepared for the mass registration that soon followed. This activity, which was at its peak during late November and December, coincided with a rush by the states to pass unemployment compensation laws before January 1, 1937, swamping the staff of the Bureau of Unemployment Compensation. That rush had been precipitated by a postelection Supreme Court decision validating the New York law, and by the refusal of the board to ask Congress to permit taxpayers in states without approved laws to obtain rebates on their Title II taxes for 1936.

Chairman Winant returned to the board under a special limited appointment to help it complete its organization, straighten out certain personnel snarls, and advise the President on fitting the functions of the Social Security Act into the administrative reorganization plan which was then being presented to Congress. By the close of this period, having accomplished his objectives, he had resigned, and Arthur Altmeyer was named chairman and became the dominant personality in shaping board administration. Murray Latimer was nominated by the President as the third member, but the Senate took no action. Its failure to confirm was reported to be due to the feeling that he was a Democrat. Since Altmeyer and Miles were Democrats, the approval of Latimer would violate the provision of the Social Security Act which limited representation from any one party to two members. The President later withdrew the Latimer nomination and substituted therefor the name of Professor George E. Bigge, a Republican, whose nomination was confirmed.

Difficulties with the Civil Service Commission over personnel matters continued. The board was dissatisfied with the results of the special examination for administrative officer for which it had asked in the summer, and which at the board's request was rushed through in the autumn. But the "expert" problem revived when the board sought that means of staff expansion for its field establishment, particularly for Old Age Benefits. The Civil Service Commission clinched its case by obtaining an opinion from the Comptroller General supporting its contention. A harvest of thistles from the expert clause was reaped by the board at the end of this period, when Senator Carter Glass secured the support of his colleagues in holding up the board's appropriation until the House would agree to a provision requiring senatorial confirmation of the appointments of higher-paid experts. That episode, which terminated in victory for the Senator, also led to propitiatory consultation ("clearance") with senators and congressmen before making field staff appointments.

Public Assistance

There was no need to urge states to adopt old age assistance legislation, and to some extent programs for aid to the blind and to dependent children were swept along with the aged-pension current. Even before the regular sessions of state legislatures which began in January 1937, there were forty-two states and the District of Columbia with approved plans for aid to the aged, and twenty-seven each with approved programs for aid to the blind and to dependent children. The problem of the bureau and the board was to obtain adequate state administration. This in turn was primarily a matter of professional nonpolitical personnel. Beginning in July 1936, when the board had to find its way through the troubled political waters engulfing state welfare administration in Kentucky and Illinois, the board committed itself to a requirement that states must incorporate in their administrative plans adequate standards of personnel for state and local staff. But when these were not lived up to (and it was easy for governors to agree to paper standards and then disregard them) certain minor sanctions were added to exhortation. But on no occasion did the board resort to its power to discontinue to certify the state for a grant.[21] Yet in many states there was doubtless considerable return from the skillful persuasive efforts of Frank Bane, Miss Jane Hoey, and her field officers.

The field staff of the bureau was increased gradually, until by early 1937 there were at least one, and often two, representatives in each of the twelve regions. Their concern with improving administration reached into methods as well as personnel, and in this respect their work became a teaching activity. For knowledge about the legality and honesty with which grants were actually given out to individual recipients, they had to wait for data turned up by the auditing crew, which grew slowly to large proportions but which was still too small to catch up with the enormous number of state payments. Friction which began in the spring of 1936 because auditors persisted in becoming independent administrative critics led to a shake-up in the Bureau of Accounts and Audits in January 1937, and to a new plan for articulating field auditing with public assistance field needs.

At the end of this period, with state legislatures reconsidering their old age assistance legislation, the acute problem of finding revenues with which to support the state and local share of these systems was becoming evident.

---

[21] The grant to North Carolina for the blind was revoked, but that was due to failure of the law to meet the requirements of the Social Security Act and not to inadequate administration.

Field agents theoretically had nothing to do with this question but actually they were ears for the board, which was seriously concerned with the prospect. This was all the more true because states like Colorado and California were boosting the pension for the aged above the $30 maximum, of which the federal government would pay half, and were prepared to pay flat-rate monthly pensions regardless of the financial need of the individual. What effect would this have on social work standards? What would this movement do, if it expanded, to the modest annuities under old age benefits, scheduled not to start until January 1942? With these questions the board was concerned, though it found no satisfying answers and took no action regarding them.

Unemployment Compensation

The associate director of the bureau directed staff studies, during the summer of 1936, to perfect revisions of the January model bill for unemployment compensation so as to overcome the complicated record and report procedure required by the earlier plans. This was perfected by November and ready for incorporation in the new legislation born during the special sessions of state legislatures at the close of the year. Many of the earlier laws were also revised in the sessions of early 1937. The legislative phase of the bureau's work was pretty well completed by the end of this period, because acceptable legislation seemed assured by that time in all but three states. It was fitting that late in March 1937 the Supreme Court should accept cases from Alabama which involved the constitutionality of that state's unemployment compensation law as well as of Titles VIII and IX of the Social Security Act.

So heavy were the demands for advice during December 1936, when state legislative activity was at its peak, that the bureau could not meet them with experienced advisors. It was a period of hectic and fatiguing activity, and there was the added difficulty, all through these winter sessions, that the Employment Service representatives were lobbying at cross-purposes with the representatives of the board concerning the character of a desirable state administrative organization. This conflict brought to a head the issue of reconciling the policies of the two federal agencies and the need to get ready for benefit payments early in 1938. The result was a signed agreement late in February 1937 between the board and the Secretary of Labor, creating a coordinating committee whose decisions would be binding upon the Employment Service and the Bureau of Unemployment Compensation.

The policies connected with the making of grants tended to increase the board's detailed control over expenditures of the state agencies. This irked the New York and Wisconsin officers, but most of the states appeared to welcome the tight rein with which the Washington bureau drove its budget control. The revised forms sent out by the board in December 1936 reflected this desire for increased budget restraint.

At the end of the period, however, the process of reviewing grant requests still lacked adequate methods. No one at Washington yet knew enough about the actual state administrative problems to do a sure-footed reviewing job. The urgent need was for a good field staff, but it was proving very difficult to find the right kind of men for this work.

Although the legal prohibitions in Title III concerning the board's relation to state personnel were identical with those in Title II, the bureau worked out a standard personnel classification and job specification plan for state unemployment compensation staff positions. This was made available to the states in the summer of 1936, but there were few requests. Aside from the few states with well-established general merit systems, there was slight interest at that time in the inauguration of formal merit systems for these new state units. Working through the Association of the State Unemployment Insurance Commissioners, the board tried to generate interest in personnel standards, but little response was secured until the March 1937 conference when a moderately enthusiastic endorsement of the merit system and methods of implementing it was obtained.

Old Age Benefits

The developments in the Bureau of Old Age Benefits during the summer are difficult to trace because, with the director almost completely absorbed by his duties with the Railroad Retirement Board, much of the planning for registration and staff organization was scattered among the board members, the field organization commitee, the coordinator, and individual members of the bureau staff, which was still at that time a mere skeleton organization.

Even as the board decided to undertake the registration task itself, grave doubts were voiced by the chairman of the field organization committee, who had been in active charge of plans for the enterprise, about whether personnel could be recruited in time. But the order was given to get ready for the permanent organization of the headquarters staff, 89 district offices, and enough of the primary and secondary branch offices so that the board would have 202 enumeration centers ready for operation in November.

Negotiations were started at about the same time for space in which to house the huge recording job and to process the application forms for the 26,000,000 accounts expected from the registration. There was no structure available in Washington, and after fruitless effort to obtain a new building, the board late in July leased three floors of a large warehouse structure in Baltimore. Here were installed in the autumn a great battery of IBM machines, and upwards of 2,300 machine operators and checkers trained to handle the processing job as rapidly as cards came in from the field.

During July, the Treasury agreed to furnish lists of employers compiled from its internal revenue files, which the board might use in making its preliminary census of the numbers and location of workers so that application forms could be quickly and accurately distributed in November. In August, a considerable force was set to work copying these names onto cards which the board ultimately did not use.

While the procedure for conducting the registration and operating the record office had been well projected by late July, the board's belief in its own ability to get ready to do the job was increasingly shaken. Conversations were started then with the Post Office Department, first to secure its cooperation and then to get it to take over the whole job. It was not until September 15 that, under prompting by the President, the Post Office acceded to the full wishes of the board. By that time the board had received the resignation of Director Latimer and appointed the former coordinator as head of the bureau. But it had chosen a Philadelphia businessman, Roger Evans, to supervise the registration job. He took over the task of perfecting with the Post Office the procedure and the preparatory instructions, while the Post Office organized itself to handle the job simultaneously with its Christmas mailing rush. At about the same time, agreement with the Treasury was reached on the use of its sanctions for obtaining employer cooperation, and on the regulations it would issue concerning tax and information returns under Title VIII. The final regulations required employers to file applications for identification numbers with the Post Office not later than November 21, and employees not later than December 5.

While the Post Office was perfecting its plans (largely using instructions written by Evans) the board's Informational Service was getting huge quantities of forms, leaflets, and posters printed and ready for distribution at every enumeration center. It was also distributing short movies that had been under preparation for some months. The regional offices were getting ready for active participation. The Personnel Division worked night and day to recruit the Baltimore record office employees. But the schedule of opening up field offices for the bureau, which the board had authorized on September 26, had to be drastically curtailed. It had called for a total of 554 field offices by January 1, 1937. It soon became evident that this number was not needed, but more important was the sheer inability to staff that number. The civil service register for administrative officers was not delivered to the board until December 2, over two weeks after registration had started. Although the Civil Service Commission loosened up the expert clause for finding field officers, it limited the number to about 100, and the board was compelled to assign members of its headquarters staff temporarily, to open up in time the 56 field offices in the cities where the Post Office maintained its central accounting offices. The latter were in charge of assigning the account numbers for all except the first-class post offices.

The Post Office began the distribution of employer application forms on November 16. In anticipation of this, each mail carrier had compiled a list of employers on his route to whom he would give forms. This was the basis for the later distribution of forms for employees, because each employer was asked to indicate the number of his employees. The registration process went through without apparent difficulty despite its coincidence with the Christmas postal rush, but it soon became evident that it could not be completed as quickly as expected. Accordingly, arrangements were made for the Post Office to continue the job. By February 15, 1937, a total 23,647,000 applications for account numbers from employees had been received.

So successful had the work been that the board induced the Railroad Retirement Board to let it and the Post Office handle the registration of the Retirement Board's clients. This was carried through after January 1, 1937.

The board had expected to take over the continuous account number assignment work by January 1, 1937, but its inability to expand its field staff made that impossible. On March 1, 1937, it had a total of only 100 field offices open, so that the Post Office agreed to continue to run this part of the board's work until June 30, and after that to assist on a curtailed basis. Because the board estimated that 3,000,000 new accounts a year would be opened up, the Post Office agreed to continue to have permanently available the application forms for both employers and employees.

The total cost of this work, for which the Post Office billed the Social Security Board in June, was $5,700,000. How good a job had been done was not really known at the end of this period. So far as the errors of copying in the typing centers were concerned, the work could be regarded as reasonably well done. But other errors, such as duplicate registration, failure to locate employees, etc., would not show up for some months.

Title II of the act entitled persons reaching age sixty-five after January 1, 1937, and the estates of insured wage earners dying after January 1, 1937, to 3.5 percent of their wages as lump-sum or death benefits, respectively. This was the provision which necessitated the creation of field offices before the payment of monthly benefits in 1942. The procedure and forms for filing claims and processing them had not been fully developed by January 1. The application forms were sent to the field in February, where officers reacted very critically because of the complicated and expensive requirements made necessary by the law. Actually only twenty-seven claims were filed, and eight had been approved by the Bureau of Old Age Benefits by the time this study ended (March 31, 1937).

The resignation of the head of the bureau shortly after the first of the year had precipitated a staff reorganization which was taking place during the closing weeks of this period. Friction within the bureau, which had been growing in the summer and became acute in the autumn and winter, had led to intervention by board members and finally to a staff shake-up. The assistant executive director, John J. Corson, was detailed to the bureau under the new head, LeRoy Hodges, to help perfect its structure and procedures.

It will be seen that during the eighteen months under review the Social Security Board made definite headway. It had created and staffed a nationwide organization. It had made large sums of money quickly available to the states for the needy aged, blind, and dependent child population. In fact, the sums for the aged alone estimated in February 1937 to be spent that year exceeded the amounts estimated by the Committee on Economic Security by some $30,000,000. The board had witnessed the enactment of unemployment compensation laws in all but three states and had played a very important part in helping the states to formulate these important measures. It had, with the aid of the Post Office and the Treasury, carried through the first important preliminary step for carrying out its duties as the administrator of a national system of old age annuities.

Its members were keenly aware that there were many difficulties ahead; but it was trying to complete and perfect its organization and methods to meet them.

.2.

PROBLEMS OF BUDGET AND
ORGANIZATIONAL STRUCTURE

PREPARING THE FIRST ESTIMATES AND
CRYSTALLIZING THE ORGANIZATION

ORGANIZATION CHART NO. 1 IS QUICKLY ALTERED

As soon as the Social Security Act was passed, Altmeyer had undertaken the work of preparing an appropriation estimate for the Third Deficiency Bill for the 74th Congress. In this he was aided by Merrill Murray and the rump staff of the Social Security Committee. To aid in thinking about administrative needs they prepared a chart of the proposed organization for the Social Security Board which was called chart no. 1 and was the basis upon which the board, when it was appointed, began its thinking about organization patterns and budget. It was necessary to plan these two phases simultaneously, because the estimates for administration had to be made on the basis of particular tasks for particular divisions, bureaus, or offices under the board. The District of Columbia unemployment compensation administration was immediately lopped from the chart and budget, because Congress had transferred this from the board to a special local commission.

Under this original organizational pattern the board work was to have been concentrated into four line divisions (plus the District of Columbia office) and four staff divisions. There were also to be nine regional offices reporting directly to the executive director. The line divisions were designated as Unemployment Compensation, Old Age Benefits, Aid to Dependent Children, and Old Age and Blind Assistance. The staff divisions were Legal, Research and Planning, Auditing, and Administration.

When our study began, three of the four line divisions were grouped into one unit called Federal-State Relations, and the fourth—the Division of Old Age Benefits—was not started except for the very recent employment of Elwood Way as assistant director. He had begun the discussion, with Seidemann, about account numbers for registering employees, and was trying to sketch out an organizational structure for the purpose of submitting budget estimates. Only the Legal Division was organized then, although certain of the tasks to be embraced by the Administrative Division were being directed or performed by Bane, Seidemann, Sorrels (of the Civil Service Commission's staff) and members of the board. It had already been decided to split the federal-state relations unit into two, one division to care for the administration of unemployment compensation and the other, the public assistance division, to supervise all the other grants-in-aid.

Seidemann said that one of his first efforts was to expand the number of regions contemplated from nine to twelve, and to add district and branch offices in order to provide for administering the old age benefits. He proposed one hundred district offices, one thousand full-time branch offices, and two thousand part-time branch offices. This scheme, with slight modifications, was later used in projecting the permanent organization, after Colonel E. J. McCormack and his regional establishment committee had carried out their investigations of regional and local organization.

Unknowns Make First Estimates Very Difficult

To estimate appropriation needs was exceedingly difficult at this time because of the total absence of experience. As Seidemann expressed it, he and his staff were making guesses and trying to guess high enough, for it would be just too bad if they should not include sufficient funds for operating the act, since there would be no other sources from which money could be obtained. He indicated that to estimate the costs of administering old age benefits was easier than estimating for public assistance and unemployment compensation, because the whole nation would be covered by the system of old age benefits, whereas in the case of the other functions no one could foresee how many states would pass laws and prepare administrative plans conformable with the terms of the Social Security Act. This statement was made the day before the completion of the first Seidemann budget.

Bane and the board also felt the insuperable difficulty of making accurate estimates, but Bane went even further in pointing out the impossibility of foreseeing with accuracy the magnitude of the first job in administering old age benefits, that of registering the employees and probably employers, and the consequent difficulty of knowing how many field offices or how large a staff to plan for. At the time he was speaking the board had not yet approved a state unemployment compensation act, although it was considering the Wisconsin act; it had decided against the Massachusetts law and had approved that of the District of Columbia. The few other states with unemployment insurance laws (Washington, Utah, California, New Hampshire, and Alabama) had not yet made formal applications for approval. While inquiries were being made concerning the eligibility of state laws for aid to the needy aged, to the blind, and to dependent children, no one could foresee in the middle of November how many such acts would be passed or how rapidly the legal obstacles to approval, which were imbedded in some of them, would be removed.

THE FIRST BUDGET REQUESTS FOR FISCAL 1936 AND 1937

Nevertheless, a letter was sent to the Acting Director of the Budget on November 23, 1935, covering the first complete estimates of appropriations required for the fiscal year ending June 30, 1937, and for the balance of the fiscal year ending June 30, 1936. These two estimates are summarized in their major purposes as follows:

	Balance of fiscal 1936	Fiscal year 1937
For administration		
Washington office	$ 1,826,618	$ 10,280,934
Field offices	619,941	6,800,936
	$ 2,446,559	$ 17,081,870
Registration for assignment of account numbers (nonrecurring)	3,522,050	5,274,230
Grants to states	52,000,000	157,000,000
	$57,968,609	$179,356,100

It was indicated in this estimate that in the fiscal year 1937 the board would employ in its Washington office as permanent staff 2,121.5 persons, of whom 1,059 would be used for administering the Bureau of Old Age Benefits. The permanent field staff was estimated at 3,398, of whom 2,800 would be assigned to the Bureau of Old Age Benefits. This would make a total permanent organization of 5,519.5. During the period of registration there were to be added 2,481.5 persons in the Washington and field organizations together. The summary pointed out the need for a large field organization, particularly during the first two years. It also emphasized the fact that the board hoped to

unify the national identification for Social Security account number with that of the states and with the perpetual inventory of unemployed persons now maintained by the U.S. Employment Service. If this can be accomplished it means that the account number assigned to an individual will serve the requirements of the several agencies and will facilitate the interchange of information. The use of such a system would also relieve the employer of reporting one number to the state agency and another to the federal agency for the same individual.

The chairman indicated the regret of the board that it had had no opportunity to present these estimates personally so that it might explain certain needed phases of the work which would not be evident on first consideration. The concluding sentence of the letter read: "I want to assure you, however, that these estimates have been prepared after careful analysis of our problems and that the amounts now requested are considered essential to the successful operation of the administration of the Social Security Act."

Drastic Changes in Organization Plans, November 22, 1935, Chart

Along with the letter of November 23 went a revised chart of organization, marked "tentative" and dated November 22, 1935. (We have called this chart no. 2, and the chart dated December 4, 1935, chart no. 3.) By this time very important changes had occurred in the plans for the board's structure: first, the office of coordinator made its appearance as a position outside the control of the executive director and reporting immediately to the board; second, the former divisions of aid to dependent children and old age and blind assistance were amalgamated into one bureau; third, a new unit called Informational Service was added to the staff; fourth, there had been a reallocation of functions between the auditing bureau and the business management (called in the earlier chart, administrative) division, by which the important functions of accounting and budget were transferred from the business to the auditing division, renamed Accounts and Audits.[1] The Informational Service was left blank as to functions, although the description contained in the covering letter of November 23 briefly indicated its work in general terms.

Above all these changes was the significant shift in title from *division* to *bureau*. This had been motivated chiefly by the need to offer higher salaries in order to secure the desired persons to head these units. By using the designation *bureau* larger salaries, it was hoped, could be obtained from the Civil Service Commission. It is significant, too, that in this revised chart the regional structure was changed. Twelve offices were proposed, each to have representation from the three line bureaus and the bureaus of Research and Statistics,

---

[1] *Statistics* replaced *planning* in the name of the new Bureau of Research and Statistics, as a genuflexion to the rising antipathy among businessmen toward the word *planning*.

Accounts and Audits, and Informational Service. The chart showed one hundred district offices under the Old Age Benefit Bureau and beneath them an unnumbered designation of branch offices. The latter were to maintain contact with employers and employees and to provide special services for the claims division of the bureau.

A week after this first letter of transmittal, a revised summary of the estimates for the fiscal year 1937 was sent to the Bureau of the Budget, together with detailed estimate sheets and supporting schedules. In the covering letter of November 30, it was pointed out that the tentative organization chart sent with the previous letter was being revised and that a copy of the revised chart would be submitted at the earliest opportunity. This revised estimate provided for a total appropriation for the fiscal year ending June 30, 1937, of $179,319,800, which was $36,300 less than the preliminary estimates transmitted the week before. The differences between these two estimates are therefore negligible. It was pointed out that $1,500,000 had been set aside for payment of death claims under section 203(a) and an identical sum for payments to aged individuals not qualified for benefits as provided in section 204(a), and the suggestion was further made that if the Secretary of the Treasury had already submitted estimates for these two items, this sum should be excluded from the board's estimates. A significant explanation of the large request for old age benefit purposes was contained in the statement that the major work of the fiscal year would fall between October 1, 1936, and June 30, 1937, and that the board expected to complete the task of assigning account numbers to 26,000,000 employees before January 1, 1937. It was stated that probably a maximum of 15,000 persons would be employed by the board during this first period, and that as soon as registration and assignment had been completed the temporary forces would be released, leaving a total permanent staff for all purposes of about 8,200 on June 30, 1937, of which number 5,200 would be in the field. The total estimate for registration costs given in this letter was $8,796,280, of which only $5,274,230 was asked in this estimate. It was the intention to request that the balance be incorporated in the First Deficiency Bill for the second half of fiscal 1936 "in order that we may initiate this phase of the work in the last half of the current fiscal year."

Certain items concerning salaries set up in this first proposed budget are of interest from the standpoint of organization. For example, it was proposed to pay the executive director and the coordinator $10,000 each. An item was included for an assistant executive director at $8,000 and two assistant coordinators at $6,500. The director of the Bureau of Old Age Benefits was classified for the same salary as the executive director. A general actuary was to be employed in that bureau with a compensation of $9,500, and a chief actuary at $8,000. The total amount proposed for the Bureau of Research and Statistics was $426,195. It is interesting to see how this item was expanded after Walton Hamilton was appointed and before the final estimates for 1937 were sent in to Congress. Similarly, it is interesting to notice that the amount proposed for the Informational Service totaled $131,756, which was a modest request compared with the sum asked four months later. The salary scale included in this estimate for regional officers showed $4,600 for the top officer and $3,800 for the assistant regional officer. This was another item which was markedly altered before the board's thinking about a regional organization was completed. The itemization for personnel services in the Bureau of Old Age Benefits was very abbreviated compared with that in the March budget after Latimer had worked the organization plans over thoroughly.

December Revision of Estimates for Fiscal 1936

The itemized November estimates were withdrawn by the board after the Bureau of the Budget indicated that it did not intend to itemize proposed expenditures for submission to Congress in the printed budget made up in December. One reason for this withdrawal was that during December the board appointed a number of important bureau heads, and with their assistance it was possible to make better estimates. Another reason was the decision reached on December 17, to submit alternative estimates for the balance of the current fiscal year (ending June 30, 1936) based on different hypotheses. The first hypothesis was that the Third Deficiency Bill (H.R. 9215, 74th Congress, 1st Session) would not be enacted into law. On that assumption, the amounts called for during the balance of the year totaled $63,307,127, divided as follows:

Administration	$ 2,510,847
Registration for the assignment of social security account numbers	8,796,280
Grants to the states	52,000,000

This figure for grants to states was based upon the assumption that they would become effective as of January 1, 1936, with the exception of grants under Title III (for unemployment insurance administration). These grants were further subdivided into the following items:

Old Age Assistance (Title I)	$30,000,000
Unemployment Compensation (Title III)	4,000,000
Aid to Dependent Children (Title IV)	15,000,000
Aid to the Blind (Title X)	3,000,000

This request represented a reduction of $29,500,000 from the amounts authorized for grants to the states in the first year by the Social Security Act.

In this letter the following commitment was made as to the time when registration of employees for old age benefit account numbers would be made. After indicating that this work should be completed before January 1, 1937, it said:

It is necessary, therefore, to complete assumption of this work prior to June 30, 1936, if possible, and it is probable that the maximum number of persons employed during the fiscal year 1936 may reach a total of 10,000. Approximately 6,650 of these employees are temporary force retained for that purpose and will be released. The permanent employees as of June 30, 1936, will approximate 3,350, of which 1,450 will be in Washington and 1,900 in the field.[2]

Another covering letter of the same date for another set of estimates was transmitted. This second document was based upon the hypothesis that the Third Deficiency Bill, which had not been passed in August 1935, would be enacted into law without change early in 1936. The total of this estimate for the balance of the fiscal year ending June 30, 1936, was $10,302,761, divided into two items: administration, $1,506,481, and registration for the assignment of account numbers, $8,796,280. In each letter it was stated that the board would sometime later submit for the appropriation bill a draft of proposed provisions deemed necessary for organizing and operating the board's activities. This second estimate was of course comparatively small, because of the assumption that items for grants to the states would be adopted as part of the Third Deficiency Bill.

On December 27, 1935, the chairman addressed two other letters to the Director of the Budget to supplement those of December 26. One contained an estimate of the amount required in case grants for public assistance and unemployment compensation should be made retroactive to July 1, 1935. It was pointed out that since the adoption by Congress of the Social Security Act, a number of states had passed legislation with the expectation that federal grants would be made to the states at a date "prior to the time when appropriations may not be made available by the Congress for the matching such grants without special provision. Such special provision is not required for Title III [unemployment compensation administration], since grants under that part of the law are now effective as of July 1, 1935, whenever given the appropriation." It was declared that the amounts which the Social Security Act authorized for the first year would be insufficient to meet the requirements, if all grants were made retroactive to July 1, 1935. The board was careful to indicate that it was making no recommendation concerning retroactive grants, merely submitting the information so that the President would

[2] It is interesting to compare this projection of speed of organization with the facts when June 30, 1936, arrived. By then there were 748 employees in the entire establishment.

know the sums required to match state funds on the basis of the July 1 date. The itemization in this letter was as follows:

Old Age Assistance (Title I)	$40,000,000
Unemployment Compensation (Title III)	6,675,000
Aid to Dependent Children (Title IV)	20,000,000
Aid to the Blind (Title X)	3,510,000
	$70,185,000

The other letter of December 27 was similar in form, but presented data based upon the assumption that Congress might make grants to the states retroactive as of October 1, 1935. Here the required amounts were as follows:

Old Age Assistance (Title I)	$34,000,000
Unemployment Compensation (Title III)	4,925,000
Aid to Dependent Children (Title IV)	17,250,000
Aid to the Blind (Title X)	3,500,000
	$59,675,000

The revisions made by the board did not cover the proposed estimates for the fiscal year ending June 30, 1937, which were allowed to stand as submitted on November 30. There was transmitted, however, a revised description in the justification sheets of the various units of the board's organization. These had been drafted with the cooperation of the new bureau heads and were nearly as complete as those which accompanied the budget sheets submitted later on March 17, 1936, except for Informational Service and the regional establishment.

ACTION BY THE BUREAU OF THE BUDGET AND THE PRESIDENT

On January 6 Seidemann submitted to Chairman Winant information he had just received about the action of the budget bureau on the board's estimates for the balance of fiscal 1936. According to him, the budget bureau on January 4 had submitted to Congress a total estimate of appropriations for that year of $34,910,000, or a reduction of $28,307,000 from the $63,307,000 requested by the board.[3] The reductions were distributed as follows:

Grants-in-aid	$18,090,000
Administration	1,511,000
Registration	8,796,000
	$28,397,000

[3] Seidemann's tabulation contained an adding error of $90,000.

This last item represented an entire deletion of the sum requested. The budget bureau's proposal was $27,215,000 less than the amounts proposed in the Third Deficiency Bill of the preceding year. Apparently, the Bureau of the Budget made its cuts without discussing with the board the effect of its reductions on any particular item.[4]

On January 8, the day following the decision invalidating the Agricultural Adjustment Act, Chairman Winant and Daniel Bell, Director of the Bureau of the Budget, had an interview with President Roosevelt about the proposed appropriations for the Social Security Board. Winant presented to the President the problems connected with the amounts asked for grants. These figures were based upon the latest information accumulated by the board of what the states proposed to spend for public assistance purposes. They were much higher than the figures for the first year's operation included in the Social Security Act. However, that law intended that the federal government should match the grants which the states were willing to make for these purposes. It had been impossible to anticipate correctly what would be required in the way of federal funds until state intentions were known. It was agreed that the President would authorize Winant to explain to the congressional appropriations committee the reasons for this request which the board had made. He was also to be permitted to explain the administrative needs of the board and the justification for the sums requested to get so large an organization started. Winant agreed to drop out the item, included in the proposed 1936 budget, for registering account numbers for old age benefits. It will be recalled that the total sum for this purpose had been split between the estimates for 1936 and those for 1937. But in view of the special doubt thrown by the Supreme Court's decision of the preceding day upon the validity of old age benefits, Winant thought that this item should be withdrawn until the President and his advisors should decide what their strategy with reference to the Court's decision would be. At this meeting with the President and the Director of the Budget it was also agreed that the estimates for fiscal 1937 would be withheld until February. A bill would then be drafted and pushed containing not only the appropriations for the fiscal year ending June 30, 1937, but also a supplemental grant for the balance of fiscal 1936 in addition to the estimates for that year then being transmitted to Congress by the President. This supplemental grant was to be for general administrative purposes and for the beginning of registration for old age benefits.

[4] This is the statement made by Seidemann's assistant, Clearman, in a note dated January 9, 1936, attached to a table showing the sums allowed by the budget bureau for grants-in-aid.

The Board Is Heard by the House Committee

Seidemann arranged a meeting between the board and the clerk of the House Committee on Appropriations, Mr. Shields, late in December, in order to plan in advance the strategy of the congressional hearings. The hearings before the House committee were set for January 8. In anticipation of them, a table was prepared showing the supplemental amounts needed for the fiscal year ending June 30, 1936, provided the deficiency estimate submitted to Congress by the Bureau of the Budget on January 4 should be embodied in an appropriation act and modified as now recommended by the board. This table indicated that an additional sum of $1,130,799 would be needed for administration in the Washington offices, and for the field offices a total sum of $375,682, or a grand total for administration of $1,506,481. This would be in addition to the $1,000,000 retained in the Bureau of the Budget's proposals for board administration. To meet the problem of money to match state funds and for state unemployment compensation administration, the board estimated that $18,090,000 more would have to be appropriated before the 1936 fiscal year expired. These items were distributed as follows:

Old Age Assistance (Title I)	$ 5,340,000
Unemployment Compensation Administration (Title III)	1,750,000
Aid to Dependent Children (Title IV)	10,000,000
Aid to the Blind (Title X)	1,000,000

The total supplementary sum was thus estimated by the board at $19,596,481.

On January 9, the House Subcommittee on Appropriations heard the board defend its request and explain its work. Curiously enough, although there were one or two facetious remarks about the Supreme Court decision of three days before, no serious attention was paid to the question of the constitutionality of the board's functions. Instead, the discussion assumed that the work of the Social Security Board would go forward. Not a single member of the House committee raised the issue of constitutionality as an objection to appropriating the sums asked. The basis on which the committee reached its conclusions about sums for social security was a percentage multiplication of the items that had been included in the original Third Deficiency Bill of the preceding session. The committee said in effect, you have five months in 1936 to go, so we will take five-twelfths of the items in the Third Deficiency Bill and allow you that, except for administration. They left intact the $1,000,000 for administration, on the theory that as a new organization the board needed extra money to get started. The committee did not recognize the validity of the estimates made by the board for grants to the states, even though these were based upon the states' own figures as to intended expenditures for public assistance purposes, and even though the principle declared by the Social Security Act was that of matching state funds. They did agree, however, that if the funds of the board for these purposes began to run out before the fiscal year was up, the board could bring in a deficiency request for $10,000,-000 more. Table 1, on page 48, gives the summary comparisons between the sums allowed by Congress, those in the President's budget, and those in the earlier deficiency bill.

During the House committee hearings Winant and Altmeyer explained that the board had arrived at the estimates submitted the preceding summer for the Third Deficiency Bill without staff assistance and that, as a matter of fact, the estimates had been submitted before the board had had a formal meeting, although its members had been appointed. These were really the estimates which the Bureau of the Budget had been considering in its recommendations at this time.

Very early in the hearings, while discussing the item for administrative expenses, it was brought out that the board's request for $2,110,500 had not been seriously studied by the Bureau of the Budget, which had instead simply retained the old figure of $1,000,000 in the Third Deficiency Bill, in order, as Seidemann put it, "to give us the money immediately." The board had the understanding with the budget bureau that it could come to the bureau again, which would then make a recommendation to the appropriations committee.

Another important fact elicited in the hearings was the inaccuracy of the budget bureau's recommendation for grants-in-aid to the states. Here, again, they had simply used the old deficiency bill estimates, which had been prepared before there was any real knowledge of what the states proposed to do. The board had discovered since beginning operations that the sum for old age assistance should be increased and likewise the amount for aid to the blind and for unemployment compensation administration, but that the amount recommended for aid to dependent children could be cut to less than half. These modifications were based upon requests received from the states. The board's judgment of needs was based upon the fact that it had by January 1 actually approved thirteen state plans for public assistance, and twelve more were then pending. It was thus in a position to estimate the future in terms of what twenty-five states proposed to do. But it was apparently not easy to make the committee understand why the board's new estimates were so different.

Altmeyer's testimony made it clear that the figure for unemployment compensation administration was based on a percentage (for the beginning years, 10 percent) of the total amount expected to be collected by the federal government under Title IX of the Social Security Act.[5]

In justifying the request for administrative expenses as against the original million-dollar item, Altmeyer explained that the increase was due to his failure

---

[5] *Second Hearing, Supp. Appr. Bill for 1936*, p. 110.

TABLE 1 *Estimates and Appropriations for the Social Security Board, Fiscal 1936*

	Amounts included in H. R. 9215 as it failed Senate, 74th Congress, 1st Session	Revised budget estimates submitted to 74th Congress, 2d Session	Amounts recommended in revised estimates accompanying bill	Increase or decrease, in accompanying bill, from budget estimate	Increase or decrease, in accompanying bill, from H. R. 9215
Salaries and expenses	$ 1,000,000	$ 1,000,000	$ 1,000,000		
Grants to states for old age assistance	37,312,500	20,700,000	24,660,000	+$3,960,000	−$12,652,500
Grants to states for unemployment compensation administration	3,000,000	1,660,000	2,250,000	+590,000	−750,000
Grants to states for aid to dependent children	18,562,500	10,300,000	5,000,000	−5,300,000	−13,562,500
Grants to states for aid to the blind	2,250,000	1,250,000	2,000,000	+750,000	−250,000
Total	$62,125,000	$34,910,000	$34,910,000		−$27,215,000

to see in the preceding summer how rapidly the board would get into the old age benefit work, and to his underestimate of the number of regional offices that would be required. The appropriations committee had difficulty following his argument because it did not clearly understand the difference between old age benefits and old age assistance. Altmeyer also explained the item covering the payment of claims under old age benefits which would have to start on January 1, 1937, or as soon as the taxes under Title VIII became effective. He said that these would number about a thousand a day. Part of his explanation is contained in the following statement:

The character of those claims is this: When a man has reached the age of sixty-five at any time before 1942, who has not earned $2,000 or more since January 1, 1937, he is not eligible for a benefit in 1942 and he gets a refund on the payments he has made. If he dies prior to 1942, his estate gets a refund. So that there are these numerous small claims but aggregating in the total, if I recall, about $2,000,000.

At this point Mr. Seidemann interjected, "$3,000,000."

It was also brought out during his testimony that no member of the board had up to that date, January 8, received any salary for his services, despite the fact that Miles had qualified in September 1935, Winant on October 14, and Altmeyer on October 16, and despite the further fact that all three had been on the job since early in September and had had meetings from that time forward. They were asking in the appropriation act the right to pay their salaries from the time at which they had officially assumed their duties.

The committee seemed to be much impressed with the problem of the vast record system required for old age benefit administration. Mr. Taber was especially concerned with seeing that the Treasury and the board did not set up a complete duplication of records. The board, through Chairman Winant, stated very emphatically its intention to work out a cooperative arrangement with the Treasury by which the two agencies could use much of the same data and avoid undue duplication.

THE FIRST APPROPRIATION ACT, UNEMPLOYMENT COMPENSATION NOT RETROACTIVE

On February 9, 1936, Congress passed the deficiency bill (P.L. 440, 74th Cong.) containing the fiscal 1936 appropriations for the board. Two days later the President signed the bill, which made money available at once for the board's needs. The act made the grants-in-aid to the states for public assistance purposes available from February 1, 1936. Nothing being said, however, about the grants under Title III (unemployment compensation), the board had assumed that the provisions of the Social Security Act would govern and that grants for unemployment compensation administration in the states might begin with July 1, 1935. It had not wanted to set forth a stipulation of this sort in the appropriation bill lest it call attention to this retroactive feature, and so it chose the easier course of silence. However, no sooner was the bill passed than the question was raised: Are these funds for unemployment compensation administration available for grants to states for such administration on July 1, 1935, and before the passage of the act? Wilbur J. Cohen, who was present during the drafting of the amendments to the Third Deficiency Bill which were incorporated in this new appropriation act, called attention to the failure of the amendments of Leonard J. Calhoun, assistant general counsel, to make clear provision for payments back to July 1935. But the board decided to take a chance. On the basis of the provision in the Social Security Act and of the conversations that had gone on with the states, Cohen felt there was a moral obligation to pay from that earlier date.

To clarify this point, the board solicited and secured a ruling from Comptroller General McCarl, who on February 28 released a ruling which stated in part:

The amount appropriated for grants to states to assist them in the administration of their unemployment compensation laws is available for such uses *only* *prospectively* from the date of appropriation, February 11, 1936, and not for reimbursing the states for expenditures theretofore made or for liquidating obligations theretofore incurred.

Thus came the ironic conclusion that the board's caution made moneys for unemployment compensation administration available eleven days later than moneys for public assistance administration.[6]

Further Changes in Organization Plans, December 1935

Let us go back to the matter of general organization. The final pattern, in the large, had been completed during early December. In the chart approved by the board on December 4, the functions of the Informational Service were filled out, and included the answering of "inquiries of employers in regard to their functions and obligations," the acquainting of "the twenty-six million beneficiaries with their rights and the reasons for payments," the education of the general public, the issuance of publications, and the operation of a library. This list of functions was increased at the expense of the Bureau of Business Management, or, as it was called in chart no. 1, the Administrative Division. As conceived in the first plan, publications and library were lodged in that division. The title of the Informational Service had originally been intended

[6] For the sequel to this in the June 1936 appropriations act see pp. 63-64ff. below.

to read *Publicity,* but was changed as part of the effort to obtain a higher salary grade for the man to be placed in charge of that unit. The board had discovered that it could not secure the minimum salary of $8,000 it felt it required for the chief of that bureau, or $6,500 for his first assistant, unless something were done to distinguish the work of this unit from the usual publicity work found in other federal agencies. The care of the library might more appropriately have been given to the Bureau of Research and Statistics, had it not been for the need to boost the salaries of the chiefs of the Informational Service. Even this series of maneuvers was not sufficient to secure the desired objective, so that when Resnick came on the job and classification sheets for his position were being prepared, it was found expedient to include additional duties not listed on the chart. Among these was the preparation of rules and regulations issued by the bureaus and the board.[7]

The effect of the various reallotments of internal functions led ultimately to the resignation of James V. Bennett from the headship of the Bureau of Business Management. When Bennett accepted the appointment at the urging of Bane, he had understood that he would become the chief administrative officer of the board. He doubtless had in mind the scope indicated in the first chart as embraced under the Administrative Division. He had scarcely accepted service with the board before vigorous discussion occurred over the location of the budget function. Seidemann, with the support of Chairman Winant, held out for the moving of the budget office from Business Management to Accounts and Audits. Seidemann's reason was given in an interview of December 6, and was substantially as follows:

The business manager's is merely a housekeeping job. The business manager will find space, purchase supplies, etc., and control personnel. He will not be a general manager coordinating the work of the staff on behalf of the executive director. The budget ought to be consolidated with the accounting work, because the operation of the budget data for the administration of the budget after the appropriation bill has been passed will be hampered unless the accounting is under the same control. The accounting forms determine the accessibility of budget information and if the two are separate there will be constant friction. This has been the experience of states which have made a separation of these two functions.

The chairman thoroughly approved of Seidemann's analysis and was joined by Altmeyer, so that despite the contrary view entertained by Bane and Bennett, the board lifted the budget job from Business Management and gave it to Accounts and Audits. Bennett was not convinced by this action

---

[7] See the discussion in chapter 7 under "Personnel Management Problems: The Expert Clause."

and showed McKinley a number of organization charts of other federal services, none of which made this combination of auditing and budgeting. He felt that the man who made up the budget must be in a position to convince each division or bureau of the validity of his judgments. To do this he must know their tasks rather intimately and in a certain sense act as a general manager for them. This he believed was not the job of an auditing and accounting section. Bennett at this time (December 20) indicated that the board did not appear to know yet whether it was going to make the Business Management Bureau a mere service bureau or a real bureau of business management, acting for the executive director in coordinating the administrative activities of all the bureaus. In accepting Seidemann's proposal in regard to the budgeting function, it appeared to have fallen into the former choice.

REVISING AND DEFENDING THE
1937 BUDGET ESTIMATES

Even before the deficiency bill was passed on February 9, 1936, the coordinator and his assistant, Clearman, were at work again on the revision of the board's appropriation request for the fiscal year ending June 30, 1937, plus the supplemental budget needs for the rest of fiscal 1936. During the fourth week in January, he sent out requests to each bureau head to revise his estimate of needs and to plot his administrative requirements upon a month-to-month basis.

By this time, all of the bureau heads except one had come on the job and, with more staff aiding them, were in a better position to know what their needs would be than they had been early in November, when Seidemann's estimates for fiscal 1937 were first prepared. The coordinator was hopeful that the Bureau of the Budget would act rapidly and present a bill in which both the 1937 estimates and the supplementary items for 1936 would be incorporated. He felt that the $1,000,000 which had been allowed by the House Appropriations Committee for administrative expenses in fiscal 1936 would be utterly inadequate if the board's organization proceeded as rapidly as it ought. Therefore supplemental funds for the last of fiscal 1936 would have to be granted the board. This was his view on January 29. A month later the estimates were still unfinished because the bureau heads were so slow in getting information to him. In some cases he had been compelled to go ahead and construct the budget estimates himself. Moreover, the work on the administrative charts showing the detailed anticipated organization which the bureaus had been asked to prepare had not been completed.

THE NATURE OF THE MARCH 17, 1936, ESTIMATES

It was not until March 17 that the estimates for fiscal 1937 and the supplemental estimates for fiscal 1936 (based on the needs from April 1 to June 30) were ready for the Bureau of the Budget. On that day the board transmitted to the bureau a set of documents showing the detailed estimates, plus a new set of justification sheets. This new financial document combined the needs for both years into one proposal, and it was intended that moneys appropriated for either year might be used in the other, so as to give more flexibility. The covering letter referred delicately to the oral understanding reached at the time of the board's hearings before the House Appropriations Committee concerning supplemental estimates for 1936. The following statement summarizes the strategy in presenting these new figures:

On the summary sheet of Form 3a showing the totals for each of the two fiscal years, the amount appropriated in the Third Deficiency Bill is subtracted from the estimate for 1936 showing a balance of $3,055,292. This amount is added to the amount for the fiscal year ending June 30, 1937, in the first column, giving the total additional amount needed for 1936-37, which we recommend be appropriated in one lump sum for the fiscal year ending June 30, 1937, and that the total amount be made immediately available upon passage of the bill, and further that the amount appropriated for "registration and assignment of Social Security account numbers" remain available until expended for the registration of employers and employees, or initial wage records of persons entitled to benefits under Title II of the Social Security Act are set up to receive periodical entries of wages.

The requests for the three main subdivisions were as follows:

	1937	*1936*
Administration	$ 20,386,496	$ 2,293,836
Registration and assignment of account numbers	14,082,984	1,761,456
Grants to the states	157,000,000	33,910,000
	$191,469,480	$37,965,292

Grand total for both years: $229,434,772, less the amount appropriated in the Deficiency Act (P. L. 440, 74th Cong.) $34,910,000.

Total additional appropriation request for 1937 and 1936: $194,524,772.

This combined request was $7,917,925 less than the revised total of the original estimates sent in during November and December of 1936. The difference was due to certain changes which are indicated as follows:

Decreases	
Grants to states	$18,090,000
Federal old age benefit claims	3,000,000
	$21,090,000

Increases
Administration	$ 6,123,915
Registration—social security account numbers	7,048,160
	$13,172,075
Net decrease	$ 7,917,925

The covering letter explained the administrative increase by pointing out that estimates for 1937 had been increased along the line, while there had been slight decreases in the anticipated requirements for 1936. It pointed out that the new estimates had received the benefit of the more accurate preparation made possible by the appointment of heads for all the bureaus. It noted that the largest increase was for the Bureau of Old Age Benefits and explained this on the ground that:

1. The Social Security Board, rather than the Treasury, is to furnish all information report forms.

2. The decision has been arrived at that the Board will attempt to distribute to all persons affected, literature on the operation and terms of Title II of the Social Security Act. These two items account for the increase in printing costs.

3. The division of functions as between the Bureau of Internal Revenue and the Board, has placed certain burdens upon the Board, particularly in the way of checking information returns which had not been anticipated at the time of the original submission.

4. The original budget made inadequate allowance for travel expense and did not take into account the fact that agents of the Board would necessarily, during the initial stages, have to investigate and perhaps initiate a large number of claims.

5. The decision has been reached that prior to placing men in the field for duty beginning on January 1, 1937, they will be called in three to four months in advance of that date for a period of intensive training.

As a matter of fact, the general increase in estimates for administrative expenses was partly the direct result of Seidemann's desire to boost the figures, as shown by his repeated requests to bureau heads to increase their estimates. This fact contributed directly to the large sums asked for by the Bureau of Informational Service and the Bureau of Research and Statistics. It is probable that this campaign for estimate padding which Seidemann and Clearman carried on was facilitated by the inattention of the bureau heads to the budget-making job. In a number of bureaus a subordinate worked with Clearman, with little supervision by the bureau head. The absorption of the bureau directors in the job of getting their organization set up probably explains this neglect.

The large increases in the figures for registration expenses were said to be due to the board's agreement with the Treasury to register employers, of whom there were estimated to be from two to three million. It had earlier been assumed that there was already available in the Treasury an adequate list of employers and that any expenses required to complete it would be borne by the Treasury. The board indicated that the best information from other government agencies argued for the work of registration to be done by the board itself, "despite the fact that some organizations already possess a field staff which might conceivably have been used." The other cause of the large increase in this item was the decision on the part of the board to couple with registration the effort to give out literature to employees advising them of their rights and how they might protect themselves under the Social Security Act.

The covering letter pointed out that these new figures provided for the equivalent of 11,191.9 full-time positions with the board for the fiscal year ending June 30, 1937, and 1,360.8 for the fiscal year ending June 30, 1936; that there would probably be a maximum of 15,000 persons employed during the registration period, but that when this was completed the release of temporary employees would leave a permanent staff at the end of the fiscal year 1937 of 9,400, of whom 5,400 would be in the field. Since it was impossible to predict in advance how fast the work of registration could be carried out, emphasis was placed upon the need for including the 1936 and 1937 sums in one lump appropriation to be made immediately available. The board's intention to secure the services of the U.S. Employment Service and the National Reemployment Service for the registration task was also indicated.

The President's Vacation Causes Delay
Leading to Important Changes in April 14 Estimates

Hearings on this request were held before the Bureau of the Budget on March 18th. It was impossible, however, to discuss these estimates with the President before his vacation during the latter half of March, and it was approximately a month later before the board's needs were considered by the President and the Bureau of the Budget. As a consequence of this delay, it became desirable to submit another revision that would reflect changes in the board's situation wrought by this lapse of time. In addition, the board had modified some of its former judgments on the language which ought to be included in the appropriation bill, particularly that relating to certain proposed exemptions from the civil service and classification acts. In the documents submitted to Budget Director Bell on March 17, there had been included a revision of certain language in the appropriation bill which was of considerable importance and which is quoted below:

Salaries and expenses, Social Security Board.

For three Board members and other personal services in the District of Columbia and in the field including field offices, and all other authorized and necessary administrative expenses of the Social Security Board . . . including attorneys, experts, an Executive Director, a Coordinator, a General Counsel, a Chief Actuary, and heads of Bureaus established by the Board, all of whom may be appointed without regard to the Civil Service Laws and their compensation may be fixed without regard to the Classification Act of 1923 as amended; provided, that with the exception of not to exceed five positions, the compensation so fixed shall not exceed the rates of compensation determined by the Board to be prescribed for comparable duties by the Classification Act of 1923 as amended and in no event may the compensation of any position exceed the compensation authorized for members of the Board . . .

This provision was an echo from the controversy with the Civil Service Commission, which was then at its height and had left the board feeling very sore.

By the time the revised figures of April 14 were sent to the budget bureau, it was becoming increasingly evident that the rate of expansion of the board's staff was very much slower than had been expected. Moreover, the uncertainty of securing additional funds had been a contributing factor to the slowing down of the expansion, for it became obvious that new moneys for the board's anticipated use on April 1 would not be available until sometime in May. For this reason if for no other, a revised set of figures was required for the balance of fiscal 1936. In the covering letter for the new figures, Acting Chairman Altmeyer pointed out that since writing the letter of March 17 a new item in the cost of administering the act had been discovered, namely,

that in making payments on death under Title II where there is no estate it may be necessary to consider creditors' claims, and further, that in some cases creditors may be the persons to whom payments must be made under the law of the state where the individual was domiciled at the time of his death.

For this newly discovered task a new item of $1,544,765 was included. He further stated that an opinion from the Comptroller General about this presumed function of the board was being requested, and that in case Congress should pass amendments simplifying the administration of Title II the board would ask for the elimination of this increase. The new total increased the anticipated 1937 expenditures for administration to $21,931,261. No change was proposed in the figures for registration or for grants to the states in that year, nor in the supplemental estimates for fiscal 1936.

Between March 17 and April 14 a number of other facts had developed which were of concern to the budget-making process. One of the most important of these was the discovery that the estimates formulated by the Bureau of Public Assistance for grants-in-aid to the states for the balance of fiscal 1936 had been made up with an oversight of the last quarter. Winant was reluctant to go back to the budget bureau and confess this error, but suggested instead that the language of the appropriation bill be changed by inserting a sentence which would make available the total grant money for both 1936 and 1937. Seidemann argued that while this could be done, no one knew when the next deficiency bill would go up to Congress, and if, as was very likely, it should not be passed until some time in June, the board could approve allowances only to the extent of the balance on hand. Payments that it would ordinarily make the first of April or shortly thereafter would have to be held in abeyance until the deficiency bill should be passed. He also raised the question as to whether or not the money for fiscal 1937, if made available in fiscal 1936 also, would carry the board until it could get a deficiency bill through, say, by the middle of February, 1937. It was finally agreed that Seidemann should try to secure from Jones of the Bureau of the Budget the insertion of a sentence which would make this money available in 1936 as well as in 1937. This was following the pattern adopted for administrative funds.

During this same period (between March 17 and April 14) certain other items were reconsidered or amplified by more data. One of these had to do with the proposed creation as a unit outside of the executive director's office of a position entitled Director of Agencies, at a salary of $6,500, with a headquarters staff of seven other persons and a field staff of assistants to oversee the regional work. When the board questioned this item, Seidemann explained that in the future Bane would not be able to handle the regional offices in addition to his other work, and so this office had been created to undertake that responsibility. Both Altmeyer and Winant objected to this setup, especially to the direct implication of a large special staff in Washington supervising the regional directors in the field. Altmeyer vigorously opposed the idea of "superregional" offices located in Chicago, San Francisco, and Washington. Seidemann admitted that this section in the estimates had been set up as an afterthought. He confessed that it was wrong, and that the Bureau of the Budget should now be advised to include this item in the office of the board which also embraced the items for executive director and coordinator. In view of the fact that this section of the appropriation estimates had been set forth separately when the board sent its estimates on to the Director of the Budget in March and that the justification sheet for this office had described it rather clearly, it is difficult to understand how the board permitted it to get by. The most charitable explanation is that the board's thinking about the regional setup underwent rapid modification between February and the middle of April and that Seidemann and Clearman, in working out the budget, did not keep pace with these changes of view, and so no one had caught this discrepancy until after March 17.

At the board meeting when the discussion just summarized occurred

(March 24) Winant indicated his anxiety about the slow rate at which the board's staff was being enlarged. He pointed out that the board was spending large sums of money for grants-in-aid to the states through the public assistance and unemployment compensation bureaus, and questioned whether it had sufficient people in its auditing bureau to check these expenditures. He felt that the three operating bureaus should be asked to work out charts of expansion to aid the other service bureaus in working out expansion charts of their organization. The board therefore agreed that (1) each bureau chief should prepare a chart of the personnel anticipated for his organization, and (2) each bureau chief should prepare a flow chart indicating at monthly intervals the number of persons he contemplated employing in the various grades, and plotting this out for the next six months, or until January 1937. It was felt that upon this basis the personnel officer, Albert Aronson, could know in advance what personnel he must provide for. It would also be possible for the board to keep a chart of its actual accomplishments in persons employed which it could compare with the charts anticipating the future. The board asked that these projections be made up for submission on April 2. The head of each bureau was asked to send in a revision of his justification sheets on a unified pattern so that there would be consistency in the document when it was finally filed with the Budget Director. Apparently the Budget Director had cautioned the board to fit its revised budget into the one submitted in March, rather than make up a wholly new document.

In the interval between March 17 and April 14, a number of discussions were held with the legal staff over the newly discovered costs of administering section 205 under Title II, and the proposed increase of more than $1,500,000 to take care of it. The board was rather concerned over the fact that this discovery had come too late for mention in the original estimates submitted in March. Altmeyer was disposed for a time to let the matter go. Instead, he suggested requesting the opinion of the Comptroller General, and advising the Bureau of the Budget and the Appropriations Committee that in case his opinion required this new duty the board would have to put in a supplemental estimate. The discussion on April 11 indicated some feeling that there was enough velvet in the estimates as they stood to take care of any such additional expense if necessary. But Seidemann, quoting Latimer, argued that a supplemental estimate should be made. The result was that the board sent a letter to the Bureau of the Budget making the additional request.

HEARINGS BEFORE THE HOUSE COMMITTEE

On April 22, the board received notice that the House Appropriations Committee would hear the board's estimates at 2:45 the following afternoon, and sent a hurried call to all the chiefs of staff to meet with the board on the morning of April 23 to talk over the strategy to be used. In opening this meeting, Chairman Winant announced that he wanted every bureau director to be present to defend his own estimate, but that since the Budget Director had made certain eliminations, the coordinator should go through the estimates as they would be presented to the House committee. Various details in the estimates were threshed out and suggestions for changes made, but the chairman emphasized that the meeting should stick to the appropriation bill as submitted and justify it without proposing changes. It was agreed that the chairman would make the opening statement, but when it was proposed that Altmeyer would handle the $23,000,000 item for administrative expenses, he balked, saying he could not defend it because he did not have enough information to justify the additional $2,292,000 for the rest of fiscal 1936, and that he thought the facts presented in the estimates did not show the need for this amount of money. It was agreed that the chairman would point out in his opening statement that nearly $1,500,000 could be saved by amending section 205 so as to simplify the payment of benefit claims. It was finally agreed not to mention the possibility that the estimates for registering employees or for setting up the recording system for old age benefits might be too high. Both Altmeyer and Miles wanted to admit to the committee that the estimate of $1,293,000 for administrative expenses for the rest of fiscal 1936 was no longer accurate because it had been predicated upon availability of those funds by April 1, and the delay now made it excessive, so that only a part of it would be needed. Altmeyer also insisted that the item of $3,000,000 for registering employers was too high. But Seidemann disagreed with him. Clearman was called into the meeting, and he advised against admitting that the board might not need all the money requested in the 1936 budget. He said that his conversations with the bureau directors since they submitted their estimates had shown that most of them had underestimated what they would need for travel, printing, and communications. He said also that this underestimated amount was about the amount asked for in 1936 in the original estimates, which now appeared to be excessive because of the time left. It was decided not to use this argument either.

The meeting recessed without any definite strategy being agreed upon but with the expectation that, in addition to the board, Bane, Seidemann, Clearman, Eliot, Calhoun, Bennett, Way, and Resnick would attend the hearings.

As a matter of fact all the board members, the executive director, and the business manager felt that this set of estimates was high. Winant admitted that mistakes had been made, but laid most of them to Clearman who, he said, had tried to be crafty and had slipped in a number of items that were hard to defend. For example, his estimates of costs for space were far above normal costs. Seidemann, for the sake of safety, he thought, had probably overestimated a number of needs. Bennett felt that the budget had been without effective scrutiny from any one mind familiar with the probable needs of all the bureaus. He thought, for example, that the request of the Bureau of Research for nearly a million dollars, which exceeded the total appropriation for the Bureau of Labor Statistics, was almost preposterous. Bane, too, regarded the request as clearly more than needed. As a result of this lack of confidence in their own figures and a "conviction of sin" about some of the requests, it would have been difficult to make a convincing presentation before the House committee had the latter been fully adequate to its inquisitorial duties.

A week of hearings was given to the Social Security Board. The lack of political sense displayed by Seidemann and Resnick complicated the problem of defense. Seidemann, in explaining the sum asked for registering employees, blandly stated, according to Winant, that there would probably be need for 22,000 employees during October. Winant reported that it seemingly never occurred to Seidemann that anyone could connect this with the election in November. Resnick committed a similar *faux pas* in defending his appropriation by describing a big movie project (which, by the way, had not yet been approved by the board) and his organization of speakers.[8]

Yet it was a much more inquisitive House Appropriations Committee that had to be faced by the board than that of January. In his opening remarks Winant struck a conciliatory note by showing how a million and a half could be saved if Congress would pass an amendment to section 205 of the Social Security Act, to eliminate the legal complications in the payment of death benefits. Before the hearings were over, this subject was pretty thoroughly explored, particularly when the estimates for the legal staff were under discussion. Calhoun presented a detailed exposition of the task involved in administering this section. At the request of the committee he filed five different possible amendments.

Early in the hearings, Altmeyer was called upon to defend the board's employment of experts. It is very interesting that in his defense he fell back, as did Bane and Chairman Winant later, upon the Civil Service Commission as the guarantor that these appointments, as well as those of attorneys, were being handled in a meritorious manner. This testimony had a very different ring than did the discussion which had gone on within the board and between the board members and the Civil Service Commission staff a month or so earlier. It was also in distinct contrast to the disdain of the Civil Service Commission evidenced by the board in the drafting of the first proposals for this appropriation bill as submitted to the budget bureau on March 17.

Altmeyer had the chance to express his opinion that the board's estimates exceeded their probable needs for administration during the rest of 1936. He

---

[8] These statements do not appear in the printed record of the hearings.

pointed out that because the appropriation would not be available for the board's use until approximately June 1, it would now be possible to eliminate certain expenditures that the board would have made had it possessed the money. Because these delays had slowed the rate of expansion, the personnel estimates, as they stood in the proposal coming from the board and the Bureau of the Budget, were higher than necessary. At the request of the committee, he submitted a table showing the possible reductions in the 1936 estimates that might result from the foregoing factors. This table indicated that instead of the additional $1,293,836 requested for April, May, and June, the board could now get along with $621,598.

In the scrutiny of requests for administrative expenses and for registration, Representative John Taber of New York, Republican, led the attack. He was well seconded by Woodrum and Chairman Buchanan, although the latter were not so determined that the personnel estimates should be drastically cut. It was noticeable that in the discussion of old age benefits, the members of the House committee were frequently confused as to how this task differed from the other line functions. Latimer made a lucid exposition of his plans of organization, both for the registration job and for the permanent organization of the Old Age Benefits Bureau. It was very difficult, however, for the committee members to understand the need for an actuarial staff in his bureau, in view of the Treasury's actuarial duties. It was also hard for them to visualize the problems of record-keeping which the bureau would have to meet, and why it could not merely use the Treasury records for its purposes. The committee was quite insistent that registration data for assigning account numbers could be had from the Census Bureau as a result of the 1935 census of manufacturers. But when the census people, through Latimer, made it clear that their information had been collected under a pledge of secrecy, even with regard to other federal departments, most of the committee retreated from that position, although the chairman insisted to the last that he could see no reason why this information should be kept confidential.

Only one particularly vulnerable phase of the estimates was fully exposed by the committee hearings. That was the amount asked for rental. Here the space estimates that Clearman had made were finally shown up for what they were. Seidemann pretended to misunderstand a good many of the questions on this point, but Bennett finally blurted out the fact that the space estimates for the Washington offices averaged $2.50 a square foot, including maintenance, while Bennett's statement showed that the board was then paying $.80 a square foot, which together with maintenance brought the cost to $1.15.

When the estimates for the Bureau of Research and Statistics were under discussion, a concerted effort was made by some committee members to secure from Hamilton an admission of the excessive cost of that activity. They particularly insisted that Hamilton's organization was duplicating the work carried on by the Bureau of Labor Statistics and the Federal Reserve Board. Hamilton asserted that his plans were being carefully developed in cooperation with Lubin's organization in the Department of Labor and with the Central Statistical Board. He emphasized that the primary function of his group was not to gather statistics, but to reinterpret data collected by other governmental and private agencies so as to serve the needs of the social security functions.

The committee was particularly interested in and yet uncritical of the proposed regional office setup, alike as to number of staff, functions, and salaries.

One final episode during the hearings is worthy of special mention, the colloquy between Chairman Buchanan and Bane and Seidemann concerning the process by which the board's estimates had been prepared. The chairman apparently wanted to find out what action had been taken on the estimates after Seidemann had worked them over. He also asked whether or not the board had reduced any of the estimates, and how much reduction they had made. Bane was evasive in the one case and could not recall in the other. Seidemann then intervened, and attempted to lead the discussion on a back track over the procedure used in dealing with the bureaus, but the chairman stuck to his point. What did the board do? And how much did it cut? Seidemann, driven into a corner, replied as follows:

I do not have the aggregate, but I recall that the office of the general counsel was reduced materially. And we cut other bureaus. We increased a number of the estimates because possibly the bureau chief, having just entered upon duty, was not thoroughly familiar with the whole problem. I can assure you, Mr. Chairman, that the budget estimates before you represent an estimate based upon the mature judgment of all of us at the time it was presented to the Bureau of the Budget.

At that point the chairman let the matter drop.

BUCHANAN "PROPOSITIONS" WINANT

After the hearings were finished, Chairman Winant became anxious about the situation and on the first of May went over to see Chairman Buchanan. He learned from him that the committee would probably slice the $15,000,000 requested for registration to $12,000,000, and that they would cut by 25 percent the $23,000,000 asked for administration. Buchanan also said that they would cut Research rather drastically and would include a provision making it impossible to transfer funds from one item to another. Winant tried to persuade Buchanan to change the cut to not more than 20 percent and to give to the board the right to transfer funds allotted one bureau to another bureau in case of need. He insisted that the board could not stand the 25 percent cut and that it needed flexibility because of its newness as an organization. Buchanan did not give a commitment to Winant about the total which would be recommended for public assistance grants, but did say it would be possible to transfer between grants. Winant tried to reemphasize to him the fact that the precise sums needed would depend altogether upon what the states were willing to match, and that there was no way to accurately foretell that.

Toward the close of the interview Buchanan intimated that he would like to have one of the board's regional offices in his home town, Austin, Texas. He offered to try to get favorable consideration for Winant's request concerning the board's appropriation if Winant would try to get a reconsideration of the regional office in the southwest so that it could be located in Austin.

Overlooking the commitment already made by the board to Oscar Powell for appointment as regional director for that area and location of the regional office in San Antonio where Powell lived, Winant impulsively agreed to Buchanan's plea for a *quid pro quo*. But when he returned to his office regrets assailed him. He was sailing to Europe in a day or two, with a staff party, to study European social insurance experience. Contritely he called Bane to his office, confessed his sin, and asked Bane to straighten out the situation. With loyal good nature Bane undertook this delicate diplomatic task. The outcome of his efforts was that the regional office was left in San Antonio, while Buchanan was placated with a district office in Austin.

THE APPROPRIATION ACT PROVISIONS

It was not until late in June that the appropriation bills were passed and signed by the President, so that only a few days of the fiscal year 1936 remained when the new funds became available. As the appropriation measure finally stood, it provided for a total grant to the board of $187,800,000, distributed among the following items:

Administration	$ 18,400,000
Grants to the states	
Old age assistance	85,000,000
Unemployment compensation administration	29,000,000
Aid to blind	8,000,000
Aid to dependent children	35,000,000
	$157,000,000
Registration for account numbers	$12,400,000

It provided that of the total for administrative purposes, $600,000 was to be made immediately available; that grants-in-aid to the blind, to dependent children, and to the aged might go back not earlier than March 31, 1936;

and that the money for state unemployment compensation administration could be allotted back to January 1, 1936.

This last provision was the result of pressure by those states which had unemployment compensation administrations before February 11. As has already been explained, the states had been promised grants, going as far back as July, 1935, for those that had had approved administrations in operation at that time. But they had been euchered out of these expected funds by the failure of the board to restate explicitly in the first appropriation bill the provision on this point embodied in the Social Security Act, and by the subsequent ruling which Comptroller General McCarl had made. In his testimony before the House committee Wagenet had explained the situation in the following statement:

We have been asked by the state agencies now operating, or, rather, by the representatives of those agencies in conference here in Washington, to secure, if possible, the total amount of money the states have paid so far in setting up and maintaining their administrative agencies. The deficiency appropriation bill took effect February 11, 1936. The states were greatly disappointed in that. They had already asked the Board for their funds going back to the dates on which they set up their agencies last fall. They finally asked the Board in conference here in Washington, last month, to see if the appropriation bill could be so worded as to give the administrative costs as of January 1.

It will be seen from this summary that Congress cut out the entire amount of supplementary grant-in-aid money requested for the balance of 1936 but left the estimate for grants for 1937 precisely as requested. However, it made these funds available for the last quarter of 1936, and in the case of unemployment compensation, for the last two quarters. The reductions in administrative funds from the sums requested for the two years totaled $4,286,332. (This was exclusive of the $1,544,765 which had been added in the request for the newly discovered duties of administering section 205 and which it was understood Congress would take care of by amendment. The amendment was not passed.) The total reduction for these purposes (exclusive of the section 205 item) was $41,634,772 or slightly less than 20 percent.

PREPARING THE ESTIMATES
FOR FISCAL 1938

PRELIMINARY DISCUSSIONS AND INSTRUCTIONS

The process of preparing the board's budget estimates for the fiscal year 1938 started with an executive staff meeting on August 6, 1936 (which Frase attended). The deadline for board estimates fixed by the Bureau of the Budget was September 15. Consequently it was decided that all estimates from the bureaus must be in the board's hands by August 25, so that it might have a week for revisions. It was agreed that the director of the Bureau of Accounts and Audits should set up a time schedule for each bureau, so that all estimates would not pour in on the last day. Bane and Hughes urged all bureau heads to give the estimates their personal attention, to avoid the situation of the preceding spring when directors came to the board for additional requests after the estimates which they had submitted had been acted upon. There were no detailed instructions or general fiscal policies stated, either at this meeting or subsequently, for the guidance of bureau heads in preparing estimates, nor were any limits indicated for these preliminary estimates.

After they had been submitted, the executive director and his assistant discussed them separately with each bureau director and made small reductions. The amounts eliminated were insignificant and were more than equaled by subsequent increases decided upon by the board itself.

On August 31, the board discussed the estimates in a preliminary fashion with Bane, Corson, and Hughes. Bane summed up the total situation by saying that the bureaus had increased their requests by approximately 75 percent over the previous year. Hughes explained that out of the $1,000,000 appropriated in the First Deficiency Bill, of February 1936, a great deal of equipment was purchased which was in storage and had not been used, and the board had turned back some $50,000 of that sum to the Treasury. The $600,000 made available for the fiscal year 1936 in the 1937 appropriation had not been touched by June 30, 1936, but was being used in the 1937 fiscal year.

Miles believed that the board ought to include everything in its budget estimates that it could possibly justify; Winant, however, thought that there ought to be a very careful check on the estimates. Bane suggested that the bureau directors be asked to defend their budgets at the board meeting on the following day; that after the board had decided on a gross budget, it should authorize Bane, Corson, and Hughes to work out the details. The board members agreed to this procedure and further decided at this time that only the chairman and the executive director should appear before the House committee.

THE BOARD REVIEWS THE BUREAU ESTIMATES

The Bureau of Unemployment Compensation

The first bureau budget to be considered on September 1 was that of the Bureau of Unemployment Compensation. Murray and Batzell represented the bureau; the estimate submitted asked for $674,733 for personal services covering 202 positions, distributed as follows:

Director's office	6
Service Section	45
Division of Administrative Grants and Procedures	54
Grants section	
Procedure section	
Division of Legislative Aid and Approval	36
Division of Liaison	18
Field Division	43

Murray argued for more personnel for the procedure section of the Division of Administrative Grants and Procedures and for more regional and field personnel. He thought that 20 technical advisers in Washington would be adequate if there were a field representative of the bureau in each state; the estimate called for 43 field representatives, who would be sufficient for servicing the states considering unemployment compensation measures during the coming year. Nevertheless, he requested an increase in the Field Division to 52.

Chairman Winant attempted to arrive at some percentage estimates comparing the cost of administration with the sum of unemployment compensation taxes to be collected during the following year, approximately $500,000,000. Batzell stated that they were collecting figures on the cost of administration but that there would be no means of making a more adequate computation until there had been a great deal more experience. Altmeyer then recommended an increase in the items requested by Murray; and Miles countered with the proposition that the entire budget for the Bureau of Unemployment Compensation be increased by 20 percent. He based his proposal on past experience with the House Appropriations Committee. The board approved both suggestions. The final estimate for the Bureau of Unemployment Compensation (approved on September 9) provided for a total of 242 positions and an expenditure for personal services of $795,225.

The Bureau of Public Assistance

The next bureau reviewed was the Bureau of Public Assistance. May and Roseman appeared, to defend an estimate of $467,800 for the salaries of 159 people distributed within the bureau units as follows:

Director's office	10
Plans and Grants Division	32
Policy and Procedures Division	20
Technical Training Division	8
Special Studies Division	23

Technical Service Division	30
Field Division	36

May stated that the $467,800 requested was rock-bottom. A large cut had been taken in the field staff, and if any increase were allowed they would prefer to expand the field staff rather than the Special Studies Division. The board then proceeded to inquire about the work projected for the various divisions, and especially what seemed to be an overlap between the Policies and Procedures Division, the Technical Service Division, and the Special Studies Division. In view of the fact that the civil service classifications then set up would have to be retained, it was decided to transfer the Technical Service Division (office management) to the Office of the Director, and to call the Special Studies Division the Administrative Surveys Division. May requested an increase of 12 people in the field and regional staff. The board approved this increase, and also a 20 percent increase in the total budget for the bureau. This budget action increased the number of positions to 202 and the amount for salaries to $621,900.

The Bureau of Federal Old Age Benefits

The following estimate for the Bureau of Federal Old Age Benefits was considered on September 1, proposing an allotment of $19,124,660 to cover 9,926 positions:

Office	Number of Positions	Amount for Personal Services
Departmental	3,016	$ 5,537,260
Director	30	116,280
Administrative Division	164	263,980
Accounting Division	99	211,080
Claims Division	418	999,500
Field Service Division	65	165,200
Records Division	2,240	3,601,220
Field	6,910	13,767,400
Claims Division	1,005	2,231,500
Records Division	2,456	4,639,500
Field Service Division	3,449	6,896,400

The discussion of this projected huge establishment consumed most of the time of the following three days, and was punctuated by the acceptance of the resignation of Murray Latimer as director and the final appointment of Henry Seidemann to his place.

In addition to the $19,000,000 asked for personnel, the bureau was also requesting $8,000,000 for equipment and supplies. These great sums were justified as necessary to operate the Records Division and the field offices. The plan envisaged 1,000,000 annual postings, with punching performed in

64 field offices located in juxtaposition to the collection centers of the Bureau of Internal Revenue. Thereafter the cards would be transmitted to Washington, checked, tabulated, and then posted to individual ledgers. Under this division would also be produced statistical records, recording of the original information from employees (SS-5), the creation of a central case-record file of employers, and a numerical and alphabetical file of employees. For this alone it was estimated that a total of 4,696 people would be needed, of whom slightly over one-half would be located in the field offices.

The plans of the bureau were predicated upon its need to make a great many investigations of the accuracy of the information returns from employers. This at once raised the question of whether the Bureau of Internal Revenue would permit the board's field staff to contact its taxpayer clients. The chairman and Altmeyer were obviously apprehensive about the attitude of Treasury people; but Latimer insisted that the board would have to make its own investigation of information returns, since the Bureau of Internal Revenue only made investigations when complaints were made, while the board, on the other hand, would have to explore any error or discrepancy which it discovered in the records. Beach, who had been representing the Bureau of Old Age Benefits in its contacts with the Treasury, felt that no objection would be raised if the board could present a plan showing that it was not conflicting with the tax collecting function of the Bureau of Internal Revenue.

For a time it appeared that the board would hold up the estimates for this bureau until it could obtain an agreement with the Treasury defining the nature of the wage record investigations to be made by each agency. Both Altmeyer and Bane expressed their belief that an intelligent budget could not be constructed until this issue was determined. Bane further felt that the board ought also to know what the Post Office and the Treasury were going to do in connection with registration, before final figures were attempted. Bane suggested a tentative approval so as to allow alterations prior to the October hearings before the Bureau of the Budget. While the board at first agreed to this procedure, it changed its mind and decided to go ahead. Before approving estimates, however, it ordered the bureau to cut its proposed personnel list by 1,000 positions. In so doing it estimated that this would reduce the total budget request by about $2,800,000, bringing the total request to about $24,000,000 as against the $27,000,000 requested. Latimer and Seidemann protested, but the board stuck to its guns, though permitting the bureau chiefs to distribute the cuts where they wished rather than from the field staff alone. Altmeyer made the remark during the discussion that he thought the estimates were about 50 percent too high, because he believed that the bureau would probably not spend half the 1937 appropriation.

The final estimate for personnel alone, approved for submission to the Bureau of the Budget, called for 8,926 positions costing a total of $17,171,-402.[9]

The Office of the General Counsel

In its estimate, the Office of the General Counsel asked for $1,305,000 for 403 positions. A vigorous attack against the number of lawyers requested was launched by Altmeyer and seconded by Miles. When the assistant general counsel defended the estimate by asserting that one out of every fifteen or twenty claims filed with the Bureau of Old Age Benefits would present a knotty legal question, Altmeyer countered with the proposal that an agreement with the Treasury lawyers on some of these legal points would cut the board's legal costs in half. The board agreed to reduce the number of lawyers to 175, and its final approved estimate conceded 260 positions costing a total of $876,620.

The Bureau of Informational Service

The estimate of the Bureau of Informational Service was approved as submitted. It asked for $438,720 for 161 people distributed as follows:

Director and Associate Director	18
Business Information	12
Press Service	18
Education	8
Inquiry	21
Library	17
Radio, Motion Picture and Exhibits	10
Press Digests and Reference Files	6
Publications	23
Regional Director	4
Regional Staff	24

The director of the bureau was apparently the only chief who accepted seriously the instructions of the executive director to keep estimates down to actual needs. His request made no increase over his 1937 budget. In return for this conservative estimate the assistant executive director was understood to have promised that the estimates would not be cut. It may be noted here, however, that when the Bureau of the Budget later slashed the board's total estimate, Informational Service was cut as deeply as the bureaus which had markedly increased their requests.

[9] It may be recalled here that early in 1936 when the cry was being raised that the board was creating a vast bureaucracy, the board asserted that no more than 7,500 persons would be needed to administer the Social Security Act.

The Bureau of Accounts and Audits

With the reservation that it was difficult for him to make an estimate for the Bureau of Accounts and Audits without knowing the plans of the Bureau of Old Age Benefits, Director Hughes offered an estimate of $1,062,279 for a staff of 437 distributed as follows:

Director	7
Constructive Accounting Division	14
Budget and Accounting Division	75
Field Auditing Division	222
Administrative Auditing Division	86
Administration and Payroll Division	22
File Section	11

The board's interest centered in the work of constructive accounting. Chairman Winant was concerned with furnishing the states with accounting advice. He was told that the top men in the Field Auditing Division were also constructive accountants and could be expected to give aid on accounting problems, in addition to auditing, especially for public assistance duties. The question of bureau organization was thus precipitated, because Altmeyer proposed that if this was the case and if the Constructive Accounting Division was actually confining its work to unemployment compensation matters, it ought either to be renamed or transferred to the Bureau of Unemployment Compensation. The director's defense was that this setup was the old way to get a high enough classification and salary from the Civil Service Commission to make it possible to employ a good man for the supervision of constructive accounting.

The board agreed, at the suggestion of the executive director, to increase the estimate for personnel by $100,000 so that the Constructive Accounting Division might raise its staff from 14 to 38 positions.

The Office of the Board Proper

When the estimate for the boards' office was discussed, Corson explained that it allowed for the present staff plus 3 additional secretaries and 5 positions for certain political incubi not wanted by the bureaus. The estimate of $97,300 was approved without change.

The Office of the Executive Director

The estimate for the Office of the Executive Director was also approved without change. It proposed $140,520 for 46 people, organized into four units as follows:

Office of Executor Director	10
Assistant Executive Director	5
Internal Operations	22
Field Operations	9

Regional Offices

Bane asked for $524,840 for a regional staff of 250. He pointed out that the main question was whether the various regional representatives of the bureaus should be placed in the regional office budget or not. He recommended that this be done because of the psychological benefits to be derived from setting the regional offices up as complete operating units. The estimate presented alloted $40,000 per regional office for a skeleton staff which would include a regional director, an administrative assistant, and stenographic and clerical help. The board approved the estimates but directed that in presenting them to the budget bureau and to Congress the regional staffs of the other bureaus be included in the regional offices request.

The Bureau of Research and Statistics

Director Hamilton asked for $843,650 to pay the salaries of 276 employees scattered among eighteen organizational units in the Bureau of Research and Statistics:

Economic Studies Division	28
Analysis and Planning Division	7
Legislation and Administration Division	10
Review of Manuscripts Division	5
Industrial Relations Division	6
Statistical Studies Division	24
Public Assistance Statistical Division	30
Unemployment Compensation Statistical Division	16
Old Age Benefits Statistical Division	10
Statistical Service Division	36
Reporting Division	9
Research Cooperation Division	3
Materials and Resources Division	7
Education Division	8
Clerical Service Division	33
Consultants	3
Public Assistance–Field	16
Unemployment Compensation–Field	16

The Bureau of Business Management

Director Mitchell and associates of the Bureau of Business Management defended salary estimates of $1,502,001 for the following organization of 908 people:

Director	7
Service Division	718
Chief	6
Administration and Travel Section	13
Statistical and Drafting Section	11
Procurement, Property and Supply Section	102

Printing and Duplicating Section	111
Stenographic Section	175
Correspondence and Review Section	300
Personnel Division	183
Director	
Classification Section	
Analysis Section	[not specified]
Placement Section	
Appointment and Payroll Section	
Field	

After a considerable discussion of the work of the correspondence and review section, the estimates of the bureau staff were tentatively approved and the executive director authorized to compare them with the budgets of the other bureaus and to see that they were adjusted in accordance therewith. The only change made before final approval on September 9 was an increase of $100,000 for salaries in the office of the director.

In summarizing the story of budget estimate preparation for 1938 up to this point it may be said that much more orderly procedure had been developed than had been possible during the preceding spring. Moreover the board was better informed about organization and people and gave the estimates a much more systematic scrutiny. The executive director's office also played a more important part in advising on bureau needs, although it had not yet assumed the stature of a thorough budget staff agency. Some drastic reductions were made by the board, but these were confined to the Bureau of Old Age Benefits and the Office of the General Counsel, where the obviously inflated figures made even Miles critical. It is fair, nevertheless, to say that the principle of budget padding won out quite decisively. The board itself arbitrarily increased the bureau estimates for Unemployment Compensation and Public Assistance by 20 percent and made a blanket addition of $100,000 to the figures for Accounts and Audits.[10] This decision to play a game of financial hide-and-seek with the Bureau of the Budget and Congress had important repercussions. The Bureau of the Budget and the congressional committees suspected that the board's estimates were inflated, even though they were not always sure just where and how much. The board invited the blind slashing which it was to receive.

---

[10] This statement oversimplifies the process used. The board rescinded its blanket 20 percent increases for the two bureaus a few days later, but transferred to the executive director the right to review and increase these budgets by that amount. That right he used, so that the final figures were 20 percent more than the bureau directors had requested.

We turn now from the budget for administrative purposes to the estimates for grants-in-aid to the states which had been prepared by the bureaus of Public Assistance and Unemployment Compensation.

Estimates for Public Assistance Grants

1. Old Age Assistance. When these were presented to the board, the executive director explained that three possibilities had been considered:

    a) 25 percent of the persons over sixty-five years of age in the country to be covered and the board to pay $15: total federal share, $367,000,000

    b) 20 percent of those over sixty-five to receive old age assistance and the board to pay $12: total federal share, $241,000,000

    c) 15 percent of those over sixty-five to receive old age assistance and the board pay $10: total federal share, $150,000,000

It was pointed out that the highest average total payment for old age assistance per recipient for any state in the month of June was $25.26 and that the average payment for all states then cooperating with the board was $18.00. Several hundred thousand people were receiving old age assistance under plans approved by the board—but only 12 percent of the population was over sixty-five. It was further shown that 37 percent of the eligibles were receiving aid in Oklahoma, and almost that many in Texas. The board chose the middle estimate, approving the budget of $241,000,000 for grants for old age assistance.[11]

2. Aid to Dependent Children. For this, three alternatives were also presented:

    a) Assuming that 5 percent of all children under sixteen years of age in the United States would receive aid and that the average payment by the state would be $14: total federal share, $112,000,000

    b) Assuming that 4 percent of the children under sixteen would receive an average of $12: total federal share, $77,000,000

    c) Assuming that 3 percent of the children under sixteen would receive an average of $10: total federal share, $48,000,000

The board in this case, also, approved the middle estimate of $77,000,000.

3. Grants for Aid to the Blind. The Bureau of Public Assistance pointed out that there were no statistics of blind population in the United States and

[11] It is interesting to note that the statistics of September 1937 showed that 19.2 percent of the population eligible on account of age for old age assistance were then receiving it, and that the average state amount was $18.97 a month. Thus of the three alternatives presented, the board had chosen the one which most closely approximated the situation which developed.

that it was necessary to estimate these figures. Pennsylvania and Wisconsin, which had had blind-pension laws for some years, had determined that 8 of every 10,000 persons were blind. The three alternatives presented for this grant were:

    a) Four out of each 10,000: total federal share, $10,000,000
    b) Six out of each 10,000: total federal share, $15,000,000
    c) Eight out of each 10,000: total federal share, $19,000,000

The board approved the middle estimate of $15,000,000.

In reviewing the total approved estimates for public assistance grants, the spokesman for the bureau pointed out that the board would probably be about $10,000,000 short in its 1937 appropriation. This would mean a request to Congress for a deficiency bill unless the 1938 appropriation act was passed early in the session.

Grants for Unemployment Compensation

Associate Director Murray asked $46,500,000 for grants, under Title III, to administer state unemployment compensation acts (as compared with the $29,000,000 granted in 1937). There was not much discussion of this estimate. It was noted that the Treasury would probably collect $200,000,000 in Title III taxes in 1938; that by January 1, 1938, twelve states would pay benefits; that on April 1, 1938, two more states would pay benefits; and that on July 1, 1938, still another state would pay benefits, bringing the total to sixteen paying benefits during 1938. The board approved the proposed estimate.

On September 9, the board approved the revised budget estimates for transmission to the Bureau of the Budget. The total, including grants to the states, had been cut from $527,769,000 to $396,275,000, a cut of $131,-494,000. By far the greatest part of this reduction was made by accepting the middle estimate for public assistance grants rather than the maximum. The reduction in personal services was from $27,000,000 to $24,000,000.

DRASTIC CUTS BY THE BUREAU OF THE BUDGET

On October 5, 1936, the board had its hearing with the budget bureau. The manner in which this hearing came about was not calculated to help the board. Toward the end of September, Leonard W. Ahern of the budget bureau had met Director Hughes on the street and in a casual way had suggested October 5 as the date for reviewing the board's estimates. Sometime later Ahern also mentioned this date to the associate director of the Bureau of

Accounts and Audits. Neither officer told the executive director. On the morning of October 5 the board was in session, when a telephone message was received from the Bureau of the Budget which said that the bureau had been waiting for a half hour for the board to appear. Corson and Hughes hurriedly gathered up some materials and hastened over to the Budget office where Director Bell and a committee of three, of which Ahern was the most important member, were meeting.

During that morning session the public assistance and unemployment compensation grants-in-aid were discussed rather casually, because neither the staff of the budget bureau nor that of the board had any sure basis for criticizing or defending these particular estimates. At the afternoon session the estimate for board administrative expenses was considered. Ahern was particularly critical of the sums requested for the bureaus of Research and Statistics and Informational Service (probably because of a greneral prejudice against these types of governmental activity), and of the large amount for the Bureau of Old Age Benefits. At his request Director Seidemann, Hamilton, and Resnick were called into the meeting to defend the estimates. However, the subsequent discussion was not detailed or searching and the hearing closed late that afternoon. It also developed during this hearing that the budget bureau would insist on separate itemization for printing and binding.

On two later occasions, the Bureau of the Budget requested and received additional information on mechanical record-keeping and the cooperative arrangements of the Bureau of Research and Statistics with other government research agencies.

Acting Director Bell wrote to Acting Chairman Altmeyer on November 13, 1936, announcing the decision reached by the Bureau of the Budget:

The estimates of appropriations submitted by you for the fiscal year 1938 pursuant to Budget circular No. 340, dated January 19, 1936, together with the hearing of representatives of the Board appearing before the Committee of the Bureau of the Budget, have been given careful consideration. The total amount which has been determined for inclusion in the 1938 budget for the Board is $256,000,000 distributed by appropriate titles as follows:

Salaries and expenses	(a)	$ 12,000,000
Printing and binding		1,000,000
Grants to States (Old Age Assistance)		150,000,000
Grants to States (Unemployment Comp.)	(a)	29,000,000
Grants to States (Aid to Dep. Child.)		54,600,000
Grants to States (Aid to the Blind)		10,000,000

(a) Together with any unexpended balance of appropriation for the fiscal year 1937.

There is enclosed herewith a schedule of approved changes in appropriation text for the 1938 budget.[12]

It will be appreciated if, not later than November 18, 1936, revised schedules of obligations be submitted, in duplicate, so as to conform to the amounts above indicated.

The bureau also cut out a provision in the appropriation text submitted by the board which would have allowed it to make transfers between all appropriations for grants to the states (unemployment compensation as well as public assistance), on the grounds that an administrative agency should not be given too much flexibility in the apportionment of funds appropriated to it. In order to protest this drastic action by the budget bureau cutting the estimates from $35,444,000 for salaries and expenses to approximately $21,500,000 (figures which included the estimated 1937 carry-over), Winant and Corson conferred with Ahern a day or so later.

On this occasion Ahern insisted that the board could not possibly use the amount requested by the Bureau of Old Age Benefits, and he pointed out that the estimate for this bureau carried sums for personnel and business management functions which duplicated those of the Bureau of Business Management. He also continued his attack on the requests for the Informational Service and the Bureau of Research and Statistics. Nevertheless, he did relent a little. Before leaving, Winant secured a promise from Bell to increase the estimate for administrative expenses from $12,000,000 to $15,000,000 plus the unexpended balance from the 1937 appropriation. Director Bell wrote to Winant on November 20, confirming this agreement:

In my letter to Mr. Altmeyer of November 13, 1936, I informed him that the 1938 budget allowance for "Salaries and Expenses" would be $12,000,000

---

[12] Before this letter, the board had no indication that the Bureau of the Budget would approve an estimate based upon the use of unexpended balances. Such a procedure was contrary to the usual policy of the bureau because it complicated their record-keeping. But, as it developed in the subsequent hearing described in the following passage, the bureau thought it justifiable in this instance, in view of the large surplus which the board would have and its probable effect as an incentive to save money during the fiscal year 1937. The board agreed with the budget bureau that it would probably have an $8,500,000 carry-over from its 1937 appropriation for administrative expenses and a $17,500,000 carry-over from its 1937 appropriation for grants to the states for administration of unemployment compensation. Corson, who made this estimate of $8,500,000 carry-over, was severely criticized on this score by Seidemann, who felt that the board would have no carry-over whatsoever and probably would have to ask for a deficiency appropriation in the spring of 1937. The actual carry-over, increased, of course, by the board's subsequent action in allotting many ordinary expenses like those of the Informational Service, the Bureau of Business Management, and the regional offices to the wage record appropriation, amounted to $12,800,000.

together with any unexpended balance of the appropriation for the same purpose for the fiscal year 1937. This is to advise you that upon reconsideration the amount allowed has been increased by $3,000,000.

The board decided not to protest further this reconsidered judgment of the Bureau of the Budget. Its conclusion was communicated to Mr. Bell by the executive director in a letter of November 23, which read in part:

In accordance with instructions, we are submitting herewith revised budget estimates for the Social Security Board for the fiscal years 1937 and 1938. In our opinion, as we have previously advised you, it will be extremely difficult, if at all possible, to effectively administer the Social Security Act during either of the fiscal years 1937 or 1938 within these estimates, even with the most rigorous economy.

These revised estimates submitted on November 23 were almost solely the work of John Corson. Because it was necessary to act rapidly and the executive director was out of town, Corson took the figures home with him one night and cut each bureau almost in direct proportion to the total reduction in administrative expenses. There were some variations from this procedure: the reductions in the estimates of the bureaus of Research and Statistics and Informational Service were slightly more severe than the others.

CONGRESS AND THE BOARD'S
1938 ESTIMATES

Before the first hearings of the Subcommittee of the House Appropriations Committee on December 18, Corson prepared a very detailed justification of the board's budget estimates. The arrangement of this bulky multilithed document was suggested to him by W. A. Jump, the budget officer of the Department of Agriculture, who knew the peculiarities of this particular House subcommittee because it also reviewed the budget requests for the AAA. The most important feature of the new arrangement was the elimination of personnel totals which always seemed to have the effect of leading some member of the committee off on a long discussion obscuring the real functions and budget needs of the agency.

HEARINGS BEFORE THE HOUSE COMMITTEE

The first hearing before the House subcommittee was on December 18. The board adopted an entirely different strategy than it had used on the two previous occasions. Instead of sending a circus parade of board members and bureau directors, it was decided to assign the task of presenting the board's estimates to Chairman Winant, Bane, and Corson. Buchanan of Texas, chairman of the Committee on Appropriations, attended the entire session.

The printed record of the hearings shows that the board made a much better presentation than it had ever done before. After a brief general statement by Winant, Bane and Corson handled most of the questions. There can be little doubt that the advance submission of a detailed justification in documentary form simplified the procedure a great deal. In the case of all three public assistance grants Woodrum, chairman of the subcommittee, drew out by questioning the fact that the board had submitted larger estimates than the budget bureau. Throughout the hearing it was apparent that the board was greatly aided by the sympathetic attitude and questions of Chairman Woodrum of Virginia, an old personal friend of Bane. The requested appropriation for old age assistance was a very conservative one, which Bane made clear in the following statement:

The last Congress appropriated for this title $85,000,000. Our request for this year is for $150,000,000, or a $65,000,000 increase.

This request of $150,000,000 is based upon the assumption that 15.7 percent of the estimated total number of persons 65 years of age and over in the United States will receive old-age assistance during the fiscal year 1938, and that the average monthly payments made by the States to individuals from Federal, State, and local funds will be $19.

The Census advises that on January 1, 1938, the estimated total number of persons 65 years of age or over in the United States will be 7,988,000.

Our experience to October 1936 demonstrates that approximately 12.6 percent of the estimated population 65 years of age and over were receiving old-age assistance in 40 of the jurisdictions with plans approved by the Social Security Board.

I might state that for the 6-month period of this current fiscal year, for the first two quarters, from July 1, 1936, to January 1, 1937, the Board has made grants to States of $59,289,612.68. This, you will see, is well over half of the amount which was appropriated last year, namely, $85,000,000.

You gentlemen also understand that the Social Security Board has very little power to curtail expenditures for old-age assistance.

The act provides that the Social Security Board shall match funds, dollar for dollar, that are expended by the States for old-age assistance. The right to determine the number of persons who are in need and the right to determine the amount of assistance to an individual person who is in need are reserved to the States. This means that the State, to all intents and purposes, determines the amounts expended. The Federal Government is obligated under the act to match the amounts expended, dollar for dollar, irrespective of what the amounts may be. . . .

The discussion on aid to dependent children and aid to the blind was of much the same nature but more brief; the interest of the committee, as on previous occasions, seemed to center upon old age assistance.

In respect to the request for grants under Title III (unemployment compensation administration) the board was on much shakier ground, even though its position had been strengthened considerably by the passage of legislation in about twenty states during the preceding month. The coverage of employees in the thirty-six states possessing laws was approximately 85 percent of the total estimated coverage for the entire country. Nonetheless it was not easy to justify the detailed factual statements in a request for $46,500,000. The board had received an appropriation of $29,000,000 for the current fiscal year, and even a very liberal estimate of grants for the last two quarters would only bring the total expenditure from this sum to $11,500,000. The following exchange between Mr. Wigglesworth of Massachusetts and John Corson brought out the most definite justification the board was able to offer in support of its request:

MR. WIGGLESWORTH. What I am trying to get at is this: How accurately can we estimate this item that we are now discussing? You have made an estimate of $46,500,000. What is the basis of that estimate?

MR. CORSON. We have based it upon estimates of the coverage in the States. For example, the first 16 jurisdictions with laws approved under title IX accounted for 38.8 percent of the estimated number of employed workers subject to unemployment compensation. Those States which have recently adopted or seem likely to adopt unemployment compensation laws within the next several months include a number of workers which would bring this coverage up to 64.6 percent of such workers. In estimating the number of workers to be covered in States which do not now have approved laws, the estimated coverage is based upon the minimum coverage specified by the Social Security Act; however, it is likely that some of the States will follow the example already set by certain other States and elect to provide more complete coverage.

It is upon this estimate of the probable coverage that we have based this request for $46,500,000 for grants to States for unemployment compensation administration.

Most of the hearing time was consumed in a discussion of the items for salaries and administrative expenses, particularly in connection with the Bureau of Old Age Benefits. The committee immediately concentrated its questions on the total number of employees requested, their civil service status, the number of lawyers and experts, and the nature of regional and field offices. At the request of the committee, Director Seidemann was asked to explain the field offices of the Bureau of Old Age Benefits. The committee, as on previous occasions, seemed to have the greatest difficulty in understanding the differences between the regional offices and the field offices. To further complicate the situation, Seidemann forgot his instructions not to draw distinctions between district and branch offices, with the result that Chairman Winant intervened to say that no distinction should have been made between them; that they were all field offices.[13] As a result of this extended discussion on field offices, the board was compelled to include in the record a list of the field offices then open and the ones proposed for future opening. This list undoubtedly gave rise to a large number of conflicts with congressmen and senators, who noted that their home towns were not included and who brought pressure on the board to change its location plans. Among those towns not included on the list was Lynchburg, Virginia, over which the important dispute with Senator Glass was already beginning.

Subsequent discussion dealt with a request for an item of $10,000 for staff expenses for attendance at meetings and another $10,000 for the payment of transportation and per diem to persons called in to consult and advise the board. These particular items seemed to be of special interest to the House committee during this entire session of Congress, as indicated by the printed hearings on estimates of other departments and agencies.

The assignment of account numbers was lightly skipped over, as were proposals for amendments to the act. Despite difficulties made by Seidemann the board was well satisfied with the hearing. The committee was, on the whole, very sympathetic with its request. The chairman of the subcommittee, Mr. Woodrum, closed the hearing with the statement:

I do not mind saying, individually, that I am very much pleased with what the board has done, and particularly appreciate your fine justification that has been furnished to the committees. It is one of the best justifications I have seen.

A month later the subcommittee called Bane, Corson, and Seidemann in once more for supplementary information. Meanwhile the board had proceeded in its discussion of proposed amendments and decided to ask that the appropriation act specify that the money for all three public assistance titles be used for grants to *needy* individuals. The board had already had a good many perplexing moments over some public assistance plans which leaned in the direction of universal, flat old age pension grants, and it was quite concerned about the apparent tendency for this type of state law to spread. Director Jane Hoey had suggested that it would be wise to head off this movement by amending the Social Security Act to provide that federal matching funds be available only for assistance to needy individuals. Rather than raise this question in

[13] The Board had previously agreed to allow Bane to organize the hearing before the House committee as he pleased, and Seidemann was not included in the lineup. Seidemann came to him shortly before the hearing and pleaded that he be allowed to come along on the ground that he knew the details of old age benefits as no one else did.

connection with proposed amendments to that act, which would undoubtedly get a good deal of publicity, the board decided that it would be wiser strategy to put such a provision in the appropriation act. Consequently, the chairman of the board wrote on January 5 to Budget Director Bell and Mr. Woodrum as follows:

The question has been raised whether Federal grants under Titles I, IV and X of the Social Security Act are limited by the Act to assistance for individuals who are in need. The Board believes that the Act was intended to and does so limit such grants. Thus Section 1, dealing with old-age assistance, provides expressly: "For the purpose of enabling each State to furnish financial assistance . . . to aged needy individuals, there is hereby authorized to be appropriated. . . ." Similar provisions appear in the first section of Title IV dealing with aid to dependent children (Section 401), and Title X, dealing with aid to the blind (Section 1001). The argument that grants under these titles are not limited to needy individuals is based on the fact that there is no mention of need in the other sections of the titles.

Previous appropriation acts have expressly limited grants under Title IV to "grants to States for the purpose of enabling each State to furnish financial assistance to needy dependent children," but have made no express mention of need in connection with grants under Titles I and X. The pending appropriation act follows this language of the previous acts. In order to clarify this situation, the Board suggests that the language of the pending appropriation act with respect to grants under Titles I and X be modified as follows:

"Grants to States for old-age assistance: For grants to States for assistance *to aged needy individuals,* as authorized in Title I of the Social Security Act. . . ."

"Grants to States for aid to the blind: For grants to States *for the purpose of enabling each State to furnish financial assistance to needy individuals who are blind,* as authorized in Title X of the Social Security Act. . . ."

The language suggested is, as will be noted, virtually identical with the wording of the first sections of the respective titles.

These suggestions were accepted by the Bureau of the Budget and the House committee, and appear in the social security board section of the Independent Offices Appropriation Act for 1938.

On Thursday, January 27, Bane, Corson, and Seidemann were called to appear before the House Subcommittee on Appropriations once more, apparently at the request of Congressman Wigglesworth of Massachusetts. Wigglesworth took up the greater part of this short meeting, but two other members of the committee, Dirksen of Illinois and Houston of Kansas, also participated. Chairman Woodrum of Virginia was again very helpful in answering questions for the representatives of the board and in steering the questions into less embarrassing channels.

Wigglesworth went over most of the board's activities, concentrating attention, however, on the details of grants for public assistance and the extent of the board's control over state operations. He also touched again on grants under Title III, civil service status of personnel, experts, the Bureau of Old Age Benefits, the Bureau of Public Assistance, and the Informational Service (particularly in regard to the number of press releases, speeches, and motion picture and radio activities). From the printed record of the hearing it appears that Congressman Wigglesworth's questioning was not designed to embarrass, but rather was the expression of a real interest in the operations of the board.

This could not be said of Congressmen Houston, Dirksen, or Johnson of West Virginia. All three of these gentlemen had a particular interest in personnel problems, which Johnson expressed very frankly as follows:

Some of these gentlemen may be a little bit unsympathetic to this but we Congressmen have to go back every few years to be elected; and these things confront us about this patronage business. I am not sure that I am in full sympathy with this.

I have five set-ups according to your arrangement in West Virginia. I would like to know whether it is the purpose of this Social Security set-up to bring into my State—and I know that there are plenty of people to fill those jobs if it is possible—whether you are going to exhaust West Virginia to get proper help in these regional offices.

Johnson was particularly concerned about the small number of people in West Virginia who had taken examinations for administrative positions in the field offices of the Bureau of Old Age Benefits, and tried to pin Bane down definitely to a pledge that no employees would be hired for the West Virginia offices who were not natives of the state.

Dirksen of Illinois tried to draw out the board's policy on a proposed amendment that would reimburse the thirteen states which had not passed unemployment compensation laws in 1936. (Illinois was one of these states.) Bane furnished the board's standard answer:

Some time prior to the time when these 20 additional States enacted unemployment compensation statutes the Social Security Board was asked whether or not it would recommend an amendment providing for the earmarking by States of funds received and reserving those funds for expenditure within the respective States if and when they passed unemployment compensation laws. The position of the Board at that time was that it would not recommend such an amendment.[14]

[14] This was, we think, the last public statement on this question made by representatives of the board before it reversed its policy and acquiesced in a joint resolution to deposit 1936 collections to the Unemployment Trust Fund accounts of those states in May 1937.

THE HOUSE COMMITTEE MAKES FURTHER CUT

Despite the friendly attitude of the House Appropriations Subcommittee and of the subcommittee chairman, Woodrum, in particular, on February 1, the main committee reported out an independent offices appropriation bill containing recommendations for the Social Security Board that made further drastic cuts.

While it approved all of the grant-in-aid items as submitted by the Bureau of the Budget, it reduced the administrative expense figures by $5,000,000. But this reduction, it explained, was not done "for the purpose of impairing or diminishing the activities of the Board, but in the belief that the Board will not be able to recruit its personnel as rapidly as it anticipated." The committee noted that it was counting the unexpended balance of the 1937 appropriation estimated at $8,377,202. This, together with the direct apppropriation of $10,000,000, would give the board a total of $18,377,202 for administrative purposes. This was double the expenditure which it was estimated that the board would actually make during 1937. "It is believed the sum provided is all the Board will be able to expend judiciously during the fiscal year 1938."

When the board met the following day, Corson furnished it the following summary analysis on the effect of the additional cut made by the committee:

Appropriations, salaries and expenses, 1937		$18,400,000
Allotments to January 30, 1937	$8,610,000	
Estimated savings from allotments	350,000	
	$8,260,000	
Probable unexpended balance as of June 30, 1937		10,140,000
Appropriation recommended by House Committee		10,000,000
Funds available for fiscal year 1938		20,140,000
Budget request, salaries and expenses, 1938		23,377,202
Deficiency		*$3,237,202*
Percentage reduction		*13.8%*

This indicates the probable funds available for this year if the Committee's recommendations stand.

It will be seen that the estimated carry-over from the 1937 appropriation was now boosted to $10,140,000 from the estimate of $8,300,000 submitted to the budget bureau and accepted by the House Appropriations Committee.

The board, on learning that Representative Woodrum was prepared to stand by the record and to recommend a supplemental appropriation the following year if it was needed, decided not to enter any protest against these additional cuts. Mr. Woodrum publicly went on record to this effect on the floor of the House on February 3:

We find in this bill the Social Security Board, set up to administer that great humanitarian purpose of the President and the administration, to look after the needy people of this country. They are just now beginning to come into full operation, January 1, 1937. The committee cut their appropriation for administrative expense $5,000,000 under what the Budget estimated. I am perfectly frank to say to you, and I want to make it a matter of record, I am afraid we cut them pretty deep, but we hope they will be able to get through on the amount of money we have allowed them, which is $18,377,202 for administrative expenses. I have had the matter up with the Board. They have been to see me since this bill was reported. Of course, they were disturbed that the committee had cut $5,000,000 off of what the Bureau of the Budget allowed them. I went over the thing with them and pointed out that even allowing them $18,000,000, we were giving them twice as much for 1938 as they had in 1937. They splendidly and very graciously said I might state to the Congress that they would do the best they could with the funds we had allotted to them. But, of course, if we find we have cut them too deep, we will still be here to meet whatever needs they may have for appropriations. That is a new activity. The Social Security Board, I believe, is as big and as comprehensive as all the life insurance companies in America put together. Just think of that. That is the kind of an organization we have set up. Of course, it will cost money. It will be a mounting cost of money, but we must see that there is no dissipation of funds or that there is no more appropriated than is necessary to do the job we have given them; but having given them the job, we must pay the freight as we go along.[15]

Even Mr. Wigglesworth of Massachusetts, ranking minority member of the Committee, seconded this sentiment:

Mr. Chairman, I have no intention of offering any amendment by way of reducing the sum made available in this bill for the Social Security Board. The work of this Board is too important, too vital to millions of our people. I have been in hearty sympathy with its objectives from the outset. One of the most vital matters confronting us at this time is the proper solution of the problems by which the Board is faced. Moreover, while every cent requested has been allowed for annuity payments a substantial reduction has been recommended in the costs of administration as compared with the Budget figures. It may be that the reduction has been too great. You have heard the fine attitude of the Board presented by the chairman of the subcommittee this morning. If it proves that the cut is too deep, the way is of course always open for an increase through a deficiency item.[16]

[15] The *Congressional Record*, Feb. 3, 1937, p. 956.
[16] *Ibid.*, p. 981.

SENATE HOSTILITY; CARTER GLASS AND HIS PATRONAGE GRUDGE

When the bill reached the Senate, it appeared at first that the board would not be faced with the necessity of appearing before the Senate Appropriations Committee. Chairman Carter Glass had written on February 2 that the committee would be glad to arrange to hear the representatives of the board if the board so desired, but he did not indicate that the committee on its own initiative intended to ask them to appear. The board was not displeased with this prospect, Chairman Winant writing Senator Glass on February 4 as follows:

Thank you for your letter of February 2. The Social Security Board has decided after careful consideration not to request the Senate Committee on Appropriations to make any changes in the language of the independent offices appropriation bill for the fiscal year 1938, as reported to the House of Representatives on February 1. A severe reduction of the Board's budget request has been recommended by the Committee on Appropriations of the House, but the Board will endeavor to conduct its operations within the funds provided under this bill.

The experience of succeeding months may make manifest that this severe limitation of financial support will impair and seriously curtail necessary activities of the Board. The House Committee on Appropriations recognizes this possibility and its chairman referred to it on the floor yesterday. If this proves to be the case it will then be necessary to submit a request for a deficiency appropriation. In the meantime the Board will conduct its affairs with the same measure of economy as has permitted substantial savings from the appropriation for the current fiscal year. The Board, hence, makes no request at this time for a hearing before the Senate Committee on Appropriations. We will be glad, however, to supply the Committee with any additional information or materials that may be desired.[17]

Some further incident seems to have occurred in the feud then in progress between Senator Glass and Frank Bane, because a week later, on February 10, Bane, Corson, and Aronson were called up to testify before the committee.

Before describing the hearing it will be well to discuss briefly the main outlines of Senator Glass's difficulties with the board. These were two-fold, one having to do with a patronage appointment and the other with the location of a field office.

Early in the summer of 1936 Senator Glass called Bane and asked him to appoint a certain Miss Snead as an expert in public assistance. In the view of Bane, Aronson, and Miss Hoey, she lacked the experience to justify expert

[17] *Hearings before the Subcommittee of Committee on Appropriations of the U.S. Senate, 75th Congress, 1st Session (H.R. 4064),* page 58.

status.[18] Bane and the board did not want to offend the Senator, who had not troubled them before with patronage requests. They therefore passed the buck to the Civil Service Commission, confidently expecting that Miss Snead would not be qualified, but the Senator apparently brought his influence to bear on the Civil Service Commission because the lady was quickly approved as an expert.

The board then decided that although it would have to accept Miss Snead, it would not give her an expert position or pay her a salary of $3,200. The personnel officer suggested appointing her, pending examination, at a salary of $2,000 in the Bureau of Public Assistance, and wrote to Senator Glass saying that she had been given a position. The commission, however, refused to confirm an appointment pending examination, because it had eligibles whom it could certify. It insisted that Miss Snead would have to be employed as an expert at $3,200 or not at all. A second attempt was made to appoint her, pending examination, in the Informational Service, but the commission balked at this as well. Bane by this time felt himself so definitely committed to Glass that he expressed his willingness to pay the woman's salary out of his own pocket if a position could not be found for her. Finally he appealed to Aubrey Williams, who agreed to put her on the Works Progress Administration payroll at $2,000 and detail her to the Social Security Board.

Miss Snead's subsequent history with the board was substantially as follows. After she had finished the in-service training course, nobody could be found to take her and so she was sent back to the training course once more. At the end of this second period of education she was assigned to the educational division of the Informational Service, but so much disturbance resulted that she was sent back to the training course for the third time. All during this period she continued to complain to Senator Glass about the treatment she was receiving, to wit, that she was being paid only $2,000, when she had confirmed as an expert at $3,200, and that she was not being treated as a bona fide member of the staff.

This Snead affair alone was sufficiently embarrassing in dealing with the aged and irritable senior senator from Virginia, but it was complicated further by the incident of the Lynchburg field office. One of the office sites for which the board had authorized the director of the Bureau of Business Management to secure space early in September 1936, when the board was still planning on having 606 field offices for the Bureau of Old Age Benefits, was Lynchburg, Virginia, Senator Glass's home town. After the budget bureau in October had drastically reduced the board's estimates for 1938, the board

[18] She had worked for the District of Columbia welfare organization and been released, and she had also at one time engaged in the real estate business. Aronson's office investigated her record and reported against an expert classification.

revised its plans and for two months assumed that it would be able to provide for only 287 field offices. Among the 319 offices thus eliminated was the one in Lynchburg. Accordingly, the contract for space there was cancelled and the furniture shipped elsewhere. When Senator Glass inquired about this action he was told that the budget cut had made it necessary to reduce the number of field offices by more than half.

In January 1937, however, acting upon revised figures submitted by the Bureau of Old Age Benefits, the board decided that it could afford 397 field offices, including the one in Lynchburg. Senator Glass was then notified that there would be an office in Lynchburg. It was easy because of these circumstances for the Senator to believe that he was being discriminated against, and he publicized this incident in the hearing before the Senate Appropriations Committee on February 28 in the following words:

> In other words, I may say to the committee that it is my very definite conclusion that the Board acts as it pleases; and when a Senator is so unfortunate, as I am, as to become persona non grata to the Board, it proceeds to punish him.
>
> In other words, you originally had an office, in my town. They secured the available space in the public building there. They shipped the furniture to my town; and when I become persona non grata to some of the people there, they abolished the office, and shipped the furniture away to another town in the State; and when I brought the matter to the attention of the Board I was told that the reason of it was that they did not have funds to carry it out, and afterward I was told that they had sufficient funds to carry it out . . .
>
> It was a rather peculiar circumstance that my home town should have been selected when I was in a controversy with members of the Board because of what I regarded as objectionable arbitrary action . . .
>
> I do not know how clearly other Senators or Representatives in Congress make a case, but it is perfectly clear to me that what was done in this particular case in Virginia was done out of spite—nothing else on earth.

These incidents furnished the emotional atmosphere in which the questioning of Bane, Corson, and Aronson took place when on February 10, 1937, they came before the Senate Appropriations Committee, of which Glass was chairman. The committee was unsympathetic; the board did not have a single friendly inquisitor. As usual, committee interest centered on matters of personnel in Washington and the field, the location of regional and field offices, and publicity activities. The questioning was unusually petty and browbeating in nature, giving no real heed to the important character of the board's functions and its problems. When Chairman Glass laid bare his quarrel with the board and his anger over the treatment of his "expert" female client and his home town's claims for a field office, the committee became especially interested in the board's use of the expert clause. It requested the board to submit a list of all experts, their titles, salaries, and legal residences.

When on February 15 Chairman Glass reported the independent offices bill out of the Senate Committee on Appropriations, the report carried a reduction in the sum for grants to the states for unemployment compensation administration of $15,000,000, and two other items which read:

Salaries and expenses (salary of executive director reduced from $9,500 to $9,000 per annum) [19] $10,000,000

It is recommended by the Committee that the following be included in the bill: "Provided further, That no salary shall be paid for personal services from the money herein appropriated under the heading 'Social Security Board' in excess of the rates allowed by the Classification Act of 1923, as amended, for similar services: Provided further, That this proviso shall not apply to the salaries of the Board members. Provided further, That none of the funds herein appropriated under the heading "Social Security Board" shall be used to pay the salary of any expert or attorney receiving compensation of $5,000 or more per annum unless and until such expert or attorney shall be appointed by the President, by and with the advice and consent of the Senate." [20]

Despite all the board could do in soliciting senatorial support to defeat the Glass amendments, the Senate passed the bill as it has been reported by the committee. The fight then shifted to the Conference Committee, where the bill was deadlocked until late in June.

While the story of the ultimate solution of this conflict—one of the most dramatic issues faced by the board—falls beyond the period of this study, the later developments may be briefly told. Glass, with the support of a good many conservative southern Senators, consistently refused to give way unless Bane or Personnel Officer Aronson were sacrificed. The board proceeded to make concessions of various kinds, mostly in the nature of political appointments in field office positions. The Senator reduced his demand to the sacrifice of Aronson—not so much that the latter was held personally at fault (because he was merely carrying out the policy of the board) but as a token of the board's submission. The board refused to make this concession and the whole independent offices appropriation bill was threatened with indefinite suspension beyond the beginning of the fiscal year (July 1). Finally the House acceded to the Senate amendments. In this form the bill was signed by the President on June 28, 1937.

The summary financial history of the board's budget for 1938 is shown in table 2.

[19] Glass's way of getting even with Bane, whom he believed had double-crossed him. He later apologized for this meanness.

[20] The Central Statistical Board had also incurred Senator Glass's displeasure, with the result that in this same report the Senator recommended the deletion of the entire appropriation for that agency.

TABLE 2 *Summary Financial History of the Social Security Board's Budget for the Fiscal Year 1938*

	Bureau Estimates	Board Estimates	Budget Bureau Estimates	House of Representatives Estimates	Senate Estimates	Final	Actual Expenditures[a]
Administrative Expenses	$ 37,749,197	$ 35,653,292	$ 16,000,000 8,300,000[b]	$ 11,000,000 8,300,000[b]	$ 10,000,000 8,300,000[b]	$ 10,500,000 12,500,000[c]	$ 19,958,477
			24,300,000	19,300,000	18,300,000	23,000,000	
Unemployment Compensation Grants	46,500,000	46,500,000	29,000,000 17,500,000[b]	29,000,000 17,500,000[b]	15,000,000 17,500,000[b]	19,000,000[d] 20,000,000[e]	
			46,500,000	46,500,000	32,500,000	39,000,000	41,910,919
Old Age Assistance Grants	367,000,000	240,650,000	150,000,000	150,000,000	150,000,000	150,000,000[e]	182,198,734[f]
Grants for Aid to Dependent Children	112,000,000	77,189,000	54,600,000	54,600,000	54,600,000	54,600,000	25,498,282
Grants for Aid to the Blind	19,000,000	14,717,000	10,000,000	10,000,000	10,000,000	10,000,000	5,161,249
Total	$583,249,197	$414,708,292	$285,400,000	$280,400,000	$265,400,000	$272,100,000	$274,727,661

a Data from Third Annual Report of the Social Security Board, pp. 140–41.
b Estimated carryover.
c Actual carryover.
d This includes an additional $3,500,000 appropriation approved May 25, 1938.
e $18,000,000 was made available for fiscal year 1937.
f Includes funds transferred from dependent-children and aid-to-the-blind appropriations, unexpended balances of 1937 appropriations, and funds made available in advance from the 1939 appropriation.

DEFICIENCY APPROPRIATION FOR OLD AGE ASSISTANCE

At the first hearing with the Bureau of the Budget on October 5, 1936, the board had pointed out that its fiscal 1937 appropriation for old age assistance ($85,000,000) would be insufficient. The bureau counseled against a deficiency appropriation request until the board had more accurate estimates, in the belief that it would be possible to get the fiscal 1938 appropriation adopted early in the session and make that available for grants for the fourth quarter of fiscal 1937. In January, even before the board got snarled up with Senator Glass, it became apparent that there would be a serious deficiency in the old age assistance funds. On January 29, 1937, the board requested the Secretary of the Treasury to transfer $2,000,000 and $12,000,000 respectively from the 1937 appropriations for aid to the blind and aid to dependent children, to be used for expenditures for old age assistance.

On January 30, the board wrote to the Director of the Budget that it had already made grants of $78,527,210 under Title I out of a total appropriation of $85,000,000 for the fiscal year, and submitted further details on the required expenditures for the balance of the fiscal year. The chairman's letter continued as follows:

Mr. John J. Corson, Assistant Executive Director, I believe, discussed this matter with you by telephone this morning. Upon your suggestion to him, the Social Security Board will not ask that you present this request to the Congress for inclusion in the first deficiency bill. In order, however, that funds may be available in order to meet the requests of States for grants for old-age assistance to the fourth quarter of the current fiscal year, we will appreciate your early consideration, with representatives of this Board, of this request.

Detailed figures were submitted on February 4 in a memorandum to the Budget Bureau, based on the actual expenditure up to January 13. The estimated expenditure for third- and fourth-quarter grants was as follows:

	Old Age Assistance	Aid to the Blind	Aid to Dependent Children	Total
Additional for third quarter	$ 8,580,233	$ 544,411	$ 2,717,647	$11,642,291
Fourth quarter	41,114,188	2,501,695	10,793,962	54,409,845
	$49,694,421	$3,046,106	$13,511,609	$66,052,136
Unencumbered appropriation balance as of Jan. 13, 1937	5,294,362	4,955,679	25,275,222	35,526,263
Deficit or balance	$44,400,059 (deficit)	$1,909,573	$11,763,613	$30,525,873 (deficit)

On February 4, Bane wrote Bell requesting the formal consideration of a $30,000,000 supplemental appropriation for old age assistance for the fiscal year 1937.

The bureau delayed action on this request until the end of February 1937. Then it suggested that the board postpone its request for a deficiency appropriation and instead use money from the anticipated fiscal 1938 appropriation for the fourth quarter of fiscal 1937. It believed the language of the proposed appropriation act would permit this. This would avoid the need of a deficiency appropriation request until January 1938. When this suggestion was made, the Senate committee had already reported out the 1938 appropriation measure, but of course the board had no idea that the Glass amendments would produce a four-month deadlock. Accordingly, it was disposed to accept the budget bureau's plan.

But this situation was complicated by the fact that the board had already submitted to the budget bureau its proposed amendments to the Social Security Act. These amendments included provisions to (1) put all public assistance grants on a fifty-fifty matching basis for administrative expenses as well as assistance; (2) raise the federal share of aid to dependent children to one-half; and (3) increase the grant matchable in aid to dependent children from $12 to $18 on second and subsequent children. It was estimated that these changes would require an additional appropriation of $36,700,000 in the fiscal year 1938. In view of this fact Altmeyer on March 2 wrote the Director of the Budget as follows:

Your Mr. Ahern recently mentioned to our Assistant Executive Director, John J. Corson, the possibility of not including in the last deficiency appropriation bill any amount to cover the deficiency on the appropriation for grants-in-aid during this present fiscal year, since the appropriation in the pending Independent Offices Bill is available for use during this fiscal year, as well as during the next fiscal year. If the substantive changes now under consideration are approved you might plan to take care of the increased cost of these changes as well in the first deficiency bill next year, rather than in the last deficiency bill this year. However, in making such decision the possibility of exhausting the funds prior to the time that Congress could act next year should be given thorough consideration.

In the next few days it became apparent that to follow the proposal of the budget bureau would probably involve the board in serious difficulties the following year, unless Congress should act on the regular 1939 appropriation bill during January or by early February 1938. Consequently Altmeyer again wrote Bell on March 10, reviving the suggestion that a deficiency appropriation be obtained in 1937:

This office has been informally advised that you contemplate withholding presentation of this estimate to the Congress. In view of the small unexpended balance under this appropriation, the Board is desirous that the estimate be submitted to the Congress at the earliest possible date.

As of February 28, 1937, there was an unexpended balance in the current appropriation for old-age assistance of $10,734,170.58. There still remain two

States for which grants for the third quarter have not been made. Based on estimates of the Bureau of Public Assistance, the total grants to such States for the third quarter will be $305,812.50, which will reduce the available balance to $10,428,358.08. The estimated requirements for the fourth quarter amount to $41,114,188. With an available balance of only $10,428,358.08, there will be an estimated deficiency somewhat in excess of $30,000,000.

The appropriation for the fiscal year 1938 as requested and passed by both houses of Congress is $150,000,000. If the deficiency of $30,000,000 for the fourth quarter of this year is defrayed therefrom, there will remain a balance of $120,000,000 left to meet the requirements of 1938. According to recent estimates of the Bureau of Public Assistance, this amount would not be sufficient to provide grants for the first three quarters of the fiscal year 1938. It is not impossible, therefore, that the entire 1938 appropriation might be exhausted prior to passage by Congress of a deficiency bill in 1938.

Under the circumstances it appears inadvisable to rely on the funds provided by the pending appropriation bill for the fiscal year 1938 to cover the requirements for grants to States for the last quarter of the fiscal year 1937. The Independent Offices Appropriation Bill, which contains the appropriation for 1938 is still in conference and, while it may be passed in the near future, there are, as you know, certain controversial items therein which might so delay its final enactment that the funds provided therein would not be available in time for grants covering the fourth quarter of the fiscal year 1937.

Before it received an answer to this letter from the Bureau of the Budget, the board was asked by the Bureau of Public Assistance for advice on the policy to be followed on state requests for funds for the fourth quarter of 1937. The board directed that these requests be put through as they came along, in the usual manner. But its anxiety caused it, through the chairman, to write letters on March 20 to Chairman Glass of the Senate Appropriations Committee and Congressman Woodrum, chairman of the House Subcommittee on Appropriations, pointing out the deficiency of the 1937 old age assistance appropriation and asking advice as to the course of action to be taken in securing these funds. These chairmen replied that no deficiency request had been sent to them but that they would be glad to take prompt action on such a request as soon as it was submitted by the budget bureau. Attaching copies of these replies, Chairman Altmeyer wrote Bell on March 29 to request once more that the Bureau of the Budget submit such a deficiency request to the Congress.

By that time the situation was becoming quite serious because the fourth quarter, beginning April 1, was only a couple of days off. Therefore on March 30 the board reversed its decision of March 12 concerning the fourth-quarter public assistance requests from the states, and directed that estimates for the total amount of these fourth-quarter grants be made, but that the states be notified immediately by telegram that grants would be made only for the *first month* of the quarter pending the passage of the 1938 Independent Offices Appropriation Bill.

Finally, on April 1, Budget Director Bell came through with a definite statement refusing to approve the submission of a deficiency appropriation for old age assistance:

When the Board's estimate for a supplemental appropriation of $30,000,000 for old-age assistance was received in this office, it was given careful consideration. In view of the fact that the Independent Offices Appropriation Bill for 1938 contains an item of $150,000,000 for old-age assistance and that the appropriation language thereof provides that expenditures may be made from this item to meet the requirements of the last quarter of the fiscal year 1937, it is not believed that the supplemental item should be transmitted to Congress at this time, and particularly so since the Board is considering amendments which would, if approved, require an additional supplemental item or an adjustment of the estimate which you submitted on February 4, 1937.

As the proposed amendments are still under consideration, I am of the opinion that it would be advisable to delay the further consideration of supplemental estimates until the proposed amendments have been cleared, especially since there can be no assurance that the supplemental item transmitted to Congress at this time would be approved prior to the end of April. Furthermore if the item were to be submitted as a joint resolution it might not be approved in time to be of any advantage.

Because of the possibility of the Independent Office Appropriation Bill being approved prior to the date on which action might be obtained on either a supplemental estimate submitted in the usual way, or as a joint resolution, I am of the opinion that we should await action on the Bill now in conference. Such action, of course, will necessitate furnishing the States at this time with but a portion of the funds requested for assistance during the last quarter of this fiscal year, the amount alloted to be supplemented by funds from the regular appropriation as soon as the Independent Offices Appropriation Bill for 1938 is approved.

The board notified the states on March 30 that they would receive grants covering only the month of April, because of the delay in passage of the Independent Offices Appropriation Bill. These one-month grants began on March 31, when grants to nine states were made.

The crisis was resolved in the following way. On May 27, Congressman Woodrum introduced a joint resolution appropriating $18,000,000 to the board for payments to the states for old age assistance, and a second resolution deducting this sum from the old age assistance appropriation contained in the 1938 bill. These two resoutions were adopted by the House on May 27, and by the Senate on May 28. It was not until June 18 that the House concurred in the Senate amendments to the Independent Offices Appropriation Bill, and June 28 before that bill was signed by the President.

USE OF THE BUDGET FOR
ADMINISTRATIVE CONTROL

The second aspect of budget management is the systematic control of expenditures after appropriations become available. This was almost wholly neglected by the board throughout the period under review. When the board, in February 1936, received its first belated appropriation covering the last five months of the fiscal year 1936, it spent the money freely in the desire to accelerate the construction of its organization. This was a period when attention was centered upon expansion, rather than control of the purse strings for management purposes. It is true, however, that expenditure control did develop in a left-handed incidental manner as a part of the board's detailed consideration of individual appointments recommended by the bureaus and the executive director. The scrutiny which the board gave to appointments became a partial substitute for a systematic budget control activity. Such a substitute is only usable in a rapidly expanding organization. When the board's staff should settle down to a fairly constant level it might be confidently expected that general budget control as a tool of central management would be recognized for its intrinsic importance.

Those expenditure allotments of the fiscal 1937 appropriation which became available in July 1936 were authorized by the board upon the basis, almost entirely, of the estimates which the board had approved in the spring. The board did not have a budget officer, through failure of the salary it could offer to lure the men of its choice from their existing employments. But Assistant Executive Director Corson would have been glad to function as a center of expenditure control had the board been willing to lodge that duty with the executive director's office. As is shown earlier in this story he did take over the budget officer's duty of preparing expenditure estimates and defending them before the Bureau of the Budget and Congress, but explicit control of expenditures was denied him. The net result was a period of expansion directed primarily by the wishes of the directors of the bureaus.

When the Bureau of the Budget drastically cut the expenditure requests of the board for the fiscal year 1938 there ought to have been some incentive to institute a more systematic expenditure control system, because its cuts were coupled with a provision in the bill which would make available for 1938 any money for 1937 which the board did not use. Thus the less it spent from October 1936 (when the budget bureau wielded the axe) to June 30, 1937, the more it would have available for use during fiscal 1938. That this was not sufficient incentive may have been due to the amount of "velvet" in the appropriation item of $12,400,000 for the conduct of registration and for setting up the initial accounts for posting wage records. It should be noted, however, that in fiscal year 1937 the board did not spend $12,500,000 of funds appropriated for administrative expenses, and that in fiscal 1938 this item had been reduced to $3,000,000. Many items of regular establishment costs were charged to this fund, including a considerable part of the salaries of the regular staff of the Bureau of Informational Service.

It may be said in conclusion that the board was not hampered by lack of money in doing the things it wished to do during this beginning period. Practically no important project had to be abandoned or was seriously curtailed for lack of funds.

.3.

THE FIELD ORGANIZATION

PRELIMINARY STUDIES AND PLANS

The Determination of Regional Areas and the Selection of Headquarters Cities

Organization chart no. 1 had merely indicated that there would be nine regional offices, in which a representative would be placed from each of the board's line and auxiliary staff divisions. It did not include any suggestions for a subregional organization, even for the administration of the wholly federal function of old age benefits. Seidemann had quickly insisted that for this activity a district and a branch scheme must be provided. M. Tixier gave emphasis to Seidemann's recommendations. He thought that there must be more regional offices than the chart suggested, in order to reduce the amount of correspondence within any one region and in Washington.

Serious study of the problem of decentralization was launched by the board on December 2, 1935, when it formed the Field Organization Committee, with Dr. W. T. Stead of the U.S. Employment Service as chairman and Col. E. J. McCormack and R. B. Harris as representatives from the board's staff. Stead was selected because of his experience in helping organize the field services for the Federal Reemployment Service. The committee had the benefit of the study on regionalism which had just been published by the National Resources Committee,[1] as well as the judgment and experience of the administrators of some twenty other federal agencies. They made particular use of the Federal Reserve organization, the Post Office Department, the National Employment Service, and the large insurance companies. They made no special study of the experience in field organization of the Insurance Division of the Veterans' Administration, which might have given cogent information, particularly for the projected field units of the Bureau of Old Age Benefits.

---

[1] *Regional Factors in National Planning and Development,* December 1935.

The committee compiled maps and tables showing transportation and communication facilities and the number of compensable population in the different sections and urban centers of the United States. It had been instructed at the beginning of its work that in designing regional areas it was not to divide any state. On this point an animated argument developed between members of this committee and the National Resources Committee staff, whose recent study had declared for a principle of regional boundaries not restricted by state lines.[2]

The committee had also to keep in mind that because agriculture had been exempted from both the old age benefits and the unemployment compensation provisions of the Social Security Act, large areas in the Middle West and the Far West would be of little immediate importance in carrying out the board's functions. Headquarters cities for all field units would have to be selected with this fact in mind.

The committee had no instructions from the board concerning the distribution of authority between regional manager (a title later changed to director) and the field representatives of the operating bureaus or the district offices of the Bureau of Old Age Benefits. It therefore had to make its own assumptions about what the duties of the regional office and field representatives should be. At this time, with the exception of Miles, the board members seemed to think of the regional manager as a high-class office clerk who would take care of such matters as transportation, supplies, office space, and services for the field staff of the various bureaus. However, by the time the committee made its report on January 29, 1936, the board had shifted toward a view of the regional director as a very important functionary in the whole administrative scheme. The report reflected this point of view in stating that "coordination of activities of the service bureaus, cooperation with state authorities and boards, field supervision, claims, investigation, education and developmental work, selection and training of personnel, space procurement, and such special functions as may be assigned by the Board" would be the principal tasks of the regional director. It also proposed that "regional officers will not have the authority to originate policies but will supervise the execution of such policies and procedures as the Board may indicate." So far as the field plan for the Bureau of Old Age Benefits was concerned, the board assumed that the district office manager would be in charge of the branch offices within his district and that he would be administratively responsible directly to the headquarters bureau staff at Washington.

The recommendations of the committee were based upon the assumption that a gradual development of the field organization would make it possible to secure a better adaptation to administrative needs. They proposed that not

[2] *Ibid.,* p. ix and chap. 15.

all units of the field plan be started immediately but that three regional offices should be set up first, and then the number expanded, as experience indicated, to nine and ultimately to a total of twelve.

The first three headquarters proposed were for Washington, D.C., serving the southeastern and eastern states; Chicago, serving the middle western states; and San Francisco, for the Rocky Mountain and Pacific Coast area. It justified the selection of Washington, rather than New York, for the eastern states by pointing out the advantage of using this as a model unit which could be very closely observed by the board and made to serve as a proving ground for developing procedures and training people who would then be assigned to other regions. In addition, Washington had the advantage of being more conveniently located than New York for serving the southeastern states. The fact that Chicago and San Francisco were natural regional headquarters had been made clear by the report of the National Resources Committee, which showed these cities to be already regional headquarters for sixty-six and seventy-three national agencies, respectively.

The committee proposed to open a second group of offices: Boston for the New England area; New York City, for its state; Atlanta or Birmingham for the southeastern states; Dallas for Texas, Oklahoma, Arkansas, and Louisiana; St. Paul for Minnesota, the two Dakotas, and Montana; and Denver for the Rocky Mountain states of Wyoming, Utah, Colorado, and New Mexico, as well as the prairie states of Nebraska and Kansas.

As a possible final step the redesign of the areas to twelve regions was suggested. New Jersey would be added to New York, Pennsylvania and Delaware would be given to the Washington area, North Carolina would be detached from Washington, D.C., and included with the other six southeastern states with headquarters at Atlanta, and Chicago would be restricted to the service of Illinois, Wisconsin, and Indiana. A new regional office, to be opened in Columbus, would take care of Michigan, Ohio, and Kentucky. The realignment for the territory of St. Paul would include Minnesota, the two Dakotas, Nebraska, and Iowa. There would be created a new regional office at Kansas City, Missouri, to care for Missouri, Kansas, Oklahoma, and Arkansas. The office at Dallas, Texas, would be restricted to Texas and Louisiana. The Denver office would be confined to Colorado, Wyoming, Utah, and New Mexico. The San Francisco office would take care of California, Nevada, Arizona, and Hawaii. A new regional office would be created in Seattle for the territory including Washington, Oregon, Idaho, Montana, and Alaska.

This twelve-region plan proposed two new regions in the Middle West and one in the Far West. It was pointed out that the experience of persons familiar with the Far West indicated that a horizontal grouping of states paralleling lines of transportation and communication would prove more workable than a vertical combination, with Montana and Idaho attached to Denver and Washington and Oregon to San Francisco. The report quoted the study of the National Resources Committee indicating an apparent natural grouping of regional office headquarters in the United States, with the 1300 regional offices belonging to eighty-two nationwide agencies concentrated in a relatively small number of cities: San Francisco, New York, Chicago, Denver, Atlanta, the Twin Cities, Seattle, St. Louis, Portland, Baltimore, Kansas City, Los Angeles, Detroit, Cincinnati, Pittsburgh, and Omaha. The committee endorsed the idea that by selecting its headquarters for regions from this list of cities, the Social Security Board would be serving "the dual purpose of promoting the cooperation and integration of field agencies dealing with similar problems, and of capitalizing on the experience of other agencies in working out their own problems of regional location." Chairman Stead had been particularly impressed with the cogency of arguments presented by Mr. Frederick Delano and Mr. Charles W. Eliot of the National Resources Committee, that while the regional boundaries for the board's purposes might properly vary from those suggested in the special study of the National Resources Committee, it was highly important that the central offices for the regions be located at the regional centers indicated in that report.

The committee proceeded upon the assumption that there should be at least one district office in each state. The remaining forty-nine offices were assigned to more heavily populated states upon the basis of "population density, compensables to be served, transportation and communication facilities, and other factors." The committee recommended locations for 308 primary branches within the districts and 177 secondary branches, and deferred the location of the additional branch offices to future experience. In locating district and branch offices the report was concerned with the work load falling on each office and with following as closely as possible the location of the offices of the U.S. Employment Service. The ninety-seven district offices selected, and all but 398 of the branch offices, were in cities having district offices of the Employment Service. The report called attention to the fact that the U.S. Employment Service was then operating 336 branch offices and that the board could draw from the experience of that service in making its choices for further branch elaboration of its own field structure. The report also noted that, with a few exceptions, the locations of the proposed district field organization coincided with the locations of collection offices of the Internal Revenue Bureau of the Department of the Treasury, and for the exceptions the report proposed the establishment of branch offices. In many instances the district offices were to be located in capital cities, but those capitals which were not of sufficient consequence for all the functions of the board were to be assigned primary branch offices. This concern with capital cities grew out of the recognition that the public assistance and un-employment compensation tasks of the board required effective cooperation with the states, and for that purpose capital city locations were of particular importance.

The committee found it difficult to use criteria which would suit all of the three line-functions that constituted the substance of the board's job. As a matter of fact, the major criteria used were the numbers of employees and employers whose records would have to be kept in connection with tax col-lections and for whom claims for old age benefits or unemployment compen-sation benefits would be lodged. Studies of transportation facilities and the convenience of travel from one center to the surrounding territory were also important in guiding the committee. While economic homogeneity was re-garded as important for unemployment compensation, it had little significance for the other two functions and was thus sacrificed in designing regional boundaries and determining regional centers.

When the board received this report, it called in the committee to explain its recommendations. On February 14, 1936, the board approved the parts of the report relating to regional areas and offices (with certain modifications) but took no action upon the proposals for district and branch offices. About the time this report was submitted, the board had decided to open up all regional offices simultaneously, thus ruling out one of the committee's major recommendations.

Why this decision was made is somewhat obscure. Miles had from the beginning of the talk about regional offices been anxious for their early establishment, and had expressed his conviction that men of business experi-ence should be hired as soon as possible and trained to open up the regional offices. Altmeyer later explained that the decision to start all twelve offices simultaneously was required by the need for good public relations, a need which was not confined to three centers but existed all over the country; therefore why piddle along with a gradual process? Winant's conversations, together with confidential information from another informed source, gave the impression that the decision was partly motivated by the desire to block the political maneuvers of Miles, and led to the hypothesis that Altmeyer and Winant felt the congressional pressure for regional offices to be so strong as to be difficult to resist, and that they therefore combined to block Miles by deciding at once where they should be located and who should get the chief regional jobs. On one occasion Miles strenuously argued for a regional group-ing which would make Little Rock, Arkansas (the capital of his own state) the logical regional center. Altmeyer countered with the contention that if that grouping were justified, then Milwaukee, Wisconsin, was a logical center for the region for which St. Paul had been recommended as headquarters. Chairman Winant intervened in this wrangle by solemnly suggesting that for New England, Boston was passé and obviously Concord, New Hampshire, should be chosen as the regional headquarters. This episode brought Winant and Altmeyer together in a gentleman's agreement to support the committee's report on locations and regional boundaries.

However, at the final consideration of the report on February 14, the board modified the committee's report in a number of particulars. The night before this meeting, Miles had summoned his political aide, Douglas, to prepare a criticism of the committee's report for him. Douglas stayed up all night working up critical data and argument. He was particularly convinced that the report had erred in its regional boundaries for the southwest and south central areas. He thought it a great mistake to tie Texas and Louisiana together; that instead Louisiana should be joined with Arkansas and Missouri; that the choice of Denver was ill advised and that instead Salt Lake City, as the center of railroad, airline, and highway transportation, should be chosen; that Michigan should be thrown with Indiana and Illinois; and that Pennsylvania, New Jersey, and Delaware should not be linked together. His report for Miles was used in the discussion the following day.

The board also invited Senator Black of Alabama to discuss the location of a regional office for the southeast. Black urged a regional office at Birmingham instead of Atlanta. He was told that the committee had discussed the possibilities of these two cities in more detail than any others in the entire country. Senator O'Mahoney of Wyoming had requested a chance to discuss the desirability of Cheyenne, and Miles tried to reach him by phone so that he might appear and press his case before final action was taken. The final motion as adopted accepted the committee's report, with these exceptions: Birmingham was selected in place of Atlanta as the regional center for the Southeast, Cleveland instead of Columbus for the Michigan, Ohio, Kentucky region, and Houston instead of Dallas for the southwest region. The committee proposal for a twelfth region in the Pacific Northwest, with Seattle as its center, was discarded. The board created an additional eastern region with Philadelphia as its center. This permitted detaching New Jersey from New York and making New York State a region by itself.

There were three causes for the changes from Atlanta to Birmingham and from Columbus to Cleveland. The first was the pressure of Senator Black; the second was the committee's own hesitancy when it had discussed these two cities, because Birmingham's industrial activities gave it some valid claim to recognition; the third was related to another regional patronage dispute. Miles wanted as regional manager of the Columbus office a particular person whom Winant did not like. Winant gave way on the southeastern office at

Atlanta in favor of Birmingham, in order to be in a better position to deny Miles' demand in the North and to take the regional headquarters from Columbus to Cleveland.[3] Altmeyer was convinced that Cleveland was nearer the center of the employee population than Columbus and was a better location.

We may conclude the story of regional locations by running ahead to one other episode which occurred some weeks later and which concerned a change in boundaries and headquarters for the southwestern area. On March 27, 1936, the board modified its action of February 14 by detaching New Mexico from the Pacific Coast region, joining it to Texas and Louisiana, and moving the regional headquarters from Houston to San Antonio. At the same time it rescinded its decision to locate a headquarters in Cleveland, and moved back to Columbus. These decisions were made after consulting the Field Organization Committee. But while the committee approved the change from Cleveland to Columbus (this having been the committee's original recommendation), it strongly disapproved the southwestern proposal. Two varying interpretations of this action were given. Winant claimed that he had never felt happy about the detachment of New Mexico from Texas. He had disapproved the inclusion of Oklahoma with Texas because this would give an opportunity for Miles to insist upon putting the regional office at Oklahoma City, and run the danger of getting the board into politics. If New Mexico were joined to Texas, San Antonio would be nearer the center of the region than Houston, with better railroad connection. Another reason for his attitude, Winant explained, was that Oscar Powell, whom he regarded as a very unusual man and whom he wanted for regional manager, would probably not take the place if he had to leave San Antonio, his home. Miles and Bane both declared that the change was made to satisfy Winant's desire to get Powell.

This was the snarl created by Winant's impulsive agreement to Congressman Buchanan's proposed trade of influence, a softening of the proposed budget cut for fiscal 1937 in return for the relocation of the board's proposed regional office in his home town, Austin. It should be added here that the board had already made so firm a commitment to place its southwest regional office in San Antonio, that Powell had gone ahead to dissolve his partnership in legal practice to be able to accept the board's regional directorship.

[3] This decision to go to Birmingham created a personnel snarl. Negotiations had been carried to virtual completion with A. Steve Nance, president of the Georgia State Federation of Labor, to accept the regional directorship in the Southeast. He lived in Atlanta and had agreed to accept on the understanding that the office would be located there. The board neglected to notify him of its change, and on May 13 proceeded to appoint him. The promise to Senator Black was felt to be more important than the retention of Nance. Consequently Nance declined, and B. F. Ashe, president of the University of Miami, became the first director at Birmingham.

PLANNING THE FIELD ESTABLISHMENT AND THE
DUTIES OF THE REGIONAL DIRECTOR (MANAGER)

After concluding its report on regional areas and office locations, the Field Organization Committee turned its attention to determining the functions of the field establishment and the duties of the regional manager.[4] To clarify this problem it prepared a memorandum which it sent to the heads of all bureaus and made the basis for a discussion on February 5. This memorandum was designed to focus the discussion on "(a) the relationship of the different types of field offices to the central office in Washington, (b) the relationship of the different types of offices to one another, namely, region to district, district to branch, etc., (c) the relationship of the different types of offices to state governments and the public, (d) the functions and duties of the directors of regional offices, the representatives in regional offices of the several bureaus, and the managers in district and branch offices." The committee stated its own hypotheses about the regional office in practically the same words that it had used in its report to the board. In addition it included the following ideas about cooperation between the manager and the bureau representatives:

Cooperation with the manager of the region is required for securing coordination with other bureaus; that is, the legal representatives would inform the manager of the region as to their actions, particularly those of possible regional effect, but the regional manager would not attempt to direct the legal representative. The Informational Service Bureau representative would regard closely the wishes of the manager of the region concerning publicity and all other matters pertaining to his department, but the policy of the Informational Service Bureau representative would be determined in Washington. Assignment of speakers, special articles not issued from Washington, and other activities of possible regional consequence, shall be submitted for consideration to the manager of the regional office. The relationship of the other bureau representatives to the manager of the regional office shall be the same as in the two instances cited above, regarding all matters pertaining to the work of their respective bureaus. Among the definite problems of the manager of the regional office within his regional office are cooperation with the regional representative of the Bureau of Business Management, in the assignment of space within the regional offices, and the enforcement of rules and regulations for the proper conduct of the office, provision for the reception of state officials and representatives as well as the public, including their proper guidance to bureau representatives to secure for them the information sought, and follow-ups on such calls and correspondence. In all matters of policy connected with operations within the territory of the

---

[4] Stead, who had turned over to McCormack active direction of the committee, resigned from it on February 12, and McCormack became chairman in name as well as in fact. R. U. Wilder was assigned to the committee on February 1.

regional office, whenever any irreconcilable differences of opinion develop between the manager of the regional office and the Bureau representatives, the manager of the regional office shall have the authority to suspend action on the matter until specific instructions have been received from the Board in Washington. The manager of the regional office shall provide for the handling in this same manner of correspondence from state officials or representatives and private individuals, including the acknowledgment and disposition of such correspondence.

The committee also gave its view of the kind of people who should be selected for the regional managerships. This view clearly implied a person to represent the board in public relations contacts. The memorandum further suggested relations between the regional manager and the district office organization. Because it was clear that in that situation the problem of old age benefits was paramount, the suggestion was made that the manager of the regional office make his contacts with the district office "only through or in conjunction with the regional representative of the Old-Age Benefit Bureau," except as he might be commanded to execute specific duties assigned him by the board.

The committee asked each bureau director for a memorandum indicating his space requirements, describing his notion of the functions of each member of the regional personnel, and commenting on the problems of field organization.

The staff meeting at which this memorandum was discussed was attended by a few people from the outside, of whom Stead of the Employment Service and a Mr. Renshaw of the NRA were the most important. As related to McKinley by Col. McCormack, the only serious challenge to the memorandum of the committee about the functions of the regional manager was made by Helen Bary of the Public Assistance Bureau, who objected to the control suggested over the field representatives of the Public Assistance Bureau. A day or so later Latimer quoted with approval the consensus of the meeting, as expressed by Renshaw, that there should be a regional manager with power to control the representatives of the different bureaus but with the explicit understanding that if he ever exercised it he would be fired.

These matters were discussed frequently during the spring by the bureau heads. On the whole they were very skeptical about the entire regional plan, because they disliked the creation of a regional officer with control over their own field representatives. Even the board's committee had dealt very tenderly with the jurisdiction of the regional directors over the district and branch offices of the Old Age Benefits Bureau. Both the committee and the head of that bureau, Murray Latimer, assumed that the administration of this federal function was unrelated to the two federal-state services and would be directed from Washington. Such field representatives as would be located within the region by this bureau would function in the nature of inspectors rather than administrators. The operating field unit would thus be the district, which in turn would supervise the branches. In addition to general skepticism about the proposed regional establishment, the bureau heads regarded the move to set up field offices as premature, because they could not see what functions the regional directors could profitably exercise at that stage in the board's experience. On March 11, less than a week before the beginning of the first training course for the executive assistant to the regional director, Bane held a meeting of bureau chiefs at which the question of what the regional offices would do was discussed. With one exception, there was consensus that the board should proceed slowly in opening up the regional offices. The one exception was Wagenet, head of the Bureau of Unemployment Compensation, who vigorously supported the early establishment of regional offices, affirming his belief that the only way their activities could be developed was by putting people out to learn by making mistakes. Within a short time he had changed his mind, and he became throughout the remainder of the period studied the most persistent obstructor of the regional scheme.

LAUNCHING THE REGIONAL ORGANIZATION

SELECTING THE FIRST REGIONAL OFFICERS

No sooner had the decision about regional areas and headquarters been taken (on February 14) than the board instructed Bane to prepare plans for selecting employees. Miles had been itching to start the hiring process two months earlier. His mind was fully made up to put a different type of person in charge of the regional office. Rather than the academically trained specialists who had been sought for top positions in the Washington headquarters, he wanted businessmen whose experience and personality would make it easy to deal with politicians and employers and to interpret the field specialists to the people of the region. This point of view, with some slight modifications, was pretty largely accepted by the other members of the board by the end of March. As late as February 29 Winant had said that the board was undecided just when to set up the regional offices, or what degree of authority the regional manager should have over the field staff.

On this point the board had blown hot and cold. All the NRA people had told the board that it must have one person in charge. The public needed someone who could answer any questions that would arise. It did not like to be shifted to three or four people. Winant was undecided as to what was wise.

Altmeyer suggested that the executive assistant, at least, should come from the federal establishment, so that the regional office would possess a knowledge of federal routines and practices. He urged Bane to canvass the people being released by the NRA. Bane selected a committee composed of McCormack, Aronson, Bennett, and Clearman to interview prospective candidates for regional offices and to recommend a group for training, with the expectation that from them both regional managers and assistant managers would be ultimately chosen. The committee canvassed NRA prospects and selected a preliminary list, practically all of whom had been identified with the Bureau of Foreign and Domestic Commerce before they went to the NRA. There were also some with this same background but taken from the Agricultural Adjustment Administration, then apparently folding up.

Bane made a report on March 4 telling the board that the committee was planning to employ a number of these prospects at an early date. It was also planning, if the board approved, to open up regional offices at New York, Washington, Chicago, and San Francisco by the first of April, or by the fifteenth at the latest. He asked the board to decide whether or not it intended to request of the President exemption from the regular civil service requirements for the initial appointments to the regional executive positions. If it did not so intend, Bane did not want to bring in any people not already possessed of civil service status. The committee had in mind to begin each regional office with a skeleton staff consisting of the manager, if possible; if not, an assistant manager; an information representative; and the necessary clerical assistance. Later, specialists would be added. Miles protested at the opening of offices a few at a time and the board agreed that all regional offices should be set up at once.

By March 10, the committee had interviewed about thirty people and had asked half a dozen to come in to meet the board. It had also worked out a tentative plan for a minimum staff, and a training plan to start on March 16 and to run for two weeks. The committee was shooting at April 1 as the opening date.

Bane asked the board about his authority with reference to the regional executives. He also asked it to decide what authority the regional manager should have over the field representatives of the bureaus. Miles answered Bane's second question by saying that the regional managers should be so competent that they should have authority to remove people in their organizations. Altmeyer declared that he had been swinging more and more to the idea that the board must depend upon the regional managers to run the office, although this should not preclude bureau specialists from carrying on direct communication with the bureau directors in Washington through the medium of the regional office. He thought the regional manager should take up any conflict with the executive director, not with the bureau head.

In an interview a few weeks later (May 4, 1936) Altmeyer gave Frase a more complete statement of his views on the functions of the regional managers, which were, in summary:

They should respond to local requests for speeches and discussions of the board and its work and should be able to meet individual requests for information. They should have the knowledge and the personality to do effective public relations work. This is urgently needed. Other government agencies, by confining their attention to the regular publicity channels and personnel, have made a mistake which the board does not want to repeat. The regional representative of Mr. Resnick's bureau will not be able to do this kind of thing. He is a technician for publicity, not a public relations person. Were the board to rely upon the regional Informational Service representative, it would lay itself open to the charge of propaganda. This is not so true of the regional manager, who speaks directly for the board. After the bureaus have been sufficiently organized to send staffs to the regions, the regional manager will undertake to coordinate the activities of all the bureaus operating in the region.

In crystallizing the board's judgment on this question of the regional manager's powers, it is probable that the field organization committee's subcommittee on forms and procedures for regional offices played an important part. Before this subcommittee could go very far in preparing a manual, it was necessary to determine its own assumptions about the relations between regional directors and bureau field staffs. As explained by William Galvin, chairman of the subcommittee, there were two schools of thought: one felt that the regional director should be a kind of office manager, with responsibility for mandatory decisions left to the bureaus in Washington; the other school, which dominated the committee, thought the regional director should be a director in fact as well as in name. The people of the subcommittee who had this second view were the most influential in determining the board's policy, and their judgments were incorporated in the memorandum handed to the regional directors by Bane when they departed to begin their work. The subcommittee was composed largely of men who had been field representatives in the Bureau of Foreign and Domestic Commerce and in the NRA.

By March 11, plans for a training program for the first group of candidates for high regional executive positions were well under way.[5] The people selected for the course were all employees of other federal agencies, and most of them had been with the field service of the Bureau of Foreign and Domestic Commerce and with the NRA or AAA. It was expected that these

[5] An account of the in-service training programs is given in the discussion of personnel management procedures, chapter 7.

people might make good executive assistants to the regional directors. By the time the training program was completed, the board had concluded it would be unwise to send them out before the regional directors had been selected.

When the board confronted the task of developing a second training program, for the regional directors, it made up its mind to choose if possible outstanding local people, and to attempt to open up the regional offices the first of May. Winant said, on April 4, that the board then had four or five properly qualified people in line for these positions. He wanted a different type of person than the Bureau of Foreign and Domestic Commerce group then taking the training course. The board already had Mrs. Anna Rosenberg for New York. She had been an outstanding person in the NRA organization, and the board had taken her over, together with her staff in the New York office, some weeks before.[6] She was said to be an excellent contact person, able to reach important people and organizations, and had already been used by the board to help the governor of New York secure changes in the public assistance laws to conform to the requirements of the Social Security Act. For New England, Winant at that time had John Pearson in mind, and for the Southwest, Oscar Powell. All of these people, in Winant's view, possessed standing in their communities, unusual social insight, and the personality to represent the board.

Because of this decision to use, for regional directors, local people of standing who would ordinarily lack civil service status, it appeared to the board necessary to secure an executive order exempting the positions from the regular civil service requirements. The board asked Bane and Bennett to undertake negotiations with the Civil Service Commission looking toward approval of such an executive order. On March 27, Bennett reported the upshot of his conversations with the civil service commission people. He had indicated the kind of functions the regional directors would perform and the sort of experience they should be able to present in order to meet the standards and qualifications that the commission would be inclined to impose. He had discussed the idea that these exempted candidates should be required to establish their qualifications by means of noncompetitive examinations. He reported that the commission would probably be much more liberal in establishing such standards for noncompetitive appointments than they had been in determining qualifications for experts. He closed his memorandum by urging the desirability of this noncompetitive approval by the Civil Service Commission. His chief argument was that because the board intended to

[6] On February 24, McKinley was told that the board had already engaged Mrs. Rosenberg and placed her on the payroll. She was said to be close to persons highly placed in the Democratic Party, and on that account her office staff and spacious NRA quarters were taken over lock, stock, and barrel months before the other regional headquarters were opened up.

exempt only the initial appointments, the positions would by such an arrangement remain in the competitive service and the persons initially appointed, even though noncompetitively, would acquire a classified or competitive civil service status "which would make them eligible for transfer or promotion and likewise give them a status under the Retirement Act." Bennett also indicated his feeling that such a plan would assure the selection of properly qualified candidates, and would facilitate the approval of this proposed executive order by the Civil Service Commission.

Nevertheless, the board did not accept Bennett's suggestion but proposed an executive order without any tests. This action the Civil Service Commission disapproved. Inasmuch as it had become practice for the President to require both the approval of the Civil Service Commission and that of the budget bureau before he would issue an order, the board had to back down.

The proposed executive order, as finally drawn, went further than the inclusion of the twelve regional office managers. It also provided for exempting from the competitive provisions of the Civil Service Act and rules the initial appointment of a confidential clerk or secretary for each member of the board and for the executive director, the coordinator, the general counsel, and each of the seven bureau directors. In each case, however, noncompetitive tests to establish requisite qualifications could be made by the Civil Service Commission.[7]

The original request for the order was made to the Civil Service Commission on March 31. Approval was not obtained until the order was revised. On April 17 it was sent for approval to the Bureau of the Budget, and subsequently its legal form had to be passed upon by the Attorney General's office. It was therefore not until May 7, 1936, that the President issued the order. In the meantime the board went ahead with its plans for selecting directors for the regional offices on the assumption that the order would be issued.

To attract the talent desired, the board decided to pay good salaries. The schedule established on April 8 was as follows:

New York	
Philadelphia	$7,500
Columbus	
Chicago	
Boston	
San Antonio	$6,500
San Francisco	

[7] The board had originally wanted to exempt an additional position of this type for each of the board members and executive heads. Here, again, it had been advised that the Civil Service Commission would not stand for two such places being exempted.

Washington
Birmingham
St. Paul　　　　　$6,000
Denver
Kansas City

THE DIRECTORS ARE SENT OUT TO OPEN THE REGIONAL OFFICES

The first group of six regional directors were given a training course of eleven days, and then on the first of May were sent out to open up their offices, guided by a set of instructions about their duties and the organization of their offices. The instructions, "Administrative Order No. 11," consisted of two pages of items, of which the following are the more important:

II. Each Regional Director shall be the representative of the Social Security Board and shall be the responsible director of all activities of the Board within the region to which he is assigned.

III. The Regional Attorney and regional staff representatives of each of the bureaus shall be appointed by the directors of the respective bureaus. The Regional Director will have the right in respect to the appointment of each individual who is to serve on his staff, first, to recommend potential employees to the respective Bureau Directors, and secondly, to protest to the Executive Director the appointment of any individual to serve on his staff who in his opinion is unsuitable for service as a member of his staff.

V. The representatives assigned by the bureaus of the Regional Offices are to represent within the region their respective Bureau Directors subject, however, to the supervision of the Regional Director.

VI. The Regional Attorney and specialists assigned to Regional Offices by the Board's bureaus will be subject to the control of the Regional Director so far as their relationship with State and local governments and public are concerned. They will be under the control of their respective Bureau Directors with respect to all technical matters.

VII. Representatives of the Board's bureaus operating from Washington within a region or district shall inform the Regional Director as to their itineraries, plans, and instructions.

Moreover, in so far as practicable these representatives shall keep the Regional Director at all times informed, either directly or through Washington, of results of their activities within the region.

VIII. The traveling field staffs of the Board's bureaus will be so organized as to correlate their activities in detail with the field organization of the Board and the twelve Regional Offices. These traveling representatives and auditors will utilize the Regional Offices as their headquarters.

IX. All communications between Washington and any member of a staff of a Regional Office shall be routed through the Director of the Regional Office, or copies shall be simultaneously forwarded to him when direct routing is impossible. Similarly all communications between specialists assigned to the staff of a Regional Office and the Washington office of the Social Security Board shall be routed through the Regional Director.

X. It is incumbent upon the Regional Director, by staff meetings, conferences and communications, to coordinate the activities of the Regional Staff to effect maximum efficiency.

XI. The Regional Director shall refer all technical matters requiring special knowledge or knowledge probably within the province of the specific bureau, to the proper specialists, or in the absence of such specialists in the region, to the Bureau Director in Washington.

XII. All appointments of members of the regional staff with public officials, the press, as well as speaking engagements, shall be made through or with the approval of the Director of the Regional Office.

XIII. The district offices and branch offices, within a region, whose activities will primarily be concerned with the administration of Title II of the Social Security Act, shall be supervised and their activities coordinated by the representatives of the Bureau of Federal Old-Age Benefits assigned to the staff of the Regional Director. While the direct supervision of these district and branch offices shall be the function of this staff member, he will at all times be generally supervised by the Regional Director.

When Frase discussed the task which lay ahead with John Pearson, a few hours before he left for his New England assignment on May 1, Pearson called attention to paragraph VI of his instructions, saying that he thought it still left very much to be cleared up. The illustration which had been given to him and his associates that day was the following. When a field representative of the Public Assistance Bureau, for example, is about to contact a state official, the regional director may advise against doing that because of some delicate political situation. The field person must accept that advice. But when that person has been authorized to make the visit, what a field representative tells the political officers about the technical problems of the bureau is solely within the province of the field agent and his bureau superior. Pearson felt rather shaky about this lack of clarity but concluded there was no way to solve the problem save by trial and error.

The new regional directors were:

San Francisco. Richard Neustadt had been with the NRA, the Federal Employment Service, and for a short time the Bureau of Unemployment Compensation. Wagenet intended to use Neustadt as the field representative for his bureau also.

San Antonio. John Oscar Powell had no previous training or experience in public administration. He was an attorney with a very sympathetic attitude toward the social program of the board.

Kansas City. Edward McDonald had been connected with the Oklahoma State Highway Commission and according to Miles, who was his sponsor, came with high recommendations for competence from the U.S. Bureau of Public Roads.

Boston. John Pearson had a wide background of activity in public affairs, although not specifically in the field of labor relations. He had been director of the New Hampshire Foundation.

Philadelphia. William L. Dill, formerly state tax commissioner of New Jersey, had been the Democratic candidate for the governorship of New Jersey, opposing Harold Hoffman. He was selected also because of favorable recommendations made by Louis Brownlow and William J. Ellis, commissioner of the New Jersey Department of Institutions and Agencies.

New York. Mrs. Anna Rosenberg was formerly administrative assistant to one of the leading members of Macy Brothers. While she had had no professional training in welfare work, she was said to have had ample contact with welfare and labor situations, and in the judgment of the board was well oriented to her task.

On May 13, four more regional directors were approved:

Cleveland. Benedict Crowell, onetime Assistant Secretary of War and more recently regional and state director for the NRA in Ohio.

Chicago. H. L. McCarthy, dean of the College of Commerce, DePaul University, former director of the regional labor board, and labor arbitrator.

Minneapolis. Fred M. Wilcox, for twenty years a member of the Wisconsin Industrial Commission (twelve years as chairman), and recently for three years executive director of the Wisconsin Conference of Social Work.

Birmingham. A. Steve Nance, president of the Georgia State Federation of Labor.[8]

Both McCarthy and Wilcox were suggested by Altmeyer. With Crowell's appointment, the regional office in Columbus, Ohio, was moved back once more to its original position in Cleveland. On May 19 the board appointed the remaining two regional directors:

Denver. Heber Harper, from 1922 to 1927 chancellor of the University of Denver. Subsequently a faculty member of various universities and a research worker.

Washington. G. R. Parker, former businessman, exporter, and regional director of the NRA.

[8] See note 3 above for an explanation of Nance's failure to accept and of the appointment of B.F. Ashe in his place.

Thus shortly after June 1, 1936, all of the regional directors and their executive assistants were on the job, and a considerable number of regional attorneys had been appointed (on the basis of Mr. Eliot's selection, without the advice and consent of the regional directors concerned).[9]

The attitude of the bureau heads toward the regional offices was summarized on May 4 by Mr. Galvin, the chairman of the subcommittee on regional organization, as follows. For Business Management, the executive assistant to the regional director would act. It was still a little uncertain how the Bureau of Business Management would exercise control over this person, in view of the fact that he was not selected by the head of that bureau or subject to his discipline. With regard to public information, Resnick was expected to place representatives in the regional offices as soon as possible. He told the directors before they left Washington that he would expect his field men in the regional offices to follow headquarters instructions with respect to publicity originating in the Washington headquarters for general public information. With regard to stories originating within the region, he would expect the regional director to exercise a good deal of influence in determining how they should be handled. For the Bureau of Old Age Benefits, no change in projected relationships had been made since Latimer's memorandum on April 3. Miss Hoey was still adhering to her intention to operate Public Assistance only through four regional headquarters and to make little use even of these until she had more field staff. Wagenet was still uncertain what the relationships between his Unemployment Compensation people and the regional directors should be. He was of the opinion, however, that it should be possible to operate within the framework of instruction VI of the memorandum to the regional directors.

OPERATION OF THE REGIONAL ESTABLISHMENT BEFORE REGISTRATION

The course of development in the regional and field staff of the board before the assignment of benefit account numbers in November, 1936, is difficult to trace. The most important question was, of course, the nature of the relationship between the regional director and the various representa-

[9] On June 9, Bane told Frase that every region had its director chosen and space obtained for its offices. Equipment was then on the way from Washington and in most cases the offices were actually set up, although not far enough advanced to be ready for business. But this could not be delayed more than a few days more.

tives of the Washington bureaus, particularly the bureaus of Public Assistance, Unemployment Compensation, and Old Age Benefits. The board had not defined these relationships in detail when the regional directors were sent out, nor did it do so at any later date. It preferred—as in so many other cases—to allow relationships to crystallize slowly, by concrete action in particular cases of conflict between the regional directors and the field staffs and between the regional directors and the bureau chiefs in Washington. Naturally, the tendency was for things to work out somewhat differently in each regional office, according to the personalities involved.

SLOW COMPLETION OF REGIONAL STAFF—SUMMER 1936

For the first two or three months, the regional directors had little to do and they had a slender staff with which to do it. After two months (by August 1, 1936) there were:

7 offices with a regional attorney

7 offices with an Informational Service representative

1 office with an Unemployment Compensation representative

7 offices with a Research and Statistics (public assistance statistics) representative

There were no representatives of the bureaus of Old Age Benefits, Public Assistance, or Accounts and Audits in any regional office, though the latter two bureaus had a considerable staff in the field, working out of Washington.

By November 10, 1936, just before registration started, this picture had changed. There were now:

8 offices with a regional attorney

11 offices with an Informational Service representative

4 offices with an Unemployment Compensation representative

12 offices with a Public Assistance representative

11 offices with a Public Assistance statistics representative

1 office with an Old Age Benefits representative

The Bureau of Accounts and Audits still had no regional representatives, although by this time the field auditing staff (for public assistance payments in the states) had reached very sizable proportions.

This simple tabulation gives a rather graphic indication of the way in which certain bureaus were subtly sabotaging the board's ambitious regional scheme by simply neglecting to recruit and appoint a regional staff. Wagenet frankly had no intention of appointing any regional representatives, because he did not want to give the regional directors a chance to interfere with his direct relationships with the states. He preferred to have state officials come to Washington themselves—or, failing that, to send out members of the bureau staff direct from Washington. (The Unemployment Compensation representative in New York was appointed because Mrs. Rosenberg insisted on one. The other three noted for November 10 were all either temporarily assigned, or resigned to take positions with state unemployment compensation agencies.) Miss Hoey had held out for some time, but finally capitulated and designated members of her field staff as regional representatives. Hughes consistently maintained the position that his field auditors did their work in the state capitals and in the county seats, and that except where the regional office was also a state capital there was no reason whatsoever for them to spend any time in the regional headquarters. He further contended that he didn't want to tie down any group of auditors to one region but preferred to have them available for work in any state at any time. His auditors went out in large crews to clean up one state at a time. Latimer continued to be suspicious of the regional arrangement. He wished to keep the regional director from exercising any control over the projected field offices of the Bureau of Old Age Benefits. That attitude and his preoccupation with the Railroad Retirement Board, plus the fact that the Bureau of Old Age Benefits was only a skeleton planning organization until November 1936, resulted in failure to designate any regional representatives of this bureau until Seidemann came in as director in September; and he appointed only one such representative before November.

The general counsel was quite willing to appoint regional attorneys, even though he was not sure what they would do. He had in fact submitted, and the board approved, a complete list of twelve even before all the regional directors had been appointed. If there were not twelve regional attorneys from the start it was because of declinations of appointments or because some of the regional directors—like McCarthy, Neustadt and Powell—saw no need for one. Miss Helen Jeter, who was directing the Division of Public Assistance Statistics of the Bureau of Research and Statistics, proceeded to appoint her field staff as quickly as possible in order to begin the process of getting adequate statistics from the states. She did not hesitate to name them as regional social statisticians, because there was not much danger of any great amount of interest and interference by regional directors in that dry field. Resnick, as usual, was the one bureau director who took the board's statement of policy with complete seriousness; he set about appointing regional Informational Service representatives as soon as they could be recruited, and turned them over to the direction and supervision of the regional directors with practically no strings attached.

Summarizing the situation that prevailed during the summer of 1936, it may be concluded that the regional directors had little to do, except general public relations activities, and that they were regarded rather distrustfully by the bureau directors in Washington.[10] This distrust was not at all surprising, because most organizations start out with a tendency toward strict centralized control.[11] Moreover, although the Washington bureau directors had been in office for only six months or so, they had already come to regard themselves as old hands at the social security game and placed no confidence in these rank newcomers, none of whom had any name or standing as social security experts. The regional directors themselves understood this situation, at least in part, but it would not have been human for them to have accepted it passively. Many of them were vigorous men, anxious to play an important part in this big new activity. Even in the few cases in which the regional director himself was not so active, the executive assistant supplied the ambition.

These executive assistants were to present a special problem of considerable importance. They had been recruited and trained before the selection of the regional directors themselves, at a time when the role of the regional offices was not clear either to the board or staff. Were the executive assistants to be assistant regional directors or chief clerks concerned with housekeeping details? The board was not sure; the executive assistants naturally leaned in the direction of increased responsibility and policy decisions; the bureau chiefs in Washington and the bureau representatives in the regional offices wished them to have as little power and influence as possible.

The board's attitude toward the regional plan during the first couple of months after directors were sent out was largely determined by Altmeyer, for Winant was in Geneva most of that time. From the start, Altmeyer had been more favorable toward decentralizing the board's activities than had Winant; and this feeling may have been strengthened by the fact that at least four of the regional directors were his men and several more had been

[10] What the regional directors were doing during the summer of 1936 may be illustrated concretely by the functions of one of the more dynamic personalities occupying this office, McCarthy of Chicago. In July he recounted his activities as the following: (1) preparing a semimonthly summary of public opinion trends toward social security in his region, (2) making speeches to groups interested in social security, (3) contacting state executives performing functions connected with the board's work, (4) discussing problems of public assistance with the field agent of Miss Hoey's bureau, (5) reading letters sent from Washington to persons within his region, (6) answering inquiries from employers, particularly about records required for old age benefits, and (7) interviewing applicants for jobs. The last activity consumed more time than any other, notwithstanding the fact that there were very few jobs in prospect.

[11] British Ministry of Labor officials have noted this tendency in British experience. During the first years of the nationwide system of unemployment insurance and public employment offices, Headquarters insisted on making all decisions; but as time went on the divisional offices were given more and more authority and discretion, particularly in the day-to-day functions of supervision, control, and inspection of local offices.

agreed upon between him and Winant.[12] At any rate, Altmeyer frequently made the statement that it was the declared policy of the board to decentralize its activities to the maximum degree possible. At the first meeting of the board with the executive staff and the bureau directors (on June 17, 1936) he consistently maintained this position.[13] The following is a summary of that discussion:

Regional offices. Altmeyer asked for any questions that the bureau directors might have with regard to Administrative Order No. 11, which set forth the role of the regional directors. Murray Latimer objected that there was a contradiction in this order as far as his bureau was concerned. On the one hand, the district offices were to report directly to Washington; and on the other hand, the regional representative of the Bureau of Old Age Benefits was to have a supervisory function over district offices in his region. He and Altmeyer discussed this question at some length without arriving at any satisfactory conclusions, and the matter was postponed for further discussion between these two, since it did not particularly interest the other persons present. Altmeyer insisted that the difference of opinion was entirely a question of words, whereas Latimer thought there was a double responsibility implied which could not be carried out in practice. He suggested that the function of the regional representative of the Bureau of Old Age Benefits should be similar to that of a bank examiner who would go around and check on the operations of the district offices but would have no authority to order changes. He would merely report his findings to the Bureau of Old Age Benefits and the bureau would take whatever action it chose. At this point, Miles brought up the general question of lines of authority, indicating that in his mind they should be similar to those of the army, with the operating bureaus as the fighting forces and the service bureaus as the service units operating under the chief of staff (executive director) and a general (the board). If any inspector were set up, he would like it done entirely in the open, in order not to follow in the habits of the Interior Department and its extensive spy system.

Hughes explained that as far as his field staff was concerned, he considered it their duty to report their findings of facts and orders to the bureau, which would in turn refer this information to the board for whatever action they chose to take. He did not bring up the question of the relation of the field offices to his field auditors at all.

Miss Hoey insisted that her field staff would have to go into a state that was new at the game and stay on the spot while an organization was being set up.

---

[12] The selection of regional directors seemed to have been about as follows:
Winant: Powell and Pearson
Altmeyer: Wilcox, McCarthy, Crowell, and Neustadt
Altmeyer and Winant: Ashe, Parker, and Harper
Miles: McDonald and Dill
Required to accept: Rosenberg
[13] These meetings were suggested by Altmeyer but after the first two were held very spasmodically, and never developed into significant discussions of board policy.

The regional directors would not have sufficient knowledge of the field to be of any assistance, and so the field staff of the Bureau of Public Assistance could not in any sense be responsible to them. Altmeyer concurred in this point of view, suggesting that this was the difference they were aiming at in making the distinction between technical and administrative duties.

According to Altmeyer, the general idea of the board in setting up these regional offices was to decentralize the administration as much as possible, but details would have to be worked out in the course of time.

Miles thought that probably the preliminary function of the regional director was to get acquainted with the local situations in the states in his area, in order to be able to pass this information on to the other representatives of the board going into any of these states for particular purposes. Seidemann, looking at the matter from the point of view of procedure, seemed to think that the way to work this problem out was to have orders transmitted from the executive director to the regional directors, who in turn would give them to the other members of the regional staff.

Latimer vs. Altmeyer on the Powers of the Regional Director

This discussion did not satisfy Latimer as to the relationship between the regional representatives of Old Age Benefits and the regional directors. He believed that the district offices should be directly responsible to the Bureau of Old Age Benefits in Washington and be subject to no administrative direction or control by the regional directors or the regional representatives of the Bureau of Old Age Benefits, as contemplated in Administrative Order No. 11 (quoted above on pp. 110-11). To him several paragraphs, and particularly paragraph XIII, gave the regional director too much control over field offices.[14]

---

[14] Part of Latimer's concern may have been due to the fact that, in addition to his doubts about the need for regional directors at all, he was not in favor of the use of an executive director but preferred to have each board member responsible for a certain number of activities. In an interview some months after he left the board on December 11, 1936 he sketched his point of view, summarized as follows: "Latimer believes that the board's form of organization has been unsatisfactory: a division of the responsibility between the board members themselves is a better solution than an imposition of an executive director between the board and the bureau chiefs. Latimer believes that the executive director system in the Social Security Board has never worked effectively and never can work. Bane's chief duty was to authorize travel, and even this simple job was complicated by the fact that authorization would be made by the board directly. When Bane was requested to sign a travel order, he would have no knowledge of the board's action. The cumbersomeness of this system is demonstrated most clearly in the set up of the regional organization. Latimer insisted from the very beginning that it was impossible for the control of field offices of Old Age Benefits to be exercised through the executive director and the regional directors. He remembers

Altmeyer asked Bane, on July 3, to confer with Latimer in order to secure a revision of the administrative order which would satisfy them both. Corson discussed the question with Latimer, and they each submitted a draft for the revision as follows:

In response to Mr. Altmeyer's request of July 3, the following proposed revision of Paragraph 13 of Administrative Order No. 11 is submitted for your consideration. The revision of this paragraph is based upon two presumptions:

(a) That it is the intent of the Board to decentralize its activities insofar as it is administratively practicable by placing responsibility and authority in the hands of the Regional Directors; and

(b) That effective administration demands that responsibility for supervision and control be definitely assigned.

Corson	*Latimer*
13. A technically qualified representative of the Bureau of Old Age Benefits, assigned to each regional office staff, shall:	13. A technically qualified representative of the Bureau of Old Age Benefits, assigned to each regional office staff, shall:
(a) *be responsible* for the efficient operation, the relationships with the public, and the coordination of the activities of all district and branch offices within the region, in accordance with policies laid down by the Bureau of Federal Old Age Benefits, *to the Regional Director;*	(a) under the *general administrative supervision and direction of the Regional Director,* be responsible for the efficient operation, the relationships with the public, and the coordination of the activities of all district and branch offices within the region, in accordance with regulations, procedures, and instructions issued by the Bureau of Federal Old Age Benefits.
(b) continually examine and report on the methods, practices and details of the handling of all technical matters involving enumeration records, wage records and benefit claims, and correspondence relating thereto, to the Bureau of Federal Old Age Benefits and simultaneously submit copies of such reports to the Regional Director for the purposes of information;	(b) in conformity and in the light of regulations, procedures and instructions issued by the Bureau of Federal Old Age Benefits, continuously examine and report on the methods, practices and details of the handling of all technical matters involving benefit account number records, wage records and benefit claims, and correspondence relating thereto, to the Bureau of Federal Old Age Benefits and simultaneously submit copies of such reports to the

very vividly the board meeting held just after the regional directors had been sent out into the field; he was called in and found the board anxiously searching around for ideas as to what the regional directors should do."

Regional Director for the purposes of information;

(c) perform such additional duties as may be assigned by the Director of the Bureau of Federal Old Age Benefits under the general supervision and direction of the Regional Director.

(c) perform such additional duties as may be assigned by the Director of the Bureau of Federal Old Age Benefits under the general supervision and direction of the Regional Director.

13. Branch offices shall be within the administrative jurisdiction and report directly to their respective district offices. Information reports relative to enumeration record, wage records, benefit claims, and correspondence related thereto will be routed from the branch offices to the district offices and from the district offices to the Bureau of Old Age Benefits, except that when necessary branch offices may communicate directly with the Bureau.

13. Branch offices shall be within the administrative jurisdiction and report directly to their respective district offices. Information, reports and inquiries relative to enumeration records, wage records, benefit claims and correspondence relating thereto will be routed from the branch offices to the district offices and from the district offices to the Bureau of Federal Old Age Benefits. When necessary branch offices may communicate directly with the Bureau, giving the district office simultaneously a copy for its information. The Bureau shall communicate and issue instructions directly to district offices, except when necessary, instructions may be sent directly to branch offices.

The board (Altmeyer and Miles) was agreeable to Latimer's draft with the proviso that the words "general administrative supervision and direction of the Regional Director" in subsection 12(a) be changed to "under the immediate supervision of the Regional Director." Thus the conflict remained unresolved. Altmeyer and Corson wanted to give the regional director some real control over the representative of the Bureau of Old Age Benefits, and consequently over the district and branch offices; Latimer, on the other hand, wished to have the district office act as a supervising unit, with only an inspectional function given the regional representative and no real influence or control in the hands of the regional director. When Latimer received word of the action of the board he conferred with Corson once more with the following result (memorandum from Corson to Altmeyer of July 4, 1936):

I discussed with Murray Latimer last evening the revision of Administrative Order No. 11 which you and I discussed yesterday morning. He asks that three changes be made. They are indicated in the following draft.

．　　．　　．　　．　　．

Mr. Latimer states that immediate supervision in governmental classification terminology means detailed and specific supervision such as is usually accorded to clerical workers. He suggests the substitution for the term immediate supervision of the term general supervision. After considerable discussion, he agreed that the term general supervision implies the usual or customary control exercised over a subordinate by a superior officer vested with authority and the right to inspect the subordinate's work and to command his activities.

In view of the meaning which Mr. Latimer implies to the term general supervision and with the understanding that this meaning is agreed upon, I see no objection to the substitution of the term general supervision for the term immediate supervision. I believe that the term general supervision thus carries the meaning that the Board desired. Accordingly, I would recommend that we revise Administrative Order No. 11 as stated above with these changes as recommended by Mr. Latimer and give prominence to the definition of the term general supervision.

Mr. Latimer requests the insertion of the word "general" in the first line of paragraph 14 to distinguish between specific field activities such as the handling of individual claims and general instructions and policies of the Bureau for the administration of its field activities. I think that such a distinction deserves to be made.

May I have your criticisms at your convenience?

In its meeting of July 15 the board acceded to Latimer's wishes in the matter of terminology, but the question was by no means answered definitely.[15]

[15] The revised Administrative Order No. 11 was dated July 20, 1936, and contained sections for the other technical bureaus as well as Old Age Benefits. Thus the provisions relating to the Bureau of Unemployment Compensation stipulated that its regional representative should perform "such duties as the Director of the Bureau may assign, including handling of matters referred to him by the Regional Director. In the performance of these duties the representative shall be subject to the general supervision of their respective bureau directors with respect to all technical matters. . . . By the term 'general supervision' is meant the usual or customary control exercised over a subordinate by a superior officer. . . . Representatives of the Board's bureaus operating within a region or district shall report to the Regional Director their itineraries and plans. . . . All communications between Washington and any member of the Regional Office shall be routed through the Director of the Regional Office, or copies shall be simultaneously forwarded to him when direct routing is impossible. Similarly all communications between specialists assigned to the staff of the Regional Office and the Social Security Board shall be routed through the Regional Director. . . . The Regional Director shall refer all technical matters requiring special knowledge or knowledge probably within the specific bureau, to the proper specialists, or in the absence of such specialists in the region, to the Bureau Director in Washington."

Revised Administrative Order No. 12 (of September 21, 1936) raised the status of the regional director further by providing: "With reference to communications not of a confidential nature from bureaus and offices of the Social Security Board in Washington to a State agency or any other official or person not an employee of the Board situated in a region, a copy for the information of the Regional Director will be made and sent with the original to the Mail Room. The Mail Room will detach the extra carbon and route it to the appropriate Regional Director."

The regional representatives of the Bureau of Old Age Benefits were to be "under the general supervision of the Regional Director," with general supervision defined as "the usual or customary control exercised over a subordinate by a superior officer." This little tiff over words might have developed into a continuing struggle between Latimer on the one hand and Altmeyer, Bane, and Corson on the other, because the disagreement over the fundamental principle of organization would have had to be settled one way or another when specific cases arose. However, Latimer was soon to leave the position of director of the Bureau of Old Age Benefits, and Seidemann was to be so occupied with the details of registration that no further revision of Administrative Order No. 11 was made during the period of his directorship.[16]

The Executive Director Supports the Authority of the Regional Director

The actual day-to-day job of dealing with the regional directors and thus, by making decisions on individual cases of conflicting authority, filling out the general language of Administrative Order No. 11, devolved upon the Office of the Executive Director. John Corson and William Galvin came into Bane's office at about the same time, but Corson rapidly took over control of the regional organization, leaving to Galvin the routine jobs of correspondence control, space, equipment, personnel, and housekeeping details.[17]

The Field Organization Committee under McCormack, which had done most of the planning of the regional organization, transferred its attention to the problems of locating field offices for the Bureau of Old Age Benefits and to making plans for the conduct of registration. Thus Corson became a key figure in the development of the regional organization.

[16] We shall have occasion to refer again to this order, which remained the formal basis for the lines of authority in the field service, in connection with the recommendations made by Donald Stone and Wayne Coy in a report to the executive director in October 1936, and the actual relations between the regional directors and the field offices of the Bureau of Federal Old Age Benefits which came about during, and as a result of, the assignment of account numbers work in December and January. The later development was to demonstrate that the words of Administrative Order No. 11 were capable of justifying a far greater degree of control by the regional directors over the field offices than was anticipated by either Altmeyer or Corson in the summer of 1936.

[17] The 1937 budget provided for a director of agencies in the Office of the Executive Director, at a salary of $6,500 a year, but this proposed organization never came about. Instead Corson, as assistant executive director, continued to handle regional matters with the assistance of Galvin, and later of Parker, regional director, whose headquarters were in Washington, D.C.

With almost all of the bureau directors reluctant to trust anything to the regional directors and most of them taking their own sweet time about appointing regional representatives, Corson could not do much in a positive way to increase the authority of the regional offices. His own position (and even Bane's) was not yet strong enough to permit him to order bureau directors to start using the regional offices. Nevertheless there were a great many less dramatic ways of building up the regional offices (and as a consequence the Office of the Executive Director as well). Corson had been state director of the NRA in Virginia, and he believed that a large degree of regional autonomy was very desirable and should be promoted, perhaps until the board's regional offices should have as much power as the regional offices in the Bureau of Public Roads. In conversation with the observer he cited his own experience as state director of the NRA for Virginia. People come in to a regional director or a state director for answers to specific questions, and every time the director admits ignorance or refers the matter to Washington his effectiveness is weakened. In addition to this fact, the director actually wishes to increase his authority and is reluctant to refer any matter to the central office for fear that he may be regarded as a weak sister or a person who can't make up his own mind. Corson thought, however, that there would be slight difficulty in getting regional directors to seek and follow the advice of their technical staffs on technical subjects. He was sure that most of them would be eager to obtain as much advice as possible because they realized their ignorance in the social security functions. Corson's role exposed him to criticism from all sides—from regional directors, regional representatives, and bureau directors—but he stuck to it.

One of the means of increasing the power of the executive director's office was the paragraph in Administrative Order No. 12 ("Procedure to govern Correspondence with Regional Offices") which provided that all outgoing correspondence to the regional offices should clear through the Office of the Executive Director and that carbon copies of incoming correspondence from the regions should be directed there also. Through a special correspondence review unit (supervised by Galvin) it was possible for the executive director's office to learn the nature of the relations between the Washington bureaus and the regional offices, and the extent to which the former used the latter.

A second and even more important method of defining the authority of regional directors was the settling of conflicts which arose between regional directors and regional representatives of the bureaus. From the very first, Corson followed the policy of deciding all such cases in favor of the regional director. (It was not nearly so easy to uphold the regional director in a conflict with a bureau director in Washington.) In a review of experience during the first month he recounted two episodes showing how the executive director had backed up the regional director. Thus in the Philadelphia office,

Director Dill ordered the regional attorney not to confer with the legislature over certain pending bills. The lawyer protested, but Bane upheld Dill. From California came a letter from the State Director of Public Welfare saying that she wanted no dealings with underlings and would therefore ignore the regional director and his office. Bane tactfully insisted that she deal with the board through Neustadt's office.

Early in July the executive director developed a "Regional Letter," a biweekly summary of instructions from his office to the entire staff of the regional offices (part A) and a collection of the most important internal news items for information purposes (part B). To the letter were attached important forms, copies of significant letters on policy questions sent out by the board, copies of internal revenue decisions on Titles VIII and IX taxes, the Comptroller General's decisions, directories of field personnel, and other similar information. In short, this letter formed the most important source of instruction and information to the regional offices, taking the place of a comprehensive regional and field manual. It also offered added opportunities to the executive director for inquiring about matters in the several headquarters bureaus, thus furnishing occasions for issuing instructions designed to build up regional autonomy. Despite a complete lack of authority in any formal action of the board, one issue of the regional letter carried the statement that executive assistants would take the regional director's place in the latter's absence, and in the course of time this practice became firmly established.

It should perhaps be emphasized at this point that the regional letter was used to accomplish gradually a result that might have been reached much more quickly by the issuance of a regional and field manual at the time when the regional directors were appointed. A rather shrewd analysis of this situation was made by a junior assistant in the coordinator's office early in June, 1936. He pointed out that the conflict between the coordinator and the executive director had prevented the issuance of a field manual, and that meanwhile the discussion of the role of the regional offices and the various people in them had proceeded so far over a period of several months in staff meetings and various conferences of bureau directors that it was already practically impossible to iron out various conflicts. If the field manual had been started three months earlier when the whole matter was still in a formative stage, the bureau directors might have committed themselves to a policy more or less directed by the executive director or the coordinator.

Corson considered frequent conferences of regional directors in Washington to be the most important single means of promoting the effective operation of the regional offices. As a result of his experience as field officer (state director for the NRA in Virginia) and at headquarters (assistant director, NYA) he believed that small changes in policy at headquarters either escape notice or seem too trivial to call to the attention of field officers, but accumulate over a period of time until they result in major shifts in policy. He planned therefore to bring the regional directors to Washington every two months or so for a two- or three-day conference—even though the cost of such meetings would amount to five or six thousand dollars. The first of these conferences was called for July 16, 17, and 18, 1936.

Frase attended the first two full days of this conference. None of the fundamental problems, such as the place of the regional office in the board's plan for administration and the relationship between the regional director and his staff, were touched upon.

Although this first conference did not clarify these basic questions, it did permit the directors to catch up with board developments since they had been sent out into the field. It also furnished an opportunity for the directors to complain about their treatment by the heads of the Washington bureaus. These complaints dealt with the following items: (1) that certain bureau directors had no confidence in the regional scheme and no intention of using the regional offices, (2) that the regional directors were not consulted in the appointment of staff for the regional offices, (3) that the regional offices did not receive carbon copies of letters sent to officials and other persons in the region, (4) that directors were not consulted about quarterly grants for public assistance and unemployment compensation, (5) that there was not enough work to justify a regional attorney, (6) that there was too much red tape in making small purchases for the regional offices, (7) that the regional directors were not kept informed of the general policies of the board nor of the role they were expected to play.

So far as getting any definite information on the role of the regional offices from either the members of the board, the executive director, or the bureau directors, this conference was a rather complete failure. Altmeyer and the executive director attempted to reassure them that their function was significant and that the board favored increased decentralization. On the other hand, the bureau directors, particularly Wagenet, Latimer, and Hughes, did not commit themselves to any further use of the regional offices than had already been made, which was little enough.

On the other hand, Corson believed that the conference was well worthwhile, even if it accomplished nothing more than getting the regional directors better acquainted with the Washington staff, and developments and changes of policy which had occurred since their appointment.

After the conference, Corson found it necessary to go around to the bureau directors and jack them up on certain laxities which had been pointed out by the regional men. He believed that the bureau directors were slowly being brought around to using the regional offices and getting over some of their earlier suspicion and refusal to cooperate. As an example of this hopeful trend he noted that the procedure in making appointments to regional offices had been corrected; that nominations were being referred to regional directors for checking and concurrence before final appointments were made.

THE STONE-COY STUDY OF THE FIELD ESTABLISHMENT

We are fortunate in having an additional review of the regional situation in its relation to the rest of the organization, done by outsiders specially trained in administrative analysis. It was made in the autumn of 1936 as part of a report requested by the board from Donald Stone, of the Public Administration Service. Stone was assisted by Wayne Coy, Indiana's welfare administrator. Their report was handicapped by two factors: first, they were unable to visit the regional offices, and second, the plans for the field offices of the Bureau of Old Age Benefits, while well developed as to location, size, and number of the offices, were still tenuous as to the nature of actual field office operations.

Each investigator wrote a separate memorandum, but they agreed that the first and most important step for the board to take was to set up a strong director of field services in the Office of the Executive Director. They found that the stumbling block to a regional plan was the relationship of the Bureau of Old Age Benefits and its field offices to the regional director and his staff. Coy recommended that the regional director have a very tangential relationship to the Old Age Benefit field service:

It would seem that by terms of Administrative Order No. 11 the regional directors would exercise the same "general supervision" with respect to Federal old age benefits as to unemployment compensation and public assistance. The Bureau of Old Age Benefits has a direct administrative responsibility for this title of the Act in contrast to the advisory, consultative and supervisory responsibilities of the Bureaus of Unemployment Compensation and Public Assistance to the State agencies administering these titles of the Act.

Because of the direct administrative responsibility of the Bureau of Old Age Benefits, it is recommended that the field service of this bureau have full administrative responsibility with respect to its district and branch offices and without regard to the general supervision of the regional director, as defined in Administrative Order No. 11. The primary responsibilities of the regional director with respect to this bureau would be in public relations and assisting when requested in other matters. The initiative for his participation should issue from the Bureau of Federal Old Age Benefits.

Stone, on the other hand, was not willing to accept the implications of this recommendation which would, in effect, have removed the old age benefit program from any real connection with the regional offices. This in turn would have weakened the case for assigning representatives of the auxiliary staff bureaus to the regional offices, because there would not have been enough work to justify them. Further, it would have required the establishment of these same auxiliary functions in the district offices of the Bureau of Old Age Benefits.

With this insight into the implications of Coy's recommendations, and sensing a responsibility to offer suggestions for making the regional organization scheme work without major modifications, Stone presented two alternatives without really recommending either:

This straight line problem of administration of old age benefits raises the question of subordination of the service (staff) functions to the bureau management in the field. If the regional directors do not serve as a stage in the direct line of administrative responsibility flowing from the Washington office of the Bureau to the district and branch offices, then special measures will need to be taken to integrate personnel, accounting, legal, statistical, and other staff services with the district and branch organization. In some instances the various staff technicians attached to the regional offices can provide the necessary services. In other cases where such staff services form a day in and day out part of the administration of the district and branch offices, they will need to be set up as a part of the district and branch management. Management must control its tools if it is to be effective or responsible.

The alternative is to place the district and branch offices under the management of the regional directors, so that orders from the Old Age Benefit Bureau in Washington will be channeled through the Director of Field Services to the regional director and on down the line—a rather unsatisfactory procedure. In view of the present development of regional offices, it may be desirable to compromise with both of the above approaches, at least during the early stages of the old age benefit program.

In effect Coy recommended that the regional director have nothing to do with the old age benefit field program; and Stone recommended that either the auxiliary staff representative in the regional office should service the field offices of the Bureau of Old Age Benefits or that the field offices should be placed directly under the regional director. Apparently, none of these recommendations had any particular effect on the thinking of the board, because they came at a time when it was completely absorbed in a last minute rush to get the assignment of account numbers under way. Seidemann, of course, was in favor of Coy's alternatives; and the Office of the Executive Director leaned toward Stone's second proposal. The ultimate decisions were to come about not through the careful reconsideration of the whole problem of regional and field administration but rather as a result of fortuitous circumstances which placed a large degree of responsibility for supervising the field offices during the registration period in the hands of the regional directors and (what perhaps was even more important) their executive assistants. This denouement resulted from the failure of the Bureau of Old Age Benefits to recruit its own regional representatives in time.

In analyzing the relations of the regional office to the other bureaus, the Stone report was more positive. It found that almost without exception the bureaus had been "making every effort to find ways and means of 'going around' the Regional Directors." As a general remedy it proposed the establishment in the executive director's office of a director of field services who would be given final power to resolve conflicts between regional directors and the bureaus. The more positive duties of this officer were further listed as:

(1) Give content to the field job, including the regional directors, the bureau directors and the bureau representatives; (2) interpret intra-staff relationships and staff relationships to Regional Directors in the regional offices; (3) clarify relationships of bureau representatives to their respective bureaus for their directors; (4) bring about understanding between bureau directors and Regional Directors with respect to bureau problems in the field; (5) coordinate and supervise the relationships between regional office staff members and state governments. Other duties of such a person would include personnel in the regional offices, budget in these offices, a continuing review of administrative practices in these offices and the establishment in them of uniform office practices.

Stone further suggested that the board might adopt a more vigorous policy in offering services to the states through its field representatives. This would take the form of model administrative and operative procedures; suggestions by the field staff on details of technical procedure and practice; establishment of an understanding on the part of the states that the board had these advisory and consultative services available; and the setting up of a service on personnel standards and administration to be available to the states upon request.

Thus in regard to the more clear-cut issues of the use of the regional arrangement by the Bureau of Unemployment Compensation, the Bureau of Public Assistance, and the service bureaus, Messrs. Stone and Coy made recommendations which skimmed rather lightly over the detailed and fundamental questions involved, leaving most of them to the wisdom of a proposed director of the field service. Perhaps they could have done no more without severely criticizing either the bureau directors who had not conformed to the board's avowed policy of decentralization or the board itself in setting up so hurriedly a scheme involving so many difficulties in operation. The old question remained: Was the regional director an important official with real autonomy and broad authority or was he a figurehead and office manager? In October 1936 he seemed much closer to the latter than to the former— despite the fact that the original salary scale had been boosted very considerably, from an original range of $5,600–$6,500 to a range, by July 15, of $6,500–$7,500.

THE FIELD ESTABLISHMENT AT THE CLOSE OF REGISTRATION

CHANGES BEFORE AND DURING REGISTRATION

The detailed story of the evolution of the field establishment for the Bureau of Old Age Benefits is given separate treatment elsewhere. Before September 1936, the board had planned to use this bureau's field offices for the big registration job. It had consequently approved the establishment of 90 district locations, 312 primary branches, and 184 secondary. Had it been possible to recruit employees from the existing civil service registers or through the expert provisions of the act, it is probable that 90 district offices would have been opened up during the summer of 1936. The need to await the result of the examination for administrative officer given in August, the registers from which were not available until December, made postponement necessary. When on November 5, 1936, the board decided to open up 56 field offices to help in the registration job that the Post Office was undertaking, it had to detail temporarily a large number of people from its Washington office to do this. During the heaviest part of the registration in December there were thus only 71 field offices open.[18]

Immediately before the opening of these 56 offices, there developed a running conflict between the executive director's office and the chief of the Bureau of Old Age Benefits over the extent to which field offices would be controlled by the regional representatives of the Bureau of Old Age Benefits and by the regional directors. Seidemann insisted that the district offices report directly to Washington, with the regional representative acting merely as a kind of inspector without direct supervisory power. Bane and Altmeyer wanted the

[18] After the Post Office had agreed to undertake the registration and the board's administrative budget estimates for 1938 had been cut by the Bureau of the Budget, there was a long series of changes both in the number of offices and the opening schedule. There would be no particular purpose in describing the details of these various changes; but the fact that there were at least five of them indicates how frequently the board changed its mind on the function of the old age benefits field service as it became apparent that the Post Office would handle the job at least until March 31, 1937, without any assistance from the board. The number (397), location, and salary schedules for the field offices were not definitely agreed upon by the board until January 22, 1937.

regional representative to be in the direct line of administrative authority from Washington, with a considerable amount of control over him by the regional director. At a board meeting on October 9 it had been agreed that the claims attorneys in the field offices of the bureau would report on legal questions to the regional attorney. At the same meeting Altmeyer, with the concurrence of Miles, had rebuked the attempt of the chief of the bureau to reopen the board's decision that the regional representative of the bureau should have full authority to oversee and supervise the field offices within the region. But the matter was reopened two months later when Seidemann complained that the regional directors were interfering with the registration job. Even though he had designated the executive assistant in each regional office (except in two cases) as his bureau's representative, he considered that their authority was distinctly limited. This time the board partly conceded his demand by agreeing that the regional directors should inform postmasters that they were to refer all questions connected with assignment of account numbers to the Post Office Department in Washington. It also left to Seidemann and Bane the clarification of other differences of opinion on the lines of responsibility of regional offices.[19] Three days later Seidemann submitted another memorandum to the board recommending that all claims adjudications be handled in Washington rather than in the field and regional offices. There were strong arguments in support of this proposal; namely, that the claims work would be rather light in the beginning, centralized adjudication would be cheaper, uniform standards and practices could be built up, and the advice and consent of the General Accounting Office could be readily obtained. The board agreed to this plan for the first six months, on condition that the bureau study and report on the practicability of decentralization of the claims work at the end of that period.

THE REGIONAL OFFICE SITUATION EARLY IN 1937

At the end of December 1936, the observers began a series of brief regional office inspections in order to learn how these problems looked from the field,

[19] Whether as a result of this conference or not, the instruction in Regional Letter No. 12 (November 21, 1936) that weekly reports from field office managers "be submitted in duplicate (to the Regional Director), the Regional Director forwarding the original copy, together with his comments, to the Director, Bureau of Federal Old Age Benefits" was changed on December 5 to provide that in conformity with Administrative Order No. 11, "weekly reports being prepared by field offices of the Bureau of Federal Old Age Benefits will be routed directly to the Director of the Bureau in Washington. Two copies of all such reports will be simultaneously sent to the regional office, one each for the Regional Director and (Acting) Regional Representative."

and also to get some first-hand knowledge of the progress of the registration enterprises. It must be remembered that at this time the registration was still under way and that consequently this activity was uppermost in the minds of the regional directors and most of the members of their staffs. These field visits continued in January and early February until seven of the twelve regional establishments had been observed: Boston, Cleveland, Chicago, Kansas City, Minneapolis, Denver, and San Francisco.

While each regional office had its peculiarities, certain general tendencies in the evolution of the field situation could be discerned at this time. It was clear by January 1937 that the mass registration job, the peak of which had been comfortably passed, had hoisted each regional director into a position of administrative leadership for the Bureau of Old Age Benefits. The failure to create a district field staff of its own for all the essential cities, plus the inexperience and lack of prestige of many of the district office representatives, and perhaps most crucial of all, the designation of the director's executive assistant or (as in San Francisco) the director as the principal representative of the Bureau of Old Age Benefits, led to this result. Once having tasted power in this function, and having discovered that the tasks were not so technical and abstruse as to baffle their intelligence, the directors appeared to be in a strategic position to retain this initial and unplanned advantage. Because the executive assistant was in most regions becoming the regional director's alter ego, and in other cases was even more clearly his subordinate office manager, the allocation to the executive assistant of temporary regional authority over old age benefit duties made this task in effect a regional director's function. That officer had been given so little to do during the first six months of his tenure that he pounced upon this registration job as a real opportunity to serve the board and to justify the existence of his establishment.

In doing this he further cemented the close relationship begun with the Informational Service representative during the tail end of the 1936 election campaign. In every office that officer had become, in effect, as closely identified with the regional director as was the executive assistant. This development would probably have come in the course of time, but its early and complete arrival was doubtless the result of the unexpected attack by the Republicans upon the Social Security Act, catapulting the board into an intensive publicity campaign that for the first time made full use of the regional establishment, particularly in combatting the organized payroll-stuffing maneuver of Republican employers. Following on the heels of this affair came the big publicity campaign necessary to prepare the millions of workers and employers for the assignment of account numbers. Here again the need for the regional directors (in some cases all of the regional staff pitched in) to help the Informational Service man do his stuff, and for the two together to scan the regional horizon for publicity opportunities and problems, brought an intimacy that appeared to be complete and lasting. The general failure of the Washington head-quarters of the Informational Service to keep in close touch with its regional representative on policy questions also helped to throw the latter into the embrace of the regional director.

There was a similar cause contributing to the unexpected drift toward regional control of Old Age Benefits. The struggle for power within the headquarters of the bureau which had been going on since September, and the disorganization consequent upon this unfortunate circumstance, were clearly reflected in the field situation at this time. Reports were almost unanimous that the regional representative of the Bureau of Old Age Benefits could not obtain satisfactory communication with his Washington chiefs. Letters and even telegrams went unanswered, or when answered, replies were evasive or in other ways unsatisfactory. One regional director reported that the only way he could really make contact with the Washington office was to send a telegram saying that at a certain time he would call Washington on the phone. In another region the Old Age representative had received instructions about carbon copies of letters and other small routine matters, but nothing about his relationships with the district offices. Consequently he had taken the initiative in exercising close regional control over them, calling them in for regional conferences to discuss their problems, developing a set of regulations for the conduct of correspondence, public relations, and office management. There being no adequate supervision of the district offices from Washington, the regional representative had stepped into the breach. By January 1937 he was already closely cemented to the regional director and was likely to stay there unless the board itself should blast him out.

It is interesting to speculate on what effect the difference in background between the regional representatives for the Bureau of Old Age Benefits and the Bureau of Public Assistance may have had on the evolution of regional office powers. Most of the executive assistants had been in the field organization of the Bureau of Foreign and Domestic Commerce and after that in the field establishment of the NRA. The permanent regional representative of the bureau in two regions visited came from the field services of other old federal agencies. These men had been used to accepting the general administrative control of a superior regional officer, and the problem of working out a modus vivendi in their relations with him and their Washington chief did not seem difficult to them.

But the field people of the Bureau of Public Assistance were generally recruited from state, local, or private welfare agencies. They regarded their functions as professional and therefore difficult for the layman to understand. They and their Washington chief knew the part that politics had played in state and local welfare administration and were probably suspicious of any regional director who had been associated with politicians before his appointment, fearing lest he interfere with their task of elevating the state public assistance agencies above the miasma of party or fraternal spoils. The field representatives therefore entered the regional establishment prepared to fight for their bureau's freedom. But wherever the board had chosen as regional director a socially intelligent person with insight into his function and with the qualities of group leadership, this suspicion was rapidly melted away. Thus the promise of success in the field operation of public assistance under the regional pattern was directly proportional to the personal qualifications of the regional director. Fortunately, the board had chosen wisely in at least four of the seven regions visited, so that the Public Assistance regional officers there had fewer complaints about the regional office setup than they had about their relations with the Washington office. In the other regional establishments the relationships were either covertly suspicious, contemptuous, or hostile. Where the executive assistant was assuming the functions of the regional director's alter ego, this dislike was transferred to him, or in the other four offices was directed toward him alone because he did not possess the talents of the director. Only in one of the seven regions did the executive assistant at this time appear to have the qualities that would permit him satisfactory fulfillment of the implied relationships with the representatives of Public Assistance or Unemployment Compensation.

Unemployment Compensation had so few regional representatives assigned at that time that no conclusions can be drawn from this slight experience.[20] It was generally known within the bureau, however, that Wagenet wanted to keep the state people coming to Washington until enough experience had accumulated so that policies could be fixed in advance of regional decentralization. He therefore still wanted to bypass the regional establishment. There were a number of instances where his office, like that of Miss Hoey, had even bypassed its own field representatives by dealing directly with state officials, without first clearing with its field agents. These episodes cut the ground from under the feet of the bureau's field force. They were doubtless the result of the inexperience of the headquarters staff with the many new problems of their organization, and perhaps, even more, the lack of preceding experience in handling a field organization of nationwide extent. None of the bureau directors on the board's staff had been possessed of such experience before assuming their posts with the board. They had to learn how to handle their field forces at the same time that they were learning appropriate policies

[20] Thus in January 1937 there were no regional representatives of this bureau in the regional offices at Philadelphia, Washington, Birmingham, Chicago, Minneapolis, San Antonio, and San Francisco. In Cleveland the regional representative who had been sent out during the preceding autumn resigned early in January. In San Francisco, Boston, and Chicago the regional directors had been designated the regional representatives for unemployment compensation.

for their bureaus to adopt. This double task was bound to produce unfortunate administrative snarls. Both the Children's Bureau and the Public Health Service avoided these troubles because, in the case of the former, the directing staff was familiar with national agency field organization techniques and could apply them even to a new field staff with a minimum of wire crossing, and in the case of the Health Service both headquarters and the augmented field force were already used to similar tasks and relationships.

The field auditors had been sent out from Washington with few instructions as to how to do their job. The chief of the bureau felt that instructions would be appropriate only after a period of trial and error. By the time these field studies were made the difficulties arising between the auditors and the Public Assistance field staffs had led to a shake up in the Bureau of Accounts and Audits. Formerly many auditors had made their way from state to state ignoring the regional establishment, scattering upon state and local officials gratuitous comments about the administration of public assistance functions. The board, early in January 1937, had agreed upon a working relationship between the field staffs of the two bureaus.[21]

Even before this agreement some of the auditors had seen the importance of close cooperation with the field staff of the Public Assistance Bureau, though unfortunately many had not. But late in January the signs were clear that this gap in articulation was being narrowed. Whether it would be susceptible of complete closing without a radical change in bureau structure, splitting the auditing function and throwing part of the field job to the Bureau of Public Assistance and part to the Bureau of Unemployment Compensation, was an interesting speculative question.

The most questionable staff assignment to the regional office was that of regional attorney. The general counsel, despite his early skepticism about the utility of regional attorneys, speedily secured their appointment by the board and sent out a number of them early in the summer of 1936. Sometimes he did not consult the regional director—an act which violated the express procedure the board had approved. These attorneys had all been cleared politically, but some of them were not well regarded either by the director or their other regional colleagues. While in some regions there was considerable legislative activity in social security problems (particularly unemployment compensation) in which attorneys could be of service, a number of them knew too little about the nature of these matters to be helpful. They had been given a variety of busy-work jobs not at all implicit in the nature of the

---

[21] For a full discussion and the nature of the agreement, see "The Bureau of Accounts and Audits and the Comptroller General," chapter 4, p. 197.

legal profession. How will they be kept busy when the state legislative activity ceases? was the question being asked by the ablest regional directors.

It was difficult to tell at this time whether the regional geographic pattern would lead to undue cost or friction in administration. The only obvious disadvantages then evident were found in the Rocky Mountain area, although there were some complaints that the three regions centering at Cleveland, Chicago, and St. Paul had inappropriate groupings of states. Even in the vast region directed from Denver, the disadvantages of inadequate north-south railway connections were alleged to be decreasing because of the growing use of long distance telephonic communication and the airplane. The Denver staff insisted upon the paramount importance of cultural homogeneity arising from common mineral, grazing, and irrigation-farming activities and from the sparse distribution of population characteristic of the whole area from the Canadian boundary to Mexico. Whether this was an exercise in self-deception to justify powers already attained could only be determined later by careful study of operating experience.

Complaint was general that regional directors were not given sufficient authority to control the operation of the regional budgets, and that clearance with them in the employment of minor (and sometimes major) personnel was overlooked by the Washington bureau chiefs. The directors were irritated by their lack of authority to meet by transfers small, urgent expenditure needs not foreseen when the budgets were prepared. For these needs they were re-quired to obtain advance clearance from the Bureau of Business Management in Washington. Thus the need of the Informational Service representative for a newspaper cut essential to publicity for an important regional meeting required a telegram sent nearly across the continent to authorize an expendi-ture of $1.50! Washington had forgotten a number of times to notify regional or field offices when people were being dispatched to the field, sometimes for regional staff assignment. There were a number of occasions when men walked into the regional or field office to report for duty without any ad-vance notice to or request from the officer in charge.[22] One would expect these irritations to disappear as the routines of field management were better established and the habits of bureau heads adapted to them.

The director of one of the regions most remote from Washington insisted that his judgment of the rate of expansion of regional staff and field offices for the Bureau of Old Age Benefits ought to be used by Washington. In addition to his difficulties in fighting off the permanent assignment of a regional attorney for whom he could see no sufficient need, this director had

[22] By formal vote on January 8, 1937, the board decided to allow regional directors to pass on all prospective candidates for field office positions.

not been consulted about the expansion of district and branch offices. He had recently been overruled in regard to one office for a state capital which he felt was not necessary. Four other offices about which he had not been consulted were to be opened within another state in his region. His first notice of the board's decision in these cases came through a press release. He felt not only that this procedure laid the board wide open to political pressure in the appointment of field staff, but that the board was hurrying unduly the proliferation of a field establishment for which the need was not yet in sight.

The New York and Washington regions were not typical. In the first case the region was composed of a single state. This gave the appearance of creating a special unit to supervise the operations of the New York Department of Public Welfare and the Division of Placement and Unemployment Insurance. Miss Hoey tried to relieve this by giving her New England regional representative the added jurisdiction of New York. The executive director of this region was appointed two months before the rest; she was a relatively independent agent whose high political connections were believed to give her pretty much what she wanted from the board. Thus she retained in her new position nearly all her former NRA staff, most of whom were still on temporary appointments. Having only one state and knowing most of the state officials, the regional director handled directly a large part of the contact work.

Because the New York officials who headed Unemployment Insurance regarded their state as *sui generis* and their own insight into the job equal if not superior to that of the board's staff, they dealt directly on important matters with Washington rather than through the regional representative of the Bureau of Unemployment Compensation.

The region centering in Washington, D.C. (region 4) was also peculiar. The regional field representatives of the various bureaus tended to go directly to their respective national bureau chiefs, thus eliminating the function of the regional director as coordinator. The director spent most of his time from September 1936 to the end of the period, not in the regional office at Washington but in Bane's office, where he worked as an assistant to Corson.

As one reviews these first months of regional and field experience it becomes clear that the regional scheme was beginning to play an important part in administration, particularly where the directors were men of insight and high calibre. So far as field staff relations were concerned, the system was working with remarkable smoothness where this directorial competence was distinct, and badly or poorly where the top regional officer lacked these qualities. Could or would the inferior directors develop the indispensable competence and leadership qualities to win the respect of their field associates and facilitate rather than impede the work of the latter? Would the Washington bureau leaders develop trust in the regional establishment and work through it rather than covertly around it? Would the regions be given more control over personnel and budget for their areas? Would the federal function of Old Age Benefits profit administratively by regional supervision? Would regional directors chosen because of local residence and a public relations emphasis regarded as important in 1936, and regional staffs cleared with local senators and congressmen, tend to thwart or twist national policies of the board, because of local friendships or loyalties, long after these special considerations had ceased to be of crucial importance? These are questions for which certain answers could not be found within the brief experience covered by this study.

.4.

THE ADMINISTRATION OF
GRANTS-IN-AID FOR THE AGED,
DEPENDENT CHILDREN, AND
THE BLIND

THE FIRST GRANTS AND THE
ESTABLISHMENT OF THE BUREAU
OF PUBLIC ASSISTANCE

In turning to the substantive program assignments entrusted to the Social Security Board and its collaborating federal and state agencies, we must keep in mind the desperate situation which existed for the aged, the blind, the unemployed, and other dependent members of the American community when the 1935 act was adopted, and which confronted the board when it began to function. There were no accurate data about the economic dependency of the 6,500,000 persons over sixty-five years of age enumerated in the 1930 census and comprising 5.4 percent of the entire population of approximately 122,000,000. The Committee on Economic Security, in its January 1935 report to the President, noted that in 1934 about 700,000 of the aged subsisted on grants from the newly established FERA. It guessed that the numbers of aged then receiving some form of public charity exceeded 1,000,000. An additional 180,000 persons, mostly over seventy, were being helped by some form of public pension, which under the state old age assistance laws of that day averaged $19.74 per month.[1] A somewhat smaller number received some aid from veterans' pension and public retirement programs, and perhaps

---

[1] Committee on Economic Security, *Report to the President,* Jan. 15, 1935 (Washington: G.P.O., 1935), Appendix tables 14 and 15, pp. 68–69.

150,000 aged were getting pension money from industrial and trade union pensions. The report further stated:

The number of aged without means of self-support is much larger than the number receiving pensions or public assistance in any form. Upon this point available data are confined to surveys made in a few states, most of them quite a few years ago. Connecticut (1932) and New York (1929) found nearly 50% of their aged population (65 and over) had an income of less than $25 per month; 34% in Connecticut had no income whatsoever. At this time a conservative estimate is that at least one half of the approximately 7,500,000 people over 65 years now living are dependent.

Children, friends and relatives have borne and still carry the major cost of supporting the aged. Several of the state surveys have disclosed that from 30 to 50 percent of the people 65 years of age are being supported in this way. During the depression this burden has become unbearable for many of the children, with the result that the number of old people dependent upon public or private charity has greatly increased.[2]

The Townsend movement had developed such strength by the time the Social Security Board was appointed that the board's assignment to allocate grants for the aged to the states and to see that proper systems for state and local administration of these federal relief funds were inaugurated was the most pressing of all its many programs. The political heat turned upon Congress and the elected state officials by organizations of oldsters was redirected to the board and its public assistance staff. The Huey Long filibuster in the Senate, which killed the federal appropriation for this and other public assistance programs in the late summer of 1935, increased the urgency of a flying start for distributing grant moneys to the states just as soon in 1936 as the new Congress could provide legal authorization.

While the special New Deal federal work programs to relieve unemployment had begun to assuage the most acute distress, the estimated proportion of nonagricultural workers who were unemployed in 1935 averaged 32.2 percent among the states and the District of Columbia. The industrial states of Michigan, Pennsylvania, and New Jersey were in the deepest trouble, with 45.9, 40.2, and 38.8 percent respectively, and the two rural states of Arkansas and Arizona were not far behind, with 39.2 and 38.5 percent. For those types of workers customarily covered by unemployment insurance under contemporary West European laws, the percentage out of work in the United States that year was estimated as 39.2.[3]

The COEC report pointed out that even in 1929, when the stock market boom was at its peak and paeans to prosperity were a part of most political

[2] *Ibid.*, p. 24.
[3] *Ibid.*, Supplement, tables 5 and 6, pp. 4–6.

oratory, 44 percent of the gainfully employed (exclusive of farmers) had annual earnings of less than $1,000 and 70 percent received less than $1,500. Throughout the golden twenties, it declared, "the number of people dependent upon private and public charity steadily increased." [4] But the President's statement to Congress in June 1934, from which stemmed the "charter" for this committee's study, had included an assignment broader than that of finding cures for the two social ills cited above. It was to seek to find "some safeguards against misfortunes which cannot be wholly eliminated in this man-made world of ours." The committee therefore used its staff to examine misfortunes associated with industrial and nonindustrial accidents and with crippling illness, all of which are expressed not only in pain but in incapacitation for work and the earning of income. It was the latter—income—which the report insisted was the most nearly all-embracing as a foundation for economic security:

A program of economic security, as we envision it, must have as its primary aid the assurance of adequate income to each human being in childhood, youth, middle age and old age—in sickness or in health. It must provide safeguards against all the hazards leading to destitution and dependency.

A piecemeal approach is dictated by practical considerations, but the broad objectives should never be forgotten. Whatever measures are deemed immediately expedient should be so designed that they can be embodied in the complete program which we must have ere long.[5]

The committee regarded its major recommendations only as a substantial beginning, not a complete program. To push the latter, it said, might unduly delay any action at that time.

We must keep these facts and these affirmations of the President's committee in mind as we examine the beginnings of the program, activities, and aspirations of the Social Security Board in our account of its first eighteen months of planning and operations.

The administration of federal grants to the states in behalf of the needy, aged, dependent children, and blind were, as indicated elsewhere, grouped together under one organizational unit ultimately called the Bureau of Public Assistance. When this study began on November 15, 1935, the staff of that division consisted, aside from stenographic aid, of Helen V. Bary, Alvin Roseman, and Ivan Asay, all borrowed from other New Deal agencies by whom they were then being paid. They were busily at work answering inquiries pouring in from the states concerning the sufficiency of existing and proposed state laws, and concerning administrative requirements under the public assistance portions of the act (Titles I, IV, and X). There was no

[4] *Ibid.*, p. 2.
[5] *Ibid.*, p. 3.

uniformity in the data accompanying state requests for grants-in-aid; a great deal of the staff's time was consumed in personal interviews with state representatives who were asking the same questions over and over again. It therefore seemed important to get some standardization of the appropriate information and to shortcut the process of answering inquiries. Consequently the staff, with the help of Mr. Seidemann, was attempting to whip into shape a series of forms to be sent out to all the states for their use in submitting laws and administrative plans.

A few state administrators and public welfare experts met privately in the Labor Building on November 27 to discuss these proposed forms with the Public Assistance staff. Representatives from the Children's Bureau were brought in to attempt to consolidate the information requested by the Children's Bureau and by the Social Security Board. That attempt was not successful, since the Children's Bureau felt that it required a good deal of additional data on the administrative proposals of the states. The grants supervised by the Children's Bureau, insisted Dr. Martha Eliot, who spoke for it, would be used not to assist individuals but to build up generalized services, and on that account its needs for information were somewhat different. This meeting, and the subcommittee activities which developed from it, considerably aided the board's staff to whip into final form standardized application blanks for public assistance money.

When these forms were sent out on December 3, 1935 (to all states and territories eligible for public assistance grants), they were accompanied by an invitation to the state agencies in charge of administering the public assistance money to send delegates to meet with the board and the Children's Bureau representatives in Washington, on December 14 and 15, to talk over the problems involved in preparing acceptable state plans. The board and its staff hoped this meeting would speed up the arrival of state plans and help to get them through before December 31, 1935, which by the terms of the Social Security Act was the last day the board would approve applications for public assistance grants for the first quarter of 1936.[6] The staff felt itself almost overwhelmed by the difficulties involved in meeting that deadline. By getting all the state people together, it seemed possible to answer at one time many of the questions that would consume weeks to answer individually. It was also the desire of the staff to become personally acquainted with the state people and to demonstrate to them that the board and its representatives were anxious to aid the state in getting started.

[6] This was the interpretation the board gave the Social Security Act at the time. Later, it decided that quarterly grants could be certified after the beginning of the quarter (see "The Bureau of Accounts and Audits and the Comptroller General," chap. 4, p. 197).

The volume of work to be done before December 31 is indicated by a few statistics compiled by Asay and incorporated in a memorandum dated November 19, 1935:

Present Status of the Analysis of Pub. Asst. Law

Type of law	Memo sent to Legal Div.	Laws remaining to be analyzed		Memo returned from Legal Division
Old Age	11	26*	38†	
Blind	7	21	42	
Dependent children	11	35	38	[no information given]
Administrative Organization	3	10	46	
Totals	32	92	164	

* Assuming only the number of laws actually in existence.

† Assuming that one will be analyzed for each of the forty-eight states and the District of Columbia.

These figures do not tell the entire story of the burden of work to be handled. Some of the analyses made by the Public Assistance Division (it was not called Bureau until some weeks later) had to do with bills rather than laws. Therefore subsequent analysis would be necessary if those bills were enacted into law, since changes would usually be made during legislative consideration. Asay estimated that something like one hundred bills or laws would have to be considered by the board before January 1. In addition, the plans for state administration would have to be considered, which meant a terrific burden for the small staff then at work. And finally, when the public assistance people had finished their review, the lawyers would begin their independent examination of the legal adequacy of both the proposed bill or law and the proposed plan of administration. The lawyers were exceedingly slow and were regarded as a bottleneck, notwithstanding the fact that Eliot and his staff were greatly overworked. He was frequently ill under the strain, as were other members of his organization.

During this period Miss Bary and her staff could give very little attention, through field trips, to the state administrative arrangements actually under way or in contemplation. While a few trips were made, three people could not do field work and also handle the central office job. Consequently the staff was compelled to rely for knowledge of state administrative and financial facts upon information which they, as professional public welfare administrators, already possessed or could get by correspondence or through the assistance of their friends in WPA and FERA. The FERA had collected a great deal of information about the financial ability of the states and the nature of their welfare administrative staff. This information it had freely passed along to the staff of the board. It was also compiling, at that time, a full digest of all state laws embodying public assistance functions.

These cooperative activities were exceedingly helpful. Nevertheless, the board's staff felt itself seriously handicapped in not having its own field organization to help the state administrators work out plans that would conform to the administrative and legal requirements of the Social Security Act.

This is the background for the decision to hold the December 14–15 meeting with the state representatives. That meeting lasted all day Saturday and a very long Sunday morning. It was attended by delegates from forty-two states and territories. Bane, Altmeyer, Miles, Eliot, Seidemann, and Miss Jeter represented the board, and Miss Lenroot spoke for the Children's Bureau. Altmeyer, Miss Lenroot, and Bane sketched out the general requirements of the Social Security Act as they related to the board and the Children's Bureau. In the morning session Bane tried to center the discussion on the kind of welfare organization which should be created by the states to handle the public assistance tasks effectively. The state representatives explained their various organization structures. Bane particularly called on delegates from such states as New York and Maryland and from the District of Columbia, in which very effective organizations were then operating. During the afternoon meeting Bane tried to center the discussion on the type of local organizations which should be set up, and also to explore what activities state supervision over local organizations should include. Again the states related what they were doing and described their local situations. There gradually emerged from the discussion certain significant problems of state supervision over local administration and certain conclusions about the essential minimums of state control. The Sunday meeting concentrated upon explanations of the forms which the board had sent out and answers to questions arising therefrom. It brought out a great many technical points which otherwise might have taken weeks of correspondence to clarify. Each delegate was, of course, particularly interested in asking questions about his own state situation. Before the meeting adjourned, it was announced that the board people and the Children's Bureau staff would be glad to confer individually with the delegates during the following week. The Children's Bureau also scheduled group meetings for those state people particularly concerned with the child welfare and crippled children provisions of the Social Security Act.

This December conference was highly successful in making clear to the state representatives the anxiety of the Social Security Board and of the Children's Bureau not to dictate, but to cooperate, with them. It was also valuable to the board and the Children's Bureau to discover the many differences in state administrative organizations and welfare policies. It is also clear that many questions which were asked could not yet be answered, partly because they were legal questions for which no one yet knew the answers, and partly because the total situation surrounding the problems would have to determine their ultimate answers. There was plenty of give-and-take in the discussions, with a tendency for the various state representatives to think somewhat narrowly in terms of their own peculiar experience.

Many individual consultations between the state people and the staff of the Social Security Board were held during the three days following the conference.

Miss Bary felt that the meeting had been quite worthwhile: first, because it had seemed to dispel the fear of federal dictation and the idea entertained by many state people that the board expected to set up many meticulous or unreasonable requirements; second, because it showed some of the states (in particular Arizona, North Carolina, and perhaps Oregon) that they could probably qualify for federal funds, whereas they had thought that they were out of the running; third, because it greatly expedited the submission of state plans. Eight plans came in on the day following the conference.

Bane, in a post-conference review, said the board had hoped to get a consensus from the state people that state welfare organization should be unified for the handling of the three types of grants-in-aid (for the aged, dependent children, and the blind). It had also hoped to secure agreement that state supervision over local administration must cover the following items: (1) a financial audit; (2) standards and specifications for local personnel; (3) administrative rules and regulations; (4) the setting up of a state field-supervising force. Shortly after the conference Bane, on behalf of the board, wrote each state representative a letter which included an assertion that such a consensus had been reached at the meeting.[7]

During these early months the board did not give its staff any explicit statement of administrative principles to use in trying to help the states fulfill the terms of the Social Security Act, which in all the aid titles read, "provide such methods of administration (other than those relating to selection, tenure of office, and compensation of personnel) as are found by the board to be necessary for the efficient operation of the plan." While no ruling had been given the staff, nevertheless the three people working on this task developed certain well-understood criteria which they used in their recommendations to the board concerning state plans: firstly, that there should be a single unified state welfare agency, either a board or a single officer, handling one or more grant-in-aid programs; secondly, that the administration should not be handled by an elected officer. Two of the people in this group had received their training in welfare administration with the American Public Welfare Association, under Bane. The third member was also a professionally trained welfare

---

[7] Resentment was privately expressed by some of the delegates over Bane's attempt to pin the state people to an approval of the board's conception of state supervision—especially the item relating to local personnel standards.

worker whose point of view on administrative matters harmonized very closely with that of the association. Thus in the consideration of state administrative plans an unwritten elementary code of administrative principles was in operation from the beginning. The conference served to fortify and amplify these criteria.

During the second half of December, when the state plans were being pushed through as rapidly as the staff could go over them, the board prescribed certain explicit standards for state supervision in instances in which the administration of grants was entrusted to local agencies: in such states, the plan must include provision for a state audit, for the right of the state to adopt rules and regulations to govern local action, for the state to fix standards of local personnel, and for state field supervision.

In these legal stipulations and principles of formal organization, the board was expressing a set of ideas that must, for want of a better name, be called political in character. Because it was highly sensitive to the opinions of those groups which were then pushing for gratuities to the aged and because it appreciated their potential political importance—particularly that of the Townsend movement—it was extremely anxious to start the flow of federal funds for these needy aged as rapidly as possible. It wanted to counteract what appeared to be an increasingly powerful demand for the Townsend and similar proposals. Moreover, it was keenly aware of the expectation of many of the state relief committees, and of governors and state legislators, that the Social Security Act would ease the state relief situation. It realized that the states, disappointed by the failure of the Third Deficiency Bill the preceding August, were hoping for and in some cases gambling on the possibility of the release of federal funds as soon as Congress should reassemble. These political considerations, together with the genuine sympathy of the board members for the distressed aged, underlay a decision not to erect too high a standard of state administration to start with. To have brought the state programs up to such a standard would have retarded the rate of approval, for it would have required special reports and assistance by a field staff, and perhaps in some cases even statutory changes.

The philosophy of Miss Bary and Bane fitted well with this sense of political requirements. It was Miss Bary's general conception of federal-state relationships that the big task ahead was not primarily one of coercion. Rather, it was an experiment in educating the people of the states, counties, and towns to want to do an effective public assistance job. She believed that no matter how tight the laws or rules, state people would get around them if they were sufficiently determined to do so. On this account the board must, she believed, place most of its reliance upon a properly trained field staff which would approach its task with a feeling that its function was to educate and aid state and local administrators rather than to snoop and punish. There can be no doubt that this philosophy and this sense of political realities tinted the vision of the staff as well as that of the board. The board, in at least one case, Missouri, even went to the extent of approving a state plan which the staff had decided would not do, and the ghost of this action was to rise up and walk not many months later.

The professional welfare people in the other Washington agencies closely concerned with the work of the Social Security Board indulged in a good deal of discussion about this attitude of the board towards the states. Some of the people in the Hopkins organization felt that the board was very definitely on the downward path, and making a fundamental mistake in policy from which it would never be able to recover. Also, of course, the attitude of the Children's Bureau toward state plans was in marked contrast to that of the board. In those states which expected to turn over to local governments a part of the administrative responsibility for public assistance, the board was inclined to pursue a laissez-faire policy, and to let the states decide what units of local government should exercise that responsibility. In many of the New England states, it permitted the use of the town for such purposes, despite its typically small size. In those midwestern states having both county and township governments the board did not require, as it might have, that counties should be the local agents for the state welfare bodies. Again, in some states, local welfare functions were split between a number of county agencies, or between the county and town. The board might have required the unification of these local welfare structures so that all forms of public assistance could be handled by the same agency. But here, too, it pursued a flexible policy, as Miss Bary explained, in order not to disturb those recently created local agencies which were doing good work, particularly in the field of child welfare.

These attitudes of the board and the staff, plus lack of time, led to the approval of a large number of state plans which were not all that the staff or the board desired. As a consequence, the board coupled its first approval, in most cases, with conditions which were set forth in letters to the states. The official minutes of the board for December 31, on which date a very large number of plans were approved, indicate some of these conditional stipulations. In accepting the Missouri plan for old age assistance the board asked for "additional data including rules and regulations having to do with administrative procedure." The Pennsylvania plan for aid to the blind received approval "with the understanding that detailed rules and regulations will be developed immediately." A similar clause for the Iowa and Vermont plans for old age assistance said, "Subject to additional information to be secured during the first quarter." New Hampshire had a corresponding condition attached to all three assistance grants, as did Wyoming, Nebraska, Maine, and Idaho. The same conditions were attached to a grant for the blind in North Carolina, to plans for dependent children and the blind in

Arizona, and to plans for the aged in Delaware and for the aged and the dependent children in Alabama.

When the deadline of December 31, 1935, was reached, eighteen states had plans for at least one of the public assistance grants approved by the board, and there were a number of other plans pending but requiring supplementary information. A table dated January 15, 1936, prepared by the Public Assistance Bureau, showed the approval of fifteen state plans for old age assistance, ten for aid to dependent children, and eleven for aid to the blind. By that time there were still pending nine submitted plans for old age assistance, eight for aid to dependent children, and six for aid to the blind. On that date forty-one states, two territories, and the District of Columbia had legislation for old age assistance, or general enabling acts for such plans. There were only seven states without any legislation, all of which, except South Dakota, were in the southeast section of the United States. Thirty-seven states and the District of Columbia possessed either legislation or general enabling acts for aid to the blind, and forty-six states, two territories, and the District of Columbia had laws relating to aid to dependent children. The two states without legislation for dependent children were Georgia and South Carolina.

On January 13, 1936, Miss Jane Hoey became head of the Public Assistance Bureau, though for some time she continued her work for the New York Welfare Council on a part-time basis. Her point of view towards this function of the board coincided almost precisely with that which had influenced the staff work thus far. She was convinced that the general approach of the board toward the states ought to differ from that of the FERA. She did not believe in beating people into agreeing, and instead put her faith in education to be carried on by an adequate, properly trained and oriented field staff.

Her associates at this time were very anxious for the elaboration of the field organization and of the central office staff, because of the pressing need of the states whose plans had been approved—a need for advice on initial procedures and problems of administration. There was a constant stream of requests for this kind of service, which led to the feeling by some of the staff that one of the first tasks to be undertaken should be the compilation of an advisory manual of procedures. Questions were also pouring in about the meaning of certain terms in the laws. For example, what constituted "desertion" or "permanent absence from home"?—important questions in administering assistance to dependent children—and what was the board's definition of blindness? Problems of this kind could not, of course, be solved by the staff except in the form of advice to the board, and the board was reluctant to answer without more knowledge, and more time to consider the probable results of its answers.

One of the most important of these questions and one which received a good deal of discussion during the succeeding months was the question of what constituted a "fair hearing"? This phrase occurred in all the titles relating to grants. It was intended to assure the applicant for aid an opportunity to have his case reviewed by another representative of the state administration, in case he should be denied assistance by an inferior official. Must the phrase be interpreted in accordance with judicial decisions, or could it be given a new content more closely linked to the necessities of good administration while at the same time safeguarding the rights of the individual? The legal staff had been inclined to interpret the phrase as requiring customary common-law trial safeguards. The public assistance staff, on the other hand, contended that in order to safeguard the applicant from arbitrary decisions it was neither necessary nor desirable to surround the work of a new administrative organization with the costly and time-consuming procedural arrangements of a common-law trial. They were convinced that a large number of people would contest the denial of their petitions by local administrators because their distressing experiences had unbalanced them emotionally and inclined them toward the nursing of grievances. Ultimately the public assistance staff, with the support of Altmeyer, requested that if the words "fair hearing" had to be interpreted in traditional common-law procedure, then the board ought to secure an amendment to the act which would substitute the phrase "fair review" for "fair hearing." During March 1936 the matter was debated at length, and the board decided to send an interpretative letter to the state administrators. A letter was drafted urging the use of every possible means to avoid resort to hearings, by careful attention to such matters as reinvestigations. The draft also laid down the essentials of fair hearing as interpreted by the courts, but in a manner so strictly legal and traditional, stressing the elements of proper notice, opportunity to produce testimony, to cross-examine witnesses, and so forth, that Altmeyer opposed it strenuously. He was afraid that it would lead to legalistic distortions of administration. Consequently the letter was never sent (although the board first approved it), and instead, such interpretations as were given to the phrase were made orally by the staff of the Bureau of Public Assistance during their discussions of administrative plans with state administrators.

All through this period, members of the staff were spending a great deal of time with people from the states who were proposing to change earlier state laws to conform to the provisions of the act, including the stipulations about proper administration. Miss Hoey found that many of their proposals were attempts to build their laws around or away from particular people. If there was some person or officer in whom the state representative had special confidence, he wanted to word the act so as to throw the responsibility on this individual. If he was moved chiefly by antipathy, the opposite desire was manifest. Miss Hoey's policy during this period was not to draft laws for such persons but rather to make suggestions.

There was at this time a great deal of speculation by state welfare administrators about whether or not Congress would make the first appropriations for grants-in-aid retroactive to the preceding summer or autumn. The board, too, was in suspense on this point until after its hearings with the House Appropriations Committee, which indicated the intention not to make the appropriations retroactive.

With the reconvening of Congress early in January 1936, the Townsend drive received added publicity and during that month and February appeared to be on the upswing. Edwin Witte of Wisconsin urged the board to take a liberal and nonmeticulous attitude toward the task of getting funds into the states for the needy aged. As a result of this insistence, every administrative rope had been greased to make the funds for approved state plans for public assistance available as soon as Congress passed the appropriation act. Seidemann and his associates had arranged with the Treasury and Comptroller General to give these funds right of way. As a consequence, on February 14, three days after the law was signed by the President, checks were on their way to twenty states and the District of Columbia; all had then qualified for one or more public assistance grants. The total payments were $3,182,825.80 for assistance to the aged, $395,696.56 for the blind, and $689,174.18 for dependent children. For this expedition the board received a good deal of favorable publicity.

SPECIAL LEGAL PROBLEMS ENCOUNTERED IN APPROVING STATE LAWS

Specific legal problems were bound to arise in the consideration of the varying state laws and administrative arrangements. The board made every effort to find a cure for obstacles that could be removed without new legislation, relying for that purpose whenever it reasonably could upon rulings by the state attorneys general, and on rules and regulations of the administrative agencies. But some of the defects were beyond remedy short of statutory changes. A few typical problems which claimed the board's early attention are described below.

MAY A PRIVATE INSTITUTION CONSTITUTE A STATE AGENCY?

In connection with Maryland's application for funds for the needy blind, the question of what constituted a state agency (required by the Social Security Act to receive federal funds) had to be answered. The Maryland

Workshop for the Blind, a private organization, had been used by the state for a good many years to perform its charitable activities for blind people. The Social Security Board was confronted by requests from the state of Maryland to adopt this private agency for the administration of federal funds. On March 2, Miss Hoey asked the board for a definition of a public agency. On the advice of Tate, of the General Counsel's Office, the board decided that the Maryland Workshop was not a governmental agency, and this view was also adopted by the Children's Bureau.

The Use of Contracts to Obtain Statewide County Compliance

The first Utah plan for the administration of public assistance grants was interesting, because of the device in it used to bridge a gap in the law in order to make the state eligible for federal funds. The state law did not make the participation of counties mandatory throughout the state. To achieve this objective, the administrator, with the active cooperation of the governor, worked out a system of contracts between the state and the counties, under which each county became obligated to provide funds and carry on the administration of the public assistance function. Every county was induced to sign this contract, and through informal conversations with members of the board and its staff, the Utah officials learned that such an arrangement would be acceptable. When Miss Bary made her field trip early in April, she stopped in Utah and looked over the situation. She wanted to make the public assistance grant to that state retroactive to cover February, since all the counties were actually carrying out the public assistance program in January, even though not all the contracts were signed until the middle of February. The state people were very anxious to extend their health work, in particular the nursing program, and the retroactive grant would make it possible for them to do so. Miss Bary commented on the peculiar situation in Utah where some lusty Mormons, over sixty-five years of age and eligible for old age assistance, had young children eligible for dependent children grants. The attorney general was also struggling with the legal questions involved in plural families now deprived by law of a father; if they were in need were they legally entitled to aid?

Legal Problems with Oregon, Delaware, Wyoming, and Idaho

During March, when there was pending before the board an application from Oregon for a grant for old age assistance, the board had Tate of its legal staff summarize the decisions it had taken previously on a legal problem like that presented in the Oregon case. Inasmuch as this and the related decisions throw light on the point of view with which the board approached its task in dealing with the states, it seems worthwhile to summarize the legal problem presented and the way in which it was analyzed and decided.

The Oregon statute restricted old age assistance to persons who had lived in the county of application one year. This restriction obviously conflicted with the terms of the Social Security Act. However, another provision set forth the fact that Congress was then considering legislation relating to old age assistance and that it was the declared public policy of the state of Oregon to cooperate with the United States Government and its agencies. The statute then went on to say that the State Relief Committee was designated

to prescribe and enforce rules and regulations made or approved by the United States government or any federal agency or administrator, for the purpose of carrying out any of the provisions of a federal law, any rule or regulation for old age assistance, and to do all things necessary or required in coordinating and cooperating with the federal government or any of its agencies in carrying out and administering the provisions of this Act.

The Oregon Attorney General advised the board that because of these last provisions, the State Relief Committee could lawfully make additional rules and regulations to supersede any provisions in the statute that contradicted the requirements of the Social Security Act. Accordingly, the State Relief Committee had adopted a ruling waiving the county residence one-year requirement. It had also passed a regulation providing for prompt payment to the United States of half the amount collected from the estates of recipients of old age money. This requirement of the Social Security Act had not been met specifically before in Oregon statutes.

Somewhat comparable problems had been presented earlier in the act creating the Delaware Old Age Welfare Commission. The act contained a residential requirement contradicting the Social Security Act standard, and it also provided for outside relief. There, too, the attorney general of the state had given an opinion that under the general provisions of a later law these contradictions could be ignored by the administrative agency. The board had approved the Delaware plan on the ground that "an opinion of the state Attorney General should be accepted on questions involving the interpretation of state legislation."

The board had likewise approved plans of Wyoming for aid to dependent children and aid to the blind. There, existing state laws had been modified by rules and regulations of state administrators under the authority of a broad delegation of legislative power to the state executive. The same situation had been present in two of the Idaho public assistance plans.

In view of these precedents, the board approved the Oregon plan despite the fact that its legal staff held a good many doubts about the validity of the Oregon program.

When Does a Plan Legally Begin Operations?

When the Arkansas plan for the three grants-in-aid was presented to the board with memoranda from the Bureau of Public Assistance and the Office of the General Counsel, a discussion ensued about an important legal point on which, again, the lawyers and the administrators differed. The Arkansas administration had asked for a grant beginning the first of February, but the Bureau of Public Assistance reported that before March 1, grocery orders or payments in kind, in lieu of cash, had been given in two counties. Therefore the grant could not begin until March, when the facts seemed to indicate that all the counties would be on a cash basis.

The real issue turned on the question of whether or not the Arkansas plans were legally in effect before March 6, on which date the executive committee of the state had adopted the necessary resolutions concerning residence, payment to counties from the state, and fair hearing. A month earlier, however, that committee had brought up these resolutions, read them, and given them to the field staff to be taken out into the state and abided by. They had waited until March 6 before final adoption, in order to see if Washington would approve the resolutions as meeting the federal requirements. Williams, of the legal staff, advised the board that if it were willing to accept the statement of Arkansas's chairman that Arkansas had operated under the plans from March 1 forward, the board could approve the plans as of that date. The board decided thereupon to approve the three Arkansas plans effective March 1, 1936. At the next day's meeting, Eliot reopened the subject by commenting adversely upon Williams's opinion and raising the whole question of the kind of evidence concerning the operation of state plans which should be used by the board in certifying grants to the Treasury. After a sharp remark by Altmeyer that it was rather late for the general counsel to be raising this question, Eliot was requested to prepare a memorandum on the subject for the board. On April 10 he presented a statement dealing with the evidence available from each of the states then asking for retroactive grants.

Eliot recommended that reimbursements for Arkansas date from March 6, despite evidence that the state was actually operating according to the submitted plan before that date. He took the position, which Tate supported, that the Arkansas plan did not become legally effective until March 6. Tate admitted, in response to a question by Winant, that if the board should certify a grant for Arkansas from March 1 there would probably be no serious results. Miss Hoey insisted that it had been the understanding of her bureau that the Arkansas plan would be approved as of March 1 and that she, with Williams of the General Counsel's Office, had so informed Andrews, who represented the state of Arkansas. Therefore it would be very embarrassing, now, to tell him that Arkansas could not be reimbursed for funds spent before March 6. As a matter of fact, the Arkansas administrators had been asked to submit an estimate of their expenditures for the period dating from March 1.

During the course of the discussion, the question of the board's right to reimburse states for payments upon the basis of an accrual estimate rather than actual payments arose. Eliot took the position that accrual payments were out and that only cash payments could be matched. Hughes, of the Accounts and Audits Bureau, was called in on this matter and asked whether or not the phrase "expended during such quarter," under Title I, section 3a, meant cash disbursements only. He gave the opinion that usually the term *expended*, as the General Accounting Office had used it, meant cash actually paid out. When asked point-blank about the Arkansas problem, he told the board that he believed it could reimburse Arkansas on an accrual basis. He said that where the records of the board showed that it had given due deliberation and made an honest effort to weigh the factors involved, there was small likelihood of any difficulty arising from the General Accounting Office. Thus the advice of the lawyers and that of the accounting expert were contradictory. On April 14, the board decided to grant Arkansas funds for old age assistance to match state payments beginning on March 1.

NORTH CAROLINA PLAN FOR AID TO THE BLIND, APPROVAL REVOKED

The North Carolina plan for aid to the blind was first approved on December 31, 1935, and the state notified of the approval on January 6, 1936, in a letter from the chairman of the board to the executive secretary of the North Carolina Commission for the Blind. Subsequently, a grant of $3,324 was made for the months of February and March. The plan was set up on the basis of legislation passed in 1935 providing for the vocational training of blind persons, granting them monthly stipends out of which they paid both their living and training expenses. The state commission had only a very small appropriation for this purpose, but most of the counties turned over relief funds to the commission for these expenditures.

The Public Assistance Bureau asked a ruling from the board on the policy which should be followed where conditions originally attached to grants had not been fulfilled. Miss Hoey declared that the plan had been wrongly approved in the first place and had not been complied with since its approval, but that nevertheless she thought the North Carolina administration was good enough to work the matter out ultimately.

There had been a considerable amount of correspondence and two field visits to North Carolina, and in general an attempt to put the plan on a more satisfactory basis before the matter should come up for consideration before the board on June 2, 1936. On that date, the bureau reported that the law was not mandatory on all counties and that the attorney general of North Carolina had furnished an opinion, on May 20, that the plan did not and could not conform to the requirements of the act. The bureau suggested that the plan be terminated at the end of the fourth quarter (June 30), and asked the board for the procedure to be followed in carrying out this termination, especially the requirements for a hearing. A letter signed by the chairman was sent that same day to Dr. Roma Cheek, executive secretary of the North Carolina Commission for the Blind. The letter was not very definite and was largely a request for more information about the fourth quarter. Without mentioning the word *hearing* it did suggest that Dr. Cheek come to Washington, if she cared to do so, to present the case for the plan to the board.

Dr. Cheek replied that she had supplied all the information possible and did not see any good reason for coming to Washington, though she would be willing to do so if the board requested it. On June 13, Acting Chairman Altmeyer wrote that the board expected to meet on June 19 for a final decision on the plan, and specifically asked whether a hearing was desired, in accordance with section 1004. By June 19 no reply to this last letter had been received, and the board agreed to receive the recommendations of the Bureau of Public Assistance and the Office of the General Counsel at its next meeting, and then to take final action on this plan.

At that meeting, the bureaus of Public Assistance and Accounts and Audits and the Office of the General Counsel recommended that a grant of $1,100 be made for the fourth quarter, but only after an audit of previous expenditures. The Bureau of Public Assistance further recommended that the approval of the plan be withdrawn for subsequent quarters, because the law was not in operation in all political subdivisions of the state nor mandatory upon the counties. The Office of the General Counsel supported this recommendation and stated that "the Board's letters to the state agency on this subject, dated June 2 and June 13 respectively, constituted reasonable notice and also for a hearing as required by Section 1004." These recommendations were approved, and the board formally withdrew approval of the North Carolina plan for aid to the blind as of the end of the fourth quarter of the fiscal year 1936.

The last letter from Dr. Cheek appearing in this case indicated the cooperative attitude of the North Carolina commission and the ease with which this single termination of approval of a public assistance plan was accomplished. (Incidentally, neither the governor of the state nor any other political officer was consulted by the board at any time.) Dr. Cheek's June 16 letter to Bane stated in part, "We appreciate so very much the Federal funds which we have received and although they have not been sufficient to aid in all counties, they have been of invaluable assistance to the blind receiving them because relief grants in our state are far from adequate."

This case was a consequence of the haste with which state plans had been pushed through during the second half of December 1935. The original approval was later recognized by both state and federal agencies as having been a mistake.

A FIELD STAFF GOES TO THE STATES, BUREAU ORGANIZATION LAGS

THE FIRST FIELD INSPECTIONS

All through February and into the first part of March, the public assistance division worked with practically the same small staff it had had from the beginning (save for the addition of Miss Hoey). There were no people in the field except when Frank Bane or some member of the office staff, and especially Miss Hoey herself, made an excursion to one of the states. The systematic advice, on home ground, that would have been possible with an organized field staff was not being given. The urgent need for this was made vividly clear during the second half of February, when McKinley went to New England to see how the states were getting started on their administrative tasks for all phases of the social security program. An eagerness for advice on technical problems of procedure, personnel, and general organization was manifest in nearly every state visited. The fact that he had frequented the board's office made him a constant target for countless requests for information and suggestions. This was not true of the work of the Children's Bureau nor the Public Health Service, which had already sent their field staff to the New England area. No field staff from the board, however, had been around. McKinley had some difficulty in disclaiming any responsibility for board administration. On his return to Washington, he reported his experiences to Miss Hoey and found that she was disturbed at the failure to get her people out into the states, but was working hard to secure staff for this purpose.

It was not until the middle of March 1936 that the bureau organized its first systematic field trips, and made a rapid survey of the administration of public assistance funds in the states launched on the new programs. Three field representatives and Miss Bary left Washington for this purpose. Miss Bary covered Nebraska, Wyoming, Colorado, Utah, Idaho, Washington, Montana, and North and South Dakotas. Mrs. Kathleen Lowrie was to visit New Mexico, Arizona, Mississippi, and Alabama. Ernest F. Witte was to cover Illinois, Michigan, Wisconsin, Iowa, and Missouri. Miss McChord was to go to Maine, New Hampshire, Vermont, Connecticut, and Rhode Island. These field trips were made in company with members of the Bureau of Accounts and Audits (except in the case of Miss Bary). It was believed that if people from the two bureaus went together they could reinforce one another in their inquiries, minimize disturbance in the state offices, and obtain a more rounded picture of the state situations. Miss Bary was gone for over a month.

Miss McChord was able to cover only four states because of the floods then menacing New England. She visited Rhode Island, Maine, New Hampshire, and Vermont, and returned quite discouraged about what she had found. In Vermont, the director of old age assistance had told her, with considerable pride, about the uniquely meritorious system Vermont had adopted for investigating the cases of applicants for old age moneys. They had found it the best practice to call on the groceryman or the drugstore proprietor or the merchant to ask about the aged applicant, instead of sending a social worker out to talk with him. This, the director contended, was a much more reliable way of finding out about people, since it made use of the merchants' judgments, and they knew about the ability of such people to pay their bills. Miss McChord felt that anyone who could boast of such a practice would strain her educational powers. In Maine, the head of the welfare department was anxious to keep his own hands on the administration of relief for the aged but was uninterested in what was being done, and rather competently, by his officer in charge of the children's section. A duplicate set of local districts for state administrative purposes was being organized, and the head of the department had not considered any plan for unification. She found the New Hampshire situation spotty, with the work for dependent children being poorly done, while the officer in charge of the task of relieving the aged wanted to build up a good staff and do a good job. The situation in Rhode Island was extremely discouraging. The people directly in charge of the public assistance functions wanted to live up to their responsibilities, but at every point they had been blocked by the political spoils system. The administrator for aid to the aged, and his assistant, had appealed to Miss McChord to go to Governor Greene and tell him that they could not function because they had no qualified staff. This she did, after she had told them what she was going to say and had secured their approval. The governor expressed great surprise that his staff had not appealed directly to him, although he and she both knew they had been in to see him and that he had done nothing about it. Then the governor is alleged to have said, "Why doesn't the Social Security Board lay down the requirement that we must have trained people? Then we would get them." Miss McChord reminded him that the Social Security Act prohibited the board from such behavior.

The reports about the middle western states, where Ernest Witte made the first visits, were equally discouraging. In Missouri, which was the worst state, Witte found the situation so bad that he recommended in his statement to the board that the grant be withheld unless the Missouri outfit "cleans out its administration and obeys the law." Here was a clear case in which he felt that the terms of the Social Security Act were not being fulfilled. The entire administration was dominated by Boss Prendergast of Kansas City. After Witte's return, the Missouri people were called in to Washington and many hours of talk ensued in the endeavor to get them to voluntarily change their methods of administration. In addition to that, a letter was sent to Missouri (and to all the other states in which difficulties had been discovered), pointing out what the administrative troubles were and suggesting what should be done to remove them. Moreover, the board made its second-quarter grant for a two-month period only, withholding moneys for the third month pending action by the state in response to the request for changes in state administrative program and practice. This same tactic was used in handling the other states in which most difficulties had been discovered. The board was anxious not to resort to revocation until all other efforts had failed.

In the case of Missouri, the board at length decided to send Miles out to "talk turkey" to Prendergast and his people, to whom the real responsibility for the Missouri situation was clearly traceable. Witte reported that one of the troubles during his first field trip to Missouri was an allegation by the people there that certain aspects of their administrative setup to which Witte objected had been approved earlier by Miles, whose approval they quoted. Witte felt that if the board members were to indulge in such field activity, it would be impossible for the professional field organization of the Public Assistance Bureau to function. He was skeptical about the prospects ahead if the three board members and Bane went around the country doing field work with the state officials.

An amusing example of Missouri administrative technique was a rating system for determining the degree of need of the aged. This was the joint product of the chairman of the Missouri board and his executive officer, both of whom were officials in a livestock association and connected with the horse-breeding industry. They had worked out their rating system on a set of schedules similar to those used in rating livestock for shows, and were exceedingly proud of this objective technique as a contribution to the science of public administration. As late as April 28 Miss Hoey had been unable to convince them that it should be discontinued.

The total absence of a paid local investigating staff in Missouri threw an impossible burden on the state administrative staff (also inadequate in numbers and training), so that resort to some mechanical formulas had become almost inescapable unless funds could be found for employing new people. One obstacle to adequate personnel was an interpretation by the Missouri attorney general limiting salary expenditures to a small portion of the federal grant for administration. There was also difficulty in securing agreement from the state administration to use proper standards for the selection of the proposed investigating and field supervising staffs.

The Iowa administration of moneys for the needy aged was described by Witte, on April 22, as eaten up by overhead. The three members of the commission spent their full time in listening to the human tales of woe and going over the details of cases. This cost the state around $15,000, so that there was not enough money left to employ supervisors. The state director, although a political appointee, was able and desired to do a good job, but his funds were eaten up by his board. Witte felt that these difficulties could have been prevented if the Social Security Board had had a staff in the field early enough to help the states prepare their plans, or even, perhaps, had it been there when administration was being started.

The Iowa situation, in Witte's view, illustrated the ill consequences of the hasty approval which the board gave to some state plans for public assistance. The Iowa plan, he asserted, never called for a proper field staff, and so the board could not complain that the plan which was approved was not being administered.

In Wisconsin the problem was one of county funds. Wisconsin was the only state of the four reported upon by Witte in his first field trip which had adequate personnel standards for its administration. But some of the counties were not living up to the mandatory provisions of the Social Security Act, apparently having no money with which to meet the public assistance requirements for old age. The state officers appeared to believe that the board had no jurisdiction over the actual administration of the mandatory clause other than to see that the plan provided by state law should be in existence in all counties. When Witte taxed them with the fact that the plan was not actually operating in some of the counties, they contended that this was none of the board's business. After Witte's report, the board turned the Wisconsin problem over to Altmeyer, who felt sure that Wisconsin had plenty of money tucked away which could be used for the mandatory provisions of the Social Security Act. This proved to be the case.

Among the other difficult spots revealed by this first general inspection was the situation of grants for the aged in Mississippi, as reported by Kathleen Lowrie. Mississippi enacted a new law in the latter part of March, with a small appropriation act which permitted a meager staff. Mrs. Lowrie recommended that, since the law fulfilled the requirements, an initial grant should be made, but that it should be conditioned upon an understanding that trained social workers would be employed as county supervisors and a trained social worker employed as case consultant in the state office. The board should offer its aid in the training program "so that their assistant administrator will not feel too helpless as the sole field supervisor."

Another very bad spot which came to light about this same time was in Pennsylvania. When the board had approved the Pennsylvania plan for assistance to the needy blind, Chairman Winant had written the secretary of the State Department of Public Welfare a covering letter containing recommendations about improved methods of administration upon which he indicated the board would base its considerations of future requests for the renewal of the grant:

The Social Security Board hopes it will be possible for you to make definite improvements in the methods of administration embodied in the Pennsylvania plan. Among the steps which we consider to be most necessary are the following:

1. The Board believes that it is extremely desirable that the present state field staff be increased in number to permit more definite supervision over the administration of aid to the blind by the local boards than your department had been able to maintain in the past. Visits to local boards should be made more frequently than is indicated in the plan and arrangements should be made for the state supervisors to act as case consultants, especially in regional areas.

2. The Board believes that the practice of placing the responsibility for the actual administrative work upon unpaid local boards is not desirable. It is suggested that a paid staff should be employed to administer aid to the blind in each county. In rural areas, where caseloads are small, one worker might be able to carry the work for several adjoining countries.

The field investigator, Miss Amy Tapping, reported on March 30 in a memorandum to Miss Hoey that the Pennsylvania field staff had not been increased, and that two of the six members had been replaced for purely political reasons by less efficient people who could not comply with the minimum standards which the state itself had set for field representatives. She also pointed out that the plan for the employment of paid staff in each county had not been put in operation, there being twelve counties without paid staff. She reported that on March 24 the newly appointed secretary of the Department of Welfare had placed the Division of Grants and Pensions under the supervision of a deputy who was without any previous training or experience, except the secretaryship of the Women's Division of the Pennsylvania State Democratic Committee. She asserted that there were increasing evidences that members of the local county boards were being replaced by political appointees and that staff members were being superseded by people with the proper political endorsements without regard to professional qualifications. Finally, the report stated that "an effective administration of assistance to the blind is jeopardized by an insistent lowering of personnel standards and by a disregard for the need of a qualified staff."

In the far west, Miss Bary took a more optimistic view of the state administrative arrangements in Idaho, Montana, and Washington. She had nothing but praise for the progressive spirit and vigor with which the Idaho people were doing their job. In Washington an even more advanced department of welfare was functioning, despite the fact that the supervisor of public assistance had been appointed for political rather than professional reasons. His assistant, a trained worker, had brought him into line on policies. The chief difficulty in Washington was the mistake of the state administration in trusting to the statement in the Social Security Act that federal payments to supplement state moneys for aid would begin on July 1, 1935. Washington began its payments at that time and then, in the spring of 1936, found itself short of money. Its fairly generous average for grants to the aged contributed to this difficulty.

In Montana things had been pretty bad, but Miss Bary reported a "new deal" as a result of the housecleaning which the new governor had just accomplished. She found the governor and the new commission very anxious to straighten out their social security program and to obtain not merely the money which the board could release to them but also its help and guidance. They also wanted to coordinate all three programs and gear them into general relief administration.

During this trip Miss Bary aided groups in Nebraska, Colorado, and Nevada that were considering legislation and administrative organization. She found a good many objections to the plan of administration that the Nevada people were intending to present to the board. The chief executive of the State Board of Pensions and Relief (who was also the WPA administrator) seemed confident that Senator Pittman could put anything across in Washington, no matter how shoddy it might be. Miss Bary stepped up their plans for supervision of the counties, to which direct administration of the funds for the aged was to be entrusted. The plan also contemplated no contribution by the state toward administrative expenses or toward assistance funds. During Miss Bary's conference the administrator agreed to put on several field persons, claiming that he could use WPA money for that purpose.

There can be no doubt that these first field visits made it crystal clear that the heart of the problem of state administration was personnel. Wherever the field staff discovered difficulties, it was the personnel situation which was at fault. This was related directly to the prohibition in the Social Security Act against interference by the board with matters relating to the selection, tenure of office, and compensation of personnel. The field staff was nonplussed time and time again because of this provision in the law. Miss Hoey had even felt it necessary, when state plans were being submitted, to refrain from inquiring into the precise character of the duties performed by each member of the staff and into his previous experience and training.[8]

These trips also revealed some startling facts about the amount of assistance being granted to individuals. In Mississippi the average grant for the aged was discovered to be $3.65. Having no relief moneys, that state was using the funds for the aged for relief purposes wherever possible, so as to spare the money which they had, very small in total, for aid to dependent children. The situation in Missouri was somewhat comparable. There were no FERA funds. There was a huge list of applicants for old age assistance, and the policy had been to dole out small sums to each person. In effect, these two states and others were dividing wholly inadequate assistance among the largest possible number of people. There can be no doubt that this policy contradicted the intent of the Social Security Act. Certainly the aged in these states had been much better off when they were on direct relief under FERA. However, the board was in this dilemma: if it insisted upon the states making grants sufficient to permit each applicant to live on a decent relief standard, there would be thousands of needy aged and dependent children cut off with absolutely no assistance whatsoever. This was the result, first, of the failure of the states to make provision for relief funds, and second, of the decision by the national government "to get out of this relief business." Either the board would have to insist upon adequate standards of relief in making its grants to states, or it would have to bring to the attention of the President and Congress the urgent need for the national government to resume its general relief activities in those states which could not afford or would not perform this task themselves. The danger was looming that the Social Security Act might become the instrument for the development of an unbelievably inadequate relief system for the aged poor and for dependent children.[9] It seemed to McKinley that this was the most important social development to emerge from the first six months' experience of the administration of the public assistance grants-in-aid.

[8] This information had been demanded by the Unemployment Compensation Bureau from the state administrators of unemployment insurance.

[9] Altmeyer raised this issue at a meeting of the board on March 26, when the Ohio problem was being discussed.

It was almost inevitable that a number of states whose plans had been hurriedly approved in the December-January rush to start public assistance funds flowing would later be found wanting in the complete fulfillment of their plans. As information began to trickle in, showing failures in this or that particular, the board and its public assistance staff were faced with the question of how closely they should hew to the letter of the law. This issue had to be faced as soon as applications for grants for the second quarter (the fourth for the fiscal year 1936) came up for consideration. Miss Hoey brought it before the board at its meeting on April 7, 1936. She wanted to know what the board intended to do in those cases where her field staff had discovered that the state administrations were not functioning in accordance with the approved plans. Winant suggested that the board certify for the quarter but make its grant on a monthly basis and write at once to those states that had not complied, thus giving them due notice until the end of April. He suggested also that a hearing be scheduled for April and that the states be promptly advised of the date. To this General Counsel Eliot objected that under the law the board was presumed to tell the Secretary of the Treasury when to make payments, supposedly at the beginning of each quarter. If the board should hold a hearing and discover that it had to withdraw certification for a particular state, there was nothing in the law about notifying the Secretary of the Treasury to hold up payment. After some discussion, the board requested the General Counsel, the Bureau of Public Assistance, and the Bureau of Accounts and Audits to work this matter out and make a report to it. The report appears not to have been made, or at least not to have been formally considered by the board.[10]

On April 29, memoranda were presented to the board from the Bureau of Public Assistance and from the General Counsel's Office, dealing with the subject of noncompliance with the state plan. In this discussion Miss Hoey pointed out that noncompliance usually fell into one of three categories: (1) noncompliance because of physical hazards, such as bad weather, which prevented the state field staff from getting into the counties; (2) noncompliance because of lack of time in which to complete the procedural arrangements which set the administrative machinery in motion (for example, in those counties where there was a large Negro population, it took a long time to establish correct ages for administering old age assistance); (3) noncompliance caused by the failure of funds in certain counties. Both the legal and public assistance bureaus agreed that for the first few quarters the board ought to be lenient in determining compliance. The Bureau of Public As-

---

[10] Nevertheless, Miss Hoey told McKinley that the board had in the case of Missouri made a grant for only two months of a quarter, holding the third month back as a weapon to use in securing compliance.

sistance believed that the board would not be able, before July 1, to judge which states had counties that were not to be a part of the plan by the third quarter. This, it said, was due to the long time it took to get under way in all the counties. Because of the physical, climatic, and personnel difficulties involved in getting a plan completely under way, and because of the delays in securing proof of age, residence, and so forth, the board agreed not to hold hearings or withhold grants from a state for the second quarter in which the plan was in operation.

Tate, of the General Counsel's Office, recommended that the board should not hold any hearings on state plans for the second quarter of its experience, excepting where those plans clearly had no proper foundation, as in North Carolina. Further, he recommended that the state not be told that the board intended to be lenient. Altmeyer insisted that any concessions should be upon a consistent basis which the board could defend. He also appeared to feel that noncompliance because of physical difficulties or lack of time to get started should not be held as a justification for the withholding of grants. Winant appeared to support, with unimportant verbal modifications, the policy proposed by Miss Hoey. It was agreed at the conclusion of this discussion not to adopt any formal policy except for the guidance of the Bureau of Public Assistance. Miss Hoey suggested that where noncompliance was due to the failure of counties to find funds for fulfillment of the "statewide" provisions of the Social Security Act, she be permitted to negotiate with the state officials to get funds into these counties, and where she was not able to accomplish that, she should come back to the board with recommendations.

BUREAU ORGANIZATION PROBLEMS, SPRING OF 1936

Certain internal problems of organization in the Bureau of Public Assistance emerged during the latter part of the spring of 1936. Most of these could be traced to the slowness with which the staff for this unit was augmented. It became increasingly difficult to perform the work of the bureau promptly and in ship-shape form. Time and again its representatives came to board meetings to present recommendations concerning state plans when the facts relating to the state situation had not been fully ironed out with the lawyers, and as a consequence the plans were not ready for final board consideration. The board itself became aware of this problem, and on April 7 the chairman commented upon the need for more people in the bureau and the need to speed up its activities and to give it ample opportunity to check carefully its recommendations in the handling of the large sums that were being awarded on the basis of its work. He proposed at that meeting that the board should employ Howard Smith, the accountant who had been engaged as a member of the staff to help in the Ohio investigation. He wanted Smith to help train auditors and speed up auditing activities, so that the board's public assistance grants to the states could be more certainly accounted for.

Inside the headquarters staff there was great admiration for Miss Hoey's unusual gifts in dealing with the policy problems and in handling the state people, but there was some dissatisfaction with her failure to organize the staff so as to secure better administrative results. She had not definitely allocated duties among her headquarters people. Gradually they had agreed among themselves on a rough distribution of functions. This lack of clear organization within the headquarters was reflected in the relations with the field staff and the states. There were complaints that correspondence did not receive prompt attention from the Washington office. One member of the field staff related that on his first trip he had written back to the bureau for advice and had received no reply until he sent a caustic telegram. There was also some feeling that the first field force was handled upon too individual a basis, without the benefits of group conference and the sharing of experience.

How far the failure of Miss Hoey to work out the proper distribution of duties and responsibilities within her staff was due to any desire she might have had to keep responsibility in her own hands, how far it was a consequence of the demands upon her time which prevented her from deliberating upon this question, and how much it was the result of failure to get additional workers (which in turn was related to difficulties of classification and civil service examination) it was impossible to say. Certainly, however, her headquarters group felt itself doing a rather sloppy job. One of her most intelligent assistants expressed the opinion late in April that because of the hectic situation in which they were working, the public assistance people were missing a great opportunity to evaluate the policies embodied in the decisions which they had been making. No one had time to do this and so no one really knew, aside from the consciousness of a general desire to secure decent standards for state personnel, what trends were being created by the decisions about state plans. This same person felt that headquarters relationships to the field staff had not been well worked out because there had not been staff or time enough to do a good job. For example, a policy like that which Witte had advocated, to refrain from calling state people to Washington unless the field representative covering that state was also present, could not be carried out by a short-handed bureau. As an illustration, it was necessary for the board to take action concerning the Pennsylvania administration of aid to the blind without the presence of Miss Tapping, the field agent who covered Pennsylvania, because she was at that time out in the Far West.

At the end of April, McKinley discussed the staff situation with Miss

Hoey, who did not appear to share the sense of difficulty which seemed to prevail among her assistants. She did complain that the central staff had not been expanded as rapidly as she had wanted, because of trouble with the Civil Service Commission, which did not approve the grades she felt were appropriate and necessary to secure the talent she needed.[11] She gave, as an example of her problem, the failure to get for the head of the Educational Service a grade sufficient to attract a good person from one of the university faculties of social work, which was the kind of person she required. The job would be planning and organizing institutes for training people on the board's staff, or the staffs of the state and local administrative agencies. She was convinced that it would be impossible to get a proper person for less than $5,600, but the highest the Civil Service Commission was willing to go was $4,600. As far as field staff was concerned, Miss Hoey believed that the six people she then had (this was April 28) were taking care of the problem fairly well. She had three more signed up to join the staff on May 15. On the whole she felt that the field work was being elaborated with sufficient rapidity to care for the urgent needs. They were not only checking up on the administration of plans that had been put into operation, but were also aiding in the preparation of plans about to be submitted to the board by those states which had not yet qualified.

POLITICAL "HOT SPOTS"
KANSAS, OHIO, COLORADO, AND KENTUCKY

Because the concept of old age pensions had such wide public sympathy and interest, state political leaders and their backers were either beating the tom-toms on behalf of pensions for the aged or had ridden to power on that issue. The board therefore confronted a few systems of state administration already established whose architects had designed them not so much for efficient service to the aged as for continuing aid to the elected. In a few of them, the administration was so obviously inefficient that in making the initial grants the board was faced with the alternative of demanding drastic changes or perpetuating systems of administration which would not conform to the letter

[11] Miss Hoey refused during this period to make use of special examinations, under the classified service, to expand her staff. While this would have taken some time, had she asked for them when she came on the job adequate lists might have become available during the summer of 1936, if sufficient pressure had been put on the Civil Service Commission.

or spirit of the act. In other cases legal defects in state legislation were ignored by the governors and their political assistants, who hoped to "bull through" their applications by pressure and obtain board approval.

KANSAS AND THE LANDON BOOM

Plans for the three public assistance grants were submitted by Kansas under date of January 7, 1936. The paper set-up for administration seemed excellent. John G. Stutz, State Emergency Relief Committee director, who would become the state administrator for these grants in case the Kansas plans were accepted, came to Washington about the middle of January and spent a number of days attempting to get the board's approval. During the discussions about the power of the state to fulfill the legal obligations of the Social Security Act, intimations came to the board from Senator McGill of Kansas (who was not of the same political party as the governor) that the facts were not as Stutz had represented them. The chief questions that arose were, first, had all the counties funds with which to do their part in fulfilling the plans? The state had no funds to use for taking over the obligations of defaulting counties. Stutz was reported to have categorically asserted time after time that all the counties had the money required to do their part. Second, did the state have the authority to supervise the county administration of social security funds? Again Stutz, with the backing of the Kansas attorney general, declared that the state had ample power even to the extent, if necessary, of removing county officials. The board began to receive telegrams from the county officials of different counties declaring point-blank that they would not put up the funds for this purpose. With these evidences of the falsity of the declarations made by Stutz and the attorney general (who were in this affair the direct representatives of Governor Landon) the board could not accept the Kansas plans without violating the terms of the Social Security Act. Yet the board was in a very tight hole. It had on previous occasions made a generous interpretation of the act for certain states whose plans had not quite fully conformed to the literal requirements of the Social Security Act. But in no case had a state come forward with three plans, all of which failed to fulfill important legal requirements. Moreover, the board was fully aware of the delicate political situation involved. Already it was apparent that Governor Landon was becoming the leading Republican aspirant for the presidential nomination. The board had freshly in mind the episode of the Treasury and its prosecution of Messrs. Raskob and Dupont over their 1929 income tax returns. Winant and his associates felt very strongly that the board did not want to get itself into the position the Treasury had occupied, that of appearing to persecute political opponents. On this account, the board was very desirous of accepting the

Kansas plan and turning over the Kansas allotments for all three purposes. If, however, it did this for Kansas, it would have to accept similar violations of the act for other states.

After nearly a week of conversations between Stutz and Miss Hoey and her staff, and Stutz and the board members and Bane, Miss Hoey and Bane finally induced Stutz to admit the truth about the Kansas situation. But still the board was in a state of uncertainty over the course it should pursue. At nearly every meeting from January 24 until February 11, when the matter was finally disposed of, the Kansas problem was debated and various "outs" discussed. At the morning session on January 31, the board voted to disapprove the Kansas plan and to dispatch a letter to Stutz on that day setting forth the reasons. In the afternoon session, the case was reopened and Bane was asked to rewrite the letter according to new suggestions, and to present it at the next meeting of the board. At the next meeting, on February 1, further discussion occurred, with Miles attempting to phrase the message to Stutz. At the conclusion of the discussion Altmeyer was assigned to prepare a letter stressing three points: (a) the program would not be in effect throughout the state; (b) there was no way of assuring money payments; and (c) there was no assurance of state supervision. At the next meeting, on February 4, Winant reported a long distance telephone conversation which he had had with Governor Landon since the last meeting. The board agreed that Bane should go out to Kansas and confer with Landon as soon as possible, and postponed further action until Bane's return. Bane went out shortly after this meeting and explained the situation to the governor and his committee. Commenting on Bane's trip to Kansas, Winant said he wasn't sure it had been justified. Judging from the press clippings after Bane's return, he thought that Bane's friendly manner and good humor in talking the situation over had obscured from some of the people there the fact that he was saying that the board would not accept the plans.

Bane reported to the board meeting of February 11 that he had talked with Governor Landon, Akers, chairman of the Kansas Emergency Relief Committee, and Stutz, the director. He proposed to the board that it adopt a motion that it could not approve the Kansas plan for the aged, blind, or dependent children. A debate as to whether or not the board wanted to establish the policy of disapproving any plans ensued. Eliot interpreted the act as giving the board only the duty of approving plans and not of disapproving them.[12] Miles proposed that the board by unanimous action disapprove the Kansas plans "on the grounds that they do not comply with the minimum provisions of the Social Security Act."

[12] The same legalistic point had been raised in the consideration of unemployment compensation laws.

The action finally taken was as follows. The board decided that the Kansas plans did not comply with the provisions of the Social Security Act, and instructed the executive director to prepare a letter for the signature of Chairman Winant to the director of the Kansas Emergency Relief Committee stating the position of the board. A letter bearing the date of February 18, signed by Chairman Winant, was dispatched to Stutz and read, in part:

We regret to advise you that these plans do not meet the following requirements of the Social Security Act:

(1) That a state plan shall "provide that it shall be in effect in all subdivisions of the state, and, if administered by them, be mandatory upon them."

(2) That assistance to the aged, aid to dependent children, and aid to the blind shall consist of money payment.

(3) That there shall be a single state agency to supervise the administration of the plan.

In other words, the plans submitted by you are not in accordance with the specific provisions of the Social Security Act designed to establish on a statewide basis, and not on a county option basis, all new forms of public assistance, usually called "pensions" to supplant so far as possible the older types of poor relief. These conclusions are based upon the information you furnished the Board. You stated very strongly that a county would have the right to decline to participate in a state plan and instead elect to furnish public assistance to all needy individuals, including the aged, dependent children, and the blind, in the form of grocery orders, supplies, and other necessaries rather than in the form of money payments. You also stated that the executive order of the Governor dated December 20, 1935 does not give supervisory power to the Kansas Emergency Relief Committee with respect to funds supplied by the counties. Since the plans as submitted provide that the funds for granting assistance and which could be used for matching federal funds will have to be supplied by the counties, it follows that the executive order does not give the Kansas Emergency Relief Committee supervisory powers with respect to a very substantial part of the state program.[13]

In a conversation about ten days later, Chairman Winant declared that the board's chief desire in the Kansas situation was to prevent it from becoming the basis of a Republican attack on the President. Up to that time, he felt, the board had succeeded. He thought he had made Landon understand by telephone before Bane's trip that the board had no power to approve the Kansas plans for public assistance without violating the law. However, he did not feel certain that a hue and cry distorting the facts would not be raised at any moment. No such episode did occur, however.

[13] It took two more board meetings to get this Kansas letter polished to the satisfaction of all board members.

TIDYING UP OHIO

No sooner had the Kansas difficulty been surmounted than another political hot spot had to be handled. Early in the third week of February Governor Davey's representative, M. L. Brown, arrived in Washington to demand acceptance of the Ohio plan for old age assistance. From Miss Hoey's account of this episode, it would appear that Brown first went to the board members and demanded approval of the Ohio plans. The members of the board were already advised of grave charges against the Ohio administrators, particularly those resulting from an investigation by Colonel Sherrill, formerly city manager of Cincinnati. However, they sent Brown on to Miss Hoey and awaited a report from her. He repeated his demands to her and told her that the board was willing. She told him point-blank that until the administration was changed, she would not recommend the approval of the plan.

He was furious and demanded an explanation. She told him she had a large number of complaints from citizens in Ohio who knew what the facts were, setting forth the grossly ineffective administrative arrangements. In his anger he asked her why the board didn't come out and investigate the administration itself, whereupon Miss Hoey took him up, knowing that he didn't want it done. In both these actions, namely the refusal to recommend the plan for approval and the accepting of the obligation for an investigation by the Public Assistance Bureau, the board backed Miss Hoey up. She had done this not only because of her conviction that the Ohio situation was extremely bad, but also because of her belief that it might have a salutary effect on the other states.

At the board meeting on February 17 Miles had brought up the Ohio situation and discussed it at considerable length. He had talked with Colonel Sherrill about his findings, and he and the other board members had discussed the state plans with Brown. The board agreed to consider the Ohio question at its next meeting, with Brown and Miss Hoey present. But before the meeting the following day the challenge to investigate Ohio had been made and accepted, so the meeting was largely given over to a discussion of how the investigation would be conducted and who would do the job for Miss Hoey. As she was shorthanded it was proposed that Ewan Clague, who had but recently joined the Bureau of Research and Statistics as assistant director, but whose experience in the WPA and other welfare agencies qualified him to direct such an enterprise, should lead the Ohio expedition. Members of the board were rather perturbed at the prospect because they were uncertain of the board's legal power to inquire into the personnel aspects of state administration. Altmeyer felt it would be good strategy to have a formal request from the Ohio people for the board to come out and make a study. After some discussion, it was agreed to call Brown by telephone and ask him to write the board "relative to his suggestion of a few days ago, asking the board to make a study of the administration of old age assistance in Ohio." The job of getting in touch with Brown was turned over to Miles, whose fraternal relationship to the Eagles made him the appropriate contact man for this enterprise. It was further agreed that upon receipt of this letter from Brown, the Bureau of Public Assistance should go ahead and send its representatives to Ohio. An invitation came in the form of a telegram from M. L. Brown, acting administrator for the Ohio old age assistance law, but it asked the board to send businessmen to investigate. Miles said that this telegram had been dictated by Governor Davey. Since the board would not sent a delegation of businessmen, it decided, against Bane's desire, to write Brown the names and professions of the staff it proposed to send. Bane felt that to take this line was to admit the right of a state to dictate to the board its investigatory personnel. Winant insisted that because of the way the invitation had been secured, and the conditions attached, it was necessary to tell the Ohio people who were coming so that they might protest if they wanted to. It was decided to send Clague, assisted by Helen Jeter, Alvin Roseman, Keith Tindale (Bane's assistant), and an accountant, H. L. Smith, the latter retained on a per diem basis because he was not a regular member of the board's staff.

No protest having been lodged by the Ohio people, this staff left for Ohio on February 26. The official case for the investigation made by the Bureau of Public Assistance was presented in a memorandum to the board dated February 18, part of which read as follows:

The Bureau respectfully recommends that the Board consider the following points before taking action on the Ohio plan:

a. Numerous protests in writing and verbally have been received from groups of representative citizens in Ohio, which indicate very great dissatisfaction with the present methods of administration in the Division of Aid to the Aged in Ohio.

b. Old age assistance is now being paid to almost 22 percent of the 1930 population of eligible age in Ohio. The experience of other states seems to indicate that approximately 15 percent of persons of eligible age will ordinarily qualify for such assistance on a need basis if adequate investigations are made. The fact that the proportion of population of eligible age receiving assistance is one third greater than the experience of other states, seems to justify raising a serious question as to the efficiency of the present administrative methods.

c. The Sherrill Report indicates that aproximately 50 percent of the 167 cases investigated by the Sherrill Committee had never been visited in their own homes.

d. In June, 1934, when Mr. M. L. Brown, the present Acting Chief of the Division of Aid for the Aged, was in charge of that Division, applicants for old age assistance were required to state their political affiliations on the application blank. The Sherrill Report states that only after vigorous protests from the Hamilton County Advisory Board was this requirement waived for Hamilton County. The state forms used after this time did not require the applicant to indicate his political preference.

e. The chief of the Division has informed members of the Social Security Board's staff that the pressure of approving 36,000 applications, in the first six months of operation, resulted in the acceptance of a number of ineligible persons. However, he also made the statement that aid has been discontinued in only 10 percent of the cases which have so far been accepted for aid and that 5 percent of these discontinuances were because of death. This would seem to indicate that no serious effort has been made to weed out ineligible cases.

f. The lack of adequate qualifications for both investigatory and supervisory staff raises serious questions as to whether a good administration can ever be developed under the present set-up.

The Bureau of Public Assistance, therefore, suggests, because of serious doubts concerning the efficiency of the methods of administration and the possibility that persons who are not eligible may be receiving old age assistance and those who are eligible may be excluded from the list of recipients, that a brief study of the Ohio administration be conducted before the Board considers the approval of this plan. This procedure has been suggested by Mr. M. L. Brown, Acting Chief of the Ohio agency. Ohio is a pivotal state, and, according to reports which have come into this office, the inadequacies of its present administration are widely known. If the Board were to put money into this state and then, because of the administrative inadequacies, be compelled to withdraw federal funds, serious results might ensue both for Ohio and for the Board.

The report further objected to the qualifications for local personnel selected by the county boards, which had been prescribed by the state civil service commission and which read as follows:

I. At least five years experience as owner, operator, or manager of a successful business enterprise, or in a position giving contacts with results in successful public relations or in a position requiring skill in consummation of successful business transactions, and

II. Must also possess a good personality, decided initiative, and an aptitude for investigational procedure.

As a matter of fact, Ohio had undergone a reaction against social workers which enabled the Eagles to control almost the entire administration of the old age assistance function. This was the nub of the Ohio situation.

After three weeks of study Clague presented a summary report to Bane under date of March 24. In addition to examining and appraising the methods of accounting and of statistical reporting, and surveying the organization and methods of operation of the state and county administrative offices, the staff systematically interviewed state and county officials indirectly concerned with the administration of the old age assistance program, and the officers and staff members of other welfare agencies concerned with this function. Certain counties were selected for detailed studies. Another phase of the investigation consisted of

a special sample survey of cases selected at random from the files in the state office of the Division of Aid to the Aged. The case record for each of these individuals was read in the office and a summary prepared of the information contained therein. . . . Then, entirely independently, this individual was interviewed in his own home by a member of the staff who obtained similar information, as though from a new case. Finally a detailed point by point comparison was made between the original record and the data obtained by our investigators.

The major findings of the survey related not to corruption, but to inefficiency born of ignorance and incompetence. There had not been as much deliberate distortion and political partiality as the Sherrill report had indicated. As a matter of fact, it was the impression of the board's investigators that the Sherrill report was not a good piece of work, that Sherrill had been "tipped off" to selected cases which were not typical. Roseman felt that one of the contributing difficulties in the Ohio situation was the bad reputation which had been made for social work by the social workers operating in that state during the depression. They had made so many mistakes of tact and judgment in handling people that there was a general revulsion against the whole genus of social workers.

Following the reports by the survey staff, the Public Assistance Bureau recommended certain changes, to be required as conditions of approval of the Ohio plan. These were specific organizational devices and procedures to remove the difficulties presented in the summary of finding. When this came before the board, together with Clague's report, on March 24, Miles declared frankly that he did not see how the board could approve the plan. Nevertheless, the Bureau of Public Assistance recommended approval of the Ohio plan if the recommendations which it had submitted were put into effect by the Ohio officials. It should be kept in mind that Ohio was asking for a retroactive grant covering the first quarter ending on March 31, which was only seven days away. The Public Assistance Bureau felt that the board had in that circumstance considerable leverage to induce the Ohio people to make immediate changes. As Miss Hoey was more anxious to get constructive results from the investigation than to show up the Ohio administration, she proposed that before the plan was approved by the board, someone go out to talk with the governor, put before him the findings of the board's investigators, and secure assurance from him that these points would be corrected. The discussion was continued at the meeting of March 26. Again Miles flatly declared that on the basis of the information on the Ohio plan he would disapprove it. Bane pointed out that if the board wanted to secure action in time to reimburse Ohio for the present quarter, the thing to do was to send out a very small group to Ohio to spend a day with Governor Davey and Brown and get them to agree to the changes in administration outlined in the Public Assistance memorandum. Miss Hoey insisted that a decision be made concerning the first quarter on the basis of a conference with Governor Davey. Bane said that for the current quarter's approval, the board might draw up its mandatory requirements and suggestions, send some-one to Davey on March 30 for conference, and bring back his written agree-ment which, if satisfactory, could be made the basis for approval of the plan on the thirty-first.

He further proposed that the matter should be handled by writing in the form of a letter the conditions which the board wanted Davey to accept, and which under the law the board could require, the letter to be taken along to Ohio for the governor's signature. Bane emphasized the fact that this whole situation was entirely different than those of states in which the board had only paper plans not yet operating, because in Ohio a plan had been operating for a year and had had a thorough investigation of exactly how it worked. Finally, Miles proposed that he as an individual and an Eagle, and not as a member of the board, call Frank Haring (an Ohio Eagle officer) and advise him of the board's investigation and the situation develop-ing therefrom. Miles would ask Haring to get Governor Davey and Mat Brown together to agree to the requirements which the board proposed. This proposal was accepted. It was further agreed that Bane and Miss Hoey would work out the details and handle the affair for the board in accordance with the view expressed at this meeting. What followed can best be told from Jane Hoey's account as recorded by McKinley from an interview on April 1:

As a result of the investigation, which revealed not corruption but unbelievable inefficiency in financial practices, in case work, etc., as well as very weak structural organization arrangements, she and Bane prepared a memorandum for the board, analyzing the things which needed to be done. In this memorandum, they deliberately stressed the kind of faults which would appeal to the business mind, for the politicians in Ohio are business men. For example, they pointed out the utter inadequacy of their accounting system. They also stressed the failure to actually check many of the statements made by the applicants which the law required to be checked before grants should be made. They used terminology, phrases, which were common in business, and avoided wherever possible in this memorandum social worker patois.

Then Bane and Miss Hoey went to Ohio to put up to Davey and his admin-istrator, Brown, what they must do if they wanted to secure a grant before the first quarter expired. When Bane and Miss Hoey reached Ohio they put their demands in the form of this memorandum squarely up to Davey, and he at once confessed that these things obviously should not have happened and ought to be corrected. They told him that if he would incorporate the suggestions of this memorandum as part of the Ohio plan of administration for which he was voluntarily asking, they would go back to the board and urge the board to approve the Ohio administrative scheme, retroactive for the first quarter. This was on March 30, and any chance to make the grant cover the first quarter would lapse on March 31 at midnight.

Both Governor Davey and Administrator Brown agreed 100 percent to all of the specifications which Miss Hoey and Bane had written out. They also agreed on stipulation from Bane and Miss Hoey that they would give out no publicity on this affair and the board would make no public statement about it until the matter had been closed by the board. When Miss Hoey returned, she instructed Resnick to watch every Ohio paper for any statements to see that Davey lived up to this agreement.

As a result of the changes in their administrative arrangements which they have thus pledged themselves to make, she and Bane both felt that it was wise policy for the board to grant their application. To turn them down would have meant no gain and only a row, and stubborn resistance to any future attempt to teach Ohio better administrative techniques. But by securing an express pledge to institute the essential administrative changes, a definite step forward has been taken, for they know that if they renege on these promises, Ohio's grant will be cut off at succeeding quarters. As a matter of fact, they asked Bane and Miss Hoey to send out to Ohio a staff to institute the modifications in auditing, etc., to which they had agreed. Miss Hoey is sending out three people to put through these changes.

In connection with the problem of qualifications for personnel, the memorandum which Miss Hoey and Bane presented to Davey stipulated qualifications that had been in use prior to the time the Eagles had come in and wrecked the welfare organization. Thus the board got around the odium of civil service requirements by using Ohio's own experience. Miss Hoey feels that this whole episode and how it has been unsnarled has taught her organization a great deal about the technique of dealing with state politicians. If you can find a kind of language which they understand in which to express your demands or your requests for change, you stand a pretty good chance to get somewhere. She is using this episode with each member of her field staff as a part of their education for their job in dealing with state officials.

COLORADO

During the latter part of February 1936 Governor Johnson of Colorado, supported by the two leading Denver papers, began a publicity campaign in derogation of the Social Security Board for not approving the three plans submitted by Colorado for grants-in-aid to the aged, to dependent children, and to the blind. This campaign had been undertaken without taking up with the board the questions that had invalidated the Colorado plans. Winant interpreted it largely as a strategic attack to weaken Senator Costigan, a supporter of Roosevelt who was to come up for reelection in 1936 and who would be opposed by Johnson. Senator Costigan inquired of the board concerning the Colorado situation and there was a general discussion at the board meeting of March 4. A letter appears to have been sent to Governor Johnson that week advising him of the difficulties present in the Colorado plans and of the need for more information. However, on March 12 Governor Johnson sent a telegram to President Roosevelt which read as follows:

Colorado's crippled children, blind and aged still awaiting promised benefits under the Social Security Act. They have been very patient but as the weeks slip by they are losing hope. Colorado has met every requirement of the Social Security Board. We have had our share of funds ready for nearly a year. We cannot understand why our Wyoming neighbors receive benefits that are denied us when the Colorado and Wyoming set-ups are identical in every respect. Our Attorney General has made two trips to Washington and has upheld our statutes in several lengthy opinions and I have conferred with the Board personally twice, but we are unable to get either an approval or a rejection. Please help us.

This telegram was turned over to the board by the President and the following reply was suggested:

I have your telegram relative to the failure of your state to participate in the benefits of the Social Security Act. I am advised by the Social Security Board that it has been cooperating with you in an attempt to revise the legal methods under your existing state laws whereby your state could qualify for federal aid in granting assistance to the aged, the blind and dependent children. I am further advised by the Social Security Board that it is summarizing in a formal notification to you today the legal and administrative difficulties in the plans you submitted. I appreciate your concern and know you will want to take immediate steps to correct such difficulties.

Governor Johnson also communicated with the board in correspondence dated March 14.

The Bureau of Public Assistance and the legal staff presented to the board on March 12 memoranda dealing with the Colorado situation, and they were discussed on that and the following days. The board prepared a letter dated March 16 restating its reasons for not approving the Colorado plans and emphasizing its desire to assist the states in securing approval. It pointed out that because of this desire, the board had repeatedly examined the documents submitted by Colorado but had not been able to find its way clear to approve them. It was not insisting upon the opinion which the board's lawyers held, that the Colorado legislation underlying its plans was invalid because of the delegation of certain powers to the State Relief Committee, but it did insist that there were other important shortcomings. One was the existence of two conflicting statutes dividing the authority over the administration of old age pensions between the State Relief Committee and the county courts. The presumed legal right of the State Relief Committee to deprive the county courts of their function in this matter was contradicted by a decision of the Supreme Court of Colorado.[14] In addition, the board pointed out that the county courts still retained their jurisdiction with regard to mothers' pensions, so that the

operation of the plan for aid to dependent children would duplicate, to a considerable extent, the functions of the county courts under the Colorado mothers' compensation statutes. This would mean that there would be two agencies in the state of Colorado for administering aid to the dependent children.

The letter also stated that no method had been proposed in the Colorado plans for avoiding duplication and conflict between the State Relief Committee and the county agencies in administering funds under the three grants-in-aid. It also insisted that in handling aid to the blind, there would be duplication between the work of the State Commission for the Blind and the State Relief Committee. The concluding paragraph read as follows:

For the reasons given above, the Social Security Board cannot properly approve of the Colorado plans. As you know from our previous correspondence and discussions, we have expressed doubt on a number of other points, but have resolved these doubts in your favor. However, future legislation ought to clarify all doubtful points. Knowing of your desire that Colorado shall secure the benefits of the Social Security Act, we are confident that you will wish to take appropriate action. Needless to say, we shall be only too glad to cooperate with you to that end.

At the time this letter was dispatched, Miss Bary, who was on her way to the Far West, was commissioned to stop off at Colorado to make clear why the board could not approve the Colorado plans and what must be done to bring them within the scope of the Social Security Act.

Commenting on the Colorado problem on March 17, Miss Hoey said that while Miss Bary's visit had produced an immediate call for a special legislative session to amend the Colorado laws to meet the social security requirements, that might not change the administrative set-up in Colorado, which she had found to be exceedingly poor. The end of the Colorado story came on May 4, 1936, when the board approved plans for all three grants-in-aid.

---

[14] The attorney general of Colorado had given an opinion to the governor that these conflicts had been legally reconciled, but the board's legal staff felt sure that this was not the law.

Politics and public assistance for the aged were intertwined in Kentucky in the summer of 1936. On June 29 Kentucky submitted its application for the approval of its program for aid to the aged, but the documents were incomplete, and requests for further information delayed immediate presentation of the plan to the board for consideration.

The Democratic national committeewoman for Kentucky sent Miles a telegram on July 29 which said that Governor Chandler, who was a candidate for renomination in the August 1 primaries, had a few days before appointed 240 old age assistance investigators (2 from each county) to help him win the election. The following day, July 29, Bane talked with Governor Chandler and his commissioner of welfare, Wallis. Chandler asked that the board either approve or disapprove the Kentucky application for a grant by noon, July 30. Chandler had also phoned the President, asking him to bring pressure on the board to approve the Kentucky plan; but the President's office referred him back to the board. Chandler was reported to have said that he did not "want anything from the Social Security Board but money," and to have threatened to go to the President again if he did not get it. Farley also called Miles, but merely asked that the Kentucky situation be studied and such action taken as would be appropriate.

The documents on the Kentucky plan, and the analysis by the Bureau of Public Assistance and the legal staff, did not give the board a clear-cut basis for either approval or disapproval. At the meeting on July 30, the material submitted by Miss Hoey showed that the Kentucky law provided for a real department of public welfare, with a fund of $2,500,000 for payments to the aged.

The weakness of the plan was the lack of personnel standards (but the board at this time had not yet reached a decision as to what it would do about insisting on minimum standards for state personnel). The law provided only that the director of the Division of Public Assistance should be a person thoroughly experienced and trained in welfare work. Welfare Commissioner Wallis had written to the bureau, on July 16, that he was setting up ten standards for personnel which included such items as "physical fitness, . . . mental capacity to understand the old age assistance laws, . . . ability to make clear to applicants the conditions of eligibility, . . . ability to systematize and expedite work." His general supervisor of the Division of Public Assistance had written further on July 17:

Frankly we know and are aware of the fact that a number of our present appointees will not be able to perform the work to the satisfaction of this administration. . . . Some, therefore, we expect to eliminate themselves, but we have the Governor's assurance that we may release them as rapidly as they are discovered to be unable to perform efficiently the work which has been given to them. Eventually, we believe we will be able to meet the qualifications which we know are necessary. . . .

Although the Kentucky Department of Public Welfare had not definitely outlined its plans for administration or submitted rules and regulations, this was not regarded as an insuperable obstacle to approval. Miss Hoey's bureau concluded its digest with the statement:

The Kentucky law seems to establish a basis for a sound old age assistance program. . . . it is believed that an unusual amount of assistance and supervision will be needed by the state agency if it is to establish an efficient administration. . . . the most serious defect apparent in the plan is in respect to personnel. Not only is the basic method of recruitment open to question, but the state agency is now burdened with some 240 workers who apparently were selected quite hastily on a geographical basis and without due consideration to their qualifications. . . . the only method of enforcing standards seems to be to dismiss workers after they have been appointed.

The general counsel reported that the copy of the law which had been sent in was not certified and that no regulations had been received. However, the Kentucky commissioner of public welfare had telegraphed, on July 29, that rules and regulations would provide for a fair hearing and the prompt payment to the United States of one-half of the recoveries from old age assistance estates. The general counsel considered that the plan provided a sound legal basis for approval if the promised rules and regulations were made.

The board was on the spot. The staff reports indicated the Kentucky plan had met the legal requirements, and aside from its personnel arrangements the administrative organization met the technical administrative standards. If, however, the board approved, it would appear to be condoning Chandler's wholesale political appointments; if it disapproved it would appear to have reprimanded the governor on the eve of the primary election. Regional Director Crowell was called into the board meeting and his opinion solicited. He informed the board that his regional attorney and his executive assistant had attended a meeting on July 15, when Chandler addressed the 240 political appointees to the Kentucky department staff and told them that their retention depended upon the efficiency of their work as judged by Commissioner Wallis. It was his opinion that if the board made a grant to Kentucky it would do so knowing the political situation full well, and that the Kentucky personnel had been selected upon a political basis. He counselled against being stampeded into approval of the plan.

Upon Winant's suggestion, the board decided to evade the issue by taking advantage of the fact that on July 13 it had written a letter asking for additional information, to which a reply had not been received, and it could therefore say it had been impossible to reach a decision by July 30. Accordingly, the following telegram was sent to Chandler over Bane's signature:

Presented matter of Kentucky plan to the Board this morning as per my statement to you yesterday. Presented also telegrams from Mr. Wallis. Board is of the opinion that Kentucky plan is not complete as set forth in detail in our letter to Mr. Wallis of July 13, 1936 to which we have not to date received an answer. Understand from Mr. Wallis that letter was lost in his office but that he is now assembling necessary material which is to be here Friday. As soon as this information arrives will again present matter to the Board.

Following this action, the board at the same meeting reached a major policy conclusion. It decided that from that time forth, despite the limitations in the Social Security Act, it would try to obtain decent standards in the hiring of state workers to administer the public assistance grants-in-aid. Accordingly it unanimously agreed "that a state plan must include minimum objective standards for personnel."

The board again considered the Kentucky plan on August 7, 1936. The documents submitted by the Bureau of Public Assistance and the Office of the General Counsel had been modified. The digest of the Kentucky plan prepared by the Bureau of Public Assistance was substantially the same as the one previously submitted on July 30, with the following exceptions:

(1) The number of district offices for state administration had been reduced from forty to sixteen; and (2) the rules and regulations submitted provided in paragraph twenty-one that employees would be chosen in accordance with the requirements of the Division of Personnel Efficiency of the Department of Finance. The recently enacted Reorganization Act for the entire state government provided that this Division of Personnel Efficiency should prepare examinations for recruitment of all state personnel hired after September 1, 1936. The Commissioner of Welfare, Wallis, had further written a letter of July 30 that the field staff "shall be trained in the technical phases of social service work."

Geoffrey May, chief of the grants division, reported orally that the big problem involved was the actual working out of the paper plan. Their personnel problems, however, were partially cleared up, because on September 1, when the new state reorganization act would go into effect, there would be established a state civil service system for all state appointees. But the law would not apply to those now in office, particularly the 240 employees recently appointed by the governor. Even though Miss Hoey stated that they had not yet received an agreement on objective standards for personnel, May recommended the approval of the plan.

The General Counsel's Office reported that although the regulations still did not entirely conform with its suggestions, this would not necessarily preclude the approval of the plan.[15]

Altmeyer remarked that so long as the state had not agreed to objective minimum standards for personnel he would not approve the plan. The board then agreed that it would approve the plan if the state would apply the standards in their new civil service law to the employees who were now in the State Department of Public Welfare as well as to all future employees.

This arrangement was evidently agreed to by Kentucky, because Commissioner Wallis announced to the newspapers that he had received the following telegram from Frank Bane:

The Social Security Board today approved the Kentucky plan for Old Age Assistance in accordance with understanding as set forth in our letter on August 7th. Letter to you today.[16]

The official letter approving the plan was not sent until August 18.[17] It pointed out

that the approval of the methods of administration of the plan was based on the facts before the Board, including the understanding mentioned in our letter of August 7, that all personnel engaged in the administration of the plan—present employees as well as those to be employed in the future—will be subject to minimum objective personnel standards to be made effective September 1, 1936, as provided in the State Reorganization Act. It is also expected that an adequate administration and field supervisory staff will be provided to insure efficient administration.

THE IMPROVEMENT OF
STATE ADMINISTRATIVE STANDARDS

The Bureau of Public Assistance, almost from its inception, became interested in improving the standards of administration in the states, primarily though not entirely in terms of accepted practices of social work. It must be remembered that the bureau was staffed from top to bottom with profes-

[15] It was obvious that the state would be perfectly willing to make the regulations suggested by the General Counsel's Office in regard to payments from the states and fair hearing, and that these legal matters did not particularly affect the decision of the board.

[16] *Louisville Courier-Journal*, August 9, 1936.

[17] Official board announcement of the approval of the plan was made in a press release on August 13, 1936.

sional social workers, who tried to lead the states to accept the standards of that profession. In practice, these standards were almost entirely concerned with personnel questions—getting trained social workers rather than political appointees in state agencies.

The method of accomplishing this purpose was essentially pacifistic and persuasive rather than belligerent and coercive. Thus, great weight was given by the bureau to the building up of a capable field staff to advise and help the states. It shrank from using more stringent means of controlling state administration. One of the headquarters assistants summarized the bureau's policy and experience late in July 1936.

He declared that direct negotiations and personal influence exerted by the field staff and by the Washington staff of the Bureau of Public Assistance was much more effective with the states than threats to reduce grants. Miss Bary had already achieved a number of points in her dealings with governors in western states, and Miss McChord in New England was likewise very successful. In the case of Maine, where the governor flatly refused to carry out the provisions of the agreement he had made with the board as a condition for grants to Maine, it had been necessary to have Miss Hoey go up for a personal conference with him. Confidence was felt that the governor in the long run would fall into line. The mere reduction of grants would not produce the desired effect, because in the first place it would take assistance away from the people who needed it, and in the second place merely reduce the scale of operations rather than improve their efficiency.

This field staff was gradually built up during the spring and summer of 1936, but was not definitely assigned to regions. During the interim period it was often necessary that the bureau continue to rely on the diplomatic skill of Frank Bane and Jane Hoey, both of whom spent a great deal of time traveling about the country conferring with state officials and governors.

On July 30, the board took a stronger stand on the state personnel question by deciding that in the future it would not approve public assistance plans which did not provide for personnel standards. The episodes which led immediately to this decision arose in Illinois and Kentucky cases. They illustrate the board's caution in bearing down and its reluctance to invoke the extreme power of terminating grants. But even before these cases, there had been other instances where the problem of original approval of state plans had been inextricably entangled with the issue of personnel standards. The more important of these cases follow.

INDIANA

The need to secure better personnel standards for state and local administration induced in this case a roundabout technique of control. During March, when the legislature was formulating the Indiana law for old age assistance, Bane went out and persuaded the sponsors to include a clause providing for the merit system in the employment of state and local personnel. There was already in the measure, however, a restriction requiring county residence for county workers which it was almost impossible to delete, despite the fact that such a restriction would make it very difficult, particularly in the poorer and less populous counties, to get adequate staff. Nevertheless, through the influence of one of the friendly social worker groups, another provision was incorporated into the measure which stated that if competent people were not available in any county, that county might then employ staff residing elsewhere. It seemed probable that the Public Assistance Bureau would be increasingly inclined to resort to the assistance of friendly professional groups in the endeavor to overcome this fundamental administrative obstacle. It seemed likely also that the bureau would adopt the policy, which the Unemployment Compensation Bureau had been pursuing, of securing data about personnel when state administrative plans were proposed, and that it would make suggestions on state classification and salary standards. If it was proper for the Bureau of Unemployment Compensation to do this, it was certainly appropriate for the sister bureau to demand similar information and to make similar suggestions. However, such a tactic could have little efficacy when a state had its organization already set up and insisted on staffing its offices with partisan or incompetent people.

TEXAS

The Texas primaries then occurred in July. In the spring of 1936, the Texas administrators of old age assistance were attempting to use the old age funds as a means of keeping the governor and his crowd in office. They had broadcast news soliciting applications and promising to pay not less than $30 a person and to not be restricted by the qualification of need in making grants. As a result, they had on hand at the close of April one hundred thousand applications. To handle these in accordance with the promises made by the governor's administration would have cost the state $60,000,000 a year. The staff of the old age assistance administration had been recruited largely from political workers, broken-down sheriffs, and the like. Miss Hoey on a trip to the state early in the spring was informed that two people on the staff had been drunk ever since they were appointed. She had discussed the problem of staff qualifications with the state administrator, and he had indicated his willingness to accept her proposals for new appointments, but not to disturb those already chosen. (Another obstacle to approval of the Texas plan had been the lack of proper organization of the state office.) At the board meeting on April 21, Roseman presented a memorandum from the

Bureau of Public Assistance recommending the approval of the Texas plan for old age assistance. This recommendation was made despite the fact that Miss Hoey had made no headway in persuading the Texas people to discharge incompetent people already employed. The board approved the Texas plan.

ILLINOIS

When Illinois presented a request for the approval of its plan for old age assistance, the bureau recommended disapproval in a memorandum that was considered by the board on March 24. The Illinois law had been enacted over the governor's veto. According to Miss Hoey, it went much further than any other state law in restricting the state's influence over local administration. Despite the fact that the administration of this act was to be entrusted primarily to the counties, the law said explicitly that the state administrators were to have nothing to do with setting the qualifications for local employees. In Miss Hoey's judgment, the Illinois plan constituted in effect a collection of county plans, instead of a single state plan. The other specifications of state supervision which the board had set up as conditions for approval, namely, that the state should have authority to make rules and regulations, conduct audits, and secure a fair hearing on the decisions of local administrators, were met by this Illinois plan. Thus the board came face to face solely with the issue of control over personnel. There had been plans presented before in which the state's right to determine standards for the selection of local employees had been quite tenuous, but there had been no previous case in which the act contained a specific prohibition. The board asked its legal counsel whether the prohibition in the federal act concerning the board's jurisdiction over the selection, tenure, and compensation of personnel covered the staff of local units. The lawyers announced that the prohibition applied to both state and local personnel. They declared that the board had no legal power to disapprove of a plan because of conditions of tenure or qualifications of local people. An immediate decision on this issue was postponed, partly because of the political situation in Illinois at the time. The campaign for primaries was then under way, and there was a fight on between Governor Horner and the regular Democratic organization which had repudiated him. The board therefore felt that any publicity given to the Illinois application would at once become the object of political advertising. The board also wanted to see more clearly how the Illinois problem fitted in with precedents created by its action on other state plans. Not until May 5 did it make up its mind what to do. In the meantime conversations went on between the board's staff and Governor Horner and the Illinois administrative people. Governor Horner and Bane had a conference on April 30 and prepared a draft letter, upon the basis of which the governor proposed to call a special session of the legislature. Bane, in presenting this matter to the board on May 4, pointed out that the question before it was whether, in view of the clause in the statute concerning personnel, the board ought to take the position that the state develop, promulgate, and put into effect such procedures and administrative methods as would enable the state to be certain that agreements it might make with the board would be carried out. Bane expressed his own opinion that since the state was delegating to the counties its authority to select personnel, the board could require that the state have something to say about the qualifications of the agents to whom it was subcontracting this function. Altmeyer confessed that if the Illinois plan were one calling for state administration, the board could not say anything about the qualifications of state employees, but he insisted that, since the Illinois plan was a state-supervised one, it must contain the elements of supervision. To this the board's lawyers replied that where the state retains provision for fair hearing, it has a check upon the locality. They reiterated their view that the Social Security Act gave the board no power over local personnel. On May 5, the board agreed (by a two-to-one vote, Miles voting in the negative) to disapprove the Illinois plan for old age assistance and to send a letter to Governor Horner along the lines which had been suggested in Horner's and Bane's conversations. Thus the board overruled its own lawyers and supported its administrators in insisting upon a definition of state supervision embodying the right to specify qualifications for local personnel engaged in administering public assistance grants-in-aid.[18] Since this decision was likely

[18] On the same date Eliot submitted a memorandum to the board pointing out that it had already approved several public assistance plans which did not give the state agency the power to set up minimum personnel standards for the counties or localities: "It has been argued that the Illinois plan should be disapproved because under it the state agency would not have the power to prescribe the qualifications for minor county personnel (there is apparently no argument that the state agency should prescribe the qualifications for more responsible personnel). . . . In at least three instances the Board appears to approve plans in which the Board has no more power than does the state agency in Illinois."

The three states mentioned by Eliot were (1) Wisconsin, in which all three plans for public assistance had been approved, although section 49.51 of the Wisconsin Statutes of 1935 provided in part: "The administration in counties of all laws in this state relating to old age assistance, aid to dependent children and blind persons shall be vested in the officers and agencies designated in the Statutes to administer these forms of public assistance. The County Board shall have the authority to provide assistants for such officers and agencies and to prescribe their qualifications and fix their compensation." (2) California. In San Francisco, Los Angeles, and Alameda Counties, public assistance personnel was recruited in accordance with county civil service regulations, and the State Department of Social Welfare had no control over these activities. (3) Massachusetts. According to the Massachusetts law, cited by a

to become an important precedent, the argument in support of it contained in the letter of May 8 to Governor Horner is quoted below:

You are already aware of the defects in the plan in regard to the provisions of the Social Security Act concerning opportunity for a fair hearing and the prompt payment to the United States of amounts collected from estates. The Board believes, after further consideration, that these defects should be corrected in the Illinois law, as Illinois presents a permanent legislative plan rather than a temporary interim plan awaiting legislative sanction. We are also of the opinion that the methods of administration are not such as will secure adequate supervision and efficient operation.

The Social Security Act specifies that a state plan must either provide for the establishment or designation of a single state agency to administer the plan, or provide for the establishment or designation of a single state agency to supervise the administration of the plan. The Social Security Board deals with the state rather than with the local administrative units, and it is apparent that the state agency must be in a position to assure the Social Security Board that old age assistance will be administered to all parts of the state in conformity with the specific provisions of the Federal Act, and in conformity with the provisions of the state plan.

Under the Illinois plan all funds which will be used for the payment of old age assistance and for the costs of administering this aid are to be furnished by the state and federal governments. Despite this fact, the state agency does not appear to have supervisory powers which will enable it to discharge its function adequately. It has little to say concerning the organization of the work and nothing to say as to the experience and efficiency of the local employees whom it pays and upon whom rests the major responsibility for carrying out provisions of the state plan. In addition to these administrative difficulties, the five-year county residence requirement may also exclude legal residents of the several counties from participation in this public work. No other state has submitted a plan to this Board which contains provisions so restricting in nature and so hampering to effective operation.

In order to meet the points noted above, and in order to assure adequate supervision of administration and effective utilization of state and federal funds, we believe the Illinois law should be amended to enable the state to prescribe minimum qualifications for the employees of the local county welfare units who are responsible for the expenditure of state and federal funds in the administration of old age assistance. Such an amendment would not preclude the County Commissions of Public Welfare from selecting any person who meets such qualifications. Since the counties do not bear any part of the cost of old age assistance or of administration, the present county residence requirements for

---

January 16 memo on the Massachusetts plan from the Bureau of Public Assistance, the state agency had no control over the personnel standards of the towns which administered the plan.

local employees should also be modified to permit the employment of any legal resident.

With these changes, there would be assurance that sufficient administrative supervision with respect to the operation of the state plan rested with the state agency.

Governor Horner accepted the decision of the board without much question and proceeded to ask the legislature to amend the Illinois law to conform to the suggestions of the board. In urging immediate action on these amendments of the law, the governor announced that he considered the board's requirements "fair and reasonable" and in line with what had been done in other states.[19] Not all of the state legislature agreed entirely with the governor, and there was a good deal of opposition by down-state Republicans, who opposed state control of county personnel. "The Federal Board has announced that a Federal grant cannot be made until the State eliminates the requirement that prospective employees, under the Old Age Assistance Act, must have lived five years in the county. Down-state legislators have publicly announced that this provision is for the purpose of giving jobs to residents of their counties and of excluding professional social workers from outside. Many have indicated that they will not accede to the Board's demand on this point, because they believe it exceeds the Board's powers." [20] Some of the state legislators went so far as to propose a resolution calling upon the state attorney general to file mandamus proceedings in the U.S. Circuit Court for the District of Columbia to force the board to approve the Illinois law.[21] Nevertheless, amendments providing for minimum objective standards for county personnel and a fair hearing before the state department were approved by the Illinois legislature on June 19, and the amended plans submitted to the board.

The board considered the Illinois plan once more on July 6. The general counsel submitted a memorandum approving the plan in consideration of the recent amendments. The Bureau of Public Assistance concurred, pointing out that the Department of Public Welfare now had the following powers of supervision over county welfare departments: audit, prescription of minimum qualifications for personnel, and the promulgation of rules and regulations binding on the counties and policed by a supervisory field staff. Bane outlined the status of the plan, including the recent amendments enacted by the state legislature, and added that the state of Illinois had submitted a letter to the board outlining minimum personnel standards. Although these did not fully meet the standards of the board, they had been discussed with the Illinois

[19] *Springfield Register,* May 13, 1936.

[20] *Chicago Tribune,* May 20, 1936, as digested by the Bureau of Informational Service.

[21] *Springfield Journal,* May 20, 1936.

people who had agreed to submit a further letter incorporating them. Miles asked that this further letter outlining personnel standards be included as part of the Illinois plan. On July 31, the board notified the state of its formal approval of the plan for old age assistance.

Meanwhile Ernest Witte, the field representative of Public Assistance in that region, had conferred often with the Illinois officials to get them to put the personnel standards of the plan into effect. However, they paid so little attention to his suggestions that he telephoned Miss Hoey on August 4 requesting that the grant for the current quarter be held up until Illinois would agree to the necessary changes. Bane put the grant on the board agenda for August 7. Miss Hoey reported at that meeting that the state had not made its personnel standards effective, and recommended that Bane go out to Illinois to talk to the governor about it. The board accepted Altmeyer's suggestion that the grant be approved but the state not be notified until Bane had talked with Governor Horner on August 10. After a conference on this date with Bane, Witte, and McCarthy (the regional director), Governor Horner promised that all present and future members of the Illinois old age assistance staff would be selected and retained on the basis of merit. Personnel examinations were promised not later than October 15, 1936. During the balance of the quarter several more field visits were made by the staff of the Bureau of Public Assistance; and Bowen, the director of the Illinois Department of Public Welfare, appointed as technical assistant to the superintendent of old age assistance someone who had been recommended by the head of the American Public Welfare Association.

On October 7 the board approved without discussion a grant for the second quarter ending December 1, 1936, acting on the recommendation of the Bureau of Public Assistance, which had hopes of improvement at that time. Miss Austin, chief of the field division of the bureau, reported that the "Governor has been most cordial, ready to listen, but quite reserved in his response to suggestions made."

From November 7 to 13 Witte inspected the Illinois state office and reported that the personnel examinations had been put off until January 1; that no recovery from estates of recipients had been instituted; that no hearings had been held, though 756 requests had come to the state office; that gross inefficiency prevailed and no substantial improvements in administration had been made. The board took no formal action, but on December 16 a study of the administration of old age assistance in Illinois was started under Witte, with the board's approval and the governor's consent. On January 11, Witte requested that the grant for the third quarter be held up, pending the completion of this study. On January 26, 1937, the board had before it a preliminary report by Witte which described the situation in Illinois briefly as follows:

1. *Personnel qualifications:* None set up for State and county employees. Appointments to Division of Old Age Assistance made only after approval by the Democratic employment office with little or no regard to education, previous experience in public welfare, or personal fitness for the position. The Director of the Field Staff has had no previous work in public welfare administration.
2. *State Office Administration:* Confusion, lost effort, suspicion and failure to work effectively. No adequate definition of procedures. Arbitrary decisions regarding county functions.
3. *Field Services:* Inefficient; working on few written instructions; hinder efficient county offices.
4. *Method of Review:* Arbitrary decisions on the approval or disapproval of assistance and determination of amounts in State office. No follow-up service on grants.
5. *Reimbursement from Estates of Deceased Recipients:* No procedure yet established.
6. *Fair Hearings:* 700 requests held in State Office without even letter of receipt to applicants or county offices.
7. *Manual for County Offices:* None. Few and unsatisfactory bulletins. Tardy handling of correspondence.
8. *Physical Set-up of County Units:* Very inadequate, often in jury rooms and parts of judges quarters.

The board decided not to hold up the Illinois grant on this occasion, but to try warning the state once more. During its meeting on February 26, 1937, Bane announced that Governor Horner had told two of the board's representatives that the necessary changes would be made. There was no further action in the Illinois case before the close of the period studied, but a brief sketch of the sequel will round out the episode. After several more warnings, the board decided to select Illinois as the first state on which to apply the sanctions authorized it by the Social Security Act. A hearing was called for late July 1937, after which the Illinois grant for the first quarter of the fiscal year 1938 beginning July 1, 1967, was formally suspended. There were several counts in the indictment made by the board, the most important of which were no personnel standards, lack of fair hearing, financial discrepancies, and lack of adequate accounting procedure (the last based on a field audit report). The case was so clear that after several weeks, Illinois capitulated with much grumbling and threat of reprisal. Thus after eighteen months of substantial failure by Illinois to comply with the standards of Title I, the board applied its full authority to compel state compliance.

STATE MEDICAL EXAMINATION TO DETERMINE BLINDNESS

In the administration of aid to the blind one very important step in advancing state administration was taken during this period. This had to do with making adequate medical examination and treatment a regular part of state procedure. The employment of Miss Ruth Blakeslee in April 1936 was the signal for this advance. At the time of her employment no state required adequate medical examination for recipients of blind grants. State commissions in charge of assistance to the blind had grown up on a semipublic basis out of private charity, and were almost wholly devoid of scientific or uniform standards of administration. Miss Blakeslee, who came to the board from the Federal Emergency Relief Administration, had had considerable experience in this field, and in cooperation with the various national associations concerned with the problem of blindness, the American Public Welfare Association, and the Public Health Service proceeded at once to work out standard requirements.

After considerable effort, the Bureau of Public Assistance was able to get the board to consider this matter. On June 2 Altmeyer requested the bureau to submit a memorandum for the next board meeting. This was to contain recommendations regarding policies the board should adopt in making grants for aid to the blind, including a definition of blindness, in order that the board might decide these questions before July 1, 1936. Because the Bureau of Public Assistance had done a considerable amount of preliminary work on this question, it submitted a procedure to the board on June 16, which had already been cleared with the principal national associations concerned with aid to the blind, and with the Public Health Service. The salient items in this carefully prepared memorandum were:

1. A review of the state practices showed that there was no uniformity in the definition of blindness; that at least seven states had no definition and that in some states persons with very slight defects in vision had been receiving aid as "blind" persons. A number of states had requested that the Board make a definition which the states could use in enacting legislation.

2. The Board should adopt a definition of "blindness." In so doing it should notify the states (a) that they must define "blindness," using therefor the definition of the Board as a guide; (b) that about each blind person the states must record, upon a uniform blank, information essential to a program of medical treatment for improving vision; (c) that examinations should be made only by qualified physicians; (d) that the cost of such examinations should be considered a justifiable administrative expense.

3. A program for prevention of blindness, after joint formulation by medical authorities and societies promoting this work, should be given to the field staff for discussion with the state agencies. Also, a program for vocational rehabilitation and employment of the blind, prepared in cooperation with the other federal agencies interested, should be given to the field staff.

4. A plan of cooperation with the other federal agencies was suggested to include:

a. A specialist in ophthalmology from the United States Public Health Service to work with the Board on this program, his travel expenses, only, to be met by the Board; a medical specialist to review the activities of the states in their aid to the blind, so as to stimulate constructive programs of cure and prevention.

b. If facts show much childhood blindness there should be a joint program of prevention developed by the Children's Bureau and the Public Health Service.

c. Fuller utilization of services of the Federal Bureau of Vocational Rehabilitation for blind persons.

d. Utilization of Bureau of Vocational Rehabilitation and the Employment Service in development of methods of placing blind handicapped persons in employment.

The definition of blindness tentatively suggested had been prepared by Dr. Carl Rice, ophthalmologist on the staff of the United States Public Health Service.

When these questions were considered, Tate represented the Office of the General Counsel and Miss Hoey the Bureau of Public Assistance. Preliminary discussion between these two bureaus had already brought out the fact that the lawyers were very dubious about the board's power to make any such requirement. Tate stated at the board meeting that the act contained no definition of blindness and that its legislative history indicated no definition except that the states were to establish their standards as to the blind. The question was whether the board or the state agency, or both, should define blindness. He recommended that the board should decide whether the definition adopted by a state was reasonable, and if it was, should accept it and then see that the state adhered to it. As an alternative the board could suggest to the state a definition of blindness.

In addition to the question of the legality of such a requirement there was also a "political" question involved, that is, the dispute between the optometrists and ophthalmologists. The procedure suggested by the Bureau of Public Assistance would turn these examinations over entirely to the medical profession, and a vigorous protest by the optometrists was anticipated. Miles supported Tate, believing that the board should start out by giving the states a maximum definition of blindness without regarding any particular methods for determining the degree of blindness until sufficient experience had been accumulated to check the states' methods and determine whether they were sound. Altmeyer, on the other hand, was in favor of sending the states a definition approved by the board and requiring them to demonstrate the reasonableness of any variation from this standard. Miss Hoey insisted that it would be a very poor administrative practice for the state not to attempt to advise and assist in curing or improving blindness, or to go on paying assistance to persons who might be cured. Her argument was that it would be possible to make this requirement of the medical examination and recommendations for treatment on the basis of Section 1002(a)(5), which deals with methods of proper administration. The discussion terminated with a general agreement that the definition and methods of determining blindness should be put on the basis of suggestions to the states; the Bureau of Public Assistance was advised to revise its recommendations in order to submit them to the board at its next meeting.

The resistance of the General Counsel's Office proved so strong, however, that the revised recommendations were not actually written until August 13, and not considered by the board until September 15. Meanwhile, the board had confirmed arrangements with the Public Health Service whereby Dr. Rice of the latter organization was to be detailed to the board as a consultant on this problem. At the meeting on September 15, at which the Bureau of Public Assistance was represented by May, Roseman, Miss Blakeslee, and Dr. Rice, and the General Counsel's Office by Tate, the bureau submitted the following revised recommendation prepared by Miss Blakeslee:

A report on an eye examination will be submitted in duplicate by an ophthalmologist or a physician skilled in diseases of the eye for each individual for whom blind assistance is approved under the provisions of the state plan. Social Security Board Form No.— is provided for these reports. A state form which will furnish the same information may be used. The original form will be incorporated in the case record and the duplicate sent to the state office for review and approval by a state supervisory ophthalmologist. Reports with regard to the items on this form will be requested from time to time by the Social Security Board. These forms may also serve to make possible a coordination of state plans for assistance to the blind with those relating to prevention of blindness and vocational training and placement.

In general, visual acuity of 20/200 or less with correction has been considered as economic blindness, meaning that a standard object which can be identified at a distance of 200 feet by a person with normal vision can only be identified by an economically blind individual at a distance of 20 feet.

A description of the peripheral field is required on this form only if it is accepted as a factor in economic blindness in the approved state plan and then only on individuals who have a visual acuity of more than 20/200, and who by rough test show a marked field defect. An individual with visual acuity of more than 20/200 in the better eye with proper correction is usually not considered blind unless there is a field defect in which the peripheral field has contracted to such an extent that the widest diameter of visual field subtends an angular distance no greater than five degrees.

The following information shall be obtainable from the report which shall be signed by the examining physician:
1. Diagnosis of eye condition causing blindness.

2. Etiology of eye condition.
3. Visual acuity in Snellen notations with and without correction.
4. Description of peripheral visual field where indicated.
5. Prognosis.
6. Recommendations as to medical or surgical treatment of eye condition and as to re-examination.
7. Recommendations as to medical or surgical treatment of condition causing eye pathology.

Continued grants of assistance to a blind individual should be contingent upon a report of re-examination not less than once in two years, when the original eye examination record indicates eye condition may change.

The expense of the eye examination to determine eligibility for aid and for recommended re-examination may be considered as justified administrative costs and may be charged against the five per cent federal grant for administration.

The applicant should not be expected to pay the examination fee, and payments to individuals may not be conditional upon his payment of such costs.

Tate of the General Counsel's Office still opposed making this procedure a requirement, although he had receded a little from his previous objections, admitting that there was some legal basis for a requirement though in his judgment it was not fully satisfactory.

Miles was not present at this meeting. After Chairman Winant had suggested eliminating the phrase *economically blind* because of different interpretations which might be placed on the word *economically*, and several other minor changes had been made, the board approved the form and procedure as requirements for its approval of state public assistance plans for the blind.

It was not until October 21, however, that the Bureau of Public Assistance had prepared the printed instructions and report form for the states. It was November before these forms and instructions were actually sent out to the states with the following letter:

I am enclosing a copy of instructions regarding procedure in determining blindness, together with form PA 701, Physicians Report on Eye Examination. The procedure outlined should apply to all applications for Aid to the Needy Blind accepted or rejected on or after December 1, 1936, and its applicability extended to the group of applications previously accepted as it can best be handled over a period of time.

We suggest that you consult with the regional representative of the Bureau of Public Assistance for your state regarding these procedures.

If you should decide to adopt the Federal Form PA 701, we will be glad to supply copies of them.

The dates mentioned in the above letter were not rigidly insisted upon by the bureau, a considerable amount of leeway being allowed in order that the states might adjust themselves. Furthermore, the states were informed that they might submit more liberal definitions if they so desired. Miss Blakeslee's point of view was that, since this whole question was a new and unexplored field, the states ought to be encouraged to experiment with various procedures and definitions in order that further progress might be made. The bureau did insist, however, on (1) an examination by an ophthalmologist, and (2) employment of a supervising ophthalmologist by the state for the approval of all state plans for aid to the blind. The field staff was at all conferences instructed on bureau requirements for plans, and Dr. Rice made his services available to the states as a consultant. By January 1, 1937, seven states had appointed supervising ophthalmologists.

The anticipated resistance by the optometrists to this requirement was not long in developing. About a month after the states had been notified of the new procedure, the American Optometrists Society had appointed a lawyer to fight the constitutionality of the requirement and had hired a lobbyist, Dr. Deiken, to fight the provision both with the board in Washington and with the states. Dr. Deiken frequently called on Miss Blakeslee to protest the board's action and to threaten retaliation. She in turn endeavored to educate the lobbyist herself rather than turn him over to the Public Health Service, which had been delegated the responsibility of contacting the medical profession. Her position was that, whereas it might be permissible for the states to employ an optometrist to test the eyesight of recipients of aid to the blind in certain circumstances, the responsibility of the board was such that it had to insist on medical examinations as well, in order to enable the state and federal governments to deal with the prevention and cure of blindness as well as the payment of assistance to persons who were found to be blind.

The opposition of the optometrists never came to a head in a serious incident of any kind, even after the Ophthalmology Section of the American Medical Association went on record at their convention in January 1937 as favoring the board's procedure.

Before the convention of the optometrists in May 1937, the board had succeeded in shifting the field of battle to the states. With the efforts of the field staff and the cooperation of the national associations concerned with blindness and the American Public Welfare Association, the provisions for aid to the blind in most states were modified in the legislative sessions in the winter of 1937 to provide for the requirements that the board had developed the previous autumn.

The question of enforcing the board's suggestions, or similar requirements, in the state laws and plans had not developed far enough by the end of this study to make any judgment on the effect of the board's action in this realm possible. The field auditing staff of the Bureau of Accounts and Audits had been so busy completing the preliminary audits of old age assistance payments that it had not begun to audit payments for aid to the blind. Consequently it was not possible to obtain a detailed account of the extent to which the states had actually put this new procedure into effect. The Bureau of Public Assistance had followed a consistent policy of moving ahead slowly in advising and consulting with the states rather than cracking down. States on the whole did not resist the adoption of the new procedure. Even by autumn 1937 some results of the board's action were evident. Before November 1936 no state had used examinations or employed a supervising ophthalmologist. By September 1937 all states with approved plans for aid to the blind used a procedure which called for medical examinations under the supervision of an ophthalmologist.

Slow Development of General Policies

It is hard to determine the effectiveness of a gradualist approach toward the improvement of state personnel standards and administrative practices, pursued through exhortation and a soft-spoken field staff. Even though by the end of 1936 Miss Hoey expressed considerable satisfaction over the progress made, the situation as a whole was extremely difficult to appraise. We paraphrase her oral summary:

A good deal of heartening progress has been made in the past year in many states, but in many others there has been none whatsoever. Rhode Island has been cleaned up a little bit. Ohio will not improve until Governor Davey leaves. He will continue to make agreements with the board and not live up to them. There may be some slight change for the better in Ohio if the injunction against the Civil Service Commission is turned down. Missouri has improved a great deal. Texas is a little better than it was, and the governor says that he wishes that he had accepted the board's suggestions of personnel standards, because he would have protected himself against many job-seeking groups. There has been no great progress in Kentucky. Colorado is trying to get the board to turn down the scheme which was recently ratified as an amendment to the constitution, but there seems to be some doubt as to whether Colorado would have any old age assistance plan at all if the board refused to approve this scheme. After months of dickering, Pennsylvania finally decided that they would get nowhere in negotiating with the board on personnel standards and have apparently knuckled under, putting Karl De Schweinets in and taking over a great many people from the relief organization.

The states have been gradually getting the idea that the board has no interest in securing jobs for particular people and merely wants to build up personnel standards in the states, and this has made dealing with them easier and much more fruitful.

There were other indications that a field staff in itself was not the complete solution to the problem and that it might be necessary to set up more definite standards and to insist upon them. This is implied in attitudes expressed by two of the most thoughtful members of the Division of Grants in January 1937. The summary of their observations reads:

The weekly field reports now come in to one individual and are then routed around to various members of the staff, including Miss Hoey and heads of divisions. They end up ultimately with four individuals in the Division of Grants, each of whom has, roughly, one quarter of all the country. The thought was that these individuals would bring together all the knowledge which the bureau had on the situation in these super regions and would be available to other people in the bureau when any question involving a state was up for consideration. In actual practice the scheme has not worked out very well, because these four people are regarded as a part of the Division of Grants rather than a service unit for the whole staff, and their time has been taken up very largely writing summaries of state plans and other more or less routine duties. Instead of calling these people in to the board on problems involving states with which they are supposed to be familiar, the field reports and other information are dug out of the files. Furthermore, no system is set up whereby suggestions in the field reports regularly act as stimuli to action on the part of the bureau; they are merely filed away and the information is available when and if needed. This arrangement will probably be modified in the general reorganization of the bureau which is now contemplated. After a Division of Policies and Procedures was set up it was discovered that there was no unit for formulating policy, and this led to a reconsideration of the function of the bureau as a whole.

.   .   .   .   .

A pattern of attitudes in dealings with state officials has grown up in the Bureau of Public Assistance which is not satisfactory. The bureau never wishes to commit itself on policy and therefore never praises or compliments the state on what it is doing or has done, but either criticizes or grumblingly accepts a plan or proposal. This is exemplified in the present situation in Idaho, whose public assistance people are fighting desperately against the Townsend crowd and getting no support from the Social Security Board. Rather than continuing the unpleasant fight in the state, they may give up and accept the Townsend idea because of lack of support from Washington. Miss Hoey cannot do unaided the job of smoothing down the feathers and spreading oil on troubled waters that is required. The job is too big, and moreover, the usual relationship between a state and Washington is with the grants division of the bureau or the field staff. The field staff tries to do what it can, but it in turn cannot give binding decisions, and confines itself largely to making criticisms and suggestions rather than following the practice of praising those constructive things that have already been done.

In February 1937 Frase talked to May, chief of the grants division, about the same matter. His record of that conversation is as follows:

In answer to the observer's inquiry as to whether the board contemplated codifying its requirements as laid down in many individual decisions for general distribution to the states, as is done by some of the agencies administering grants-in-aid programs, May said that no such action was contemplated. However, there is an attempt being made by Corson and his staff to cull all possible sources, including board documents and letters, for policy decisions, in order that they might be codified and distributed to the field staff, which is often unaware of the nature of the decisions that have been made.

Many decisions on policy are made and become accepted in a rather unobtrusive manner. The board has followed the practice of deciding each case as it comes up rather than attempting to lay down any general principles. This means in actual practice that drawing the general principles from such specific decisions and their application to still other cases has devolved upon the Bureau of Public Assistance and more specifically the Division of Grants. The Office of the General Counsel, and Tate in particular, objected to this practice and was reluctant to give approval to many actions which they considered to be of doubtful legality under the act. Through constant repetition, however, Tate has now gotten to the point where he readily affixes his signature when an action is contemplated which is in line with precedents. In very doubtful cases he is given the opportunity of protecting himself by attaching a note that though he personally does not approve the action taken, it is in accordance with board policy as expressed in certain prior actions. There are an increasing number of cases of this kind, among them questions of Indians and Confederate veterans, which are decided by the Bureau of Public Assistance without referral to the board.

Perhaps it was inevitable that definite standards and procedures would be hard to achieve in the administration of a grant-in-aid relief function, and that efforts were properly centered in promoting personnel standards. There were some indications, however, that this was not necessarily the case, and that the board could have been prodded into more systematic action. The formulation in June 1936 of a definite procedure for presenting public assistance plans and grants to the board did not come about until the board insisted upon it. The same was true of the revision of this procedure in December 1936. It was only during the summer of 1937 that real plans were under way to codify the policies of the board and to issue them in the form of definite instructions to the states.

In fields further removed from the political question of personnel, the Bureau of Public Assistance was able to make much more decisive headway. Some of the most important was made in new public assistance legislation in the states, especially during the legislative sessions of 1937. Armed with the model bills drawn up by the American Public Welfare Association in cooperation with the bureau, the field staff, with the support of the association, was able to bring about a considerable improvement in state welfare legislation during the winter and spring of 1937. Many temporary plans were replaced with permanent legislation, and a considerable number of state departments of public welfare were created. Since most of this activity occurred after the close of this study it is not recorded in detail.

THE BUREAU OF ACCOUNTS AND AUDITS
AND THE COMPTROLLER GENERAL

Auditing played a very large role in the development of policy in public assistance. The relationship between the auditors who reviewed state expenditures for public assistance and the field staff of the Bureau of Public Assistance was a constant source of friction, and many of the board's most definite policy decisions in regard to public assistance grants to the states resulted from these conflicts, either in the field or in Washington.[22]

The inclusion of field auditing in the Bureau of Accounts and Audits was one of Seidemann's contributions to the organizational structure of the board. The staff of the Bureau of Public Assistance would have agreed for the most part with the analysis made by Robert Lansdale upon his return, in January 1937, from an extensive field study of the administration of public assistance in the states. He had concluded that the Social Security Board's organization for auditing was fundamentally defective. A separate auditing bureau was, in his view, incompatible with the best administration by the board. He held that an independent auditing group was a constant danger to the public assistance function, because the auditors would urge state practices which, while convenient for the auditors, were incompatible with the best performance of public assistance. He cited the situation in Wisconsin, where the state supervisors of public assistance had been spending their time out in the counties teaching the county people how to do a constructive job. The board's auditors, however, urged them to change their practices and instead to emphasize the review of county cases in Madison. The auditors naturally wanted all the records in one spot because it made their job easier, and they did not realize how bad this would be for administrative operations in public assistance. Lansdale felt that the failure of the field auditors to contact the regional representatives of the Bureau of Public Assistance as they entered the states was damaging good relations with the states and counties.

[22] Decisions on a number of unemployment compensation grant policies were also precipitated by questions raised by the Bureau of Accounts and Audits, and these are discussed in chapter 5. There was not, during the period studied, any field auditing for Unemployment Compensation.

During the early months, however, the chief influence of the Bureau of Accounts and Audits upon public assistance policies related to the legality of various grants. In many instances, particularly in respect to board decisions on the public assistance grants, the Bureau of Accounts and Audits acted as an outpost of the General Accounting Office. A. J. Hughes, director of the bureau, had come from the General Accounting Office and he took a very firm stand, particularly in the early days, against the approval of grants which seemed to him of doubtful legality. He had no particular sympathy for the "social worker" viewpoint expressed in the Bureau of Public Assistance but emphasized a "sound" legal basis for public assistance, particularly in regard to verifying the money available from the states and local units for matching purposes. This brought him into many conflicts with the Bureau of Public Assistance, the General Counsel's Office, and the board itself, and led to his eventual demotion.

Hughes's attitude was well expressed in an interview on June 12, 1936, when he hastily reviewed the experience of the first eight months. When he joined the board he had found it very anxious to make a big splurge by announcing quickly the first grants to the states. It thus wanted to rush the grants through as rapidly as possible when the appropriation act was passed. He had advised it to proceed with the utmost caution because it was entering a new field in which there were as yet no guidelines. His advice had been ignored, but he believed that history had proven him more correct than he had anticipated. Thus he cited the case of Maine, which he said was given $85,000 upon the basis of promises that the board was not legally justified in accepting. It would take nine months to clean up the Maine situation. Montana was another example. Its plan had been sent in five months before but had been kicking around in the Bureau of Public Assistance, whose people were fussing about personnel standards and other social work principles. When political pressure was suddenly exerted, the bureau sent the plan to Accounts and Audits for quick approval, but Hughes had refused on the grounds that the file must be carefully examined and that such action was contrary to the established procedure.

These remarks are cited without further exploration of their accuracy, simply to indicate the differences in orientation of these two administrative entities toward the public assistance functions of the board.

Only a few of the many specific examples of conflict over public assistance grants need be recited.

The Backdating of Estimates

One of the clearest cases concerned the making of estimates by the board in order to certify public assistance grants to the states. Sections 3(b)(1) and (2) of the Social Security Act provided:

The Board shall, prior to the beginning of each quarter, estimate the amount to be paid to the state for such quarter under the provisions of clause (1) of subsection (2), such estimate to be based on (a) a report filed by the state containing its estimate of the total sum to be expended in such quarter in accordance with the provisions of such clause, and stating the amount appropriated or made available by the state and its political subdivisions for such expenditures in such quarter, and if such amount is less than one half of the total sum of such estimated expenditures, the source or sources from which the difference is expected to be derived, (b) records showing the number of aged individuals in the state, and (c) such other investigation as the Board may find necessary.

The Board shall then certify to the Secretary of the Treasury the amount so estimated by the Board, reduced or increased, as the case may be, by any sum which it finds, that its estimate for any prior quarter was greater or less than the amount which should have been paid to the state under clause (1) of subsection (a) for such quarter, except to the extent that such sum has been applied to make the amount certified for any prior quarter greater or less than the amount estimated by the Board for such prior quarter.

The bureaus of Public Assistance and Accounts and Audits and the Office of the General Counsel held a conference early in April 1936 on this point, and agreed in a joint memo to the board that it was not necessary for the board to make the required estimates before the beginning of the quarter in question. The board approved this recommendation, but the Bureau of Accounts and Audits decided afterward that in order to avoid any question by the General Accounting Office it would be safer if the official minutes should date both estimates and certifications prior to the beginning of the quarter. This policy was thus followed by the board until June 29, 1936.

In view of the later reversal of its opinion, there is some reason to believe that the Bureau of Accounts and Audits was not moved entirely by fear of the General Accounting Office. Hughes seems to have disliked the board's policy of delaying grants that spring, because of his belief that the board was indulging in this device to bring pressure on the states to accept its point of view on matters which he regarded as the states' own business. He also felt that some of the delay was caused by staff inefficiency in the Bureau of Public Assistance. At any rate, his opinions were influenced by his desire to secure an earlier date for making the quarterly estimates and grants.

The other bureaus were not satisfied with this back-dating arrangement. Consequently, on June 18 Bane called a meeting of representatives of the Bureau of Public Assistance, the Bureau of Accounts and Audits, and the General Counsel's Office to thrash out the question. They reached the same agreement as in April, that is, that the law did not require estimates prior to the quarter. This time Bane, to be sure of tying them down, asked the General Counsel's Office and the Bureau of Accounts and Audits for a written memorandum confirming the decision. Tate, the assistant general counsel, submitted his the same day, remarking that this had been the position of his office all along. Hughes delayed a bit longer, but finally retracted his earlier position, stating that more careful study of the law led him to believe that since the board's action in making the estimate was dependent on receiving the state's financial figures and upon other circumstances out of its control, it could not be required to make its estimate before the beginning of the quarter to which the estimate applied. The whole tone of his communication was very similar to that of the Comptroller General's decisions —authoritative and legal. The Board received his memorandum on June 29 and voted to discontinue its policy of backdating estimates.

CAN THE STATE MATCH GRANTS WITH OTHER FEDERAL AID MONEY?

A more extreme case of conflicting attitudes developed in connection with the certification of a grant to New Jersey for old age assistance for the fourth quarter of fiscal 1936. The board had approved the New Jersey plan and on May 20, after recommendation by the Bureau of Public Assistance, had authorized the certification of a grant of $234,450 for the fourth quarter. On May 22 Hughes submitted a memorandum objecting to this grant and saying that his bureau would take no further action toward preparing the necessary vouchers until a certain question had been cleared up. $142,500 of the $158,250 which was to be made available by the state as its matching money was federal money transferred to the Emergency Relief Administration of New Jersey. Hughes stated: "It is a well established fact that money which is granted to a state under a federal act cannot be used as state moneys for matching purposes under another federal act." He declined to recommend payment, pending a ruling from the Comptroller General which he urged should be secured. Meanwhile, Corson had submitted the Hughes statement to the General Counsel's Office, and Tate of that office replied that he thought it was perfectly feasible to use state moneys derived from the Federal Emergency Relief Administration to match the board's funds; that other government departments had accepted this, and that there were no opinions of the Comptroller General which prohibited this action. However, he had no objection to submitting the whole question to the Comptroller General and believed that it might be well to do so if the board desired to stop this practice on the part of the states, because the Comptroller General was inclined to rule against the expenditure of federal funds in all doubtful cases.

The board discussed these memoranda at its May 26 meeting, at which both Hughes and Tate were present. After lengthy discussion it appeared that both Miles and Altmeyer (Chairman Winant was absent in Geneva) were very dubious about the legality of allowing FERA funds to be used for matching purposes. Hughes stated, however, that if Bane had the written assurance of the state that its matching money had been appropriated by the legislature for this purpose, he would withdraw his objection to the board's authorization of the grant. It was agreed to request a telegram from the New Jersey commissioner of public welfare covering this point, and not to hold up the grant to New Jersey if he advised that the money used for matching was state funds which had been kept entirely separate from federal funds apportioned to the state.

When the telegram came, it stated:

Item $142,500 listed in New Jersey plan as allocated to old age assistance by Emergency Relief Administration is money regularly appropriated by New Jersey Legislature for relief in New Jersey and is not in any sense in whole or in part contributed by the federal government. It is not mingled in a combined federal-state account.

No decision was reached on the specific point of matching grants in whole or in part received from another federal agency, but the board agreed to request a direct opinion from the Comptroller General on this point. When this was obtained it upheld the legal view taken by Hughes, as is shown in the following:

On June 17, 1936, the Comptroller General ruled that under the Social Security Act only those funds may be matched which are made available by the state after eliminating all federal funds contributed to and used by the state for the same purpose for which the grant is proposed to be made under the Social Security Act. Under this decision, the Social Security Board, in making payments to the states under Titles I, IV and X of the Social Security Act, may not match funds derived from another federal agency such as, for example, funds derived from the Federal Emergency Relief Administration.

REIMBURSEMENT TO U.S. GOVERNMENT OF MONEY
COLLECTED FROM AGED

A controversy over the reimbursement to the federal government of amounts collected by the states from recipients of old age assistance came up to the board as a result of a clash between the Bureau of Accounts and

Audits on the one hand and the Bureau of Public Assistance and the Office of the General Counsel on the other. The Bureau of Accounts and Audits had instructed its auditors to notice all repayments to the states made by recipients of old age assistance, in order that one half of these sums might be deducted from future grants. This policy was adopted without the knowledge of the Bureau of Public Assistance, but it came to the notice of that bureau through Miss Bary, who was then on the field staff in the far-western states. Subsequently Miss Hoey sent a memorandum to Hughes on July 28, 1936, which read:

> Miss Bary tells me that our auditors in the state of Washington have taken the position that Section 2(a)(7) [23] of the Social Security Act refers not only to collections made from the estates of deceased recipients of old age assistance but also repayments made by recipients during their lifetime.
>
> Several months ago the General Counsel's Office informed us that their interpretation of this section was that we were entitled to reimbursements only for collections made of the estates of deceased recipients, and we have been advising the estates accordingly.[24]
>
> Will you please advise us of your opinion on this matter.

On receipt of this memorandum Hughes replied on August 12:

> The Section of the Act referred to deals only with the collections made by the states from the estates of deceased recipients. However, there are other federal acts (regulations) which govern expenditures of federal funds, and it is on the basis of such laws (regulations) that we have instructed our field auditors that any recoveries made by the states from recipients during their lifetime, for any reason whatsoever, one half of such recoveries must be repaid to the federal government, in the same manner as recoveries made from estates as specified in the Social Security Act.
>
> Our auditors are instructed to check for such items and where refund is not made by check, such items must be included in the statement of difference, to be

[23] Section 2(a)(7) provided that a state plan for old age assistance must provide that "if the state or any of its political subdivisions collects from the estate of any recipient of old age assistance any amount with respect to old age assistance furnished him under the plan, one half of the net amount so collected shall be promptly paid to the United States. Any payment so made shall be deposited in the Treasury to the credit of the appropriation for the purpose of this title."

[24] The Bureau of Public Assistance had issued instructions to the states December 3, 1935 (schedule AA, page 8), interpreting section 2(a)(7) of the act as follows: "This requirement does not extend to amounts collected from the recipient himself or by proceedings against his property during his lifetime." The Bureau of Accounts and Audits should have been aware of this interpretation, but evidently did not check it before issuing instructions to its field auditors. The incident is just one illustration of the general lack of coordination and cooperation between the two bureaus.

deducted from future grants. These instructions are based on Comptroller's decisions with respect to the accounting for federal funds.

If your people have instructed the states otherwise, such instructions should be countermanded. I would suggest that in the future, before such advice is given to the states, we be given a chance to protect you on such questions.

Two months later, in a memorandum to the board on October 19, Hughes shifted his grounds somewhat from the firm stand he had taken with the Bureau of Public Assistance:

Recoveries from recipients of public assistance during their lifetime should not be confused with the recoveries from estates of recipients. No mention is made in the Social Security Act of recoveries that might be made during the lifetime of recipients. *Instructions to our auditors are based on an informal opinion of the Comptroller General's Office which was obtained during a discussion of audit procedure to be followed by the Social Security Board, in auditing grants to the states. This opinion held that payments to states, especially those made by the Social Security Board, which are made in advance, remain Government funds until such time as final audit has been made;*[25] and that our auditors should examine the records and where it is shown that recoveries have been made from recipients of public assistance, the Government is entitled to recover its proportionate share of such recoveries. . . . It seems logical to assume that where the states do recover any portion of the moneys paid out as public assistance in which federal funds are involved, repayment should be made to the federal government for its proportionate share of such recoveries.

Because the Office of the General Counsel and the Bureau of Public Assistance disagreed with his interpretation in regard not only to old age but to all three forms of public assistance, Hughes requested a ruling from the board. The views of the general counsel were expressed by Tate in a memorandum to the board which read in part as follows:

It should be pointed out, however, that under Sections 3(b), 403(b) and 1003(b), the Secretary of the Treasury is authorized and directed to pay Federal funds to each state for use as assistance under an approved state plan. These funds are paid on certification by the Board. The expenditures by the state, upon fraudulent representations of applicants or by mistake, might properly upon recovery be considered reason why future estimates should be increased or decreased in accordance with provisions of Sections 3(b)(2), 403(b)(2) or 1003(b)(2) of the Act.

I believe the provisions discussed above are the only ones bearing on the problems which Mr. Hughes presents.

I am aware of no opinion of the Comptroller General which would extend the requirements of these provisions. . . .

Mr. Hughes states that "it seems logical to assume that where the states do

[25] Italics added.

recover any portion of the monies involved, repayment should be made to the federal government for its proportionate share of such recoveries." This might be considered a valid assumption of moral responsibility, aside from the legal implications of the Act, were it not for the fact that Congress, having stated the duties of the state and the federal government in this respect, would seem to have intended that they should not be extended.

This whole question was discussed at the board meeting of October 23, 1936, where it developed that Altmeyer, Miles, Bane, Tate, and Hughes all had different ideas as to the policy that ought to be followed.

In the absence of any general agreement on the ruling to be adopted, the board decided to ask for a ruling from the Comptroller General, and the following letter was subsequently sent to him:

It has come to the attention of the Board that, in several of the states which have public assistance plans in operation, which were approved under Titles I, IV, and X of the Social Security Act, monies may be received by the state in connection with the plan, by recoveries from recipients of assistance, or their property, or otherwise.

Section 2(a)(7) of the Social Security Act requires as a condition of approval by the Board that a State Plan for Old Age Assistance provide that, if the state or any of its political subdivisions collects from the estate of any recipient of old age assistance any amount with respect to old age assistance furnished him under the plan, one-half of the net amount so collected shall be promptly paid to the United States.

The Board has adopted the interpretation that this requirement does not extend to amounts collected from the recipient himself, or by procedure against his property during his lifetime. By the same reasoning as that leading to this interpretation the requirement would not extend to collections made after recipient's death from property which did not become a part of his estate for probate purposes.

Under Sections 3(b), 403(b), and 1003(b), the Secretary of the Treasury is authorized and directed to pay federal funds to each state for reimbursement on expenditures for assistance made by the state as assistance under an approved plan. Federal funds are paid upon certification by the Board. It would seem that, upon the theory of reimbursement implicit in the Act, the monies when paid become state monies. The expenditures by the state, upon fraudulent representations of applicants or by mistake, might properly upon recovery, be considered reasons why future estimates should be increased or decreased in accordance with the provisions of Sections 3(b)(2), 403(b)(2), or 1003(b)(2) of the Act; but neither these sections nor any other provisions of the Act make specific provision for payments to the United States or for adjustments on account of any other monies received by the state.

Thus two questions are raised in connection with these provisions: (1) Does Section 2(a)(7) of the Social Security Act apply to any collections made by a state other than collections from a decedent's estate, for example, recoveries from recipients of old age assistance, or from their property, during their lifetime, or recoveries from the property of recipients after their death where such property did not become a part of the estate: (2) is the United States entitled either to receive an actual payment or to make an adjustment downward in the state's quarterly estimate (in cases other than those where payment to the recipient was induced by fraud or mistake) on account of any collections by the state or other funds received by the state in connection with the plan, in spite of the fact that there is no specific provision under Titles I, IV, and X for such payments or adjustments.

We would appreciate an early opinion from you on these questions.

The Comptroller General answered on November 30, 1936, in part as follows:

The term "estate" appearing in Section 2(a)(7), *supra,* is not defined by any provisions of the Act. Its meaning is not always uniform in the law in that in certain cases it has been held to refer to the estate of a decedent and in others to the estate of a living individual. In view of these facts the precise meaning of said term can be ascertained only from the context, or the circumstances under which it is used, and said term, therefore, should be construed in a sense which will tend to accomplish rather than to defeat the purposes of the act. The broad purpose of the grants to states for old age assistance is to enable the state to furnish financial assistance to aged needy individuals who because of their impecuniosity may be receiving aid from the state under an approved state-aid plan. Where it develops, therefore, that an individual in receipt of such aid possesses an estate of such amount as would, under the state-aid plan, constitute a bar to old age benefits [*sic*], it follows that payments received by the beneficiary in such circumstances constitute improper payments thus giving rise to a right in the state to recover back such payments. The evident purpose, therefore, of section 2(a)(7) of the statute, *supra,* is to provide for payment to the federal government of a share of all such recoveries, because a portion of the amount of the improper payments on account of which the state effects a recovery from the estate of the recipient was paid from federal funds granted to the state. That appears an equitable adjustment and for the purposes of the act it becomes immaterial whether the estate from which collection is made be that of a living recipient or of one since deceased.

With respect to your second question, a careful reading of the act discloses that the adjustment provided for under section 3(b)(2), *supra,* is not intended to cover the matter of reimbursement to the federal government provided for under section 2(a)(7) under the act. The adjustment provided for under said section 3(b)(2) relates only to estimates for the "prior quarter" and, of necessity, must have reference to estimates for the "prior quarter" in respect to errors in calculations, correction of data, such as the number of recipients, amounts payable to each and such like, whereas the collections authorized under section 2(a)(7) would not necessarily relate to the "prior quarter" but, to other quarters as well. The provisions of section 2(a)(7) are mandatory in that "one-half of the net amount so collected shall be promptly paid to the United States" and that any payment so made "shall be deposited in the Treasury to the credit of the appropriation for the purposes of this title." These mandatory provisions must be taken as requiring a separate and distinct accounting to the federal government for its share of the collections made by the state under said section 2(a)(7) of the act. Such accounting, unquestionably, will afford a better record than if the collection were considered as a basis for any adjustment under the provisions of section 3(b)(2) of the act such as that suggested in your letter.

Of course if data has been obtained of state collections which have not been accounted for, the share of the United States in such collections would be properly for deduction from the next payment to the state and the amount so collected be transferred to the credit of the proper appropriation if necessary.

This opinion complicated the situation still further. May pointed out at the board meeting of December 2 that the Comptroller General had not only succeeded in ignoring questions propounded by the board but had made rulings which apparently ignored the clear intent of the act and made effective administration almost impossible. He had interpreted section 2(a)(7) of the act in a way that limited it to cases where payment by the states to the recipient was not made in accordance with the requirements of the state plan, whereas the section was definitely intended to provide for reimbursement to the federal government in cases in which the state plan contained provisions for collecting from the estates of recipients. In the second place, he had interpreted sections 203(b)(2), 403(b)(2), and 1003(b)(2) to mean that adjustments in subsequent grants had to be made in the immediately following quarter, whereas the act plainly stated that these adjustments might be made "for any previous quarter." As General Counsel Eliot, who had helped draft the Social Security Act, remarked in a memorandum some time later:

I can say from my own experience that this language was very carefully inserted into the Act so that the Board would be able to make adjustments six months or possibly nine months after the original error was made. We were perfectly aware that the Board would be several months behind in getting accurate audits, and, therefore, framed the Act so that the adjustment would not have to be made in the quarter immediately following the quarter in which the error was made. The Comptroller General, without any explanation, has disregarded the language of the Act, and given us the impossible task of making adjustments in the quarter immediately following the quarter in which the error was made. This is impossible administratively and not in accordance with the wording of the Statute.

At the board's request, Tate discussed these discrepancies with the General Accounting Office, with the result that McFarlane of the GAO informed him that the board could ignore any sections of the opinion of November

30 which were not satisfactory. After discussing the question again on January 5, 1937, the board decided to ignore the entire opinion, except for that part which defined the word *estate* in section 2(a)(7) as applying to the estates of living as well as deceased recipients of old age assistance. Thus, in this case, the original position taken by Hughes had been upheld by the board; but his original question had long since become a matter of secondary importance compared with the problem of unsnarling the tangle that the Comptroller General had created by his obiter dicta. On January 22, 1937, the Comptroller General replied to the board's letter of January 9, stating that this interpretation of the decision of November 30, in the light of subsequent discussion between the staffs of the two agencies, was correct.

The lack of understanding not only of the purposes of the act but of the relatively clear language of the sections concerned was in this case so flagrant that the general counsel felt compelled to submit a memorandum to the board members asking them to exercise the utmost discretion in submitting further questions to the Comptroller General. After tracing briefly the history of the case, he said:

This is not the first time that the Comptroller General has made an absurd ruling with respect to our Act. Heretofore, we have asked the Comptroller General for a modification of his ruling, and finally have come out with something that was more or less workable, although highly illogical. Probably that could be done in this instance too.

Experience shows that when the Comptroller General's opinions are sought by the Board they are quite likely to be wholly erroneous. Furthermore, as practically all the Government departments have long realized, a Government agency can carry out its law under reasonable interpretations of the law without any fear that the Comptroller General will step in, except in cases where there is obviously a serious question of interpretation. On the other hand, if the Comptroller General's opinion is asked, it is always a heavy likelihood that regardless of the law the Comptroller General will say that certain money cannot be expended.

This is a rather frank statement of an unfortunate situation that has long been the source of trouble to the operating departments of the Government. May I respectfully suggest that the Board seek the Comptroller General's opinion only where it is absolutely necessary and where there is a serious ambiguity in the wording of the Statute?

Whether or not as a result of this suggestion, the board did not request any further opinions from the Comptroller General on points concerning public assistance grants, but it did continue to ask for opinions relating to the forms and procedures for the payment of lump sum and death claims under Title II.

Retroactive Public Assistance Grants

The episode of the retroactive public assistance grants was probably the most vivid example of the difficulties the board encountered in trying to use the Comptroller General to settle internal disputes and to pull its chestnuts out of the fire. Several of the state public assistance laws provided that when an application was approved, assistance would be paid the applicant from the date on which his application was filed. Since some states were greatly in arrears in approving applications, many applicants would thus be entitled, in their first assistance checks, to payment for several months. At a board meeting on June 22, 1936, May of Public Assistance brought up the question of whether the board would match such retroactive payments made by the state to individuals. This problem was particularly important in Missouri, which at that time had a plan coming up for the board's approval. There was no great amount of discussion on the problem at that board meeting; the board merely agreed that it was now following a policy of matching payments back to February 1, 1936, and that under the Appropriation Act of 1937 it could match payments back only as far as April 1, 1936.

On the strength of this board action, which was transmitted to the Bureau of Public Assistance, the bureau wired its field representative in Missouri on June 23, 1936, as follows:

Federal funds granted for quarter ending June 30, may be used to match state funds disbursed during the quarter for old age assistance payments incurred back to February 1, but not earlier. Federal funds to be granted for quarter ending September 30, may be used to cover payments incurred back to April 1, 1936, but not earlier.

The Bureau of Accounts and Audits questioned the interpretation contained in this telegram, and as a result, a conference of representatives of the two bureaus and of the Office of the General Counsel was held shortly thereafter. In this conference the Bureau of Accounts and Audits opined that the board had complete legal authority to match all retroactive payments made by the states to individuals for any month as far back as February 1, 1936. The Bureau of Public Assistance was anxious to stick to the policy outlined in its telegram of June 23, that is, that the language of the Appropriation Act prevented the board from matching retroactive payments for the period before April.

As the general counsel stated in a July 24 memorandum to the board which sketched the discussion at this meeting, there did not appear to be any sound basis in the Social Security Act or the Appropriation Act for either of these interpretations. He suggested the alternative (which he had already offered at an earlier date) that the board rule that it would match state payments to individuals for the month in which the state actually approved the grant to the individual, or for the immediately preceding or immediately succeeding month. He recommended that if the board did not see fit to accept this suggestion, it should ask for an opinion from the Comptroller General. Hughes explained to Frase a good many months later that the board was committed to Missouri officials to approve retroactive payments to individuals, because its advice had been asked on this question before the Missouri law was passed. If the board should decide that it could not match these retro-active payments, it would place itself and the Missouri officials in a very embarrassing situation. Hughes had suggested that the only thing for the board to do was to go ahead and match payments retroactive to February 1, 1936 (the date on which the first appropriation became available), and not to ask for an opinion from the Comptroller General which might result in the board's hands being further tied.[26]

The board discussed this question at great length at its meeting on July 24. Eliot's suggestion was unfavorably received, because it would not only have made the retroactive payments in Missouri impossible but would also have resulted in an equally embarrassing situation in Texas. The Texas law provided that when an individual's application was approved, he would re-ceive payments back to July 1, 1936; but the volume of applications was so large that it would probably be a year or more before all of them were in-vestigated and approved. These two states were the ones most vitally af-fected; there were several others in which the situation was similar, though the amounts of money involved were smaller. Bane pointed out that if the Comptroller General did not allow retroactive payments, Texas would either have to amend its law or put on a large number of extra workers to pass on applications. The board finally decided to allow the Comptroller General to make a decision. The Office of the General Counsel was instructed to prepare a draft letter, and the Bureau of Public Assistance to submit a tabula-tion showing the amounts of money involved in the several states affected.

On August 14, the board reviewed these two documents. The Bureau of Public Assistance reported that eight states had such laws, and that if the board approved retroactive payments by the state back to the date of ap-proval of the state plan, an additional federal grant of $4,494,000 would be required for the fiscal year 1936, and $15,778,400 for fiscal 1937. If Eliot's proposals were accepted, the additional cost to the federal government would be $1,626,000 for fiscal 1936 and $7,751,000 for fiscal 1937. After making several minor changes, the board approved the draft letter to the Comptroller General, the most important sections of which follow:

[26] This was the only case we know of in which Hughes advocated restraint in appealing to the Comptroller General. In this instance he was in favor of the expenditure in question.

The question is before the Social Security Board whether, and to what extent if at all, the Board may hereafter cause to be matched by federal funds, payments made by a state to individuals during a particular month *for* or *on account of* prior months. The matter is of fundamental importance and requires, in the opinion of the Board, consideration by the Comptroller General.

Six state laws upon which are based plans approved by the Social Security Board, contain provisions for retroactive payments to individual applicants. For purposes of convenience the problem which has been raised will be discussed as it applies to grants-in-aid for old age assistance provided for in Title I of the Social Security Act. Any conclusions arrived at would, however, be equally applicable to grants for aid to dependent children under Titles IV and X.

For instance, an aged person might make application on the first of April, and an administrative delay might cause the approval of the application to take place not before August. Assume that the state agency then decided that the applicant was entitled to $30 a month. The state might pay him $150 in August, the payment being made "for" April, May, June, July and August.

As is shown by Section 2(a)(1) of the Social Security Act, Federal grants to the states shall not take into account "so much of such expenditure with respect to any individual for any month as exceeds $30." In the example just given, may the Board properly recognize that the payments by the state were "for" the months of April, May, June, July and August, or must the Board rule that the payments having been made in August were made "for" August, thereby limiting the state to a much smaller sum? Or, in view of the fact that many states do provide for retroactive payments, and often find it difficult to keep from falling as much as two months behind in giving assistance, may the Board properly rule that a payment in a given month may be deemed "for" that month and "for" the two immediately preceding months, but that the payment in August, for instance, cannot be said to be made "for" any period prior to June 17?

The whole approach to the problem of old age assistance in the Social Security Act would seem to indicate a general purpose to grant aid to those states which make regular grants to aged needy individuals, rather than to states which delay payments for six months or a year, during which time the aged person may have suffered or died. On the other hand, the necessity of making constant investigations of the needs of every applicant inevitably results in some delay to the state in making payments. The Board has in the past recognized this necessity in considering estimates and certifying grants to the Secretary of the Treasury. *In this connection the question arises whether it would be a reasonable regulation, within the power of the Board to make rules for the proper administration of the Social Security Act, and in recognizing the problems of state administration, to recognize an old age assistance payment as being made "for" the month in which it was made, or for one or both of the immediately preceding two months.*[27]

Although Public No. 440 and Public No. 739 authorize "payments" for a quarter prior to that in which the payments are made, "excepting payments for any period prior to the quarter in which the plan was submitted to the Social

---

[27] Italics added.

Security Board for approval," the reference seems to be to grants by the United States to a state and not to payments by a state to individuals. The application of the Appropriation Act to this problem does not seem clear.

In view of the importance of the problem, the Social Security Board requests the Comptroller General to furnish it with an opinion on the questions raised.

On September 5, 1936, the Comptroller General replied in part as follows:

What is stated in the above quotation is applicable to the question now submitted,[28] that is, of the $150 expended by the state in August there may not be considered for matching by federal contribution more than $30, the federal contribution being one-half of that sum, and no portion of the $150 could be considered as applicable—insofar as the federal contribution is concerned—to the months preceding the month in which the payment was actually made—the amount "expended" by the state.

The fact that the appropriations provide for federal payments to the states for quarters preceding the quarter in which the federal payment is made does not change the above rule, the appropriations have reference to payments by the United States to the state and not to payments by the state to individuals. [Comptroller General Opinion No. A-80185, September 5, 1936.]

The Comptroller General had merely taken an earlier, January 23 decision on public assistance grants and applied it to the new case, apparently without considering either the administrative problem involved or the statutory provisions of the Social Security Act and the Appropriation Act (which were, it must be admitted, very ambiguous). The board, of course, was not at all pleased with this communication, because it would prevent any retroactive payments whatsoever; that is, if a state should delay making a payment to an individual for as little as one month, the board would not be able to match the payment of that month. Considering the stage of public assistance administration in most states, such insistence on prompt action would have heavily penalized applicants in many of them. Eliot was thereupon instructed to submit the question once more for reconsideration, which he did in a letter of September 26, pertinent sections of which follow:

Upon receipt of your letter of September 5, 1936, in reply to our letter of August 25, 1936, we felt that our letter had not stated completely the questions confronting us, and, therefore ask your permission to resubmit these questions, which are of great practical importance to us in dealing with the states under the Social Security Act.

The problems which have arisen in connection with matching state expenditures may be stated separately as two questions, though in many respects they are very similar.

First, a number of state plans have been in operation for some months, with regular monthly payments of old age assistance being made by the state to

[28] A previous opinion of his on another matter.

qualified aged persons. In a number of these states, the state old age assistance plans themselves provide for payment being made in August, for instance, with respect to the applicant's need in July. It is sometimes the practice, on the other hand, for August payments to be made with respect to the applicant's need in August and sometimes with respect to his need in September. In many instances, these variations are required by state law and accord with customary accounting procedure. Also it sometimes happens that the state necessarily falls a month or two behind in making its payments to these aged persons. For example, sometimes reinvestigation of the person's need causes a delay of a few weeks. Sometimes there is a delay occasioned by some technical defect in the state's quarterly application for a grant from the United States. Under these circumstances, may the Board match the disbursements made during a given month to individuals for their support in a month (or months) immediately preceding or following the month during which the disbursements are made, assuming of course, that the rate of payment has not been in excess of $30 per month.

Second, there are some instances where payment with respect to an earlier month might be made in a state which was just getting its old age assistance plan into effect. For instance, the state old age assistance law might, by its own terms, come into operation January 1, with rights to assistance accruing therefrom. The state might find it impossible to complete the enormous task of examining every application for assistance in less than several months. It might not be until June or even later that the state felt itself to be in a position to begin making payments. Under these circumstances, would the Social Security Board be justified in authorizing a grant to the state to match the disbursements made during a given month to individuals for their support in the months preceding the month during which the disbursements are made, assuming of course that the rate of payment has not been in excess of $30 per month.

While if a state made a payment to an aged person in one month and said that the payment was "for" a month long past, it would seem to be questionable whether the intent of the Social Security Act, for regular monthly assistance, was being carried out; still the practical situation is that in a number of states it has been found impossible thus far to make the payment during the month for which assistance is being granted. In other states the state plans themselves call for payment in one month "for" the month just passed or the month to come. In these states every effort is being made to carry out the full intent of the Social Security Act and it is in our relation with these states that the problems presented above assume significance which warrants, we believe, our resubmission of these questions.

Not only did the board send this letter, but Eliot and Calhoun talked to some of the staff of the General Accounting Office about the problem, and on September 27, the Comptroller General submitted a revised decision:

Your submission of August 20, 1936, submitted the case of an aged person who filed application on the 1st of April but administrative action delayed the approval until August, when it was approved and payment made in August for

$150, reported to cover the months of April, May, June, July and August, at the rate of $30 per month. In the decision to you of September 5, 1936, it was stated:

> ... of the $150 expended by the state in August there may not be considered for matching by federal contribution more than $30, the federal contribution being one-half of that sum, and no portion of the $150 could be considered as applicable—insofar as the federal contribution is concerned—to the months preceding the month in which the payment was actually made—the amount "expended" by the state.

Said statement must be considered as made in the light of the facts in the particular case there involved.

While the law provides for payments to the states "for each quarter" on the basis of expenditures to be made by the state "during such quarter," the limitation with respect to the computation of the maximum amount payable "for" or "during" the quarter is upon the rate of the expenditure with respect to any individual "for any month." That is to say, the $30 limitation relates not to the amount expended in a particular month but to the amount expended for any particular month.

Accordingly the quarterly payments to the states by the federal government are for adjustment upon the basis of one half of the amounts expended by the state during said quarter as old age assistance, not in excess of $30 per month with respect to any individual, for the period covered by the state payment, provided that in no case shall payments by the state for any period prior to the month in which the first payment was made by the state to the individual be considered. The decision of September 5, 1936, is modified accordingly.

General Counsel Eliot interpreted this decision to the board:

> The Comptroller General has revised his opinion with respect to retroactive payments under Titles I, IV and X.
>
> His first opinion holds that, with respect to *initial* payments of assistance by the states to needy individuals under the state plan, no retroactive arrangement may be recognized by the Board. In other words, where the plan is newly established, and the first payments are made in August and supposed to cover the four preceding months, we will not be able to match payments for those preceding months. This is in line with the earlier opinion.
>
> However, the new opinion states that where, at some time *after* regular payments by the state to needy individuals have begun, the state makes a payment in one month designating all or part of it as being for some different month or months, the Board is to match these payments.
>
> Presumably, in the case where the plan has already been in operation, prospective payments by the state would be entitled to recognition for matching purposes as well as retroactive payments.
>
> This modification of the original opinion is entirely in accordance with the remarks of Mr. McFarland of the General Accounting Office when Mr. Calhoun and I talked with him on September 15. I do not see any legal justification for

the distinction which the new opinion draws between administrative delays before the first payments of assistance and administrative delays after regular payments have begun. However, I doubt whether it would be wise to attempt to get a further liberalization of the original opinion.

Eliot may not have been particularly interested in getting a revision of this opinion, because it confirmed in large measure his original suggestion of not matching retroactive payments for long periods, in the cases of Missouri and Texas. The board felt much the same about it. It wanted to avoid the nuisance of matching these retroactive payments, and to conserve the very considerable sums involved, and it was willing to put the responsibilty for this policy on the Comptroller General.

The amusing part of this episode was still ahead. The Bureau of Public Assistance had wired Missouri and Texas of the Comptroller General's decision; the following day May came into the board meeting to say that Missouri wanted to know what the effective date of the Comptroller General's decision was. A few days later a letter was sent to the General Accounting Office requesting this information, but weeks went by and no answer was received. Hughes then got permission from the board to go over to the General Accounting Office to find out informally where the matter stood. One of his friends in that office told him that if the Social Security Act was to be interpreted so as not to allow the matching of state retroactive payments, the decision would naturally govern from February 11, 1936, the date on which funds were available under the board's first appropriation. Hughes then explained that the General Accounting Office had misinterpreted the law in its decision and that insisting upon February 11 as the effective date would cause a great many difficulties. Several days later this friend telephoned Hughes and said that the General Accounting Office had given instructions to the auditing department not to concern itself with grants retroactive to any date earlier than September 26, 1936, but that it would not let the board have anything in writing to this effect. In order to be perfectly sure where he stood, however, Hughes got in touch with a friend of his in the auditing department and discovered from him that a memorandum had actually been sent to that department instructing them not to apply the decision in question to any case before September 26, 1936. Hughes transmitted this information to the board on December 2, 1936, and the states concerned were notified of it.

THE PROBLEM OF A FIELD AUDIT OF STATE PUBLIC ASSISTANCE EXPENDITURES

The question of a detailed field audit of all public assistance expenditures by the states is one of the most puzzling episodes in the board's history.

Evidently it was decided quite early in the spring of 1936 that, at least for the first year, every payment made by a state operating under an approved plan would be audited by the bureau's field auditing staff. Hughes consistently maintained that this detailed audit had been stipulated by the General Accounting Office. Whether this was actually the case Frase was never able to find out, but several persons who were acquainted with the practice of the General Accounting Office expressed a belief that it was very unlikely. Among these was Bachmann, chief of constructive accounting on Hughes's own staff. Similar expressions of doubt were made by several members of the staff of the Bureau of Public Assistance, which bureau believed on the whole that a sample audit would be sufficient. Certainly no other federal aid agency had ever undertaken such an extensive auditing program.[29]

The field audit of public assistance expenditures was pushed forward as rapidly as personnel could be recruited.[30] At first it was hoped that all states might be covered by June 30, 1936, but this proved to be impossible. The field auditing staff did grow from 27 on July 31 to about 110 in December 1936 and 125 in March 1937.

The lines along which the audit was to be conducted were not, however, made very clear during this early period. Except for the Social Security Act itself, some general governmental regulations, and the state legislation, the field auditors had no guides to policy. Walsh, assistant director of the bureau, explained this lack of explicit direction in a training school lecture in June 1936:

No definite policy has been set up for field audits with regard to public assistance because the bureau is just feeling its way, trying to determine from experience what are some of the things that have to be watched in auditing the expenditures by states of federal funds for this purpose.

One of the regional auditors seven months later described the situation as follows:

The auditors were sent out without any very specific instructions as to how to do their job, save for knowledge of a few treasury regulations. As a result, they have had to find their own way. At the conference in Washington, January 11-16, 1937, when all regional auditors were called in by the board, they learned why they had not received more and better instructions. The national office did not know just what the job involved, and they were waiting, before issuing

[29] According to V.O. Key, *The Administration of Federal Grants to the States* (p. 119), the Children's Bureau at about the same time had 5 field auditors, the Bureau of Public Roads 34, and the USES 6. The Social Security Board's auditors at this time numbered 110.

[30] This was not very rapidly, because of the difficulties of securing competent auditors. (See the discussion of personnel in chapter 7.)

instructions, for the auditors to come back and tell what they had run into and how they had met their difficulties.

The difficulties resulting from having uninstructed field auditors out in the states did not become apparent in Washington until the Bureau of Public Assistance established, early in the fall of 1936, a permanent field staff with headquarters in the regional offices. Then it was discovered that the auditing crews (which seldom came into the regional offices) were, in addition to helping local officials improve their recording processes, advising states about all manner of public assistance matters, often in directions contrary to the policy of the operating bureau. Late in the fall, as a result of unceasing complaints by the Bureau of Public Assistance, Hughes finally agreed to appoint regional auditors, but he complied more with the letter than the spirit of the agreement. This continuing source of friction led in January 1937 to Hughes's demotion to assistant director of the bureau and his replacement by Banning, a man with long experience in federal accounting. A conference of all the regional auditors was then called for January 11–16, 1937, at which time Corson and May outlined the nature, and more particularly the limitations of their duties. Corson stressed two points: (1) that the auditors were not to discuss general administrative matters with local and state officials, and (2) that they were to make their findings in the counties available to the public assistance representatives in the regional offices, rather than sending them to Washington and letting the facts filter back to the regional representatives of the Bureau of Public Assistance after the reports had been consolidated and rewritten in the Washington office of the Bureau of Accounts and Audits. Following this meeting, more definite policies were promulgated which culminated in an administrative order by the board defining the duties and interrelation of its field officers. A series of institutes in several regional offices were also used to instruct and clarify the functions of the field auditing staff. Finally, the relationships between the bureaus of Public Assistance and of Accounts and Audits were expressed in a written agreement approved by the board on February 2, 1937.

Although no judgment could be made at the close of this study about the results of these clarifications and new understandings, the conflict between the two bureaus—which probably would not have occurred if auditing had been made a function of the Bureau of Public Assistance—seemed to be on the way to a satisfactory solution.[31]

Without extensive field observation, it was impossible to judge the net result of the extensive auditing job undertaken by the board. Hughes complained to Frase in April 1937 that despite the comprehensive field audit of

[31] In at least two regional offices, Boston and Minneapolis, this conflict had ironed itself out earlier through informal agreement.

public assistance payments which had been done and was continuing, the board had as yet made practically no use of the information gathered. Only two complete reports on states had been made, and only one of them had been used.

.5.

UNEMPLOYMENT COMPENSATION

LEGAL PROBLEMS RAISED BY
THE FIRST STATE LAWS

A handful of states were waiting on the doorstep of the board when it was well enough organized to give systematic consideration to the legal sufficiency of state unemployment compensation acts. With the exception of Wisconsin, these acts had all been passed late in 1935, when the inducement of federal legislation which would pay the state administrative bills and enforce state tax sanctions led to a quick response from a few forward-looking state legislatures and governors. During the performance of this duty of scrutinizing and approving the first state acts, the board came upon a number of interesting and important legal questions concerning which its decisions were likely to constitute precedents that would bind its hands in dealing with the flood of laws ultimately expected. It therefore proceeded with great circumspection. As an introduction to our administrative history of unemployment compensation we give a brief account of a few of these major legal issues.

WISCONSIN

The Wisconsin law for unemployment compensation had been passed in January 1932, over three years before that of any other state. It was submitted to the Social Security Board late in September 1935, but the board withheld its approval for two months. The impression prevailed among the Wisconsin administrators that the board's delay derived from its unfavorable attitude toward the reserve plan of unemployment insurance.

There was probably another and controlling reason for this delay. The nature of the Wisconsin act raised two issues of policy having to do with how it might be made to conform with the Social Security Act provisions. The first of these related to the stipulation in section 108.03(1) of the Wisconsin law which provided for the payment of benefits "in such place and in such manner as the commission may from time to time approve or prescribe." The second question was the propriety of paying benefits in the form of wages for work in unemployment relief projects. In order to make this first part of the Wisconsin law conform with the requirements of the Social Security Act, under section 903(a)(1), that benefits would be paid through the public employment offices, the Wisconsin commission passed a rule that benefits would be paid through public employment offices or such other agencies as the commission, with the advice and approval of the federal Social Security Board, might designate. As pointed out by the board's attorneys, the board had the alternative of tentatively approving any agency the state commission might designate, without regard to the rules and regulations, or of considering as a part of the law the rules and regulations issued, and withdrawing its approval of the Wisconsin act when such rules and regulations were so altered as to constitute a failure to meet the requirements of the Social Security Act.

With regard to the second question, the Wisconsin commission, by a rule, declared its intention to exercise its discretionary power concerning relief projects as one method of paying benefits only when, upon the advice and approval of the Social Security Board, the commission should find that the payment of benefits in the form of relief wages was consistent with the requirements of the Social Security Act. The Social Security Act did not specifically define the term *benefits*, although it modified the term by linking the word *cash* with *benefits*. In the absence of a definition of this word, the General Counsel's Office suggested to the board that there would be some legal justification for a finding that benefits, particularly in the form of wages, constituted compensation. It pointed out further that if the board made such a finding it would be necessary for it to approve, as agencies through whom benefits would be payable, the state or any political subdivision which was paying such benefits in the form of wages to unemployed individuals employed upon public relief projects approved by the Wisconsin commission under section 108.25. Were it to take that course, it could again avoid the need of approving rules and regulations issued by the Wisconsin commission as a part of the Wisconsin law.

As explained by Eliot, the board believed that the term *benefits* ought not to include work relief payments, but it did not say so in its decision. It abstained in order to give itself a chance to change its mind, if in the future that should be wise. Had it defined benefits to exclude payments of relief, it might find itself caught at some future date. From the point of view of the board, the other matter of policy involved in the Wisconsin law was whether it should ask a state to modify its statute by administrative orders which could then be used as a basis for approval. The danger of that policy lay in the possibility that the board would be overwhelmed by the need to scrutinize continuously the whole volume of rules and regulations being issued by the state unemployment compensation administrative authorities.

The board's approval was given to the Wisconsin act on November 27, 1935, and was couched in the following terms: "On the basis of the statute and the definite rules and regulations submitted, the Board approves the Wisconsin Unemployment Compensation Act." Eliot insisted, in a conversation with McKinley, that this did not constitute a precedent, because it carefully refrained from giving the specific reason for requesting supplementary administrative rules. While it is true that this action was not a precedent which could be used by other state agencies in their negotiations with the board, so far as the definition of the word *benefits* was concerned, it apparently did constitute an important precedent, because the board used it as a basis for its approval of rules and regulations issued by the Wisconsin commission. In that sense it appears to have undertaken an obligation to watch all changes in such rules and regulations, for unless it did this the basis for its original action might be undermined. Certainly, in dealing with state plans for public assistance it soon found itself in the position of securing abridgements or modifications of statute by administrative rules and regulations, and thus took on the burden of watching a large volume of delegated legislative activity.[1]

The problem of how benefits should be paid in Wisconsin was raised again in the spring of 1936 when the Wisconsin commission, facing the need to begin benefit payments the first of July 1936, requested permission from the board to make such payments by a number of alternative methods. On April 29 the Wisconsin commission came to Washington and met with the board to discuss this application, though at this time they had whittled down their request to a single alternative to the use of the employment offices. That alternative was to pay benefits by mail. During the discussion, Wagenet declared himself opposed to this procedure, chiefly because he wanted a close contact between the employee and the employment office. After the discussion of a possible experimental period of one year, the Wisconsin people withdrew from the meeting and an executive session of the board and its staff ensued, in the hope that an immediate decision might be given. Bachmann of the

---

[1] It is probable that it would have been compelled to assume this burden in any event, because of its statutory obligations relating to the assurance of certain standards of administration. See the discussion on pp. 282-83ff.

accounting staff, who had been handling the accounting practice for all the states with approved unemployment compensation plans, told the board that the Veterans' Administration had had difficulty in paying by check through the mails, and he thought other organizations had had similar experiences. The board was unable to make up its mind until May, when it approved mail payments for an experimental period.

MASSACHUSETTS: REJECTION AND SUBSEQUENT APPROVAL

There was transmitted to the board on September 19, 1935, a request to approve the Massachusetts Unemployment Compensation Act, which had been adopted early in 1935. On November 11, the board decided that it could not approve the measure and so notified the chairman of the Massachusetts commission, indicating as the reasons for this rejection a number of provisions in the Massachusetts act whose meaning was not entirely clear to the board and about which further information was needed. The board's action was based upon section 19(c)(2) of the Massachusetts act. That provision related to the hours, wages, and working conditions of jobs offered to unemployed persons when these were substantially less favorable than those offered for similar work in the same locality. To a clause permitting an employee to reject such an offer of work, the Massachusetts law had attached the stipulation that the wages or working conditions so offered must depress "unduly wages or working conditions."

Commenting on the Massachusetts law, the board's letter stated that "it would be possible for the commission to deny benefits to an employee because he refused work, even though his refusal was due to the fact that wages, hours, and other conditions of the work offered were substantially less favorable for him than those prevailing for similar work in the locality. Because this is possible under the Massachusetts act, that cannot be approved under Section 903(a) of the Social Security Act." [2]

The Massachusetts legislature met in January 1936, and on the thirty-first of that month enacted amendments removing this objection and smoothing out a number of details, actions which made the law more fully acceptable to the Social Security Board and took care of certain administrative requirements of the Massachusetts people themselves. Among the changes that were made was a provision for making the exemptions from coverage the same as those in the federal act, and providing for the postponement of detailed payrolls for employers until 1937, by basing the employment record

[2] The rejection of the Massachusetts law was never made public, a fact of some embarrassment to the Informational Service in dealing with newspaper reporters during January.

upon which benefits were to be paid on the employment experience beginning with January 1937. On February 4 the board approved the Massachusetts act under Title IX.

THE UTAH REJECTION

During the 1935 session of the legislature, Utah passed an unemployment compensation act that was out of line with a number of requirements of the Social Security Act. Utah communicated with the board during the autumn of 1935, and at that time the board offered to help the state meet requirements. Pursuant to that offer, Eliot drafted a letter to be sent to the assistant attorney general of Utah suggesting various ways in which the law might be made acceptable to the board. At the board meeting on March 2, 1936, this letter was discussed, and Wagenet asked the board to take action on it, since it involved an extreme interpretation to be given the state act in order to make it conform to the Social Security Act. During the discussion, in which Murray, Bane, and Wagenet participated, it seemed clear that the Eliot letter if accepted represented at best a patching-up process applied to a bad statute. Wagenet was opposed to sending Eliot's letter, for he felt that the law was too out of line to be cured by administrative action. Miles appeared to be hopeful that the governor of the state could solve the problems by means of regulations, but the discussion brought out the fact that the law did not go into effect until the governor so declared, and that he had taken the position that he would make no declaration until he was certain that the board was going to approve it. Murray told the board that the Utah industrial and labor commissioner did not want the board to approve the law as it stood. At the following board meeting (March 4) Miles presented a memorandum proposing the rejection of the Utah law, and Wagenet endorsed Miles's position. Action was postponed, however, pending the return of Altmeyer, and the matter was not finally settled until the meeting of March 13.

It was Altmeyer's position that the board should advise the Utah people to call a special session of the legislature and correct the state's law by legislative action. It was finally decided that Eliot should write a letter to Assistant Attorney General Huffaker of Utah, with whom he had been in correspondence, stating that after full consideration he could not recommend the approval of the Utah law to the board. Wagenet was also instructed to write a similar letter to the Utah industrial and labor commissioner.

THE NORTH CAROLINA REJECTION

During the closing days of the 1935 session of the North Carolina legislature, the General Assembly passed an act turning over to the governor and council blanket authority designed to permit North Carolina to take advantage of the anticipated federal legislation on unemployment compensation. The governor and council were authorized to set up a state agency to administer unemployment compensation with full right to promulgate rules and regulations and with "full right in said agency, commission or department of government to receive contributions from the government of the United States, employers, or from other sources . . . ; with full right in said commission, agency or department to suspend any and all rules and regulations in whole or part in conformity with federal legislation on the subject."

Governor John C. B. Erhinghous, early in the board's career, asked for approval of this North Carolina act as the basis for North Carolina's participation in unemployment compensation administrative grants and the federal Unemployment Trust Fund. But the board had postponed giving an answer until the governor should come in person and present in detail his plans for administration, even though the board was pretty certain that the state law did not comply with the Social Security Act. During the delay a misquotation concerning the North Carolina law, from a talk by Winant, was given wide newspaper circulation in the state, much to Winant's embarrassment.

The matter was brought up at the board meeting of March 24, 1936, by Altmeyer, who read a letter from John B. Andrews, of the American Association for Labor Legislation, commenting adversely upon the North Carolina law.

Altmeyer asked that the board record some appropriate action on North Carolina. He did not think it fair to give the governor of North Carolina a chance to say that the board had not made a ruling on the North Carolina law. Out of this discussion came authorization for Bane to talk to General Counsel Eliot by long distance phone (Eliot was on vacation) and get the facts up to date as Eliot knew them, and to then invite the governor to meet with the board early the following week. Bane followed his instructions and arranged a meeting on April 1. At that time Governor Erhinghous and his attorney general, Sewell, met with the board. Eliot was also present. The governor sketched the history of this legislation in North Carolina and pointed out that the important thing was the board's interpretation of the word *contributions* as defined in the Social Security Act under section 907. He urged that an interpretation be given the words *required contributions* which would not restrict it to taxes but would include voluntary contributions by employers. The governor had all along taken the position that payments to a state fund, made voluntarily by an employer without the employer being subject in any way to provisions requiring reports, payment at particular times, and so on, might be deemed contributions within the meaning of section 907(f) of the Social Security Act. If voluntary contributions were defined as "payments required by a state law," it would enable the employees of employers making such contributions to obtain benefits under the law.

Eliot later told McKinley that in supporting this position Erhinghous even went back to Latin derivations, insisting that upon this etymological basis the phrase included voluntary payments. He argued that if the board insisted upon a narrower definition, it would very materially restrict the movement for nationwide unemployment insurance. Altmeyer asked Erhinghous whether, if the board should accept this view about the North Carolina law and so approve the act, he thought the United States Treasury would give the North Carolina employers the 90 percent offset against the federal tax. Erhinghous replied that that was the business of the Treasury Department and should not concern the board. He asked the board to go along with North Carolina and certify the law to the Treasury Department, leaving it to the Treasury to decide whether or not *required contributions* was applicable to the North Carolina position.

Attorney General Sewell supported the governor's position. Miles asked the governor whether he could make the contributions mandatory upon North Carolina employers. The governor thought he could.

After the governor and the attorney general had departed, the chairman asked the general counsel if there were legal objections to the request which the governor had made. Eliot replied that there were legal objections: (1) "The accepted legal interpretation of the word *require* is such that there is no possible way of agreeing to Governor Erhinghous's interpretation, except by straining almost beyond the limit all interpretations and statutory evidence available on this point; (2) if Erhinghous's interpretation is adopted it will not have a leg to stand on." Eliot pointed out that to accept the governor's interpretation would very seriously endanger the constitutionality of the Social Security Act.

Eliot reported to the board that he had been trying unsuccessfully every day for the last week to get a reply from the Treasury Department to the board's letter of February 11, 1936, asking for an interpretation of section 907(f). However, he had learned informally that the Treasury's opinion on this question was in accord with the board's. Altmeyer expressed the opinion, which appears to have been accepted, that the way to handle the affair was to get the Treasury decision in a form that could be made public and then advise the governor that the board concurred in it.

The matter rested until March 5, when Eliot reported that the reply from the Treasury to the board's letter about an interpretation of 907(f) was not worded appropriately to send to Governor Erhinghous. He submitted a new draft letter to the Treasury asking for a more restricted and specific definition, and the department's opinion of the validity of Erhinghous's construction of the word *require*. Winant signed the letter, and Eliot was asked to take it personally and to do everything possible to get a reply from the Treasury Department within a week.

Apparently Eliot was at least partially successful, for on the following day, March 6, Winant addressed a letter to Governor Erhinghous in which he stated that the reply from the Treasury showed the governor's construction to be untenable. "The opinion of the Secretary of the Treasury states that credit against the excise tax imposed under Title IX of the Social Security Act may be allowed only for payments to a state unemployment fund which are made by an employer who is subject to a state law and is compelled by that law to pay contributions at such times and in such manner as may be prescribed. It follows that under Title IX of the Social Security Act, credits will not be allowed for payments not required by law, but required as a condition precedent to employer's employees receiving unemployment compensation."

This manner of handling the North Carolina problem permitted the board to lean upon the prestige and legal authority of the Department of the Treasury. It reduced, somewhat, the heat generated against itself as the agent for a novel program in which many states joined under economic and political duress rather than through conviction.

THE NEW YORK LAW AND TITLE III

New York was one of the states waiting, when the board was set up, with unemployment compensation acts to be approved under Title III of the Social Security Act. There was, however, considerable delay in securing its initial grant for administration, because of certain difficulties in meeting the legal stipulations under Title III. This illustrates the fact that a state might meet all of the conditions set forth in Title IX and provide for an excellent plan of administration as indicated under Title III, but still be held up through the failure to meet certain other requirements of the act. In the case of the New York statute, there was no provision explicitly giving an individual whose claim for unemployment compensation might be denied, an opportunity for a "fair hearing" before an impartial tribunal.

To prevent undue delay, Winant proposed that the matter be solved by securing a declaration from Glen Bowers, the New York administrator, that he would promulgate a rule to meet the fair-hearing requirement. If this commitment were made, Winant felt the board could find the New York law acceptable under Title III, and certify the grant. Miles agreed to that proposal, and Eliot was authorized to get in touch with Bowers to secure this action. As a consequence, on March 10 the board authorized the Secretary of the Treasury to grant New York approximately $280,000 to administer the New York law during the third quarter of fiscal 1936.

STATE TRUSTEEING OF EMPLOYER CONTRIBUTIONS

When McKinley was in New Hampshire on February 17, 1936, he learned that the employers of that state had been permitted to pay their contributions into a trust fund for which the state administrator was acting as trustee. He found also that a number of employers had placed their contributions in escrow with New Hampshire national banks (one Massachusetts bank was also used). The escrow arrangement made it impossible for either the state unemployment administration or the employers to secure those funds until the conditions of escrow should have been fulfilled. The reasons given for this arrangement by the New Hampshire administrators was that the employers feared the unemployment compensation act would be declared unconstitutional. They did not wish to be caught under such circumstances with their money in the hands of either the state or federal governments.

This arrangement seemed on its face to violate the provisions of Title IX of the Social Security Act, which in section 903(a) says that "all money received in the unemployment funds shall immediately upon such receipt be paid over to the Secretary of the Treasury, to the credit of the Unemployment Trust Fund established by Section 904." It had been discussed when New Hampshire had first applied for an administrative grant, but Chairman Winant thought that the request had been withdrawn. The actual approval was apparently given by the chief of the bureau after assurance of the legal validity of the arrangement had been given by the general counsel. Winant was distressed that the proposal had been approved and that he had not been informed about it; he regarded it as contrary to good administrative policy even though the trustee plan was to terminate January 15, 1937. Altmeyer was more complacent, feeling that the plan was legally valid and not touchable under the board's control over administration.[3]

During the month of April 1936 the board began to undergo a change of mind about this feature of the New Hampshire administration. This was the result, partly, of Winant's dislike of the arrangement and his feeling that he had been misled in connection with the original approval. More important was the filing of a similar request from New York early in April, which asked the right to hold its employers' contributions in escrow and withhold

---

[3] This episode was one of the reasons for the board's insistence upon the development of a more thorough and standardized procedure for the handling of future administrative grants for unemployment compensation.

payment from the federal treasury until the constitutional issue should be decided.

By this time, also, the board was aware of an exchange of letters between the Treasury Department and the State of Wisconsin (discussed below) that safeguarded the state's contributions in the event the court should invalidate either the Social Security Act or the state laws.[4]

On April 7 Wagenet presented a memo to the board on the payment of employer contributions in trust, and a general discussion of the problem in New Hampshire and New York ensued. Winant clearly indicated his hope that the New Hampshire people would be persuaded to discontinue their trustee arrangement. He even suggested that perhaps New Hampshire should be limited to January 15, 1937, and that New York be told that the board was working out a method to get New Hampshire to reconsider its arrangement. Eliot still insisted that the scheme came within the terms of Title IX and that the only possible basis for withdrawing it would be to employ the provision in Title III relating to the administrative arrangements under which the payment of benefits must be assured.[5]

---

[4] It seems curious that the board did not know until March 6, 1936, when Seidemann informed it of these letters, that Secretary Morgenthau had several weeks earlier guaranteed the state's right to the return of moneys placed in trust with the federal treasury for unemployment compensation purposes. Yet as late as March 4 a lengthy discussion occurred at the board meeting about the tale being spread by the National Association of Manufacturers that the states could not get their money back from the Treasury if the court should invalidate either federal or state law. Eliot and Murray, at this meeting, proposed that the board should make a specific request of Secretary Morgenthau on this point. At the close of the discussion the board instructed the general counsel to prepare a letter to the Treasury asking for clarification of this question. This was more than six weeks after Wisconsin had received such a letter from Morgenthau.

[5] In discussing this matter on April 21, Eliot gave as justification for his opinion the fact that the fund created by the New Hampshire employers under the trust agreement, even though administered by the state treasurer, was legally distinct from the unemployment fund as defined by the Social Security Act. The definition said that the unemployment fund was a special fund established under a state law and administered by a state agency for the payment of compensation. Since the terms of the escrow agreement clearly withheld this money from the state agency for the purpose of paying compensation, it was not, in Eliot's view, an unemployment fund. From the strict legal point of view, he thought it impossible to stop the use of this device to prevent employers' contributions from going into the United States Treasury. It is interesting to note at this point the view of Edwin Witte, director of research for the Committee on Economic Security, which had drafted the law. When told of the New Hampshire arrangement and of the interpretation given by Eliot's office, he expressed astonishment. He thought that the plain intention of the drafters clearly prohibited any such arrangement.

Wagenet hoped that some way would be found to stop this practice, even if the board had to reverse its decision on New Hampshire. Altmeyer declared that the board had to either permit New York to go ahead or else revoke the approval given New Hampshire. It was finally agreed to inquire into the New Hampshire experience and get the facts on how the practice had been working. On the basis of these facts the board might be justified in considering reversing its stand on New Hampshire and then drafting a letter to New York.

At the board meeting on April 11, Wagenet presented the proposed letter to be sent to Bowers of the New York Unemployment Insurance Administration concerning the board's opinion about contributions in trust. At the same time another letter for New Hampshire was discussed. There was some difference of opinion between Eliot and Wagenet over the reasons that should be given in the two letters, and it was finally agreed that these two staff members should get together and work out the letters and report back. During this discussion Eliot again suggested that the objection might be based upon improper administration.

The matter hung fire until April 28, when Commissioner John B. Andrews of New York came to Washington and waited in the outer office while the board, with the assistance of Wagenet and Murray, attempted to reach a decision. Altmeyer reported that Marion B. Folsom, representative of the Eastman Kodak Company, had called him by phone and indicated his surprise that the board should be concerned by this question. Altmeyer had told him that the board was opposed to the trustee procedure "because of the psychological atmosphere of uncertainty which it created." Wagenet urged the board to take a position opposing the trustee arrangement.

The board agreed to take the stand that this procedure was not contemplated in the act; that it was permitted in the case of New Hampshire because at the time there had been no Treasury ruling; that the board felt it had worked very badly; that consequently the board was opposed to it. Andrews was invited in to meet with them and present his case. The board then advised him of its opposition to this procedure for the reasons mentioned above. It was agreed to give no publicity to this meeting or this decision.

Immediately following this action, the Bureau of Unemployment Compensation presented a request for certification of an administrative aid grant for New Hampshire for the fourth quarter of fiscal 1936. Because of the contribution in trust arrangement, the board decided to postpone action on New Hampshire until the following week. On May 5, it approved a grant for New Hampshire for the fourth quarter after being informed by Winant "that the situation in New Hampshire had now been cleared up." What that statement meant is difficult to understand, for New Hampshire continued its established practice of trusteeing contributions.

STATE PAYMENTS TO FEDERAL UNEMPLOYMENT TRUST FUND
THE INTERPRETATIONS AND REGULATIONS OF THE TREASURY

It may be well here to notice the arrangements made by the United States Treasury for handling the moneys received by the states from their taxes for purposes of unemployment compensation. The Treasury's arrangements and interpretations of its relationships to the states were made clear in connection with Wisconsin's January 6 request for information, addressed to the Secretary of the Treasury. In that request, Administrator Paul A. Raushenbush indicated that Wisconsin had a fund of $7,000,000 known as the Unemployment Reserve Fund. In addition to collections already made, the collections coming in during the succeeding six months were expected to reach a total of approximately $8,000,000, although some of the contributions were not covered by the Social Security Act. The letter set forth the Wisconsin administration's understanding of the legal rights with these moneys in case they should be deposited with the United States Treasury. It indicated the belief that Wisconsin could make deposits in that trust fund even if the Wisconsin Unemployment Compensation Act were not approved under section 903 of the Social Security Act, or in case at some future time it should cease to be approved under that section. "It is our present understanding that the right balance standing to the credit of Wisconsin's 'Unemployment Reserve Fund' at any time would and could be released to said fund, or in case any final court decision on the Wisconsin act should so direct, or in case Title IX of the Social Security Act were finally invalidated."

The letter further declared that deposits made to Wisconsin's account in the United States Unemployment Trust Fund would be made subject to the understanding set forth in the letter, and that the commission would mark Wisconsin's checks "for deposit only to the account of the Wisconsin 'Unemployment Reserve Fund' in the Unemployment Trust Fund of the United States."

A reply was sent to Wisconsin on January 21, 1936, by Secretary Morgenthau. While his letter indicated general accord with the interpretations of the Social Security Act given by Raushenbush, it said, "I do not believe that the Department would be justified in accepting moneys deposited on any condition not contained in that Act." The most important parts of this letter were as follows:

It is the opinion of this Department that funds may be accepted for deposit in the Unemployment Trust Fund, whether or not the state law under which the funds in question were collected has been approved or certified by the Social Security Board in accordance with Section 903 of the Social Security Act, and whether or not some part of the funds were collected prior to the enactment of the Social Security Act, and whether or not the contributions have been made with reference to services the wages for which are not included within the measure of the tax imposed by Section 901 of the Social Security Act.

It is the opinion of the Department, moreover, that that portion of the Unemployment Trust Fund for which a separate book account is maintained for the Industrial Commission of Wisconsin, would not be subject to withdrawal by any other state agency, but would at all times be subject to withdrawal when duly requisitioned in proper form by that Commission or its authorized representative or representatives. It would presumably become the legal duty of the Commission and of such representatives to make such requisitions for the entire balance in the event that the Wisconsin legislature or a final court decision should so direct or in the event that a final decision of the Supreme Court of the United States should declare section 904 of the Social Security Act invalid. In any of these contingencies, or in any other, the Department of the Treasury, in accordance with its interpretation of the law, will honor requisitions duly made, to the extent of any balance standing to the credit of the Book Account for the Industrial Commission of Wisconsin. I may add that the Fund will be set up as a special deposit account, and that payments from it will not require the approval of any officer outside of this Department.

The same letter outlined a different procedure for handling state checks than that which had been proposed in Raushenbush's communication. That procedure was substantially as follows. The states would draw their checks on the federal reserve banks serving their regions (in case of Wisconsin, Chicago). Checks were to be forwarded to the bank for collection and credit in accordance with instructions which were issued simultaneously to the governors of the various federal reserve banks. As soon as the check deposited had been collected, the reserve bank was authorized to forward to the state agency a duplicate certificate of deposit which would constitute the agency's initial receipt. The triplicate of the certificate of deposit was to be returned to the depositor, which in the case of Wisconsin would be the state treasurer. "As soon as this department receives advice from the Federal Reserve Bank of the making of such a deposit, we will forward to you a certificate that such amount has been deposited, in the Unemployment Trust Fund, to the credit of the appropriate bank account." The Treasury's standard letter of procedural instructions to the several federal reserve banks in handling the states' deposits was in complete conformity with Secretary Morgenthau's assuring letter of January 21, 1936, quoted above.

The Wisconsin authorities replied to Secretary Morgenthau indicating that he had fully disposed of the questions raised in the Wisconsin commission's letter of January 6. They said, in part, "In view of your clear-cut explanation and interpretation of Section 904 of the Social Security Act, we are entirely satisfied to make deposits in the Unemployment Trust Fund pursuant to your letter, . . . in accordance with that section." The letter also announced that Wisconsin's first deposit for this trust fund would be sent to the Federal Reserve Bank of Chicago, on Monday, January 27, and would be in the amount of $4,000,000. It enclosed a copy of the resolution adopted by the Industrial Commission on January 22 "promptly after receiving your air-mail letter of January 21" which directed the state treasurer of Wisconsin to issue checks for this purpose.

It may be interesting at this point to note the treasury's arrangements for handling the federal Unemployment Trust Fund. These were set forth in a memorandum, which, when shown to McKinley on February 28 by Mr. Collins, was being kept confidential pending agreement with Comptroller General McCarl, agreement which was subsequently obtained. In it the Treasury made provision for payments from the fund upon order by the state. It provided for an issuance of monthly statements by the Treasurer to the Commissioner of Accounts and Deposits. The Commissioner was then to send this statement together with all checks received during the month to the Comptroller General. It also set up certain instructions as to the kind of investments in which the fund should be placed, and it made provision for an audit of the earnings of the fund, together with the allocation of interest to each of the state divisions of the fund. It was the obvious intention of the procedural arrangements to keep the Comptroller General's hands off the administration of this fund and to restrict his authority simply to that of audit. This scheme for administration followed the practice of other trust funds which, as to withdrawals, are exempt from the usual appropriation procedures.

In interpreting the Treasury's plan for handling these moneys, Collins, Assistant Commissioner of Accounts and Deposits, said that the Treasury did not deal directly with any employer concerning the taxes he was paying into the fund under the state laws. This was a matter for the state agency itself to handle. The Treasury would deal only with the state agency. He volunteered this explanation, because the Federal Reserve Bank of New York had sent on an inquiry from Hurwitz of the New York Unemployment Compensation Administration about whether the Treasury, through the bank, would receive checks for state unemployment compensation taxes direct from employers.

EARLY INABILITY TO HELP
NEW STATE ADMINISTRATIVE AGENCIES

STAFF SHORTHANDEDNESS AND FIRST STATE CALLS FOR HELP

On November 15, 1936, the staff assigned to the board's unemployment compensation job consisted of a very few people (in addition to Altmeyer), with Merrill Murray and Wilbur J. Cohen carrying the brunt of the work. And because Murray was also being used by the board for its general administrative purposes and for public relations work, this meant that the time available for thinking about the administrative problems of the states which had just passed unemployment insurance acts was limited indeed. As a matter of fact, Murray and Cohen were giving most of their time and effort to advising state groups interested in the enactment of new legislation for unemployment insurance.

One of the first complaints about the board which McKinley heard on arrival in Washington had to do with its failure to develop suggestions for administrative rules and regulations and for reporting, to help the states start their unemployment compensation administrations. This complaint came from Meredith Givens, who was then helping the board find personnel. Givens had recently accepted a position as head of the research and statistics division in the New York unemployment compensation organization and was spending only part time with the board. He may have been expressing the disappointment of Glen Bowers (his New York chief), who had received no assistance on these difficult problems. Givens was impressed by the urgent need for such advice for the District of Columbia, New York, New Hampshire, Massachusetts, and the three other states which at that time were trying to set up their unemployment compensation administrations.[6] New York had already drafted its forms for employers to report wages and hours. The state administrator had just sent them out. While the forms were said to be tentative, they had actually been passed upon favorably by the advisory council to the state administration, and were expected to be final. They were being withheld from final approval chiefly because a meeting of the Republican state convention was soon to take place, and the New York administrator wanted to avoid any political discussion of them.

At about this time, McKinley asked Altmeyer why the board was not more concerned with unemployment compensation administration. He replied that the board felt the most urgent question to be settled was that of the registration of employees, which would be useful both for contributory old age benefits and for unemployment compensation. The board, he said, wanted to key the old age benefit registration procedures and forms to the unemployment compensation symbols and records.[7] Both Altmeyer and Winant seemed to feel that the board would have ample time to go ahead with unemployment compensation administration problems as soon as they had settled the initial

[6] California, Alabama, and Oregon. Washington was making no move to start; neither was Utah, which had a defective statute. Wisconsin had been under way for two years.

[7] It is interesting that the decisions concerning the registration for old age benefits were not made until nearly eight months later.

questions relating to old age benefit administration. Perhaps M. Tixier's emphasis upon meshing the record systems for both into one unified plan was responsible, in part, for this attitude. Certainly Tixier stressed the need of curtailing duplicate reports from employers. Nevertheless, his memo of November 22 insisted that the employee registration should be postponed until January 1937.

The District of Columbia officials felt that the board had been of no assistance to them. Corporation Counsel Prettyman had taken the initiative in attemping to secure from the board suggestions about rules and regulations for promulgation at the beginning of the District administration. He reported, however, that the board's staff was too busy with other things. As a result, the District commissioners had made use of the services of Reagh and Shepherd of the Treasury Department, who had worked out for them a system of payroll reporting. (The District commissioners abandoned that plan, however, because of the expense involved.) Later a private organization of comptrollers and accountants in Washington, D.C., proposed a scheme of payroll reporting which the administrators took as the basis for the plan ultimately adopted. The formulation of rules and regulations was almost entirely the work of Prettyman and John Marshall, the District insurance administrator.

Prettyman indicated on December 13 that he had never been able to see the chairman of the Social Security Board about the District's problems. He said that he and the other District people did not want to thrust themselves upon the board, and were "waiting for the board to show a desire to discuss the situation with the District."

The board's expert on forms and reports, Elwood Way, said on December 11, 1936, that Hurwitz of the New York administration had recently asked him to come up and help work out forms which would tie the old age benefit scheme to unemployment compensation; but Way had not been able to find time to do this.

The anxiety of the New Hampshire employers and state administrators to prepare for the administration of their unemployment insurance act, which was to become effective January 1, 1936, led them to use a private organization to get started. They obtained the services of Professor C. A. Kulp, a member of the staff of the Committee on Social Security of the Social Science Research Council, who went to New Hampshire and worked out report forms, procedures, and general methods to be followed. Before going to New Hampshire, he prospected the Social Security Board's staff for aid, with but scant results.[8] His suggestions were used (with small changes) to set the

[8] John Pearson of the New Hampshire Foundation, who was the chief stimulus for effective administrative organization in New Hampshire, had come to the board for help in October. He too had found it unprepared.

New Hampshire system going. New Hampshire was the first state after Wisconsin to begin the collection of contributions. The board had played no part in this enterprise.

During the second week of December 1935, T. Morris Dunne traveled across the continent from Oregon, for advice from the board on how to proceed in making rules and regulations and designing reports for the new unemployment compensation act which Oregon had just passed, and which was soon to go into effect. Three weeks before Dunne came to Washington he had scarcely heard of unemployment compensation and knew nothing about it. As a member of the Industrial Accident Commission of Oregon, to which body the legislature had added the unsolicited task of unemployment compensation administration, Dunne urgently needed information and advice. During his stay in Washington he had conversations with Bane, Lambert McCallister of the legal staff, and Keith Tindale (Bane's administrative assistant), but he was unable to talk with anyone qualified to advise him about forms and procedures and the interpretative regulations for the Oregon statute. While the board people had been very kind and anxious to aid him, they had been unable to actually furnish any of the technical assistance which he required.[9]

Dunne's view of what the board might contribute to states facing the inauguration of unemployment compensation administration is indicated in the following paraphrase of an interview on December 12, 1935:

The Social Security Board could do its greatest service to the states right now if they would send someone out in the field to advise the states which have passed laws on unemployment compensation how to proceed with the making of definitions elaborating the statutes which they must enforce. The same representative ought likewise to help them set up the report forms to be required of employers and employees. Both these are important right now so that all the states get off on the same basis, so far as that is possible, and so that the national unemployment compensation picture will have some degree of uniformity about it. This is more urgent than the problem of old age benefits because the job of immediately giving answers to employers and employees is upon the states that have adopted unemployment compensation acts.

When Murray returned from Minnesota, he expressed the opinion that the problem of interstate coverage (which very much bothered Dunne) could not be solved by anyone until more was known about the extent and nature

---

[9] At the time of Dunne's visit, Murray was away from Washington advising the Minnesota legislature about the provisions of bills on unemployment compensation then being considered. Cohen, his chief assistant, had been compelled to take a vacation on account of illness due to overwork, and Walter Couper, the most recent technician added to the staff, was in Vermont advising the state legislators there on the substance of bills being considered.

of interstate employment. This was a matter for research during the coming year, and an item for that purpose had been included in the proposed budget. He and Altmeyer had come to the conclusion that the federal government would have to step in and, by agreement with the states, finance the care of employees in this "no man's land." He said that while there ought to be legislation by Congress at the coming session to fill this gap, it would probably be inadvisable to try to get it. Murray felt that the District of Columbia, and states like New Hampshire and New York which wanted to start their payroll tax collections in January 1936, should for the first year simply ask for summary payrolls. He was intending also to advise Alabama to do this. During the coming year, it would be possible to study the payroll report methods of employers and devise proper systems. He thought that perhaps the better employers could be trusted to keep the individual accounts of employees, rather than have the states do it.

Near the close of December 1936 the board began to recruit a staff of accountants to assist the states in working out their report forms. Altmeyer showed considerable concern that this job be tackled at once. It was the plan, he said, as soon as the board's accountants had crystalized their ideas, to call a meeting of the state unemployment compensation administrators to try to secure uniformity and standardization of report forms.

Even after the board's technical staff was sufficient to begin this work, there was considerable hesitation in offering services to the states, lest the board be saddled with the responsibility for all the administrative sins that might ultimately be committed by state administrators. Stanley Rector, who had been loaned to the board by the Wisconsin Industrial Commission, probably had more appropriate experience than any other member of the board's staff. He felt that the board should simply give consultative service on the basis of a written agreement setting out the limits of its advisory functions. Moreover, in giving advice, the board should have a number of alternative systems to suggest and should not urge the selection of any one system. He indicated that this was the approach being taken by Bachmann, who was then (February 8) working out suggested accounting systems for the states. Rector himself was developing tentative plans of organization for state agencies. He had one specifically for Alabama, which was a more simple scheme than those for the larger states.[10]

During the 1935 Christmas holidays a meeting was held in New York City, where the American Economic Association and the American Statistical Association were holding their annual sessions. Some of the problems of employer reporting, rules and regulations, and procedures for state administra-

[10] Miss Kathryn Fenn had already drafted forms for Alabama, and shortly afterward went to Montgomery to help set up the administration.

tion of unemployment compensation were discussed. This meeting was attended by Chairman Winant and several of the staff of the Unemployment Compensation Bureau. At that time Bowers, of New York, put to Winant the question of the board's inability to help the states get started. Winant, so Bowers later asserted, admitted that the board was unprepared to help.[11]

WAGENET'S ARRIVAL AND THE
GENERAL ORGANIZATION OF THE BUREAU'S WORK

The first head of the Unemployment Compensation Bureau, R. Gordon Wagenet, came on the job the last week in December 1935. He had been a regional director of the National Labor Relations Board, and had had a successful career before that as a negotiator and administrator in the field of employer-employee relations. He had no particular knowledge of unemployment compensation and no experience in its administration. This last handicap was, of course, characteristic of most members of the staff, since there was only one state in which an unemployment insurance law had been in operation before the adoption of the Social Security Act. There were in the United States a number of people attached to the universities or to research institutions who had rather ample knowledge of the provisions of European unemployment insurance statutes; but the administrative aspects of European unemployment insurance experience had received little attention by American students. Besides, there was no reason to assume that such knowledge, if possessed by such students, would be joined with the administrative competence required to take effective charge of a federal bureau.

Wagenet's conception of the immediate task before him was expressed to McKinley on December 30. He felt that the first job was the proposed model unemployment compensation bill. Work had been going forward actively on this measure during December, and on the twenty-seventh a meeting of a group of employers had been held to discuss the first draft of the proposed bill, and on the following day a similar conference with labor leaders took place. This model, or as it was later called "draft," bill was designed to supersede the draft bill prepared by the Committee on Economic Security the previous spring as the basis for state legislation. Once the bill was whipped into final shape for distribution to the states, the next task would be the

---

[11] On February 10 Bowers expressed to McKinley a belief that the board would never act in time to help the states. He reported that at the meeting in Washington January 23 (see below, page 238) when the New England, New York, and Wisconsin delegates met with the board and the Unemployment Compensation staff, nothing of importance to help the states had been offered by the board. He thought that the board was afraid to "stick its neck out."

preparation of forms and procedures needed to launch the state administrations. Wagenet said he was trying to recruit staff for this purpose, but was being delayed by the slowness with which the Civil Service Commission was approving his selections.

He differed with Murray about the advisability of collecting payroll report data during 1936. He felt that it was impossible to postpone the collection of detailed reports from employers pending a research inquiry into American employer practices. As he expressed it, "There isn't time enough to do this. States are already starting, and something must be got under way." After that, the bureau should build up its legislative field service so as to help the states enact legislation.

Wagenet's plans for organizing the bureau followed closely those already worked out tentatively by Murray, his assistant chief. He expected to have one division assigned to legislative service to the states, another on grants and procedures, a third on administrative advice on forms, procedure, and so forth, and a fourth to work out the coordinating arrangements between the unemployment insurance agencies and the employment exchange services. This was the theoretical organization pattern adopted and justified in the budget request, but as a matter of fact only two of the divisions functioned fully during most of the period studied. As will be shown later, the division charged with liaison with the Employment Service, after a few months of fruitless effort by a very small staff, became a subunit in the Division of Legislative Aid. The Division of Administrative Aid did not come fully to life until late in 1936.

A BRITISH EXPERT'S VIEWS

It may be worthwhile to indicate at this point the views on administration of a distinguished British authority, Ronald Davidson, who spent some time during December 1936 and early January 1937 giving advice to the board and its staff. Davidson had been in America for some months teaching at the University of Chicago. His distinguished career in the British Civil Service as an administrator of unemployment compensation made his opinion of peculiar interest. He expressed concern that the board seemed unable to get started on the preparation of suggested forms and procedures for the states. He felt that the talk then current in some of the states to the effect that employers should be permitted to keep individual records for employees boded ill for the administration of unemployment compensation when the time for benefit payments should arrive. In a good many cases it would be necessary to go back five years to secure the data needed to determine what benefits should be paid. People seemed to forget, he said, that the problem of administration "will be centered on the 40 percent or perhaps even a smaller minority of employees who are employed intermittently." For such people, who make the real administrative difficulties, the problem of record-keeping is very complicated. It cannot be left to employers over any extended period of time. He felt that the attitudes in the United States towards the administration of unemployment compensation were too much influenced by the Wisconsin system. That system, in his judgment, was so highly theoretical that it could not work out administratively.

Davidson was also concerned by the backwardness of state administration. He thought there was a special problem in that connection of which people were not aware. Unemployment compensation sets up contractual rights which the employee may enforce through the courts. Therefore if laxity in state administration exhausts the funds, the employee has a right to demand his rights by a court action. Also, if a partisan administration should be inclined to take a niggardly view of definitions or to exclude certain people from compensation to which they were entitled, the matter may be taken into the courts. Thus, he thought that because of the low efficiency and the political partiality of many state administrations, an extraordinary amount of litigation might ensue as soon as the time for benefit payments arrived.

Davidson was also skeptical about the prospects of success in administering so complicated a scheme of benefit payments as the American laws required. The British practice of paying substantially the same benefits for all employees regardless of wage rates made a much simpler problem of administration. While payments in accordance with wages earned is fine in theory, it placed a great burden upon administration. Before many years rolled by, the system, in his view, would have to be changed to something approximating the British practice. Finally, he was dubious about the solvency of the unemployment funds, first because the collections would not be adequate as a result of poor collection machinery, and second because the payments were likely to be too generous, owing to liberal interpretations of eligibility.

ASSOCIATION OF STATE UNEMPLOYMENT OFFICERS

On invitation of the board, delegates from the northeastern states met in Washington on January 23, 1936, to discuss the problems of unemployment compensation administration. The agenda, prepared by Wagenet and Murray, centered on six major topics: (1) definitions of employment for purposes of contribution; (2) variations from the exemptions provided in the federal act; (3) uniform payroll reporting; (4) feasibilty of cooperation between states and federal government in individual employee records; (5) required information for administrative grants; (6) coordination of registration numbers for unemployment compensation and old age benefits. The meeting was attended by delegates from Massachusetts, New Hampshire, Connecticut, Maine, New York, and Wisconsin.

Merrill Murray's summary of the discussion which occurred is as follows:

1. Definition of employment. This was the problem pointed particularly at the employees who work in more than one state. The desire was to make a definition which would be the same in each of the states and facilitate the obtaining of coverage by such employees. The statement contained in the proposed draft bill being prepared by the Unemployment Compensation Bureau of the board seemed acceptable to most of the delegates.

2. Differences of coverage by the state and federal laws. The variations that exist in the unemployment compensation acts as to the number of employees an employer must have before he becomes subject to the unemployment compensation taxes were regarded as undesirable. It was the consensus of all delegates that the state laws should be changed to a coverage of employers employing four or more persons. It was also the opinion that the federal act should be changed from eight or more to four or more.

3. The taxation laws designed to support unemployment compensation should be standardized so as to exempt employees' salaries above $3,000. The states agreed to make such changes in their laws and to ask the board to recommend to Congress a similar change in the federal Social Security Act.

4. The registration number question. The use, in the proposed registration number which was explained by Elwood Way, of a number to indicate the age of the employee was objected to by some of the states. An objection was also raised to a question on the proposed registration card concerning race.

5. The consensus of the meeting was that the employee registration task in the states having unemployment compensation should be turned over to the state organizations.

6. Uniformity of report forms. The group agreed that the summary forms to be asked of employers should be identical for all the states, but that the detailed reports should be allowed to vary, since no two laws were precisely the same.

7. Sample forms for applications by the states for grants-in-aid for the administration of unemployment compensation were presented to the group by Mr. Wagenet's bureau. These were discussed but no serious changes were suggested. The only important suggested change was that concerning the keeping of a journal of vouchers. This is being taken up by the bureau in considering the revision of the forms.

8. A future conference to be held in the middle of February 1936 in New York was agreed to. To this conference are to be invited all the states with acts. Mr. Glen Bowers is to be the chairman of this conference, which is not to be regarded as a Social Security Board affair.

Wilbur J. Cohen reported that while no definite conclusions had been reached, the meeting, which had rather been designed primarily to build good relations with the states, had been fairly successful in attaining that purpose.[12] This meeting and a second conference during February in New York were the beginning of a formal organization which was perfected at a conference March 23 and 24 in Washington. At that time, at the suggestion of Seidemann, the Association of State Unemployment Insurance Officers was organized. The name is somewhat deceptive, because the federal agencies concerned with the activities of these state departments were also members. This was made very clear in the appointment of the first executive committee, composed of Hurwitz of New York, McCartin of Massachusetts, Wagener of Wisconsin, Eager of New Hampshire, Marshall of the District of Columbia, Dr. Stead of the United States Employment Service, Dr. Lubin of the Bureau of Labor Statistics, and representatives to be named from the Unemployment Compensation Bureau of the Social Security Board. The New York meeting, which had been called by Bowers, was explained in his letter of invitation dated January 31, 1936, to the governors of the states, as follows:

At a meeting with members of the Social Security Board held in Washington a few days ago attended by representatives from New Hampshire, Massachusetts and New York the question of coordination of state activities in unemployment insurance was discussed. Particularly the question of administrative procedures was raised.

All those present felt that there are important opportunities for constructive work between the states themselves, as contrasted with procedures which would leave entirely to the federal Social Security Board all matters of unification and coordination of state activities. With this point of view the members of the Social Security Board and its staff agreed.

It was therefore suggested that a series of conferences of representatives from interested states, attended by representatives of the Social Security Board, might be of great advantage.

To the New York meeting were invited representatives from the following states, which were then either setting up unemployment insurance agencies or were contemplating the enactment of laws which would require such agencies: Alabama, California, the District of Columbia, Illinois, Indiana, Kentucky, Louisiana, Maine, Maryland, Massachusetts, Mississippi, Missouri, New Hampshire, New Jersey, New York, Ohio, Oregon, Rhode Island, South Carolina, Tennessee, Texas, Utah, Virginia, Washington, and

---

[12] At the close of the meeting, some of the delegates wanted to know if the board would pay their expenses from the grants to be made for defraying administrative costs. One delegate presented an expense account for $75, which the Comptroller General's office deducted from the balance of a $100 income tax which he still owed the Treasury.

Wisconsin. In addition to the states, the United States Employment Service and the Social Security Board were asked to send representatives. When the meeting convened on February 21, delegates were present from Alabama, California, Indiana, Massachusetts, New Hampshire, New York, Utah, Virginia, and Wisconsin. The most important question discussed was the problem of avoiding duplication in the coverage of employees working in more than one state. No conclusion was reached, but a committee was appointed which made a preliminary report and was asked to present a further report at the next meeting. The other items covered at the New York meeting related chiefly to the problems of account numbers to be assigned employees and employers and to the information to be given the Social Security Board in making application for a grant of administrative funds for unemployment insurance.

At the March 1936 meeting in Washington, when the organization was perfected, the matter of a uniform number system for employees was again presented, and there appeared to be a consensus that the plan proposed by the Social Security Board through Elwood Way was acceptable.

When the question of uniform payroll forms was presented by Seidemann and Bachmann, who advocated the standardization of payroll forms for various types of employers, there was almost unanimous objection from the state officials. They were of the opinion that any attempt to prescribe payroll forms would be resented by employers. They also questioned the feasibility of a standard form which would provide payroll information that the employers would want while at the same time giving the data needed for unemployment compensation. The state representatives took the position that they should confine themselves to prescribing the minimum payroll information employers would have to provide for unemployment compensation purposes. They should leave the form of the payroll entirely to the employers.

Perhaps the most valuable part of the meeting was the testimony of each state representative on progress in the work of getting his administration under way. There was a general exchange of experiences in meeting difficulties. This was very useful at this stage of administration. The Social Security Board people also raised the question of standardizing personnel qualifications and employment office organization. These problems were commented upon in the light of each state's existing practice, but no definite conclusions were reached.[13]

The board and its staff looked upon these conferences of state compensation officials as so useful that Altmeyer announced at the March 1936 meeting the board's intention of making generous travel allowances in the ad-

[13] The questions of personnel and the attitude of the association toward it are discussed more fully in chapter 7.

ministrative grants to the states, to encourage the state administrators to attend the meetings.[14] During the following twelve months the conferences (with increased membership) were held three times (July in Crawford Notch, New Hampshire, October in Madison, Wisconsin, and March in Washington), and the discussion as well as the action of the officers of the association became increasingly independent. It played a part of growing importance in influencing the board on questions of administration, in the development of standards for state legislation, in facilitating the growth of incipient standards of state administration, and in working out plans for state reciprocity in the payment of benefits for migrating workers. Following is a summary of those questions that tended to constantly recur in the discussions of this association, and the extent to which they had been resolved by March 1937:

1. Contributions for interstate workers. A definition of employment had finally been agreed upon which, if adopted, would more or less automatically allocate workers to either one state or another.
2. Account numbers. The board had finally secured permission from the Treasury to turn over duplicates of the old age benefits registration cards, with account numbers, to the state unemployment compensation commissions.
3. Statistical requirements. Although the board had approved one set of statistical requirements for state agencies as early as May 29, 1936, they had not yet been promulgated at the conference in March 1937. Instead, a promise was made to submit a preliminary draft of the requirements to the states by May 1, 1937, for criticism. A uniform system of occupational classifications had been worked out, and arrangements were made for experts of the Bureau of Research and Statistics to install them on request.
4. Payment of benefits to migratory workers. No detailed arrangement had been made for meeting the problem of benefit payments to (a) workers who moved to another state and became unemployed after having built up benefit rights in one state; (b) workers who would be eligible for benefits only on the combined employment records in two or more states. At the March 1937 conference, Murray submitted a proposed amendment to the Social Security Act which would empower the board to act as agent and coordinator for agreements between the state commissions to act as each others' agents in paying benefits. State officials considered this plan far too ambitious, and it was agreed only to work out a system whereby the first group (a) of employees would be handled. The second state would merely take registration for benefits determined by the first state under its own laws.
5. Personnel standards. The board had endeavored to encourage the states to set up personnel systems on a merit basis, and had offered its services in so doing. Nevertheless relatively little progress had been made, and the con-

---

[14] This practice was like that of the U.S. Public Health Service in subsidizing attendance at the meetings of the State and Territorial Health Officers' Association.

ference of that date in Washington in March 1937 went on record as favoring the merit system and requesting the technical help of the board on examinations and classification. The first resolution of the committee on personnel standards, inspired by the board, calling for a college-trained personnel officer for each state agency and a uniform system of classification (but not of compensation) for all state agencies, was voted down.

6. Contributions and records. By the March conference no decision had been reached on uniformity of records and contribution procedures, although it appeared likely that most states would go over to the quarterly reporting procedure of the January, 1937, edition of the board's draft bill.

ADVISING THE STATES ON
UNEMPLOYMENT COMPENSATION
LEGISLATION

CONTINUED USE OF MODEL BILL
DRAFTED BY THE COMMITTEE ON ECONOMIC SECURITY

The story of the board's activity in influencing state legislation on unemployment compensation is the sequel to that of similar work started by the Committee on Economic Security. The COEC prepared a model draft bill for the states that was largely the work of Paul Raushenbush, who headed the Wisconsin unemployment compensation administration. That bill was used to answer inquiries from state groups interested in securing laws which would conform to the requirements of the Social Security Act and furnish a proper basis for state unemployment insurance.

The state of Washington had copied that model bill almost verbatim. New York had asked for advice on unemployment insurance from the COEC, but had its own ideas on which its law was ultimately based. Professor Herman Feldman of Dartmouth College was chiefly instrumental in drafting the New Hampshire law, although he had come to Washington and spent a couple of days discussing policy and legal provisions with Merrill Murray and other members of the staff of the Committee. In Massachusetts the supporters of legislation paid no attention to the Committee's model bill but followed New York and New Hampshire as their guides.

During the interval between the adoption of the Social Security Act and the establishment of the Social Security Board, Murray had gone to Alabama and had taken part in the drafting of a bill which became law on September 14, 1935. The Utah people had asked for advice which had been given by letter, but they largely disregarded it in the final measure enacted. In the case of California, a voluminous long-distance correspondence had been carried on between Murray and the California group pushing unemployment insurance. At the last moment, certain amendments had been inserted which allowed the state administrative agency to permit companies to contract out their insurance.

The original Ellenbogen Unemployment Compensation Bill for the District of Columbia had been drafted with the aid of Murray and had been based upon the model pooled unemployment compensation bill prepared by the Committee on Economic Security. In the Senate this bill was completely revised at the insistence of Senator King of the Senate District Committee. Murray took a prominent part in this redrafting. Wilbur Cohen asserts that criticisms developed during the enactment of the District bill served to show the necessity for revising the committee's model bill.

As a result Murray, with the assistance of Thomas Eliot and a staff of NRA lawyers, began work in the autumn of 1935 on a careful redraft of the previous model measure. This redraft was well under way by the middle of November 1935. Because the staff was small, however, and burdened with other duties, progress on it was then very slow. Murray was being used to contact state legislative groups for the public assistance functions as well as unemployment compensation. He had recently been in Illinois and Nebraska and found that the attitudes toward unemployment compensation in the states were changing. Whereas a year before there had been many appeals for advice and information, now there appeared to be resentment if advice was offered, and there was much talk about federal "dictation." This attitude had been present in Nebraska despite the fact that each house of the legislature had passed a resolution inviting Murray to come out and help them. The manufacturers were taking a strong stand to prevent the adoption of unemployment compensation. Murray had just received reliable information that in Illinois the Manufacturers' Association was quite willing to lose its 1 percent tax for the sake of helping to defeat the establishment of an unemployment compensation system.

During the first part of December 1935, Murray spent ten days in Minnestoa working with both the labor people and the Manufacturers' Association in the endeavor to get their separate proposals near enough together to secure enactment of a desirable measure. One of his assistants, Walter Couper, was in Vermont during this same period on a similar mission. All during this time the staff attempted to keep abreast of proposals being introduced in the state legislatures, making analyses of proposed amendments to see if they conformed to the requirements of the Social Security Act and to good practice. They were also giving advice, by correspondence, to officials and laymen in the states. At the close of 1935 there were eight states with acceptable laws, and three more—Mississippi, Indiana, and Rhode Island—adopted laws during the first three months of 1936.

PROMULGATION OF BOARD'S "DRAFT" BILLS, JANUARY 1936

Early in January the first edition of the revised draft of what was formerly called the Model Unemployment Compensation Bill was mimeographed, and copies were first distributed at the Columbia, South Carolina, meeting of the American Association for Labor Legislation in January, which Wagenet, Murray, and Winant attended. The revised draft was the fruit of months of study and discussion. Certain errors in copying the text were discovered, and this held up general distribution of the document until the end of January. It was no longer called the "model" bill, but was the "draft bills for state unemployment compensation of pooled funds or employers' reserve account type." The insistence upon the word *draft* in place of *model* was the result of the board's anxiety to escape the odium of "dictating" to the states.

The publication was not one draft bill but two draft bills, and as finally issued these were entirely distinct. Numerous alternative provisions were suggested in both measures. Even the administrative organization was presented in terms of alternatives. For the reserve draft bill a special alternative was suggested which provided for partial pooling of contributions.

As an accompaniment to this document went a revision of the pamphlet on actuarial factors in state unemployment compensation plans, to supplant the similar document issued in September 1935 which had been based upon the old model unemployment compensation bill. It was designed particularly to guide the state legislatures in deciding upon the dates of contribution, the amount of benefit payments, and the length of waiting periods. The discussion in this pamphlet was, of course, based upon the standards suggested in the new draft bills.

As indicated, this document had not only received the study of the legal and technical staff of the board; it had also been criticized by groups of employers known to be sympathetic to unemployment insurance and by representatives of the labor unions. Thus it was issued with the assurance that it would receive the backing of both of these forces.

Altmeyer had high hope that the new definition of employment contained in this draft measure would narrow the number of people excluded from coverage because of the problems of interstate employment. This was one of the questions constantly recurring in connection with the advice sought by states when they were supplementing their acts by interpretative rules and regulations. Altmeyer expected that it would eliminate the practice of duplication in coverage, as well as reduce the numbers left in the no-man's-land between state jurisdictions. During the discussion in New York on February 21 and 22, 1936, when the state unemployment insurance administrative officers met, important questions were raised concerning the adequacy of the new definition, but it still remained to be seen how far the interstate coverage problem had been solved.

The legislative aid division had taken an active part in the formulation of unemployment insurance legislation in Indiana and in Mississippi. It had also sent staff members out as far as Colorado. But during most of 1936, interest in unemployment compensation legislation on the part of state legislatures was at a low ebb. The attitude of most employers, labor unions, and state officials seemed to be that the unemployment compensation features of the Social Security Act would be declared unconstitutional. Employers were therefore not greatly interested in recovering for state compensation purposes 90 percent of the federal tax under Title IX of the Social Security Act. Activity was also reduced because most state legislatures did not meet in even-numbered years. Wherever there was some local pressure for passage of such legislation, employers shifted their tactics from opposition, to taking the initiative in pressing for individual employer reserve or partial pooling types of state laws. Whenever the board's staff pointed out the inadequacy of these employer promoted schemes, they aroused the opposition of the employer groups.

This was well illustrated during the enactment of the Indiana law early in 1936, when the bureau's representatives incurred the wrath of the General Electric Company, one of whose accountants, Mr. Cliff, had drafted a bill for unemployment compensation and spent six weeks before the session formulating his scheme and building up his connections with the legislators. As a result, the bill which the board's staff helped the governor's advisor to draft had been drastically modified by the Cliff substitute bill, after it got into the legislature. It was reported that during consideration, Cliff was on the floor of the houses and was permitted to discuss the measure with the freedom of a member of the legislature, whenever questions were raised. Nevertheless his proposal, which included very low benefit payments to unskilled workers, was defeated. Later he went to Ohio and threatened to fight the board's draft proposals in every state. Later in the spring there was considerable activity in Kentucky, where the State Federation of Labor (and particularly the United Mine Workers) seemed to have made a deal with the employers to accept an employer reserve unemployment compensation bill in exchange for a better workmen's compensation law. The situation in Ohio was still uncertain, with a great deal of employer opposition, and the Pennsylvania Democratic House had passed a law that seemed likely to be killed in the Senate.

On June 6, 1936, South Carolina passed a law based upon the board's January draft bill. There was little opposition to the legislation itself, but a controversy did develop in the legislature over who was to administer the law and dispense the patronage connected with it. The Senate wished to put the administration under the State Industrial Commission of five members (which had only the Workmen's Compensation Law to administer). In view of the composition of this Industrial Commission, the board pressed for the appointment of an independent unemployment compensation commission. The House was agreeable to this arrangement, but because it had been having a disagreement with the governor over state highways, it insisted that the members of the unemployment compensation commission be appointed by the legislature, and in this form the bill finally passed.

During June, the governor of Louisiana came to Washington, anxious to patch up the feud between the Roosevelt Administration and the Huey Long machine. He expressed his willingness to pass any kind of unemployment compensation law that the board wanted, and took back copies of the January draft bill with him. A pooled-fund law based on it was pushed through by June 29. There was one incident in the passage of this Louisiana bill which influenced the work of the Bureau of Unemployment Compensation with other state legislatures later in the year. Even though the governor's office was in constant telephonic and telegraphic communication with the bureau in Washington, when this law was finally passed it was found that it could not be approved because "Unemployment Trust Fund" had been used in the place where "Unemployment Compensation Administration Fund" should have been used. It was necessary to pass another statute correcting this error. As a result of this experience, the bureau decided that in the future it would be necessary to have its representative on the spot when bills were going through the legislatures, to see that no mistakes of this kind were repeated.

On August 6 Idaho passed a law, and on August 29 Utah repealed its old and defective law passed on March 25, 1935, and substituted another based on the January 1936 draft bill.

BASIC REVISION OF THE BOARD'S DRAFT BILLS

At the end of April 1936, the legislative division of the bureau had decided to design a new draft bill to supersede the January draft. The principle upon which the latter had been based was the same as that in the draft bill of the Committee on Economic Security: that unemployment compensation benefits rested upon previous weeks of employment and the employer was obliged to report the hours which his employees worked each week and the wages which they received. New Hampshire was the only state which attempted to secure complete records on each employee covered by the law in the year 1936, and in the spring of 1936 it was already apparent that the requirements of the draft bill, as demonstrated by the experience of New Hampshire, would impose too great an administrative burden on both the state unemployment compensation agencies and the employers.

The Bureau of Unemployment Compensation, particularly Associate Director Murray, were well aware that the provisions of the January draft bill were too complex for effective administration, and several alternative plans were suggested and discussed. One of these was to use a scheme, prepared for a national unemployment insurance act for the railroad industry, which provided that benefits would be based on wages lost rather than weeks of unemployment. Another was the principle proposed by Cliff, of the General Electric Company, which provided that employers would report quarterly total wages earned by each of their employees and the total number of weeks worked during the quarter. Benefits would be one-thirteenth of the second-highest quarterly earnings during the previous year. The second of these plans seemed most feasible to the Bureau of Unemployment Compensation, and a considerable period was spent by Cliff and the staff of the bureau in trying to work out some modification of his plan for incorporation in the new draft bill. This cooperation was partly the result of the merit of the scheme and partly an attempt to divert Cliff from his lobbying activities with state legislatures. The bureau's criticism of the Cliff plan had been that its plan of benefit payments seemed less favorable to the lower-paid employees than the provisions of the January 1936 draft bill.

During May 1936, Cliff agreed to abandon his legislative activities if the board would incorporate his plan into a new draft bill. A series of compromises was worked out, and a start was actually made by Couper of the Bureau of Unemployment Compensation on a new bill based upon his plan. Each time it was submitted to Cliff that gentleman raised additional objections, and finally there were no elements for compromise left. If the Bureau of Unemployment Compensation had continued to work with him, the result would have been nothing but the original Cliff plan. By the first of June Cliff had ceased his cooperation with the bureau and had started working with a group of employers in New York on his own draft.

There was one other reason for pigeonholing the quarterly report scheme at this time: the Bureau of Unemployment Compensation and the Bureau of Internal Revenue had not yet decided whether employers would be required to report monthly, or quarterly, under the old age benefits provisions of the act. (Late in June it was decided that employers would be required to pay taxes under Title VIII monthly, but to furnish quarterly information returns on the wages earned by individual employees.)

Toward the middle of July 1936, Murray told Frase that an almost completely revised draft bill was going to be taken up with the state administrators at their conference in New Hampshire late that month. It was based on the Cliff scheme of quarterly reporting. Murray believed that it would enormously simplify the burden on employers but would be resisted by the statisticians and the research people, who wanted to get as much statistical information as possible from the employer reports, even to the number of hours worked by each employee. Cliff's original plan contemplated only the reporting of total wages of each quarter, and would not have enabled the employment compensation agencies to determine the amount of overtime work. Murray believed that the compromise plan basing benefits on one-thirteenth of the quarterly wages in the highest quarter of the previous two years would do away with most of the difficulties in existing state unemployment compensation laws and retain most of their advantages, without imposing a heavy administrative burden on both employers and state agencies. He felt that a simplified reporting procedure had to be worked out if the principle of paying benefits in accordance with previous earnings was not to be sacrificed to a flat-rate benefit scheme like that of the British. He had not yet succeeded in getting board approval of this quarterly scheme, because Wagenet was afraid that it would be less fair to the employee than benefits based on full-time weekly earnings.

At the conference of state officers in New Hampshire, Murray presented his plan in detail to a committee composed of Smith of New Hampshire, McCartin of Massachusetts, Scott of Louisiana, and Dunne of Oregon. Frase's impression at the meeting was that the state people seemed unable to comprehend the importance of this matter. Smith of New Hampshire, the one person who had had experience with the maintenance of employee records on the full-time weekly wage scheme, was the only exception. Murray and Smith tried to push through a recommendation by the committee in favor of the quarterly reporting reform, but the committee preferred to recommend that it be studied further. The conference as a whole voted to accept this recommendation of the committee. Wagenet looked upon the idea a bit more favorably when he learned that the state officials were not strongly opposed to it.

Work was continued on the new draft bill, and by the first of December mimeographed copies were available for distribution in the states which were considering unemployment compensation legislation during December 1936. As has been explained elsewhere, because of the favorable action of the Supreme Court in upholding the New York unemployment insurance law in November 1936, and the board's announcement in that same month that it would not recommend to Congress that states passing laws in 1937 would have their 1936 taxes under Title IX rebated to them, there was a great rush of legislation during December. A great many states adopted the new quarterly report system then and during the first three months of 1937. In fact, by the end of March it appeared that practically all of the states had either shifted or would shift to the quarterly system.

In its concentration on the evils of the reporting system incorporated in the January 1936 draft bill, the Bureau of Unemployment Compensation had almost entirely neglected a related problem of employer reporting, namely the procedure for reporting part-time work for the payment of partial unemployment benefits. Many states had adopted the provisions of the earlier draft bills, that partial benefits would be paid for workers on part time. This problem was fortunately brought to the attention of the bureau in January 1937. Paul Raushenbush, director of the unemployment compensation division of the Industrial Commission of Wisconsin, pointed out that if employers reported only the total wages for each employee for each quarter, the state agency would have no means of knowing when employees were only partially employed, and no basis for paying partial benefits to them. Wisconsin had kept to its original scheme of paying total benefits on a termination report supplied by the employer when the worker became unemployed; and the current reporting of low earnings for the payment of partial benefits. Therefore it was not directly concerned with the problem. New York brought it up later in January 1937, because they were planning to urge their legislature to change over to the quarterly system. The Bureau of Unemployment Compensation was given several days by the New York officials to suggest some method whereby employers would report partial unemployment on the quarterly scheme, but at the end of this period the bureau was forced to admit frankly that it had no solution to the problem. Subsequently, the New York Division of Placement and Unemployment Insurance submitted amendments to the New York law which provided for the shift to quarterly reporting, but they themselves had not succeeded in working out any reporting procedure for partial unemployment at that time. When this study came to a close at the end of March 1937, no procedure had yet been evolved for paying partial unemployment compensation benefits, although several states which were scheduled to start benefit payments on January 1, 1938, had such provisions in their laws.

THE SCRAMBLE FOR STATE LAWS, THE END OF 1936

From August to late November 1936 only one state, Texas, adopted an unemployment compensation law. In the autumn of that year it seemed almost certain to the board that the bulk of new state legislation would have to wait until the forty-three state legislatures should be in session in the year 1937.

Then came the decision of the Supreme Court on November 23 upholding the New York Court of Appeals in validating the New York unemployment compensation law. There had already been considerable sentiment in Congress for legislation which would enable the states that did not adopt laws during 1936 to obtain a refund of the 90 percent of tax collections under Title IX, in case they enacted laws during 1937. But the day following the high court's pronouncement, the Social Security Board announced that it would oppose such legislation. An epidemic of special legislative sessions broke out in the states, and in the scramble which followed a total of eighteen laws were adopted during December. By midnight on December 31, 1936, there were thirty-six states with unemployment compensation laws. Members of the Social

Security Board held themselves in readiness until the stroke of midnight the last day of the year, to take action on state legislation, but this turned out not to be necessary.

The Bureau of Unemployment Compensation was swamped with demands for assistance in putting through state legislation, and it was necessary to send out staff members who had had no previous experience with this type of work, because Murray and Couper could not handle it alone.

The bureau's difficulties were not lessened by the fact that the director of the United States Employment Service had ordered the state employment service directors to work with the state legislatures to make sure that state employment services were designated the official recipients of Wagner-Peyser funds, rather than the state unemployment compensation commissions.

In Iowa, for example, Regional Director McCarthy was requested by Murray to work with the legislature, because there were no staff members from the Bureau of Unemployment Compensation available. When McCarthy arrived in the state capital he found Wilcox, the regional director from Minneapolis, in whose region the state of Iowa was located, already there, but Wilcox soon departed and McCarthy remained to handle the situation. The only point on which any controversy developed (frequently true in the passage of this legislation) was the location of the administrative agency. McCarthy wanted to make sure that unemployment compensation and the employment service were kept together, but he regarded the labor commissioner as a rather incompetent individual and therefore advised the setting up of a new agency headed by a part-time board. The commissioner of labor naturally put up a fight and had his friends in the legislature attack McCarthy for meddling in state legislation, asserting that McCarthy had no business in Iowa anyway because it was not in his region. The labor commissioner also protested by telegraph to the Bureau of Unemployment Compensation in Washington, and Murray wired back that McCarthy had been sent to Iowa only because they were short of people and he was the only person available.

Meanwhile John Gross, the newly appointed unemployment compensation representative in the Denver regional office, had been asked to stop in Iowa to work on unemployment compensation legislation on his way to Denver. He found that the committee had accepted McCarthy's plan for keeping unemployment compensation and the employment service together. McCarthy explained to Gross that he had recently discussed this matter with Wagenet and Altmeyer and they had urged him to press for this type of state agency, which was a part-time per diem commission with a full-time executive. When the labor commissioner telephoned Washington, Murray called Gross and insisted that what the bureau really wanted was a full-time paid commission of three; so Gross had to go to the committee the next morning and unsell the idea which McCarthy had induced them to adopt. Both McCarthy and Gross were very much upset about the way in which the bureau had refused to back up their field agents and had made them look ridiculous to the state legislatures.

There were similar situations in other states, because of the conflict between the bureau and the United States Employment Service. In Montana, the state officials decided that the state commission which was to administer both unemployment compensation and the state employment service should be the official agency for Wagner-Peyser purposes. Gross helped them draft a law on this basis, but was called by Wagenet's office and asked why he had not designated the state employment service rather than the commission. He told them that this was not his affair, that the state people wanted it and that he proposed to follow their wishes. What had happened was that news of the proposal had got to the United States Employment Service representative and he had wired Director Persons, who immediately got after the board.

In addition to conflicts with its own field staff, the bureau also got into difficulties with the Office of the General Counsel, which naturally regarded bill-drafting as its own special province. In addition to the unemployment compensation lawyers in Washington, there were attorneys in many of the regional offices with very little to do and eager to get into this field. In Ohio one of the lawyers from Washington, after working for two days with the legislature, was suddenly called back by the Bureau of Unemployment Compensation and replaced by one of its own staff. There was a similar situation in the Minneapolis regional office. The regional director felt that the staff member from the Bureau of Unemployment Compensation who was sent up to work with the Minnesota people was much less capable of handling the technicalities of this legislation than his regional attorney who had been requested to stay out of the picture. He was even more annoyed about the developments in North Dakota, where there had been a steady procession in and out of the governor's chair for the past two or three years. Regional Director Wilcox had gotten in touch with Governor Langer, the incumbent at that time, and Langer had shown a great deal of interest in the legislation. Wilcox then sent Miss Harrison, his regional attorney, out to North Dakota to talk to the governor and several groups of interested people. Wilcox felt it was necessary to do something about bringing these groups together quietly and reasonably before the legislature came into session, when the whole matter might be thrown into the political arena. But after Miss Harrison had been there for two days the Bureau of Unemployment Compensation wired Wilcox to have her withdraw, because one of the Washington staff was going to handle the legislation in North Dakota.

In Delaware the manufacturing interests attempted to take advantage of the provisions of Title IX of the Social Security Act which allowed employers to make use of the maximum offset of the federal tax under state laws providing for merit rating. By incorporating provisions in the state law that contribution rates might be reduced to zero when a certain reserve had been set up, and by putting in a waiting period of ten or twenty weeks with very low benefit rates, it would be possible for the employers in a state to escape almost entirely from both federal and state taxes for unemployment compensation. Jerome Frank and others had foreseen this danger when the Social Security Act was being drafted, but this was the first time that there was any real attempt to use these loopholes. The general counsel was of the opinion that the only thing the board could do would be fight for the defeat of the bill in the legislature, because if it were passed it would have to be approved. It developed that the bill was not to pass until 1937, and by that time these objectionable provisions had been eliminated.

Considerable legislative activity continued in the first few months of 1937. By the time the Supreme Court upheld the unemployment compensation provisions of the Social Security Act and the unemployment compensation law of Alabama, late in May 1937, twelve more states had passed laws, bringing the total to forty-eight. Thus the effort of the Bureau of Unemployment Compensation to get state legislatures to pass laws which would not be dependent upon the constitutionality of the federal act was wasted. There were, however, eight states with such laws, including the large states of New York, New Jersey, and Pennsylvania. Several other states took a compromise position urged by the bureau when it was impossible to get them to pass completely independent state laws. This compromise consisted in a provision that the law should be temporarily suspended in the event the federal law was held unconstitutional, until the state legislatures had had time to meet and decide what action to take.

Practically all of the later laws were pooled fund with or without merit rating. Another variation which seemed to be regarded favorably was a law providing for five-sixths employer reserve and one-sixth pooling. This type of law was adopted in Kentucky, South Dakota, Indiana, and Nebraska. The official position of the board and of the Bureau of Unemployment Compensation was still one of neutrality in judging the respective merits of the pooled fund and the employer reserve laws, but unofficially the entire bureau was in favor of a pooled fund and had really exerted its influence to secure the passage of that kind of legislation.

THE PROCESS OF MAKING
ADMINISTRATIVE GRANTS TO THE STATES

By the time the board began to prepare for the making of grants to the states for unemployment compensation administration, there were some six states whose laws had been approved as conforming to Title IX of the Social

Security Act. These were Wisconsin, New Hampshire, California, Oregon, Alabama, and the District of Columbia.[15] It must be recalled, however, that for a state to be eligible for federal money for administering its unemployment insurance system it had also to conform to the requirements of Title III. This was the title that required methods of administration "reasonably calculated to secure full payment of unemployment compensation when due." It also required a "fair hearing" opportunity for individuals denied payments; it stipulated the payment of all moneys received "in unemployment trust fund of such state, immediately upon such receipt, to the Secretary of the Treasury to the credit of the Unemployment Trust Fund. . . ." Thus it appeared that the states would have to run the gauntlet of federal approval for their acts twice, even though in the second approval the matter most emphasized was the plan of administration.

DELAYS IN INITIAL GRANTS, PROBLEMS OF STATE PLANS

Wagenet's staff began to work out the forms to be used by the states for submitting their plans for approval under Title III very early in January 1936. On February 8 Rector indicated that the work was going forward rather slowly. The board as a whole had not discussed the proposed forms, and the prospects of making grants as speedily as for public assistance purposes were not good.

It was not till March 4 that Wagenet reported his bureau ready to make recommendations for grants to the District of Columbia, New Hampshire, and New York. He also had, on that date, estimates from California and Wisconsin. Nevertheless, the board was not ready to grant the sums recommended that day, because the procedure which had been followed by Wagenet did not satisfy it. The board insisted that recommendations be brought to it with clearances from the General Counsel's Office and from the Bureau of Accounts and Audits, together with papers for the board to sign, constituting the finding and the certification to the Treasury. As a consequence of this discussion, a staff committee was appointed to work out the forms.

The first grant was for New Hampshire and was given on March 5, 1936, an allotment "strictly for internal bookkeeping use" of $44,188.32 for a period from February 11 to March 31, inclusive.

Within the staff of the Bureau of Unemployment Compensation there was considerable criticism of this delay. Both Cohen and Rector felt that the delays resulted chiefly from the board's dilatoriness in approving the application forms. They felt that even though the forms were not perfect, they would

[15] Washington had not submitted its law for approval, because the governor had appointed no board to administer the act.

have been satisfactory for the first grants had they been accepted a month earlier. The result, according to Cohen, had been to make a number of the states angry. They had been given hope that they would receive money much earlier. It is true that at the New York meeting of state officials on February 21, one or two minor changes had been made in the proposed forms, but the corrections accepted at that meeting had not actually been incorporated in a revised edition of the forms, but were handled by separate letters. Rector and Cohen may have been particularly sensitive on this matter because of their close relationships with the Wisconsin unemployment insurance people.

In asking for data for determining the initial payment, the board indicated by letter to each of the state administrators its intention to temporarily waive the factors, listed in the act under section 302, upon which allocations to the states were presumed to be determined.[16] The essential paragraph read as follows:

The board must necessarily secure from the state relevant information on which to base its determination of proper and necessary costs. However, it is planned to make an initial payment without particular reference to the factors that later must be taken into consideration. The State of _____ may now apply for this *initial* payment. It is to be borne in mind that this initial payment is without reference to the determinants that the Board must necessarily use in making all subsequent allotments. The states are specifically warned against considering this first and special payment a basis for making extensive commitments, and to forego any expansion in personnel or equipment except that which might be indicated by the essential administrative tasks of the period in question.

The letter also notified the state that it would be asked to send an accredited representative to Washington within the next few weeks, fully authorized to deal with the board in all matters pertaining to administrative grants and to sign such memoranda or agreements as might be deemed necessary. "The purpose of this conference will be to place before the Board relevant information that will allow the formulation of a plan for allocation of administrative expenses pursuant to the specifications set out in Title III. Such procedure is necessary in case of each state before any grant subsequent to the initial and special grant can be made." The board asked each state to furnish, by the time of that conference, information on the proposed administration, giving among other things a full description of the entire setup, broken down into its various subdivisions, a classification of the personnel, and an account of the duties of each staff member together with specifications for each position. It asked for the salary ranges, actual and prospective, together with the salaries of other departments in the state government whose employees had comparable

---

[16] These factors were: (1) population of the state; (2) estimated number of persons covered by the state law; (3) such other factors as the board might find relevant.

classifications and duties.[17] It requested information about recording and accounting systems, and cost comparisons of mechanized, semimechanized, and manual record-keeping. In addition to these eight types of information, the letter served notice that beginning with the next (fourth) fiscal quarter, the board would have to have estimates of coverage in order to make allotments for the quarter.

This letter was pretty largely the work of Stanley Rector. The information sought by it was later analyzed by another employee of the bureau, Miss Ruth Reticker, in order to discover the kind of information which had actually been obtained. One conclusion which her analysis made clear was that the questions were too general in character.[18]

In making the initial grants Altmeyer, to whom the board looked for advice on such matters, told Wagenet that he should refuse any grants for placement functions, and that he should tell the states that they were not to ask for expansions. It was clearly stated that the grants for this quarter were to be emergency grants, not to be considered as precedents. The details of the process involved in making the actual allocations were handled by Wagenet personally. There is no written record, however, of what considerations he used in paring down the requests.[19]

The effective scrutiny of the state requests took place at the individual conferences with state representatives. There it was possible to go behind the written breakdown of items and discover the precise reasons for the figures

[17] This is the kind of detailed personnel information which the Bureau of Public Assistance had failed to request, because of its belief that the act forbade the board to obtain it.

[18] Data was also supplied on forms UC101 and UC102, which became until late in 1936 the standard written basis for the submission of estimates for each quarter. These were to be submitted twenty days before each quarter's beginning. The estimates were broken down into the following categories: (1) salaries and wages, regular and temporary; (2) travel expense; (3) office maintenance and expenses (telephone and telegraph, postage, printing and binding, repairs and alterations, light, heat and water, office supplies, and other office expenses); (4) rentals (office space); (5) office equipment (purchases); and (6) other anticipated expenses (including service contracts, etc.).

Salaries for each individual, listed under either the permanent or temporary category, were to be given on a supplementary form, and details of all purchases of equipment and all anticipated expenditures over one hundred dollars were to be listed on supplementary schedules. The state was also required to submit a statement of contributions receipts for the previous quarter and a statement on coverage for the current quarter.

[19] It was particularly difficult to make any close estimate of the necessary cost for the first grant to a state. In fact, the experience all during the year 1936 showed that in most cases, state agencies were not able to spend all the money allotted them by the board during the quarter and that there was usually a very substantial unexpended balance.

presented. The only state which received exactly what it requested without modification was Wisconsin. The New York estimate was reduced by approximately $6,000. It is only fair to say, however, that this reduction was due primarily to the fact that the original New York estimate had been based upon the period beginning February 1. This had to be changed to February 11 because of Comptroller General McCarl's ruling.[20] Paul E. Batzell, the assistant administrator heading the Division of Grants and Procedures, declared that the New York estimate was very well done, having been carefully and intelligently prepared. The New Hampshire request, which was the first to be granted, was reduced only slightly. There can be little doubt that New Hampshire was treated with less scrutiny than the other states. This was partly because of the emergency situation there: New Hampshire had began operating the first of January, and the legislature had made no allocation of funds for administrative purposes. It was also a result of the inexperience of the board's staff.

The request presented by the District of Columbia was slashed from $30,000 to $12,000. This change, as well as nearly all the other important deductions that occurred in state applications for the first and second quarters, does not show in the board's records. In order to save face for the state administrators, each state was permitted to withdraw its original estimate and prepare a new application. The old papers were destroyed. There were a number of unjustifiable requests in the first estimates, of which California's was probably the most flagrant.

California's proposal for the first quarter came to nearly $300,000. Typical of this estimate was the printing request of $25,000. When pressed by Rector to explain what they were going to do with this money, the California representative indicated they were going to print 500,000 copies of their state law. When he was asked to whom they were going to give them, he replied that there were 250,000 employers subject to the act. This figure was so out-

---

[20] For full discussion of McCarl's ruling see pp. 49-50. It may be of interest here to note that in one of the letters accompanying the first application for a grant for unemployment compensation administration, the California commission called attention to the explicit promise which had been made at the time the California bill was before the state legislature, that no provision need be made by the state for financing the administration of the state law. The letter alleged that promises were made that the federal act would be retroactive on this point, and furnish all the funds for the cost of state administration. It also said that the California commission felt that there was a moral obligation on the part of the Social Security Board, despite the ruling of the Comptroller General that money from the appropriation act would not be available to the states before February 11, 1936, to supply funds for the earlier state administrative costs. It suggested that the board should sponsor a bill providing for such a retroactive appropriation as a means of keeping faith with the states.

rageously out of line with all the known information about the ratio of gainfully employed workers to employers that it was drastically pruned. California's first census of employers showed less than 21,000 employers. The
state's automobile expense request had included very expensive cars, and they
had also asked for costly and elaborate statistical machine equipment.

DIFFICULTIES IN FINDING CRITERIA,
POLICIES OF HUNCH AND HORSE SENSE

The estimates for the second grant (fourth quarter of the 1936 fiscal year)
followed quickly on the heels of the first. This time there were not as many
flagrant cases of guessing, although California again came in with a grandiose
scheme. It asked for an elaborate regional organization with a staff of three
people for each region. It also included the cost of purchasing automobiles and
the cost of providing a large supervisory staff in the central office. All told,
the reduction in the California estimate was from approximately $180,000
to approximately $82,000. On April 22 Frase had a fairly full description from
Wagenet of the method he had used in analyzing the estimates and in deciding how much money to allot the state administrations. He had used the
detailed breakdown of personnel very effectively. He found that a number
of the states, up against political pressure to start out with a full-fledged
staff, were glad to have the Social Security Board as an excuse to drop
unneeded employees and to raise the standards of training and experience.
For example, in the case of Massachusetts he cut out thirty-seven employees
who one of the responsible state administrators agreed were unnecessary. He
felt that this breakdown of information had virtually enabled him to set the
personnel standards, notwithstanding the prohibitions in the Social Security
Act. Up to that date there had been no kickback from his procedure.

Another policy insisted upon at this time was that equipment should be
bought on the installment plan. There were two reasons for this policy, despite
the fact that it would increase ultimate cost of equipment by about 10 percent.
The first was that the plan reduced original outlays and thus eased the demand
for board money, which was not expected to be entirely adequate for this
year. The second was that it permitted the return of equipment to the equipment company in case either the federal or state act should be declared
invalid. In each case in which machine equipment had been asked for, Bachmann, the accountant, had been sent out to look the state situation over and
advise the state people concerning the type of machines that should be used.

Batzell, chief of the Grants Division, who during the second period relieved
Wagenet of most of the scrutiny of state budget requests, had taken the position when requests for the last quarter of fiscal 1936 were reviewed that
statistical reporting should be a by-product of the accounting procedure, and

that therefore additional expenditure for equipment to handle statistical reporting was not justified.[21]

As a matter of practical administration at this period, it was impossible to base quarterly grants for administrative purposes on the population of the state or the number of persons covered by the state law (as indicated in section 302(a)(3)) because the state laws varied so much in their requirements. The factor of the number of employers covered by the state laws was not considered at all. Even as late as April 1937 Batzell explained that it was still not possible, in making the grants, to take much account of population in the state or the coverage of the law. At that later date the ten states with the greatest population were, in order, New York, Pennsylvania, Illinois, Ohio, Texas, California, Michigan, New Jersey, and Missouri. The first ten states from the standpoint of employer coverage, however, were, Pennsylvania, Michigan, New York, Minnesota, Ohio, Arizona, Arkansas, New Jersey, California, and the District of Columbia.

He remarked that at some later time the bureau hoped to balance the three factors mentioned in section 302(a) so that it would be possible to determine what weight each ought to carry, but in the initial stages it was impossible to do anything but meet the urgent necessities of each state. Thus the statements submitted by the states on the coverage of the state laws, while interesting, played no real part in determining the size of grants.

There was disagreement within the bureau over the normative value of Wisconsin's administrative experience, for judging the suitability of proposed state expenditure items. The bureau had full information about Wisconsin's costs. But the director believed that Wisconsin's experience could not be used with accuracy (1) because Wisconsin had been operating for over two years, and had in addition, as a by-product of its long history of social legislation, a large amount of information about state industrial conditions, and (2) because its law was so different from that of other states. Information like that already known in Wisconsin would have to be collected by the unemployment compensation agencies in other states, and as a result their costs would be different.

THE BEGINNING OF TIGHT BUDGET CONTROL OVER THE STATES

When the first grants were made, a letter of notification from Wagenet to the states announced that any unexpended sums remaining at the end of the quarter would be taken into consideration in the making of the next

---

[21] Many months later, the people in the Bureau of Research and Statistics who were concerned with securing minimum statistics from the state unemployment compensation agencies discovered that, partly because of this policy of the Grants Division, the equipment installed in state agencies was not adapted to compiling statistics at all.

grants. It also notified the state agencies that if they desired to exceed estimated expenditure in any one of the main segregations, they ought to secure the board's approval. Taking all the states together, a considerable sum granted for the first period was unexpended at the end of that quarter.

The New Hampshire trustee fund episode precipitated a request by the board, early in March 1936, that the affected bureaus work out a complete procedure for handling unemployment compensation grants which would insure that all issues had been cared for and that all documents were in order when the board took final action. This procedure required the participation of the Office of General Counsel and the Bureau of Accounts and Audits and their close cooperation with the Bureau of Unemployment Compensation. Under the procedure developed, Accounts and Audits submitted a statement giving the unexpended balance remaining in the appropriation to the state, while the general counsel certified that the state law was then meeting the legal requirements of section 303(a) of the Social Security Act, which covered such items as methods of proper administration, payment of benefits through employment offices, and fair hearing.[22]

After these statements were secured, the entire docket for the state was submitted to the board, accompanied by the recommendations of the Bureau of Unemployment Compensation.

The board could, of course, make still further adjustments in the grant, but in actual practice it accepted the recommendations of the Bureau of Unemployment Compensation. When the board had made its findings, the grant was approved and a voucher for the appropriate amount sent to the Secretary of the Treasury for certification. The state was notified of the amount of the grant for the quarter, on a form which listed the amount allotted for each of the six major categories of expenditure.[23]

[22] A technical point arose in August 1936, when California asked for a retroactive grant covering the period from January 1 to February 10. The question was whether the board must certify that the state law met the requirements of this section not only on the date of certification but also during the period for which the grant was made. The board was then making three types of grants: for an entirely past period, for an entirely future period, and for a period partly past and partly future. While California claimed that its law included all the provisions required by section 303(a) during the requested period, the board was afraid that if its certification was based on that fact it might be precluded from making a retroactive grant to a state whose law might not meet all of the requirements of section 303(a) for a past period. Rather than seek a Comptroller General's opinion, it finally decided to make the certification on the basis that all requirements had been met. But this decision arose to plague it in January 1937, when Ohio asked for a retroactive grant although its law did not clearly meet the standard for fair hearing required by section 303(a), and the state's attorney general had not cleared up the ambiguity by a formal opinion.

[23] Evidence of a tightfisted policy towards the states is revealed in the board minutes of June 5, 1936. Wagenet proposed a detailed checklist to be attached to one

Although no formal instructions were issued to this effect, the Bureau of Unemployment Compensation gradually extended its control over quarterly state budgets to include subordinate items within the general categories. This aroused some resentment in the states, particularly in New York. In fact, in July 1936 Bowers, executive director of the New York Division of Placement and Unemployment Insurance, asked the attorney general of the state for an opinion on the legality of the board's action in cutting items out of the New York quarterly requests.[24] According to Anna Rosenberg, regional director for the board in New York, Governor Lehman asked her to consult with the state attorney general on the matter, and as a result of their conference the attorney general handed down a decision giving the board full authority to reduce state budgets in this way. Bowers was not satisfied, and at the interstate conference in New Hampshire late in July 1936 still maintained that the board did not have this power. Later that month when he and Hurwitz discussed their problems with the board, he stuck to this position. During

---

of the forms sent in by the states, to compel the state to list in detail the equipment it had actually purchased and the money it had asked for equipment. Altmeyer at first objected to this as too picayunish, but Wagenet insisted that he wanted a continuous property inventory and that it would be easier to install at the beginning than sometime later. He asserted that the Employment Service did not start with this property control but later wished that it had. It was several months before the board's inventory scheme was working smoothly.

[24] The growth of this resentment was noted as early as May, when Wilbur J. Cohen averred that the attitude taken by Wagenet, Batzell, et al., when reviewing requests for the first two quarterly periods, had become a source of ill feeling on the part of the states because of the picayunish character of their scrutiny and because of an attitude of suspicion they manifested toward the states. He felt that Batzell and Miss Fenn were taking away practically all the states' responsibility when, for example, they held up a request because the number of reading lamps did not check with the number of desks requested.

While in New York late in April, Cohen listened in on a conversation between the New York administrators and Batzell concerning the New York request for administrative funds for the fourth quarter of fiscal 1936. One item of the request had been for a desk costing fifty dollars. Batzell put on a rather hard-boiled attitude, asking just what they proposed to do with that desk. New York had also included an item for a contract with Dunn and Bradstreet to assist in watching for firms about to become insolvent but still owing employer contributions. Batzell insisted that New York scale the contract down to a very brief period. He had demanded price details on another item. Cohen said that Fritz Kaufman, one of Bowers' assistants, had told him in a very excited manner when they had met; "My estimate came within three cents of the actual price." Kaufman seemed greatly relieved and elated at this demonstration of accuracy in preparing the financial request.

The New York administrator's difficulties did not end when the board had finally made the grant; the comptroller of New York State took the same meticulous attitude toward Bowers' organization that Wagenet had taken.

this meeting it developed that a particularly sore point was the questioning by the Bureau of Unemployment Compensation of the use of a direct telephone line between the New York City and Albany offices of the New York division. Wagenet pointed out that New York had had this tie line installed for three months before putting it in their quarterly request for funds, and that even so it had been allowed for the current quarter, with a request from the bureau that it be justified for the subsequent quarters.

New York and Wisconsin resented every form of control by the Social Security Board more strongly than most of the other states. They felt that they knew much more about unemployment insurance than the board's staff in Washington, and that they should have a free hand. It was easy to understand this attitude. They were dealing with operating problems. Both were civil service states with competent people not only at the top but throughout the whole organization. Many of the other states, particularly those that had started late and received real assistance from the board in making up their first forms and getting administration started, did not feel unduly constrained by the board's review of their quarterly budgets. Walter Matscheck told Frase in January 1937 that during his recent visits to the unemployment compensation agencies in Texas, Louisiana, Mississippi, Alabama, and South Carolina, relationships between these state agencies and the Bureau of Unemployment Compensation seemed very amiable. They were willing to take not only advice but orders from Washington, and felt that detailed budget control helped them do their own jobs. In Alabama, one of the officials said that the close scrutiny given his quarterly requests by the Bureau of Unemployment Compensation made him more careful in setting up his administrative machinery and do more thinking about the problem.

Another and rarer point of view was expressed in February 1937 by Robert Watt, the labor representative on the Massachusetts Unemployment Compensation Commission. Watt was an out-and-out exponent of federal administration of employment legislation and other labor legislation, because he had no confidence in the competence of most state officials or in their ability to resist pressure from employer interests.

By the end of the summer of 1936 the bureau had had enough experience with the states to feel that it could extend its budgetary and other controls without precipitating any open revolt.

The Perfection of Board Procedures and Policies for Control

When Winant appointed a Committee on the Control of State Expenditures in September 1936, composed of Asay of Public Assistance, Kimball of

Unemployment Compensation, and Clague of Research and Statistics, the larger part of the committee's time for the next two months was spent upon this problem as it applied to unemployment compensation. The administrative grants for public assistance were so small (5 percent of the total federal grant for the aged and blind, and actual administrative costs in the one-third matching grant for dependent children) that interest naturally centered in the more significant problem of control through a 100 percent federal grant. Besides, the board had already come to the conclusion that it could not withhold any of the 5 percent administrative grant in old age and blind assistance without withdrawing approval of the entire state plan. As one of the research staff pointed out in a memo to Clague on the subject:

In dealing with unemployment compensation, it was assumed that the Board looked forward toward exercising a large measure of control. In the case of Public Assistance, *per contra,* it is assumed that the desire is to establish a real federal-aid activity, in which the states, carrying on activities in which there is less need for uniformity than in the case of unemployment compensation, and with which they have already had considerable experience, are to be made primarily responsible.

This was a concise statement of the way in which the board and most of its staff looked upon the differences between public assistance and unemployment compensation so far as federal control was concerned.

In the recommendations on unemployment compensation submitted by the Committee on the Control of State Expenditures, budget control was stressed above everything else. The staff of the Bureau of Research and Statistics had recommended less drastic budget control to the committee and more emphasis upon consultation and cooperation with state officials, but the representatives of the Bureau of Unemployment Compensation (both of them from the Grants Division) insisted that recommendations of the committee must provide for control of state budgets item by item. This view prevailed with the committee.

Its principal recommendation was that "the Board should immediately adopt a specific policy requiring state unemployment agencies to adhere to their budgets as approved by the Board, except where prior permission to transfer funds from one item or category of the budget to another, or to an item not contained in the approved budget, is obtained from the Director of the Bureau of Unemployment Compensation."

The other recommendations were subordinate to this principal recommendation, and were designed to make it effective:

a.   State requests for funds should be submitted in such detail as the board prescribed, and well in advance of the period for which they are requested.

b. State budgets should be drawn up jointly by representatives of the state agency and the board, after the latter had made a "personal administrative survey" of the operations of the state agency.

c. Adequate current control of expenditures should be required, either through the general state fiscal machinery or a responsible financial officer of the state unemployment compensation agency.

d. Unencumbered balances at the end of each quarter should not be available for expenditure in the succeeding quarter without reallotment by the board or authorization of the director of the Bureau of Unemployment Compensation.

e. States should be required to submit regular quarterly reports on expenditures of Title III grants.

In its supporting arguments, the committee stated that it considered an itemized quarterly budget the only method whereby the board could fulfill its responsibility, under Title III, which limits unemployment compensation administrative grants to expenses necessary for proper administration by the state. Experience had shown, in numerous specific cases, that state agencies could not be relied upon to limit their expenditures to items necessary for proper administration. Limiting control to expenditures within certain broad categories would not effect the desired result, because the sums involved in some of these categories would be so large as to permit the purchase of items not necessary for proper administration without exceeding the total allowed for those categories. At least the principal expense items, particularly salaries and equipment purchases, had to be itemized in considerable detail, although this might conceivably vary according to the arrangements which the board had with each state.

Submission of budgets in advance was necessary to implement the major recommendation, in order that funds might not be spent or obligated prior to the board grant. Other federal agencies administering grants-in-aid activities had found that personal cooperative contact in the preparation of state budgets facilitated the process; it minimized conflicting opinions, provided an opportunity to give administrative advice to state officials, and constituted an important method of securing information about actual administrative practices in the states.

The committee recognized that no amount of detailed budget control by the board would in itself be sufficient to secure proper administration. It was equally necessary that either the state comptroller or similar official or a responsible financial officer of the state unemployment compensation commission maintain continuing control over expenditures in accordance with the approved budget. If this current state control should not prove effective it might be necessary for the board to go still further, either to deduct from subsequent budgets amounts spent improperly, or to adopt some far-reaching form of control such as the stationing of an unemployment compensation representative in each state to act as a comptroller for the state agency, or the stationing of an actual disbursing officer in each state as is done by the National Guard.

Since the bureau already required expenditure reports, the committee recommended merely that the states be officially notified that these reports were board requirements.

The foregoing report was submitted by the chairman of the committee on November 19, 1936, but was not considered by the board until December. Meanwhile the Bureau of Unemployment Compensation, with the assistance of the Bureau of Accounts and Audits and the Executive Director's Office, drew up revised instructions and forms for the submission of state budgets for unemployment compensation, in line with the recommendations of the committee. The board considered the committee's report and its proposed forms and instructions on December 15 and approved both.

The instructions (UC-501) were divided into four sections. Section A (General Instructions) provided that:

1. State budget requests for grants under Title III should be based on the federal fiscal quarter.
2. The new forms would supplant all previous forms prescribed by the board.
3. The state agency should submit its request for a grant with the appropriate regional director of the Social Security Board at least thirty days prior to the quarter in which such request applied.
4. The state would be notified of its grant on form UC-105, and that no expenditure or encumbrances would be made if not specified on that form, except by approval of the director of the Bureau of Unemployment Compensation.
5. Additional funds must be authorized through a supplementary grant.
6. State unemployment compensation agencies should designate an employee to handle fiscal affairs and maintain accounts which would supply the information required by the Social Security Board. Vouchers for the expenditure of funds handled under Title III must be approved by the chief executive of the state unemployment compensation agency and filed in the administrative office of the agency, subject to audit by the Social Security Board. State laws and rules and regulations on expenditures were to be observed, together with such additional requirements as the Social Security Board might prescribe.

7. The state unemployment compensation agencies should submit quarterly reports of expenditures and encumbrances not later than thirty days following the close of the quarter.

8. The unencumbered balances shown on the quarterly expenditure reports should not be expended or encumbered until realloted by the Social Security Board.

9. State agencies which had not submitted certain documents and data required should submit them on the receipt of these instructions.

Section B of the instructions furnished directions for the preparation and submission of the budgets on the appropriate forms. The forms were amplified to include one for personal services; one for equipment purchases; one for current expenses, broken down into supplies, communications, travel, transportation of things, printing and binding, advertising, heat, light and water, rents on premises, and repairs and alterations; one for expenditures in each office of the state agency; and one for the expenses of the state employment service in the administration of unemployment compensation. Section B also provided that the state furnish full information on state purchasing regulations, travel regulations, fiscal practice and regulations, and bonds required of state employees.

Section C applied to the certifications to be submitted in connection with the requests for grants under Title III. These included persons authorized to certify information or documents furnished to the board, certification by the Attorney General designating the person to whom payment of funds granted was to be made, monthly statements of the number of employers and employees covered by the state laws, and several statements concerning the current legal status of the law (these will be discussed separately).

Section D prescribed the expenditure reports to be submitted on appropriate forms, to parallel categories and items in the request for grants.

The statements and certifications required of the state agencies on the legal status of their laws were really not control through budget procedure, but control by the Social Security Board of the interpretation of the state acts. In theory, this had been the practice of the board in both unemployment compensation and public assistance before these instructions had been issued, but the practice was extended at this time. The state was required to certify:

1. That either no court decisions or orders affecting the state law had been issued or only those submitted to the board had been issued.

2. That the state attorney general had issued no opinions affecting state unemployment compensation laws or that only the opinions submitted had been issued.

3. That either the state agencies had issued no new or revised rules and regulations or that only those submitted had been issued.

4. That the state law had not been changed or amended by the legislature or only those amendments submitted had been enacted.
5. That no general interpretations had been issued or only those submitted had been issued.

It was further provided that the state agency should furnish the board, on issue, three copies of all decisions and orders, attorneys generals' opinions, amendments, rules, and notifications of general interpretations. And lastly, states were required to submit all contemplated rules and regulations, in order for the board to determine how such rules and regulations would affect the state laws in relation to Title III or Title IX of the Social Security Act.

The requirement that states submit in advance all contemplated rules and regulations aroused more resentment in some state agencies than the greater budgetary control incorporated in the new regulations. When Frase talked to the staff of the Wisconsin Division of Unemployment Compensation early in January 1937, shortly after the issuance of these instructions, they indicated that the board was going too far; so far, in fact, that the state administration was being taken over. As far as Wisconsin was concerned, however, the matter was evidently ironed out later, because the state continued to administer the law pretty much as it saw fit. Board requirements were set up in such a way that the Bureau of Unemployment Compensation had almost complete discretion as to whether it would attempt to control the administration of the law through rules and regulations, or would leave it to the state agency. In at least one case, the board did rule that the state agency could not require the signature of a discharged employee on termination reports.[25]

---

[25] The Bureau of Unemployment Compensation and the board both took very strong positions in administering the unemployment compensation program in a manner which would raise labor standards wherever possible. One of the most important decisions of this kind had to do with the use of severance reports by the California Unemployment Compensation Commission. On December 4, 1936, Regional Director Neustadt telegraphed Wagenet that the use of severance reports signed by the employees in California was likely to have an adverse effect upon the legal standing of workers in an optical strike. The courts had refused to recognize strikers as employees, and Neustadt felt that if they signed these severance reports they might lose any legal claim to being employees. He also feared that, in order to be rehired, employees might be forced to sign statements that they had quit or were discharged during a temporary layoff.

Wagenet on the next day telegraphed Neustadt to inform the California commission that employees would not be required to sign severance reports. At the same time he sent a memo to Bane explaining the situation, pointing out that the bureau thought a good case could be made for holding this practice a violation of section 303(a)(1) "since it constitutes a method of administration which is not 'reasonably calculated to insure full payment of unemployment compensation when due.'" This matter was taken up by the board in a meeting on December 8, and it was officially determined that requiring an employee's signature on a severance report violated section 303(a)(1) of

The procedure for handling unemployment compensation grants within the board was not materially changed as a result of these new rules and procedures. The request for grants, in many cases prepared by the state agencies after consultation with bureau representatives, were sent first to the Division of Grants of the bureau where, after the computations had been checked by the Bureau of Accounts and Audits, adjustments and deductions were made by the grants service section under the direction of Mr. Batzell, chief of the division.[26] There five men each handled a group of states with which they were presumed to be familiar. The other section in the Grants Division was the grants processing section, with a staff of about the same size. It handled the necessary clerical work, preparing the papers for submission to the board and preparing forms for the Bureau of Accounts and Audits and the General Counsel's Office.

The general counsel certified that the state statutes and all rules and regulations, amendments, opinions, and interpretations issued by the states were in conformity with the provisions of sections 903(a) and 303(a) of the Social Security Act. The Bureau of Accounts and Audits was responsible for the checking of expenditure reports, submission of field audits of these reports, the completeness and accuracy of all the documents submitted to the board, and the preparation of the public voucher for the grant. A notice of the grant as approved by the board was sent to the state agency and the board's regional office.

---

the Social Security Act, because it constituted a method which was not reasonably calculated to insure full payment of unemployment compensation when due. It is interesting that the positive language of section 303(a) requiring "such methods of administration as are found by the Board to be reasonably calculated to insure payment of unemployment compensation when due" was construed to have a negative meaning as well, giving the board power to disapprove administrative practices which accomplish other purposes.

In January 1937 the board formally announced a general ruling that state agencies might not require employees to sign severance reports. This was the only general ruling relating to the requirements imposed by the board on state unemployment compensation agencies which was issued in the form of a press release during the period studied. This public announcement also stated that such severance reports would be an infringement of section 303(a)(1).

[26] It very frequently happened, particularly with nearby states and others like New York which resented the board's financial control, that state officials would come to Washington to discuss each quarterly grant with the bureau in order to iron out differences. In fact almost without exception, Wisconsin and New York officials came to Washington to discuss every quarterly grant made during the year 1936. The grant procedure called for submission of state estimates at least thirty days in advance of the quarter for which they were submitted, but very few grants were made until after the quarter had already started.

The scope of board control through this budgetary procedure is indicated by the following excerpts from a letter to the acting director of the Arkansas unemployment compensation agency in connection with their first grant, made for the third quarter of the fiscal year 1937:

With reference to the general operating organization of your agency, outlined on Form US 101A, and submitted with your budget, it is understood that your organization is to be set up in substantial accord with the suggestions contained in the booklet issued by the Bureau of Unemployment Compensation of the Social Security Board, under title "State Unemployment Compensation Agencies —Organization and Personnel."

The general sections of this organization as shown by Form UC-101A are the following:

> Office of Director
> Office of Assistant Director
> Office of Legal Counsel
> Public Relations
> Compensation
> General Accounts
> Research and Statistics
> General Office

Assistant Director

It is understood that the Assistant Director is to assume the active direction of the Compensation section, along with other appropriate duties. Undoubtedly, the position of Assistant Director, under this set-up, is next in importance to that of the Director.

Coordination: As directing head of the Compensation Section, the Assistant Director should be in a position not only to coordinate the internal work relating to employer records, employee records, and field auditing, but to maintain contacts with employers. These contacts, of course, will involve not only the collection of delinquent contributions, but the handling of cases of doubtful status and liability.

Training of Personnel: The Assistant Director will also be charged, as the organization develops, with the responsibility of seeing that the field auditors are properly trained. This training is of the utmost importance and should involve training in the specific accounting problems to be encountered and in a knowledge of your law, as well as careful instruction with respect to the proper approach to be made to employers. As indicated in the booklet on organization referred to, it is probable that some of the field auditors may be selected from the temporary personnel that will be needed for the determination of employer's liability in the initial stages.

Supervisor of Contributions

The position of Supervisor of Contributions is primarily one of internal operation, and the individual performing the functions of this position will be called upon to exercise direct supervision over the mechanics involved in employer records, employee records and field auditing. Such an individual will have an accounting education and experience and have the capacity to direct recording and auditing procedures with effectiveness. In fact, the Supervisor of Contributions should be an accountant next in capacity to the Chief Accountant.

Chief Accountant

The Chief Accountant, who heads the General Accounts section, is the principal fiscal officer of the agency considered as an administrative unit. While the functions of the General Accounts section are separate from those of the Compensation section, it is evident that there must be close cooperation between the two sections. For example, in the initial installation of the recording equipment and procedures relating to employers and employees, the Chief Accountant will, of course, assist in such work. In the daily operation of the two sections, however, there will be a fairly clear-cut separation, as suggested in the booklet on Organization and Personnel above referred to. The Chief Accountant, as suggested therein, will be called upon to handle the cash operations of the agency, the detailed accounting for the expense of administration, and the control accounts of the unemployment compensation fund and the administration fund.

Legal Counsel

It is understood that the Legal Counsel and the Public Relations Representative will function in most cases by direct contact with the Director. That is, it is not contemplated that these two offices will be in the nature of operating sections.

Research and Statistics

The functions under Research and Statistics and under the General Office will, of course, follow fairly closely the suggestions in the booklet on organization referred to above.

Appointment of Personnel

It is understood that the Personnel will in the first instance be appointed upon a temporary basis, and that permanent appointments are to be made under the provisions of Section 11(d) of your Law, which provides for the holding of examinations under the state Civil Service Commission.

With reference to the various categories of expenses shown on the budget the allotments were made by the Board without any change whatever from your estimates. Of course, we realize, that such initial estimates on the part of the states submitting first budgets are necessarily rough estimates. Therefore, the amounts allotted are not to be considered sums that must be spent, but merely maximum amounts that are allowed. Unquestionably, it will be found, as your organization gets under way, that it may be advantageous to depart somewhat from the details as specified in the supporting schedules of your budget. It will be well, in such a case, to advise this Bureau in advance of such proposed departures so that approval may be forwarded to you by return mail, or by telegraph, if the case is urgent.

Particularly, it is believed that savings may be effected in the matter of equipment, through the obtaining of bids for the various items.

We understand that a further study of the bonding requirements is being made and that information will be given as soon as a decision with respect thereto has been reached.

Of particular value in considering budgets and expenditure reports will be the following of instructions *UC-501* and related instructions. You will doubtless wish to instruct the appropriate executives accordingly.

We enjoyed very much seeing you in Washington. Be assured that the Division and the Bureau desire to assist in every possible way in setting up the agency for effective functioning at the earliest possible date.

Thus at the end of the period studied the board was exercising a very considerable amount of control over state agencies—very largely through the process of making grants, although some controls depended on other specific powers or on general influence. Even so, about the first of February, 1937, Batzell told Frase that the adjustments made on state estimates were still of a rather rough and ready nature. Items were cut out of state requests. But there was no really adequate standard for budgetary control, because the staff of the bureau in Washington did not yet know enough about the actual problems of administering state unemployment compensation laws or the local situation in each of the states. A field staff was urgently needed, but it was proving very difficult to find the right type of man, "a mature person with a wide range of experience and good judgment who could get along with state officials and command their respect." Some of the regional directors had proven of assistance because of their knowledge of state situations, particularly those with some technical knowledge of unemployment compensation as well.

The net effect of this control from Washington is hard to gauge. Certain obvious extravagances were eliminated in some states; and the mere requirement of submitting budgets probably had a salutary effect. On the other hand, the state agencies were hardly ever able to spend the money allotted to them as fast as it was doled out. Federal estimates were just as far out of line. The board received an appropriation of $29,000,000 for Title III grants for the fiscal year ending June 30, 1937, and by the end of March 1937 it was apparent that even though more laws were passed than had been expected, the total expenditure for the year would approximate only $9,000,000.

THE DEVELOPMENT OF SPECIAL GRANT POLICIES

Perhaps the most important of grant policies developed during the period related to the payment of expenses of other state agencies which performed services for unemployment compensation agencies.

Grants for State Civil Service Agencies

In the request for the fourth quarter of fiscal 1936, New York included a reimbursement to the state civil service commission for holding examinations on behalf of the compensation organization. This is the first time that allotments for that kind of state overhead were requested. However, the board decided not to make a grant for this item. It was thought that approval for such items should be made only when there was a definite assignment of personnel at an established salary to work full time for an unemployment compensation administration; for example, approval might be given for the salary of an attorney assigned from the Department of the Attorney General for such work.

Grants to States for Auditing

A decision on the extent to which the accounts of state unemployment compensation agencies would be audited by the board, or be audited by states themselves, was not reached until early in 1937. Only a few states were actually collecting contributions during 1936, and they had not reached the stage where auditing could accomplish much—there were too many employers not reporting or delinquent to justify this activity. Most grants included sums for auditors, but most of these were for accountants in the central offices of the states, or for field men whose duty it was to get employers to report and pay contributions and to teach them how to fill out the necessary forms. Wisconsin was the only state which had been collecting contributions long enough to have reached the stage of sending auditors out to compare, from employers' books, contribution reports and payments.

Nevertheless, the question was raised in connection with some of the grants as early as 1936. In August of that year, Murray reported that the proposed unemployment compensation law in Utah provided for an audit to be paid for by the board. The board decided to ask the state to eliminate this provision and to discuss the matter when the first grant was requested. This was done. At the same board meeting Murray requested that the general question of allowing expenses for audits on the state unemployment compensation agencies be deferred until more information was available.

The Committee on the Control of State Expenditures, already referred to, and the staff members of the Bureau of Research and Statistics who worked with it, went into the question of auditing by both federal and state officers. In their report described above submitted on November 19, 1936, it was stated that, although the Bureau of Accounts and Audits was expecting to conduct regular quarterly field audits of the accounts of state unemployment compensation commissions, too much could not be expected of this type of control; if it were discovered after the fact that states had not adhered to their budgets, the withholding of the misused amounts in subsequent grants might result only in crippling the state agency.

During December 1936, Wagenet and Batzell had conferred with Hughes, Director of the Bureau of Accounts and Audits, to decide what these federal quarterly audits should accomplish. According to Hughes, Wagenet regarded the federal audit as a check on the operating efficiency of the state agencies, rather than a simple inquiry into the legality of their expenditures. He wanted the federal auditors to check not only the state expenditures of Title III grants but also each benefit payment made, and even go back to the employers' books to see whether the states had been doing a good job of collecting their own payroll taxes. Hughes pointed out that there were already over one hundred auditors in the field checking state public assistance expenditures, and this contemplated scheme for unemployment compensation would require an even greater auditing staff, for budgetary reasons an impossibility. So they agreed between them that the federal field audit for unemployment compensation would consist primarily in a check on the expenditure reports of the state agencies, to see that they had spent administrative funds granted by the board properly, and only an occasional sample check of benefit payments and contribution collections.

Having worked out the general plan in advance, Wagenet then requested, in a memorandum which was considered in the board meeting on December 19, 1936, that the board express its policy on the scope of the board's audit. In this memorandum he assumed that the board would audit the expenditure of Title III funds and would audit contributions and benefits of the state agencies, but not go back to the employers' books. Also, he requested approval of the bureau practice of not granting funds, save in exceptional circumstances, for work performed by other state agencies including state auditors and comptrollers for auditing state unemployment compensation agencies. Finally, he noted that the bureau had not conferred with or accepted the recommendations of state auditors and comptrollers in regard to record keeping. The board requested Wagenet and Hughes to confer and submit a joint proposal on this whole question of auditing.

Hughes and Wagenet in a December 22, 1936, memorandum proposed that:

1. The state unemployment compensation agencies themselves audit employer books for unemployment compensation contributions.
2. The state audit collections by the state agencies.
3. Federal audits in addition to state audits of the unemployment compensation fund be made in each state.
4. Informational checks by federal and state auditors of the federal Un-

employment Trust Fund—payments, withdrawals, and balances—be made.

5. Federal auditors audit benefits paid out by checking on state withdrawals from the Unemployment Trust Fund.

6. The state audit benefit payments to individuals and that federal agents make spot checks.

7. The administrative fund be audited primarily by federal auditors, and if the state were also to make such audits, the expense thereof not to be paid by the board.

In a meeting of December 26, 1936, the board agreed to accept these recommendations in principle, but requested that the two bureaus check with the Treasury to see what it proposed to do in the way of audits, so that duplication might be avoided. This was done, and on February 18, 1937, Wagenet and Banning (the new director of the Bureau of Accounts and Audits) submitted a report. A conference with the Bureau of Internal Revenue officials had revealed that the board could make little use of the contemplated field checks of employers' books by the Bureau of Internal Revenue, because federal and state laws varied on taxes and coverage; the extent of field audits and the matter of verifying payrolls in the Bureau of Internal Revenue were left to the discretion of the individual federal revenue agents; the examination of employers' records for Title IX taxes would be made in connection with a similar examination for corporate income tax, and would be spread over the statutory period for the tax return (one year); and finally, only about 150,000 employers' returns under Title IX would be examined during 1937 by the agents of the Bureau of Internal Revenue. There was, however, an opportunity for states to examine employers' tax returns under Title IX (form 940) in the sixty-four field offices of the Bureau of Internal Revenue, but it would probably be necessary for the states, in addition, to make their own audits of employers' records on an extensive scale.

Conferences with the commissioner of accounts and deposits of the Treasury revealed that he was already furnishing the Social Security Board with a regular monthly report of deposits, withdrawals, interest, and balances for each state in the Unemployment Trust Fund of the Treasury; this monthly statement should agree with the statements furnished to the board by the state unemployment compensation agencies; and the auditors of the board could make use of this monthly statement and even have recourse to the records of the commissioner of accounts and deposits in case of discrepancies between his statements and those furnished by the state agencies.

Wagenet and Banning concluded that the information revealed in the conference with the Treasury officials did not materially change the recommendations submitted on December 22, 1936, and they requested that the procedure outlined therein be approved. They further recommended that:

1. The Bureau of Accounts and Audits make audits at such times and in such manner as it deems necessary, of the state unemployment compensation funds transferred by state agencies to and from the federal Unemployment Trust Fund, payments to and from state budget accounts, and of state unemployment compensation administrative funds including the employment service accounts.
2. State unemployment compensation agencies audit all other accounts and fiscal operations.
3. Where the Bureau of Accounts and Audits had undertaken a complete audit as enumerated in (1) above, the board not grant funds to the states under Title III for a similar or duplicate audit.
4. This recommendation not affect the board policy reached in January, 1936, that no funds be granted under Title III to state agencies other than the unemployment compensation agencies, except in exceptional circumstances.

The recommendations were accepted by the board, and the field auditing staff made a start at checking the quarterly expenditure reports. Meanwhile, the Bureau of Accounts and Audits had been reorganized to provide for an unemployment compensation division and a public assistance division, and unemployment compensation auditors were sent from state to state for the relatively simple job of checking state expenditures reports. By the end of the third quarter (March 31, 1937) the board had made a total of ninety-three quarterly grants to states under Title III, but only twenty quarterly reports of state expenditures had been checked by the unemployment compensation auditing staff.

Grants for Law Libraries in State Agencies

A minor point in connection with proper expenses for state unemployment compensation agencies was the question of whether the agencies needed law libraries. New York had requested $1,500 for this purpose in their first request in fiscal 1937, and the bureau had cut it out. When the state protested, Wagenet requested an opinion from the General Counsel's Office and, in a memorandum of August 7, 1936, submitted the question to the board. The general counsel thought it a proper administrative expense. Wagenet recommended to the board that state agencies not be granted funds for building up law libraries, since facilities were available in the state capital. Requests for this purpose from New York, California, and Massachusetts were then before the bureau.

In the board meeting of August 14 Tate, representing the general counsel, said he thought this item was a proper administrative expense, but recommended against it in the New York case, except perhaps for a state annotated code and one or two other books. It was decided that the two bureaus would determine what law books were permissible, and the states would be notified accordingly. In the subsequent grant to New York for the second quarter of fiscal 1937, on October 5, 1936, the state's original request of $1,500 for law books was allowed.

Interest on Funds Granted by the Social Security Board and Held by the States

In February 1937 the Bureau of Accounts and Audits brought up the question of whether interest earned on funds granted by the Social Security Board for public assistance and for unemployment compensation administration and held by the state in banks should be considered as part of the federal grant and subject to restrictions set up in the act as interpreted by the board. The problem was not a particularly important one and the amount of money involved was small, but the procedure by which the board arrived at a policy had certain interesting features.

The accountants had to have some instructions on interest earnings in order to account for every last penny in their audit reports. The bureau, in a memorandum to the general counsel on February 10, 1937, raised a whole series of questions and possible alternative answers in connection with interest earnings and certain other small funds affecting grants for unemployment compensation. General Counsel Eliot's replies were in essence as follows:

1. Interest. The better legal position would be to find that interest on funds granted to the states under Title III belongs to the states because, once granted, the money itself is state money. But the intent of Congress in regard to this matter was not clear and he was willing to make a persuasive legal argument in favor of whatever position the Bureau of Unemployment Compensation might wish to recommend.

2. Penalties and fines under state laws. On the other hand, the disposition of penalties and fines was governed entirely by the provisions of state laws. If they formed a part of the state unemployment compensation fund it would be obligatory to deposit them in the federal Unemployment Trust Fund in the United States Treasury.

3. Interest on state contributions. Interest on contributions under state laws accruing before deposit in the federal Unemployment Trust Fund forms a part of the state unemployment compensation fund and must be sent to the United States Treasury.

On April 13 the board accepted the joint recommendation of Banning, Wagenet, and Eliot that "the Board rule that interest earned on grants-in-aid made under the Social Security Act be considered part of the balance of such grants-in-aid subject to reallotment by the Board, and such interest shall be accounted for and audited in conformity with this determination." [27] This decision was taken despite the four briefs written by the general counsel of the Treasury Department on the legal status of grants-in-aid, and submitted by Eliot to the board. The general tenor of these briefs was to the effect that once granted, the moneys belonged to the states, "although held by them in a relation similar to a trust for particular purposes." It was a far cry from that position to the one taken by the board, but there was small chance that the states would dispute the board's decision, because the amounts involved were so small that they would not be worth a quarrel.

CONTROL OF STATE PERSONNEL ADMINISTRATION
THROUGH GRANT POWERS

The question of what control the board had over state personnel was first raised in connection with the administration of public assistance grants, and has been discussed in the chapter on public assistance. In unemployment compensation there were only a few states that had laws in 1936, and of these California, Wisconsin, New York, and Massachusetts had state civil service merit systems. Even in the states which did not have civil service, there did not seem to be much of a tendency to appoint administrators solely on the basis of political affiliation, partly because the job was generally recognized to be a technical one which required knowledge and real ability.

During the summer of 1936 the question of board control over state unemployment compensation staff came to the fore. In connection with Massachusetts' unemployment compensation grant for the fourth quarter of fiscal 1936, the board on June 2, 1936, raised the question of whether the Massachusetts unemployment compensation commissioners were devoting full time to their work, for which each was receiving approximately $7,000 a year, the full-time salary. Batzell had reported that these men had announced when they took office that they did not intend to give up their regular positions, and that he thought that they were not actually devoting full time to their work on the commission. The possibility of asking the Massachusetts attorney general whether or not these commissioners were required to devote full time to their duties was discussed, but it was concluded that the Social Security Board could not deal directly with the attorney general of Massachusetts, and would have to get the information from him through the Massachusetts commission. That fourth-quarter grant was made without settling this question and without investigating more thoroughly whether the board had the power to limit state salaries.

[27] In the board meeting of March 26, Miss Hoey requested that the same policy be adopted for the public assistance grants.

Meanwhile, Mrs. Mary Hutchinson of the staff of the Bureau of Unemployment Compensation had been drawing up an organizational plan, classification scheme, and requirements for individual jobs in state unemployment compensation commissions. This material was mimeographed for the use of any state agencies that might request it. But at this time there were few requests. One, however, came from Indiana, where the law required the setting up of a merit system and the holding of examinations for the selection of personnel for the state unemployment compensation agency. Mrs. Hutchinson spent four weeks in Indiana trying to arrive at some arrangement that would be satisfactory both to the board and to the Indiana officials. Two staff members of the Public Administration Service in Chicago were called in to work with her as advisers in laying out a merit system for both the Indiana Department of Public Welfare and the Unemployment Compensation Commission. People from the Public Administration Service sided with the Indiana officials in trying to get board approval for the holding of these examinations by the Personnel Division of the Unemployment Compensation Commission. With their professional background in personnel work, they wanted to see a continuing personnel unit established, one which would have duties and responsibilities beyond that of merely conducting examinations and setting up registers. A committee was appointed consisting of one person each from the State League of Women Voters, the State Employment Service, and the Unemployment Compensation Commission, and the first two of these were in favor of having examinations conducted by an impartial agency. The whole series of negotiations was particularly difficult because the Democratic machine was very strong in the state, so strong in fact that at that time 2 percent was being deducted from the pay checks of all state employees for the campaign fund of the Democratic party. The board took the position that an impartial committee ought to be set up to write the examinations and hold them, and refused to cooperate unless this was done, because otherwise it might find itself in the position of being held responsible for the Indiana Commission's selection of employees without being at all sure that the work would be well done.

Finally, after four different sets of rules and regulations had been proposed (each set clinging to the idea of having the Unemployment Compensation Commission give the examinations) a compromise was arrived at which was made part of the rules and regulations of the commission. A personnel committee was appointed, with one person each from the State Employment Service and the Unemployment Compensation Commission and with an impartial chairman, a professor of government at Indiana University. Mrs. Hutchinson fought throughout for a completely impartial commission and was afraid that a compromise would not prove effective as a continuing arrangement, because if the other two members of the committee ganged up on him the chairman was likely to resign and be replaced by a more "reasonable" individual. The specifications drawn up by Mrs. Hutchinson for the Indiana commission corresponded pretty closely to those suggested by the board in its earlier mimeographed bulletin. At the Interstate Conference on Unemployment Compensation held in Madison, Wisconsin, in October 1936, Executive Director Jackson of the Indiana commission expressed some doubt about the system his state had adopted. At the same time he recognized the need to attract good people into the state service and to convince the public that theirs was not a fake merit system.

At the Interstate Conference on Unemployment Compensation held in Crawford Notch, New Hampshire, late in July 1936, a committee on personnel standards composed of the chairman of the Mississippi commission, the director of the United States Employment Service, the director of the Bureau of Unemployment Compensation, and Mrs. Mary Hutchinson submitted a report which was approved by the conference. The report read as follows:

Whereas it is the unanimous opinion of your Committee on Personnel that the Bureau of Unemployment Compensation has a very definite responsibility and is very definitely concerned with adequate personnel performance in the various states: and

Whereas the importance and magnitude of this problem cannot be dealt with in the short space of time allotted to this Committee and to this Conference;

Therefore, your Committee on Personnel begs to submit the following as recommendations for consideration during the interim between this conference and the next conference of the State Unemployment Compensation Commissions, and for discussion at the next conference of these Commissions:

1. That the State Unemployment Compensation Commissions recognize the responsibility of the Social Security Board for adequate personnel performance in the various states, and that they further recognize the responsibility of the said Board to make personnel audits in the states in connection with budget grants:

2. That the State Unemployment Compensation Commissions welcome the advisory service of the Social Security Board in:
   a. Preparing a suggested statement of personnel classification which shall include standard grades, terminology, description of state jobs, etc.;
   b. Preparing a statement for the suggested development of a complete personnel program for the state agencies, preparation of rules and regulations to cover classification, selection, compensation, personnel records, promotions, demotions, transfers, discharges, etc.;
   c. Preparing a statement for the suggested development of a program of training, covering the groups of state employees which should be considered as within such training program and for which subjects training programs should be instituted;

>   d. Preparing an outline report of procedure followed by the State of
>   Indiana in establishing a merit rating system.

Your Committee feels that these matters are of sufficient importance to require close study on the part of all states interested therein, and recommend that they be considered and passed upon at the next conference of the Unemployment Compensation Commissions, in the light of the statements and of the report above mentioned which, it is suggested, should be supplied to the state Commissions as far in advance of the next conference as is possible.

The principles approved in this report were those which the board wished to have adopted, but nothing really concrete was accomplished. Mrs. Hutchinson told Frase after the conference was over that she believed the board would have to go very slowly, perhaps draw in its horns completely, in giving assistance to the states in setting up personnel standards and merit systems. There was only one state person, Wheeless of Mississippi, on the personnel committee, and the recommendation brought forth by that committee was not at all representative of the attitude of the state officials. Mrs. Hutchinson believed that unless the board proceeded very carefully in this field, state unemployment compensation officials would bring "interference" to the attention of other state officials and state legislatures, with the result that the board would be charged with interfering in activities clearly excluded from its jurisdiction by the parenthetical clause in section 303 of the Social Security Act. She felt, further, that if the state unemployment compensation commissions were to work with the board in setting up merit systems for staff selection, they would be subject to criticism from governors and members of the state legislatures.

Nothing further was done until the meeting of the Interstate Conference on Unemployment Compensation in Madison, Wisconsin, late in October 1936. At that meeting only two members of the committee on personnel appointed at the New Hampshire conference were present, and no written report was made. Wheeless suggested instead that a standing committee on personnel be appointed to continue the recommendations made at the New Hampshire conference. He also made a few vague gestures in favor of the merit principle, but the discussion which followed indicated that, except for those states with existing civil service laws, there was not much active support for the principle of merit selection. The situation in each of the states is indicated by the following summary of the minutes of that conference:

The chairman then called upon the representatives from the various states to indicate whether or not they had a civil service set-up. Alabama had not, nor did their unemployment compensation law provide for the selection of staff on a nonpartisan basis. California had had a full-fledged merit civil service system for many years. All of the employees with the unemployment compensation commission of that state were subject to the civil service law, but at the outset there were not eligible lists for a few positions, and therefore temporary appointments were permitted for about forty people. The California law provided that an examination must be conducted within six months of the time of such appointments, which could continue only for that period. Mr. Hyde outlined, upon request, the nature of examinations given for new classifications necessary for the unemployment compensation work. Idaho's law provided for staff on a nonpartisan merit basis. Massachusetts had civil service which, however, made no provision for key positions. Those positions were filled on a noncompetitive examination. Temporary appointments were made in Massachusetts in the absence of eligible lists; they, however, had to be terminated on the fifteenth of November and appointments made from the civil service list. Approximately 13,800 had taken the examination, of which 2,500 had passed. Of the number passing, approximately 200 were veterans and 40 disabled veterans. Since under the law these latter went to the top of the list, regardless of the fact that they had merely reached a passing mark, it was probable that better qualified people beneath them could not be reached. New Hampshire had no civil service, but, since the law provided for personnel on a nonpartisan basis, the division prepared and gave examinations for its own merit system of personnel selection. New York had a long-established civil service. In the absence of eligible lists, provisional appointments were made but specifications had to be drawn for the position to be filled, and the Civil Service Commission decided whether the applicant was qualified for a provisional appointment. Rhode Island, in carrying out the responsibility for a nonpartisan basis, made probationary appointments for a period not to exceed ninety days. At the close of the probationary period the immediate chief of the appointee offered recommendations, together with reasons, to the board. The hope was expressed that eventually there would be a civil service system of some sort. The Rhode Island representative warned of their experience with the weighing of educational experience. Mere statements of an applicant that he had graduated from an educational institution were accepted without verification, and it was found that they were given undue weight without proper investigation. Mr. Fuchs urged some method of granting an equivalent value to self-educated applicants so that they too might be given consideration. In Wisconsin "substantial equivalents" were accepted for educational qualifications. South Carolina stated that "in the absence of a civil service commission they have proceeded by using horse sense in selecting the men they have selected so far." Part of the personnel have been appointed temporarily, with the understanding that they must pass a merit examination. Utah planned to give full application to the merit rating system provision in their law. Oregon was without civil service but hoped to profit by Indiana's experience and to adopt a similar program. In Wisconsin all positions were filled from examination. All personnel from the top down was subject to civil service.

As in so many other cases, the personnel problem was brought up concretely in connection with grants under Title III. The New York officials insisted that the board had no power to pass upon the size of state unemployment compensation salaries once it had decided that the duties of a position were necessary for proper administration; and they had convinced the board's regional representative for unemployment compensation in New York that their interpretation of the Social Security Act was correct. Walter Gellhorn, the regional attorney in New York, was of a different opinion, as he indicated in a letter of October 16, 1936, to Assistant General Counsel Tate. Gellhorn's interpretation of the act was as follows:

The parenthetical clause in Section 303(a) relating to personnel means only that the Board cannot withhold a grant because the state law does not contain provisions on personnel such as civil service provisions which the Board might consider desirable. Section 302(a) which provides that the Board shall certify amounts necessary for proper administration provides an independent grant of power which includes that of refusing to grant money for excessive salaries.

He requested an authoritative statement from Tate to show the New York officials or to use as he saw fit.

Tate's letter in reply of October 20, 1936, confirmed Gellhorn's interpretation. This correspondence formed the basis of a discussion at the board meeting November 10, 1936. The general counsel pointed out that the question involved referred only to the federal payments for state personnel and that, for example, if the state wanted to pay a clerk $50,000 a year the board was perfectly justified in granting $1500 for this position and allowing the state to pay the balance if it wished. Wagenet was somewhat dubious about an interpretation of the law which would give the board too much control over state personnel; he was afraid that the board might not like to accept this responsibility when in reality it would have very little control over the development of personnel standards. Miles was in favor of extending control only to the extent necessary to eliminate fraud or anything clearly unnecessary or wasteful. It was finally decided to ask Eliot and Wagenet to consider the question further and bring in a joint recommendation at some later date.[28]

After a month of discussion, Wagenet and Eliot finally reached an agreement on the interpretation of the act with respect to the board's control over state unemployment compensation salaries. They submitted their recommendations in a memorandum of December 14, 1936, of which the following is a digest:

[28] It is interesting to note that on July 30, 1936, the board ruled, in connection with a discussion of personnel standards for public assistance in the state of Ohio, that a state public assistance plan must include minimum objective standards for personnel. No mention was made of unemployment compensation at that time, but the board later took the position that it had on that date meant this statement of policy to apply to unemployment compensation as well as to public assistance, even though as we have seen, the question as it related to unemployment compensation was still in the discussion stage as late as November 1936.

1. Section 302(a) is concerned solely with the cost of proper administration, which must be based upon the three factors enumerated, i.e., population of the state, an estimate of the number of persons covered by the state laws and of the cost of proper administration of such laws, and such other factors as the Board finds relevant. Thereafter the Board in making grants must consider the cost of compensation of state personnel in connection with proper administration. If a state wishes to pay $10,000 for a $2,000 clerical job, the Board is not required to make a grant for this sum, but it can grant what it thinks necessary for the proper administration and allow the state to make up the remainder from its own funds if it so wishes.

2. Section 303(a) on the other hand covers only the certification of state laws for payment. Under Section 303(a)(1) the Board cannot consider provisions of state laws relating to personnel, but Section 303(b) provides for the cutting off of federal funds if the provisions of the state law under Section 303(a) are not complied with.

On the basis of this joint memorandum, the board decided it did have the power to pass upon the compensation of state personnel, and proceeded on that basis. In a subsequent grant to New York State, for example, the salary of one of the assistant industrial commissioners working for the Division of Placement and Unemployment Insurance was considerably reduced.

Nevertheless the matter was by no means closed. At the Interstate Conference on Unemployment Compensation held in Washington March 17–20, 1937, the Committee on Personnel Standards, composed of Hatfield of South Carolina, France of Rhode Island, Langley of Idaho, and Knerr of Utah, submitted a report which was torn to pieces when presented to the whole conference. The first committee recommendation included a proposal that all state agencies adopt a uniform personnel classification scheme to be set up by the board, and that they employ a college-trained personnel officer. The report had been written largely by Mrs. Hutchinson. It was unfortunate that neither the chairman nor the other members of the committee were strongly in favor of the proposal. After the conference rejected the original recommendation (despite the support of the merit principle given by those states with civil service laws) the committee submitted a second recommendation with far fewer teeth in it. This was adopted by the conference even though resisted by the consistent opponents of personnel standards, of whom there were a number among the state administrators.

The conference finally recommended that each state unemployment agency

1. establish a modern merit system by which to select all personnel except director and legal counsel; that the chairman of the conference with the cooperation of the Social Security Board choose a committee of experts to prepare a modern plan of procedure for selection of personnel on a nonpartisan basis, such plan to be circulated among state administrators for consideration and adoption at the next meeting of the conference.

2. assign and, if necessary, train an experienced staff member to establish job classification plans, job specifications, and uniform compensation. That the state agencies take advantage of the offer of the Social Security Board to give training for this work.

3. have a qualified personnel officer on its staff.

4. try to attract qualified personnel, make promotions on the basis of performance as tested by a service rating, thus building up a permanent career staff, insulated from party turnover.

5. require only one year state residence for employment.

6. supplement a written examination with an oral examination to determine character, personality and general ability.

Not a great deal more was done by the board to control personnel standards, before the end of the period studied. Later, McKinley learned that the board had decided to bring as much pressure as possible upon state unemployment compensation agencies, through its control over administrative funds, to set up systems of merit selection and equitable classification. A complete personnel system was set up in Oregon with the cooperation of Chairman T. Morris Dunne of the Oregon commission, and this was also contemplated in several additional western states. A number of other states sent their personnel officers to Washington for a brief period, to be trained in classification work in the personnel division of the board. Shortly after the close of this study, one of the men in the classification section of the personnel division reported that he had recently made a trip to several of the eastern states to help set up classification schemes, and had also surveyed the Connecticut Unemployment Compensation Commission to determine what salaries the board would allow.[29]

THE DEVELOPMENT OF ADMINISTRATIVE
ASSISTANCE FOR THE STATES

The bureau continued its comparative neglect of administrative aid for the states until the fall of 1936. With the creation of a Division of Administrative Aid at that time and the transformation of the Division of Liaison with Employment Service into a subsection of that unit, a real start was

[29] Technical personnel service furnished the states increased during the spring and summer of 1937. In the fall, due in part to other reasons, a State Technical Advisory Service under the former director of personnel, Aronson, was set up in the executive director's office to handle the problem for both unemployment compensation and public assistance.

made in giving systematic administrative advice to the states. Early in 1937 a model organization plan for a state agency and model forms for contribution collection were ready for distribution. The continued slighting of administrative service for the states had been the result of lack of staff, the pressure of other activities, and, partly, the reluctance of the director of the bureau to develop a field staff which might come under the influence of regional directors. Even when in 1937 such advice was systematically offered, Wagenet preferred to have the state officials come to Washington rather than to send men out into the field. The account of the resistance to the use of a field staff is thus in considerable measure the story of why this service to the state agencies was slow in developing.

FIELD STAFF OF THE BUREAU DIRECTED FROM WASHINGTON, BYPASSES REGIONAL OFFICES

The use of the regional offices and a field staff by the Bureau of Unemployment Compensation is a relatively simple story. It might be summed up in the statement that the bureau made as little use of the regional offices as the general commitment of the board to a regional organization would permit. This was as true at the end of the period as it was in the beginning.

In June 1936 Frase talked separately with Wagenet, Murray, and Batzell about the relationship of the regional organization to the work of the bureau, and found that they all had pretty much the same point of view. Batzell felt that the bureau could not contemplate using the regional staff to any considerable extent, either at that time or in the more distant future. His reason was that decisions on grants had to be made in the Washington office in order (1) to insure conformity to the established policies of the bureau, (2) to keep in constant communication with the General Counsel's Office, which approved the administrative rulings of state agencies, and (3) to use the information of the Bureau of Accounts and Audits. He looked upon the field or regional staff as an intelligence service, running back and forth between the states and Washington, to keep the Washington office informed of the latest local developments. He believed that the real adjustment of grants to local situations would have to come about through conferences between state administrators and the Washington staff on each quarterly budget.

Wagenet at this time, though rather uncommunicative about his attitude toward the regional organization of the board, hinted strongly that he was entirely at sea as to how the field staff of the Bureau of Unemployment Compensation could be fitted into the board's regional pattern. The bureau was proceeding very cautiously and sending its field staff direct from Washington rather than through the field offices. He felt that it was much more difficult for the Bureau of Unemployment Compensation to use a field staff than it was for the Bureau of Public Assistance, because the former was organized internally in Washington on a functional basis and the latter on a regional basis.

Murray was not quite so sure that the work of the bureau could not be fitted into the regional pattern, but he considered that the most immediate use of the regional offices for the time being would be to furnish information and build up political contacts which could be used whenever unemployment compensation bills or amendments came up in the state legislatures. He was not nearly so sure that the functional division of the Bureau of Unemployment Compensation into three major divisions of grants and procedures, legislative aid, and cooperation with the Employment Service would work out; there was need for constant conferring between these divisions. The whole function of the Bureau of Unemployment Compensation was so closely tied together that it seemed probable that eventually the bureau itself might be divided into regional units and come to depend to a considerable extent upon trusted representatives in the regional offices.

At a conference of regional directors held in Washington around the middle of July 1936, it was apparent that the regional directors particularly resented the refusal of the Bureau of Unemployment Compensation to use their services. Pearson, regional director at Boston, stated this belief quite bluntly when he said that in his opinion certain bureaus did not cooperate with the regional offices because they had no confidence in the regional scheme and had no intention of using it. Mrs. Rosenberg complained that while the New York State Division of Placement and Unemployment Insurance had fulfilled its part of this bargain by sending her copies of all letters addressed to the board, she either did not receive letters from the board to the New York Division or received them so late that she was forced to obtain information about them from the New York officials or the governor.

When Wagenet addressed this meeting he was evidently on the defensive, and spent most of his time describing the proposed field manual for the Bureau of Unemployment Compensation and outlining the functional division of his bureau. He did state, however, that unemployment compensation representatives would be appointed within the next ten days in all those regions which had unemployment compensation laws. Meanwhile certain regional directors, including Neustadt, McCarthy, and Pearson, were appointed acting regional representatives for unemployment compensation. On the same day that Wagenet was making this statement to the conference of regional directors, his associate Murray told Frase that as far as the Bureau of Unemployment Compensation was concerned, the regional directors would not be given any authority for a long time to come, because of their lack of knowledge in the field of unemployment compensation.

The bureau was exceedingly slow in appointing regional representatives, and when the observers visited several of the regional offices late in December and early in January 1937 there were relatively few unemployment compensation representatives on the job. The situation with regard to the use of the regional offices by the Bureau of Unemployment Compensation as late as January 15, 1937, may be gathered from the following summary of an interview with Wagenet:

Wagenet was rather pleased by the observer's statement that the Bureau of Unemployment Compensation seems to have kept its activities free from influence by the regional directors to a greater extent than any other bureau. He explained that it was a well thought-out policy. Whenever the regional directors came in to talk to him about it he would always assure them that he wanted their cooperation in his part of the program, and would outline certain specific activities that he thought they might do. This proposal of specific activities, combined with his insistence that many of these tasks were highly technical in nature, succeeded for the most part in scaring off the regional directors into less difficult fields. Meanwhile, he has conducted most of his dealings with state people either directly through Washington or through field representatives directed from and responsible to Washington.

Probably the best solution to the problem of cooperation with the states will be to have a field man in each state. It is important for the Washington office to keep informed about what is going on in all the states, in order to function effectively in giving technical consulting service and in controlling administration through grants of funds. In the poorer states, the representative of the bureau might come pretty close to administering the state law, or at least to determining the lines along which it should operate. The main difficulty with this plan would be to secure the people for these jobs. There is not enough money provided in the budget for this many field workers, but it will be easier to get money than to find the personnel.

At that time Wagenet indicated, further, that the bureau had followed the practice of inviting administrators of the new state laws (passed late in 1936) to come down to Washington for a week or so for consultation on the problems involved in setting up their agencies. This practice was followed partly because of the lack of field staff and partly because the arrangements seemed to the bureau to lead to better relationships with the states:

The state people like to come to Washington and talk to the heads of the organization, and do not resent advice received in this way as much as they would suggestions offered by a field staff. The Washington staff works with them for the few days that they are in town, and they take away with them material which has been prepared to aid the states in setting up administrative systems. Many of them go away much impressed with the work of the bureau and the necessity for constant advice from technical people on the staff. Then if there is any need for a continuing service in the field it can be met on the basis of requests from the states themselves.

When Frase talked to several regional directors in January 1937, all of them seemed to feel that the Bureau of Unemployment Compensation had been particularly uncooperative and had carried on its relationships with the states in a rather high-handed manner. The regional directors kept pushing for submission of both public assistance and unemployment compensation requests for quarterly grants through the regional offices. This pressure was finally successful and Administrative Order No. 23, as revised on March 13, 1937, provided:

1. Instructions to states for submitting . . . quarterly budgets or expenditure reports for unemployment compensation will henceforth contain the direction that (1) the original and all copies of such . . . budgets and expenditure reports, and (2) a carbon copy of any communication (by telegraph or mail) to the Social Security Board or its bureaus in Washington concerning such . . . budgets or expenditure reports, are to be sent to the Regional Director of the Social Security Board in the appropriate region.

The administrative order provided further that the regional director would retain one copy of the state budget, in order to study it and submit his recommendations to Washington after consulting with the regional representative of the Bureau of Unemployment Compensation. The regional director was also authorized to receive one copy of the grant allotted to the state and to retain permanently one copy of the quarterly expenditure reports.

That this routing of budget requests through the regional offices was more in the nature of a formal concession than an actual extension of power may be gathered from the following provision of the same administrative orders:

3. The Regional Director, through the appropriate Bureau representative, will obtain from the state officials such additional information as may on occasion be specifically requested by: . . . the Bureau of Unemployment Compensation as to unemployment compensation budgets or expenditure reports. *Under no circumstances will the Regional Director, the Regional Director's staff or the Bureau representative volunteer information to the states as to the content or sufficiency of estimates, statements of expenditures and accompanying material, budgets, or expenditure reports unless so requested by the appropriate Bureau.* Answers to inquiries of the states will be made only in accordance with instructions outlined by . . . the Bureau of Unemployment Compensation and confined to such inquiries as can be effectively answered in accordance with such instructions. All other inquiries will be referred to Washington . . . the Bureau of Unemployment Compensation, and copies of replies thereto will be sent to the Regional Directors. These provisions shall not preclude the Bureaus from communicating directly with the states.

4. If a state is delinquent in submitting its . . . budget or expenditure report, the Regional Director will, through the appropriate Bureau representative, after a lapse of . . . ten days prior to the quarter in the case of budgets for unemploy-

ment compensation administration, and forty-five days succeeding the end of the quarter in the case of expenditure reports for unemployment compensation administration, make inquiry of the state *except when requested not to do so by the appropriate bureau.*

5. After the Social Security Board has taken official action in relation to a grant . . . the Bureau of Unemployment Compensation . . . will notify the appropriate Regional Director of such action by telegram including therein the official date of release to the press previously determined by the Informational Service. If a grant has been made, the Regional Director will promptly communicate the information to the proper state officials and to the Regional Informational Service representative, notifying them when so requested by the Bureau that the grant is subject to conditions of which *the Bureau will inform the state.*[30]

CONSTRUCTIVE ACCOUNTING SERVICES TO THE STATES

While this function was formally located in the Bureau of Accounts and Audits as a separate unit, it was really a part of the administrative advice which the board planned to furnish the states in the field of unemployment compensation. In actual practice the unit was more or less suspended between the two bureaus, and never functioned effectively for either. Murray's judgment below, given to Frase on July 16, 1936, was to be more than confirmed by the experience of the following months:

As originally planned the Division of Constructive Accounting would have been a part of the Bureau of Unemployment Compensation, with perhaps a similar division in the Bureau of Public Assistance. Adherence to a short-sighted view of functional division of activities led to the placing of this division under the Bureau of Accounts and Audits, probably because of the word *Accounting* in the title of the division. Several months of experience has shown that the work of this division is much more inherently tied up with the activities of the Bureau of Unemployment Compensation than it is with the Bureau of Accounts and Audits. Practically no assistance has been given to the states in setting up adequate accounting procedures; the division has not had enough experience on which to base recommendations to the states, and the personnel of the division have been drawn off into other activities.

The board had almost from the very beginning considered that one of the valuable services it would offer the states would be advice on accounting and record-keeping procedures for public assistance and unemployment compensation, particularly for the latter. But as late as May 1936 not much had

---

[30] Italics added. Even after the issuance of this administrative order, for several months thereafter, there was no evidence of a more extended use of the regional offices or a field staff by either the Division of Grants or the Division of Administrative Aid.

been done, except to make plans for a large "constructive accounting" section in the Bureau of Accounts and Audits. The organization chart of the bureau then provided for a constructive accounting section of one chief (CAF 13), seven senior (CAF 12) and four constructive accountants (CAF 11) responsible directly to the director of the bureau. The chief, Bachmann, and four senior constructive accountants had been appointed at that time, but only Bachmann was spending full time on the job. During the spring and summer of 1936 he visited practically all the states which had unemployment compensation laws, but he seems not to have worked out any very definite plans or procedures for the state agencies.

Seidemann, who was very largely responsible for planning the arrangements for the accounting work of the board, expressed to Frase, about the middle of July 1936, his annoyance that no substantial progress had been made in advising the states on their records and procedures. He felt that the board ought to send a constructive accountant into each state which had an approved unemployment compensation law or plan, to make a survey of their needs. Three different systems would probably be needed for states of different sizes and different types of laws. The actual installation of mechanical equipment would be handled by the business machine firms, who were willing to spend a great deal of time and money on these contracts, as evidenced by their patience in New Hampshire. But as yet Bachmann and his men had failed to put their recommendations for alternative systems for Unemployment Compensation or Public Assistance into writing.

The status of this constructive accounting service was brought before the board on July 14, 1936, in connection with the request of the Massachusetts Unemployment Compensation Commission for a grant of $1250 to contract with a Boston firm of accountants to set up records and procedures. Wagenet outlined the nature of the request in a memorandum to the board of that date. In it he pointed out:

1. that on July 6 they asked for $1250 for this work by telephone and that he replied that the constructive accountants of the board would undertake the job instead.
2. that Miss Fenn of the Bureau of Unemployment Compensation and Stewart of Accounts and Audits went to Boston on July 8 to survey the problem and report on the situation.
3. that McCartin, of the Massachusetts commission, in a letter of July 10, agreed to this work being done by the board if it would be finished by August 7, and outlined what the job would entail. It involved the preparation of:
   a. All necessary forms
   b. Complete instruction for employees

    c. Manual of instructions for personnel of the commission

    d. Flow charts

    e. Floor plans and layouts

    f. Organization and procedure charts

    g. (Temporary) system of employer-account numbers

    h. System of accounting with banks

    i. Follow-up service to insure effective operation of the system

4. his own recommendation that this understanding, in a more definite form, be approved, and that in view of the needs of the states for such services the constructive accounting staff ought to be increased.

Hughes, of the Bureau of Accounts and Audits, also submitted a memorandum at this board meeting questioning the legality of such use of appropriations. He thought that the board had no legal right to spend its appropriation for this sort of service to the states, and thought that at the very least the matter ought to be submitted to the Comptroller General for an opinion. He pointed out that several months earlier he had raised this question with Bane, when the Bureau of Public Assistance requested constructive accounting work for the State of Ohio in connection with the board's special investigation of old age assistance administration. Bane had agreed that there was a legal question involved, but the matter had not been brought before the board. In the Ohio case the solution had been to use regular public assistance field auditors to do the job. But if the board decided that it had the authority to furnish such services to the states, Hughes requested that certain other related policy decisions be made. The Indiana unemployment compensation agency was given a grant to employ local accountants to set up forms, records, and procedures after conferring with accountants of the board. Would further grants of this kind be authorized? Was there not the possibility that the board would be severely criticized for taking the bread out of the mouths of local accounting firms by insisting on doing such work itself? Finally, if the board decided to undertake such services for every state which requested them, the recruitment of additional constructive accountants was urgently necessary.

After considering these memoranda (only Altmeyer and Miles were present) Altmeyer expressed great surprise that Hughes should question the board's authority to use constructive accountants as it had planned. But Hughes stuck to his argument. He was quite certain that the board did not have the authority to furnish this service to states for old age assistance, because the administration grant was limited in the act to 5 percent, and it could be construed as going beyond that figure. Even in the case of unemployment compensation there was considerable doubt about the legality of such a procedure. He said that members of the General Accounting Office staff had intimated that the Comptroller General would probably rule that the Social Security Board appropriation was not available for this work. Hughes recommended that the constructive accountants work up alternative systems in Washington and that the field auditors suggest these tentative systems to the state authorities.

Miss Hoey remarked that the states did want detailed advice on these matters. Almeyer was sure that the board had full authority to furnish such services under section 702 (which directed the board to study the whole question of social security legislation and administration). The board *agreed* that it had the power to furnish this service, and so notified Hughes, Way, and Hoey, and that it would approve the Massachusetts request. That settled the matter for the time being, but it is interesting to note that on July 22 the board approved an unemployment compensation grant to Massachusetts, for the period from July 1 to September 30, which included $500 for a special survey of accounting services and business machines.[31] By August, the Massachusetts commission had decided to delay the installation of business machines until October, because the automatic feed for ledger cards which The International Business Machines Corporation had developed would be available at that time. When Indiana attempted to keep provision for local accountants in its budget request for the second quarter, it was informed that the board would furnish the services if they were required. Nine hundred dollars was cut from its budget.

On August 4, 1936, Bachmann told Frase that he was devoting himself entirely to constructive accounting for unemployment compensation. The work in public assistance was so simple that it could be left to the field auditors, who were working with the states anyway. Besides, he had had a run-in with the Bureau of Public Assistance which encouraged him to avoid all future contact with the "social workers" there.

The question of the relation of the board's constructive and other accountants to the business machine companies, when it came to advising state agencies, particularly in unemployment compensation, was always very ticklish. In fact, it was probably a major reason why the board never really succeeded in helping the states with these technical problems. Bachmann was suspected by the IBM representative of being partial to the Burroughs bookkeeping machines, because of their lower cost and because of his alleged indifference to the collection of statistics, one of the major selling points of IBM punch card machines. The observers were, of course, completely in-

---

[31] There was a widespread impression that, for his own purposes, Governor Curley of Massachusetts was pressing for the purchase of one company's equipment. The board evidently was willing to allow this grant for the purpose of employing unbiased consultants to decide the question, in order to thwart Curley's alleged aims and to prevent the possibility of unpleasant charges of graft and corruption in the Unemployment Commission of Massachusetts.

competent to pass any judgment on the merits of the respective types of business equipment and can only report the ideas of the technicians with whom we discussed these matters. There seemed to be no agreement, even among them. Bachmann was certainly in favor of bookkeeping machines, and he was relatively indifferent to statistics. He once remarked that he considered the IBM punch card equipment unsuitable for the Old Age Bureau's central records office in Baltimore and thought it cost twice as much as necessary. Mr. King, the sales representative for IBM on social security matters, complained of Bachmann's activities in the states and was inclined to blame him for loss of business in South Carolina, Mississippi, Texas, Utah, and other states.

The representatives of business machine companies were certainly tireless in their efforts. At every conference attended by state unemployment compensation officials they could be found standing around in the lobby, eager to strike up a conversation with any state or federal official who might even remotely influence decisions on the purchase of equipment. They were always extremely courteous to the observers and willing to spend an unlimited amount of time explaining the mysteries of business machines. At the slightest encouragement they would drag us off to inspect the machinery set up in their Washington offices.

It is difficult to draw any conclusions about this business machine controversy in the field of unemployment compensation, except to say that the board seemed so afraid of being drawn into it that the staff of the Bureau of Unemployment Compensation never did become familiar with the problem. The constructive accountants presumably knew something about machines, but they were not very well informed about the technicalities of unemployment compensation administration. Besides, they were part of another bureau.[32]

[32] Two additional bits of evidence turned up after the period covered by this study. Walter Couper, in April, was given a special assignment of one month's duration to go into the question of business machines thoroughly, and he came out with some definite conclusions and recommendations (Bachmann had resigned by this time). But this assignment may not have arisen solely from the bureau's interest in the problem of the business machine. The other repercussion from the earlier neglect in advising state unemployment compensation agencies on equipment and business machines came from the board's statisticians, in the late spring of 1937. In April and May, when the unemployment compensation statisticians of the Bureau of Research and Statistics began conferences with state statisticians and researchers, to find ways and means of actually collecting and compiling the unemployment compensation statistics which the board was to require of states, they found that much of the accounting equipment and procedure adopted earlier by the accountants was simply not adapted to the furnishing of this statistical information. Both the federal and the state statisticians began to realize that they had been sleeping at the switch several months before when equipment was being chosen, and about all they could do now would be to improvise means to get as much information as the machines would allow.

The board members themselves took a particular interest in the constructive accounting service. We have already related how, during the budget discussions in September 1936, they had, of their own volition, added another $100,000 for this purpose.

During the first three months of 1937 there was no substantial progress made in constructive accounting for unemployment compensation. In December 1936, Bachmann told Frase that he and his staff were still going slowly in setting up two or three model systems for the states to adopt. Then, in January 1937, Hughes was demoted to the rank of associate director of the Bureau of Accounts and Audits, and Paul Banning, from the Bureau of Internal Revenue, was appointed director. After the new director had gotten into the swing of his job, the Bureau of Accounts and Audits was reorganized into two main divisions, Public Assistance and Unemployment Compensation, each with a constructive accounting and a field auditing section. When Bachmann resigned in March 1937 Altmeyer tried to get Wagener, chief accountant for the Unemployment Compensation Division of the Industrial Commission of Wisconsin, to take his place as chief constructive accountant for Unemployment Compensation, but Wagener declined to accept. Then Wilbur, a young accountant from the Wisconsin State Budget Bureau, was appointed, but he was put to doing special studies for Banning.

When Frase talked to Hughes in April 1937, the former director summarized the constructive accounting situation for Unemployment Compensation. He said that very little had been done in furnishing states with consultant services to help them set up accounting and record keeping systems and that even less was being done at that time than before. Two of the constructive accountants—Carl C. White and Leonard L. Tucker—had been doing regular public assistance field auditing; Bachmann had quit and James Peebles, the only good man on public assistance systems, was temporarily filling the place that Tyler had vacated. The man in charge of constructive accounting had been for some time doing special studies for Banning.

As far as unemployment compensation was concerned, Hughes felt that there was considerable doubt whether the board had much of a function to perform in the field. The unemployment compensation record-keeping systems had to be built around particular types of equipment. If the board decided which kind of record system it wished to recommend, the equipment companies, which had the best experts in the field on their staffs, could design a system to do the job. That was what was done with the board's own old age benefits record system in Baltimore. The equipment companies would be glad to try new systems and develop new machinery to do the unemployment compensation job, if the board would only give them some idea of the problems to be solved.

RELATIONS WITH THE
UNITED STATES EMPLOYMENT SERVICE

APPREHENSIVE ATTITUDES OF USES OFFICIALS

The United States Employment Service (a federal-state system of employment offices serving regular employees) was already operating under the rejuvenating impulse of the Wagner-Peyser Act grant-in-aid system when the Social Security Act was enacted in 1935. W. Frank Persons, its New Deal director, had pulled it out of the desuetude into which it had fallen since World War I and had organized a parallel but distinct placement mechanism to register and place on the various work projects set in motion by the Roosevelt regime the millions of unemployed.[33] This National Reemployment Service, while financed independently, solely by the federal government, had been administratively unified in seventeen of the twenty-six states that by 1935 had taken advantage of the Wagner-Peyser grants for creating state employment exchanges.[34] Persons was proceeding cautiously in the remaining nine states, because of the political difficulties surrounding the state employment service in most of them. Thus in Massachusetts, for example, the head of the state employment service was a James M. Curley appointee, too weak to resist the insistent pressures of the governor, and therefore Persons would not merge the Reemployment Service with the state service even though the officer in charge of the national system in that state was competent to handle both.

The creation of the Social Security Board put Persons and most of his leading associates on the defensive. The new agency, with far more money to dispense to the states and with its valuable connections to employment offices administering unemployment insurance benefits, was bound to be viewed with suspicion by a competing bureaucracy, which saw itself eclipsed in size and prestige.

But these suspicions were rationalized with considerable cogency. Persons and his director of federal-state relationships, Miss Mary La Dame, were fearful of the spread of a state pattern of administrative organization like that which had been early projected for New York, where the unification of unemployment compensation and placement functions was contemplated.

---

[33] See Arthur W. Macmahon, Gladys Ogden and John D. Millett, *Administration of Federal Works Relief,* for an account of the Employment Service in work relief placement.

[34] On July 31, 1936, there were nine states where no such unification had occurred. These were Massachusetts, Pennsylvania, Ohio, Virginia, Illinois, Missouri, Oklahoma, Minnesota, and Colorado.

Although at the top level the New York plan proposed a director for each of these two divisions of its work, in the regional, district, and local offices direction and operation were to be amalgamated under a single administrative officer. In the view of Persons and Miss La Dame this would mean the inevitable subordination of job placement to unemployment compensation. They felt that the throng of people seeking insurance benefits in the offices used for employment would make it very difficult to carry on placement tasks, and that the antipathy of many employers to unemployment compensation would expand to cover the employment service if it were to be controlled by the same official. It had been a difficult and uphill job to create employers' confidence in the employment offices and to induce them to use these services. To couple the two functions might, therefore, be fatal to the further development of good placement relations with employers.

Miss La Dame also believed that the training and personal qualities required for successful placement officers differ markedly from those needed for compensation officials. To succeed in the former task involves knowledge of a wide variety of vocational skills, personnel policies in industry, and labor conditions, while the compensation job calls for the capacity to apply fine distinctions of rules and procedures in particular situations. Both greatly preferred the current Wisconsin administrative pattern, under which there was unification at the highest level for the formulation of compensation and placement policies, but in which the field operations of the two services were kept entirely distinct.

A minority point of view within the Employment Service was held by the director of research, Dr. W. T. Stead, who felt that the compensation function would inevitably become more important than placement; therefore, the only way to keep the latter from starving to death was to place it in close relation to compensation administration.

TENSIONS OVER ACCOUNT NUMBERS, REGISTRATION AND THE "DRAFT" BILLS

Even before the emergence of the basic problem of correlating the administration of unemployment insurance and placement, there developed a number of important issues of joint concern to the board and the United States Employment Service. Early in the consideration of the board's duties, the question of an identification number to be used by both the Bureau of Old Age Benefits and the state unemployment compensation agencies was raised. The Employment Service had its own account number which, by the time of the board's appointment, had been assigned to nearly twelve million persons. We have described elsewhere the interesting story of the selection of the employee account number system by the board. Here it is sufficient to note that the officials of the Employment Service were not able to accept the logic of the Social Security Board in scrapping the Employment Service system and developing an entirely new scheme.

Another related matter upon which disagreement developed was the question of using the Employment Service for the mass registration for old age benefits ultimately scheduled for November-December 1936. The board early asked the service to work out plans and cost estimates for holding this registration. While early in the winter of 1935–36 Persons appeared to acquiesce reluctantly to such a plan, he was convinced that it would not only jeopardize the placement function but would also cause increased expenses. Even if the Social Security Board should reimburse the Employment Service, it could not fully cover the extra cost to his organization. In planning his budget estimates for the fiscal year 1937, Persons proposed to withhold estimates for these extra expenses until after the regular appropriations for his organization were made. This strategy was dictated by his feeling that the opposite course would jeopardize the normal functions of his service and by the limitations of the Wagner-Peyser Act, which does not explicitly authorize appropriations to aid in the administration of unemployment compensation. When those estimates for a supplementary appropriation were presented to the Bureau of the Budget, that agency disapproved them. When he finally made up his mind to refuse the board's request, Persons' argument was that the President expected a marked pick-up in employment during the winter of 1936–37, and Persons did not want to undertake any task that would interfere with performing the placement functions such an upsurge would require. Having just emerged from the burden of relief job placement, he wished to make a real beginning as an agency for private placement.[35]

It seemed to McKinley that in this matter of using the Employment Service for the assignment of account numbers, the officials of the Social Security Board were so concerned with the necessity of getting the job done so as to save their own skins, that they had little patience with the protests of other agencies that taking on this emergency job would seriously interfere with their primary activities. One person close to Acting Chairman Altmeyer said

[35] The judgment of history probably would be that Persons was right in making this decision—even if the reason which he gave was not the real one for turning down this job of registration. The Post Office Department with its 42,000 offices was able to take the additional job of registration in its stride, without interfering with the peak operations of the Christmas period. The Employment Service would have been swamped, and a less effective job would have been done for the Social Security Board. Besides, the anticipated increase in private placements did take place. The total for 1936 was 1,510,000, a 36 percent increase over 1935. In December, the month in which the bulk of the social security registration took place, more private placements were made by the Employment Service than in any other December in its history; over 172,000 as compared with only 60,000 in December 1935, an increase of 185 percent.

early in June 1936 that he thought it would not matter if the activities of the Employment Service were seriously handicapped by conducting the registration, that the Employment Service had no standing anyway; and that it would be preferable to have the Employment Service suffer rather than have the registration of the Social Security Board impaired! It is easy to understand how any indication of this attitude by the Social Security Board in its dealings with the United States Employment Service would irritate the latter organization.

When the board's January 1936 draft bills for state unemployment compensation were being prepared, Persons and his aides sat in with the board's staff and participated in framing the sections relating to organization. They insisted on keeping the placement and unemployment compensation functions in the states so distinct that placement would not be obscured by compensation. They wanted to fend off the dangers implicit in the New York scheme, including the difficulties of cost accounting in an amalgamated state administration. When the draft bills were finished it was clear that the Wisconsin theory advocated by Persons had won out. In addition, section 12 of both draft bills smoothed the way for the acceptance by states of opportunities and obligations under the Wagner-Peyser Act.

Quite apart from the difficulties of harmoniously resolving these issues were the personal frictions growing out of special relationships within the Department of Labor and between some of the board's members and the heads of the Employment Service. These apparently increased the tensions inherent in the federal organizational pattern and the separate legislation upon which it rested.

ABORTIVE EFFORTS TO HARMONIZE FUNCTIONS

In an effort to minimize conflict and to further the development of a state program in which mutual interests were closely joined, Dr. William T. Stead proposed that a coordinating committee of top people from the two agencies be established. It would include one Social Security Board member, Persons, and such other members as the two agencies might designate. Below this committee, subcommittees of lesser staff members could work out technical details for the various plans. This suggestion was not accepted.

In designing the organization for his bureau, Wagenet included one unit which he called the Division of Liaison on Compensation and Placement, to be headed by an associate director and to contain, by January 1937, seventeen other staff members.[36] The board attempted to secure as head of this divi-

---

[36] Murray had opposed this. He felt that so ticklish a problem would have to be handled by someone with more authority.

sion Miss La Dame, who had been in charge of one of the divisions of Person's organization. Instead, however, Mrs. Mary Hutchinson was selected in January, and for some months she was the only person assigned to the division, although she had the occasional assistance of Rector, Neustadt, and other members of the staff. While the problem of organizing placement work in relation to compensation was clearly a matter of very great concern to both of these national agencies, no common agreement was reached on this question for over a year.

This failure to work out a prompt, joint program was not the fault of Mrs. Hutchinson, who submitted to Wagenet on January 28, 1936, a memorandum setting forth the major problems of coordination with the United States Employment Service which ought to be tackled at once. She called attention to the important part in the administration of unemployment insurance which could be played by the United States Employment Service, and insisted upon the great difficulty in surmounting the administrative problems that lay ahead. She therefore asked "that immediate steps be taken to bring the Social Security Board and the United States Employment Service into coordination so that the program of development may be planned now and gotten under way during 1936. It is therefore recommended that a coordinating committee, composed of at least two members from the Social Security Board and two members from the U.S.E.S. to be appointed by the Board and the Secretary of Labor, respectively, whose function it shall be to draw up a program for correlation of the two authorities into a system for the administration of the state unemployment insurance acts." The memorandum urged that plans be speeded so that the Employment Service would experience a minimum of impairment to its placement function, which had been making notable progress during the preceding two and one-half years. The attention of the proposed coordinating committee was called to eight major questions which ought to be acted upon by the board and the Employment Service before the commencement of benefit payments.

THE PROBLEM OF JOINT COSTS IN THE STATES

One very important issue jointly discussed during these first months was the part which the board should play in financing placement services within the states, and what formulas should be used for this purpose. This problem was discussed at some length by Persons during the meeting of the state unemployment insurance administrators with representatives from the board's staff in New York on February 21 and 22, 1936. On the second day of that meeting, Persons made it very clear that he was extremely anxious to preserve the Wagner-Peyser controls over the placement service, while Wagenet danced gingerly around the question of whether or not the board, in its grants for the administration of state unemployment insurance services, should permit the inclusion of any items for placement expense. At the same time, some of the states insisted that they were faced with the need to integrate in their administrative structure certain aspects of placement organization, and that they needed for this purpose more money than was obtainable under the Wagner-Peyser law.

In Stanley Rector's memorandum on administrative grants, prepared for the board at this time, there was included a discussion of employment office expense. The legal hypothesis which he espoused was that the Wagner-Peyser Act should not be deemed to have been modified by the Social Security Act, unless the legislative intent of Congress to do so was clearly implied. He presented the argument that the additional employment offices needed because of the recent adoption of state unemployment laws should be set up in the manner indicated in the Wagner-Peyser Act. He pointed out that the Wagner-Peyser Act provided for a system of national employment offices *"and for other purposes."* It did not designate the specific functions of the employment offices, and any item that could reasonably be related to the objectives of the employment office would seemingly fall into the designation of employment services as used in that act. Rector also found support for his view in section 5(a) of the law, which stated that the sums to be made available after 1938 were to be such sums as Congress might deem necessary. "This means that under the language of the Wagner-Peyser Act there will be sufficient authorized appropriations at the time benefits become generally payable to meet any and all necessary expenses of employment service units, whereas if these additional services of employment service units are to be accounted the responsibility of the state administration of unemployment compensation, there is an upper limit of $49 million to cover not only these additional expenses of employment service, but all other expense items of the state employment administration."

Rector, however, noted that the board might find that considerations of policy would make "necessary the assumption of additional burdens imposed upon employment services as an administrative cost item to be allowed for as defined in 302(a) of the Social Security Act." In that case he declared that the only function placed on the board which could be reasonably required of it over and above the federal burdens assumed in the Wagner-Peyser Act would be related to the needs of the states to pay benefits. He pointed out that with the exception of the state already in operation, Wisconsin, the employment service relation to a state compensation act would not come into effective operation until two years had elapsed and benefits had become payable.

He admitted that there would be expenses prior to benefit payments time to get ready for that activity. Wisconsin was the only state where the problem must be met immediately. He did not indicate in this memorandum what criteria the board should use in considering to what degree, if any, these preparatory expenses were to be considered.

Rector told McKinley privately that, except possibly for very limited overhead allocations to start the needed organizations in the states, the Social Security Act should not be charged with the expense of placement service. The Wagner-Peyser Act had not been repealed by the Social Security Act, and it had no ceiling on the amount of money which might be appropriated for placement purposes, whereas the total expenses of unemployment insurance administration under the Social Security Act had been definitely limited to $49,000,000.

The position set forth by Rector was not accepted by the board. During March, 1936, Mrs. Hutchinson and Mr. Neustadt prepared two memoranda on the proper basis and methods for determining the allocation of monies for the administration of unemployment compensation through public employment offices. In these memoranda they used Wisconsin as an example, since the Wisconsin people had already made known their desire for monies for this purpose, and were requesting something over $8,000 to be used in connection with placement activities in preparation for the payment of benefits beginning on July 1, 1936.

The first of these two memoranda suggested two alternative policies for assuming part of the cost of the placement organization, but made no special recommendation except that in the case of Wisconsin, whatever the ultimate policy adopted, a grant should be authorized at once for the last quarter of the fiscal year ending June 30, 1936, to survey the situation and to prepare for the prompt and adequate administration of benefit payments. The Wisconsin officials had objected to the suggestions contained in the first memorandum on the grounds that they would require expensive and confusing bookkeeping. They countered with a proposal that the board pay the entire budget of the Wisconsin State Employment Service over and above the maximum allocation of Wagner-Peyser funds from the United States Employment Service, plus a like amount appropriated by the state and local governments. They insisted that a rule requiring the state to match the maximum allocation of Wagner-Peyser funds was necessary in order not to punish those states which assumed fullest responsibilities under the act and to reward those that shirked their responsibilities in matching Wagner-Peyser funds. If that contention were accepted, the board would pay about 40 percent of the employment service costs in Wisconsin despite the fact that the actual use of employment service offices in that state had been chiefly confined to domestic servants and agricultural labor, classes of employees which were excluded from the unemployment insurance coverage. Wagenet had been trying not to commit himself on this matter as long as it was possible to hold off.

The second memorandum by Hutchinson and Neustadt made it clear that no state, even when it had fully utilized the federal grant available from Wagner-Peyser funds, had created a public employment service that would be able to administer adequately the load of compensation and placement. It said that while there were thirty-seven states affiliated with the United States Employment Service, only eleven had matched to the fullest possible extent the federal grants available to them. It interpreted the intent of the Committee on Economic Security as requiring the assumption by the board of this extra cost of employment service, and quoted Professor Witte's testimony before the Ways and Means Committee to buttress that interpretation.

Early in April 1936, New York presented an application for grants for the fourth quarter of fiscal year 1936 which included a request for $40,000 for additional regional supervisors for the Division of Unemployment Insurance and Placement. While New York would not begin the payment of benefits until January 1, 1938, Bowers and Bryce Stewart were apparently determined to set up from the very start a fully coordinated administrative mechanism for insurance and placement. They insisted that it was necessary to begin expansion at the earliest possible date, and they needed Social Security Board funds for that purpose. When members of Wagenet's staff broached this matter with Dr. Stead, the latter urged that New York's request be considered in the light of general policy. He indicated that it was time to bring together the proposed joint-laision committee, but this apparently was not done.[37]

At the board meeting on May 9, 1936, Wagenet recommended the granting of $30,000 to New York, despite the fact that there had been some feeling within his own staff that New York ought to have exhausted its opportunities under the Wagner-Peyser Act before it asked the board for money. The board approved his recommendation, but a few days later apparently doubted its judgment, because it sought further assurances from Bowers in New York that the expanded regional and supervisory staffs would, during the coming quarter, devote their time largely to insurance rather than placement duties.

Shortly after this initial grant to New York, the board approved a similar grant to Wisconsin. In doing so, an effort was made to treat each case on its merits, without setting policy precedents. The board and its bureau were shying away from a statement of policy partly because of a desire not to interfere with the program of the United States Employment Service in building an effective national system of employment exchanges. The service was unwilling to accept the Wisconsin proposal (namely, the payment by

[37] As late as April 16, 1936, the coordinating committee recommended by Mrs. Hutchinson on January 28 had not been formed, although Dr. Stead had been designated as the representative from Persons' organization.

the board of all extra placement costs after the state had matched its full allotment of Wagner-Peyser money) because it felt that a number of states ought to do more than merely match the Wagner-Peyser allotment.

New York received another allotment of $32,000 for its expanded staff in the grant for the first quarter of the 1937 fiscal year, but New York wanted to reach a permanent agreement about the future handling of grants for these purposes. Consequently, Bowers and his associates met with the board on July 31, 1936, to thresh out the problem. The issue, as presented by Bowers, was one of a fair accounting in providing services using common facilities and personnel. The actual administration of unemployment compensation must occur in some degree within the organization of the state employment service. Bowers requested "that you permit us the latitude of matching expense with expense when such expense is incurred by employees of different agencies and if so we will assume the responsibility and ask that you have a member of your staff check that we are not disproportionately using facilities provided from unemployment insurance funds in this common administration at headquarters and other offices." He also proposed that the cost of personnel be divided between the two agencies according to some agreed upon percentage. He agreed to abide by an apportionment to be made by the accountants of the Employment Service and the Social Security Board. He also wanted the board to agree to finance the expansion of employment offices according to a schedule beginning January 1, 1937, even though benefits would not be paid until the following year.

The board was willing to work out a consolidated budget for the balance of the year under which an agreed plan for apportioning expenses between the two services would be made. But it did not commit itself to paying for a large expansion of employment service offices. These small gains were kept by New York until July 1937 when the first grants for an expanded employment service were formally made.

THE CULMINATION OF FRICTION, ENDING IN ENFORCED AGREEMENT

Despite this modest progress in the peaceful adjustment of issues between placement and insurance, the hostility between the two federal agencies made staff collaboration very difficult. Mrs. Hutchinson, acting chief of the Bureau of Unemployment Compensation's division of liaison between Unemployment Compensation and the Employment Service early in the summer of 1936, had abandoned all her activities in this field. During the fall, all cooperation between the technical staffs of the two agencies came to a virtual standstill. The only exception was the cooperation of two individuals in writing procedure manuals, and this was the result of the interest of one of them in the Employment Service and his personal conviction of the necessity of cooperation rather than any official encouragement given to him. Even this small amount of cooperation between two individuals far down in the administrative hierarchy was brought to an end late in 1936.

The staff of the Employment Service were more worried about this situation than was the staff of the Social Security Board, because they realized that the funds available to the Social Security Board for 100 percent grants to the states gave it the whip hand in the situation. One Employment Service officer told Frase late in November 1936 that several directors of the state employment services had hinted strongly that as soon as the Social Security Board began to make grants for employment service purposes during 1937, they would tell the United States Employment Service where to get off. Nor could these state directors be blamed; they realized that the grants from the Social Security Board would be several times as large as the matched grants of the United States Employment Service, and their eyes were glued on the main chance. About the middle of December, Edgar Young, Persons' assistant, made the same analysis to Frase. It was evident that he and his chief were closely following the board's policy in making grants to states. He quoted the exact amount the board had granted for the administration of the employment service in Wisconsin for the previous quarter and the percentage of the grant to the total cost.

During the special state legislative sessions in the last two months of 1936, which were called to pass unemployment compensation laws, the picture of "cooperation" became a caricature. Staff members of the Bureau of Unemployment Compensation were attempting to secure administrative arrangements which would put unemployment compensation and the employment service in the same state agency, either in an independent commission or in the state's department of labor. (The Social Security Board's draft unemployment compensation bills of September 1936 designated the state employment service as the official agency for the receipt of Wagner-Peyser funds, but the January 1937 edition—which was earlier issued in mimeographed form in November and December 1936—made the state department of labor or the state unemployment compensation commission the official agency.) On the other hand, Persons had ordered the directors of state employment services to lobby for state employment services independent of unemployment compensation bureaus, or at least employment services which were themselves the official agencies for receiving Wagner-Peyser funds.

Early in 1937 the board began to go over Persons' head in order to secure the integration of unemployment compensation activities both in Washington and in the states. The time had come when this matter could no longer be postponed. States which would begin to pay benefits on January 1, 1938, had every reason to expect that they would receive funds at least six months in advance to make possible the expansion of employment offices and the recruitment and training of staff to carry out these new duties. July 1, 1937, was a deadline for another reason. The affiliation agreements between the United States Employment Service and state employment services ran from July 1 to June 30, and for the states which would begin benefit payments in 1938, it was necessary to include provisions relating to unemployment compensation in these agreements.

On December 19, 1936, Wagenet addressed a memorandum to the board requesting advice on how to proceed in relation to the United States Employment Service. He pointed out that the director of the USES had often said, both in public and in private, that the service should be kept entirely separate from the administration of unemployment compensation in the states. A paraphrase of his further statements follows:

1. The director of the United States Employment Service opposed any coordination of these two activities on the grounds that it would harmfully affect placement work because of
   a. Pressure for the placement of benefit recipients
   b. The retardation of the mobility of labor
   c. The likelihood that employers would extend their aversion to unemployment compensation to the employment service as well.
2. The director of the United States Employment Service had refused to allow unemployment compensation offices to be located in the employment offices in Pennsylvania.
3. The director of the United States Employment Service had directed the heads of state employment services to lobby against the proposals of the Bureau of Unemployment Compensation in state legislatures.
4. The director of the United States Employment Service had insisted on dealing directly with the directors of state employment services on budget and other matters even where the state unemployment compensation commission or labor commissioner was responsible for the administration of both unemployment compensation and the employment service.

In view of these circumstances, Wagenet requested instructions from the board as to further action and recommended specifically that the drafts of the state unemployment compensation bills be changed to provide that the state labor departments or unemployment compensation commissions constitute the official agency for all dealings with the federal government.

On February 2, 1937, Wagenet submitted another memorandum to the board outlining a far-reaching solution to the problem of coordination. He proposed an agreement between the Secretary of Labor and the Social Security Board to cooperate in helping the states coordinate the administration of unemployment compensation and the public employment service through uniform policies drawn up by a coordinating committee of the department and the board, to be mandatory upon the United States Employment Service and the Bureau of Unemployment Compensation. This proposal was predicated upon the assumption that the board would require that unemployment benefit payments, which would begin in thirty-two states in January 1938, should be paid through public employment offices. It pointed out the important additional responsibilities which these new functions would thrust upon the employment offices, and reviewed the attitudes of the board up to that date in looking forward to this joint enterprise. It concluded with a plan for joint action between the board and the Department of Labor, suggesting that coordination of policy was particularly necessary with regard to the problems of finance, organization, plans, methods of administration, procedures, premises, standards of operation, statistics, and training.

After a considerable amount of discussion during the month of February, this proposal was submitted to the Secretary of Labor on February 20, and accepted by her on February 23. Further details were elaborated in an agreement dated March 30, 1937, signed by the chairman of the board and Secretary of Labor Perkins:

The recommendation made on February 20, 1937, to the Secretary of Labor being mutually acceptable is hereby adopted by the respective parties and agreed upon as the policy of the Board and the Secretary with respect to services rendered state employment services.

To give force and effect to this policy the Social Security Board and the Secretary of Labor agree further as follows:

I. Joint Federal action will be pursued in assisting states in the administration of state employment services as an integral part of the state unemployment compensation system.

II. The coordinating committee shall be responsible for effecting and directing the cooperative activities of the Bureau of Unemployment Compensation and the United States Employment Service in rendering assistance to states in the administration of the state employment services to meet the requirements of the state unemployment compensation system.

III. A representative of the Social Security Board and the Department of Labor shall constitute the coordinating committee, to which all matters of legislation and administration relating to the Employment Service and Unemployment Compensation shall be referred for decision before action is taken by the United States Employment Service or the Bureau of Unemployment Compensation.

IV. The Social Security Board and the Secretary of Labor agree that all decisions of the coordinating committee shall be countersigned by the Social Security Board and the Secretary of Labor and all action by the Bureau of Unemployment Compensation and the United States Employment Service shall be in accordance with such decisions.

V. If no decisions can be reached by the coordinating committee, the matter shall be referred to the Social Security Board and the Secretary of Labor and only such action shall be taken by the Bureau of Unemployment Compensation and the United States Employment Service as the Board and the Secretary of Labor shall jointly approve.

VI. All records, reports, memoranda, correspondence and other information in the possession of the Bureau of Unemployment Compensation and the United States Employment Service shall be made available to the coordinating committee.

In accordance with this agreement, Secretary Perkins appointed either Mr. Saunders or Miss La Dame as the representative of the Labor Department on the coordinating committee. On March 30, Altmeyer appointed Frank Bane as the board's representative and requested that the subject for discussion at the first committee meeting (to be attended by the chairman of the Social Security Board and the Secretary of Labor, if possible) be the administrative relationship of state employment services to state unemployment compensation authorities, particularly where the former were under the latter.[38]

---

[38] This committee did not begin to function until after the period covered by this study had ended. Wagenet, of course, knew what was going on, but Persons was not consulted until after the agreement had been signed. Public announcement of the joint action of the Social Security Board and the Department of Labor was not made until May 6, when Chairman Altmeyer gave a speech at a convention dinner of the International Association of Public Employment Services in Washington. By the end of May it appeared that the details of the joint action would be elaborated in time to incorporate them in affiliation agreements between the United States Employment Service and the state employment services for the fiscal year beginning July 1, 1937.

.6.

OLD AGE BENEFITS

PLANNING THE BUREAU AND
ITS RELATIONSHIPS WITH THE TREASURY

For the purpose of ready understanding it is somewhat unfortunate that the term *old age benefits* was used in the Social Security Act to designate what was in reality a system of contributory annuity insurance. However, because that was the legal and official term it will be used throughout this discussion.[1]

In attempting to describe the administrative experience of the Bureau of Old Age Benefits we must recognize at the outset that it had no actual operating experience until November 1936, and then its only administrative job was to aid the Post Office in assigning account numbers. The activities on which its small staff were engaged were chiefly confined to planning administrative structures and processes. As late as March 15, 1936, there were only five employees in the bureau, including Director Murray Latimer, his secretary, and the assistant director, Elwood Way. By the end of March there were two additional employees. During April the assistant regional executives, then in training, helped to project plans for a field staff and for a temporary staff for assigning account numbers, but there was no important elaboration of the administrative organization. During this same period Mr. McDonald of the Veterans Bureau was helping to plan the procedural details for the Claims Division. It should also be recalled that Latimer's services for the board were on a part-time basis, because he retained his responsibilities as chairman of the Railroad Retirement Board.

---

[1] In the amendments of 1939, *federal old age and survivor's insurance* replaced the old designation.

THE ORGANIZATION AS PROJECTED IN THE 1937 BUDGET ESTIMATES

The organization chart prepared by Latimer for working out estimates for the 1937 budget bears the date of April 1, 1936. It was projected to January 1937 and thus did not cover the second six-month period of the fiscal year 1937, or pretend to be a complete picture of the full-fledged organization. In addition, as Latimer told the House Subcommittee on Appropriations on April 24, the chart was still highly tentative and he did not want it to go into the permanent record. Following is an outline of its main divisions and subdivisions which indicates that 4,336 people were expected to constitute the staff by January 1937, with 4,572 additional temporary employees for registration and the management of account numbers.

> Director
>   46 others
> I. Records Division
>   a. Procedure, 13 people
>   b. Mechanical (exclusive of registration), 763 people
>   c. Index and file section, 243 people
> II. Actuarial Valuation Division, 59 people
> III. Field Department, 75 people
>   Field (not classified), 3062 people
> IV. Claims Division, 74 people
> V. Registration and Assignment of Account Numbers (temporary), 4572 people
>   a. Field positions (not classified), 4240 people
>   b. Personnel records, 252 people

So far as the permanent organization was concerned, Latimer believed the most important units to get started were the Records and Claims divisions.

The April budget estimates of the board proposed distributing funds for administrative purposes among the Bureau of Old Age Benefits, its subdivisions, and the rest of the board's organization. Of the $23,000,000 asked for administrative purposes, apart from the nonrecurrent special item of $15,800,000 for registration, $14,825,000 was requested for the Bureau of Old Age Benefits for its permanent establishment. To the Records Division Latimer had allotted approximately $4,000,000; to the Claims Division, almost $3,000,000. The General Field Organization was allotted not quite $7,000,000 for training and regular activities.

The Records Division was to have the responsibility for maintaining the records of the estimated 26,000,000 wage earners who would be entitled to benefits under Title II of the Social Security Act, completing the registration forms and devising a procedure for filing them, and seeing that the 3,500,000 employers responsible for filing records with the board fulfilled their obligations. The work of that division had to begin promptly on January 1, 1937. While the estimates showed 1,019 persons employed in this unit, Latimer pointed out that it was probable that by the end of the fiscal year 1937 (June 30) the staff would grow to approximately 2,000 people. He estimated that the yearly per capita cost of maintaining the records would be about twenty-eight cents, but this included items other than Record Division expenses which, if taken alone, would be only twelve cents. He told the subcommittee of the House that these figures were somewhat lower than is ordinarily estimated by insurance companies for maintaining insurance records.

Latimer expected the job of the Records Division to expand, because it was thought that ultimately the whole working population of approximately 50,000,000 persons would at one time or another engage in employment coming under the contributory annuity system. Therefore, in the course of a few years individual accounts would have to be opened up and maintained, even though intermittently, for approximately that number.

Latimer was particularly concerned with securing personnel technically competent to man the Claims Division and have it fully ready to start by January 1, 1937. Under the provisions of Title II, three types of benefits became available to persons in employment subject to the contributory annuity system. There was, first, the monthly payment for those attaining the age of sixty-five, beginning on January 1, 1942. Second, those attaining the age of sixty-five before that time were to receive lump sum payments equal to 3.5 percent of the total wages paid to them after December 31, 1936. A third type of benefit payment was to be paid to the estate of an individual dying after December 31, 1936, before attaining the age of sixty-five. Latimer estimated that there would be at least 350,000 claims a year of the first and second types, and that they would begin pouring in immediately after January 1, 1937, when they would become valid. Therefore, he required a trained and complete staff in the Claims Division.

The task of the Claims Division was further complicated by the interpretation of section 205 of Title II given by the General Counsel's Office and subsequently confirmed by the Comptroller General. In effect it made the board the administrator for the estates of persons whose death payments would amount to less than $500. The discovery by the board's lawyers of the additional duties required by this section came after the first submission, in March, of the estimates to the Bureau of the Budget. Latimer was greatly disturbed by the prospect of this additional job, and urged the board to ask for an amendment at the current session of Congress to so change the language of the act as to eliminate the extra duties.

Leonard Calhoun of the General Counsel's Office made an extended statement of the administrative problem involved in section 205 at the budget hearings on April 24, 1936. Since that section provided that the board might make payments without administration to the beneficiaries of the estates of the deceased annuitants, these payments would have to be paid

to the beneficiaries entitled thereto according to the laws of the particular state where the deceased was domiciled at the time of his death. That necessarily means a different formula of distribution for each state because the laws of each of the several states differ, at least in some particular, as to who is entitled to the property under its decedents laws. This is further complicated by the fact that under the laws of many states, before any relative is entitled to anything under the intestacy laws, either some creditors or all creditors must be satisfied. This means additional difficulty in establishing validity of creditors' claims, and in establishing the number of creditors or that there are no creditors. Thus not only is the Board precluded from uniform administrative procedure in determining beneficiaries, but will have a very difficult administrative job in finally determining the deceased person's creditors, before making payment. If the Board does not exercise the option of paying benefits before there is an administrator appointed in these 80 or 90 percent of the cases where there are these small benefits—and that ordinarily would not have an administrator; the beneficiaries either get nothing or else pay a good part of all the benefits for the cost of administering the deceased's estate. The only alternative to requiring formal administration is for the Board to act virtually as an administrator. Determination of the extent of all assets and liabilities is frequently necessary prior to making anyone a payment.

Thomas Eliot said that this problem was discovered as a result of some ten weeks of research by members of his staff who had analyzed all of the state laws relating to the handling of estates. From that study it appeared that the Social Security Act as written would make the board responsible for paying all creditors and claims before the balance of the death benefit could be paid to the heirs. This would require not only a large increase in the Claims Division of Latimer's bureau, but likewise a large increase in the legal staff. He said that when sections 203, 204, and 205 were drafted it had been the intention to follow the language used in veterans' legislation covering similar problems. (The veterans' statute provided that the veteran himself might designate the beneficiaries of his death payment.) That was not done, however, and section 205 allowed creditors to file claims against death benefits.

EARLY JOINT INTERESTS WITH THE
TREASURY IN COLLECTING TAXES AND INFORMATION

The European experts, Tixier and Davidson, with their knowledge of the European practice of unifying insurance tax collecting and administration, doubted the success of bifurcating the two aspects of administration as the

Social Security Act proposed. Both expressed great concern over the task of articulating the work of the Bureau of Old Age Benefits with that of the Bureau of Internal Revenue. After studying the situation Tixier had inclined to the view that the Social Security Board, since it was obliged to fix the amount of pensions and other benefits in accordance with the amount of wages earned, should assume full responsibility for keeping the individual accounts.

The possibility of unifying the system by giving the job of tax collection to the board was early ruled out, because the Treasury decided that since it was charged by law with the collection of taxes it could not deputize this duty to the staff of the Social Security Board unless Congress expressly authorized it. It was equally apparent that the board could not operate the system of benefit payments without receiving current, detailed payroll records. Thus it seemed inescapable that the task of collecting data would be separated from that of collecting taxes. Nevertheless, it was not fully decided until April 1936 whether the Treasury should be asked by the board to gather the information concerning individual employee accounts from the employer, or whether the board would do that itself. If the latter choice were made, the task of the Treasury would be greatly simplified. All that the Treasury would need for its tax collecting duties under Title VIII, according to Alanson Wilcox, would be a payroll summary, possibly once a month. But one of the handicaps in the board's securing information returns, as Wilcox viewed it, was the absence of adequate penal sanctions in the Social Security Act for enforcing its rules and regulations.

When McKinley discussed this problem in March 1936 with Henry Mac-Reynolds, administrative assistant to the Secretary of the Treasury, Mac-Reynolds said he understood from his discussion with members of the Social Security Board that they felt the board would have to collect detailed payroll information. He had told the board members that he was willing, if they so desired, to place in the local offices of the Social Security Board a deputy from the Internal Revenue Bureau, to whom employers might pay the tax due that department and also make a detailed return for use by the board. He was of the opinion that it might be necessary to do this, so that the board could have the benefit of the sanctions possessed by the Treasury to secure the detailed information which the board needed. The Treasury could use these detailed reports, when it cared to do so, for checking the summary tax returns from employers. He indicated that the matter had not been fully decided because there was no need for haste. This view was confirmed by Frank Mires, who was acting as the Treasury coordinator in negotiations with the board and its staff. He said that the individual employer report would go to the board's representative, who would check it against the total shown at the bottom of the tax report (which was then in contemplation). The total would be detached and turned over to the Treasury.

On March 10 a meeting of staff members representing the Treasury and the Social Security Board agreed upon a resolution dividing the administrative duties of the two agencies under the Social Security Act. The essential provisions of the agreement were as follows:

1. That the inventory of employers and the inventory of employees for the purpose of assigning social security account numbers, be made by the Social Security Board, and that the Board shall include in its estimates the amount of the appropriation deemed by it necessary to make such inventory.

2. That it be recommended by the Social Security Board that there be included in the appropriation act for the Social Security Board, a provision which authorizes the Board to repay, or prepay, out of this appropriation, any other federal agency, or agencies, such sums as may be required to pay expenses and salaries incurred with respect to services performed, or to be performed, and facilities and office space furnished, or to be furnished, by such agencies at the request of the Social Security Board.

3. That the wage records of the 26 million individual employees estimated to be subject to Title II of the Social Security Act be maintained by and be in the custody of the Social Security Board, but that the Treasury Department shall cooperate in obtaining or making available the basic payroll information and that such records shall be available at all times to the Treasury Department. . . .

John Winant transmitted this resolution to the Secretary of the Treasury in a letter dated April 8 in which he declared that the Social Security Board "is in complete accord with these recommendations, and would appreciate the views of the Treasury in the premises to the end that a mutual understanding may be presented in connection with the appropriation hearings." A reply dated April 10 from McReynolds for the Secretary of the Treasury declared: "The Treasury Department concurs in the recommendations to the effect that the responsibility for making an inventory of employers and employees and for the maintenance of the wage records of individual employees affected by Title II of the Social Security Act rests with the Social Security Board. The Treasury Department will cooperate with the Social Security Board in the establishment of such records, and it is understood that the department will have access to such records when necessary."

THE QUESTION OF A STAMP TAX SYSTEM

Some members of the board thought that the issue of the division of responsibility between the Treasury and the board for tax and information collection could be more readily solved under a system of stamp taxes, a method that had been explicitly recommended to the COEC by its academic experts. Stamp tax collection, as the British and others used it, automatically gave the information necessary for account posting and also provided a receipt for the worker. The possibility of using it in America had been one of the first questions analyzed for the board by Pierre Tixier when he was being consulted early in the winter of 1935. He dealt with it in a memorandum submitted on November 25, 1935, in which he pointed out that with contributions based on a percentage of wages, the advantages of the stamp book system were lost. He therefore advised that the periodic filed-payroll-report (information return) method be used to ascertain the wages on which benefits were to be paid. Altmeyer was not entirely convinced by Tixier's arguments; he felt that the stamp book would prove simpler for small employers and for occupations like that of longshoreman and migrant laborer in which employers were changed frequently. Most important of all, the stamps would serve as proof to the employee of the payment of contributions by his employer. The pressure of other matters was great enough, however, to push this question into the background for several months after Tixier left. Furthermore, the Treasury technicians had very early decided against the use of stamps, and their views tended to color the thinking of the Treasury's administrative staff about methods of tax collection.

On March 27, 1936, the question was revived once more with the submission, by the Pitney Bowes Postage Meter Company, of a very elaborate argument in favor of the stamp book method both for unemployment compensation and for old age benefits. This firm, which manufactured machines licensed by the Post Office Department for metering mail, had spent a good deal of money on investigating the possibilities of using a more elaborate form of meter for stamping books to be used for unemployment compensation and old age benefits. Their report on the relative merits of the stamp book system and payroll reports was compiled from a questionnaire which they had sent out to various employers. Needless to say, the employer opinion which they presented was overwhelmingly in favor of the stamp method of collecting contributions. Altmeyer again became very interested and asked for comments on the Pitney Bowes proposal from various people in the Bureaus of Unemployment Compensation, Old Age Benefits, and Research and Statistics. He himself worked out a compromise plan for using the stamp book system for small employers and filed returns for larger ones. He asked Walton Hamilton to give him a report on this idea by early May. On May 7, Winant wrote Tixier once more to get his comments on the Pitney Bowes proposal as well as a general summary of arguments for and against the stamp book method. Tixier did not reply until June 8, when Winant was in Geneva, but Winant cabled a summary of Tixier's judgment to Altmeyer before a final decision was reached on June 17. Tixier's views, in summary, were:

No doubt the stamp system would not be impossible to employ under the Social Security Act. I maintain, however, my view that, where the law assesses taxes as a percentage of individual wages, the stamp system loses most of the advantage of its simplicity.

In those European insurance schemes which I have studied on the spot, in particular those of France, Germany and Great Britain, the stamp system has actually been employed only where the taxes are not based on individual wages, but vary with age and sex as in Great Britain or are fixed for a small number of wage classes as in France and Germany.

Before you take a final decision, I suggest that you should examine for yourself the working of the stamp system, for example in Paris and in London.

Tixier's long memo on the Pitney Bowes proposal extended into the general problems of collecting contributions and foretold rather accurately many of the difficulties which would be encountered. It also anticipated some of the solutions to these difficulties which were to be adopted by the board and the Treasury Department about a year later.

Meanwhile, the Treasury had been considering the problem independently because of the necessity of preparing regulations for the collection of taxes under Title VIII. Acting Secretary of the Treasury Givens wrote to the board on May 16:

Section 807 of the Social Security Act provides that the taxes imposed under Title VIII may be collected either by monthly returns or by use of adhesive stamps. Section 808 provides that the Commissioner of Internal Revenue, with the approval of the Secretary of the Treasury, shall make and publish rules and regulations for the enforcement of this title.

In connection with the preparation of a preliminary draft of such regulations, the Treasury Department has, after careful consideration, reached the conclusion that the taxes imposed under Title VIII may be more efficiently and effectively collected by means of monthly returns. However, this Department desires to cooperate with the Board in administering the taxing power of this title, and I would appreciate the views of the Board with respect to whether the taxes should be collected by monthly returns or by the use of adhesive stamps.

Inasmuch as it would be impracticable to make further progress in connection with the preparation of the regulations and forms until I have your opinion, an early reply will be appreciated.

Bane acknowledged Givens's letter on May 20. The point of view expressed was that of Altmeyer:

At the present time there are several persons who are collecting information for the Board abroad bearing on the actual experience with various methods, and this information will not be available for several weeks. Hence the Social Security Board is not yet prepared to state whether there should be a combination of the two methods mentioned.

In the meantime, the Board would appreciate an appointment to have its representatives meet with your representatives to discuss certain phases of the problem.

A series of conferences were held, but the Treasury had evidently made up its mind in advance that it would not accept any method so far from its tradition and previous practices as the use of adhesive stamps. Mires believed that either the stamp system or the payroll system would work, that the former would be more clumsy and more expensive, and that consideration of it was revived because of the plausible argument made by the Pitney Bowes Company in their booklet. He cited the successful operation of the second railroad retirement act, which utilized the payroll method, and he recommended using a carbon copy of the payroll. Admitting differences between the two situations as to size of operations and numbers of employees involved, he pointed out that 90 percent of the social security tax would come from large employers capable of furnishing carbon copies, and that to use the stamp method because of the remaining 10 percent might cost more than the amount of taxes it would save. The stamp system would also impose a heavy and ludicrous burden on large corporations who would have to stamp fifty or one hundred thousand books each payday.

A further expression of Treasury opinion was given by Mires on June 6 in a lecture to the training school of the Social Security Board:

Under the stamp method, it was contemplated that each time a passbook was filled with stamps at the end of a six months or a year period, the stamp book would be turned in to the local office where the amount of earning registered on it would be transferred to a new stamp book. This would mean that an employee would have in his pass book at all times his total earnings up to date. This would probably mean a considerable saving on administrative costs for the Social Security Board in eliminating a large number of inquiries by individual employees as to their total earnings at any particular time. On the other hand, a great many objections can be marshalled against the pass-book method. It would mean that some employers would have to handle thousands of stamp books every pay period, which would be a very large burden upon them, particularly in view of the fact that the Bureau of Internal Revenue is very reluctant to require employers to buy or to rent any particular type of mechanical equipment. The bureau has never done this in the past and does not want to do it for this particular purpose, as in the case of stamp metering machines. It has also felt that if at each pay period odd fractions are disregarded in assessing the tax, making each stamp at least one half cent, considerable injustice may be done when the totals are added up.

The payroll report method would not involve carbon copies of payrolls, because the Bureau of Internal Revenue has never requested any information of this particular kind, involving as it does more intimate details of an employer's private business affairs than is required for the mere collection of taxes. Rather, it would involve a small card for each employee made out with an addressograph plate with the employee's name, which would also contain his serial account number. This 3″ × 5″ card could be handled very easily by mechanical sorting machines. Posting of entries in employees' individual register accounts would be easier from this 3″ × 5″ card than it would from a pass book since the stamps in each pass book would have to be totalled up. Either system, of course, requires sending either the pass book or the card to Washington or to the regional office if this system should be regionalized. A further argument in favor of the payroll report method is that the Treasury now requires employers to keep track of the total earnings of employees who are likely to receive more than $1,000 in wages during the year. These reports are sent in for use in checking upon income tax payments of employees, and it would be a simple matter to coordinate these two activities so that little more would be required of the employer than he already does in filling out forms 1099. A copy of this card showing both earning and tax could be kept by the employer, another given to the employee, one sent in to the Bureau of Internal Revenue and another to the Social Security Board. These cards would be made up by the government and sent out to the employers. Every time an employee got one of these cards he would be instructed to check his identification number against the one appearing on the card in order that an additional check might be had upon the accuracy of crediting wages received and taxes paid for each particular employee.

The final conference between representatives of the Bureau of Internal Revenue and the board was held on June 17, 1936, when the Treasury view was accepted by the board. At this meeting the Treasury accepted the entire responsibility for collection of taxes and thus won over Altmeyer. The Treasury people clinched their case by citing their success in collecting other types of taxes, such as the processing tax and taxes on soft drinks. (One official told the story of a collector of internal revenue going twenty miles up stream in the Florida Everglades to collect a tax of one cent on a hog killed by a farmer who had sold one-half of the hog.) The board's capitulation to the Treasury point of view was made official in a letter from Altmeyer to the Secretary of the Treasury on June 22, which read in part:

The Board is impressed with the advantages of the stamp system, particularly in the case of small employers and casual workers. However, the Board wishes to defer to your judgment in favor of the use of monthly returns because of your primary responsibility and experience in the matter of tax collections.

The Treasury then proceeded to prepare a preliminary draft of its regulations for the collection of taxes under Title VIII (Regulations 91) which were considerably modified before they actually appeared late in the fall.

THE LOCATION OF ACTUARIAL WORK

Another problem which raised the issue of duplication of administrative tasks between the board and the Treasury was the question of actuarial work. Latimer proposed to the board that it sponsor an amendment which would transfer from the Treasury to the Social Security Board the duty of making valuations and estimating amounts to be appropriated to the old age reserve account. It was his opinion that the board's actuaries would be in a better position to do this than the Treasury's staff. However, the board preferred to work out a mutually satisfactory agreement on the division of duties between the Treasury actuaries and the old age benefit actuaries.

When testifying before the House Subcommittee on Appropriations, Latimer had to defend his estimates of the number of employees needed for the Actuarial Division. He argued that the number was very small compared to the actuarial staffs employed by the large insurance companies. Of the 59 positions proposed, only 14 were purely actuarial. He illustrated the situation by citing the example of the Travelers Insurance Company which, with an annual income in its life department of about $100,000,000, maintained an actuarial department of 150 persons, though at times it had been as high as 200. The sum which compared with the premiums of the private companies was about five times as large as the annual life premiums of the Travelers company. The chairman of the committee insisted, however, that these comparisons were quite inappropriate, and that Latimer had no need of actuaries at all, since the rates of benefit payment had been determined by the law. He pointed also to the fact that the Treasury Department had presented an estimate of $40,000 for actuarial services. He therefore could not see the justification for an actuarial staff for the board.

But Latimer contended that the Treasury could not function in making its actuarial estimates without the data gathered and prepared for the Treasury by the board's staff. Included in the data to be sent to the Treasury was the essential information upon which to construct the mortality rates, rates of withdrawal, and rates of salary changes. It was Latimer's contention that the Secretary of the Treasury could not perform the duties required of him under section 201 of the act without the preliminary work of the Social Security Board staff. His point of view was expressed in the following interchange:

MR. LATIMER: . . . primary work cannot be done in the Treasury. It must be done in the Social Security Board, because—unless we merely duplicate all of the 26 million records—we must summarize.

MR. WOODRUM: Undoubtedly the primary work must be done in the Social Security Board, but upon what basis, upon what data and information is the Treasury going to make their estimate to submit to Congress?

MR. LATIMER: They will base it on estimates of mortality, on tables of salary change, retirement, withdrawal rates, etc.

MR. WOODRUM: It is on the records you have accumulated, are they not?

. . . . .

MR. LATIMER: Yes Sir. . . . But my point is that this job of summarization and analysis of the primary data is the function of the Social Security Board and cannot be done in the Treasury, because, apart from the actual operation of the scheme the actuarial estimates will have no meaning.

THE BOARD'S INTEREST IN TREASURY DEFINITIONS

The board was vitally concerned with the definition of many terms which the Treasury proposed to include in its regulations designed for use by taxpayers. As the Treasury broadened or narrowed definitions, so would the account-keeping task of the board be automatically affected. This mutuality of interest may be illustrated by one episode: the definition of remuneration as relating to tips.

At the board meeting of February 28 Eliot reported that the Treasury Department had just advised him by phone that it was including tips on its definition of remuneration in the regulations for the railroad retirement tax plans. Since this definition was connected with the interpretation of Titles VIII and IX of the Social Security Act, Latimer, Wagenet, Seidemann, and Murray began a discussion of the meaning of remuneration. Latimer insisted that it would be impossible to administer the Railroad Retirement Act if tips were included for purposes of benefit payments. It would also be embarrassing to have a tax levied on tips and yet not be able to pay benefits on them. He advised the board that although the taxes levied by the Railroad Retirement Act were to be collected the following week, he could stop the railroad regulations from being interpreted as including tips in the phrase "remuneration from employer."

During the course of the discussion, the board was informed that the proofs of the Treasury regulations for Title IX—including a definition of remuneration which encompassed tips—had already gone to the printer. Latimer, however, believed that if the board requested it, the Treasury might change its definition to exclude tips. Eliot thought that tips were legally excluded from the act which called for benefits to be paid on "remuneration from the employer."

The board decided to send a letter to the Secretary of the Treasury recommending that tips and gratuities from customers be eliminated in the figuring of wages under Treasury regulations concerning Title IX. Latimer left the meeting to see the Treasury people about getting tips stricken out of the Railroad Retirement Act regulations.

Altmeyer was on vacation at the time of this board meeting, and when he returned, he declared that the board had made a mistake. The Treasury

Department, however, accepted the recommendation of the board and excluded tips from wages under Titles VIII and IX.

EMPLOYEE ACCOUNT NUMBERS AND
IDENTIFICATION TOKENS

The system of contributory annuities was built upon the accumulation of taxes paid on the earnings of each employee covered. The benefits paid would be calculated upon each employee's lifetime working record. This individual accumulation began simultaneously on January 1, 1936, for an estimated twenty-six million workers. It was the duty of the board to see that a correct accounting was kept so that when retirement age was reached, each employee would receive his due under the law. To start this huge record-keeping task, it was assumed that each eligible employee would have to furnish the board with certain essential identification information and that each would receive, in return, some numerical identification which could be used by the board and the employer in keeping their records on his behalf.

When this study was begun, it was apparent that the board and its staff were deeply concerned about the payment of old age benefits. Controversy was already ranging over the kind of number system to be adopted for identifying the individual employee and his account. During discussions with Frank Bane, it was revealed that heated arguments had occurred over the question of whether the number should contain seven or nine digits. He expressed his great surprise that so much emotion should be generated over such a dry subject.

But the subject was one of genuine importance. Early in November 1935 the board, at the suggestion of Seidemann and his technical adviser, Way, had adopted a number system composed of three alphabetical digits, representing geographical areas, and five numerical digits. This action was taken without any discussion by the board staff with other federal agencies. Probably the board was unaware that other federal agencies felt themselves vitally affected by this decision. When Dr. Stead, of the United States Employment Service, learned of this decision, he indicated to the board that his service, together with the Bureau of the Census and other federal agencies, would be affected by the new numbering plan. Data collected by the Social Security Board would often be vital to statistical studies made by the Census Bureau, the Central Statistical Board, the Bureau of Labor Statistics, the Employment Service, and other federal organizations. All of these agencies were using comparable symbols keyed to machine tabulation, but their symbols were without alphabetical digits. The Employment Service had developed an identification number system for its active file of approximately nine million registrants, as well as for its inactive file of approximately ten million persons, as of November 1935.[2] The number system used for these two purposes consisted of nine digits: the first two represented the state; the second two, the county (metropolitan counties like Cook County, Illinois, and New York County were divided, each division having its special digits); and the last five, the serial numbers of identification. This number system was similar to that used by the Census Bureau and practically all other federal agencies, and was keyed for use in standard statistical machines such as the Holerith.

While the Employment Service number system had been in use only about a year, account numbers as of July 8, 1936, had been assigned to approximately twelve million persons, seven million of whom were unemployed persons seeking work. The Employment Service regarded itself as tied to this number system until the WPA should end, because it had been made the basis of the payroll plan for that organization.

As a result of Stead's warning, the board authorized Seidemann to call a meeting of representatives of all interested federal agencies, at which the problem was discussed. As a result of this and subsequent meetings, a subcommittee composed of representatives from the Bureau of the Census, the Central Statistical Board, the Bureau of Labor Statistics, and the Employment Service was appointed, with Way as chairman.

The census people insisted that the alphabetical digits be discarded. In the first place, they felt that the adoption of the alphabetical system would play into the hands of certain private machine monopolies. There were only two companies which manufactured tabulating machines designed for a combined alphabetical and numerical system, and the government had brought suit against them under the Sherman Anti-Trust Act for allegedly dividing the territory between them. Way, however, who had dealt with these companies for ten or twelve years, believed that the charges were unfounded and that competition did occur. It appeared that the use of alphabetical digits would require the purchase or rental of new equipment by all the federal agencies. Since it was the intention to use this number-alphabet system both for old age benefits and for unemployment insurance, it would place a heavy burden upon those agencies already equipped with the other types of machines. It was later discovered—and given as one of the reasons for abandoning the

[2] On July 1, 1936, the active file stood at 6,666,599, the inactive at 16,230,214, making a total of 22,896,813 registrants during the three years past. The active file stood at 9,000,000 until May, when a major reduction began.

alphabetical-number designation—that many private companies would like-wise be put to considerable expense if that system were used.

Stuart Rice, of the Census Bureau, estimated that it would cost federal agencies at least five million dollars a year to rent new machines. During the 1930 census the cost to the Census Bureau in rentals to private machine com-panies had been more than one million dollars. Another objection was that only one kind of card could be used for the alphabetical machine, and that card was manufactured by the company owning the machine. The Census Bureau also urged the advantage of using a number system that could be keyed to a new tabulating device which the bureau itself had recently pat-ented, and which its staff regarded as superior to any other machine then on the market. The bureau's machine could use any kind of paper and so escape the high, non-competitive price of data cards.

Moreover, the census people suspected that Way was allied with the ma-chine interests. It is probable that the alphabetical number system was aban-doned because of the fear that, as Way put it, a "stink would be raised" over the board's playing into the hands of the machine monopoly.

Behind these objections was the belief that the board's enumerating func-tions should be merely one phase of a universal registration plan. Rice held this point of view, which he explained substantially as follows. At the present time in America we have birth registration in practically all of the states, although it is not done with efficiency or economy. Similarly, we have a death registration system which covers nearly the entire nation. The Social Security Act will require the registration of about half the population at the time it begins work. It seems grossly wasteful in money and in informa-tion not to articulate these three registration episodes and plan them as seg-ments of a unified activity looking toward the ultimate acceptance of uni-versal registration.

The subcommittee on account numbers presented a report to Seidemann for transmission to the board on November 27. The report discussed three separate systems. The first was composed entirely of numerical digits, nine in all, designed to cover ultimately 160,000,000 registrants. It would include a serial number of four digits, two digits showing the year of birth, and a three-digit series indicating the area where registration occurred. The second num-bering plan called for eight digits and was designed to cover 100,000,000 registrants. It eliminated any indication of date of birth, giving five digits for the serial number and three digits for the area of registration. The third plan was a combination of numerical and alphabetical digits. It would use four numerical digits followed by a combination of three letters, a total of seven digits, and was designed to cover ultimately 80,000,000 registrants.

In a covering letter to the board, Seidemann stated the conclusion of the committee as follows: "Plan (1) is the choice of the committee provided the Board authorizes inclusion of the last two digits of the year of birth. If the Board decides otherwise, then its choice is plan (2)." The report indicated that the chief objections to the third plan were its greater cost and the greater amount of time it would take to punch and sort such numbers.

Seidemann urged the board to make an early decision so that states with unemployment compensation laws expecting to make an early registration of employees might use the numbering system adopted by the board. He also recorded his personal view that the year of birth ought to be included in the registration number, "because of the facility with which the accounts may be handled, and the resulting economy of operation." Seidemann later explained that if the year of birth was not included in the number symbol, the necessity of a second punch card would increase costs to the board by about a quarter of a million dollars a year.

Before the board took action on the report, Way prepared a memorandum suggesting a slight modification of the number scheme. He would retain the nine-digit number, but would make the first four digits stand for the serial number. He would also group the last five together, using the first two digits to represent age and the last three to represent area. Way proposed that a code number be substituted for the age digits, except for young people who would probably not object to their ages being known. On December 17, the board approved an account number patterned after the committee's recommendation, including an age symbol but rejecting the code suggested by Way. It agreed, however, that the registrant should have the right at any time to secure an entirely new account number, or if he requested it, to have a code symbol indicate his age.

Seidemann expressed the hope that when the board decided on the number system, it would stand pat. He was doomed to disappointment. The board had scarcely adopted its resolution of the seventeenth when Altmeyer asked for a reconsideration on the basis of an appeal by Hurwitz of New York State. He wanted a number of not more than seven digits including two alphabetical symbols. As a result, a committee made up of Way, Stead, Rice, Givens, and Hurwitz was organized. It was to convene in New York during the Christmas meetings of the American Statistical Association and was to lock itself up until it came to a *final* conclusion.

This committee at length endorsed the system which the board had adopted on December 17, although Hurwitz agreed reluctantly. Seidemann told McKinley on the third of January that he hoped that would end the matter, although he knew that Altmeyer was still reluctant to use the age designation.

Seidemann had expected that the account files for the old age beneficiaries would be arranged on the basis of the year of birth. Apparently this notion had been changed by the end of January 1936, when Way said that the plan was to use the year the registrant reached sixty-five, the age of retirement, instead of the year of birth. This would, he said, economize on the total of numbers needed, for as soon as a person reached sixty-five, his record would pass out of the file and his number be given to someone else.

On February 5, the board again considered the account number question and instructed Way to prepare a report on the comparative costs and advantages of the two methods of setting up internal records for old age benefits and whether or not age should be designated. This reconsideration was probably influenced by the objections to the age designation raised on January 23 at a meeting of New England and New York unemployment compensation delegates. Hurwitz of New York, Watt of Massachusetts, and Davie of New Hampshire had strongly protested the inclusion of age digits.

A few days later, Latimer said that Way's calculations on the effect of dropping the year of birth from the digits in the registration account number indicated that his earlier estimate of a quarter of a million dollars in extra administrative expenses was too high. If the objection to a number which showed the year of birth was fairly widespread among workers, it seemed likely that a large percentage of them would falsify the date of birth. Later, when they claimed benefits, many corrections requiring the manual sorting of thousands of cards would have to be made, a very expensive process. If, on the other hand, the incentive for falsifying age was removed, then less expensive machine-sorting would be sufficient. Thus, it would be possible to save money and expedite record-keeping by dropping the year of birth from the registration number.

As a result of these recalculations by Way and Latimer, the board, on February 14, rescinded its action of December 17, 1936, and adopted a new nine-number scheme in which the first three digits would stand for the area, the next two for the month of birth, and the last four for the serial number. The two digits representing the month of birth simply increased the number of permutations possible, and were of little importance from the standpoint of administration.[3]

When this action was taken, New Hampshire had already made an agreement with the board to use its old system for inventorying employees subject to its unemployment compensation law. It had been assigned certain area

---

[3] This two-digit number representing the month of birth was still not final. It was thrown out and a new number plan adopted on June 2, 1936.

digits and was already beginning to use age digits. It continued to do this even after the board's reversal on February 14. Latimer reported, on February 9, that New York was also willing to use numbers suggested by the board, except that it wanted to key counties into the area digits, although the board's scheme ignored county lines and divided the nation into one thousand areas. Latimer saw no obstacle to permitting New York to use county boundaries for its area digits. As noted above, the United States Employment Service, as well as a number of other federal agencies, used a system of area digits based upon county subdivisions. The New York point of view, therefore, had ample historical precedent.

In view of the board's decision to abandon the combined letter and figure scheme and to eliminate age digits, the Employment Service came to feel that its system and the one finally adopted by the board were quite similar. It therefore renewed its suggestion that the board adopt the Employment Service number plan. It argued that if this were to be done, a large and expensive part of the registration task would have been accomplished. To assign numbers to the unemployed, many of whom were already covered by the Employment Service system, was particularly difficult because the people would have to be brought to some central point for registration. One objection to the number plan in use by the Employment Service was the fact that in large metropolitan counties, like those in Chicago and New York, a single county number might have to cover about one hundred thousand people. The Employment Service answered that for such large counties, several county numbers were assigned, and it was also possible to give the states with large populations two numbers, since the state digits permit ninety-nine combinations. The assignment of two state numbers to a state like Illinois would, in turn, allow the doubling of county numbers. Dr. Stead believed that his number plan could be so arranged for Illinois as to take care of a possible compensable population in Cook County which would exceed the total present population of that county. He asserted that one billion compensables could be theoretically covered under the Employment Service numbering system. While the assignment of numbers by blocks somewhat reduced the possible coverage, it would still be adequate for the anticipated population of the United States. To these arguments the board turned a deaf ear, though as late as July 1936 Persons was still asking why the Employment Service system could not be used.

Simultaneously with the discussion over the registration number, there was considerable debate about what information should be included on the employee's registration card and what identification device should be given to the employee to indicate he had been registered. Both of these items were discussed at the first three conferences of the state unemployment insurance administrators. During the February 1936 conference in New York, the

New Hampshire administrator explained what had been done in his state for the initial registration of employees. He indicated that there had been pretty thorough cooperation between New Hampshire and the board, though one or two items of information which the board wanted had not been included in the initial New Hampshire census.

The information which the board's staff thought necessary to include on the registration card was stated by Way at this meeting. It comprised the following: address, sex, date of birth, place of birth, race, mother's maiden name, father's given name, present occupation, present employer, the applicant's signature, the date of the interview, and the signature of the interviewer. At the earlier Washington meeting in January 1936, some of the states, particularly New York, questioned the desirability of including the mother's maiden name, the father's given name, and race. Way explained that the first two items were necessary as additional identification checks, while the last item was essential to the purpose of actuarial calculations, since there were apparently important differences in life expectancies among different races. Hurwitz, at this time, objected to including the applicant's address, his employer's address, and his occupation, since all three items were not consistent throughout life but were subject to frequent change.

Another objection was raised at the New York meeting to the use of the word *race*. Way made it clear that it was included for both identification and actuarial purposes. The objections voiced in the discussion, however, were not to the facts which the item was designed to obtain, but to the word used. (Some months later it was decided to use the word *color* instead of *race*.)

A good deal of fear was evidenced, particularly by the New York people, that the identification token given to the employee would be used for blacklisting by the employer, particularly if it included the employee's name. Therefore, they felt that the only item of information on the identification token, which the employee would have to show his employer, should be the number, and even it should be changed for any employee on his request.

It is interesting to point out here that the system which had been used by the United States Employment Service for some months included all the items objected to by the state administrators. The registration card which that service had used for approximately twelve million persons included not only all these items, but coded union and religious affiliations as well. The religious designation had been included because many employers specified that members of certain faiths were unacceptable. The Employment Service took the position that it was better to send the employer people he wanted rather than to let an employee begin a job and then be fired because of religious prejudice. Stead said there had been no protest from the labor unions concerning the inclusion of age and union affiliation on the registration card. Of course, it was provided by law that these cards would not be divulged either to the employer or to the public. Similarly, the social security card given the employee would not contain all the information included on the registration form.

The identification card given by the Employment Service to the worker, which the employer could demand to see whenever the worker applied for a job, gave his age as well as his name. Probably the fact that most of the registrants under the USES and the Reemployment Service were restricted to working for PWA or WPA accounted for the lack of protest over the inclusion of age.[4]

Another phase of the registration problem intermittently discussed by the board and its staff throughout the period from November to June was the kind of identification token to be given the employee at the time of registration. At one time, Seidemann had favored the use of a small card similar to the usual credit or trade union card. However, objections were raised to the fact that such cards wear out very rapidly and are used for comparatively short terms. A proposal was made by the Addressograph-Multigraph Corporation to furnish a metal card, or token, measuring approximately $\frac{3}{4}"$ × $2\frac{7}{8}"$, made of Monel Metal, a noncorrosive substance of nickel and copper. This token would have on one side the name and account number of the employee and the name of the Social Security Board. On the reverse side would be the request: "If found, drop in the mail box, no postage required." On April 6, Seidemann and Latimer recommended to the board the use of a metal identification token made of suitable noncorrosive material. They asked the board for authority to undertake immediate negotiation of a contract with the Addressograph Corporation for the manufacture of such tokens and the equipment needed for the initial stages of registration. Their report indicated it would take 250 tons of metal to furnish the number of tokens required to complete registration, and the manufacturer of the metal would have to equip his plant with certain additional machinery, so that it would take him from a month to six weeks from the date of his contract with Addressograph to deliver the tokens. There was only one manufacturer producing this metal, on which it held a patent. Similarly, Addressograph Corporation would need additional equipment to cut, engrave, and finish the tokens.

The advantages urged in favor of this identification device were listed as follows:

1. Permanence—It would not be affected by dirt, grease, perspiration, or by the natural elements, and only to a very slight degree by time.

2. Accuracy—Various records of the Board could be imprinted from the embossed token before delivery to the employee, thus obviating the probability

---

[4] At the time of the February discussions neither Seidemann nor Way knew that these controversial items were shown on the registration and identification cards used by the Employment Service.

of transposition of numbers or incorrect spelling, as between identification token and the Board's records. It could also be used by employers in making reports, facilitating their work, and eliminating the possibility of error in either name or number.

3. Economy—If the initial cost of the metal token and the cost of heading various records of the Board with the token is compared with the initial cost of a good type of card and holder and the cost of separately typed headings on such records, the economy of the metal token is evident. It is estimated that the initial cost of the token delivered to the employee will average approximately five cents.

Four days after this memorandum was written, a conference was held in Altmeyer's office to consider this and alternative proposals. This meeting was attended by Altmeyer, Seidemann, Latimer, Way, John Corson, Miss Helen Jeter of the board's statistical staff, Isidor Lubin and an associate from the Bureau of Labor Statistics, and Karl Pribram, an expert on the Austrian social insurance system. Professors E. Wight Bakke of Yale and Douglas Brown of Princeton were also present. Altmeyer asked the group to answer two questions: (1) Was there any need for an identification token? (2) If there was agreement on the need for an identification token, what kind of device should be used? Unanimous agreement was quickly reached on the need for a token, but an entire afternoon was consumed in talking about the second question.

Lubin and his associate at first vigorously opposed the metal token device on the grounds that it would not be carried by the employee anyway and, if it were so carried, it would be of no value to the employer. Latimer and Way explained that they intended to use the identification plate at the time of registration to stamp some five different cards for each employee which would be basic to their whole record-keeping scheme. They also pointed out that since this token was to be made to fit into the Addressograph machine, it would be used by many employers in making out their payroll reports to the federal government. The cost of the token would be five cents. Lubin thereupon withdrew his objections, saying that that cost was warranted merely because it would secure accuracy in employee number and name for the board's records. He was skeptical that the token would be used by employers for payroll reports, however, since the metal was not sufficiently strong to withstand bending and mutilation. Altmeyer was skeptical about both the metal token and its proposed form. No conclusion was reached on the question of the form of token.

A week later, Way stated that the board was no nearer a decision about either tokens or registration. He had designed a token which looked something like a business card. It was his view that this metal device would probably not be used either by the very small employer or the very large industrial concern for reporting payrolls. He did feel, however, that it would be used in many moderate-sized establishments because a hand machine for stamping the number on payroll forms or on time cards had been designed which could be manufactured and sold for about two dollars. Way felt that the use of tokens for payroll reporting could be markedly enlarged by an educational campaign. Way and Seidemann were both inclined to discount the argument that the metal token smacked of regimentation or a fingerprint system. They contended that workmen and employers in industry were so much in the habit of using metal discs for identification that there was no danger of such misinterpretation.

Still, after much work by Way, the metal token plan was abandoned, and the board, early in June, decided to use a small paper card.

BUREAU DEVELOPMENT AND PLANS FOR REGISTERING ELIGIBLE EMPLOYEES

How and when to start the process of setting up individual accounts for the estimated twenty-six million eligible workers was the subject of endless discussion and study before registration actually occurred. *Registration* was the term first used to designate the organization of accounts, even though fears quickly developed that it sounded too much like *regimentation* and would thus furnish a convenient weapon for opponents of social insurance to use in drumming up adverse public sentiment. Pierre Tixier suggested *matriculation* as a substitute, but this was dismissed as too academic and "brain trusty." For a time during early spring 1936 there was an informal agreement that the word *inventory* would be used, but after some effort to give it currency in conversation it was abandoned as too obscure. Finally in the summer of 1936, the board formally adopted the substitute phrase *assignment of account numbers*. But because the verbal habits of staff members were already set, the term *registration* lived on in common discourse though it disappeared from official documents.

When Henry Seidemann was first interviewed in November 1935, he expressed the belief that the Social Security Board must speedily decide when registration was to be held. He assumed, as did most of his associates, that registration should be conducted simultaneously, or nearly so, for all the nation's eligible workers. He therefore regarded the perfection of plans for this mass enrollment as the most urgent task confronting himself and his colleagues, next to preparing the board's first budget. Dr. W. T. Stead had already been requested by the board to prepare a plan for registration, together with an estimate of cost in case the facilities of the United States Employment Service were used. His report indicated that the cost would be approximately $7,500,000 and that nearly sixteen thousand people would be needed to do the job. He proposed utilizing the existing facilities of the Employment Service, then totaling 232 state employment district offices and 490 regional reemployment district offices. There were 36 branch offices of the state employment services and 1,330 branches of the reemployment service available also.

Not long after Stead's report was made, the board created its own field organization committee. Because of Persons' intimations that the placement functions of the Employment Service would be disrupted if registration were handled through it, and because certain members of the board appeared to feel that the board itself should assume full responsibility for the registration task, it was soon assumed that the Employment Service would not be used and that the board would set up its own organization.

BUDGET DISCUSSIONS RAISE THE DATE ISSUE

In the meantime, no conclusion had been reached as to the time registration should take place. On January 3, 1936, the board approved Seidemann's letter to Budget Director Bell asking for an item in the final 1936 budget to finance the cost of registration. This would appear to indicate that the board was hoping to accomplish this job, or at least inaugurate it, before June 30, 1936. However, on February 17 the board instructed Seidemann to confer with Budget Director Bell and to follow his advice concerning the fiscal year in which the appropriation should be included.

Murray Latimer, appointed temporary Director of the Bureau of Old Age Benefits in January 1936, thought that registration ought to be completed before January 1937. His reasons, presented during budget hearings in April 1936 before the House Subcommittee on Appropriations, were that the states with unemployment insurance laws were already in need of registration, and that the job of the Old Age Benefits Bureau would be greatly facilitated if the registration were completed before January 1937. He estimated that over a million employees changed employers each month. If the board were to delay assigning account numbers until the first tax returns from employers were filed, "endless confusion would result. In the case of some large employers they possibly would prefer to file this once a year, and some would prefer to file it once a quarter and that may or may not be standardized."

THE CHAIRMAN: Do you think you are going through the entire United States and find the names and addresses of those employees and assign numbers to them between now and January?
MR. LATIMER: It can be done. There will be some, of course, whom we will not find but it can be completed substantially.
The account will then be ready to receive entries immediately after January

1st. If we wait until after January 1st to assign account numbers there will be literally hundreds of thousands of cases of uncertain identity and there will be confusion which will be hanging over the accounts for years.

Tixier had recommended that registration be postponed until January 1, 1937, and then be accomplished on a single day. The reason for this recommendation was that the workers at that time would be different from those who worked during the preceding months. This would lead to the unnecessary opening of individual accounts "upon which there will be unnecessary notations of the wages." He urged the board to register everyone throughout the country on the first of January, rather than spread the registration work over a period of weeks or months, which would lead to many duplications because of changes in occupation during that period.[5] Latimer felt that Tixier's view of the problem was inaccurate because of his European background. In Europe the practice of universal registration made it relatively easy to undertake such an enumeration in one fell swoop. In America no such situation existed and it would have been impossible, therefore, to undertake the kind of program which Tixier envisaged. Since the registration process was expected to consume a number of weeks or even months, the board could not afford to postpone it until January 1, 1937, when the payment of claims was due to begin.

Latimer felt that to carry on the adjustment of claims and registration at the same time would be quite difficult. It was estimated that there would be at least 350,000 claims a year. Latimer did not contend that account number assignment was essential for adjudicating claims. For that purpose he was expecting to depend upon data being collected from the census records, and upon investigations by the field staffs of the health services of the various states.[6] Registration would perform the vital service of proving that

[5] No consideration seems to have been given to the War Department's use of a one-day registration for establishing the World War I draft in the United States.

[6] Benefit eligibility depended upon proof of age, which could not be given for most Americans without the assistance of the Census Bureau. During the hearings on revised H.R. 9215, a deficiency appropriation bill, before the House Subcommittee on Appropriations, Mr. Austin, a representative of the Census Bureau, testified that the bureau would have to supply information on age for at least 80 percent of the applicants for old age pensions. He also pointed out that the records of the Census Bureau had not been arranged alphabetically, since the registration of births was not begun until 1915. Increased demands for census records could be expected from the Social Security Board, the Railroad Retirement Board, the Bureau of Old Age Benefits, and the pension agencies of the states. Therefore, the Census Bureau asked for $300,000 for organizing its records alphabetically, but the request was killed by Huey Long's filibuster. However, a WPA allotment was secured to start the process of putting census age-data on individual, alphabetically indexed cards. The grant was insufficient to complete the project and additional funds were asked of Congress in 1936. It was feared that unless Congress should make a recurring appropriation, the Census Bureau would bill the Social Security Board for the extra work.

employers had paid taxes for every employee for whom they were responsible under the provisions of Title VIII. Without the assigned account numbers and the information on the registration card, employers would not be able to prove, in case of dispute, that they had paid these taxes. That was the main reason for insisting upon a pre-January 1, 1937, inventory, as the registration process was then being called.

During February the idea began to crystallize that in addition to the registration of employees there should be a preliminary registration of employers throughout the country. The employers' returns would show how many workers were in their establishments and would later facilitate the work of employee registration. This view was confirmed at a meeting of employers' representatives with Latimer, Seidemann, and Way early in March 1936 in Washington, D.C. The group represented the employers of approximately one million employees, including those of the General Motors Corporation and members of the National Retail Federation.[7] Latimer and Way presented their proposals for registration procedure and for the registration forms which Way had tentatively designed. The employer representatives insisted that registration be started soon and be completed long enough in advance of the first payments required of employers in January for individual account numbers to be assigned before that time. They favored the registration of employers first (which it was estimated would take about a month) and then the registration of employees (which they thought could be completed by November 1). Prior to employee registration, the employer representatives wanted the board to send the employers a memorandum explaining registration which they could then circulate among their workers.[8] Retail store owners were willing to have registration take place in their stores, while automobile manufacturers wanted it done at some other place such as the post office, to avoid interference with manufacturing operations.

As a result of the report on this meeting submitted to the board by Latimer and Seidemann, Miles (who had been anxious all along to start the work) introduced a resolution which called for the assignment of account numbers before January 1, 1937, and preferably before the middle of October 1936, in order to "avoid confusion and protect the rights of both employers and employees." This resolution was not seconded, but the board did agree to instruct its staff to proceed with the development of plans for assignment of account numbers and to report back to the board for approval.

[7] Most of these firms were also associated with the Business Advisory Council of the Department of Commerce.

[8] See pp. 357-58 for a discussion of the spurious registration representations then being made by a minority of employers.

At the time this assignment was made, it was already apparent that Altmeyer did not want the registration to occur until after the presidential election. Miles wanted it to start at once, and Winant was undecided. It was also becoming the dominant thought of the board that registration would be performed by the board itself. On March 5, Way indicated that one reason for this attitude was the feeling that the Employment Service had contact with a minority of employers and therefore could not readily accomplish a complete job. Moreover, by adopting the proposal of a preliminary employer registration to be conducted through the Post Office Department, the board could find out how many employers there were, how many different kinds of employment, and the number and location of employees. Thereafter, the board with its own staff organization in the Bureau of Old Age Benefits would conduct the registration.

McCormack's Committee Tackles the Problem

The job of planning for registration was now turned over to the Field Committee on Organization Planning of which Col. E. J. McCormack was chairman. On March 10 he called a meeting with representatives of other federal agencies interested in this task. Seidemann presided and McCormack presented proposals for subcommittees of this interagency committee on forms and procedures as follows: (1) a committee of the whole on which were included, in addition to a large number of persons from the board's staff, one person from the Post Office Department, one from the Central Statistical Board, two from the Census Bureau, two from the Internal Revenue Bureau, and one from the United States Employment Service; (2) a locations subcommittee to decide the number and location of registration centers and the number of offices and personnel needed to accomplish registration for three different possible periods; (3) a space and equipment committee to present a report on the cost and amount of space and office furniture needed; (4) a mechanical equipment committee to prepare estimates of numbers and costs of various machines required, and the possibility of contracts for services of this sort; (5) a committee to work on the drafting of registration forms, and to determine the quantity and cost of such forms; and (6) an information committee to plan an educational campaign to secure the cooperation of civic, commercial, and professional groups and to study the possibilities of public instruction by means of motion pictures. It was also to draft instruction pamphlets for the enumerators and to supply information to employers and employees; (7) a subcommittee on instruction and training to have charge of the administration of a training school for supervisors; and finally (8) a committee on forms to determine what information should be secured at the time registration occurred. The committee of the whole was asked to decide promptly whether or not the assignment of account numbers should be undertaken before or after January 1, 1937.

At the second meeting on March 17, McCormack announced that the most urgent matter was to consider the request of the Social Security Board for advice on when registration should be held. To speed up the decision, he presented a resolution (which had been prepared in advance) calling for the immediate appointment of an executive committee of the committee of the whole. It would make recommendations directly to the board on procedures for assigning account numbers to employers and employees. This resolution was approved, the committee was named at once and, since most of the members were present, it was immediately called to order to consider procedures for registration.[9]

The discussion at this meeting centered on the two questions of whether an employer registration, in addition to the employee registration, should be held, and whether both registrations should occur before January 1, 1937. It was announced that staff members of the Treasury and the Social Security Board had held a previous meeting at which it was agreed that neither the board nor the Treasury had the legal authority to compel registration of either employers or employees before the payment of taxes was due on January 1, 1937. Therefore, it was their view that if registration were to take place before that time it would have to be upon a purely voluntary basis. It was also their consensus that the inventory of employees, when conducted, should be done by the board and the inventory of employers, if conducted, should be made by the Treasury.

Frank Mires, chief representative of the Treasury Department, said that from the Treasury's point of view it was desirable to get an inventory of the employers first, since that would aid in the collection of taxes. He and his associates also made it clear that it was not necessary for their purpose to assign an account number to employers. Altmeyer was anxious to get the opinion of the committee as to whether or not there was any need for giving employers account numbers. He opposed the idea because he felt it would complicate bookkeeping. The committee appeared ready to adopt his view when Seidemann and Latimer arrived at the meeting and presented the other side of the case. Latimer insisted that account numbers for employers would be very helpful in tracing the records of employees. He expected to use them in connection with the old age benefits records for posting information on

---

[9] It may be mentioned here that this cut-and-dried, steamroller mode of handling meetings of representatives from other agencies was characteristic of Seidemann's technique. It was manifest on many other occasions and, as Atkinson said when the organization of state insurance officers was created, "the technique was unnecessarily abrupt and tactless."

the individual employee cards. Hughes asked if it were not sufficient for Latimer's purpose that the document recording the payment of taxes by the employer be given a number which could then be used as a reference for the employee record card. Latimer replied that this was impossible because it was the present intention to use a photographic film copy summary of the employee's record card for the central records in Washington. If that plan were adopted, and it had great advantages from the point of view of space and administrative costs, there would not be in Washington a central, documented record of the employers' payments.[10]

Concerning the question of holding an employer registration, Latimer's view was that this was needed provided the employee registration was also held in 1936. If, however, employee registration was postponed until 1937, he doubted if the cost of employer registration, estimated at $3,500,000, would be justified by the results obtained.

The crucial issue of when to hold the registration for employees was disposed of in a somewhat contradictory manner. There appeared to be unanimous agreement that, from the administrative point of view, it was desirable to hold registration before January 1, 1937, but at once the question of politics complicated this objective. Leonard Calhoun of the board staff was opposed to any registration activity during the campaign. He urged that it be undertaken in December after the general election. Calvert Dedrick of the Census Bureau declared that it was impossible to separate the political issue from the technical-administrative issue. He said that it had been the experience of the Census Bureau that it could not secure the cooperation necessary to carry on a census during a presidential campaign period. Because the campaign would be warming up by the first of July and would last until the election in November, the period for registration should be either before July or during the latter part of November and December. Latimer insisted that it would take four months for the necessary mechanical equipment to be delivered. If this were true, registration could not start before the first of July. He also insisted that December was a bad month because the rush of Christmas business would make employers unwilling to cooperate.

At the conclusion of the discussion a motion was made by Newton Montgomery of the Treasury and seconded by the representative of the Bureau of Internal Revenue, which declared that registration prior to January 1, 1937,

[10] This statement is of considerable interest because of its proposal for a central record storehouse different from that envisaged by Seidemann and his associates a few months before. At that time, Seidemann had pictured the central record system in Washington as requiring an enormous building like that housing British employment insurance records at Kew. Latimer's scheme for a film copy summary of the individual accounts, based upon an administrative policy of decentralization, required much less space.

was an indispensable prerequisite for the administration of old age benefits. But coupled with that judgment was a statement indicating in general terms the political difficulties present during 1936 which made it doubtful whether such a registration should be attempted. When the motion was put, Latimer entered a vigorous dissent contending that the recommendation would leave the board just where it started and would confirm its apparent disposition to postpone registration until after the election. As a result of his protest the final report, dated March 17 and signed by McCormack as chairman, made by the executive committee to the board was markedly altered. It declared categorically for a pre-1937 inventory for both employers and employees to be carried forward as "rapidly as administratively possible." While this was less emphatic than Latimer desired, it did not have the ambiguous quality of the original motion to which he had objected.

The reasons given in the report for the recommendation of a pre-1937 inventory included the following:

The incorporation of identification numbers for all employees will be a major problem with large employers. Advance preparations must be made by these employers in order not to confuse their accounting systems and in order to facilitate the early and accurate return of tax reports. Their accounting system will need to make provisions for both the name and the security account number of every employee.

Confusion would result in the office of the Bureau of Old Age Benefits in the event that a report was received showing contributions of individuals in advance of the assignment of account numbers.

It is quite possible that employers would resent making reclassifications of all reports by account numbers several months after the effectiveness of the Act.

Post-registration would undoubtedly result in a large number of duplications of accounts in the Bureau of Old Age Benefits.

It is probable that the duplication of accounts would result in an underestimation of account liabilities since the rates of benefit accrual varies inversely with the wage, and since most duplications would occur in the lower wage brackets.

SOLICITING EMPLOYER OPINION

In the two weeks following this meeting, Latimer made an effort to feel out additional employer representatives on their views about registration. He had an opportunity to meet with the executives of various trade associations holding a convention in Washington in the latter part of March. He also discussed the question with the Business Advisory Council of the Department of Commerce, with officials of the American Telephone and Telegraph Company, and with a number of representatives from other concerns. He told McKinley that all of these groups wanted registration in 1936 and would, in fact, regard the board as remiss in its duties if it postponed registration until 1937. Latimer thought it might be wise political strategy to wait a little while until the demand from the business groups became more insistent, so that the board would have a better reason for undertaking registration in 1936. Some time earlier Latimer had opposed a 1936 registration date, believing it would result in the omission of as many as five million employees. By April 1, however, Latimer had changed his mind, having learned that the Treasury had authority to compel the registration, immediately after January 1, 1937, of any employees not yet covered.

As a means of securing a more complete census of employer attitudes toward registration, the board's Field Organization Committee prepared a letter to be sent to the officers of employer organizations throughout the country. This letter was finally approved at the board meeting of April 21, 1936, and went out over Bane's signature shortly thereafter. It stated that a number of employers had suggested that their expenses could be minimized and friction growing out of loss of time by the employee avoided, if employees were assigned account numbers before January 1, 1937. These employers were quoted as wishing the assignment to be undertaken on a voluntary basis before that date. The letter then continued:

The Social Security Board wishes to extend every assistance to both employers and employees and, therefore, is considering making facilities for this work available. The Board would welcome your suggestions and advice as to whether your members would prefer this early assignment on a voluntary basis. It would be helpful if you could indicate in your reply which month would appear to be most convenient for your members and whether in your opinion they would prefer to have the work done within their own establishments or outside of their own establishments.

The information essential to proper identification, registration and accounting procedure which will be required will probably be limited to the name, date, place of birth, mother's maiden name, father's given name, color and sex.[11]

As early as April 1 it had become apparent to Latimer that even if the board made up its mind to start registration as soon as possible, it could not really be gotten under way until late in the summer. Because of the delay in congressional appropriations, it was probable that the board would have no money with which to place the initial orders for machines and materials

---

[11] Three days after this letter was dispatched the board, defending its budget requests before the House Subcommittee on Appropriations, virtually committed itself to a pre-1937 inventory. Two days after the hearings were closed, Latimer told McKinley that he thought there was no doubt that the board would now move ahead and hold the registration before January 1937, particularly since the employer representatives with whom the board held discussions favored an early inventory.

required. These items involved a very large expense and the board could not make commitments concerning them until it was sure it would have funds to pay for them. On April 9 McKinley discussed the progress of plans for registration with Col. McCormack, who explained that his work had come almost to a standstill because of the board's inability to decide when it would begin registration.

Will the USES Do the Job?

McCormack's view at that time about the character of the organization which should be used for registration was substantially as follows. The board, in cooperation with the United States Employment Service, should undertake the task, and it should work out a plan for training its regional and district staff to do the inventory work. The Employment Service should work out the actual process of registration, which would take place in its branch offices. There should be a liaison arrangement between the ninety-seven district offices to be set up by the board and the district offices of the Employment Service. In fact, the two should be located in the same quarters to secure the best cooperation. The actual inventory, however, should be carried on by the staff which the Employment Service had used for its placement work. It seemed to McCormack ridiculous for the board to build an organization paralleling and duplicating an organization which the Employment Service already possessed throughout the United States. The board should stop the expansion of its field organization to include the district offices until the payment of old age annuities should actually begin.

Dr. Stead shared McCormack's view. He believed that registration, as a voluntary and cooperative enterprise on the part of employers, could be handled by the Employment Service. Moreover, the Employment Service was accustomed to expanding and contracting its placement organization because it had done this on three occasions during the past two years. It could furnish overhead administration with little extra cost, and it had a large staff of people trained in interviewing. Stead understood that Altmeyer had always leaned towards the Census Bureau as the agency for registration, but McCormack had come to the conclusion that the Census Bureau would have to take its registration staff from the existing lists for census enumerators, and he doubted the suitability of these people for a task which was primarily interviewing rather than enumerating.[12]

[12] Some of the members of the House Subcommittee on Appropriations insisted that the Social Security Board should economize the cost of registering employers by making use of the Census Bureau's data on employment and occupations contained in the 1935 censuses of business and manufacturers. Latimer insisted that while information from that source would be helpful and would save some money, it could not be used

Stead was inclined to discount Dedrick's assertion that political difficulties would be encountered if registration should be undertaken during the campaign period. Stead argued that there was a great difference between the board's registration task and taking a census, which requires the answering of questions employers regard as much more confidential than the information the board desired. He believed that while there might be some political kickback from registration, it would not be very important since an employer could postpone registering until 1937.

But McCormack's and Stead's views were discarded as the result of a confidential discussion between Winant and Persons on May 1, 1936. Persons told Winant that the President was looking for an upswing in industrial production during the coming autumn. Consequently, Persons wanted to get the Employment Service ready to take advantage of such an opportunity to demonstrate its usefulness. Heretofore, the service had not been used very much by private industry, and Persons wanted no obstacle to the dawning interest in government placement service on the part of private employers. He feared that if his organization undertook the task of registration, it would be too busy to develop its placement service. Winant shared Person's desire to build up the possibility of offering jobs through the placement service instead of paying unemployment insurance, and therefore concluded that the board should build its own field organization in the Bureau of Old Age Benefits in order to do its own registering.

At the board meeting of April 30, Altmeyer had asked McCormack's committee to be ready on May 5 to present to the board specific reports on the possibility of cooperating with the Employment Service in assigning social security account numbers. Altmeyer also wanted specific recommendations for alternative registration procedures, and he wanted the board to make its final decision regarding the assignment of account numbers. On May 5, McCormack submitted a memorandum to Seidemann in which he outlined the progress of negotiations with the Employment Service and several other government agencies which might be induced to cooperate with the board, but the matter was not discussed by the board at its meeting. McCormack pointed out that the Employment Service had definitely indicated that it could not cooperate, and recommended, therefore, that no further steps be taken in this direction. He also reported that the Census Bureau was not in

---

because of the promise of confidence given by the Census Bureau when the information was collected, and because of the provision in the law forbidding the Census Bureau to divulge such information to anyone, including other federal agencies. A letter was produced from Secretary Roper, dated April 13, 1936, stating categorically that the Census Bureau could not for these two reasons make available information which would identify a particular business concern.

a position to help the board; that the Works Progress Administration should probably not be urged to cooperate because of an order by the President, some months before, that emergency relief funds should not be used for projects involving the interviewing of business firms or private individuals; and that the Treasury Department could not help. He recommended that the board proceed on the assumption that enumeration would have to be conducted by its own field organization if it was decided that such an enumeration was absolutely necessary. During the balance of the month of May, the board did not arrive at any further decisions.

WHAT BUSINESSMEN THOUGHT

On May 1, the board received a letter from the Advisory Committee on Social Security of the Business Advisory Council signed by Marion B. Folsom of the Eastman Kodak Company, which stated, in part:

It is still the opinion that employers and employees should be registered as soon as possible and that voluntary registration should be permitted any time before December 31, 1936. The committee still favors the plan outlined on page three of my April 4 letter to you.

.   .   .   .   .

At the meeting of the full Business Advisory Council on the 30th I explained the proposed registration which is being considered and found the members of the Council quite willing to cooperate with the Board in launching the plan. A resolution to the effect that the Council endorses the plan recommended by the subcommittee and that the Council at the proper time would go on record publicly as endorsing the plan and urging the employers generally to cooperate in launching it was adopted without a dissenting vote. The resolution will be forwarded to you through the Secretary of Commerce.

Meanwhile, some replies had come in from the trade associations to which Frank Bane had written on April 26. On May 7, June 8, and July 2, Robert Huse submitted to the board a series of memoranda summarizing these replies. They indicated a certain cautious willingness to cooperate, but they could not be interpreted in a way which would permit the board to lean very heavily on employer cooperation in voluntary registration. As Huse stated in his memo of June 8:

I think the most that can be concluded from the results of the letter of May 1 is on the whole that the Trade Association executives desire to be cooperative with the work of the Board, and that we should continue to use them as a channel of information for their members.

Conversely, I think the results of this experiment lend weight to the position that the Board must make its own decisions, taking into consideration such evidence as there is regarding the state of business opinion, but not expecting business to be particularly articulate or helpful. Business seems quite naturally to take the position that the Board must make decisions and announce what it intends to do before business can even give consideration to the extent and form of its cooperation.

DISPERSION OF LEADERSHIP IN
BUREAU ACTIVITY, SUMMER 1936

It was difficult to follow the developments of this and other problems during May, June, and July because activity was scattered among so many individuals and committees. Latimer was so absorbed in the work growing out of litigation over the Railroad Retirment Act, that he was unable to take a more vigorous lead in directing work on the problems of his bureau. Williamson, the chief actuary who was temporarily in charge of the bureau, was not interested in administrative work and spent his energy on actuarial and insurance problems. Elwood Way, also high on the bureau personnel list, was a specialist in forms and mechanics, who confined his effort largely to such problems as account numbers, identification tokens, and employee receipts. It happened, therefore, that Seidemann and McCormack, with their enumeration and field organization committees, took a large share of the responsibility for developing plans not only for the assignment of account numbers but also for the development of the bureau organization. Altmeyer kept in touch with all the technical aspects, giving directives here and there, and carried on negotiations with Miss Perkins for Labor Department cooperation. Winant, who was trying to find a high-powered executive to act as general manager of the registration enterprise, left for Geneva in the middle of May and was gone until mid-July. His absence led to a policy of marking time on a number of important issues, while the bureau maintained only a skeleton staff. Williamson was vaguely in charge, and an assistant to Latimer was training a few new recruits to the staff. Way was making progress with plans for the forms to be used and the equipment to be employed in the central record office. McDonald, recently appointed chief of the Claims Division, was engaged in drawing up a chart of his organization. The bulk of the activity, however, was in McCormack's hands, and overall planning was the concern of the board members themselves.

Early in May, the board was so busy with the appointment of regional directors and the inauguration of its regional establishment that it did not hurry registration plans. Moreover, a Mr. O'Neil of the Equitable Life Insurance Company, whom Winant thought had agreed to direct the registration task, could not come at once to meet with the board. Toward the end of May, O'Neil concluded that he could not accept the job, and so the board determined to go ahead and reach a decision at its meeting of June 5.

During the last week of May, McCormack's executive committee of the interdepartmental committee on enumeration held a meeting at which it was agreed that until the board decided when to hold its enumeration, the co-operating agencies could not make their own plans. The group also recommended that the board conduct the enumeration itself through some 202 centers which would include 112 district offices and 90 branch offices. It stated that 12,000 to 16,000 temporary personnel would be required.

IMPORTANT BOARD DECISIONS ABOUT REGISTRATION, JUNE AND JULY

At last, on June 5, the board made a number of major decisions. These included: (1) That the director of the Bureau of Old Age Benefits complete the entire recruitment of permanent headquarters and field forces not later than October 1, 1936; (2) That the recruitment of temporary personnel needed for registration be completed by November 15, 1936; (3) That plans be made so that the work of registration might commence not later than November 9, 1936, and be completed by January 15, 1937; (4) That the board assign someone directly responsible to it who would have authority to plan registration but who would operate, for certain specific phases of the work, through other members of the permanent staff; (5) That the board at once ask the Secretary of Commerce what assistance could be given by the Bureau of the Census.

In addition, the personnel officer was ordered to move ahead at once with the recruitment of personnel; Ewen Clague of the Bureau of Research was told to report within a week on the problem of developing account numbers for employers; and Way was ordered to submit alternative plans for employee identification devices not later than June 12. The need to avoid publicity about the recruitment of so many people before the November election was emphasized by board members who wished to prevent "undesirable and incorrect connotations."

When McCormack expressed doubt that sufficient personnel could be recruited in time to complete registration, the board discussed the possibility of alternatives, but concluded that there were none. It seemed that either the Civil Service Commission would have to liberalize its definition of "expert" to speed up recruitment, or that the President would have to issue an executive order exempting appointees of the district office managers from the regular, classified, competitive civil service regulations.

About this same time, several other decisions were reached on questions which had to be settled before more extended plans could be made. On June 2, the board agreed on a new employee account number to replace that decided upon on February 14. It would eliminate the two digits representing the month, replacing them with three digits for the area number, two digits separated by a hyphen for a group number (to be used as a technical device for facilitating the maximum use of mechanical equipment and verifying the accuracy of punch cards), and a serial number of four digits. This system, designed by Elwood Way, would permit the pre-numbering of registration forms. It did not require the preparation of twelve different sets of cards on the basis of the month of birth, and it was capable of almost unlimited expansion to one hundred million accounts. Once this number was decided upon, Way proceeded, at the board's request, to draw up registration forms. These were discussed at the board meeting on June 16. There were two major forms: one was the worker's application for an account number, and the other was a permanent record card for the Bureau of Old Age Benefits from which the account number card of the employee could be detached. The application cards required of the applicant his name and address, age, date of birth, place of birth, mother's maiden name, father's name, sex, race, signature, and his present employer's address. After considerable discussion at the board meeting on June 16, Altmeyer and Miles agreed on the major outlines of these cards. Instead of a metal tag or other variation previously discussed, the employee would receive an account number card similar in size to a visiting card, with his number, name, and signature on it.

At the same time, plans went ahead for building up the field organization to conduct registration. On June 2, 89 district offices were approved; on June 22, 312 primary branch offices and 184 branch offices were approved, of which 202 would be used as enumeration centers. Altmeyer outlined the situation for the bureau directors at a joint meeting with the board and members of the executive staff on June 17. He said that it would take until approximately October 15, 1936, to organize the backbone of the permanent field staff required by the Bureau of Old Age Benefits. In addition to organizing the permanent staff, plans were under way for the recruitment, immediately prior to November 1, 1936, of the temporary personnel who would assign benefit account numbers during the months of November and December. The bureau directors were requested to advise their staffs that no publicity should be given to the recruiting of these large numbers of temporary employees, particularly before November 1, 1936. Altmeyer also emphasized that it was the responsibility of the employer and employees to apply for a benefit account number.

At this meeting Wagenet asked if any consideration had been given to the idea that employers in states with approved unemployment compensation laws might assign benefit account numbers before November 15. Altmeyer suggested that Wagenet discuss this matter with McCormack. The same question was brought up in the meeting of June 29, when the board considered McCormack's memo suggesting that the New York representative of the Bureau of Old Age Benefits work with the New York Division of Placement and Unemployment Insurance to investigate the possibilities of their handling registration in that state. It was pointed out that New Hampshire had already assigned numbers to employees for unemployment compensation and was planning to change these numbers to correspond with those of the Social Security Board. The board seemed to be of the opinion that it alone should handle the assignment of account numbers and simply supply these numbers to the state unemployment compensation commissions. This question did not, however, die out entirely, because both New Hampshire and New York were eager to complete registration in their states as soon as possible. The question was briefly discussed at the meeting of state unemployment compensation administrators in New Hampshire late in July, and during August both New Hampshire and New York pressed the board for action. There was a considerable exchange of letters and a number of personal conferences, but the board took no action.

During early summer, the board also began to take steps to secure space for a central record office necessary for processing application forms and for setting up the twenty-six million individual accounts. It was not until July 29 that it became definitely known that space in the Candler Building in Baltimore was available. Shortly thereafter, the board agreed to lease two floors in this huge warehouse-like structure, which was located downtown near the wharves.

In accordance with the board's June 5th decision to conduct registration with its own field organization, it was necessary to compile a list of employers covered by Title VIII. McCormack was assigned this responsibility, and he held a conference with Mires and Schoeneman of Internal Revenue, Copeland of the Central Statistical Board, and Wilder and himself from the Social Security Board, at which informal arrangements were completed. Then, on June 22, Altmeyer wrote the collector of internal revenue that he understood that the bureau was willing to furnish the board with card copies of a list of approximately 1,200,000 employers which the bureau's collectors were compiling. In return, the board offered to give the Internal Revenue Bureau any supplemental lists it acquired.

After a couple of weeks of further negotiation, the two agencies agreed on the kind of card on which these employer names and addresses were to be typed. Arrangements were also made to make use of certain supplemental lists compiled by the Census Bureau from non-census sources. On August 7, the board approved McCormack's request to temporarily hire eighty-seven typists, seven supervisors, thirty checkers, and twenty sorters to handle these cards. Hundreds of thousands of these cards with employers' names and addresses were actually accumulated by the board during the next two months, but they were never used because the registration procedure finally implemented provided for a much more inclusive list of 2,400,000 by simply having postmen make up lists of employers on their routes.[13]

Early in July, after conferences with the Advisory Committee on Social Security of the Business Advisory Council and representatives of the American Federation of Labor, it was decided to use employers in assigning employee account numbers as much as possible, while at the same time avoiding the risk of labor resistance. The board offered four other alternatives: (1) assignment of numbers in employers' establishments through a personal representative of the board, (2) assignment of numbers in the enumeration centers, (3) assignment of numbers by labor unions, and (4) assignment of numbers through the mail. Completed applications would be returned through the same channels from which they were received. The Business Advisory Council insisted on starting registration as soon as possible. Mr. Linton, acting chairman of the committee, wrote on July 9:

Registration: We approve the Board plan of offering facilities in the near future for the completion of employees' personal statement forms to be used by the Social Security Board in establishing the basic records of individuals and assigning individual benefit account numbers.

We strongly recommend that the Board make available as soon as possible suitable personnel to be assigned to employing units who desire to have representatives of the Board supervise the completion of their employees' personal statement forms. From what was said at the conference with you, we understand that it is not practicable to have the benefit account numbers assigned before November 15. If this continues to be the case, we urge that every effort be made to have the registration cards filled out and returned very shortly after November 15. Even if this is done we strongly doubt that the task of registration can be satisfactorily completed within the time available.

That same day the board requested Latimer to submit an outline of both the registration procedure and the operations of the central record office in setting up individual accounts. Latimer reported on July 22, outlining the procedure which was ultimately followed, except that the work was done by the Post Office Department rather than by the board's own organization. Latimer's report stated

that the original applications will be secured by representatives of the Board in a large number of enumeration centers to be subsequently known within the Board as primary branch or district offices. These applications may be secured in person where the individual will appear at the enumeration center; through the use of

[13] Since no plan was made to preserve these postal lists of employers who filed form SS-4, most of the collectors of internal revenue did use the original employer lists, supplemented by telephone directory lists, as the basis for mailing out the first tax return forms for Title VIII (SS-1).

facilities made available by the Post Office Department (either through the mail or through the local Postmaster); through an employer; or through a local labor organization.

The typing of account cards was to be done in the enumeration centers which would also return the account number cards to the employee and would ship the office record card to Washington. Duplicates (carbon copies) of typed enumeration records were to be maintained in the enumeration center to facilitate answering inquiries about duplicate accounts, lost cards, and such. Punch cards would be handled in the central records office rather than in the enumeration centers which lacked trained supervisors. There was also a detailed statement on the operations of the central record office which proved to be a very accurate forecast of the actual procedure later followed.

On July 17, the regional directors met in Washington, at which time they were informed about the progress of plans for enumeration. They were told that the assignment of benefit account numbers would be entirely voluntary, that it would begin about November 15 and be completed within sixty days, that the personnel would be recruited and trained and about six hundred field offices opened before November, that the widespread distribution of the necessary forms would begin about the middle of September, that four methods of securing the applications would be followed, and that the supervision of registration in the field offices would be in charge of a regional representative of the Bureau of Old Age Benefits under the "general supervision of the Regional Director." It was also indicated that the board hoped to secure the cooperation of the Treasury Department (in connection with the first tax information returns in January, 1937) to require employers to assign account numbers to those employees who had not previously secured them. The hope was also expressed that the Post Office would distribute application blanks and issue cards in those areas not served by the Social Security Board offices. The board also wanted the Employment Service to request each of its applicants to file for an account number and to allow its offices to be used by the board in those cities where it did not have offices.

THE POST OFFICE IS INDUCED TO CONDUCT THE REGISTRATION

The idea of using the Post Office to conduct registration was not new. In fact, early in July 1936 Altmeyer had talked with Donaldson, the Deputy First Assistant Postmaster General, with whom he was personally acquainted, about the possibility of securing cooperation from the Post Office, and had learned that the Post Office would be willing to discuss the matter informally. Meetings were held between McCormack and Wilder of the board and Donaldson and other Post Office officials, but by the end of July they had not gotten very far. Up to July 21, the Post Office had been very cooperative, but negotiations were necessarily slow because each assistant postmaster general had exclusive jurisdiction over limited activities, requiring the board to deal separately with each of them on various aspects of the problem. It also developed that the board's assumption that registration could be facilitated by the free use of franked envelopes, based on the advice of its Bureau of Business Management, was erroneous. Anything on the back of the registration card could not be franked, and separate envelopes could not be used because of rulings by the Comptroller General declaring that return penalty envelopes could be used only to facilitate government business and not for supplying information legally required of individuals.

On August 7 the board, at McCormack's suggestion, sent a detailed letter to the Postmaster General requesting his cooperation in assigning of account numbers. This letter read, in part:

> The Social Security Board, as stated in our letter of July 8, is confronted with the problem of assigning benefit account numbers to some 25,000,000 people subject to the requirements of Title II of the Social Security Act. Tentative decision has been made to inaugurate this work on or about the 15th day of November 1936.
> We feel that if this effort is to succeed the Post Office Department must be depended upon for extraordinary cooperation inasmuch as it is more closely integrated with the people of the United States than any other Governmental agency. It is pleasing to know that informal conferences on the part of Messrs. McCormack and Wilder, representing the Board, and Messrs. Donaldson, Utley, Wentzel and others of your Department, indicate that we may expect such cooperation.

Furthermore, the board wanted the Post Office Department to assign personnel in all post offices in cities where there were not board enumeration centers or field offices. (The board's nationwide system of two hundred enumeration centers covered approximately 67 percent of the registrants.) This personnel would be under the direction of the Post Office Department, but would be paid by funds from the Social Security Board. Two methods of registration procedure were suggested, but they were not mutually exclusive. The first would use employer and labor organizations; the second would use the facilities of the Post Office Department to a great extent. Under the first alternative, the board suggested that the Post Office Department distribute application forms to all employers who held post office box numbers, and forward forms to those who did not hold such numbers; deliver an employer questionnaire made out by the board which would form the basis for a list of employers covered by Title II; serve as correspondents for the board and answer inquiries at post office windows; arrange for the distribution of posters giving information on registration; supply over-the-counter service for assigning numbers; forward to the board applications for numbers received in the post offices; and provide personnel and facilities for typing account number and office record cards from application forms.

If the second procedure were followed, the burden would fall on the mail carriers, who would be asked to ascertain the number of employees on the payroll of every employer on their routes. Either regular carriers or substitutes might be used, whichever the department found most expedient.

The board further requested that space and facilities be provided in post office buildings for the assignment of account numbers to those who called in person to register or to obtain information; that the four-pound maximum weight and other limitations on first class mail packages be suspended for carrying out the enumeration; that the board be given the freest possible use of the return penalty privilege; that the Post Office supply lists of post office boxes in use; and that city carriers, rural carriers, and star route contractors make out lists of employers, their places of business, and the approximate number of their employees. The board stated that it was fully authorized under the Economy Act to reimburse the Post Office Department for all expenditures. The board's letter closed with the suggestion that the assignment of account numbers be carried out in two periods—from November 15 to December 15, and from January 2 to February 15—thus avoiding the department's Christmas mail rush.

During the rest of August there was not a great deal of progress in further defining plans for the assignment of account numbers. However, the board continued negotiating with the Treasury Department to have the latter require employers and employees to secure account numbers under its regulations. A start was also made in securing equipment for the central record office.

During this period, McCormack and Wilder continued to negotiate with officials of the Post Office without effective results. In November, Winant said that the cooperation of the Post Office would never have been obtained had he not gone to the President and persuaded him to bring pressure upon the Postmaster General. It is not clear whether this pressure was brought to bear during August, before the Post Office had agreed to a certain amount of cooperation, or in September, when the department finally agreed to do the entire job.[14]

Later in August, the board decided to replace Latimer with Seidemann as director of the Bureau of Old Age Benefits, and this was formally done on September 2. At the same time it decided to hire Roger Evans of the Phila-

[14] No evidence of presidential pressure appears in any board documents or minutes, and McCormack and Wilder seemed to believe that they were entirely responsible for securing the cooperation of the Post Office.

delphia Chamber of Commerce to act as a special supervisor of registration, but this was not done until the following month. Evans was appointed for six months as "Chief of the Division responsible for the assigning of benefit account numbers, at the rate of $10,000 a year." He was intended to be a czar overseeing registration activities. The board, especially Chairman Winant, had for some time toyed with the idea of getting a high-powered executive—probably from business—to take over the job of conducting registration. As early as May 1936 Winant was looking for such a person. Late in May, just before sailing for Europe as the United States delegate to the International Labor Conference, Winant thought he had secured a man for the job, a vice-president of a large life insurance company. This man had been rather reluctant to accept, but agreed to do so if the board of directors of his company agreed. They in turn were willing to agree if he was set on the idea. Finally, he promised to take the job if the President personally requested him to, and Winant asked the President to do this. Unfortunately, after Winant had sailed, Marvin McIntyre telephoned in place of the President, and that seemed to be the deciding factor in the board's failure to secure the services of this man.

Since Winant did not return from Geneva until the middle of July, nothing further was done about securing a czar until that time and, as the time set for the beginning of registration grew nearer, prospective appointees became more and more unwilling to take over a job in which the possibilities of failure seemed great. Evans, director of the Industrial Bureau of the Philadelphia Chamber of Commerce, was identified with some of the employers on the Business Advisory Council of the Department of Commerce who had urged the board to undertake a voluntary registration during the summer. It was Altmeyer who had the intial contact with Evans. Some time during August, Altmeyer phoned Evans in Philadelphia and asked him how he thought registration ought to be conducted. Evans answered that he thought that some existing organization, such as the banks or the Post Office, should be used. This agreed with Altmeyer's own judgment at that time. However, the board's employment of Evans created a difficult administrative situation because he was directly responsible to the board and yet under the supervision of the director of the Bureau of Old Age Benefits.

Finally, on September 4, the board received a letter from Acting Postmaster General W. W. Howes, which contained an outline of the cooperation which the Post Office was willing to give, based on tentative agreements reached in conferences with McCormack and Wilder. The Post Office agreed to distribute application forms through its central accounting post offices and its district accounting officers, and to designate employees in all post offices to provide information on registration. Postal carriers would distribute employer registration forms, check these forms, and return them to the Social Security

Board. It would also endeavor to have the star route carriers, who were under contract and could not be required to perform this function, perform this same service. The post offices would also receive applications and forward them to the board. However, in large cities it would be necessary for the board to set up its own special offices because of lack of room and extra personnel in post office buildings. The department also agreed that the central accounting postmasters would furnish information and instructions on the assigning of account numbers to the post offices in their districts, getting their information from the district offices of the board. Finally, the department insisted on being fully reimbursed for its expenditures in connection with these tasks.

From the board's point of view there were several deficiencies in this effort at cooperation by the Post Office Department. First, the plan would require the board to secure a considerable amount of space and equipment and to recruit many temporary employees in the large cities. Second, the board would be required to handle the entire burden of typing office record cards and account number cards from the twenty-six million application forms. Third, the return penalty privilege could not be granted, because it was compulsory for employers and employees to secure account numbers.

The Post Office Department was evidently under the impression that the board had, or could rapidly create, a fairly extensive field organization to handle registration, and that the cooperation of the department was being requested only to assure facilities in the smaller towns and to help with handling of an unusually large volume of mail.

In reality, the board was by then convinced that it could not handle the job alone during November and December because of the difficulties of recruiting personnel and setting up offices by that time. It would have to postpone registration beyond January 1, or induce the Treasury Department to require registration in connection with the first information returns required under Title VIII in January or February 1937. At a board meeting on September 5, Altmeyer frankly said that either the board must farm out registration or it would be in trouble. It could not possibly get its field organization into shape in two months. If the board had to do the job with its own staff, the whole business would have to be put off until January 1937. Altmeyer naturally preferred to farm out the job, and he expressed the hope that he could still get the United States Employment Service to help the Post Office Department carry out registration. In this way, the board would have more time to build up its field organization.

The board was very disappointed that the Post Office Department had refused, in its letter of September 4, to undertake the typing of record cards and account number cards. McCormack explained that the reluctance of the

Post Office was due to (1) the fact that thirty thousand post offices were without typewriters, (2) the desire to avoid crowds in the lobbies of post office buildings, (3) the high cost of having extra typists which would result in expenditures 60 percent higher than if the board did its own typing, and (4) the Post Office not desiring to take on so much extra work during its peak season. Nevertheless, the board decided to try once more to persuade the Post Office to undertake the typing duty. It drafted a letter which Altmeyer was asked to personally take to Mr. Howes. This letter expressed appreciation for "the cooperation of space and personnel which you offer" and asked reconsideration of the decision not to provide "personnel and facilities for typing office record cards and the issuance of the identification cards." It set forth the advantages to the public and to the board of having the Post Office assume this responsibility, disavowed any desire on the part of the board to shirk its responsibilities, and emphasized the magnitude of the task facing the board and its need for help. It also inquired whether the Post Office Department was prepared to send representatives to employers' places of business to facilitate the assignment of account numbers.

On the same date another letter was sent to the Post Office Department requesting that it reconsider its decision that the return penalty privilege could not be used by the board. The letter read:

There is no provision in the law which requires employees to make application for a benefit account number either in connection with the payment of taxes or the payment of benefits.

Title II of the Social Security Act places the obligation upon the employer to collect and remit the tax imposed upon the income of individual employees. Title II provides for the payment of benefits in certain amounts and under certain conditions regardless of whether or not an employee has obtained a benefit account number.

The chief advantage of the penalty privilege of the Government lies in the fact that the data thus more readily obtained will facilitate the collection of taxes as well as the examination and adjudication of claims for benefits. Other advantages to the Government are that such data would be available for the actuarial calculations required in Section 201(a), the studies and recommendations required under Section 702, and the payments required under Section 302(a).

In this letter, the board claimed that registration was entirely voluntary, in order to secure the privilege of return penalty envelopes. On the other hand, it had been negotiating with the Treasury Department to induce that department to require employees and employers to secure account numbers under regulations carrying considerable penalties.

On August 11, the chairman of the board had written to the Secretary of the Treasury asking if the department would be willing to require, by regulation under section 807(b),[15] that (1) all employees acquire identification numbers before January 1, 1937, or before the due date of the first information return required under Title VIII, or (2) that employers state the names and numbers of employees on the information returns (thus requiring employers to bring pressure to bear upon their employees to secure such numbers), and that the Treasury state under what circumstances it would excuse the failure of employers to do so, or (3) that employers file applications for account numbers signed by employees in all cases in which the employees had not themselves secured such numbers, or (4) that as an alternative to this procedure employers actually assign prenumbered identification cards to employees in connection with the filling out of the first information returns.

The board was evidently trying to get the Post Office and Treasury departments to take over as large a part of the responsibilities for the assignment of account numbers as possible. To achieve this, it was playing both ends against the middle, trusting that the Post Office and the Treasury had no direct channels of communication between them. On September 10, the day after the Post Office was urged to take on the balance of the registration job, the Secretary of the Treasury wrote to the board to the effect that his department was willing to make registration by employer and employee alike mandatory by regulation. The letter read in part as follows:

This Department would assent to the incorporation in the regulations to be issued under Title VIII of the Social Security Act of provisions necessary to effectuate the observance by employers and employees subject to such title of the procedure outlined below. Such procedure is predicated on the assumption that the Board will be in a position to receive applications for account numbers from employees prior to the due date of the first information return to be required of employers under Title VIII of the Act. The procedure is as follows:

Every employee subject to taxes under Section 801 would be required to file an application for an account number of the Social Security Board or any agency designated by the Board. The application will be filed on a form approved by this Department. Copies of such form will be distributed by the Board.

The due date for filing of applications, that is, the last date on which applications may be timely filed will, to a certain degree, be dependent upon the date the first information returns of employers under Title VIII will be due, which in turn cannot be fixed until after the Board determines the frequency with which

---

[15] "Such taxes shall be collected and paid in such manner, at such times, and under such conditions, not inconsistent with this title (either by making and filing returns, or by stamps, coupons, tickets, books, or other reasonable devices or methods necessary or helpful in securing a complete and proper collection and payment of the tax or in securing proper identification of the taxpayer), as may be prescribed by the Commissioner of Internal Revenue, with the approval of the Secretary of the Treasury."

information returns are to be filed. As suggested in our letter, consideration must also be given to the procedure and time for filing applications for employees who enter employments after the first registration takes place, or who would leave the service of their employers without having filed an application. . . .

Upon being assigned an account number by the Board, every employee would be required to furnish such number promptly to his employer. Under present plans the information return referred to above would consist of a summary sheet upon which would be reported the total amount of taxable wages paid to all employees during the period covered by the return and the total amount of employees' tax deducted therefrom. There would also be attached to, and made a part of, such return a form containing the following information with respect to each employee who receives taxable wages during the period covered by the return:

1. The name of the employee.
2. The amount of wages paid to such employee during the period covered by the return.
3. The amount of the employee's tax deducted from such wages.
4. The account number of the employee, if assigned, or, if not assigned, the reason therefore, such as 'application pending,' or 'no application filed.'

Upon the receipt of the information return in the Office of the Collector of Internal Revenue, the Collector would check the amounts reported on the monthly tax returns filed for the period covered by the information returns and then forward the information returns to the agency designated by the Board.

Willful failure to supply the information for application for an account number or on the information return subjects the person required to furnish such information with the penalties imposed under Section 1114(a) of the Revenue Act of 1926, made applicable to the taxes imposed under Title VIII of the Social Security Act by Section 807(c) thereof.

The Treasury thus indicated that it would go a considerable distance in requiring employers and employees to secure account numbers under its own regulations. It further requested the board to express its views on (1) number, kind, and frequency of tax information returns under Title VIII (with the understanding that it was opposed to making the frequency of returns contingent upon the number of employees employed by each employer); (2) whether the board desired copies of the monthly tax returns as well as the monthly information returns; and (3) the assignment of numbers to employers. The board was urged to express its views on these points as quickly as possible because the Treasury desired to put the Title VIII regulations concerning taxes (subsequently known as Regulations 91) into the hands of taxpayers early in November. The Treasury had from the first looked with considerable favor on the use of both employee and employer account numbers because it promised to facilitate considerably the collection of taxes.

On receipt of this letter from the Treasury, the board, not yet knowing whether the entire registration job could be handed over to the Post Office Department, endeavored to get the Treasury to require employers to issue numbers to their employees in connection with the tax returns for 1937. The board wanted to do this to insure that no employees had been overlooked during the "pre-registration" period. In a letter dated September 12, the chairman of the board wrote to the Secretary of the Treasury (summarized by the observer as follows):

A. The board would undertake the assignment of account numbers before the due date of the first information returns and would discuss the application forms with the Treasury Department.

B. The board thought it necessary to require employers to supply the account numbers or information on which account numbers could be issued for all employees who had not themselves secured such numbers.

C. The board desired to have copies of the monthly tax returns and wanted to know whether the Collector of Internal Revenue would verify the information returns by checking them against the tax returns and adjust them with the taxpayer before forwarding them to the board.

D. The board regretted that the Treasury Department did not wish to verify the accuracy of the information returns with the tax return of the employer, and wished to suggest that:

1. The first information return cover the period from January 1 to June 30, 1937.

2. That subsequent information returns be made at least semi-annually.

3. That combined information and tax returns on a monthly basis be permitted for all employers who wished to follow this procedure.

4. That *monthly* information returns be required of:
   (a) Employers who prove to be lax.
   (b) Employers not having evidence of payments to employees in the form of voucher checks or signed payrolls.
   (c) Employers hiring employees on a day-to-day basis.
   (d) Employers having wide fluctuations in employment, e.g., a variation of more than 100 percent between the smallest and the largest number of employees during a period of twelve months.

5. That employers required to make monthly returns continue to do so for at least six months and be required to make an affirmative showing as to why they should not continue to make monthly returns.

6. That employers must furnish employees with statement showing tax deductions.

7. That a less desirable alternative of requiring information returns on a quarterly basis be considered if the above proposals did not meet with the approval of the Treasury Department.

E. The board specifically requested the Treasury Department to approve a form (later called SS-4) for employer registration giving the number of employees and other pertinent facts about his business and to provide by regulation for the submission of this form by employers.

On September 15 the Post Office Department, in a letter to the board, agreed to take on the additional functions of typing office record cards, account number cards, and sending representatives to large employers to facilitate the assignment of account numbers on their premises. In agreeing to perform this further service, the Post Office pointed out that it would be necessary to begin immediately to work out details and prepare instructions. It was estimated that this would take from ten days to two weeks, and that another two or three weeks would be required for the Post Office inspectors to contact field personnel to supplement orally these instructions. Even with an immediate start, the field work would not begin until late October. Seidemann added that the Post Office had agreed to cooperate only if the board could reach an immediate decision and begin work that very week. Therefore, on September 18, the board formally accepted the Post Office offer and agreed to advance $500,000 to start the work.

On September 17, several representatives of the Bureau of Internal Revenue of the Treasury Department, with Newton Montgomery as their spokesman, met with the board and its principal registration staff members to work out the details of Treasury regulations for assigning account numbers, paying taxes, and filing returns. Montgomery began by saying that the Treasury would agree to all the requests made by the board in its letter of September 12, with the exception that it would insist on quarterly information returns after the first six months' period, rather than any variation in the frequency of returns depending on the size of the employer and the nature of his business. The Treasury also refused to accept the requirement that an employer give his employee a statement of the amount of taxes deducted at the time of wage payment. There was a considerable amount of discussion on this latter point, with the Treasury representatives declaring that they could not see any justification for this requirement. Altmeyer, however, insisted upon it, and the Treasury representatives finally gave in. (Confirmation of this understanding came in a letter from Secretary Morgenthau dated October 15.)

Developments during the month of October are particularly difficult to trace in detail because of the large number of decisions which were reached. Constant negotiations were carried on with the Treasury, Post Office Department, Comptroller General, and the White House to complete the plans for the assignment of account numbers, to make decisions on the time schedule, and to arrange for the printing of an enormous number of forms and their distribution to post offices throughout the country. Nevertheless, the main developments and the circumstances surrounding the most important decisions can be traced.

One of the most important decisions reached was agreement on a definite time schedule for the assignment of identification numbers to employers and account numbers to employees. The Post Office Department wanted to get started as soon as possible in order to complete the major part of the job before its Christmas rush, which began about December 10 or 15. Seidemann agreed with the views of the Post Office on this question in a memorandum to the board dated September 23, which read in part as follows:

> Pursuant to our discussion with Treasury representatives yesterday regarding the content of the employers identification form for early use via the Post Office Department, Mr. Montgomery of the Treasury today phoned our Mr. Beach expressing the opinion that the Board would probably wish to pass on the policy and/or legal wisdom of initiating any such field operations before November 3.
>
> The practical problem involved here may be summed up in the view of our representatives that the enumeration job will not be done thru the Post Office this year unless the field portion can be substantially completed before the Post Office's holiday rush. To do this, Post Office authorities are thinking in terms of the following tentative schedule:
>
> October 15—forms to be in the 1,017 first class post offices and the 57 central accounting post offices, to be printed privately because of the emergency nature of the job.
>
> October 20—begin the distribution of form SS-4 to employers from all post offices.
>
> October 31—deadline set by the Treasury Decision for the return of employer forms.
>
> November 9 or 10—begin distribution of employee forms.

Seidemann recommended that the board accept this Post Office schedule, and that a letter be sent to the secretary of the Treasury requesting that the Treasury require employers to return the SS-4 forms by October 31. The board agreed to this plan but suggested that the whole schedule be delayed two weeks, that is, that the distribution of the SS-4 be begun on November 5.

1936 Presidential Campaign Engulfs the Board

There was a fundamental conflict between administrative needs, which made it important that registration be completed before the Christmas post office rush and as much in advance of January 1 as possible, and the political situation. The presidential campaign was then entering its final bitter month, and both the Treasury Department and the board were very reluctant to start the assignment of account numbers or even to allow any widespread knowledge of the plan to reach the public. The Treasury was apparently a little afraid it was overstepping the bounds of its authority in requiring employers to secure identification numbers before January 1, when the taxes under Title VIII would begin to accrue. The board, in touch with the White House through one of the PWA officials who was part of the White House secretariat, had agreed on September 23 to submit its proposed timetable to the President before definitely deciding to adopt it.

The political situation was to get far hotter than the board suspected on September 23. On September 26, Alf Landon made a bitter speech in Milwaukee attacking the Social Security Act, and by September 29 Chairman Winant had resigned from the board in order to be free to defend the act. The prospects of employer resistance to filing SS-4 forms and aiding in the assignment of account numbers grew very serious. In fact, toward the end of the month, Seidemann proposed that the following letter be written to the Attorney General:

As you are no doubt aware, the Treasury Department, Post Office Department and this Board are preparing plans to secure identifying data with respect to all the employers who will be covered by Title VIII of the Social Security Act, and also with respect to employees who will be covered by that Title and Title II. A Treasury decision will probably be issued in the near future, pursuant to general regulatory authority of the Treasury Department, and specifically to Section 807(b) of the Act, requiring the filing of applications for identification and account numbers.

Rumors of the proposed action have spread, and we are advised by certain of our field representatives that many employers have stated that they would refuse to comply with any such requirement for fear of jeopardizing their rights to contest the validity of Title VIII of the Social Security Act.

I call this fact to your attention with the thought that you may wish to issue a public statement of the position your Department would take on the matter. If you feel that you can properly make such a statement, I am confident that a disclaimer by the Department of Justice of any reliance upon such a defense would go far to assist in the administration and enforcement of the proposed Treasury decision. The sooner such a disclaimer could be issued after the promulgation of the Treasury decision, the greater would be its effect.

While the matter is one with which the Treasury Department is primarily concerned, I take the liberty of writing you because of this Board's interest in securing the identification of employees and because of the information which has come to our attention through our field agencies. I am sending a copy of this letter to the Secretary of the Treasury.

Montgomery of the Treasury Department, the staff of the Bureau of Old Age Benefits, and Vincent Miles of the board were in favor of sending this letter. Altmeyer was of the opinion that the Attorney General would say that employers would not pay any attention to a statement he might issue, and therefore that nothing would be gained by such a letter. The same issue was raised at a subsequent board meeting, but Altmeyer remained firm in his opposition and the letter was never sent.

The board found itself thrown right into the midst of the campaign in its final days. A motion picture trailer, to be attached to Pathé newsreels and entitled *We the People and Social Security,* had been under preparation for some months, but its release was not contemplated until after the election. About ten days before the election, however, all the board's inhibitions about publicity were swept away by the payroll-stuffing campaign carried on by many employers, in conjunction with the Republican party. Starting in Cleveland and rapidly spreading throughout the country, employers distributed propaganda leaflets against the Social Security Act and the required deductions from employees' wages. About ten days before the election, Altmeyer, on suggestion from the White House, directed James Douglas, chief of the motion picture division of the Informational Service, to proceed at once to secure the widest possible distribution of the board's film. Douglas immediately proceeded to do so, driving himself from New York to Washington and distributing films all along the route. The same practice was followed in other parts of the country, using either board employees or Democratic party workers. Douglas even showed the film on Times Square, using a sound truck. Some four million people saw *We the People and Social Security* by November 3.

There was also widespread distribution of Informational Service circular no. 9, a four-page pamphlet entitled *Security in Your Old Age* which had been prepared for distribution with form SS-5. The first paragraph of this circular was changed, because social security had become an issue in the election, to read: "There is now a law in this country which will give about 26 million working people something to live on when they are old and have stopped working. This law, which gives other benefits too, was passed last year by Congress and is called the Social Security Act." Eight million copies of this pamphlet were printed before the election, of which quite a large portion were distributed. One evening, 125 members of the Social Security Board staff, including many executives, stuffed thirty-three thousand envelopes with one hundred copies each of this circular to be sent to thirty-three thousand local AFL unions throughout the country, following upon a letter sent out by William Green, president of the national AFL.

When the Democratic National Committee heard about these pamphlets, they phoned Louis Resnick, the director of the Informational Service, late one Saturday night and asked him to send a messenger to New York immediately with ten thousand copies. The messenger arrived in New York at midnight and, soon after, the committee phoned Resnick in Washington and asked him to have the pamphlets changed in several particulars. They objected to the frequent use of the word *taxes,* but Resnick explained that eight million copies had already been printed, and that a press release carrying the text of the phamphlet was going out immediately to two thousand newspapers. The committee was finally convinced that to stop the distribution of these press releases would do more harm than good. The committee also wished to distribute pamphlets at factory gates and, although Resnick pointed out that this would lead to a great deal of criticism, it went ahead and printed several million copies of a similar pamphlet of its own for distribution in this way.

A few days before the election, Wilbur Cohen, Murray Latimer, and Benjamin Cohen went to the New York headquarters of the Democratic National Committee to write speeches for Democratic campaigners, and to furnish information for the counterattack on the Republicans' payroll-stuffing campaign. When the smoke of battle cleared, it was generally agreed by board members that the Republican attack had been a blessing in disguise because it awakened the American public to the fact that there was a Social Security Act, and because it made it possible to run a quick and effective publicity campaign for registration.

PROBLEMS OF PRINTING AND POSTAGE

The Government Printing Office was in a position, in the month of October, to handle the order for three and a half million SS-4 (employer) forms and thirty million SS-5 (employee) forms, but it could not handle the job of preparing record and account number cards. This work was let out to a commercial printing company in Niagara Falls, New York, with the arrangement that the cards would be shipped directly to the 1,017 first class post offices and 57 central accounting post offices.

An additional difficulty arose in connection with the printing of the SS-5 forms, because the Post Office was still under the impression that postage would be required when individuals mailed these application blanks back to them. The board had written the Comptroller General requesting an opinion as to whether it could reimburse the Post Office for the postage in these cases. The Comptroller General replied in a manner which he evidently thought granted the board's request, but which actually succeeded in further muddying the waters:

You state that the desired data are to be furnished by employers and employees upon a voluntary basis and that the Board feels it is essential to the success of its operations that such employers and employees should not be put to the trouble and expense of furnishing postage for the return of the completed forms. It is common experience that obtaining voluntary information by mail is greatly facilitated by the payment of reply postage, and in view of the reported ruling of the Post Office Department to the effect that the return matter here involved may not be transmitted postage free there appears no objection to the use of the appropriation referred to for that purpose; it being understood that the required return postage will be affixed in such form as to be available for no other use than return of the required forms. Accordingly, the question presented is answered in the affirmative. (See 24 Comp. Dec. 111.)

In substance, the Comptroller General agreed to the reimbursement of the Post Office by the Social Security Board out of its appropriation, but definitely required that stamps be affixed to untold millions of envelopes furnished to the employee, a procedure which was, of course, out of the question. This difficulty was discussed at considerable length at the board meeting of October 8, but meanwhile the printing of the SS-5 forms, which contained instructions on the reverse side stating that they might be mailed to the local postmaster without postage, was being held up. It was finally agreed to put the question to the Post Office Department to see whether or not it was willing to take a chance on being held up by the comptroller general on reimbursement. It seemed to be the consensus that the comptroller general would not prevent reimbursement once the assignment of account numbers was an accomplished fact. It turned out that the Post Office was willing to take the risk, and the following informal memorandum of understanding was signed by Altmeyer and C. B. Eilenberger on October 8:

It is understood by the Post Office Department and the Social Security Board that the instructions to employers and employees in connection with the forms SS-4 and SS-5 will be that either form "may be handed to the letter carrier, or it may be delivered to the local Post Office in person or by messenger, or it may be mailed in a sealed envelope and addressed as follows: Postmaster, Local. In no case is it necessary to prepay postage."

It is further understood that postage will be billed to the Social Security Board with respect to all forms received except those that are delivered to the local Post Office in person or by messenger, and the Social Security Board agrees to reimburse the Post Office Department for the postage thus incurred.

At almost the last possible moment it was decided to delay the assignment of account numbers an additional week. Treasury decision no. 4704, which made registration compulsory, required that individuals who were employers on November 16 were required to file an application for an identification number with the Post Office not later than November 21. Persons who were employees on November 24 were required to file an application for a benefit account number not later than December 5. This decision was filed with the *Federal Register* on November 6 but not generally made public for several days after. (Regulations 91, for collection of Title VIII taxes, was not filed with the *Federal Register* until November 9.)

During the month of October, the board, through Roger Evans, the special supervisor of registration, worked out the instructions to be issued by the Post Office Department. Although the Post Office designated Messrs. Utley and Ellis to represent it in this matter, they left the content of the November 4 circular letter of instructions to all postmasters (entitled "Cooperation with the Social Security Board" and signed by the Acting Postmaster General) to the Social Security Board representatives. All subsequent instructions which the Post Office sent were likewise the work of the board. The only function assumed by Post Office officials was to see that the communications were couched in language which the postmasters would readily understand.

DIFFICULTIES IN ESTABLISHING FIELD OFFICES

Meanwhile, the board was trying to decide how many field offices it would open for use in the assignment of account numbers. On September 26 the board had authorized the opening, on November 1, 1936, of 56 field offices paralleling the location of the central accounting offices of the Post Office. Forty-one district offices were to be opened on November 15, 1936, and 11 additional field offices were to open on December 1, 1936, thus equaling the 64 offices of the Internal Revenue collectors. Two hundred eighty-one primary branch offices were to be opened on December 15, and 217 secondary branch offices on January 1, 1937. Within a few days, however, it became apparent that so many offices would not be required and that, in any event, it would be impossible to keep to the proposed schedule. The civil service register of administrative positions in the Bureau of Old Age Benefits was not delivered to the board until December 2. Thus, in successive steps on October 9, October 20, November 10, and December 11, both the total number of field offices was cut down and the dates of their opening postponed. In fact, on November 5 the board had no personnel available for permanent assignment to the 56 field offices paralleling the central accounting post offices. It was decided to detail members of the Washington staff to open these offices pending receipt of the administrative register from the Civil Service Commission. This would allow the recruitment of permanent field personnel, but there was some doubt as to whether the procedure would be approved by the Comptroller General.

In a letter to the Comptroller General dated October 21, the board explained its predicament, indicated that permanent assignments could be made by January 1, and asked whether it had authority to pay travel expenses and per diem allowances to persons temporarily detailed to the field posts. On October 26 a favorable reply was received, and the 56 offices were actually ready by the time the assignment of account numbers was started.

The Struggle for Power Within the Board's Staff

Even before the opening of these offices, a considerable conflict had developed between Seidemann, McCormack, and Wilder on the one hand and Roger Evans and Ernest Buhler on the other over the supervision of the field offices. One dispute arose during a discussion about the titles to be given to Evans and Buhler, who were hired on special contract for six months under the provision of the appropriation act which provided that the board might spend $75,000 for special accounting, statistical reporting, and organizational services. Seidemann believed that under this provision they could not be given administrative titles such as chief of the Field Service Division. He stated that it was his understanding when Evans was hired that his activities would be confined to the assignment of account numbers, whereas Evans and Altmeyer maintained that he was retained to handle not only this function but also the organization of the field offices. Seidemann finally lost the dispute, and Evans was given authority over both these functions. Just how this disagreement was actually worked out is not quite clear. McCormack and his co-worker, Wilder, had definitely gained power in the bureau when Seidemann was made director. Wilder, in an interview on November 24, indicated that Evans was given the "run around" on the question of supervision and direction of field offices. It was Evans, however, who handled most of the contacts with the Post Office Department after the middle of October. Wilder recounted the way in which Winant and Altmeyer had appointed Evans, and how Evans had brought along his old friend Buhler as his assistant. He indicated how difficult it had been for McCormack and himself to accept these newcomers, in whose ability they had no confidence. The internal arrangements devised to offset the influence of Evans and Buhler are suggested in the following paraphrase of Wilder's remarks:

Mr. Evans and Mr. Buhler have been given positions on the organization chart of the bureau which show them directly under the supervision of Mr. McCormack, associate director of the bureau, in charge of registration and field organization. As a matter of practice, however, Mr. Wilder, who has been placed in the Field Organization Division, must OK all material, documents, suggestions, etc., which go from Mr. Evans and Mr. Buhler to the director and associate director. If this does not happen as a part of the regular procedure, the material is sent down later from Seidemann's or McCormack's office to be gone over by Mr. Wilder.

This is also true for all matters dealing with registration, although Mr. Wilder has no formal connection whatsoever with the Registration Division.

There was also considerable friction between the Bureau of Old Age Benefits and the Office of the Executive Director, both before and after the first fifty-six offices were opened, about the extent of control of the regional directors over the field office managers. Administrative Order No. 11 had provided that the regional representative of the Bureau of Old Age Benefits should be under the general supervision of the regional director but technically responsible to the Bureau of Old Age Benefits. Distrustful of the influence which the regional director might have over the regional representatives of the Bureau of Old Age Benefits, Seidemann and McCormack wanted the regional representative to "coordinate the activities of the district offices within the region but have no supervisory powers." The board stated on October 9 that it had originally contemplated and still maintained that the regional representative of the Bureau of Old Age Benefits should have complete power of supervision over the field offices in his area. Here again it is difficult to determine just how this arrangement worked out in practice during the registration period. The Bureau of Old Age Benefits began issuing a field service letter on November 14, 1936, embodying instructions to the field office managers.[16] By December 31, when the bulk of the registration was completed, twelve such letters had been issued. Nevertheless, the regional directors in the regional offices visited by the authors late in December 1936 and early in January 1937 considered themselves completely responsible for the direction and supervision of the Old Age Benefits field staff in their regions, and this attitude was shared by field office managers. It was more or less inevitable that this should have happened, because the regional directors were not overburdened with work and naturally extended their authority when occasion offered; they were close to the field offices and available for frequent and rapid consultation. Moreover, the executive assistants in the regional offices were temporarily designated as the regional representatives of the Bureau of Old Age Benefits, and many of them were former Bureau of Foreign and Domestic Commerce employees, as were many of the men detailed temporarily to the field offices.

It was probably fortunate that the field offices did not, at least in most cities, have a great deal to do with the actual assignment of account numbers, because there were actually four groups struggling for control over them: Evans and Buhler; Seidemann, McCormack, and Wilder; the Office of the Executive Director acting through the regional directors; and the regional directors themselves.

---

[16] With the shake-up in the bureau early in 1937, this field service letter was consolidated with the regional letter from March 12 onward, and the new document was issued from the executive director's office as a regional and field letter.

HOW THE REGISTRATION WAS
CARRIED THROUGH

Before describing the actual process of registration it is necessary to discuss certain other preliminary arrangements which had been made. On September 16, the board accepted the proposal of the International Business Machines Corporation to supply mechanical equipment for the Baltimore Records Office. The Remington Rand Corporation and the Burroughs Adding Machine Company had also submitted proposals, but these were incomplete and unsatisfactory. By December 9, equipment had been installed in the Candler Building in Baltimore and some two thousand employees recruited to start the production of master punch cards containing the information on the SS-5 forms.

The Publicity Campaign

Another important preliminary step was advance publicity. The board had issued several press releases in the last few days of the presidential campaign calling attention to various forms of misleading publicity issued by the Republican National Committee and associated groups, but the first official statement on the assignment of account numbers was a press release of November 6 which outlined the procedure, carried sample SS-4 and SS-5 forms and a specimen of the social security account card, and stressed the cooperation of the Post Office Department. Several more releases were issued up to and including November 16, the day on which post office employees began distributing SS-4 forms to employers. Thirteen more press releases were issued in the period up to and including January 11 when the bulk of the assignment of account numbers took place. The following summary of an interview with Louis Resnick on December 22 gives the story of the publicity campaign:

The Informational Service was not able to make use of the traditional device of setting up an elaborate publicity plan for this registration job and getting a great deal of advance publicity on this basis, because it was not until very late in the fall that it was finally decided that the Post Office would do the job. Although the publicity for registration was more or less on a day-to-day basis, the most important fields were well covered. He estimated, as far as the newspapers were concerned, that they did about 80 or 90 percent of their full job.

By direct suggestion, and in some cases on the initiative of the newspapers themselves, the Associated Press, United Press, the Hearst chain, and many individual papers ran series of articles and series of questions and answers on old age benefits and registration for weeks at a time. In some cases the Informational Service staff actually wrote these articles and in all cases supplied the information. The contacts with Washington correspondents increased in like measure. The volume of press clippings on social security from the 340 papers covered by Press Intelligence increased fourfold from October to November. The district and regional office staffs (at that time there were ten regional Informational Service representatives in the regional offices) also did a great deal of work in both the newspaper and radio fields. The board increased the number of its own press releases and sent out three foreign language releases on old age benefits in twenty-four languages to almost the entire foreign language press of the country. These releases usually made the front page, and Resnick believes that they were responsible for perhaps a million or more of the twenty-two million registrations which have come in to date.

During the registration period there were twelve nationwide broadcasts by well-known individuals including Winant, William Green, Senator Wagner, Fannie Hurst, and Hendrik Van Loon. There were a great many local broadcasts arranged by people in the field offices all over the country and spot news releases urging people to register. An electrical transcription of questions and answers on old age benefits was sent to some four hundred small independent radio stations and used several times by each of them.

Resnick estimates that about 3,000,000 of the 3,330,000 posters printed were actually distributed. There was a great deal of delay in getting these posters out because Evans, who was handling the relations with the Post Office, had evidently given them his word that he would keep their work down to a minimum. He normally received any suggestion for publicity with a refusal, and many times when he finally agreed to put the request to the Post Office the Post Office showed no reluctance whatsoever in carrying it out. He absolutely refused to ask the Post Office to have three posters distributed to employers with the SS-4's, and would not even allow Resnick to put in his instructions to postmasters the statement that postmasters might distribute these posters to employers if they could conveniently do so. On their own initiative, however, the regional directors Mrs. Rosenberg and Judge Gill requested their postmasters to distribute the posters, and found them very willing to do so.

Resnick originally wanted fifty million copies of Informational Service pamphlet no. 9 printed and distributed, but Evans and Seidemann insisted that ten million would be ample. He finally agreed to the ten million, but at 10 o'clock the same night decided that fifty million were essential. Not being able to get in touch with Bane he finally reached Altmeyer by phone at 11:00 P.M., and got permission to go ahead with the fifty million. He rushed down to the Government Printing Office that same evening to change the order. Later it developed that people in the Bureau of Business Management were confident that the Government Printing Office could not handle this order on such short notice and arrangements were made to ask bids from private printers. One day, however, Resnick, Deviny, Mitchell, and McCauley went down to the Government Printing Office to make one last attempt to have them do the job, and after making a touching appeal to the public printer, Resnick found that he would have been willing to do the job from the very beginning.

By the time the registration was under way, the board had managed to get out three newsreel trailers which have been shown to some forty-two million people to date. Chain theatres have refused to distribute these films; before the election their excuse was that they did not want to mix into politics, and since the election the rumor is that they have refused to cooperate because some congressman from New York is said to be on the point of submitting a bill to drive the chains out of business. The board has in some cases succeeded in getting individual theatres which are members of chains to accept these films.

The one *faux pas* in preparing publicity for registration was the issuance of Treasury form 940 at the same time that employers were receiving form SS-4 from the Post Office. Form 940 was to be used for filing tax returns under Title IX (unemployment compensation) for 1936 and was, of course, payable only by employers of eight or more persons.[17] However, many small employers confused the two tax titles and assumed that it was not necessary to file SS-4's.

In view of the confusion caused by the issuance of form 940, it was fortunate that Evans had foreseen that registration might not be completed by the closing date, December 5, fixed in the Treasury decision. On November 10, Evans reached an agreement with the Post Office Department that it continue registration until December 31 and continue the issuance of forms until March 31. During the first few days of December, when it became apparent that the job would not be anywhere near completion by December 5, the Treasury Department agreed to amend its regulations to provide that SS-5's could be filed up to December 15 (Treasury decision 4720, December 11). No further extension was granted by the Treasury Department, but the assignment of numbers by the Post Office continued through most of January. In fact, on January 11, 1937, the board issued a release urging that all employers and employees who had not yet applied for identification or account numbers do so immediately.

THE TREASURY IS SWAMPED

Registration also greatly increased the volume of work in the Bureau of Internal Revenue. Employers receiving forms SS-4 and 940 began to realize for the first time that the social security taxes would soon be due, and they flooded collectors' offices, the board's regional and field offices, and the Bureau

---

[17] This was the federal tax for which a 90 percent offset was to be allowed in case the state tax or contributions were deposited in an unemployment fund under an approved state unemployment compensation law.

of Internal Revenue in Washington with inquiries. Jealous of its relationship with the taxpayer, the Treasury had all along insisted that the board keep its hands off tax matters and have no dealings with taxpayers. Nevertheless, it was practically impossible to keep tax questions separate from other types of inquiries in the field offices of the board. The following paraphrase of an interview with Roger Evans on January 8 describes the arrangements which were finally worked out, but in actual practice some of the field and regional offices were very free in explaining the tax provisions of the act and giving employers interpretations as to whether or not they were covered.

Under the agreement made in advance between the board and the Treasury concerning their respective duties, all matters relating to taxes were to be under the sole jurisdiction of the Internal Revenue Bureau.

Throughout all the discussions which have taken place, there has been continuous and explicit insistence by the Treasury representatives that the board staff should refrain from answering any questions relating to taxes under Title VIII. Nevertheless, since the registration work was started, questions began to pour into the regional and district offices of the board concerning the coverage under Title VIII. Employers and employees demanded to know whether or not they came within the terms of that title.

These questions, when referred to collectors of internal revenue, found the latter officials unable to answer them. The board's representatives were appealed to by the internal revenue collectors to interpret the law to them and to answer the questions which they, the collectors, knowing very little about the Social Security Act, felt themselves unable to answer.

Consequently, the field people of the board did answer some of these questions. Immediately there came a protest from the Washington office of the Internal Revenue Bureau. As a result of this protest, Seidemann and Evans sent a telegram on December 5, ordering all regional and field representatives, when questions concerning the jurisdiction of the Treasury or other agencies and questions concerning coverage arose, "never to do more than quote our Act or Treasury regulations verbatim and refer inquiries to agencies concerned for any official answer or more definite ruling desired. Refer requests for Treasury regulations only nearest collector."

Evans says that he, Seidemann, and Altmeyer knew that this telegram would be ineffective in taking care of the real situation. They believed that it would be impossible to answer the thousands of questions by the method suggested in the telegram, but to protect themselves against the Treasury's inevitable ill will and to bring the matter to a head, they sent the telegram out. The result of this telegram and the procedure followed as a consequence threw upon the collectors of internal revenue such a mass of inquiries which they were entirely unequipped to answer as to flood Montgomery's office in Washington with so many questions that Montgomery called up Evans, told him the Treasury was swamped, and asked his help.

Evans pointed out to him that this situation was the result of Montgomery's own insistence that the Social Security Board people should leave the question of coverage and taxation entirely alone. The outcome of this situation was that Montgomery agreed that the legal staff of the board should prepare a digest of the official rulings of the Internal Revenue Bureau, to be used by the field representatives of the board in answering questions concerning the taxing provisions of the act. He also agreed that the field representatives might paraphrase the wording of the act, or regulations and rulings, where it seemed absolutely clear that the ruling or regulation applied to a particular case. Field service letter no. 7, dated December 12, 1936, embodied the understanding between Montgomery and Evans on this question.

The reason why the legal staff of the board prepared the digest was that the internal revenue lawyers were swamped.

THE LOCAL POSTMASTERS DO THE JOB

The actual registration process was left, to a very large degree, to the discretion of local postmasters. The instructions issued by the Post Office Department on November 4 were of the most general sort. Two members of the Washington Post Office headquarters went into the field, stopping in each of the fifteen postal regions, where they met with the postal inspectors and discussed the registration job. The inspectors were to generally supervise the work at the enumeration centers, but it does not appear that many of them paid much attention to this added activity. The job was, after all, a relatively simple one for the local postmasters. By November 16 the regular mail carriers had made lists of the employers on their routes. On that date they delivered form SS-4 to those employers and then, a week or two later, collected them, checking off each employer on their original list. Then, on November 24, the mail carriers delivered SS-5 forms to these same employers on the basis of the number of employees reported on the SS-4's. The following week the employers returned the SS-5's to the post offices. Some SS-5's were mailed directly and some were filled out in the post offices, but the vast bulk were collected by the letter carriers. The 1,017 first-class post offices typed the office record cards and the social security account number cards for their own immediate postal areas, while the fifty-seven central accounting post offices did the same for the second-, third-, and fourth-class post offices within their areas.

There were, of course, great variations in fulfilling the job, from one post office to another, but on the whole the post office personnel seemed to accept the task as just another job, like the selling of Baby Bonds or the issuance of the Bonus Bonds earlier that same year. This was true also of the men on the

Post Office headquarters staff who apparently had no special interest in the social security program or the related tax job.

While on a short field trip in December and January, the authors visited several post offices in the midwest which were still engaged in registration. They thought that the local postmasters did a surprisingly good job under the circumstances. The largest post office visited was the one in Chicago where many account numbers were issued. The entire internal office procedure had been devised by the supervisor, who was normally head of the supply section in the Chicago office. Following is a brief description of the procedures used by the Chicago Post Office and noted by the authors during their visit:

The Chicago Post Office was the typing center for all the second-, third-, and fourth-class post offices in Illinois, a volume of 1,100,000 applications (900,000 had been estimated). There were relatively few instructions from headquarters and little supervision by inspectors. Mr. Smordock, normally head of the supply section, was in charge, with perhaps nine or ten other permanent employees. They were compelled to develop their entire procedure on short notice and to make a considerable number of internal forms.

Personnel was recruited from civil service lists for the most part, but the shortage of stenographers led to a considerable number of non-civil-service appointments toward the end of the period. Girls were trained by their fellows who had been employed longer; a nucleus of sixty was the start. Typewriters were rented at some seventy odd cents a week. Instead of renting desks, which would have cost about $5,000, tables of plywood were built at a cost of $900.

A late start was made, most of the applications coming in after the deadline on December 5. A maximum of 900 typists were employed but by December 29, a couple of hundred had already been laid off. In January another rush may be expected in making out numbers for the employees of all the railroad companies with headquarters in Chicago.

The procedure was rather simple. Blocks coming in from large employers were left intact and sent through in a unit. Each girl did a block of fifty at a time, after the applications which were obviously incorrectly filled out had been weeded out. Individual cards were so indicated with placards so that they could be mailed back. Each card was sent thru a verification, or checking, process.

There were a great many cards sent in by individuals, two or three hundred thousand all told.

According to Mr. Smordock, there was no interference with the Christmas business because it was handled as an entirely separate operation.

The fifty-six field offices of the board which were open at the time undertook a variety of functions, but with a few exceptions they had very little to do with the actual receiving of applications and assignment of numbers. Their job was primarily that of answering inquiries and directing people to the post offices to secure account numbers. The exceptions were in those cities where the board's field office was located in the same building as the post office. For example in Milwaukee, where the field office was located in the post office building, some of the field office staff were assigned to registration.

The process was much slower than was originally anticipated. According to the December 16 field study by the Bureau of Old Age Benefits, only 2,166,000 employer registration forms (SS-4) and 8,060,000 completed and typed office record cards had been unpacked in Baltimore as of December 16. By noon of December 16, 21,338,000 completed employee forms (SS-5) had been received by post offices and only 12,563,000 office record cards typed. In many post offices the great bulk of applications were handled after the deadline of December 5 originally set by Treasury decision 4704. On December 22, the Post Office Department reported the receipt of a total of 22,129,000 SS-5's; on February 15, 1937, it reported a total of 23,647,000 SS-5's received.

SUPPLEMENTARY REGISTRATION ACTIVITIES

Before drawing any conclusions regarding the success of registration, it is well to note that the Post Office (and the board) also conducted the assignment of account numbers to railroad employees. Early in December, after registration was well under way, it occurred to the board to assign numbers to railroad workers while the Post Office was still handling the job. Although the railroads did not come under the provisions of Titles VIII and II, a good many of them were covered by state unemployment compensation acts, and the board wished to have employee account numbers used by the state unemployment compensation administrations. Moreover, it was fairly certain that shifts in employment would bring a good many railroad employees into the general old age benefits system. The Railroad Retirement Board was glad to have the board perform this job for it, because it seemed the best way to complete registration with lowest cost and highest efficiency. On December 2, the board considered a supplemental agreement with the Post Office Department to carry out this work, but at that time there was doubt as to whether the appropriation of the Railroad Retirement Board could be used to reimburse the Social Security Board for the expenses involved. However, the idea appealed to Budget Director Daniel Bell, and he was willing to allow any funds remaining from the $12,400,000 wage record appropriation of the Social Security Board and any surplus from the Railroad Retirement Board appropriation to be used for this purpose. He agreed that if any additional funds were necessary he would support a request for a deficiency appropriation from Congress to cover the railroad registration expense.

The difficulties of finance were finally ironed out, and on December 24 the board signed a supplemental agreement with the Post Office which provided that the Post Office Department would carry out the registration of railroad employees and type up the account cards in the same manner as for the larger registration job. A special carrier registration form, designated C.E.R.-1, was worked out with the cooperation of the Railroad Retirement Board and representatives of the railway companies. Because the railroad companies whose headquarters were located in major cities agreed to handle the distribution of registration forms to their employees, the return of them to the post office typing centers, and the distribution of the completed account cards, it was possible to handle this job very easily and quickly.

For some time, consideration had been given to the idea of assigning account numbers to persons over sixty-five in order that the numbers might be used by state unemployment compensation agencies (which had no age limits in their laws). Similarly, the assignment of numbers to WPA workers had been proposed, but this was a more complex problem, because it was tied up with the use of a common account number by both the Social Security Board and the United States Employment Service. The Employment Service number was used by the WPA in all its records for payroll accounting. After the dispute with Persons over the board's refusal to adopt the Employment Service number system, which had come to a head in August, this question had been allowed to lie undisturbed. In December, the board once more wrote to Secretary Perkins to ask whether it would be possible for the Employment Service to begin preparations for using the social security account number in its records. Persons finally agreed, in February 1937, to have social security account numbers marked on the records of all applications filed with the United States Employment Service and the state employment services, and instructed all directors of state employment services to this effect. He pointed out, however, that it would not be possible to avoid using both the Employment Service number and the social security number for some time to come, at least until the WPA agreed to make the shift. Negotiations were then taken up with the WPA, but an agreement with that agency was not reached until after the period covered by this study.

It was not long after the first contract with the Post Office was signed that Roger Evans realized that the assignment of account numbers would not be finished by the first of January as contemplated in that agreement. It was clear too that the board would not be able to take over at that time, because of the slow headway it was making in expanding its field organization. Consequently, in November he reached an oral understanding with the post office people that their cooperation would continue until March 31, 1937. This understanding was confirmed by a letter to the board from the Postmaster General on December 31, in reply to a letter of Winant's thanking him for the cooperation of his department. The Postmaster General stated that "the fact that we have done a good job is a source of personal satisfaction to me and you may be assured that the Department will be pleased to continue its cooperation with your Board until the job is complete."

During January and February the expansion of the board's field organization was still going very slowly; in fact, by March 1 only forty-four additional field offices had been opened which, with the original fifty-six opened in November, brought the total to one hundred. On that date Altmeyer wrote to the Postmaster General to request him to extend the cooperation of the Post Office until June 30 on the original basis and indefinitely on a curtailed basis. He stated in his letter that account numbers had been assigned to approximately twenty-four million employees and that the board estimated that in the future, three million account numbers would have to be assigned each year to newly employed persons. Because the board's one hundred field offices were unprepared to handle the typing involved, Altmeyer requested that the Post Office continue to do this work until June 30. As for the continuing registration function, he expressed the board's opinion that it would be desirable for the Post Office to make available at all times application forms for both employers and employees. On March 20, 1937, the post office agreed to all the requests made by the board in this letter.

In June 1937 the board received from the Post Office Department the final installment of its bill for assigning account numbers. It included a large part of the cost of assigning account numbers to railroad employees, WPA workers, and persons over sixty-five. The total cost, including the purchase of equipment which was to be turned over to the Social Security Board, was $5,700,000. The estimate which Seidemann had made in October 1936 was $6,000,000, and the appropriation which the Board had received to carry out registration was $12,400,000.

THE QUALITY OF THE WORK DONE BY THE POST OFFICE

By the time this study was brought to a close, on March 15, 1937, it was not yet possible to arrive at any judgment on the completeness and effectiveness of the registration job performed by the Post Office Department, because of the lack of adequate information on the number of persons holding more than one account number. Evans estimated in January 1937 that despite provisions for checking and verifying the transfer of information from form SS-5 to the office record card, and the checking of these cards when received in Baltimore, about 5 percent of the total number of cards received in the Central Record Office in Baltimore were caught in the photoelectric cell machine and returned to the Post Office for correction. Evan's judgment was that in view of the great difficulties involved in the task, such a residual error was not too great. However, the experience of the field offices of the Social Security Board, about two hundred in number, which took over the assignment of account numbers on July 1, 1937, indicated that a check at some later date might show that the assignment of account numbers by the Post Office was not as successful as it earlier appeared to be. For instance, the manager of the Washington field office of the board told Frase in August 1937 that although some two-hundred thousand account numbers had been assigned in his area by the Post Office Department, he was handling some five hundred applications for account numbers each day. He also estimated, on the basis of the experience of his office in July 1937, that some five to eight million of the twenty-nine million applications for account numbers on file with the board were duplicates.

These duplications arose from several circumstances: some people were under the impression that the more account numbers they received the better; others thought that a new account number had to be received upon entering each new job; others lost their original numbers and either they or their employers applied for new ones; and a great many unemployed and WPA workers applied for numbers under the original registration and then secured them later through the WPA registration or when becoming privately employed. That the job was not fully completed by June 30 was further indicated by the fact that in the month of July 1937 alone, the field offices of the board issued some 1,900,000 account numbers.

There were two other major flaws in the procedure. The first three digits of the employee account number were an area code designed to identify applications as coming from one of 999 areas into which the country was divided. It was contemplated that Treasury decision 4704 and the Post Office instructions would provide that employers file SS-4's with the postmaster in the area in which his establishment was located. Although this agreement was understood by all parties, by some mistake, intentional or otherwise, the treasury decision provided that SS-4's should be filed with the postmaster from whose office the business mail of the establishment was delivered, but it permitted the filing of SS-5's with any postmaster. As a consequence, large employers with branches in different parts of the country sent out employee application forms (SS-5's) to their branches, and the employees in these branch establishments returned their applications through their national headquarters office. This office, in turn, deposited the application forms with the post office in the city in which the national headquarters was located. Thus, account numbers given to those branch plant employees contained the area designation in which the headquarters office was located. In this way, New York, Philadelphia, Boston, Chicago, and other cities used as corporation headquarters had given their area numbers to account cards from many other parts of the country. This seriously decreased the usefulness of the area number scheme and, to a large extent, also defeated the purpose of the yellow duplicates of form 702 which were designed for state unemployment compensation commissions.[18]

The other major hitch was the failure of the Bureau of Internal Revenue to get a complete list of employers for the initial distribution of the tax forms. The employer lists compiled by the mail carriers, after having served the purpose of enumeration, were in most cases destroyed rather than turned over to the collectors of internal revenue for use in distributing tax forms under Title VIII in January 1937. Just where the slip occurred in the planning cannot be determined, but it seems likely that the board and the Bureau of Internal Revenue anticipated that the SS-4 forms would be made available to the collectors of internal revenue in January 1937. But with the usual delays in having copies photostated for the Bureau of Internal Revenue and forwarding them to collectors, it was not until May 1937 that duplicates of these SS-4's actually got into the collectors' hands. Meanwhile, in January 1937 the collectors had to send tax forms and instructions to employers on the basis of very imperfect lists made up in their own offices from telephone directories and other sources.[19]

OTHER ADMINISTRATIVE DEVELOPMENTS IN THE BUREAU OF OLD AGE BENEFITS

THE BALTIMORE RECORD OFFICE

The administrative problems of operating a huge accounting factory of this type are undoubtedly great and important, but they lie beyond the scope of this study. Furthermore, the location of the plant in Baltimore made it almost impossible to keep in touch with developments there. We therefore deal summarily with this particular function.[20]

---

[18] The use of the Social Security Board number rather than that of the Employment Service for state unemployment compensation had disadvantages. The Employment Service number was based on state and county units and, had it been used for the social security account number as well, it would have greatly facilitated the process of estimating coverage by state unemployment compensation agencies for county units. It also would have given them a basis for planning expansion and establishment of new employment offices for the payment of unemployment benefits.

[19] The collector of internal revenue in Oklahoma City, Oklahoma, was the only one discovered by Frase to have secured lists of employers made up by the letter carriers for use in sending out the first tax returns in January.

[20] A visit to the Baltimore plant early in January 1938 confirmed an earlier impression: that the principal problem there was not that of setting up equipment and an

It was necessary to have this plant ready to receive the SS-5 forms sent in by the Post Office during the last week in November. The recruitment of a staff of 2,300 was a major part of the board's responsibility in this connection, since the supply and installation of machinery and equipment was taken over by the International Business Machines Corporation.[21] This company also undertook the largest part of the task of training personnel to use the equipment. The records were located in a big warehouse near the Baltimore wharves, where the board rented 120,000 square feet of space, covering three floors. When the authors visited this establishment in December 1936 there were approximately 2,200 employees, of whom 700 were trainees working under instructors and using dummy cards, but handling them precisely as the actual records would be handled. There was already a considerable nucleus of personnel familiar with punch card equipment and competent to operate it or supervise its use. In addition, many typists were being trained to operate the machines. IBM had a large staff on hand to care for the equipment as well as to train operators.

The process of setting up individual ledger cards was divided into nine steps. A block of one thousand applications and one thousand office record cards made out by the typing centers of the Post Office, and numbered consecutively, were sent through each operation together. A control unit of nine cards (one for each operation) accompanied each block through the process, with the appropriate card being removed after each operation and dispatched to the control file. Thus it was possible to tell from that file the precise stage of each block at any given time.

It would be fruitless here to describe the character of the operations. Suffice it to say that they would lead with uncanny precision to the automatic posting of the individual ledger cards upon which were accumulated notations of the tax payments made for each covered employee. That step would not be taken, however, until after July 1937, when the first payroll tax reports would be forthcoming. It was then the plan to punch the quarterly payroll record cards

---

organization to handle the vast volume of records, but of insuring that the records were complete and accurate—the job of the Bureau of Internal Revenue. The technical problem in the Baltimore office, probably difficult enough in its way, had been pretty thoroughly solved by January 1938, but the machinery for printing wage records from the payroll for the period from January 1 to June 30, 1937, was not functioning because these records had not been received in large enough volume or in a form accurate enough to justify operations. The Bureau of Internal Revenue had done fairly well in collecting taxes under Title VIII but had fallen down rather badly in getting the information required for starting employee wage records. Thus the brevity of the discussion above corresponds in part to the relative ease with which the machine operations in Baltimore were conducted because of the light work load.

[21] The recruitment of the staff is discussed in more detail in chapter 7.

from the employer returns in the sixty-four field offices which corresponded to the field offices of the collectors of internal revenue. These cards were to be sent to Baltimore where they would be automatically posted to the employee accounts.

The process of transferring information sent to the Central Record Office seemed so well designed as to be quite capable of mechanical handling. It seemed probable that such mechanical difficulties as might arise would be readily overcome. The real problem appeared to be that of securing adequate raw data from the collectors of internal revenue.[22]

Until March 15, 1937, the Baltimore office was engaged almost entirely in establishing records for each individual who had received an account number. It was not anticipated that the posting of wage records for the first six months of 1937 would start until August or September.[23]

POST-REGISTRATION ORGANIZATIONAL PROBLEMS OF THE BUREAU

Changes in Top Bureau Staff

The factional dispute which existed in the Bureau of Old Age Benefits from the time of Seidemann's appointment on September 2, 1936, through the registration period has been mentioned in several parts of this narrative.

---

[22] The board was beginning to appreciate the publicity value of this gargantuan machine-recording establishment. Already a good many newspapermen, photographers, and newsreel photographers had visited the Baltimore office.

[23] It may be of interest here to refer briefly to a record-keeping scheme much discussed by the board in the spring of 1937, after this study was completed. Mr. Harry Hoff, a consulting engineer with some experience in designing buildings for record-keeping and record-storing for private life insurance companies, was hired by the board in November 1936 at a salary of $2,000 a month, while actually employed, to design a building for its use. Hoff evidently impressed the board members greatly, because he was soon engaged in all manner of schemes for changing the organization of the Bureau of Old Age Benefits. The first of these was a plan for breaking down the records and claims work into ten units based on the last digit of the account number, the theory being that some such subdivision of work was necessary because of the magnitude of the operations. The board members, Way, and even Murray Latimer were captivated by this idea for awhile, but for some reason or other Hoff lost interest in it and began to work on a plan for the complete decentralization of old age benefit records into twelve regional record offices. This drastic step was actually approved by the board on March 30, 1937, but it was later modified to allow the establishment of twelve experimental regional units within the Baltimore plant. Hoff himself faded out of the picture in the summer of 1937. The episode, most of which occurred after the completion of this study, was the strangest in the history of the board. Hoff had never presented more than the sketchiest outline or justification for his plans. After several months he disappeared, leaving behind as a memento a half-completed decentralization experiment which, it was estimated, was costing the board fifty to eighty thousand dollars a month,

During the month of January 1937 Winant, who had returned to the board on temporary assignment, was concerned with the solution of this as well as several other personnel and organizational problems. The ultimate solution was the resignation of Seidemann in February, just before Winant's final departure. Just how or why LeRoy Hodges was selected to head the bureau was not learned. While this move cut the worst tangle, Hodges and John Corson, who was assigned as his assistant for several months, had much to learn, and no great order was achieved by the middle of March. McCormack and his followers were, however, stripped of the influence Seidemann had allowed them. McDonald was reduced to second in command of the Claims Division, under Will Hayes, on loan from the Veterans' Administration, who was made acting chief.

Plans for Handling of Claims

Under the provisions of Title II, individuals reaching the age of sixty-five and the estates of those dying after January 1, 1937, were entitled to 3.5 percent of their wages after that date as lump-sum or death benefits, respectively. This provision of the act was included to insure equity, with little realization of how large an administrative burden it would prove to be during the years 1937 and 1938. In fact, with the Post Office handling the registration job, it was this provision alone which made it necessary to establish old age benefit field offices prior to the payment of monthly benefits in 1942. As far as the authors knew, the board never seriously considered eliminating these provisions by requesting a change in the law by the Congress, at least for 1937 and 1938, although a proposal for setting up a minimum lump-sum or death payment was sometimes discussed.

The planning of the machinery for receiving and paying these claims was neglected during the fall of 1936 while the much more important and pressing question of registration absorbed the attention of the staff. Besides, the size of these payments in the first few months of 1937 was so small that most persons were not expected to find it worthwhile to file for them. We have touched elsewhere upon the struggle that went on between Seidemann and Bane as to whether the adjudication of the claims should be centralized in Washington or decentralized in the field, and have noted that Seidemann's plea for centralization was adopted for at least the first six months.

The preparation of the forms and the procedures to be followed went slowly because of the legal necessity, under the Budget and Accounting Act, of receiving the approval of the Comptroller General for the forms. Calhoun, the assistant general counsel who had handled most of the board's relations with the GAO and who was later to be placed in charge of the legal work in connection with claims adjudications, was most active in conducting the preliminary negotiations.

These had progressed far enough by December 29, 1936, to permit the board to reach a decision on claims policy which appeared in the form of Social Security Board Administrative Order No. 24 of that date.[24] It announced that the procedures, forms, instructions, and regulations for paying these small, lump-sum benefits must be based on a specified list of general principles. Listing these principles consumed a page and a half of single-spaced type. The principles detailed who could make application, how to secure sworn statements of wages paid and when and where work was performed, and how to establish dates and evidence of birth or death and identity relationships essential to justify claim payment. The order also told where to file a claim, and assured confidentiality.

By the middle of January 1937 the first draft of the claims forms was ready for distribution to certain staff members for comment. Frase happened to be in Louis Resnick's office on January 16, just as he finished looking at the draft, and observed that he was quite worried lest they prove a boomerang to the board. He felt that they were so complicated that lawyers would be needed for help in filling them out. Moreover, the board's plan to require the individual or his heir to accumulate his own wage record for the first six-month period would impose a very difficult task, particularly on widows.

The field officers' reaction was even more vigorously adverse. The western regional representative of the Bureau of Old Age Benefits expressed his dislike to one of the authors substantially as follows:

There is a great present danger that the procedures adopted by the Treasury and the board in connection with claims for death benefits and lump-sum payments will kill the incipient goodwill and become a major obstacle in the success of the board. This is due to the unrealistic policy which requires affidavits on the part of employer and employee for filling out form SS-3 for the Treasury, costing a notary fee and considerable time, and then the further affidavits when the application for claims is filed with the board, again costing notary fees for each party despite the fact that the total claim in many cases will be smaller than the notary fees. Unless this situation is changed quickly, the board is going to become the laughingstock of the country. It will be a fine issue for critics to take hold of.

Despite the rather widespread objection to the forms and proposed procedure, the board was obliged to stick to them because of the provisions of the act, other statutes governing claims against the federal government, and the requirements of the GAO. On January 26, the Acting Comptroller General approved with slight modification the adoption of standard form 1058 proposed by the board for its claims applications. On February 5, the revised multilithed forms were sent out to the regional offices.

---

[24] The Comptroller General insisted on the use by the board of an adaptation of his standard form 1058, which required notarization except for the statement of age.

McKinley happened to be in the Boston regional office the following week and found that the arrival of these forms had created a veritable tempest there, because of the fear of the unfavorable public reaction which they would create. The incident was interesting enough to justify quoting the notes written at the time:

The observer arrived at the regional office on the morning of February 8 and found a conference going on with two representatives of a large Boston utility company on the subject of claims procedure for death and lump-sum payments. This company had several claims which its employees were ready to file and evidently had been called in to discuss its reaction to the forms before any administrative use was made of them. The forms had arrived without prior notice on the preceding Saturday, February 6, and on Sunday McDonald of the Claims Division had been in town to discuss them and other claims problems.

This conference continued until noon and the reaction of the representative of the utility company was very unfavorable. He intimated his company would be willing to help individuals fill out the forms but would have nothing to do with the three questions which dealt with the amount of the estate, for fear that some liability might attach to them in terms of the penalty clause printed on the back of the forms. He also thought that in occupations in which there was considerable mobility of labor it would be impractical for the individual to determine and swear to wages received from previous employers.

After the representative of the utility company had departed, Mr. Pearson, Mr. Morton, Mr. Campbell, Mr. Thurston, and the regional attorney gathered together to discuss what was to be done about the forms. The consensus seemed to be that it would be extremely unwise to use these forms, because of bad public reaction to them. At least it was thought that if this claims procedure was to be used at all, it ought to be made clear that it was only a temporary device, pending amendment of the legislation eliminating requirement for settling claims in terms of the interstate laws of the various states, and until the wage records could be set up and used in Washington. Thereupon Pearson phoned Bane and received a rather evasive answer. Although reluctant to do so, he then phoned Winant, and Winant felt that he ought first to wait and see what the reactions of the other regions would be. With considerable reluctance Pearson then phoned New York, Philadelphia, and San Antonio and found that these offices had no particular objection to the claims forms, although Mrs. Rosenberg of New York was on a vacation in Florida and her executive assistant would be reluctant to take any action on his own initiative. New York said further that the forms were already being distributed in New York for administrative use and that the newspapers would soon have the story.

Morton then drew up an indictment of the claims procedure, emphasizing that it contradicted all the publicity previously put out during the registration period which indicated that the individual would get his benefits automatically without any further effort on his part, through the function of the wage record system in Baltimore. He pointed out further that a devastating attack could be made on the basis of widows having to tramp the streets to the previous employers of husbands in order to secure the data necessary in filing the claim. He advised strongly that either the board announce that this was a temporary procedure, pending legislative amendments, or that a statement be made that legislation was shortly to be suggested by the board to the Congress for eliminating many of the most burdensome details of the claims procedure. The Informational Service representative, in addition to sending this memorandum to Huse and Resnick, also phoned Huse and told him firmly of the objection of the whole staff of the regional office to this claims procedure.

The regional attorney was of the opinion, by reading section 203 in connection with section 208, that it was inconceivable that creditors should have to be paid out of these death payments and subsequently forwarded his opinion to Washington.

The next day Resnick phoned to say that absolutely no publicity should be given to these claims forms and that a withdrawal was being seriously considered. On the following day, Wednesday, however, the Commerce Clearing House came out with facsimiles of the forms.

But the Washington establishment discounted the protests of the field, particularly the Boston office which was considered to be habitually temperamental. While the heads of the Informational Service shared the fears of the field men, they knew that nothing could be done because of the requirements of the statutes and the time required to get the central recording procedure to function. The latter difficulty would be only temporary and the public would probably accept that explanation, but changes in the law waited on Congress. The board could not announce its request for amendments eliminating the objectionable requirements, because its proposed amendments were then being considered by the budget bureau's legislative division, and there was no way of telling if or when they would be cleared for submission to the Congress.

As one of the discerning Washington officers remarked, the irritation of the field men was partly the result of the failure of headquarters to keep them more fully informed about the reasons for its actions.

The sequel to this incident was rather significant. McKinley felt sympathy toward the attitude about these forms taken by the Boston office, believing that there was perhaps a fifty-fifty chance that the forms would be villified by some unfriendly columnist. But in this case the perception of the field staff and the professional public relations men in Washington as to the public reaction proved to be less sound than that of the technicians and administrators in Washington. Their fears proved to be entirely unfounded; there was no unfavorable comment whatsoever in the newspapers, and no reported resentment on the part of individuals filing claims.

There were actually no claims paid by the time this study came to an end, nor indeed for several weeks thereafter. Most of the spring was taken up by organizing the claims procedure in Washington and receiving the approval of the General Accounting Office on a multitude of details, including the forms for certification to the Treasury. A few claims were pushed through to approval by Seidemann just before his departure, because he wanted to crown his service as director of the bureau of Old Age Benefits with this parting gesture.

.7.

GENERAL MANAGEMENT

THE BOARD AND THE EXECUTIVE DIRECTOR

The three members of the Social Security Board decided early that they would avoid the mistakes apparently being made by the directors of the TVA, who had parceled out functions among themselves. Instead, they would confine their activities to policy problems, delegating administrative tasks to a chief administrator who would report to and be responsible to the board. As Frank Bane once expressed it, "the board decided to follow the analogy of a board of directors of a private corporation or a city council under the city manager form of government." However, there is no formal record of this decision in the minutes of the board's meetings, nor was a full, written statement of its conception of the distribution of powers between the board and the chief executive officer ever drawn up. To be sure, the bylaws adopted on November 27, 1935, contained an important statement of the executive director's relationship to the board and the staff. These bylaws provided that: (1) the executive director should attend all board meetings and, if unable to be present, should designate a member of his staff to represent him; (2) all business coming before the board should be referred to the executive director, who was to prepare the agenda; (3) state laws and state administrative plans which, under Titles I, III, IV, and VIII of the act had to be approved by the board, were to be examined first by the executive director and his technical staff, and the director was to make recommendations for the board's consideration.

Some additional light on this problem of the respective functions of the board and the executive director may be obtained from the organizational charts drawn up in the early months of the board's history. Chart no. 1 showed the following general duties assigned to the board: (1) policy formulation; (2) coordination of federal-state relationships; (3) coordination of divisions (the major administrative units into which the board's staff organiza-

382

tion was then to be divided). For the office of executive director the chart gave the following functions: (1) supervision and coordination of divisions; (2) supervision of regional offices; (3) preparation of an annual report to Congress.

The tentative chart of November 22, 1935, was prepared about a month after Frank Bane had agreed to become executive director. This second chart omitted one of the board functions shown on the first chart, namely, the coordination of divisions. This apparently was in recognition of the need to delegate all administrative responsibility to the executive director. The first chart would have confused the administrative responsibilities of these two top units in the hierarchy. When the third and final chart of December 4 appeared, it showed a further modification which concentrated policy decisions in the board's hands and administrative direction in the executive director's office. It lifted the preparation of the annual report from the latter office and placed it under the board's jurisdiction. To the executive director's office it added the function of coordination with the states. This last item would appear to have been superfluous in view of the fact that the units in the organization directly in charge of coordination with the states were, according to this chart, the operating bureaus of Public Assistance and Unemployment Compensation. Why the executive director should have a separate and distinct function in this area apart from his supervision of these operating bureaus is difficult to say. Perhaps the board members prepared this chart with Frank Bane's personality and experience vividly in mind, and were expressing their expectation and hope that he would carry on a large part of the political and public relations work with the governors of the states. Another possible explanation may have been a concern to justify Bane's classification (salary grade) with the Civil Service Commission.

Private conversations with the chairman of the board in these early months led to the conclusion that there was never a full meeting of minds among the board members concerning the jurisdiction of the executive director. On December 31, 1935, Frank Bane told McKinley that the line bureaus should not have to deal with the board through the executive director on matters involving policy; they should be able to come directly to the board. On administrative matters they should be under his orders but on policy questions not. To reach this pattern, regular staff meetings with the board were the goal, but these could not be started until all the top positions had been filled. In the spring of 1936, after a heated board meeting concerning the permanency and location of the coordinator's office, the board chairman pointed out in private conversation that the Social Security Act made the board responsible for administration, a fact which the executive director seemed to forget in constantly asking for more power.

But more important that a theoretical statement of the relationship of the board and the executive director were the personalities and habits of individual board members. In the early months of the board's existence it had been without an executive officer or other key staff members to help it build the organization. Therefore the board members, particularly Chairman Winant and Altmeyer, engaged in numerous administrative tasks. While the chairman had indicated in December his awareness of the fact that the board members were handling administrative chores, and that as soon as the bureau heads were appointed they ought to cease that kind of activity, his own personal qualities and those of Arthur Altmeyer made it difficult for either of them to break these habits and refrain from direct interference in administration.

Winant had secured his political and administrative experience in state government. As governor of the small state of New Hampshire, he kept his hands on practically everything. New Hampshire is so small that he was able to have a personal relationship with nearly every important state employee. Perhaps his most attractive and unusual quality was a talent for becoming deeply interested in, and in turn fascinating to, the people with whom he came in contact. He developed strong attachments to people whom he liked and was very cautious about dealings with those whom he did not like. These habits were well set by the time he became chairman of the board. The effect of Winant's personality on the board's administration was suggested by a statement in the Brookings Institution Report of 1932, summarizing the findings of a survey of New Hampshire state and local government, which read:

A serious difficulty in the functioning of New Hampshire's executive department is that it constantly interests itself in details of administration which should be left to the departments. . . . Much can be done by the Governor himself in making department heads feel full responsibility, confining himself to the exercise of his primary functions of leadership, policy-making, supervision, and control.[1]

These qualities of Chairman Winant not only made it difficult for him to refrain from interfering in administrative matters but also affected the functioning of the board as a group. The consumption of interminable hours in board discussion of the pros and cons of people and of problems may have been due in part to these personal characteristics. However, this is the way all boards conduct themselves. While the delay in securing key staff people was partly the result of the board's high personnel standards, it was also due in part to the cautiousness of the chairman's mind in reaching a final decision about people whom he did not know intimately. The same cautiousness was

---

[1] Interestingly enough, the report was written by Henry Seidemann, and the opinions therein expressed were fully concurred in by Frank Bane, Seidemann's associate in that survey.

manifest in the discussion of details of policy, and contributed to postponements and reconsiderations.

Altmeyer was undoubtedly the member second in influence in 1935–36. His temperament was that of the student who loves and masters detail. His technical knowledge of unemployment compensation was large. His administrative experience in Wisconsin state affairs, the U.S. Department of Labor, and the NRA had given him a knowledge of procedures which was quite superior. He also knew many people technically equipped to perform specialized administrative tasks relating to social insurance. These qualities, while contributing greatly to the information and insight of the board in creating its organization, were impediments to the restriction of the board's function to the sphere of policy-making. Altmeyer was always willing to match his knowledge of people and of administrative detail against that of Executive Director Bane and the bureau heads, and he was unwilling on many occasions to make decisions even on very detailed matters until they had been canvassed and recanvassed at meeting after meeting.

Curiously enough, in his general attitude towards the division of functions between the executive director and the board, Vincent Miles, who correctly styled himself the politician member of the board, was much more willing both to act promptly and to live up to the implications of the board's theory of its restricted tasks. The explanation for this was again the temperament and background which Miles brought to the board. He had never occupied an administrative post of large responsibility. His chief experience with administrative problems was gained as a railroad attorney, and as such he was accustomed to see administrative matters left to the railway executives. He possessed no particular knowledge of administrative procedures and techniques, and was quite willing to leave these to the executive director and the heads of the bureaus. The same traits which made him a successful politician—his love for personal relationships with Tom, Dick, and Harry and his willingness to make speeches—made it easier for him to wash his hands of administrative problems. He was of course always interested in opportunities for his friends to obtain jobs—the basic trading commodity of the politician in any country.

As the board's staff was being filled out during the latter part of January and February 1936, and the task of dealing with plans for state administration of the public assistance funds and state unemployment insurance acts became increasingly pressing, the board was compelled to drop some of the administrative activities in which it had earlier indulged. The executive director began to feel confident that the board would soon permit him the full scope of responsible activity he had expected when he accepted his office. Nevertheless, disconcerting episodes occurred frequently. Matters came up from the bureaus or the coordinator on which the director had not been consulted. Or board members interested themselves and consulted with staff members about administrative situations without his knowledge.

During this period, the executive director found himself faced with two difficulties. The first was the need to spend so much time with the board that he had little opportunity to carry on his managerial functions. The board met nearly every day and very frequently twice a day, and the meetings ran on hour after hour. The second handicap experienced by the executive director was the reliance placed by the board upon his ability as a public speaker. From the beginning Bane had been frequently away on speaking engagements or in conferences with state officials, but these were usually brief excursions. During the month of April 1936, however, Bane was away most of the time speaking on the Pacific Coast, at New Orleans, and over much of the rest of the United States. (The board in fact encouraged bureau heads and other staff members to go out on speaking engagements.) Bane seemed to accept this public relations activity in the early months because his own contacts throughout the country were much more ample than those of any of the three board members, particularly with state officials concerned with public assistance functions. These were the functions, especially old age assistance, that were political hot spots. Bane could speak on this subject without much preparation. As Winant told McKinley, "Bane is a super contact man, and it would be a shame to tie him down to a desk in Washington." Late in January 1936 Seidemann, in one of those explosive moods habitual with him at that particular time, declared that the roles of the board and the executive director had been reversed. The board, in March 1936, approved Bane's selection of a deputy, John J. Corson, who proved to have administrative gifts of a high order. The executive director nonetheless was compelled to carry on much if not most of his work as chief administrator either in absentia or after hours.

There was a lull in May and June 1936 when Bane was able to stay in Washington and give his attention to management, but this did not last. It was not until after the close of the period under review, in the late spring of 1937, that the field staff of the Bureau of Public Assistance and its director, Miss Hoey, took over the bulk of state contact work which Bane had formerly carried. John Corson's assignment at that time to get the Bureau of Old Age Benefits into high gear required Bane to stick closer to Washington. Moreover, the board decided about then to have only two meetings a week, and thus released more of Bane's attention and time for general administrative supervision.

The board consistently violated its own decision to stick to policy questions. This was particularly true in appointment of personnel. The board early reserved to itself a major role in appointments by adopting a resolution limiting the executive director and bureau heads to the selection of staff whose compensation was under the second lowest professional grade (P-2) of $2,600 a year. A large if not the largest part of the board's time throughout the entire period under study was spent in canvassing, interviewing, and selecting personnel. In the early months of its history, candidates for jobs were usually interviewed separately by each member of the board as well as by the executive director. Altmeyer, rather than Bane, played the chief role in the nomination of directors and assistant directors of the various bureaus. Chairman Winant's peculiar flair for finding and attracting good people was also frequently manifest. The role of these two board members was typified by one of the associate directors of a bureau, who said that Altmeyer had employed him while Winant had employed his chief, and he had never seen Bane before he joined the staff. The coordinator appears to have named the director and assistant directors of the Bureau of Accounts and Audits, while Bane's influence was chiefly manifest in the selection of the top people in the bureaus of Public Assistance and Business Management.

The board's great concern with appointments continued to the very end of the study in March 1937. Hardly a board meeting went by in which the discussion of the "Personnel Journal" did not occupy a large proportion of the time. The board was involved in the selection of staff for the regional and field offices beginning in the spring of 1936, and for the Bureau of Old Age Benefits. The chiefs of the bureaus of Unemployment Compensation and Public Assistance were given greater freedom in selecting staff after the top members were appointed. This was also true of the Bureau of Research and Statistics, although nominations in this area were frequently subject to veto or unfavorable discussion by the board. As related below, the board consistently used the Bureau of Informational Service as a dumping ground for the political appointees it felt compelled to hire. The concern of the board with the staff in the Bureau of Old Age Benefits probably derived from the fact that many vacancies existed there,[2] and also from the absence of effective direction in the bureau from May until September 1936: Latimer was absorbed in his duties as chairman of the Railroad Retirement Board and the board failed to replace him with a full-time director. The board seemed unwilling to trust the subordinate executives in that bureau. Thus, Winant and Altmeyer in effect took over the responsibility for running the bureau until Seidemann was named chief in September. Even then, their concern with personnel selection did not cease. The board brought in Roger Evans

[2] It was larger than all the other bureaus and offices combined, and the plan for four hundred field offices meant many jobs paying more than $2,600 a year.

to run registration, selected Hayes to do the claims work, and hired Hopf to advise on buildings, records, and organization. After Seidemann, as head of the bureau, selected as his chief aide Colonel McCormack, one of the political appointees attached to Miles, Chairman Winant and Altmeyer seemed disposed to look quizzically at any appointments Seidemann proposed. These two stuck together in opposing most of his candidates or in whittling down their salaries when opposition was inadvisable. The executive director maintained a position of neutrality in these contests over staff in the Bureau of Old Age Benefits.

After the resignation of Winant and Seidemann early in 1937, the situation was scarcely improved. McCormack, of course, had no influence with Hodges and Corson, then in charge of the bureau. Bane and Altmeyer slowly proceeded to get rid of some of the less acceptable members of the bureau staff, but Miles, as soon as he realized that Latimer would not be confirmed as the third member of the board, was strengthened in his position as the second member of what was then a two-man board.

In the matter of salaries and promotions, the sphere of activity of the board embraced the entire organization. Because the classification powers of the Civil Service Commission did not extend to the field staff, the board had large discretion in fixing and changing these salaries; but even as regards the Washington staff, the board had power over salaries. Twice a year administrative promotions, salary increases within the classification grade, which at that time were permitted at the discretion of the agency, led to long discussions in board meetings on the relative merits of particular individuals.

In these personnel questions both the executive director and the director of personnel played a relatively minor role. The latter was considered primarily a technician whose job was to get men on the payroll or to find ways around the Civil Service Commission's rules and regulations. To be sure, he investigated prospective candidates, particularly those suggested by Miles, Seidemann, and McCormack, and the information which he turned up was often of great use to Winant and Altmeyer in stopping or modifying certain appointments. When the regional offices were determined upon in the spring of 1936 and selection of executive staff for these places began, Bane and the chief of Business Management played an important part in sifting out the candidates taken over from the NRA field organization, which was being used as the chief reservoir of talent for the regional executive assistants. But board members became active proponents of candidates for the top position of regional director. This is of significance because it contradicted the understanding reached on March 10, 1936, when Bane asked the board to indicate who was to hire and fire the regional directors and their assistants. Bane understood the board to say that the regional director was to be selected by and responsible to the executive director, even though the actual appointment would be made by the board: Bane was to nominate and the board confirm.[3] But this was not the actual process. Each board member had his pet candidate, and most of the initiative in the selection of regional directors was taken by the board members.

As a consequence of the board's role in choosing and promoting particular staff people, the temptation to interfere with the details of administration continued. Each board member tended to lend his ear to staff members whom he had been responsible for appointing, and to suggest administrative decisions on which the executive director had not been consulted. In the spring of 1936 Bane was frequently embarrassed by suggestions communicated in this manner. At that time Winant worked through Seidemann, Bingham (Research), and Couper (Unemployment Compensation), and Altmeyer worked through Murray, Cohen, and Wagenet. Miles used McCormack and his field committee people.

Altmeyer was particularly interested in the technical details of unemployment compensation and old age benefits. While Winant was chairman Altmeyer played a secondary role, but when the chairman was absent in Geneva during the spring of 1936, and again in the fall when Winant resigned in order to defend the act against candidate Landon, Altmeyer assumed the active direction of administration in Winant's place. He gave orders on operating problems, through the executive director, to the staff in the Bureau of Old Age Benefits. When Winant finally left the board in February 1937 and Altmeyer became chairman, he assumed the function of director of the board. He proceeded to have surveys made by persons both within and without the organization, looking forward to the reorganization and reorientation of the work of the Bureau of Research and Statistics. Plans were also pushed for the organization of the old age benefits records system into twelve regional records offices along the lines of Hopf's suggestions. The Bureau of Accounts and Audits was recast into two divisions. Altmeyer took the initiative in all these actions, often dealing directly with the bureau or division chiefs involved, or delegating responsibility for calling meetings and getting action to Wilbur Cohen, who had become his personal assistant. The other board member, Miles, was consulted only when it was necessary to get his cooperation, and the executive director seems to have been used chiefly to carry out orders.

While Altmeyer expanded the duties of the chairman, Winant had also regarded the chairman as "head of the State" in every respect and privileged to intervene whenever it seemed desirable to him. It may be doubted whether either Winant or Altmeyer, who succeeded him as chairman, ever seriously regarded Bane as the administrative head of the organization with a distinct

---

[3] Privately, Bane expressed the attitude that without this responsible relationship he would have nothing to do with a regional organization.

administrative authority of his own. As a board member, Altmeyer acquiesced in Winant's activity as chairman, playing a subordinate role by furnishing advice on technical matters and personnel. It was Winant, as chairman, who saw the president on matters of higher politics and policy.[4] There were a number of important political questions during the first twelve months which involved the President's strategy for the campaign for reelection. Although Winant was the Republican member of the board, by virtue of his chairmanship he carried on these negotiations and spoke for the board in committing it to presidential decisions. Altmeyer, as chairman, appears not to have been so well prepared to make presidential contacts, and frequently used Secretary of Labor Perkins, his former superior, to gain access to the President. Both chairmen delegated a great deal of the responsibility for dealing with congressmen about patronage to the executive director and to Miles.

In the early months of 1936, as state laws for public assistance and unemployment compensation came in to the board and as administrative plans for their operation poured in for review and approval, there was a period during which it looked as if the board might relinquish its concern with administrative direction and become absorbed in policy questions. But that did not last. As time wore on, the number of legislative changes declined and the state administrative plans became increasingly subject to direct negotiation between the public assistance staff and state officials, while the board tended to approve the recommendations concerning these matters presented by the bureau. At the close of 1936 there was a rush of business in the approval of state laws and administrative plans for unemployment compensation, but neither of these appeared to offer a permanent policy function which would absorb the attention of a full-time board.

The social security statute rested upon the theory of a bipartisan board. But the actual operation of the board showed little connection with the theory. The cleavage within the board did not run along party lines. There was no real difference among any of the members on the basic social policies (and in fact such issues were very few) touched by the administrative process. The

---

[4] A circumstance peculiar to this period and one which greatly influenced the board members was the 1936 presidential campaign. From the early months of that year, all decisions were watched with an eye to their effect upon political psychology, and many ordinarily inconsequential matters appeared at this juncture to have special importance. Though Winant was a Republican, he was very friendly to the New Deal and he wanted to avoid any act on the part of the board which might furnish a handle for the Republican opposition. Hence the concern over the Kansas public assistance laws (discussed in detail above). This also explains the interminable discussions and the indecision shown by both Winant and Altmeyer on many of the problems involved in the registration of employees for old age benefits in advance of January 1937.

real cleavages were over appointments to the board's staff, and on this issue the lineup was usually the Republican chairman and one Democratic member opposing the other Democrat. Of course, had both Democrats been primarily professional politicians the Republican member might have stood alone. Had the Republican member been a spoils politician, he and the Democratic politician might have made an accommodation of mutual advantage even in a Democratic regime, Actually, one of the Democratic members was as much concerned as was the Republican chairman with keeping patronage politics out of the board's organization. Although the two Democrats had stood together in opposition to the chairman in the original selection of the chief executive officer, this was strictly a matter of judgment about the relative competence of the two candidates for the post. Later, one of the Democrats swung over to a temporary alliance with the defeated candidate of the chairman because, through him, certain patronage staff appointments the Democrat desired were facilitated. Yet it was partly on this account that the Republican chairman spent his last weeks of service clearing out staff patronage difficulties and in disillusion, arranging for the departure from the organization of his own former favorite.

On questions of high politics vital to the existing Democratic administration, the chairman was the dominant voice despite his Republican affiliation. It was the Republican chairman who kept in closest touch with the President, clearing matters of policy or action that might be of importance to the President's program or to his electoral success.

THE COORDINATOR

The office of coordinator as created by the board may have been a rationalization of an initial disagreement between the chairman and the other two members over candidates for the executive directorship. It seems probable that had it not been for the fact that Chairman Winant desired Henry Seidemann for that job, while the other two members preferred Frank Bane, the office of coordinator would not have been created. When Bane accepted the executive directorship he understood that the coordinator's position would be strictly a temporary one, but the chairman and Seidemann had a different understanding. This failure to communicate effectively not only led to personal irritation, but also resulted in the development of a theory to justify such an office as a permanent organizational mechanism, and in action to carry out such a theory. There was friction between the executive director and the coordinator, with echoes from their supporters in the staff and on the board, and confusion of responsibility. Even though the position of coordinator was abolished some ten months after its establishment, this early antagonism set in motion currents of attitude and activity that carried over into important decisions about organization and the selection of top personnel. It led to the growth of antagonistic cliques reaching into the board itself, to the detriment of certain aspects of the board's work throughout the period studied. Consequently, this whole episode deserves analysis.

Seidemann elaborated his concept of the coordinator's function to McKinley a few weeks after he joined the board's staff. He expressed the view that the coordinator's powers should correspond to those exercised in the American Telephone and Telegraph Company by the head of its bureau of standards. The duties of the coordinator, as Seidemann envisaged them, were to standardize forms and procedures for all branches of administration, to continuously study the ways in which procedures were actually operating, and to devise improvements. He felt that such a function was particularly important in as large an organization as he believed the Social Security Board would become. He explained that a comparable position had been set up in the Agricultural Adjustment Administration and that he had occupied it during his service with that agency, which he had helped organize. In the AAA he had attended staff meetings of the heads of the major units every morning to talk over proposals for procedures and forms. Seidemann said he had been given the right to see every such proposal before any one else did, and if he did not approve, the proposal went no further. He wanted to perform a similar function for the board. There is no doubt also that Seidemann believed that his duties included that of special advisor on personnel. He felt that because of his long acquaintance with men in the federal service engaged in business management, accounting, and personnel work he had a reservoir of information about people which should and would be used by the board in selecting many of its key employees. While he did not expect to occupy the coordinator's position for more than a few months, the function should, he felt, become a permanent part of the board's organization.

The charts drawn up by the board tell part of the story of the board's thinking about this position. Chart No. 1 (prepared by Altmeyer) made no provision for an office of coordinator. The tentative chart dated November 22, 1935, showed the coordinator's position stemming out below the board and above the executive director. The coordinator was listed as responsible for administrative methods, accounting procedures, and coordination of divisions. This last duty had been dropped from the board's functions as listed in chart no. 1 and transferred to the coordinator, where it appeared to parallel the executive director's function of supervising the divisions. Thus it split the top administrative control between these two offices. In the approved final chart dated December 4, 1936, the coordinator's position was retained in the same location, but some important changes in his functions were indicated. Instead of coordinating the board's divisions, he was given the duty of coordinating the board with other departments and agencies. These changes buttress the suspicion that the board had no very clear notions of what a coordinator's job should be and that it was really making a temporary accommodation between Seidemann and Bane so that the talents of both men might be used in getting the organization started.

That view is strengthened by the explanation which Chairman Winant gave McKinley about a month after the coordinator began work. It was made in response to a query concerning the nature of this position and was recorded in paraphrase:

Brownlow's scheme [5] provided for a single executive officer between the board and the staff through whom staff matters would pour both up and down. This was finally accepted. With regard to what kind of a man to select for this position, there was a difference of opinion between Winant and Altmeyer. Altmeyer wanted a man who would be primarily acquainted with the line activities and the nature of social security matters, whereas Winant felt that this person should be primarily an administrative, procedural, and financial expert. The final decision was to select Bane, who represented Altmeyer's view, and to use Seidemann, who had the other type of qualifications, for a temporary period to help set up the organization and the procedures. Actually Seidemann has been used for a variety of executive purposes, including that of budgeting.

. . . . .

Seidemann's title of coordinator has caused considerable confusion, both within and without the staff. Seidemann's function is that of administrative and financial consultant.

But in addition to these consultant functions, the board asked Seidemann, who as coordinator was not to have any administrative duties, to act temporarily as "Director of Bureau of Audits and Accounts until a Chief is selected." Seidemann's temporary leadership of this bureau was made formal on January 10, 1936, but he turned over the major responsibility for accounts and audits to Hughes, at first on loan from the General Accounting Office. Hughes became bureau chief in May 1936. Apparently the consulting assignment and the budget-making task soon irked Seidemann, for he complained to Winant that Bane would not use him for consulting purposes but chose to let him carry the chores of accounting and budgeting.

Seidemann concentrated his attention at that time on problems relating to the Old Age Benefit Bureau probably because of his own special interests and expectations. Winant suggested this bureau would become the most routine part of the administration, and that such a field was exactly within the special

[5] Louis Brownlow had suggested a plan of board organization to Winant.

competence of Seidemann whom he expected ultimately to become a part of that bureau. In the revised justification sheets attached to the estimates for appropriations which the board sent to the Bureau of the Budget in April 1936, the duties of the coordinator were described as follows:

The Coordinator, under the general supervision of the Board, has the duty of evolving standards of administration and the coordination of the activities of the Board with other federal departments and independent establishments on matters affecting budgetary control, accounting, auditing and business procedure. It is his duty to advise the Board relative to organization, administrative procedures and special technical equipment necessary for the efficient and economical administration of its activities; to draft and/or review orders, rules and regulations, forms and manuals of procedures to be issued by the Board and/or its bureaus and offices, and to advise the Board and Executive Director with respect to the same. To supervise the installation of a system of accounting and audit procedure to enable the Board to discharge its obligations under the Act, and to give proper control to its proprietary and budgetary acts.

The actual duties performed by Seidemann in this office up to the summer of 1936 had little bearing on many of the tasks formally assigned to his position. He was occupied during November and December 1935 with preparing the revised budget estimates for the second half of the fiscal year 1936 and with plans for the establishment of the Bureau of Old Age Benefits. He was also concerned with working out standard records which the board should require of the states in connection with the grants-in-aid for public assistance, and in coordinating them with those required by the Children's Bureau and the Treasury. He had borrowed Hughes from the comptroller general's office to set up an accounting system for the board. To that job he gave little supervisory attention because of his belief in Hughes' competence. He looked forward, at that time, to turning his attention to the drafting of rules and regulations and to the development of procedures and forms for the regional and district offices which he expected the board to set up shortly, when Congress should have provided funds. When this initial budget-making job was concluded, Seidemann began active discussions with the Treasury over the rules and regulations which it planned to issue to taxpayers coming under Title IX of the act. He was also in general charge of the board's committee on regional and district office organization, although the burden of this work was carried by a subordinate, Colonel McCormack. During the early months of 1936 he gave a good deal of attention to the problems of the Old Age Benefits Bureau, particularly to questions involved in the development of records for that agency and for carrying through the mass registration which was being projected. He likewise busied himself from time to time with suggesting appointments to the board and, in these matters, frequently clashed with the differing judgments of the executive director.[6] During March and April, with the assistance of a subordinate, he assumed the principal responsibility for preparing the budget requests for the fiscal year 1937 and for further deficiency requests for the balance of 1936.

After the congressional budget hearings, Seidemann turned his attention to the coordinator's essential functions of preparing internal rules and regulations, instructions, and manuals of procedure. His office staff at that time was quite small, consisting of an assistant coordinator, one chief assistant, one chief industrial engineer, one senior administrative officer, and six clerks and stenographers. Under Administrative Order No. 8, which the board had issued on March 8, 1936, all proposed forms were to be submitted for the coordinator's examination before being routed to the executive director for approval. On June 6, 1936, office memorandum 19 was issued. This read:

All general proposals affecting existing or proposed: (a) organizational structure, functions or procedures of the Social Security Board and the relationships between its bureaus and offices; (b) official orders and instructions dealing with matters of fundamental organizational policies and general instructions as to office procedures and methods, require prior review by the Coordinator.

This same memorandum stated that the coordinator would make recommendations on such matters to the executive director who would refer them back, when approved, to the coordinator for the assignment of form numbers. But the board was exceedingly slow in issuing rules and regulations and in developing procedure manuals which would define the responsibilities of its own staff, and of the state agencies with which it dealt, although this was from the beginning regarded as one of the principal duties of the coordinator's office. As late as June 1936 there had been no clear definition of the duties

---

[6] These clashes fanned the flames of conflict, particularly when Seidemann's candidate for head of the Bureau of Business Management was rejected and Bane's choice accepted and when, a little later, a personnel officer was chosen without consulting Seidemann. The situation was not improved when the Civil Service Commission, with which the business manager and personnel officer (who reported to the former) were the board's contact representatives, proceeded to downgrade the coordinator's classification from a $9500 to a $7500 job. On the other hand, it was Seidemann who, as noted above, had convinced the board that the budget function should be sheared from Business Management and given to Accounts and Audits—an action that was one factor in the ultimate resignation of the first business manager. He also carried on a running criticism of the personnel officer, who, he complained, was impeding the selection of staff by his special investigations and tests. Seidemann finally sent his complaints to the board in a written memorandum, alleging that Personnel was way behind in its classification of jobs and that extra classifiers must be appointed. The board hastily adopted his recommendation, but when confronted with a counter-memorandum denying point by point the allegations made by the coordinator, it withheld action and the additional classifiers were not appointed.

of the coordinator and his relationship to the executive director, the board, and the bureaus. Investigations by the Division of Industrial Engineering in the coordinator's office were going forward without specific authority so that full cooperation from the bureau directors was not forthcoming. The coordinator's personal assistant was asking the bureau heads for material to be incorporated in a field manual, but specific authorization for this had not come either from the board or from the executive director. During June and July the coordinator's activities were proceeding in this fashion without tangible results so far as Frase was able to discover.[7] The coordinator was also working with the field organization committee, although that group carried on its work with relative independence.

The question of the coordinator's function was also snarled up with the question of how permanent the position would be and its relation to that of the executive director. Bane did not think it ought to be a permanent job and raised the issue point-blank during April 1936, when the budget estimates were under consideration by the board and the coordinator's office was under discussion. For nearly three hours the board, with Bane and Seidemann present, discussed the issue. Despite the heat of this meeting, the board did not reach a definitive conclusion about the permanence of the coordinator's position. Altmeyer and Miles expressed the judgment that a full-time coordinator should not be retained as a permanent officer. Miles suggested instead, that from time to time the periodic services of an outside administrative consultant should be used to review the board's organizational procedures. Such a consultant, he felt, might have to retain several subordinates on the board's staff to keep up with procedural details.

However, the board did adopt the following motion at this meeting:

It was agreed that, as at present constituted on the chart, the office of Coordinator reports directly to the Board, but after the present Coordinator leaves the office the Coordinator will report directly to the Executive Director. It was understood that all individuals appointed to the office of the Coordinator would understand in advance that after Mr. Seidemann leaves, his successor and the office of Coordinator would report to and are under the supervision of the Executive Director.

This motion had been adopted after Seidemann's strenuous protest at the proposal that staff employed to assist the coordinator be under the direction of the executive director. So long as he remained on the board's payroll as coordinator, he objected to any detail of staff from the executive director even though they would be entirely under his immediate supervision.

[7] Both observers found it difficult during the late spring and summer of 1936 to obtain an interview with the coordinator and some members of his staff.

As a matter of fact, Seidemann continued to advocate both the permanance of the position and its independence from the executive director. The question boiled up early in August 1936 and was soon thereafter settled by abolishing the position. The issue was precipitated this time by Seidemann himself, who submitted under date of July 30, 1936, a long memorandum to the board requesting a clarification and extension of his duties and the trebling of his staff. The memorandum was accompanied by a draft of a general regulation promulgating the office of coordinator as a permanent position. This and a special essay accompanying the memorandum furnished the foundation for Seidemann's case. They were both prepared by a man who had been appointed by the board at Seidemann's request and was serving under the coordinator as chief industrial engineer.[8] The proposed regulation outlined in detail the duties and powers of the coordinator, who would report directly to the board. A paraphrase of the proposed regulations follows:

The office of coordinator, under the general supervision of the board, has the following powers:

a. Consultation with the board and executive director on fundamental policy and administrative questions;

b. Review of all phases of management, including without limitation policy, organization, procedure, facilities, and personnel, prior to submittal to board and executive director or effectuation thereof, for
1. conformity with established policy
2. administrative feasibility
3. efficiency and economy of operation
4. prevention and elimination of jurisdictional conflict;

c. Review of all rules, regulations, orders, instructions, manuals, forms, reports, bulletins, circular letters, published material prior to submission to board or executive director or the effectuation thereof;

d. Directive supervision of accounting and auditing in Bureau of Accounts and Audits and other agencies of the board;

e. Approval of procurement of all special equipment for accounting, auditing, recording, and statistics;

f. Survey of all phases of management;

g. Advice to the board on annual budget and allotments;

h. Advice to the Board concerning relations with federal, state, and local governmental agencies and with nongovernmental establishments;

i. Requesting personnel from the board for coordinator;

j. Other powers of coordination when delegated by the board; to be referred to coordinator all proposals, communications concerning matters in above list

[8] This individual was later dismissed when it was discovered that he had no industrial engineering experience to qualify him for this post, although he had been a lecturer on "philosophic problems" in Cleveland.

of duties; to secure reports on above matters from any agency when requested by coordinator.

Coordinator to recommend to the board, or its agencies, action as may be deemed desirable. On concurrence of the executive director and bureau head, such recommendations to take immediate effect.

In case of disagreement, recommendations to be docketed by the executive director with briefs from coordinator and others, and sent to the chairman of the board for the board's determination.

This essay of justification for the role of the coordinator pointed out the temporary and incomplete character of the organization chart of December 4, 1935, as it related to the coordinator's duties. It then discussed the general principles underlying the distribution of tasks among the board, the executive director, and the coordinator. A paraphrase of the analysis is given below.

There are three objectives of administration: (1) policy, or what to do, (2) carrying policy into execution, and (3) planning, observation, and technical information.

1. Policy. This is the function of the board. Since it cannot have first-hand experience, a substitute therefore is proposed: to set up an advisory council, whose members are to be chosen from outside the operating staff in order that policy formulation may be detached, nonpartisan, and impartial. If this is not feasible, then each member is to become responsible for a special area of policy, with the aid of technical and operating staff. But even if all specific tasks are delegated to others, the board will find all its time taken to make decisions based on organized and delegated observation, consultation, discussion, analysis, study, and planning.

2. Execution. The board has delegated the "production" job to the executive director. Execution is divided into two parts for the board: administrative direction and supervision by the executive director, and the observation, planning, and guidance, which is the function of the coordinator.

3. Planning and Observation. Planning here is not policy, it is planning methods of executing the policies. While all planning of execution is not the function of the coordinator, since it cannot be separated from operation of bureaus, etc., still "determinations as to planning, like all other aspects of administration, must be definitely delegated for responsibility thereof and in this sense planning must be the special area and responsibility of the Coordinator."

"Planning, as the word is used here, is in that intermediate zone between broad policy and detailed execution. Such planning as goes into the divising of Manual Procedures. Such planning, in a word, as is required for the accomplishment of the Executive Director's responsibility. Largely, this planning will be concerned with interbureau and bureau routines. The official charged with such planning will review and supplement the planning of the operating head of the organization and of each bureau."

The officer logically charged with this function is coordinator, but unfortunately the board has left his delegation of authority vague. It should lose no time in clarifying his responsibilities. While the executive director and bureau heads should normally direct personnel, that direction should accord with the procedures approved by the coordinator and, in major matters, by the board.

"The closest cooperation between the Executive Director and the Coordinator is essential. Their respective spheres of authority and responsibility are essentially distinct. The Coordinator represents the Board as to organization, methods, and procedures with the same authority that the Executive Director represents the Board as to administration, performance, and output."

The coordinator should embody his work in the *Manual of Procedures,* but before completing this he should develop procedures in the form of administrative orders, try them out, and integrate those which prove desirable in the manual. This would, of course, require the inclusion in the manual of statements of policy which the board determines.

Observation is analysis of results and comes last. It is the present greatest lack. Men at the top cannot observe because they are too far from the scene. Must have organization for observation. Is indicated on chart, but without adequate staff to function. Who really knows what is going on in the bureaus today? Perhaps executives know, but that is not sufficient, for mistakes are their mistakes. The board needs such information. Every well-organized commercial company of size has an organization for observation, unswayed by bias of departmental interests. Must be outside of operating departments in order to faithfully report and impartially analyze. For the board, this function should be that of coordinator, but he must have help.

One aspect of observation is review. It is the task of preparing recommendations for the board on all of its actions, to prompt consistency of board action.

Examination of correspondence is an important means of observation. Needed to assure consistency in administration with policy. It, too, should be under the coordinator.

At least for present, all complaints against the administration should be handled by the coordinator.

"To do his work the Coordinator must have free access to all documents and records of the Board as distinct from the rest of the organization."

This memorandum was brought up at the board meeting on August 3, 1936, but action was postponed to August 8, because the executive director had not received a copy. At the first meeting, the chairman, who heretofore had been the chief supporter of the coordinator function, made clear his feeling that Seidemann's latest memorandum pushed his duties beyond the coordinator's office. He expressed the view that this was an attempt by the coordinator to control the director's office, and that this would result in personality difficulties. At the second meeting, it was unanimously decided by the board that such coordinating services as would be maintained should be placed in the office of the executive director, effective immediately. Simultaneously, the decision was reached to offer Seidemann a new job as head of the Bureau of Old Age Benefits. However, action on these decisions was delayed. It was not until September 2, 1936, that Seidemann ceased working as coordinator and became the new head of the Bureau of Old Age Benefits, from which Murray Latimer had resigned.[9] At about the same time it was decided to employ the Public Administration Service of Chicago to make a study of the board's organizational and procedural problems, particularly in regard to the handling of grants to the states by the bureaus of Unemployment Compensation and Public Assistance. Thus the office of coordinator as an independent position came to an end.

GRAVITATION OF POWERS TO
THE EXECUTIVE DIRECTOR'S OFFICE

While the official organization plan as reflected in the chart of December 4, 1935, remained without change, actually a number of important modifications in the distribution of power did take place. These were pointed out by the Donald Stone report of October 1936.[10] That report also noted the failure of the board to define its organization beyond the chart stage:

A more satisfactory definition of the organization of the responsibilities of the several bureaus, and of the interrelationship between bureaus is needed; a chart

---

[9] That some of the conflict generated during the preceding ten months was carried over into the Bureau of Old Age Benefits is abundantly clear from the events already related in our account of the work of that bureau, and will be further amplified in our discussion of personnel management problems. Here we may note one further problem. Shortly after the August 8 meeting, at which the board resolved to make Seidemann the head of the Old Age Benefits Bureau, Winant asked him to prepare a statement for the board setting forth his ideas on how the bureau should be organized and how it should operate. Seidemann's memo proposed certain exemptions from the controls imposed on the other bureaus, and this led to action by the board, on the day it confirmed his appointment, designed to keep him and his bureau from escaping those controls. Winant communicated the board's decision in the following memorandum:

"The Director of the Bureau of Federal Old Age Benefits will have the full powers of an operating bureau Director. The memorandum dated August 31, 1936, submitted by you to the board would delegate powers beyond those already established under the policy of the Board.

It is important that the Bureau of Federal Old Age Benefits make the same use of the service bureaus and other constituted offices of the Board as do the other two operating Bureaus. That is, it shall function administratively in the same manner with respect to the Board, the Executive Director, and the service Bureaus as the Bureaus of Unemployment Compensation and Public Assistance do now function."

[10] Stone represented the Public Administration Service.

has severe limitations in indicating such responsibilites and relationships. As referred to in the report dealing with the establishment of the procedure and control division, general regulations or administrative orders should be promulgated, establishing and defining the office of the Executive Director and its divisions and also the several bureaus operating under the Executive Director. These regulations should be sufficiently precise as to leave no doubt concerning major questions of responsibility, authority, and relationships, but they should not be detailed to the extent that they will inhibit flexibility of administration and adjustment of organization within each bureau as developments warrant.

Under the authority of these general regulations, the Executive Director should issue administrative orders or office memoranda from time to time further defining the administrative procedures and requirements. In this connection, consideration should be given to the preparation of an administrative manual as formerly suggested by the coordinator. In addition to the manual prescribing matters of general administrative application, manuals of operation for the several bureaus should also be prepared. Such manuals will go a long way to remove elements of confusion that now exist in the administration. They will give added assurance that work is performed in accordance with policy and established procedure. They will facilitate unity of operation. They will furnish an excellent vehicle for in-service training and for the instruction of new employees. Finally, they will add clarity, both within and without the organization, concerning its activities and requirements.

The failure of the board to buttress the general concepts embedded in the chart with a comprehensive administrative code left the gate wide open for shifts of function and duty within the organization beneath the board, and allowed the chief executive officer, if he wished, to decide when to open that gate and what to allow through it. Bane apparently sensed this opportunity and pursued it through his assistant, John J. Corson. We have already sketched the story of Corson's policy in supporting the new regional directorate against the bureau representatives, and occasionally the bureau chiefs, with the resulting augmented influence of the Executive Director's Office in the field establishment.

Corson's talents for administration were quickly recognized. It was not long before he began to take over practically all the detailed administrative duties of the Executive Director's Office because Bane was out of town so much, and it was essential that someone give them constant attention. By June 1936 Corson was also regularly attending board meetings with Bane. He did most of the detailed working out of relationships with the regional directors. Galvin, an ex-Foreign and Domestic Commerce Bureau and NRA man whose position in the Executive Director's Office was technically equivalent to that of Corson (senior technical advisor P-5), was confined to routine matters of procuring space and equipment and of answering correspondence in connection with the regional offices.

Corson worked tremendously hard and long during the summer of 1936 and was given more and more responsibility by Bane and the board. He rarely delegated significant tasks to the other members of the executive director's staff. His duties were many and varied: he ironed out conflicts between the bureaus, made a point of talking to bureau chiefs at frequent intervals to find out what they were doing, handled the complaints of regional directors and conflicts in the field, supervised the reorganization of the central filing system of the board, directed the setting up of a control unit to inspect outgoing mail in the Bureau of Business Management, and signed enormous quantities of correspondence in Bane's name. At the same time, despite his youth (twenty-nine years) he did not antagonize either the members of the board or the bureau chiefs. Both Winant and Altmeyer placed an increasing amount of confidence in him. In addition to having real administrative gifts and working long hours, he was very circumspect about criticizing any member of the board or staff.

In August, 1936, when the board was considering the expansion of the Executive Director's Office to take over the functions of the coordinator, Corson was, on Bane's suggestion, promoted to the position of assistant executive director (August 18) at a salary of $6500 a year. Shortly after this, he took over the work on the fiscal 1938 budget. Hughes, director of the Bureau of Accounts and Audits, had directed the preparation of bureau estimates for the board during August. In fact, he and Bane had visited the Bureau of the Budget in August, and Bane had informed the people there that Hughes was the official representative of the board in such matters. When Hughes returned from his vacation, however, he found that Corson had taken over the preparation of the budget and he did not contest the issue. From then on, Corson did the entire job with little direction from Bane. In fact, he gave orders to the staff not to bother Bane with budget matters.[11]

This drift toward increased powers in the Executive Director's Office was given support by Donald Stone's report. In August, Winant had asked Bane to investigate the possibilities of having Stone make a study focusing on the board's procedure in handling unemployment compensation and public assistance grants. When the survey was actually completed it turned out to be concerned primarily with the necessity for building up and strengthening the Office of the Executive Director. Stone's report was a very able document, but its recommendations were largely confined to increasing the power of the executive director and did not dwell upon other weak spots in the administrative arrangements. Stone recommended that the informal understanding concerning the division of function between the board and the executive director

[11] See "Preparing the Estimates for Fiscal 1938," chapter 2, p. 64, for the full account of Corson's handling of this job.

(i.e., that the former be concerned with policy and the latter with administration) be laid down in the form of regulations for the information of the staff, which was somewhat confused on this matter.[12]

Stone's description of the functions of the executive director was as follows:

The Executive Director, as the chief administrative officer of the Board, is responsible for the efficient execution of the work of the Social Security program and for keeping the Board advised on the status of progress. The Executive Director thus becomes the chief advisor of the Board as well as its sole administrative agent.

To carry out the responsibilities of his office the Executive Director must divide his time between:
1. Direct administration, i.e., the establishment and coordination of the administrative organizations;
2. Technical coordination, i.e., bringing about of unity and consistency in the procedures of all branches of the organization;
3. Financial planning, i.e., determination of the program of the Board in terms of financial requirements and the control of financial operations of the organization through the device of budgeting;
4. Relations with States and Federal agencies with respect to administrative problems and plans;
5. Policies which the management finds requiring clarification or determination.

His idea of the role of the assistant executive director was sketched as follows:

In carrying out the responsibilities vested in the Executive Director, he will need to delegate authority to his executive staff. The type of delegation will depend on the nature of the responsibility affected.

With respect to questions of general administration of the Washington organization, the major part of the actual work of the Executive Director should be performed by the Assistant Executive Director. He will need to serve as the eyes and ears of the Executive Director with respect to the general operations of the whole organization as well as perform work specifically assigned to him by the Executive Director. The Assistant Executive Director should be looked upon as an integral part of the Executive Director's office and as acting for the Executive Director, rather than serving as a separate official, with separate responsibilities. In addition to handling specific matters, responsibility for which rests with the Executive Director, the Assistant can expedite administration by bringing of employees together and the resolving of conflicts of jurisdiction or opinion before conditions warrant the attention of the Executive Director. He will need to

[12] He set an expert on procedure, taken over from the disbanded coordinator's staff, to drafting such a regulation, but the board did not see fit to approve it or any like definition and demarcation of power and authority.

spend much time "loafing" in the bureaus if he is to develop the necessary relationships and harmony.

From the viewpoint of formalized organization, the Assistant Executive Director should be considered as the representative of the Executive Director—as his
"alter ego." Therefore the assistant should not be indicated on any organizational
chart as a separate officer in the line of authority, nor should formal orders provide that bureau heads report directly to him. The extent to which they deal
directly with the assistant as in the case of assistants in any organization, should
depend chiefly upon informal expressions by the Executive Director and upon
the ability of the assistant to develop the willingness of bureau officers to consider his decisions to be those of the Executive Director.

With respect to field operations of the Social Security Board and relations with
State agencies, the Executive Director will need to rely upon a director of the
Field Service Division. This division should form a unit in the Executive Director's office. The Director should serve as the administrative superior of the
regional directors and should be qualified to deal finally with most of the field
activities. Just as the Assistant Executive Director will be relied upon heavily
by the Executive Director for the effective coordination of the Washington organization, he should similarly rely upon the Director of the Field Service for
the satisfactory administration and maintenance of field and state activities.

.   .   .   .   .

Although the Assistant Executive Director should not be expected to deal
directly with most of the major questions of field determination, he should
participate as the representative of the Executive Director in matters in which
the administration of the Washington organization bears a relationship with
the administration of the regional offices.

In order to perform his responsibilities of technical coordination, the Executive
Director should rely upon a procedure and control division for the review of
all formal documents of the Board or any of its subdivisions and for correlating
the activities of the procedure units in the several bureaus. This division should
form an integral part of the office of the Executive Director.

The Executive Director must deal continuously with planning and controlling
the finances of the Social Security Board. The formulation and operation of the
budget involves policy determination at almost every stage as well as administrative decision. It is, therefore, essential that responsibility for the operation of
the budget be lodged in the office of the Executive Director. The desirability for
its location there also rests on its importance as the chief staff agency of the
Executive Director in controlling the operations of the entire organization. To
this end the Executive Director will need to rely upon a budget officer from
whom he can receive continuous counsel with respect to all budget and financial
problems and whom he can take with him to the Board for decision on questions
of policy.

Another phase of the work of the Executive Director which he cannot separate
from his responsibility of administrative management is that of final decision on
all matters of personnel. Management is essentially a matter of administration

of personnel. Therefore, the personnel agency should be maintained closely to the Executive Director. If it is not deemed feasible for the personnel officer to be an intimate part of the Executive Director's staff, the Executive Director should have opportunity for direct dealing with the personnel officer without disrupting normal administrative relationships. Due perhaps entirely to factors over which the Social Security Board has no control, the steps required for securing personnel are somewhat involved. Careful study of this problem is recommended.

Most of Stone's recommendations were ignored, both with respect to the Office of the Executive Director and other phases of the organization. A budget officer in the Bureau of Accounts and Audits had not yet been appointed in July 1937, and the assistant executive director was continuing to handle these functions. A procedure unit was set up in the Office of the Executive Director, and an increased flow of administrative orders, office memoranda, and bulletins did result, but they were more concerned with the technicalities of routine correspondence than with the delineation of responsibilities, authority, and control.

A continued growth of the authority of the Executive Director's Office, however, followed the Stone report, chronologically if not causally. The growing importance of the board's field and regional staff resulted in a considerable number of procedural problems, and a smaller number of personality and power conflicts within the regional offices between the representatives of the several bureaus on the one hand and the regional director and his executive assistant on the other. These latter had to be ironed out by some higher authority. In most cases this was done by the executive director, although some matters went to the board.

Perhaps just as important, though not as spectacular, was the increasing role of the weekly regional letter dispatched by the Executive Director's Office. This field bulletin, which first began to appear biweekly in July and was in November changed to a weekly, was divided into section A for instructions and section B for information. To an increasing extent it became the channel of general communication with the regional offices. It enabled the Office of the Executive Director to keep itself informed of the relations between Washington bureaus and the field and to control those relationships. The Bureau of Old Age Benefits also began issuing a bulletin to the staff of the field offices of that bureau about the middle of November, but its appearance was governed by the volume and necessities of administrative practice. At a much later date (March 1937) this was combined with the regional letter into a regional and field letter, which gave the office of the executive director an increased knowledge and control of the relations between the headquarters of the Bureau of Old Age Benefits and its staff in the growing number of field offices.

Another increase of duties developed with the preparation of the board's first annual report for the fiscal year 1936. During Winant's absence in the last month of the 1936 election campaign, a committee composed of Corson, Wilbur Cohen, Helen Hohman (of the Bureau of Research and Statistics), and Maurine Mulliner, secretary to the board, was appointed to prepare the annual report, which was to include a discussion of the possibility of amending the act.[13] Mrs. Hohman did most of the work of compiling statistics and preparing the first draft; Miss Mulliner supplied information from the board's central document file; and Cohen was Altmeyer's personal representative on policy. But Corson was the dominant spirit of the committee. It was he who outlined the formula for the report adopted by the committee: to call attention to all of the difficulties and problems confronting the board, but to do it in such a way as to indicate that they were not impossible to solve. This would save the board time by giving them something to shoot at. Both Mrs. Hohman and Cohen had rather ambitious plans for making this report a really first-rate discussion of problems, but as the work progressed and time grew short, they reluctantly acquiesced in the attitude of "old-timers" in government procedure that, after all, no department or agency can be expected to lay bare its soul in an annual report. Even so, Mrs. Hohman's draft was not innocuous enough for Corson; he took it home one night and rewrote whole sections of it. When it finally appeared in February—some of the delay was caused by the decision to include an appendix covering the first half of fiscal year 1937, July 1 to December 31, 1936—the document was in the best tradition of the old-line departments and agencies.

From the point of view of the administration, this incident is chiefly of interest because it portrays rather clearly the stage which the demarcation of functions at the top of the organization had reached by November 1936. A staff concerned with policy and attached to the board itself had not yet developed sufficiently to be able to prepare an annual report. The board could not do the job because it was so busy with administrative duties, although the official organization chart showed the preparation of the annual report to be one of the three enumerated functions of the board. Yet the matter was so important and so intimately bound up with questions of high policy that the

[13] Actually the committee did nothing about the amendments. The time was too short and the matter too important. The board had promised the President to submit its recommendations on amendments by December 15, and the committee had hardly gotten suggestions from bureau directors before it became necessary to draft the amendments for submission. Therefore the amendments were discussed in board meetings in November and December and drafted by Thomas Emerson of the general counsel's office. By the time Treasury approval had been secured on those which affected tax collection, Winant had left and Corson was assisting in the direction of the Bureau of Old Age Benefits. Then Altmeyer sketched his ideas for amendments, Cohen wrote them up, and Emerson drafted them.

board members, particularly Altmeyer, did not feel that it could safely be entrusted to the rather remote Bureau of Research and Statistics. Thus the committee device was used to keep the work close to the board and yet secure the services of the Bureau of Research and Statistics, through Mrs. Hohman, to do the bulk of the actual work.

One other definite accretion of responsibility to the Executive Director's Office was control over the allotment of space to the various bureaus of the board. This function was delegated to the Bureau of Business Management on the organization chart, but as the Social Security Board expanded into numerous remote and rather undesirable buildings, this bureau found that it could not settle the space problems of its sister bureaus. Claims for preferred treatment went over its head to the only two arbiters with higher status, the board and the executive director. This was such an unpleasant task for the board itself that it was perfectly willing to let the executive director handle it.

The use of a code of instructions or a detailed administrative manual did not develop into a significant device for general administrative direction and control during the period studied. There was such a medium in rather embryonic form in the administrative manual. This was merely the sum total of individual instructions under four headings: Administrative Regulations, Administrative Orders, Office Memoranda, and Bulletins. It had been hurriedly thrown together by James Bennett and Keith Tindale (an assistant to Bane) in the fall of 1935, until the problem could be analyzed more clearly and more permanent provisions made. But with procedures in the hands of the coordinator until August 1936, the hectic activity of the registration, Corson's shift to the Bureau of Old Age Benefits in February 1937, and a rather mediocre man (taken over from the coordinator) in charge of this activity in the Executive Director's Office, this temporary manual was still in use in March 1937. Too much importance cannot be given to this fact; it was as much a symptom as a cause. A real manual might have been a very effective tool of general management. The point can be illustrated by the fact that the administrative manual did not include any instruction on the methods and criteria to be used by the bureaus in preparing and presenting their budget estimates.

PERSONNEL MANAGEMENT,
THE EXPERT CLAUSE

The Social Security Act included the employees of the board under the merit system except for two groups, attorneys and experts. All its Washington employees were subject to the Classification Act of 1923. Before the board was financed by its own congressional appropriation, it depended for its personnel activity upon a number of people. As had been made clear, the board itself early became its own principal personnel mechanism, each member and the board as a group spending, from the very start, a great deal of time canvassing for staff and reviewing the qualifications of nominees. In addition, it employed Meridith Givens on a part-time basis to help it find promising candidates for key posts. About November 1, 1935, William Sorrels, of the staff of the Civil Service Commission, was detailed to the board to help it classify its people, suggest new personnel, deal with the requests of congressmen, and generally aid it in hiring staff. Even after Henry Aronson was employed as personnel director and began work in February, Sorrels stayed on, chiefly at the request of Miles, for some months. The commission also detailed classification staff to work with the board's administrators in setting up particular position classifications. Late in 1936, Sorrels returned (as will be related below) as a consultant and occupied a position which was both ambiguous and competitive with the board's personnel officer. As will also appear in the narrative, Miles' political assistant and advisor, James Douglas, likewise performed the major personnel function of interviewing political nominees and finding jobs for those whom Miles desired to place in the organization.

Early in November 1935 the board became concerned about the use of the expert clause as a result of a patronage case. A South Carolina gentleman, supported by a very influential senator and by board member Miles, was a candidate for the head of the Bureau of Public Assistance. When refused this, he was then urged for appointment as an expert. For qualifications he could show some years of activity in espousing humanitarian causes and social reform through legislation. He had no professional social welfare training and no experience as a public welfare administrator. He had some business experience. When the board dodged the issue by putting the case before the Civil Service Commission with the indication that it would take him if the commission qualified the man, to its astonishment the gentleman was qualified by that agency as an expert available for a $6,500 job. Sorrels made the initial recommendation in favor of this action. He later excused himself by saying that it was a borderline case, and that Miles told him the board wanted the man qualified as an expert and went with him to the Civil Service Commission office to argue the case.[14]

This case, and others threatening about the same time, inclined the board to seek a valid and authoritative definition of the term *expert* and to secure

[14] If this was true, it is doubtful if the other members of the board knew about it at the time. The episode is an interesting minor illustration of the confusion of responsibility which the board system permitted.

the assistance of the Civil Service Commission in enforcing it. A conversation between the board and members of the Civil Service Commission and its staff resulted in a memorandum prepared by Ismar Baruch of the Civil Service Commission, which was the basis for further discussion looking towards an agreement concerning the appointment of experts and attorneys. The memorandum came to the board early in December 1935. It pointed out that unless there was an affirmative exemption in the Social Security Act itself, the Classification Act of 1923 would apply to the board's employees with respect to salaries paid. It emphasized that the only way in which positions other than those of attorney and expert could be placed outside the merit system and the jurisdiction, therefore, of the Civil Service Commission, would be by special act of the President. Similarly, the President might exempt positions from the Classification Act.

The memorandum proposed that in the case of attorneys a noncompetitive practice be followed, which would involve the following procedure: first, each attorney position was to be classified by the Civil Service Commission in its appropriate grade under the Classification Act of 1923; second, the Civil Service Commission would determine whether or not the position in question was in fact an attorney position, and therefore eligible for an exempted appointment; third, each candidate would fill out a form, giving his education and employment history and other facts about his admission to the bar; fourth, the Civil Service Commission would then pass on the question of whether or not the candidate met the minimum standards for that grade of attorney position, "such standards being those which are usually applicable in open competitive examination." It was pointed out that a few other government agencies, notably the Interstate Commerce Commission, had made such agreements with the Civil Service Commission, even though their attorneys had been exempted by law from competitive examination. It proposed that the Social Security Board agree to this procedure or to the selection of attorneys by open competition, transfer, promotion, or reinstatement, in the manner provided by existing civil service rules.

Most of the memorandum was devoted to the subject of experts, and reviewed the history of the interpretation of this term by both the commission and the comptroller general. In the light of these interpretations, the memorandum proposed:

1. The term "expert" or "experts" refers only to authoritative specialists (a) who have had extensive educational training and/or experience in professional or technical subject-matter peculiarly related to the technical activities of the Social Security Board, which has given them a fund of specialized and comprehensive knowledge superior to that ordinarily or generally possessed by persons engaged in the same general profession or occupation; (b) whose work has established them as leaders among their associates in lines of work peculiarly

related to the technical work of the Social Security Board; and (c) who are to render planning, organizing, directing, or advising service of an authoritative character in the subject-matter represented by their qualifications.

The suggested procedure for the appointment of an expert required a list of the duties of the position, an investigation by a staff member of the personnel classification division of the Civil Service Commission, and finally, a formal certification by the Civil Service Commission approving the position for the particular grade. It was also proposed that no position would be regarded as expert if it came in a grade below grade 4 of the Professional and Scientific Service or grade 11 of the Clerical, Administrative, and Fiscal Service. This proposal meant that no position with a salary of less than $3,800 might be considered for the expert category. Finally, the Civil Service Commission would "determine and notify the Social Security Board whether or not the duties and responsibilities of the position are such as to constitute it an 'expert' position available for an excepted appointment."

Each candidate would be required to give his educational and employment history for the use of the Civil Service Commission. The commission would then determine whether or not the particular candidate met the qualifications and requirements for the particular expert position. Finally, the memorandum proposed that the Social Security Board agree to make no expert appointments without the Civil Service Commission's approval in accordance either with the foregoing stipulations or under the existing civil service rules.

At first the Social Security Board was disposed to look kindly upon this plan, except that it wanted to use the expert classification for salaries of less than $3,800. It proposed to amend the plan by lowering the limit to $3,200. The chairman of the board believed that this plan, with slight modifications, would probably serve the board's needs, although there might be some difficulty in writing job specifications that would be acceptable to the commission and, at the same time, not too rigorous for the board. The chairman and his associates were then searching the country for people for the top positions. They discovered that the board could not pay salaries high enough to attract the individuals desired unless it could secure from the Civil Service Commission recognition of the unusual importance and responsibilities attached to these top jobs. Irritations soon developed in the fixing of classifications, particularly for the top positions in the bureaus of Informational Service and Business Management.

Behind these clashes lay certain differences in fundamental attitude toward the use of civil service procedures in the selection of key people. In the first place, the board was so desirous of finding the best people in the country that it seemed to the civil service people to be trying to work outside the salary limits imposed by the Classification Act. The board saw its task as unique in importance and size. It was therefore perfectly natural that when searching for the best people it would find them already occupying positions paying more than the top salaries permitted by the Classification Act for comparable federal jobs. It was almost inevitable that it should seek approval for classifications which would appear to the commission to be out of line with similar jobs in the other federal departments and agencies.[15] Secondly, there was a profound distrust by some of the board members, particularly Altmeyer, of the adequacy of the civil service procedure for filling the key positions. Altmeyer was frank in saying that the competitive method for selecting persons to do the creative work which the board expected from its key people was not yet well enough developed to be successfully used. He viewed the board's personnel job as comparable to that of a university in selecting its faculty. It wanted creative minds not particularly concerned with tenure, and so anxious to do a good job that if they discovered that they were no longer wanted they would not care to remain. In his judgment, the problem would be even more serious from the board's standpoint when it would have to fill vacancies after the initial staff left because, under the competitive system, the board would then be restricted by the rule of three. In seeking personnel, Winant and Altmeyer did not solicit the aid of the Civil Service Commission to find properly qualified people for their key positions. Instead, they relied upon their personal acquaintances, their contacts with professional groups, and the "friends of their friends." This was not a unique procedure; many other New Deal agencies had done the same.

In contrast to the Board's attitude was the belief of the Civil Service Commission and its top staff in the adequacy of competitive techniques using unassembled examinations for the selection of second- and third-string men. They believed that the flexibility of method permitted under that examining technique (which was essentially an evaluation of an individual's training and experience) was ample to locate and select the highest talent for such positions.[16] The commission also had a basic distrust of the expert clause. This

[15] For example, Baruch cited the case of the head of the Bureau of Informational Service for whom the board wanted an initial salary of $8,000. It was contended that the subject matter which he must master and popularize was so unique that the head of this unit must be classified at that level. To Baruch, this was not convincing, because the federal service already had information people performing similar public education jobs. He compared the board's job with that of the Department of Agriculture whose information chief supervised the publicity materials for twenty-eight different bureaus and offices, many of whose publications were of a scientific character. That officer was classified at an initial salary of $6,500.

[16] Civil Service Commissioner Leonard White believed that the unassembled examination supplemented by oral examination, in which staff members of the board might be used as part of the examining committee, was adequate to this purpose. He insisted that where this technique had been used, as it had shortly before, to select the personnel officer for the Bureau of the Census, it had resulted in placing people of outstanding competence at the top of the list.

was particularly true of Vipond, the assistant chief examiner, and Baruch, head of the personnel classification section. These two men were said to be determined to do all they could to get rid of the expert clause by making it such a difficult and unsatisfactory procedure that the operating agencies would join with the commission in asking Congress to abolish it. As they saw it, beginning with the Tariff Commission Act of 1916, the expert clause had had a malodorous history. It had been greatly abused by agency after agency, because it opened up the way to political pressure which no agency, including the commission itself, had been successful in resisting. Just because it had been a "hot potato," it had been a continuous source of friction between the Civil Service Commission and every department which had used it. Finally, the commission kept in the forefront of its judgment of the board's problems its own need to treat all government operating agencies as nearly alike as possible. To accede to many of the board's importunities for high classifications, whether in the use of the expert or other clauses, posed the danger of criticism on the grounds of favoritism from many other federal agencies.

A new memorandum dated January 7, 1936, was submitted to the board after a discussion between Baruch of the Civil Service Commission staff and Bane and Bennett of the board. This revision proposed to broaden the scope of the expert clause to reach down into grades in both the professional and scientific and in the clerical and fiscal services where the beginning salary was $3,200. It also made certain refinements in definition directed toward filling the highest bureau positions. The memorandum read:

> For positions in the two highest grades of the expert group, the term "expert" will refer only to authoritative specialists of broad comprehensive training and experience whose work has established them as leaders among their associates in lines of work peculiarly related to the functions for which the Social Security Board was especially created; and who are to render planning, organizing, directing, analyzing, interpreting, consulting or advising services of an authoritative character in the subject matter or activity represented by their qualifications.

With regard to the attorneys, the January 7 memorandum provided for specific minimum qualifications for each grade and class. These qualifications were based primarily on length of experience in the active practice of law and varied in accordance with the importance of the grade. Before a promotion could be made from a lower to a higher grade, the approval of the commission was needed to determine whether or not the attorney met the requirements for the higher position.

This section outraged the feelings of General Counsel Eliot, who prepared a memorandum commenting on the parts of the proposed agreement relating to attorneys. He recommended that the board not accept the agreement because: (1) Congress clearly intended that the Civil Service Commission should have nothing further to do with the employment of attorneys, other than to see that attorneys were in fact attorneys; (2) he was unaware of any other organization where such an agreement was operative; (3) if the board signed the agreement, it would not be able to retain attorneys whenever any other governmental agency offered them higher salaries. Furthermore, he believed the following consequences would result:

As it is now proposed, it would cover all appointments which have already been made. It is probable this could be altered so that it would be inapplicable either to appointments already made or to those relating to the attorneys who have been assigned to the Board by the N.R.A. In choosing people from the N.R.A. the Social Security Board had selection from a field of about two hundred lawyers. It picked the very best of this group, some of whom are extraordinarily competent. Nevertheless, it would be impossible to keep them unless special exceptions from this agreement could be obtained, and if exceptions could be made in such cases it seems apparent that they must be secured for others as well in the future.

Eliot reviewed the effect of the agreement on a number of persons on the existing staff. In the case of one very competent person, the agreement would prevent promotion for a period of three years. In another case, a lawyer who had been employed in the Department of Labor at a salary of $5,600 would, under the proposed regulations, be eligible for a maximum of $3,200.[17] Brilliant young attorneys occupying high positions in other departments could not be employed by the board because of the very low salaries provided for in the agreement. This protest by Eliot was accepted by the board as a basis for rejecting that part of the memorandum. As a matter of fact, Baruch had included attorneys in the proposed agreement largely because of a suggestion from one of the board members. That member had expressed a feeling that the attorneys should also be freed from spoils pressure and had indicated a desire for some experience qualifications which would keep the young "whiz-bangs" from going to the top salaries too rapidly.

During January and February, 1936, disputes continued over the classification of higher positions, particularly in the bureaus of Business Management, Accounts and Audits, and Informational Service. Some of this difficulty arose from the fact that the comptroller general, whose decisions the Civil Service Commission insisted on following, had ruled that expertness applied only to what might be called line functions and not to the business management and fiscal services. These same rulings also complicated the problem of expert ap-

[17] He was receiving a much higher salary from the board, when Eliot's memorandum was written, than he had from the Labor Department.

pointments to the informational service. Another contributing factor increasing the irritation between the two agencies was the personal antagonism between the coordinator and members of the Civil Service Commission staff resulting in quarrels over classifications in the Bureau of Accounts and Audits. The classification expert detailed by the Civil Service Commission to the board did not agree with the board on a good many cases, and this led to threats on the part of the coordinator and others that the board might have to go either to the President or Congress for exemption from the commission's jurisdiction.[18] The board's delay in choosing its chief personnel officer was also a contributing factor to these irritating difficulties. In its anxiety to get its first choice for this job, a purpose not achieved after all, the board did not fill the position until February 1936. It is noticeable that after the board appointed a personnel officer, his knowledge of civil service rules and practices and his skill in obtaining results that the board wanted considerably eased the tension between the board and the commission.

Although the board did not sign the memorandum agreement, it nevertheless proceeded, during January and February, with appointments upon the basis of the terms sketched therein. But the commission was not satisfied and, on February 18, 1936, it pressed the board for a final decision, using as sanction a polite refusal to consider further requests for appointment to the expert category until the board had signed some agreement or indicated some alternative procedure which it intended to follow. This communication led to a reply on February 24 which proposed less stringent standards for experts and attorneys, use of the Civil Service Commission simply as an advisory agency, and no obligation by the board to abide by the commission's decisions.[19] This

[18] There was bad blood between Seidemann and some of the commission's staff as a result of clashes antedating Seidemann's service with the board.

[19] The counterstipulations for attorneys simply provided that the board would appoint no one as attorney unless the duties of the position to which he was assigned were actually those of an attorney requiring admission to the bar. The board also agreed to propose for attorneys only persons who, in fact, had been admitted to the bar.

Its proposed definition for experts read: "'Experts' as this term is used in Section 703 of the Social Security Act will be considered as those (a) who have had training and experience in professional or technical subject-matter or specialized activities peculiarly related to the functions for which the Social Security Board was created; (b) whose qualifications, considering length, kind and quality of training and experience would at least meet the standards for open competition for the grade and position for which proposed; and (c) who by virtue of their training and experience have acquired a fund of special knowledge not ordinarily possessed by those engaged in the same general profession or occupation."

The board proposed that the criteria for expert appointments would be essentially the same as those suggested in the memorandum prepared by the Civil Service Commission.

counterproposal was the work of James V. Bennett, who had induced the board to resume negotiations with the Civil Service Commission, which it felt was treating the board's work and problems in an unfriendly spirit. The accumulated irritations by that time had led to the board's decision to include in its budget requests proposed changes in the wording of the appropriation act to free expert appointments from the jurisdiction of the Civil Service Commission. It also wished to obtain important exemptions from the Classification Act. These intentions were not communicated to the Civil Service Commission.

Both Bane and Bennett were hopeful that the Civil Service Commission would accede to the board's counterproposal of February 24.[20] That might have happened had it not chanced that the commission read the testimony of the board's representatives before the congressional appropriations committee when the board was defending its budget requests for the fiscal year 1936. They there discovered that Chairman Winant, in response to unfriendly questions as to what the board was doing in appointing experts, had replied that the board was making its appointments in cooperation with the Civil Service Commission. The commission felt, therefore, that if the board was to make use of the commission in ducking responsibility for expert appointments, it would not accept the board's plan under which the commission became solely an advisory agency for such appointments. Consequently the commission sent, under date of March 10, a letter declining the proposals made by the board. Instead, it proposed that the two agencies enter into an agreement on terms similar to the agreement signed with the Securities Exchange Commission, or failing that, the commission was to report in detail to the comptroller general every case of expert appointment by the board in which the commission felt that the person appointed did not qualify as an expert. It asked the board for a decision as to which procedure it wanted to follow. On May 13 the board accepted the first alternative.

Thus after four months of bickering and irritation, principles relating to experts in the original Civil Service Commission memorandum were accepted, although the question of detailed specifications concerning standards for ex-

[20] Even though Bennett's position was disputed by the commission and was thus one of the causes of the board's resentment, Bennett did not share the board's emotion. His background of federal service, including work for the Classification Board and the Civil Service Commission, gave him a different perspective. He felt that, on the whole, the commission had been quite fair in its classification of top positions. He also felt that the gripes over the speed of classification work by the commission's staff were unwarranted, and that had the board had its own classification staff at that time it could not have made more rapid progress. He was therefore very reluctant to see the proposed agreement come to naught.

pertness was not included in this March agreement.[21] That remained for direct negotiation between the Civil Service Commission and the bureau heads. How smoothly this process could run where genuine cooperation was desired was shown in the experience of the Bureau of Research and Statistics in filling out its staff during this period. Shortly after Walton Hamilton became the head of this bureau, he went to Civil Service Commissioner White, told him the kind of job he wanted to do, and outlined the problems he was encountering in finding the right people. He made clear the skills which he required in his bureau and the relations of the concept of "expert" to those skills. He agreed to turn over to the Civil Service Commission every scrap of data which he obtained concerning any person whom he would recommend for appointment. What at first appeared to be a vicious circle in obtaining a staff was rather speedily broken. The commission accepted every position which he recommended down to the end of April.

This agreement with the Civil Service Commission, so reluctantly accepted by the board, became a lifesaver when the board was compelled to defend its fiscal 1937 appropriation requests before the House subcommittee during the last week of April 1936.[22] It was obvious that the congressmen were suspicious of the way in which the expert clause had been used by the board. In defense, Altmeyer, Miles, and Bane repeatedly fell back upon the board's agreement with the Civil Service Commission as a guarantee of its political purity. This may be illustrated by the following colloquy between Congressman Woodrum and Altmeyer:

MR. WOODRUM: The point has been made, and the Board ought to have an opportunity to answer it now, that while you are technically under the Civil Service Commission regulations, you are doing just as you please down there in making appointments, calling them experts whether they are or not. Is that true?

MR. ALTMEYER: That is not so. There is not a single person that we have put on the payroll who has not either been qualified by the Civil Service Commission or who has not been passed by the Civil Service Commission as an expert. There is not a single person on our payroll who has not met these requirements."

[21] As an aftermath, there remained the task of qualifying a number of people nominated by the board as experts during the month or so preceding the final phases of the agreement. It was ultimately agreed that all applications pending on March 18 would be submitted, and of these, only two or three, which the board subsequently withdrew, were not acceptable.

[22] Before submitting its requests for funds to the Bureau of the Budget, the board changed the language it had originally proposed exempting it from the classification act and giving it a free hand in the use of the expert clause. Had it retained the original language, it is doubtful if the Bureau of the Budget would have approved, because it would undoubtedly have submitted the changes to the Civil Service Commission for recommendation.

The same point is reenforced in the following interchange:

MR. MILES: The Comptroller General has the final say. He must say if these are experts. By an agreement with the Civil Service Commission, which is in writing now, we submit our proposed expert appointments to the Civil Service Commission.

.   .   .   .   .

THE CHAIRMAN: You submit the names of experts with a statement of their duties?
MR. MILES: Yes Sir. And they review them very carefully.
MR. WOODRUM: I wanted to know if that method was being scrupulously followed.
MR. MILES: Yes, Sir.[23]

In line with the policy of the Civil Service Commission to try to induce the board to call for competitive examinations for positions below bureau heads and their first assistants, the commission began, in the summer of 1936, to tighten up on the qualifications for experts. Despite this, however, the bureau heads put off the request for examinations. As late as June 1936 none of them were considering examinations for positions above the $3,200 grade. Yet no particular tensions developed during the summer because the operating and service bureau heads were fairly well satisfied with the commission and its treatment of proposed expert appointments.[24] The board's director of personnel, Aronson, felt that the commission had been quite reasonable in its attitude toward most of these requests. His principal criticism was that there was a tendency for the commission, in evaluating the question of expertness, to lean heavily on length of experience rather than on its quality and kind.[25]

In October 1936 the board was faced with the pressing problem of appointing a large number of office managers to open up, by the middle of November, field offices of the Bureau of Old Age Benefits to aid the Post Office

[23] In the course of these hearings, Bane presented figures indicating that as of April 27, the board's total staff consisted of 504 persons. Of these, 70 were experts and 29 attorneys, making a total of 99 persons, or approximately 20 percent of the board's employees, without civil service status.

[24] There were a few cases in which bureau heads were disgruntled because the commission would not qualify the appointment of personal acquaintances they wished to hire. Thus, Miss Hoey wanted to appoint a young man who had worked as her assistant in New York for a couple of years, but the commission would not admit his qualifications as an expert.

[25] It must be observed that this tendency to use quantity rather than quality of experience was of serious importance for the whole merit system. It also carried important consequences for the board when the first examination it called, that of administrative officer for the Bureau of Old Age Benefits, was made an unassembled examination and graded by the commission.

Department in the huge job of registration. The board then asked the commission for the right to broaden the definition of expert so as to include these positions. Because the Civil Service Commission was not at that time able to announce the registers for administrative officer, it conceded this request in part by providing that not more than 110 expert positions might be assigned to this bureau. When in December the register for administrative officer was announced, the board was still unsatisfied. It did not like the register, because it doubted the quality of many of the top eligibles, whose experience had been limited to private insurance work. Altmeyer insisted that the Bureau of Old Age Benefits was in reality administering a labor law and, therefore, experience in labor relations work ought to qualify, but the Civil Service Commission staff held to the view that insurance was the essential background. Because of these differences in the winter of 1936-37, and out of certain new irritations over patronage "buck-passing," the board and the commission resumed their antagonism and each made ready to appeal to the comptroller general. Early in January 1937 a letter to that officer was drafted and signed by Chairman Winant, in the endeavor to secure a favorable response to the view that it was the board's responsibility to determine the field of expertness most pertinent in choosing candidates. The letter received the terms of the law relating to exemptions from civil service laws, and the board's sparing use of these privileges. It pointed to the agreement with the Civil Service Commission under which it had been operating in the selection of experts. Then it said:

In the course of discussion with the Commission as to the exact definition of expertness in certain specific fields of the Board's activity the question has arisen as to whether the term "expert" as used applies to the individual involved or to the position which he occupies.

Therefore the Social Security Board desires to have your advice on the following questions:

(1) Are you required in connection with your duties to determine when the Social Security Board has made appointments of experts in conformity with the requirements of the Social Security Act?

(2) Does the term "expert" as used in the Social Security Act apply to individuals or to the positions which such employees occupy?

(3) If the answer to the first question is in the affirmative, is it the sole responsibility of the Social Security Board to determine the general fields of expertness which shall constitute the basis of later specific decisions as to which given individuals are experts?

(4) If the answer to the first question is in the affirmative, is it within the discretion of the Board to assign a person who is considered an "expert" to any position the duties of which are related to his qualifications as an expert and which has been properly classified in accordance with the provisions of the Classification Act?

The chairman decided to withhold this letter, however, until an informal oral inquiry by Calhoun of the board's legal staff had been made at the general accounting office. On the basis of Calhoun's report, it was decided that the comptroller general would probably support the Civil Service Commission. Consequently the letter was never sent.

In the meantime, the Civil Service Commission dispatched a letter, dated January 11, 1937, to the comptroller general. This letter pointed out the importance of defining the term *expert* which, if not defined, was liable to abuse by administrative officers hoping to get around both the civil service and the classification acts. It listed the many acts of Congress which had included expert exemption clauses and cited the decisions of the comptroller general relating to the Civil Service Commission's function in defining *expert* before questions involving its meaning could be taken to the General Accounting Office for final decision. It pointed out the consistent efforts of the commission to cooperate with operating agencies by means of written agreements. In then listed a series of questions, concerning procedure and interpretation, which had arisen in its dealing with the operating agencies of the federal government. It also suggested the answers which it felt ought to be given to these questions. Because the issues raised transcended the immediate controversy with the board as well as illuminated that disagreement, we quote the more significant items on which the comptroller general's opinion was solicited.[26]

2. Where a statute excepts "experts" from the operation of the Civil Service Act alone or from the Civil Service Act and the Classification Act, does the term refer only to persons or does it include positions?

We suggest the following view for consideration:

In passing upon expert appointments two distinct decisions are involved. The first is that the position, as such, is an expert position, i.e., it is composed of duties and responsibilities peculiar to the specialized functions for the performance of which the organization was created and of a caliber definitely requiring expert qualifications on the part of any incumbents, and therefore is available for an excepted appointment. The second is that the person proposed for such excepted appointment possesses these expert qualifications in the specialized type of work represented in that position. Favorable decisions on both points are prerequisite to any proper expert appointment.

3. Does your decision of September 15, 1936, 16 Comp. Gen. 250, apply in both of the following types of cases: (a) where "experts" may be appointed without regard to the Civil Service Act and rules, and compensated without regard to the Classification Act of 1923, as amended; and (b) where "experts" may be appointed without regard to the Civil Service Act and rules but shall

[26] Question 1 related to minor matters of procedure in approving expert appointments, and is therefore omitted.

be compensated in accordance with the Classification Act of 1923, as amended?

There appears to be some doubt as to whether the Commission has a definite authority and responsibility when "expert" positions are exempted from the Civil Service Act only and not from the Classification Act, as in the case of the Federal Trade Commission, the Tariff Commission and the Social Security Board. It is important to know whether in such cases the Commission's authority depends upon the possibility of arriving at administrative agreements with the departments, or whether it is derived from law.

The Commission believes that this question should be answered in the affirmative. The following description of the authority of the Commission is suggested for consideration: That of determining, subject to submission for the review of the general law officers of the Government, (1) whether a given position or class of positions is (a) within the purview of the Classification Act of 1923, as amended, salaries of incumbents to be fixed accordingly, or (b) within the purview of an excepting "expert" clause, salaries of incumbents to be fixed at the discretion of administrative officers; and (2) whether a given position or class of positions is (a) within the purview of the Civil Service Act and rules, incumbents to be appointed in accordance therewith, or (b) within the purview of an excepting "expert" clause, incumbents to be selected and appointed at the discretion of appointing officers.

4. May the department appoint, without regard to the Civil Service Commission Act and rules, a person who possesses expert qualifications and immediately or sometime later assign him to the work of a position in the competitive classified service?

5. May the department appoint, without regard to the Classification Act of 1923, as amended, a person who possesses "expert" qualifications, fix his salary without regard to such act, and assign him to duties and responsibilities that would cause his position to fall under the Classification Act?

The Commission believes that questions 4 and 5 should be answered in the negative.

Positions not regarded as excepted "expert" positions are not available for the employment of "experts" either through original entrance to the service or through reassignment. Persons appointed as "experts" must be assigned to "expert" positions initially and may not be reassigned to positions within the scope of the basic personnel laws, but only to other excepted positions and then under the same procedure as for original appointment thereto. Any other view would clearly permit open violations of the Civil Service Act or the Classification Act or both.

6. As a practical device in passing upon expert appointments under the agreements mentioned herein (and also in passing upon expert appointments in the Farm Credit Administration under schedule B, subdivision XII, par. 2 of the civil service rules). The view has been taken that no position is of sufficiently high grade to require "expert" qualifications within the meaning of this discussion unless its duties are sufficiently difficult or complex to warrant appraisal in CAF-9 or P-3 (the $3,200–$3,800 grade) under the allocation standards of the Classi-

fication Act, as amended. Is this a reasonable minimum level or is there sufficient similarity between the term "experts" and the terms "consulting specialist," P-6, "professional consultant," P-7, and "technical consultant," CAF-14, used in the grade definitions of the Classification Act, to warrant changing this minimum level to P-6 or CAF-13?

Attention is invited to your decision of January 18, 1934, 13 Comp. Gen. 199,200, wherein an example of an expert appointment was given as "technical agricultural experts employed as consultants or on special assignments." Also, there is for consideration the fact that the Commission and the Department of Agriculture are in the process of completing an agreement fixing $5,600 as the minimum rate below which a position will not be considered an "expert" position under the provisions of sec. 10(a) of the Agricultural Adjustment Act. This agreement arose out of a request by your office some time ago that the Commission look into the matter of expert appointments in the Agricultural Adjustment Administration.

Guidance on this question would be appreciated.

7. In your decision of July 25, 1934, 14 Comp. Gen. 70, 71, one of the descriptive phrases relative to "experts" refers to them as persons "who are not, generally, obtainable under operation of the civil-service laws and regulations." Is it a correct understanding that this clause refers to a situation in which, on account of the restricted field of qualifications required, and the consequent small number of qualified persons available, the Commission believes that it would be very difficult, if not impossible, to secure a sufficient number of eligibles through civil service examinations?

The Commission believes that this question should be answered in the affirmative.

8. Does the term "experts" as used in excepting legislation include only those who are employed for consulting or advisory service or for special assignments, of only temporary duration in any case, or may it cover permanent, regular, full-time employments, including positions in the regular organizational structure of a Government agency?

Guidance on this question would be appreciated.

If the Commission can be of any additional assistance to your office in your study of these questions we shall be glad to be of service.

The comptroller general's reply appeared to uphold the commission's views in all except one point: the suggested minimum salary level of $5,600 for experts. It read:

Where a statute expressly excepts "experts" from the provisions of either the Civil Service Laws and Regulations or the Classification Act as amended, or both, it is primarily the duty and responsibility of the particular administrative office concerned and the Civil Service Commission to determine whether a particular position or class of position falls within the exception. The jurisdiction of this office, insofar as the Classification Act as amended is concerned, extends to determining in the audit of pay rolls that the salary paid to an employee conforms with the salary range prescribed by law and regulation for the particular position to which the employee has been assigned, the fact to be assumed, of course, that the employee actually performs the class of duty embraced by the position designated on the pay roll. But where there is reason to believe that the latter is not the case then it becomes the duty of this office to question the payment in the audit. Question 1(a), therefore, is answered in the negative and the procedure suggested in question 1(b) will be sufficient for the purposes of this office.

With respect to question 2, you are advised that the term "experts" refers to both positions and persons. It must appear that the position can be satisfactorily filled only by an expert and that the person appointed to the position is such an expert.

Referring to question 3, as above stated this office is concerned primarily with the determination as to whether the salaries paid are in compliance with the Classification Act as amended. However, the decision cited in question 3 should be of assistance to the Commission in considering both types of cases described. Referring to your comments following the statement of question 3, it is the view of this office that when the administrative office and the Commission cannot agree, the determination of the Commission as to whether the duties of a position or class of positions do or do not require the services of experts should prevail. But when the Commission determines that the duties of a position require it to be filled by an expert, it then becomes the duty and responsibility of the administrative office to select a person having the qualifications necessary to fill the position, and, when the employment of experts is excepted from the terms of the Classification Act as amended, also, to fix the salary of the employee so selected.

Questions 4 and 5 are answered in the negative.

Referring to question 6, I doubt the practicability of attempting to prescribe a minimum salary rate—applicable to all services—for positions requiring the services of an expert. While in most activities of the Government a position the duties of which would not justify a rating as high as P-6 or CAF-13 would not require the services of an expert, it is conceivable that especially in some of the newer activities, there might be positions the duties of which would require employees having training or experience in some specialized field rather than general education or professional qualifications and whose services would not justify a salary of more than $3,200 to $3,800. Consequently it is believed there can be no hard and fast rule in this respect. Also, it may be that positions which required the services of experts when the activity was first undertaken by the Government later may—with respect to the subsequent filling of vacancies therein —be regarded as not requiring the services of experts.

Question 7 is answered in the affirmative. See answer to question 3.

In regard to question 8, the term "expert" as used in excepting legislation would appear to refer, generally, to positions requiring temporary services in a consultant or advisory capacity. However, the excepting legislation does not preclude the employment of an expert on a permanent basis where the position is such as to require that that be done.

With this decision to rely upon, the commission wrote on March 13 as follows:

By reason of our submission of January 12, 1937, to the Comptroller-General on the matter of expert appointments generally and his decision of January 29, 1937, we have delayed replying to your letter of January 9, concerning fields of experience to be taken into consideration in determining expert qualifications in the Bureau of Old Age Benefits.

Under that decision, the first step to be taken by the Commission in considering expert appointments is to pass upon the positions themselves. The basic facts concerning positions that will enable us to determine whether or not they are excepted expert positions, are, of course, their duties and responsibilities, i.e., the work which they involve. The next step is to draw from these facts inferences as to the qualifications requirement that would be demanded by anyone to do that work. If they are not such as to produce reasonable competition, either because they lie in a very narrow field, or are extremely exacting, or involve an unusual combination of accomplishments, the positions may be characterized as excepted.

Hence, it is not feasible to make a decision on the basis suggested in your letter. We believe, however, that a mutually satisfactory procedure would be for you to identify individual positions or groups of positions upon which the Social Security Board desires a decision as to the fields of experience from which experts might be drawn. This identification may be made by statements of duties and responsibilities or by reference to classification sheets already on file with the Commission. After a decision is reached on the status of these positions, then, as to those that are decided to be excepted expert positions, we will, as to each group of like positions, consider what fields of experience would be qualifying for the groups and advise you of our conclusions.

Here the matter rested until the end of the period covered by this study.

It is clear that out of this controversy extending over fourteen months the commission emerged as victor, but it was still disturbed by the congressional practice of inserting expert exemption clauses in statutes creating new agencies. It therefore devoted a long section of its annual report for the fiscal year 1936 to a statement of the expert problem prepared by Ismar Baruch. That statement traced briefly the history of the expert clause and argued that proponents of new legislation ought to discontinue its use, replacing it when needed by procedures available under schedules A and B of the civil service rules.

The basic objection of the commission and its staff to the expert clause was that it tended to expose both the operating agency and the commission to political pressure from members of the House and Senate since each depended on Congress for appropriations. Despite numerous experiences which should have served as ample warning on that point, the Social Security Board did not come to a full realization of this danger until it found its entire appropriation for fiscal year 1938 held up for five months by Senator Carter Glass and his colleagues while they drove through Congress a provision requiring presidential appointment and senate confirmation for all attorneys and experts appointed by the board whose salaries were $5,000 or more a year. The language of the appropriation act, as phrased by Senator Glass, made it impossible to pay the salaries of any such persons until confirmation by the Senate had taken place.

Even though all of the lawyers and experts in this category were eventually confirmed by the Senate in return for only a few patronage appointments, there were probably more political influences at work within the board during this period than at any other time in its first eighteen months. This was the result of the widespread feeling among the staff that the board had been thrown into patronage politics and thereafter it would be necessary to "play ball" with the Congress.[27]

PERSONNEL MANAGEMENT, POLITICAL PRESSURES AND PATRONAGE APPOINTMENTS

In presenting the record of patronage appointments, the authors wish to make it clear at the outset that their impression of the board's behavior in this matter was one of strenuous effort to avoid yielding to patronage pressure or compromising with selection on the basis of merit. As we have shown, the expert exemption clause laid the board open to demands which it could not always resist. The same pressures influenced the Civil Service Commission, which on at least three occasions amazed the board by qualifying people the board believed wholly unfit but whom the board, lacking the nerve to say no, had passed along to the commission in the confident expectation that the latter would relieve it of that unpleasant duty. But despite these cases and the others which we shall relate, it is our belief that the proportion of instances in which the board escaped temptation by yielding to it was remarkably small when compared with other New Deal agencies or even with the old line departments that had been given new programs without civil service requirements. There were undoubtedly a considerable number of instances in which a congressman's clients who already had civil service status were given jobs by

---

[27] In the autumn of 1937, several months after this study was concluded, a new board composed of Altmeyer, Bigge, and Dewson agreed with the Civil Service Commission that no more expert appointments would be requested. By that time all of the board's principal staff members had been appointed, and the board finally decided that the flexibility implicit in the expert clause was no longer worth the price of the patronage pressure and disputes with congressmen that seemed inseparable from the use of the clause.

the board's organization in preference to other candidates with better qualifications. Merely to possess civil service status does not assure the reign of the merit principle in competition with others similarly circumstanced. A good deal of patronage pressure is continually exerted on behalf of such people who technically are already in the federal service through merit but who actually are poorly qualified as compared with other available candidates. That the board faced this pressure and yielded to some of it we know, but we have no quantitative record of those cases, which seem to have been confined to inconspicuous stenographic and clerical jobs.

In the first months of the board's existence in 1935 the Congress was not in session.[28] Political pressures at this time impinged primarily on key positions on the board's staff. Suggestions for appointment came from Democratic congressmen, from the White House (including the uxorial branch), and from members of the board and their staff, who promoted the candidacies of personal acquaintances. Miles had made it his particular business to look up the political record of all persons nominated for staff appointments and to slap down his information with the remark that he had nothing further to say and that he would not vote.[29] Actually, he was consistently overruled on proposed political appointments by Winant and Altmeyer, with but few exceptions. Perhaps the most important appointment made for political reasons was that of a former army officer and insurance man who was backed by the American Legion and by important southern politicians. Independent investigation by the board revealed a good private employment record, and so he was appointed and given responsible work. Later he was made a very important officer in the Bureau of Old Age Benefits and became one of the most influential members of the group supporting the chief of the bureau in his conflict with the executive director's and the director of personnel. He played an important part in an internal struggle for power, in which his outside political relationships were of some significance. With the enforced resignation of his chief, this appointee was removed to a position where he could no longer affect personnel appointments, thus stripping him of weapons essential to successful internecine warfare.

[28] This eased the pressure, as did the fact that there were hardly any Democratic congressmen defeated in the 1934 election who had to be "taken care of." This was in contrast to the situation confronting other new agencies after the 1938 election, when a sizable number of Democratic congressmen were defeated. In the latter case, the agencies were importuned to place the ex-congressmen in important field positions. In one such agency, of the fifteen regional directors four were ex-congressmen or defeated Democratic candidates for congress.

[29] This summary of the situation before November 15, 1935, is based upon entries in the diary of Robert Frase, who was a personal assistant to Chairman Winant after October 9.

We have indicated in the preceding chapter how a southern gentleman was qualified as an expert by the Civil Service Commission, to the great chagrin of the board, after the board had successfully resisted political pressure to appoint him as head of the Bureau of Public Assistance. He was then qualified for a $6,500 job as an expert; but the board offered him a place at a salary of $4,600, hoping that he would refuse. He finally accepted with the expectation that he would become either a regional manager or assistant manager in one of the southern regions. For over a year he was kept doing busy work in the Executive Director's Office, the Bureau of Informational Service, and the Bureau of Old Age Benefits, apparently with the hope that perhaps he would become so dissatisfied that he would resign. He was finally temporarily assigned to a field office in one of the southern states at about the time this study ended.

Powerful American Legion support was responsible for the employment, late in 1935, of a former army officer (also unexpectedly qualified by the Civil Service Commission as an expert) who for over six months was given nothing to do except some home reading. He attended the in-service training courses and was then assigned to the speakers' unit of the Informational Service. During the summer of 1936 he was gradually broken into the job of making speeches before veterans' organizations. Despite the fact that such assignments were infrequent and his position was virtually a sinecure, his political support was regarded as too important to permit his removal.

The Vice-President was said to be responsible for the board's employment of a southern lady politician who presented a problem similar to the one just sketched.[30] After undertaking a home study course in social insurance, she was given special tutorial instruction by members of the staff and employed in the Bureau of Informational Service, whose director finally sent her to one of the regional offices. There she caused continuous grief to the regional director and to the other members of the field organization. Two college ex-presidents (one from New England and one from the southwest), each a friend of a board member, were hired during the winter of 1935–36 and also dumped into the Bureau of Informational Service, where their activities yielded return of very small value. Late in 1936 the board initiated steps looking toward their separation from the service, but final action had not been taken by the end of March 1937.

Two of the best accounting positions in the Bureau of Accounts and Audits were granted to two southern accountants as the result of pressure from Miles and certain congressmen. Neither of these men was able to function effectively in performing a very important accounting service for the states,

---

[30] Vice-President John Nance Garner had tried unsuccessfully to secure her appointment to other agency staffs.

which the board was anxious to render. Both of them remained a continuing problem through the autumn of 1936, although one of them by that time showed signs of learning his work. The unfitness of these men threw the burden of this specialized accounting duty on the shoulders of a single member of the staff, and delayed the performance of essential services (particularly for public assistance) which the board was expected to render.

The Bureau of Accounts and Audits was also the recipient of a protégé of the President. A naval officer who was a friend of a senator from one of the north-central states was killed in one of the dirigible disasters. This senator interested the President in the need of the officer's widow for a well-paying job. The President first asked the Navy Department to request an executive order exempting the lady from the competitive requirements for one of its desirable positions. But the Navy demurred, and did not make the request. Thereupon, the President's office made a similar request of the Social Security Board, and the board asked Aronsen to draw up a request for such an order. Aronsen refused, insisting that if the President wanted such an order he could make it on his own motion, and that by preparing such a request the board would make itself ridiculous in the eyes of its own staff. The order was finally initiated by the President, and the lady began service with the board on May 23, 1936.

Appointments in the Office of the General Counsel were peculiar compared with other board bureaus: any lawyer who had been admitted to the bar was eligible for appointment. The Civil Service Commission did not review their qualifications. It was inevitable, therefore, that appointments to the staff of the general counsel, including his regional representatives, would be the subject of constant pressure from congressmen, most of whom were lawyers with numerous lawyer friends. The general counsel, therefore, played ball with the boys "on the Hill," although he avowed that he was intent on getting the best possible legal staff. When reviewing the patronage situation at the close of December 1936, he insisted that out of a total legal staff of approximately eighty there were only three or four political hacks, and not many others of mediocre ability, who had been chosen because of political connections. But whatever the capacities of his staff members may have been, he followed the policy of requiring an appointee to possess the backing of at least one senator. Occasionally the board itself was to blame for poor appointments in this unit. Thus after the general counsel had persistently refused to accept the nominee of an important New England senator, that worthy was given a special hearing by the board at the end of which his nominee was appointed. This appointee was said to have been the weakest member of the legal staff.

When Congress assembled early in 1936 the pressure for political appointments markedly increased and affected the whole rank and file of the organization. It took some time to make senators and congressmen recall that they had incorporated in the Social Security Act a stipulation that the board was to use the regular merit system for all positions except lawyers and experts. In the early weeks of 1936 Sorrels, of the Civil Service Commission staff but on loan to the board, spent a large portion of his time either interviewing congressmen or answering their letters.[31] Although most of their protégés were not employed, a few were slipped in here and there if they possessed civil service status, even though their qualifications were not high. This was done to ease the forthcoming enactment of appropriations for the board. During the early months, as well as at recurrent periods, the board occasionally made "sweet compromise" with political expediency, which it justified in terms of appropriations. There is no doubt that requests by members of the House or Senate appropriations committees were treated with more consideration than those from most other congressmen. Neither is there doubt that some members of these committees were not bashful in proposing appointees. One southern senator even called attention to his membership on such a committee when writing a demand that the board find a place for an elderly lady friend of his who, though she possessed civil service status, was sixty-five years old and had passed the point of efficiency. It was difficult to refuse such requests.

But Sorrels was not the only person who was being bombarded by congressmen's friends. Bennett and Bane each spent a good deal of time listening to the stories of these people and their congressional sponsors.

Winant was spared a good many interviews with placemen by his secretarial staff, which was anxious to conserve the chairman's time for more important matters. One day in January 1936 while McKinley was waiting in Winant's office, a young man from the South came in and demanded to see the chairman. The secretary informed him that he would have to go either to Sorrels or Bennett first, but this man refused to be put off, arguing long and loudly that it took him only five minutes to see Jim Farley, but that he had been to Winant's office two or three times and had not yet been able to get an interview with him.

Because Winant and Altmeyer usually refused to entertain these political applicants and their congressional sponsors, Miles took it as his task to hear them and to try to give them the "consideration which is their due." Early in the autumn he had employed James Douglas, a fellow southerner, who while given the title of "technical adviser" was actually Miles's political aide. The Douglas-Miles technique for dealing with these political applicants was described by Douglas to McKinley. Its essentials were as follows.

When an applicant arrived, Douglas (or Miles) recorded the name and

---

[31] On a single day late in January he dictated over sixty letters to congressmen relating to requests for jobs.

a secretary in the office listened to the conversation and made notes of the interview. Later a digest was prepared which included whatever suggestions Douglas (or Miles) had made. This digest was entered in a book which Douglas and Miles kept constantly with them in order to recall the specifics of each case if the political sponsor should call. If a person returned for a second interview, a card containing the gist of the information about him was handed to Douglas or Miles before the applicant was admitted to the inner office. Most of these political orphans were simply given a little encouragement and passed along. It was understood that if a congressman really wanted a job for one of them he himself would come to Douglas's office with the prospective employee. Pat Harrison had told Douglas not to pay any attention to letters he sent over on behalf of persons whom he did not accompany. In such instances he was really passing them along to get rid of them. When he really wanted a job for somebody, he would come over and camp on the board's doorstep until he got it.

By the early part of March this interviewing job had been pretty thoroughly shifted by Miles to Douglas, who complained that the task was becoming intolerable. Often he interviewed as many as fifty people in a single day and on some days more than eighty. For a short time Douglas tried, after Aronson was employed, to send these people to the personnel officer, but Aronson's protests were such that Douglas had to take them back again. Despite his expression of distaste for this job, Douglas continued during the spring of 1936 to operate as a kind of personnel agency for political placement and became, in part, a rival to the regular personnel organization.

In addition to the instances already recited, the Bureau of Informational Service became the resting place for a number of other political appointees. One of the early cases was that of a former lady secretary to Emil Hurja, the right hand of James A. Farley. At first, she had been promised a $3,800 place. She wanted to get into the personnel office, but Bennett would have none of her; nor would other bureau heads take her on for a $3,800 job. Finally she was persuaded to accept $3,200, and Resnick placed her in charge of the inquiry section in his bureau where her energy quickly caught up with the accumulation of mail. The only complaint made about her was that she was "looking for too many worlds to conquer."

Resnick spent a great deal of time during his first months of service in interviewing political applicants passed along to him by the board, although both he and the board knew they would never be employed. The board's unwillingness to reject these applicants compelled Resnick to waste time which he sorely needed to get his organization under way. Like the other bureau heads, he had understood from the beginning that the board's policy was to disregard political claims in making subordinate appointments. But he also knew, without being explicitly told, that the board wanted him to find places for certain people with political backing. A congressman's former secretary, qualified as an expert with the help of Miles and Sorrels, had hoped to become head of the information bureau. Resnick finally gave him a post paying $3,200. A congressman, who had been very effective during the enactment of the Social Security Act, was promised a job somewhere in the organization for a relative. After this man had been flatly refused by another bureau, Resnick was made to feel that the board would like him to give the man a job so as to keep the board's pledges.

When Aronson's personnel organization got under way it became an effective brake upon the use of political pressure for appointments. Aronson was aware of the fact that mistakes had been made in the preceding period, and he was particularly anxious to develop a process of interview and inquiry which would allow no facts to escape the attention of the appointing officers and the board, while at the same time it would impress the political applicant and his congressional backer with the fairness and thoroughness of the personnel inquiry. He believed that a properly organized personnel office could impress the candidate and his congressional sponsor with its fairness and thoroughness and its concern for merit because it could show that it went carefully into the matter of qualifications, in some cases by means of supplementary tests. If a congressman did not know there was a particular vacancy, he could be stalled off tactfully by indicating the personnel officer's desire to consider the congressman's friend and his sorrow that there seemed to be no place open just then which quite suited his qualifications. The difficulty anticipated by Bennett and Aronson was that once a few political appointees got in, they would channel information directly to congressmen about anticipated vacancies. As a consequence, other political friends would be making prompt applications, sometimes even before the personnel office would have notice of the expected vacancy.

Aronson's attachment to the merit system and his unresponsiveness to politically sponsored candidates and their congressional backers was quickly sensed by Miles who, before long, began to indicate his dissatisfaction with the personnel officer. Miles was chiefly responsible for retaining Sorrels at the board's office for weeks after Aronson's organization was under way, apparently because he hoped, through this duplicating personnel unit, to keep open channels for the more favorable consideration of political nominees than could be obtained through the regular personnel staff. Already a rift was developing in the board's organization, with Miles building up a close association with the coordinator, his staff, and the Bureau of Accounts and Audits, which the coordinator had organized and whose head he had nominated. This group appeared to be kindly disposed to a number of political nominees; but when the personnel officer reported critically about them resentment was aroused which led in time to bitter antagonism. One case late in April 1936 aroused the ire of Miles so much that he complained to the board about Aronson.[32] It affected a nominee sponsored by Pat Harrison, and endorsed by the coordinator and Sorrels. Latimer, then head of the Bureau of Old Age Benefits, had been persuaded to approve the recommendation with the expectation of using the man for a field office job. Aronson's investigation showed that the principal qualifications of the nominee were Salvation Army services. When Latimer learned this he was disposed to withdraw his recommendation, and consequently, Aronson became the target of the resentment.

The regional and field office establishment was early regarded as possessed of sufficient "elasticity" to care for many of the political appointees forced on the board. A number of the cases already mentioned were ultimately destined for the field, which in all federal agencies has been particularly used to take care of congressmen's clients. With the tightening up of the definition of expert by the Civil Service Commission in the summer of 1936, the opportunities available for placement in Washington were increasingly restricted to lawyers and to the lower paid positions. In the field, however, there were a large number of jobs, chiefly for the Bureau of Old Age Benefits. Many of these field positions paid from $2,600 to $5,600, and they were also attractive because the offices might be located in the home town of the applicant. But because of the delay in making field office appointments, pressure for these positions did not become very great until mid-winter 1936–37, and became most intense after the row with Carter Glass and the Senate Appropriations Committee in February 1937. It then became the fixed policy of the board to clear all prospective field positions with the appropriate senator, and even in some cases with important congressmen. Even though the number of outright patronage appointments was probably not large, the clearance policy was a time-consuming process which resulted in delaying the opening of offices. It was also undoubtedly bad for morale.

As one reviews this phase of the board's history, it must be concluded that the total number of political appointees was probably not large. It should also be fully recognized that the board steadfastly refused to consider politics in the selection of the heads of the bureaus or, with one unhappy exception, for the key positions under the bureau directors. To put the case much more positively and fairly, the board selected exceedingly competent people for bureau posts of first and second command. Even in the regional offices, as is shown elsewhere, political considerations were not dominant in the appointment of more than one director.

The story of the board's struggle with patronage pressure would not be fair if it did not include a recognition of the fact that the Civil Service Commis-

---

[32] This was the beginning of a campaign against Aronson that greatly increased in intensity during the next winter.

sion itself, due to the elastic expert clause, was not completely above the patronage battle. While most of the staff had no political ties with congressmen and were not susceptible to patronage pressure, some entered the commission's service at a time when the route from a congressman's entourage to the commission's establishment was much easier to travel. Unfortunately, these lingering attachments seemed strong enough, upon occasion, to bend discretionary judgment toward the favorite of an old congressional friend.

OTHER PERSONNEL
MANAGEMENT PROBLEMS

Civil Service Recruitment

The board had three problems in recruiting personnel: (1) that of selective recruitment of the higher administrators and technicians, a qualitative task of key importance; (2) the mass appointment of large numbers of clerical and stenographic personnel; and (3) recruitment of manipulative employees in the lower grades. To solve the second problem it would be necessary to secure large numbers of such persons within a relatively short time. But the urgency of mass recruitment was not apparent until the autumn of 1936, nearly a year after the board took office and about nine months after it began operations under its own congressional appropriation. Before that time, the only unit of the board's organization that had found it necessary to employ a large number of lower-grade employees was the Bureau of Business Management, which on July 31, 1936, had 323 of the 942 employees of the board.[33] This bureau had experienced no particular difficulty, except in the case of stenographers, in obtaining staff through the use of existing civil service registers or through transfers from other agencies. In the case of stenographers, it became clear in the spring of 1936 that the old register had been drained of nearly all competent names, and the board's director of personnel suggested to the Civil Service Commission that the board be permitted to make temporary appointments after giving a simple test of its own, pending the establishment of a new register later in the summer. After some objection, the commission gave its permission, and the board gave tests in New York and Philadelphia which yielded about seventy-five good stenographers. These, added to the thirty or so competent people picked from the dregs of the old register or

[33] It had no experts on its staff. The Bureau of Unemployment Compensation had twenty-four out of a total staff of thirty-nine, Public Assistance had thirty-five on a staff of sixty, Research and Statistics had forty out of eighty-seven.

obtained by transfer, met the immediate needs of the board in the summer of 1936.

The real push for rapid expansion of the staff did not arise until October 1936, when the creation of the central records office at Baltimore, in anticipation of the mass registration during November and December, made it imperative to recruit about two thousand persons to man the machines in Baltimore. This job was done within a couple of months. It was made possible because Personnel Director Aronson drove his staff night and day for several weeks, actually sending several of them over to the Civil Service Commission, which was undermanned, to help handle the commission's end of the work. It required about ten thousand letters and telegrams to assemble this corps for the records job by means of transfers from Treasury, Agriculture, and other agencies, by taking junior typists from registers for punch card operators, junior civil service examiners for card comparers, and other devices.

The other area most needing large numbers of employees was that of the field offices of the Bureau of Old Age Benefits, which the board had concluded late in the spring of 1936 would probably have to handle the registration job then tentatively projected for the following November. While knowing that this would be a difficult thing to carry through, the board still approached its recruiting task largely in terms of liberalizing the expert clause, or of obtaining from the President an executive order which would exempt the field office managers from the competitive system. Meanwhile, Aronson and McCormack (the latter was in charge of the Field Organization Committee) began negotiations with the Civil Service Commission concerning the giving of an examination for these field administrative positions. Aronson tried to secure the commission's consent to a college education and a passing grade in a standard intelligence test as elegibility requirements. But he met firm opposition from the commission's staff on both points, and Altmeyer and Mc-Cormack objected to the education requirement, which they felt would eliminate good administrative material. Aronson's position in this and subsequent cases was that his proposed requirements would cut down the number of applications and yield a small register of high quality, cleared of disabled veterans and other unsatisfactory persons.

In July the board concluded that it would do everything to farm out the registration job to another federal agency, and it decided not to ask the President to exempt the district office managers from civil service requirements. Negotiations with the Civil Service Commission for an administrative officer examination were therefore speeded up, with the result that on August 24, examinations were announced for managers of district and branch field offices and equivalent positions in Washington or regional offices.[34] The closing

[34] These positions were scheduled to pay from $3,200 to $5,600 a year.

date for applications was September 14, 1936. This was the first examination for general administrative officers ever held by the commission. It was an unassembled examination based primarily upon employment experience in insurance, labor relations, or social service work, although in lieu of these experience qualifications certain allowable general experience, educational training in a college or university, might be substituted. Ten thousand persons took the examination. After a strenuous effort to rate this huge number of examinees the Civil Service Commission delivered to the board, on December 2, 1936, a register which contained about two thousand names.

The board and most of its staff viewed this register with suspicion. Aronson felt that there might be enough people selected from it, supplemented by transfers and experts in those geographical districts in which the registers were especially weak, so as to man between two and three hundred field offices. Many of the individual district registers (the examination was set up on a district basis) were clogged at the top with obviously unsatisfactory people, including disabled veterans. The slowness with which appointments to the field offices were made was partly due to the reluctance to use these registers as well as to efforts to manipulate them so as to get below the top three undesirables. Of course, part of the delay was the result of clearing appointments with the regional directors and, after February 1937, with senators. As a result of all these factors, by March 31, 1937, only six persons had been appointed from the registers produced by this examination.[35]

While most of the people in the board's organization were disposed to place the full blame for this unsatisfactory situation upon the Civil Service Commission, part of it ought to have been shouldered by the board itself. It had played a decisive part in setting up the employment experience qualifications, and it had not carefully enough discriminated between various kinds of administrative experience.[36]

Moreover, the board had held off for months before it asked for an examination, and then it demanded speed. The result was a use of quantitative measurements of experience often not relevant to the position to be filled. Length of experience turned out to be very poor criteria, sometimes even ludicrous, for administrative competence. But to rate ten thousand examinees in an unassembled examination on the basis of quality of experience was a practically impossible task for the limited staff of the Civil Service Commission. The board's concern for equity lest some non-college-graduates be excluded from the opportunity to compete, and the commission staff's aversion to intelligence

[35] William C. Hull, executive assistant, U.S. Civil Service Commission, to Robert Frase, October 4, 1937.

[36] The insurance experience allowed was too general and too heavily weighted, in Bane's opinion.

tests precluded the use of the only readily available eliminators that might have so reduced the number of candidates that careful qualitative judgments could have been used in determining the ratings of those getting over these two screening hurdles. Given these attitudes of board and commission, and the demand for speed, it is highly probable that a much more satisfactory register would have been obtained by a written assembled examination.

During April and May 1936, the Bureau of Research and Statistics initiated the first effort to develop a competitive examination as the basis for the recruitment of professional staff. This was the proposed social science analyst examination. A younger member of the staff, with the encouragement of Director Hamilton and others, began work on an examination designed to interest recent college graduates broadly trained in the social sciences, preferably in at least two fields. The support and cooperation of the Central Statistical Board in developing this examination was obtained, but this was not an unmixed blessing. The Civil Service Commission people were suspicious of that agency as a result of the active interest which it had taken in the grading of the economist examinations the preceding winter.

The prosecution of this project was so delayed that it was not until March 15, 1937, that the examination was announced (in two sections, assembled for grades P-1 and P-2, and unassembled for grades P-3 to P-6). Not until the middle of September 1937 was the assembled (written) examination held, and registers were not made available to operating agencies until the summer of 1938, fifteen months after the announcement of the examinations.

This snail's pace progress illustrates the customary difficulty of recruitment in so large an organization as the federal government, where the central recruitment agency has been habitually starved for funds, and consequently understaffed. But it was in considerable part due to other factors as well: ill feeling between the board and the commission and the relative ease with which the Bureau of Research and Statistics had used the expert clause in recruiting its professional members.[37]

Another examination was gestating in the Bureau of Unemployment Compensation. In the first half of 1936, this bureau slowly built up its higher-paid professional staff through the use of the expert clause and through transfers. Yet there was a growing realization, late in the spring, that examinations should be held in order to secure junior professional staff. While a start toward developing such an examination was made then, Wagenet, head of the bureau, was skeptical of the adequacy of civil service examinations to produce good registers for his field people and for other employees whose duties required much contact work. He also valued practical experience much more highly than ability to present an imposing paper record. He therefore held off

[37] It had fifty-four experts on its staff in February 1937.

from proposing an examination for technical analyst. During the fall of 1936 a series of conferences between members of this bureau, the director of personnel, and representatives of the Bureau of Old Age Benefits was held. The latter unit was then interested in the possibility of a joint examination for technical analyst for the two bureaus. Early in December it was agreed that an assembled examination should be asked. Long negotiations were begun with the Civil Service Commission, ending in an announcement on March 29, 1937, of examinations for associate and assistant technical analyst at P-3–$3,200 and P-2–$2,600, for the Bureau of Unemployment Compensation.[38]

The announcement showed that the Civil Service Commission, this time, had made important concessions to Aronson's views on qualitative eliminators. It allowed twenty points for a mental (intelligence) test and included in the educational qualifications, which together with experience would count for thirty points, successful completion of a four-year college course leading to a B.A., with additional credit for major courses in the social sciences. While it permitted experience to be substituted for education, it also allowed limited graduate study to be substituted for experience. A written test accounted for the remaining fifty points. Finally, an oral examination for all successful candidates was provided at the option of the board and the commission, and its passage made a prerequisite to appointment.

While the closing dates for application were April 26 to 29, 1937, the examination was not given until December 31, 1937, and the register was not made available to the bureau until the summer of 1938. But it was in 1937 that the bureau urgently needed trained personnel, particularly for field service—the states needed help in setting up their administrative structures and planning the procedures for paying benefits. Twenty-two states were to begin benefit payments in the first half of 1938. One may conclude that the Bureau of Unemployment Compensation's reliance on the expert clause, plus the usual delays in commission procedure, had precluded the effective recruitment of younger professional staff through competitive civil service techniques.

Within the Bureau of Public Assistance the dominance of the professional social worker's viewpoint allowed no compromise with the Civil Service Commission over examinations for professional positions: if examinations were to be held, graduate training in social work had to be a prerequisite for all applicants. To this the Civil Service Commission would not agree. Despite the fact that the bureau continued to be understaffed, its chief preferred to rely upon the use of the expert clause. While some might question the quality of all the personnel obtained in this way, there is no doubt that political patronage was kept completely out of the bureau. Personal friendship doubtless played its part in obtaining staff appointments, but this was the same kind

[38] The Bureau of Old Age Benefits had by this time decided not to join in the request.

of personal relationship among professional people that determines appointments on the faculties of universities and the staffs of hospitals.

The head of the Bureau of Informational Service, like his confreres, kept putting off the request for competitive examinations because he wanted to qualify people whom he knew personally or whom trusted friends recommended to him. But his resistance was not the strongest, and the board frequently used his bureau to absorb its political appointees. Consequently, the use of the expert clause instead of an early competitive examination led to a staff with many weak spots. In anticipation of the expansion of the field staff in the regional offices, conferences with the Civil Service Commission looking toward an early competitive examination were started in the summer of 1936. There was again a clash of attitudes, with Personnel Director Aronson and Huse of the Informational Service contending for a prerequisite of college graduation and a stiff assembled examination, while the commission staff held out for generous substitute experience for the college degree and an unassembled examination for the upper grades. It was reported that the commission people were afraid of offending the newspaper correspondents if they made the written questions too "intellectual." The negotiations finally culminated in an announcement, on December 21, 1936, that four grades of informational service representatives would be hired and that for each, a written assembled exam was necessary. Completion of a four-year college course leading to a bachelor's degree was required, with additional credit for majors in English, journalism, or the social sciences, but it was possible to substitute general experience for college education year for year. Because the examinations were not held until the spring of 1937 and the registers were not established until September 23, 1937, they were much too late for use in creating a field force to aid in assigning account numbers. Moreover, it became clear during the second half of fiscal year 1937 that the budget for the Informational Service would be so reduced as not to be adequate for even the existing bureau staff. Consequently, the examination appeared to be an almost complete waste of effort and money unless other federal agencies would use the register.

It early became apparent that to accomplish the task of auditing every individual payment for public assistance within the states, which the board, presumably under pressure from the General Accounting Office, had decided was necessary at least for the first year, a large force of field auditors was essential. Equally clear was the need for an examination if rapid recruitment of competent auditors was to be assured. The available auditor registers were old and clogged with disabled veterans, and the expert clause was not available for securing staff for this activity.

But personal friction between the head of the bureau and the director of personnel, and the usual difference between Aronson and the Civil Service

Commission staff about the college degree hurdle, killed the proposal for an auditor's examination. In the discussion with the commission's staff about a proposed examination, it was reported that the commission insisted that the existing registers contained some CPA's and that even a new examination would bring the disabled veterans to the top of the register. Aronson's view was that if the college degree were required it would weed out a good proportion of these veterans, and a thorough, written examination would make it very difficult for second- and third-rate veterans to qualify even with their ten-point advantage. The bureau decided to use the old register, and no new examination was called for by the time this study ended. But Aronson's prediction about the difficulties in using the old register were fulfilled. Recruitment of auditors lagged way behind the auditing tasks. Moreover, great difficulty resulted in many cases because of the ineptness of the auditors in dealing with touchy state and local officials and the professional social workers. As late as the spring of 1937, the field auditing staff was twelve million public assistance payments behind its job, and new payments were increasing faster than they could be audited by the staff of auditors then in service. The difficulty was almost entirely a matter of the quantity and quality of the auditing staff, a difficulty that the old auditor registers made almost inescapable.

By October 4, 1937, over six months after this study was concluded, the Civil Service Commission had registers for the four grades of administrative officer and for informational representative. By that time there had been six persons appointed from these registers. That is the sum total of effective results from competitive examinations under the civil service system developed especially for the Social Security Board during the first two years of its existence.

We may close this account of recruitment by noting the use made by the board of the junior civil service examiner register. This was the register built on a college graduate requirement and a written test which was in effect a liberal arts, general culture examination. It was usable for appointments to positions paying $1,620. About 269 people were taken from this list by the board during the period studied. Although the examination had been held in 1934, the director of personnel urged the extensive use of the register, taking from it a large number of people for his own division. He felt that even though the most brilliant people had been picked off, the remaining list contained very intelligent people who would be good material for future administrators and technicians. Early in the fall of 1936, when it still appeared that the board might have to conduct the registration job with its own staff, 100 persons from this register were employed as assistants and clerks for the field offices of the Bureau of Old Age Benefits. In January 1937, the board authorized the selection of 125 more to act as assistant personnel clerks in the field, positions which later developed into general assistants in field offices.

Since these people were likely to become the field office administrators of the future, the training they received on the job and the personnel policy pursued with regard to their transfer and promotion would seem to be of great importance.[39]

NONSTATUS EMPLOYEES

The lack of an intial congressional appropriation when the board was organized aggravated a problem of personnel common to many new agencies: the employment by the board of a group of people without civil service status. As has been related, the board inherited the remnants of the staff of the Committee on Economic Security, which had been recruited without regard to civil service regulations. It also borrowed heavily from the NRA and a few other federal agencies operating outside the merit system, to staff its expanding activities while it was subsisting upon its WPA grant. One of the first bits of advice given the board by the Civil Service Commission representative detailed to it in November 1935 was to stop hiring such nonstatus people. He pointed out that while a few of them might qualify as experts, the rest would either have to obtain status by passing competitive examinations called by the board or some other agency, or the board would have to obtain a presidential order exempting the nonstatus group from the usual competitive requirements. The board's immediate response was limited to a resolution, adopted November 1, 1935, to "request no more transfers from NRA to the board."

Not until late in January did the board take action pointing toward a solution of this problem, when it secured an agreement with the Civil Service Commission under which the sixty-seven nonstatus employees could be retained until June 30, 1936. In the meantime, the board agreed to replace these people as rapidly as possible with permanent employees possessed of the requisite civil service qualifications. The commission also wanted the board to agree to dismiss a fixed quota each month until the entire group was "liquidated," but Bane had objected to a plan which seemed so arbitrary.

At the end of February 1936, the head of the Bureau of Business Management reported to the board that none of these nonstatus employees had been dismissed. It was clear by this time that chances were slight that any of them would qualify through competitive examinations requested by the board, because the bureau heads were making no effective moves to set up such

[39] A later study made by the Bureau of Old Age and Survivors' Insurance (formerly Old Age Benefits) which compared the efficiency reports of this group and another group of men trained in insurance shows an outstandingly better performance by the civil service examiner group.

examinations. Pressure from a union local chartered by the American Federation of Government Employees, which some of these employees had joined, was exerted on the board to induce it to request a presidential order for a noncompetitive examination for this group. After much delay the board, which became increasingly reluctant to lose the services of these people, many of whom were among its most experienced and competent employees (although largely in the lower brackets), asked for such an executive order. The board sounded out the Civil Service Commission to discover if that agency would regard such a move as a violation of the board's January agreement. The commission indicated that it would not so regard the move, although it was opposed to the action as a matter of principle. When the order was requested in June 1936, it was referred to the Bureau of the Budget first, but that agency, which had faced a similar problem within its own organization not long before and had dismissed its nonstatus employees, refused to approve the order.

In July, the board returned to the Civil Service Commission for a supplementary agreement under which it promised to dismiss, within thirty days after the commission should certify eligibles for their jobs, those employees who had not yet qualified in competitive status or as experts. This certification occurred around July 15. Thus most of the nonstatus people left the board's service about August 15, 1936.

IN-SERVICE TRAINING

While members of the board and the executive director early recognized the need to plan for in-service training for newly recruited staff, the actual inauguration of this program was linked with the establishment of regional offices. Although the head of the Bureau of Research and Statistics, Walton Hamilton, was nominally responsible, the first training program was chiefly the work of the Field Organization Committee which had designed the regional and field office scheme. This was doubtless related to the fact that the most urgent need for organized training came when the board decided to recruit its office managers for the regional offices from the old staff of the Bureau of Foreign and Domestic Commerce, via the disbanded NRA. This first training course began on March 16, 1936, and was projected for an intensive two-week period. But when the period ended, the board continued the training, partly because two weeks did not seem sufficient, and also because it had decided that these men should not be sent out until the regional directors had been selected.

This initial training program consisted of a first week of background lectures, dealing with European social insurance experience, American social developments, and the functions of the line bureaus; a second week concerned with the Social Security Act and administrative plans to carry it out; a third week of round table discussions, reading, and class projects; and after that, assignment for temporary duty to the various bureaus or special committees (such as the one preparing a field manual). In this first training program, not only were many members of the board's staff used as instructors, but Dr. Evaline Burns of Columbia University, J. P. Harris of the Committee on Public Administration, and Professor E. D. Baake of Yale were also brought in. The works of Dr. Burns, Paul Douglas (both critical of the Social Security Act), and I. N. Rubinow were included in the basic reading.

The formal instruction consisted of two lectures daily followed by either open forum meetings or quizzes, the latter being conducted by some of the younger staff members. The administrator of the course later complained that many of the lecturers failed to follow the outline the training committee had prepared, and that two of them (bureau heads scheduled to lecture on the policies of their respective bureaus) were very poor instructors. As a justification, they said that until the board's policies were more fully developed they could not tell what their own policies would be. During the third week of round table discussions each trainee was assigned three projects: (1) to prepare a 15-minute radio talk on social security; (2) to write two 500-word book reviews; and (3) to prepare a 2,000-word memorandum dealing with the procedure to be used in organizing the work of the regional offices. Teams of trainees also visited the bureau directors, to whom they propounded questions for discussion.

This first course gave rise to conflict among the board and its staff which affected the second training program, begun on April 20, 1936, and designed for the regional directors. The theory incorporated in the first school reflected the intellectual outlook of Hamilton, Winant, and Altmeyer and was concerned with specific training set in as wide a background as possible. This meant considerable divergence in the views of outside consultants and of members of the board's own staff. This approach assumed a teaching staff of high quality and relied for loyal staff service upon the natural development of a disposition by employees to align themselves in defense of the purposes and policies of the organization for which they work.

But the other view, which to some extent colored the two-week training program for regional directors and which was espoused by Colonel McCormack, chairman of the Field Organization Committee, held that new personnel should be indoctrinated with the crystalized policies of the organization. Training should be for a concrete purpose with only such background material as was essential. It should not deal with the various philosophies of social security or with controversial matters which were likely to unsettle the trainees. The training function of the board, as thus conceived, was like that of the private insurance company in the training of its salesmen. As a consequence, Drs. Burns and Baake were not asked to participate in the second training program, though Winant disapproved of their exclusion when he later learned of it.

While this second view remained subordinate in the basic training program, with the exception noted above, it was dominant in the supplementary technical training program developed by the Bureau of Old Age Benefits (where McCormack became increasingly influential), which began to operate in May 1936. The bureau's course was planned by R. H. Blanchard, a professor of insurance at Columbia University, who designed a three-week basic training program and a six-week technical training program, but the board cut these to a total of four weeks.

Although the board, on June 5, 1936, resolved to transfer the entire training job to the personnel division, this was not carried out until February 1937. In the meantime, the Bureau of Research and Statistics continued to give the basic training course, while the Bureau of Old Age Benefits continued its technical courses.[40] A full-time instructor, Lennig Sweet, with a YMCA college experience was employed to direct the basic course, and all the newly recruited professional and administrative personnel were required to take it (after October 13, 1936). Field auditors had been exempted because the head of the Bureau of Accounts and Audits believed that on-the-job training under experienced auditors was the only way to train these men. But the board became convinced that some of the conflicts between the auditors and the field staff of the Bureau of Public Assistance could be avoided if the auditors were better informed about the relation of their work to the line bureaus and the general functions of the board. Consequently a series of short, regional office institutes was projected for the auditors, and the first institute was held in the Boston office late in January 1937.

Considerable dissatisfaction over the conduct of the training courses developed among the staff, so that in late January 1937 the board asked John Corson to investigate and recommend such changes as seemed desirable. Corson reported on February 6 that the division of responsibility for in-service training work had produced rivalry and duplication of effort, and that as then conducted the courses made an inordinate demand upon the time of the operating and service bureau staffs. He therefore proposed to consolidate all training in the Bureau of Business Management, coordinate with its Division of Personnel, change head instructors, and to use a full-time instructional staff of eight, plus clerical help. The budget proposed for this work would be nearly $43,000 a year.

The board approved Corson's recommendations despite the protests of the

---

[40] B. E. Wyatt was in charge of a half-dozen instructors trained in insurance until Seidemann took over the bureau, when he was replaced by Dr. Schurz.

Bureau of Research and Statistics, which the board refused to hear. The results of these changes could not be appraised in the short time before this study was concluded.[41]

Despite complaints over the conduct of these in-service training courses, they were a very significant administrative activity. The program was deliberately conceived as essential to developing quickly a general comprehension of function and policy, as well as to developing the more specific administrative competences needed by the continuously expanding staff, central and field. The lectures and discussions were on a high level; even the most critical trainees admitted great profit from the courses. One of the younger members of the staff, who was on the job very early and in a most favorable situation for learning the drift of events, declared that whereas it had taken him two months to acquire on his own the minimum of background information on social security, the basic training course later provided this in two weeks' time.

CONFLICTS BETWEEN PERSONNEL DIRECTOR AND OTHER UNITS IN THE ORGANIZATION

It is probable that the delay in choosing a director of personnel had created insuperable obstacles to the effective use of that officer. The board had by that time developed the habit of making personnel appointments itself; it is therefore not surprising that it should have regarded the director of personnel primarily as a technician whose chief job was to use every device possible to secure the appointment of people already determined upon by the board and the bureau directors. Most of the heads of the bureaus had never worked in an organization where there had been an operating personnel director. Therefore, it was rather difficult for the personnel director to quickly secure their acceptance of the more constructive functions of which his office was capable. Moreover, because the bureau heads were in many cases already committed to a particular candidate, they tended to resent further investigation by the personnel office which might demonstrate that the candidate was weak or that there were others available for appointment who were superior. Likewise, the director of personnel was frequently blamed for decisions by the Civil Service Commission adverse to the bureau chief's requests, or for civil service regulations which impeded the hiring of particular candidates. We have already

---

[41] Later it was reported that the effort to omit the administrators and staff technicians from the instructional job was not successful. After a short interval of reliance on full-time instructors unencumbered by administrative responsibilities, the training program again resorted to those members of the staff who were dealing with administrative and technical problems.

indicated the divergences of view between the director of personnel and some of the bureau heads over the question of holding competitive examinations for professional and administrative positions.

One of the devices Aronson developed to help the bureaus meet their greater work loads, while not antagonizing them by running counter to their demands for particular persons, was the detail section in his division. This was a pool of capable people, in the lower grades, set up under Aronson for use in the various bureaus on their request. The administrative heads soon became anxious to retain the services of these competent people.

However, a special conflict developed early in 1936 between the personnel officer and the coordinator, who was at that time taking an active interest in the organization of the Bureau of Old Age Benefits. To what extent the coordinator's discontent arose from personal disappointment over the rejection of his candidates for the highest posts in the Bureau of Business Management, within which the Division of Personnel was lodged, is a question that cannot be answered definitely. It seems probable that friction developed because of some early cases in which the personnel officer discovered information about nominees proposed by the coordinator which led to their rejection. The fact, however, is clear that within less than a month after the appointment of the director of personnel, the coordinator was complaining vociferously about the procedure for making appointments. It was the coordinator's view that at that particular stage in the board's history, the personnel officer should not conduct his own investigation of nominees but should accept without further question the people proposed by the bureau heads. We have already told about the memo which he sent to the board, early in April 1936, demanding the appointment of additional classifiers and of the refutation of these allegations which Bane presented.

When Seidemann was head of the Bureau of Old Age Benefits and allied himself with McCormack and Miles, the resentment of this group against the director of personnel soon led to such hostility that Miles began a move for his dismissal. One constant source of friction was a basic disagreement over the most desirable type of personnel to be recruited for the bureau. Mc-Cormack was a self-made man who distrusted higher education and theory. He had good connections on the Hill and a strong sympathy for candidates recommended from that quarter. Aronson believed that young people trained in the social sciences and with high general intelligence were the best kind of material for the new agency, and as the story of plans for recruitment by competition has shown, he constantly sought to persuade the operating bureaus to adopt his standards. It was almost inevitable that McCormack, Seidemann, Miles, and their associates should come to ardently dislike this kind of personnel officer. Perhaps the fact that Altmeyer, Winant, and most of the bureau heads, all of whom seemed to find places for their acquaintances, had so frequently blocked Miles in his efforts to respond to his political associates made him turn on Aronson as a scapegoat. At any rate, it was particularly convenient for such a purpose that Aronson was a Jew, and that a good many Jews had been appointed to the board's staff. This led to a whispering campaign that the board was particularly hospitable to "Israelites." This red herring produced, in the winter of 1936–37, a great deal of talk on the Hill. Another accusation which became gossip among congressmen was that Aronson had hired a lot of "Hoover" men. This doubtless referred to the ex-foreign-and-domestic-commerce staff which had been taken on by the board when it was contemplating opening up field offices, first because the President requested it, second because these men had civil service status, and third bcause they knew government routines. As a matter of fact most of these men had come directly from the original New Deal agency, the NRA.

More serious in its political repercussions was the charge that Aronson had been responsible for hiring a number of young radicals discharged from the FBI by J. Edgar Hoover. This story was said to have been spread by persons working in the board's organization. Miles brought the issue up before the board at three meetings in December 1936 and moved that Aronson be dismissed. Although Miles could not obtain a second for his motion, the affair was brought out into the open during the troubles before the Senate Appropriations Committee in February 1937. At that time, both Senator Byrnes and Chairman Glass repeated the gossip, saying that J. Edgar Hoover had told them that the board had hired a group of twelve radicals whom Hoover had fired. The facts were that seven men were employed by the board after they had participated in certain union activities in the FBI, which activities had culminated in the hanging of Mr. Hoover in effigy. Nevertheless, none of the seven men had been discharged by the FBI, although three of them had been asked to resign and their resignations had been accepted without prejudice. When the director of personnel investigated these applications, he found that the persons involved had good efficiency ratings, in most cases having been promoted within the year preceding their employment by the board. Their employment records, which were certified by the chief clerk of the Federal Bureau of Investigation, indicated that they were all eligible for transfer or reinstatement.

The personnel director's practice of investigating the background and record of all prospective employees so irritated the Bureau of Old Age Benefits group that in the fall of 1936, Seidemann made persistent efforts to set up a permanent, independent personnel division in that bureau. The last formal attempt to do this occurred on November 12, 1936, when he submitted a memo to Bane asking that all recommendations for appointments to the staff of the bureau should go directly to the executive director and then to the board, without reference to the personnel division. In his own bureau, he proposed that personnel recommendations be the work of a committee within the director's office. This request did not go through to the board, although its members were aware of it and Winant and Altmeyer were opposed to it. Bane replied to it on November 14, pointing out the incompatibility between the proposed procedure and the organization policy of the board, and noting that on three prior occasions similar requests had been made and refused. Bane also asserted that the personnel division had done a prompt and effective job. "It had recruited in a relatively short space of time an exceptionally capable staff and, as you know, upon occasions has saved us from making some serious mistakes in recruitment." He further pointed to the achievements in connection with the Baltimore record office, where, he said, the large recruitment program "is well in advance of your stated needs." Despite the rejection of this formal procedure by which the Bureau of Old Age Benefits might escape the scrutiny of the personnel division, its own special committee continued to function. An effort was also made to set up a separate classification unit instead of using the classifiers of the personnel division.

These conflicts inside the board's organization contributed indirectly to the decision which was made, late in 1937, to remove the director of personnel in order to appease Congress and to place him in a newly created position in the organization in charge of an activity which was expected to assume considerable importance. It would be impossible to say that congressional pressure was solely responsible for that action. It was argued also that he was usually behind in his work, perhaps because it took him so long to discuss and analyze problems needing decision. And he was also regarded as very unskillful in dealing with congressmen. But his basic faults, so far as some congressmen were concerned, were that he was honest, disinterested, and competent in his knowledge of personnel and his devotion to the merit system.[42]

Perhaps some of these difficulties were inevitable so long as the personnel office was a subdivision of the Bureau of Business Management, which was formally on a par with all of the other bureaus. Had Aronson's division been an integral part of the Executive Director's Office, the action of the personnel chief might have carried the prestige of the executive director. Since his function was in considerable part a negative one, so far as policy was concerned, grievances were bound to arise in the minds of other bureau people. These might have been shorter lived if it had been clear that they were based upon action taken within the Executive Director's Office. Again, the function of classifying positions is, along with budget making, one of the most important administrative management devices exercised by the chief executive. This job was formally allocated to the Personnel Division, but actually classification

---

[42] This summation of Aronson's qualities as personnel officer is based on a statement made by Bane to McKinley in January 1937, and recorded by McKinley at that time.

work was split between the Personnel Division, the Executive Director's Office, and the board. To fulfill this duty was a ticklish task, because it involved fundamental decisions relating to the organizational plans of the several bureaus. The classifier had to be guided by his own understanding of each job and the relation of that job to the total organization. It was thus a task which was very likely to displease both the operating bureau and the Civil Service Commission, for each regarded the classifier as the creature of the other. In this matter the most important difficulties doubtless occurred in the Bureau of Old Age Benefits. There, in the winter of 1936–37, the scramble for power among the various personalities and divisions led each unit to desire a hand in the field organization function. There was marked disagreement over the relationship of field officers to the headquarters divisions. There was also disagreement over the relationship of Roger Evans to the chief of the bureau and to the board. The job of the classifier from the Personnel Division was almost incapable of performance unless the Executive Director's Office could easily step in and settle these organizational issues.

PUBLICITY ACTIVITIES,
THE BUREAU OF INFORMATIONAL SERVICE

Until Louis Resnick began work with the board about the first of January 1936, as director of the informational service, no systematic attention was given to securing favorable publicity or to general public education. During these early months, Chairman Winant used a personal assistant to read press clippings and keep him informed about important publicity items. An administrative assistant performed a similar task for Bane, the executive director. The other board members lacked even such limited aid in following publicity about social security.

Winant experienced the consequences of bad publicity at the very beginning of his association with the board. At the convention of the American Federation of Labor in October 1935, he had made a speech about the International Labor Office and, in response to a request from the floor, included some brief remarks about the Social Security Board. The newspapers reported that Winant had said that the social security program was being held up because Comptroller General McCarl was refusing funds for the board even though a WPA project had been set up in the Labor Department. What he had actually said was that the project was then on McCarl's desk, and the board expected the funds to be available shortly.

During these early winter months of 1935, the board received relatively little notice in the press; much more material was printed about the Townsend Plan than about the Social Security Act. The board very seldom received newspaper men and such publicity as it attempted to get was handled by Max Stern of the Scripps-Howard organization and, to a lesser extent, by Louis Stark, the highly competent labor reporter in the *New York Times* Washington bureau. The board's extreme caution about trying to spike misinterpretations of fact is illustrated by its failure to counteract the misrepresentations of accounting and supply companies which, all through this period, were advertising their accounting and office records systems as necessary to furnish the information required by the Social Security Board.

This attitude is illustrated also by an editorial in the November 1935 issue of the *Iron Age* which stated that the old age benefits provision of the Social Security Act would cost much more than private insurance. The editorial was sent to the board by a member of Congress, who asked for an answer. Altmeyer drafted a reply, but Winant was not satisfied with it. Frase was asked to draft a revision, but Altmeyer thought his language was too strong. The matter was shuttled back and forth between Altmeyer and Frase for more than a month, with the result that no reply was ever sent to the congressman.

The need to educate the public was keenly sensed by Winant and probably by the other board members. It was referred to very frequently in conversations with McKinley, but it was difficult to secure the right man for the publicity job and to obtain from the Civil Service Commission a rating high enough to permit the payment of a salary sufficient to attract a good man. As late as December 1935, the board was still trying to obtain Max Stern, but Stern's employer was very reluctant to let him go. The board, unwilling to take a second or third choice, was patiently attempting to give Stern time to fulfill his obligations to his employers. As it turned out, his final refusal brought to naught weeks of negotiation.

After Stern declined, the board tried to attract Louis Stark, who also declined. It was largely through the suggestions of these two men, particularly Stark, that Resnick was discovered and offered the place. Louis Resnick had been publicity director for the New York Regional Plan, for the Russell Sage Foundation, and for other welfare organizations in New York City. This specialized kind of publicity work was preceded by long experience in newspaper work. Resnick accepted the position on the assumption that it would pay $8,000, which turned out to be very difficult to get because of the classification problem. Even that high salary meant a sacrifice of $2,000 in his annual remuneration, but he accepted it because of his desire to work with Winant and his attraction to the pioneer opportunity to take part in the social security program.

The European administrative experts who were in Washington during the early winter of 1935–36, Davison, Miss Foster, and Tixier, all insisted on the need for a well-organized campaign of public education which would tell the American people about the social security program and their rights and opportunities under it. Davison had spent some months in the Midwest, and he commented upon the appalling ignorance he had found there concerning the provisions of the Social Security Act. Miss Foster had been one of the original corps of lecturers organized in 1911 by the British government to prepare the way for the administration of the health insurance system. These advisors, therefore, reinforced the intention of the board to launch a comprehensive and effective educational program.

Shortly after Resnick had agreed to become publicity director, he learned that the Treasury Department intended to issue, on December 31, 1935, its instructions to all employers subject to taxes under Title IX (for encouraging the passage of state unemployment compensation acts). He felt that the announcement of this important new tax on industry ought to be accompanied by a press story from the board which would, to some extent, offset the bad taste of another tax by explaining the benefits anticipated under the social security program. He communicated this feeling to Winant, who asked him to prepare a statement for publication on Tuesday, December 31, which would set forth the work of the board up to that date and sketch the social benefits to flow from the act. Resnick suggested that this release be given out at a special press conference to be called by the board on the afternoon of December 30. But this conference was never held, and the statement was never issued. The newspapers of December 31 and January 1 carried the stories of the imposition of the new taxes, without any adequate statement of the social purposes which these taxes would serve. The board failed to begin its publicity at this important time because of a meeting scheduled at four o'clock on December 30 with the Civil Service Commission for the purpose of securing Resnick's appointment. It seemed impossible to Winant for the board to hold a press conference an hour before the Civil Service Commission should agree to the appointment of the board's publicity director. On this account the affair was canceled.

Immediately on assuming his duties, Resnick prepared a confidential outline of policy and procedure for the Informational Service. This stated that the main task of the bureau was to inform "as wide an audience as possible concerning the purposes and provisions of the Social Security Act, concerning the functions and activities of the Social Security Board and concerning the broad subjects of social security in general." It pointed out that to achieve this objective it was important to facilitate, in every possible way, the efforts of the press to secure information. For this purpose, all inquiries from the press as well as from the other media of publicity such as radio stations, movie producers, and so forth, should be promptly referred to the Bureau of Informational Service. If, after the bureau had attempted to provide the information sought, the press still desired to see members of the board or the executive director, these officers should be ready to grant interviews. Appointments for interviews would be made by the Informational Service. No member of the staff other than the board members, the executive director, the coordinator, and the bureau directors should be allowed to discuss the Social Security Act or the affairs of the board except on instructions from their respective bureau heads. The memorandum warned the members of the board and the executive staff that while they should take every advantage of opportunities to interpret the activities and problems of the board to the press they should be very discreet in speaking "off the record." Whenever a direct quotation was intended for the press, it should be sent in manuscript form through the Informational Service Bureau.

Resnick promised that all manuscripts issued to the press by the Informational Service would be submitted in advance to the board member or staff member quoted, to the executive director, or to the director of the bureau most concerned. If none of these was available, he felt that the director of the Informational Service ought to be authorized to issue such material on behalf of the board at his discretion. Another task for the director was to clear up promptly all serious misstatements or misinterpretations. The board and staff were asked to call attention at once to such misstatements and to furnish the Informational Service with the proper facts. The bureau also asked to be promptly notified of all speaking engagements and out-of-town trips by members of the board and the executive staff so that it might secure widespread publication of their speeches.

Resnick was convinced from his experience with welfare activities that the public was woefully ignorant about social welfare work. He conceived it to be his task not only to explain the social security program as clearly and simply as possible, but also to go behind the act and present the official policies justifying the program. Explanations of the law and policy, however, would not be sufficient to stop deliberate or unconscious distortion of the program and the board's activities—a distortion which he felt was already well under way. These would have to be dealt with by special devices to meet each situation.

An example of such distortion occurred in the winter issue of a trade magazine called the *American*, in which appeared a large illustration of what purported to be the registration card used by the Social Security Board. This card showed a series of detailed questions of a very personal character, together with fingerprint reproductions. Under the cut, in rather small type, was the caption "Possible registration form." As a matter of fact, nothing of this sort had ever been considered by the board, and the cut was a deliberate attempt to convey a wrong impression of what registration would involve.[43]

In its endeavor to stop racketeering by some business concerns publishing bookkeeping and accounting forms and selling accounting equipment, the board at first pursued the policy of merely making an individual denial to the concern guilty of misrepresentation that their products were required or approved by the board. When employees wrote in asking if they would be required to give such and such information or when employers wrote to find out if they would have to have a certain kind of record, the board allowed specific replies to each inquiry. Except for a release of January 17, 1936, no general warning to the public about such activities was issued. However, about this time a letter was sent by Chairman Winant to the governors of all the states advising them that the board had not laid down any requirements as to forms for employers to keep.

The board's cautious policy in these matters was due to its feeling that a vigorous broadcast of denials would arouse antagonism. One of the frauds practiced by an employer against its employees is illustrated by a questionnaire circulated during December 1935 by the Ferris Tire and Rubber Company, introduced by a covering circular which read in part as follows:

The Federal government has recently passed a bill known as the Social Security Act which becomes a law effective January 1, 1936. This provides for an old age pension at the age of 65 provided the person is eligible and also for unemployment insurance.

The questionnaire attached is to be accurately filled in by every employee for government records. It is quite necessary, for instance, that age must be accurately stated. Any information that is given inaccurately might in many ways unqualify a worker to receive benefits to which he is entitled.

The labor union membership as you will notice is also included. This is supposed to be answered for government purposes only and does not mean that you must or must not belong to such organization.

These records are strictly confidential and are not open to other employees but only to the government officials and the management. It is necessary for every employee to fill out these blanks and return immediately so the records may be set up by January 1, 1936.

This was signed by the general manager. The questionnaire had a very large number of items, including questions relating to citizenship and years of residence in this country, marital status, home ownership, number of depend-

---

[43] It was the editor of this journal, F. P. Stockbridge, who wrote a series of articles for the March issues of the *Saturday Evening Post* entitled "Social Security, or De Levee Done Bust." These articles were an interesting farrago of fact and misrepresentation by innuendo. When they appeared Resnick asked Winant to prepare a reply, but Winant wanted to get Senator Wagner to write an answer and no answer was prepared.

ents, religion, physical defects, years of schooling, graduation from high school, number of years in normal school and college, relatives employed in the same plant, and union membership, all of which the board decided were outside its purview for purposes of registration. How many similar misrepresentations occurred no one knows.

Resnick's program for handling misstatements of fact and misinterpretations was not permitted systematic application. The board decided that the Bureau of Informational Service should avoid all controversy, even to the extent of ignoring attacks on itself and the act based on misinformation. It issued instructions that it was not to be drawn into political discussions of the Social Security Act, and no speakers were to be supplied by Resnick at political meetings. The board distinguished sharply between the dissemination of information and a publicity campaign, and instructed Resnick to confine his work to the former activity. So hypersensitive was the board to the possibility of political attack that the chairman, sometime in February 1936, requested that the word *Bureau* be dropped from all references to the Informational Service.

Both Resnick and his associate director, Robert Huse, were recruited by Winant, who had led them to believe that board members would always be accessible to them, and that they would also be able to sit in on board meetings. As it worked out, neither of them ever attended board meetings, and Bane told Resnick definitely in June 1936 that this would not be permissible under any circumstances. Resnick never made an issue of this question of attendance at board meetings, or even of the reluctance of the board to discuss public relations problems with him. This inaccessibility of the board was responsible in large measure for the shifting of actual control (at least in the form of a veto) over publicity from Resnick to the Office of the Executive Director. From the beginning, all press releases and publications were cleared through Bane, and when Corson came on as Bane's assistant, he took over this job. It was not until June 1936 that an arrangement was worked whereby the board's secretary, Miss Mulliner, was to inform the Informational Service of the approval or disapproval of state laws, plans, and quarterly grants.

Other bureau directors, especially in the operating bureaus where most of the news developed, also maintained an attitude of aloofness toward the Informational Service. They seemed to view it as an outpost of the enemy (newspapers and the public generally), and therefore the less the Informational Service knew, the less danger there would be of leaking confidential or potentially damaging material. It is true that there were very few leaks of this kind compared to some other government departments and agencies, and that the Social Security Board appeared very rarely in syndicated newspaper columns, but this probably would have been true under any arrangement because the nature of the board's functions was not particularly dramatic or sensational. Even with representatives detailed to the three operating bureaus, the Informational Service often knew nothing of a development until word was received to prepare a press release. The resulting statement was usually stereotyped in style and sometimes erroneous in content. Both the editorial staff and the clerks who ran the mimeograph machines and stuffed the envelopes for mailing often worked several nights a week because of these sudden emissions. In this way, the board and its executive staff were responsible for a great deal of confusion in the Informational Service and the fact that it always seemed to be operating on an emergency basis.

The board laid down few general policies for the Informational Service, and most of these were negative. Both Winant and Altmeyer were very disturbed by criticism in the press and were thus disposed toward a policy of caution. Even though Miles and Bane were friendly to a positive and vigorous educational program which would be bound to reap some opposition and criticism, the restrictive policy of the chairman and Altmeyer ruled. This attitude was reinforced by the caution of the general counsel and the chief of the Bureau of Old Age Benefits following the Supreme Court's invalidation of the Agricultural Adjustment Act early in 1936. Before that decision, Eliot had told Resnick not to worry about the bearing of publicity statements upon the issue of constitutionality; that the Supreme Court would not be fooled by publicity devices but would look to the language of the act itself. His change of mind resulted in instructions to the Informational Service to play down the use of such terms as *insurance* and not to allow, in any official reports or publicity material, the coupling of the tax titles (VIII and IX) with the two insurance titles (II and III) lest the Court take judicial notice when considering constitutionality of the act.

Statements of approved language were formulated by the general counsel when these matters were discussed, and any publication deviating from these stereotyped forms had to be submitted to him. Latimer was particularly cagey and cautious about publicity relating to old age benefits, not only because of anxiety about the constitutionality of the Social Security Act but also because he was soon to be called as a witness in the second railroad retirement case, pending in the federal courts. He wanted to avoid questions about statements he had authorized as chief of the Bureau of Old Age Benefits which might weaken the Railroad Retirement Act in the eyes of the judiciary. Thus, super-caution had to be exercised, and every public statement relating to these titles was checked and double-checked to see that the language used was sufficiently opaque.

As has been intimated, the approach of the November 1936 presidential election sent tremors through the board's publicity policy early in the spring of 1936. For the board was then determined to keep itself entirely outside the realm of political controversy. That was one reason why it consistently ignored the misrepresentations, some of which bordered on fraud, which were frequent in magazines. This also explains its refusal to adopt the affirmative policy advocated by Professor Witte against the Townsend Plan. The board felt it could not directly engage in any publicity activity criticizing that scheme. It therefore enlisted the aid of its friends. Among other activities it stimulated to this end was a study undertaken by the Committee on Economic Security of the Social Science Research Council. Frederick Dewhurst, director of that committee, was called into the board discussions and helped arrange both for a study and for its publication by the Twentieth Century Fund. It was hoped that this analysis of the Townsend proposals would be regarded as so authoritative and free from bias as to furnish a constant source of information for all those interested in combating the Townsend movement. But the appointment of the Bell Committee in the House in the spring of 1936 relieved the board of this problem.[44]

All through this period, the Bureau of Informational Service suffered from the reputation of being poorly organized. That this was probably a correct assessment was the fault, in large part, of the board itself, because it pressed Resnick to take into his organization so many of the political appointees with which the board allowed itself to be saddled. Had Resnick possessed the force of will that the heads of the bureaus of Public Assistance and Unemployment Compensation exhibited, he might have avoided this serious staff handicap. Resnick was essentially a newspaperman, without experience in directing the work of a large staff. Despite his admirable qualities as a human being and press technician, he found it very difficult not only to select capable division heads but to delegate authority so as to obtain clear-cut responsibility. His method of operation induced him to rely heavily on small personal staff, chiefly female stenographers and secretaries. These people naturally assumed extensive authority but they had no organizational responsibility.

There was no clear-cut division or delegation of responsibility between Resnick and his associate director, Robert Huse. Resnick expected Huse to do all sorts of odd jobs, such as interviewing prospective personnel, which he himself did not care to do. Huse was also expected to fill Resnick's shoes in his absence and handle the business and trade press, and yet Huse encountered constant difficulty in keeping informed of Resnick's activities. In June 1936 it was agreed that Huse was to supervise the educational (speakers), library, inquiry, and business information divisions, and Resnick the press, regional, visual education (movies), and publication divisions.

---

[44] The technique of stimulating publicity activity through friendly channels was also applied to the press. In a number of cases, news stories were inspired by the cooperation of friendly correspondents like Louis Stark, who was used most frequently, Max Stern, Zon, of the Federated Press, and Hodges of *Labor*.

Resnick divided the bureau into seven divisions as follows:

1. Industrial Relations worked with business associations, chambers of commerce, schools of commerce, and vocational groups (like accountants, personnel officers, etc.) which rendered special services to businessmen that might impinge on the social security functions.

2. The Educational Division looked after publicity for social workers, educators, ministers, physicians, women's clubs, etc. It was to organize and direct a speakers' bureau to appear before labor, fraternal, and other organizations, such as the American Legion and the League of Women Voters. This unit was intended to handle such moving picture work as the board might undertake, but the board set up a special committee on movies, headed by Douglas, a political aide to Miles.

3. The Editorial (or Press) Division prepared and edited statements and articles for newspapers and periodicals, and for the trade press in cooperation with the Industrial Relations Division. It would arrange press conferences and interviews and handle contacts with newspapers and magazines. It was also to assist in preparing scenarios and scripts in cooperation with other divisions. The division was handled by Resnick himself until the fall of 1936.

4. The Publications Division helped the board and the bureaus in the production of all printed and duplicated reports. It helped to originate and prepare suitable publications; to control the distribution of all board publications; to edit and copy manuscripts.

5. The Inquiry Division was one of the first units organized, and began with a backlog of 3,000 inquiries. It dealt with general letters of inquiry not requiring an answer from one of the other bureaus, prepared form letters for suitable use, and maintained an information service to answer phone calls.

6. The Library Division organized and maintained the board library.

7. The Regional Division supervised the regional informational representatives.

The fact that Resnick himself handled the Press Division contributed to the absorption of his time and attention with the newspapers at the expense of other media and the formulation of a long-range publicity program. A very large proportion of his time was spent in patiently explaining the provisions of the Social Security Act to newspaper correspondents, or in seeing and talking to them even if there was no news. His theory was that if he succeeded in building up a friendly personal relationship with the Washington correspondents they, in turn, would protect him and the board from unfriendly attacks as far as they could. But the board never gave him the slightest assistance in cultivating the good will of the press. Winant held only one press conference while he was chairman, and few newspaper correspondents got to see and talk with him. However, it can be said that on the whole Resnick succeeded in establishing a very friendly relationship with most correspondents, and that the board profited by it.

As has been indicated above, the division of functions in the Informational Service was on the basis of the publicity media and not in terms of the three specific programs: old age benefits, unemployment compensation, and public assistance. When analyzed from this latter point of view, it is apparent that the major emphasis was placed on explaining the act as a whole. Most of the speeches made by high officials and board members tried to cover all three fields, as did most of the earlier articles written by the board and its staff members. Next in importance was publicity for old age benefits, partly because the board was solely responsible for this activity and partly because of the necessity of very wide public understanding in order to insure the success of the registration undertaken in the late fall of 1936. Unemployment compensation probably was next in importance so far as board publicity was concerned, but there was relatively little assistance for publicity activity on the part of the states. Although more than one state agency requested it, the Informational Service never got around to assisting them in the preparation of a publicity program. The same was true of public assistance, but discussion in local newspapers was very extensive in some states because of the political importance of old age assistance in many sections of the country.

The board had a crucial interest in the work of the Internal Revenue Bureau which, in addition to collecting taxes under Titles VIII and IX, was to act as the board's agent in collecting from the taxpayers information essential to the posting of the individual accounts which the board kept for its future old age annuitants. Of course, it also had a deep underlying interest in the efficiency of tax collection, for upon them the financing of the whole enterprise depended.

Late in 1936, a representative of the Informational Service was rebuffed by Treasury officials when he suggested that the Treasury design a simplified circular setting forth briefly the taxing provisions and their relation, under Title IX, to the state taxes for unemployment compensation. It was the Treasury's view that it had always been successful in collecting taxes without special effort at public education, and there was no use getting excited over the collection of social security taxes.[45] Coupled with this attitude was a sharp demand by the Treasury that the board keep its hands off tax questions. Thus the overtures of the Informational Service came to naught. The field representatives of the board were instructed not to deal with questions of taxation when giving information to the public.

In the field the situation was not so simple. In some cases, the local collec-

---

[45] A circular of this type was finally issued by the Treasury and the board a year or two later, and proved to be in great demand by small business enterprises.

tors of internal revenue had in desperation turned to the field representatives of the board to assist them in dealing with tax inquiries, though this was done in informal ways. In other localities, the collectors took an even more nonchalant and independent view of the tax collection problem than did their Washington superiors. Late in February 1937, however, the Bureau of Internal Revenue became somewhat panicky about the scarcity of tax returns under Title VIII. It then came to the board to ask it to arrange for a broadcast by Commissioner Helvering. This was the first time the Bureau of Internal Revenue had ever made use of such a procedure, and it did not know how to make the necessary arrangements. A second broadcast was arranged for Deputy Commissioner Russell by the board's Informational Service.

It had been the belief of the board that the Treasury was tapping, with Social Security taxes, a whole new layer of tax payers. It therefore felt that it was essential to put out as much clear and simple information as possible in order to assure approximately full collection. But until the tax returns were revealed as astonishingly incomplete and deficient, thus threatening to throw the President's budget estimates completely out of line, the Treasury people were immovable. Despite the fact that the late burst of publicity improved tax collection, the information returns under Title VIII upon which the board had to depend for posting its accounts were so unsatisfactory for the first six-month period of 1937, that posting had not yet started early by January 1938.

While the board relied principally upon newspapers, special board publications, letters, and radio for publicity,[46] the most spectacular, and perhaps the

[46] A summary of publicity activity for the period January 1, 1936, to July 15, 1936, showed the following: for newspapers and magazines, 6,750 telephone inquiries were answered, 750 personal inquiries were handled, 94 press releases were issued, 183,250 copies of press releases were mailed, 42 special articles were prepared, 4 press conferences were arranged, and 500 special reports were prepared for individual newspapers, including review, criticism, and revision of a number of articles prepared by newspaper and magazine writers; for business groups, 2,611 letters were sent to individuals, firms, and organizations, 900 telephone inquiries were answered, 342 personal inquiries were handled, 175 letters were written replying to criticisms and correcting errors about the act, and 300 trade associations were contacted about the assignment of account numbers in connection with old age benefits; for the general public, 8,000 telephone inquiries were answered, 13,100 mail inquiries were answered, and 450 inquiries were received but not yet answered; for educational and professional groups, 30,000 were contacted through form letters, 75,000 pieces of printed material were sent—23,451 in response to requests, 291 contacts were made with conferences, and 51 conferences were held with national and state women's organizations.

In addition, 25 original documents were prepared; 117 manuscripts were edited and reviewed, including speeches, press releases, and articles; 77 manuscripts were prepared for multilithing; 5 publications were prepared for the Government Printing Office; 240,000 copies of publications were mailed; 20,000 mail requests were filled; 1,100 telephone requests were filled; and 1,500 personal requests filled.

most effective, publicity activity was the production of three motion picture trailers.

The educational service which these films performed contrasts strongly with the reluctance which the board showed about producing them. James Douglas, Miles's personal aide, was authorized to work on planning the films early in April 1936. Late that month he presented a report on costs and methods of using moving pictures for educating working people in the opportunities under the Social Security Act. He had worked out a tentative agreement with the March of Time to do the film without charge to the board, while giving the latter, thru a representative, a veto over any part of it. This particular proposal fell through because the Board insisted on its right to edit after the film had been completed, but the general plan was ultimately adopted with Pathé News as the commercial sponsor. The green light was given to Douglas, by the board, on August 1, 1936, after many weeks of delay. The first film, *We the People and Social Security,* was completed a couple of weeks before the election, and its use during the last few days of the campaign has been described in our account of old age benefits. Like the other two films which were completed later in the period covered by this study, it was of a general nature, explaining the provisions of the Social Security Act and not giving any specific instructions for registration. Nevertheless, its wide distribution during the employers' payroll-stuffing campaign must have helped greatly to fix a generally favorable concept of social security in the minds of the public.

Report cards were distributed to each theater owner who showed the board films—Douglas had great difficulty in persuading the board to spend money for this—and these proved very valuable indices of popular reaction. Probably no other form of publicity used produced as good an indication of actual results as did the films. The cards also furnished fairly complete figures on the number of people who saw the films. The first film was shown to 45,000,000 people by the middle of January 1937, a member which greatly exceeded the next most popular government film—one produced by the Federal Housing Administration that was viewed by 25,000,000 during eleven months. By the end of March 1937, about 145,000,000 people had seen the board's films, and the cost per person for each viewing averaged $.00054.

The theater chains refused to show the films, in order to pressure the Roosevelt administration into abandoning its antitrust action against them, then pending in St. Louis, and also as a counter-move against the Sirovich bill prohibiting block booking. Douglas sought the aid of Will Hays, of the Motion Picture Association, to overcome this opposition, but Hays disclaimed any control over the chains, while the movie chain representatives referred Douglas back to Hays. This opposition was somewhat neutralized by the fact that many people attended second-run theaters, where the social security films were shown.

At the close of our study, other films were being planned to explain unemployment compensation and old age benefits in the guise of a romance.[47]

THE PLANNING FUNCTION,
THE BUREAU OF
RESEARCH AND STATISTICS

From the very beginning, the board was fully conscious of the need to make special provision for planning. Altmeyer's original chart proposed to achieve this by the establishment of a division with the title of Research and Planning. He proposed to give it a generous list of duties which would include research on federal and state legislation in social insurance, federal-state relationships, actuarial studies, and state administrative problems. It was also to handle the regular statistical and general informational services.[48] The chairman's consciousness of the pioneer character of the board's enterprise in America made him particularly anxious to equip it with the best talent and advice to help it chart its course across the wilderness of social unknowns that lay ahead. He was therefore fully in harmony with Altmeyer's desire to create a separate bureau of research, detached from operating responsibilities, which could penetrate beneath the surface of everday experience, observe the economic and social trends significant for the functions performed by the board, and critically scrutinize the administrative process, federal and state, used to carry out the purposes of the law. With such objective information and guidance, the board could plan its work and propose modifications of policy so as to become both administratively and socially more effective. It is unreasonable to expect in the brief period of experience under review that important results could have been obtained from such a staff agency. Yet, administrators looking for the solution of pressing difficulties and concerned with the elaboration of a social program admittedly incomplete when the Social Security Act was adopted were likely to want speedy and tangible results from the research staff. When these were not forthcoming there developed considerable impatience and criticism of the Bureau of Research

[47] Late in 1937, films showing the procedure in applying for unemployment compensation benefits were produced for twelve states. These represented one of the first, if not the first, attempts by government to furnish popular instruction about the citizen's relationship to an administrative agency.

[48] The final organization plan allocated the actuarial studies and general information duties to other bureaus.

and Statistics, the unit expected to find the answers to policy planning questions.

The board's conception of the bureau's functions, expressed largely in the language of Walton Hamilton, its first director, was given in the budget justification sheets for April 1936. The introductory paragraph read:

This bureau has as its function the maintenance of a research and analytical service adequate for the efficient administration of the law, the outlining of policies, and the careful planning for future needs of the nation in the matter of social security. It will conduct regular and special investigations pursuant to its duty of "studying and making recommendations as to the most effective methods of providing economic security through social insurance, and as to legislation and matters of administrative policy concerning old-age pensions, unemployment compensation, accident compensation and related subjects." [49]

In private conversation, Hamilton made it clear that he believed the Social Security Board occupied a strategic position for pushing back the horizons of knowledge concerning the characteristics of the American economic system, and his primary interest in his employment by the board was to take advantage of that opportunity. Something of this conception was incorporated in his testimony before the House Subcommittee on Deficiency Appropriations in the spring of 1936, when he said that one of the three major phases of the bureau's work was

a forward look on the whole problem of social security. You ought to be able to know about what the burden is going to be in a certain particular year. If there is ahead of us something in the way of depressions or of hazards that tend to make for a heavy load in taking care of the unemployed people on relief, we ought to be able to foresee conditions as accurately as we can.

As bearing on future conditions, it seems to be almost inevitable that the Board should at least give some little attention to the future of our whole system; because the more people there are employed, the less the burden of unemployment is, the more there are in old age who are able to take care of themselves, the less the burden of dependency is. Therefore, a constructive note ought to run through the whole work of the Board.

The nature of the jobs to be undertaken in the pursuit of these large objectives was also set forth in detail in the budget estimate justification:

This service will be of several types:

A. In collaboration with the Coordinator and the Bureau of Business Management, this bureau is responsible for the preparation of schedules, and the operation of statistical reporting service, including the tabulation and analysis of the

---

[49] The subquotation is from section 702 of the Social Security Act and refers to one of the duties of the board.

statistics to be collected in accordance with the Board's direct requirements under Title II and its powers to require reports from the states under Titles I, III, IV, and V. The collection of these data requires the development of a statistical staff; furthermore, the bureau must make provisions for such periodic analysis of these data as will yield maximum guidance for the several operating units of the Social Security Board and the administrators of the several state systems.

B. Additional research projects centering about related economic and social conditions and trends will be necessary in order that new developments, whether in legislation or in administration, may be adapted to realistic American needs.

C. Problems which arise from time to time will call for studies appraising pertinent European and American experience in making adjustments to these problems.

D. One function of the Bureau is the fostering of cooperation in the stimulation and coordination of research activity among other public and private agencies, such as other Federal bureaus, state research and statistical bureaus, business organizations, universities and private research foundations. Such coordination will yield results which will be significant for the administration of the Social Security Act.

E. A large number of problems will arise regarding state unemployment compensation legislation and administration. Many of these problems will be interstate in character and most of them will require research on a larger scale than the states will be able to afford. Standards of administration will have to be developed for the guidance of the states, and these standards will constantly need to be evaluated in the light of experience. Actuarial studies embracing actuarial tables for the guidance of the several states in their social insurance programs.

F. Provision will have to be made for special studies in the field of old-age annuities. While a great many of the administrative and actuarial aspects of the annuity system will be cared for in the Bureau of Federal Old Age Benefits, those problems involving the relationships of this system to other phases of social security, and especially to the old age assistance system, will require study by the Bureau of Research and Statistics.

Among the specific studies which will be undertaken as soon as personnel can be obtained, are the following:

1. Study of the problem of migratory workers and of the administrative problems arising in interstate relationships in dealing with such workers.

2. Study of the methods of employment stabilization, with a view to the establishment of experience ratings for employers.

3. In the administration of unemployment compensation, there is a serious problem of seasonal unemployment. The extent and degree of seasonality in industry will require additional study and there is urgent need for a survey of the ways in which seasonal workers have, in the past, tided themselves over their period of unemployment.

4. Part-time employment exists in a considerable number of the industries covered by the Social Security Act, and an analysis of this problem needs to be made in order to determine administrative policies in dealing with part-time.

5. The problem of the older worker, both in employment and in unemployment, needs to be studied in order to discover the way in which these older workers are affected by social security legislation.

6. The elimination of agriculture itself, and of agricultural workers from many aspects of social security, presents an urgent problem requiring intensive study. There is need for surveys to determine the way in which social security could be applied to agriculture.

7. Collaboration with the Bureau of Public Assistance in conducting field surveys of state administration of the various public assistance laws. Such surveys will have to be undertaken immediately in order to guide the Board in the determination of grants to states as well as in formulating the policies for making these grants.

8. The economic and social problems involved in the collection of the funds for social security and in the handling of the financial reserves require attention by the Bureau of Research and Statistics.

These are only a few of the studies which require work on the part of the Bureau of Research and Statistics. Such studies require field research covering the country as a whole. It will be necessary, therefore, in addition to the economists, statisticians, actuaries, and other staff required in the home office, to have a field staff located in the various regional offices. Among the latter will be regional supervisors and assistant supervisors, as well as trained workers for actual service in collecting information.

The bureau was very late in getting organized, partly because of the difficulty in detaching Hamilton from his obligation to study consumer projects associated with the Department of Labor. Winant had been particularly anxious to obtain Hamilton as head of this unit, so he was willing to pay the price of delay. But even after Hamilton was employed, a well-rounded program of actual research projects was very slow in emerging, if indeed it ever emerged. During the period studied, Hamilton's initial job was to find good research people, and he gave a great deal of time to this task for months after his appointment. In the meantime, studies dealing with the mobility of labor, the effect and incidence of payroll taxes, labor standards in state unemployment compensation legislation, trade-union unemployment insurance and out-of-work benefit plans, actuarial factors in unemployment compensation, and employer account numbers were started. From the board members and from various parts of the organization came requests for many odd jobs, research and otherwise, which had to be done. In addition, it was necessary to supervise planning for the collection of statistics by the board and the state as a product of operations.

The immediate need to set up the machinery for obtaining adequate statistical data for planning the programs of old age benefits and unemployment compensation had been particularly stressed by Tixier in his advice to the board. That advice was not followed. But in the field of public assistance statistics, through the energy of Miss Helen Jeter, whom Hamilton placed in charge, an early start was made and the task was rapidly put under way. A close working relationship with the Bureau of Public Assistance was established, and by June 1936 the first monthly bulletin of Public Assistance Statistics was issued. In July, a quarterly review was published which gave a comprehensive summary for the first quarter of the calendar year. From that time forth, both monthly and quarterly summaries appeared regularly, increasing in promptness of issue and accuracy as the regional statisticians, first sent to the field in July, aided the states in their statistical work.

Comparable progress could not be expected in compiling unemployment compensation statistics, because the activity was entirely new and, until late in 1936, only a minority of states had such laws. Nevertheless, progress was even slower than had been anticipated, even though a member of the staff was assigned in April 1936 to handle this work, under the general supervision of Clague, the associate director, who was in charge of all the bureau's statistical work. On May 29, 1936, Wagenet and Hamilton submitted a joint memorandum to the board containing some suggestions for minimum statistics to be required of state unemployment compensation agencies. The board approved these requirements at that meeting, but nothing more was heard of the subject until March 2, 1937, nine months later. The reasons for this inaction are traceable to the Bureau of Unemployment Compensation, which had the power to enforce such requirements on the states. But it was not interested in doing so because it was occupied with more pressing administrative problems. It preferred to keep "frills" like statistics to a minimum, and the Bureau of Research and Statistics was not in a position to press the matter. Clague and his assistant became engrossed with other pressing statistical problems, particularly those of employer and employee account numbers and the information returns from the two federal taxes, through which it was hoped that valuable statistics on employment might be secured. Consequently the whole matter drifted until the winter of 1937, when a slightly revised set of minimum statistical requirements for state agencies was drawn up.

But the board was not ready to approve them. It merely directed that they be submitted to the conference of state unemployment compensation administrators which was to meet about the middle of March 1937. Thus the period covered by this study ended without action on this matter. Nor were the statistical requirements promulgated by December 1937, a month before twenty-two states were due to begin benefit payments. The planning of account numbers for employers and employees, to be used for administrative and statistical purposes, by the board, the Treasury Department, and the state unemployment compensation agencies, was closely related to the question of unemployment compensation statistics from state agencies. Because federal decisions on account numbers had to be made during the fiscal year 1937, they took precedence over the decisions on state unemployment compensation statistics. Account numbers were not entirely a statistical question, nor did the Bureau of Research and Statistics play as large a role here as did other units of the board and the Treasury Department. Nevertheless Clague, the associate director, was the board's principal staff representative in the interdepartmental consideration of this question.

An account number sounds like a rather simple matter on which a decision could easily be reached by experts and action taken with relative dispatch, but like so many other problems with which the board had to deal, the necessity of securing an agreement between various kinds of experts, state agencies, the Bureau of Internal Revenue, and other federal departments required an endless series of negotiations before definitive action could be taken.

The account number for employers in many ways presented a more complicated problem than that for employees, because it involved an effort to incorporate these numbers into a statistical industrial classification scheme. A committee was set up in the spring of 1936 to make recommendations on an employer number which would include an industrial classification. Meredith B. Givens, research director of the New York Division of Placement and Unemployment Insurance, was one of the committee's members. He had earlier secured a Works Progress Administration project to work out an industrial classification for his New York division, and work was virtually completed on the main outlines of that scheme by late spring.

On June 8, 1936, Clague, as chairman of a subcommittee of this Committee on Industrial Classification, submitted a proposal to the board that the employer number for each establishment covered by the federal old age benefits and unemployment compensation provisions of the Social Security Act should consist of seven digits: two digits for the industrial group and five digits, separated by a hyphen, for a serial number (e.g., 76-43210). An additional two digits to identify the state would be added by the board as part of its internal office procedure. The groups of industries and the number allotted to each were as follows:[50]

---

[50] It was significant that the first nationwide statistical information on employment which was to be made available from the information returns of employers under the federal old age benefits program, the federal tax under Title IX, and the state unemployment compensation systems would have many of the identical deficiencies of the employment statistics gathered under the English and German systems of unemployment insurance. The most important of these was that employment statistics were available solely by industries, and unemployment statistics both by industries and occupations. So far as we know, this failure of the two principal foreign systems to provide adequate statistics of employment was never discussed by the government statisticians in this country with a view toward setting up a better system.

Agriculture	0-09		Retail Trade	53-58
Mining and Quarrying	10-14		Finance	60-62
Construction	15-17		Insurance	63-64
Manufacturing	20-39		Real Estate	65-67
Transportation	40-45		Administrative offices	68-69
Communication	46-47		Service	70-79
Utilities	48-49		Professions	80-82
Wholesale Trade	50-52			

Although the board adopted, at its June 8 meeting, the employer account number system with its industrial classification digits recommended by Clague's subcommittee, this action met with vigorous opposition, particularly from Du Brul, of General Motors, who represented employers on the Committee of Industrial Classification. Du Brul argued that an industrial classification would be meaningless for a company, like his own, which manufactured a great variety of products, unless it applied on an establishment (plant) basis, and that would mean a great deal of extra labor for employers. As a result, Clague brought in a second report late in July which recommended the recision of the earlier action. Again the board followed his recommendation. But when news of this was brought by Clague to the government statisticians (Kuznets of the Bureau of Labor Statistics and Miss Joy of the Central Statistical Board) and those from the state unemployment compensation agencies, who were in attendance at the July 1936 meeting of the Conference of State Administrators in New Hampshire, they insisted that an industrial classification scheme should be retained in the board's number plan. Meredith Givens and George Bigge, of Rhode Island, warned that if the states were to set up in their numbering system an industrial classification data-collection plan for state unemployment compensation, the board's abandonment of that idea in favor of a simpler system would force the states to abandon their position on this matter. So Clague phoned Bane and secured agreement that the board would reconsider the question again on July 29.

The lack of comparable monthly employment and unemployment statistics has been keenly felt abroad, especially in carrying on the placement and vocational guidance functions. For those purposes, it is very important for each employment office to know whether or not employment is increasing in a particular occupation as well as in particular industries. This is even more necessary for vocational guidance, a public duty which the social security system will probably eventually serve. Children ought to be warned when statistical information over a significant period indicates that a particular occupation is being displaced, or encouraged when, contrariwise, the data of employment shows a constant increase in demand for a certain skill. Or if, as in both England and Germany, the American system should incorporate training of unemployed persons for new occupations, it will be necessary to know what the trends of particular occupations have been so as to direct the training program into useful channels.

At that meeting, Clague brought in another recommendation that the board revert to its decision of June 8. In support of this change he submitted the following brief:

1. An industrial classification of employers' reports was essential from the very beginning in order to meet the administrative and legislative needs of unemployment compensation and old-age benefits. Court tests, legislative amendments, and merit rating provisions of State unemployment compensation laws and the need of actuarial data made it necessary for both the State and Federal agencies administering social security legislation to have current reports on employment in various industries as soon as possible.

2. Inclusion of industrial classification in employer account numbers is essential if the Board is to have any information as to what industries are responsible for unemployment, seasonal occupations, and reciprocal fluctuations.

3. State unemployment compensation agencies are almost unanimously in favor of an employer account number which embodies an industrial classification, the representatives of the States of California, New York, Rhode Island, Alabama, Mississippi, and Oregon presented this viewpoint very forcibly at the New Hampshire Conference. New Hampshire has been for some time using an industrial classification in their employer account numbers and is convinced that this method is the soundest one for collecting employment statistics by industries. Furthermore, if unemployment compensation statistics are to be secured by industrial classification, it is essential that the industrial classification be put in the employer account number and made part of the administrative procedure of State unemployment compensation agencies in the very beginning, particularly in view of the fact that smaller states do not have the equipment to handle an industrial classification by means of an internal office procedure because they do not use punch card machines.

4. It appears that there is sufficient time to do the job of industrial classification now. New York has practically finished its work and New Hampshire could switch from its present scheme to the revised classification very easily. These two States alone have approximately one-half of the employees insured under State unemployment compensation laws at the present time. An analysis attached to the memorandum indicated the time which would be required for this work in other States.

5. Finally, an industrial classification in the employer account number is necessary in the administration of the old-age benefits program. It is very important for actuarial studies. Since it may be some time before all States have unemployment compensation laws, and a few States may never have them, the only nation-wide statistical data on employment would be made available through employers' reports under Title VIII. Since the first employer reports under Title VIII are not due until February, 1937, there is ample time for the assignment of an employer account number embodying an industrial classification prior to that date.

In the discussion of this memorandum Latimer agreed with Clague's new recommendation, even though he thought it would delay classification in some cases until 1937. Altmeyer was afraid that the use of an industrial classification in the employer account number would force the states to use punch card business machines, but Wagenet insisted that the state representatives at the Crawford Notch, New Hampshire Conference understood the nature of the problem and were in favor of the industrial classification number. Altmeyer's chief worry seemed to be that there was danger of controversy between the board and the states over the classification of employers, but Latimer pointed out that there were only a few states which would be making such a classification in 1936 and that the Bureau of Old Age Benefits would do it later for the entire country. It was further suggested that the Bureau of Research and Statistics should organize a "flying squadron" to see that the states carried out a uniform classification which would not conflict with the classification to be made by the Bureau of Old Age Benefits.

The board finally agreed to resume its position of June 8, with the understanding that it would assign all employer account numbers after February 1937, and that Wagenet, Latimer, and Clague would act as a committee to work out a plan of cooperation with the states so as to avoid controversy and misunderstanding in the classification of employers for the two programs.

Accordingly, on August 14 the board approved a request by Clague that a field squad of the Bureau of Research and Statistics be sent to Mississippi and Alabama to help those states assign the employer account numbers embodying industrial classifications. This would test the system and the feasibility of using board workers to assist the states in this work. The New York officials had already received permission from the board to proceed with the assignment of employer account numbers there.

On October 17, Clague suggested to the board that state unemployment compensation commissions be allowed to assign employer account numbers that would include a two-digit area code as well as an industrial classification. Several state unemployment compensation commissions indicated a strong desire to use this area designation. The board, at this meeting, formally decided that the employer account number used by state unemployment compensation commissions might be different than the number assigned by the board for federal old age benefit purposes. It suggested to the states that an employer account number be assigned to each establishment covered by the unemployment compensation provisions of the several state laws, which number should consist of seven digits: two digits indicating the major industrial group and five digits for use in identifying the particular establishment within the respective groups. In those states which desired to include an area code in the number, the board suggested the use of the third and fourth digits for that purpose, provided that this did not require the use of more than seven digits or result in the exclusion of the two digits indicating the major industrial group.

After this decision, the problem of cooperation between the board and the state unemployment compensation agencies in the use of board statistics took a different form. It centered around the legal right of the board to turn over to the states the information obtained during old age benefit registration from employers on form SS-4 and the duplicate copies of SS-5 and form OA-702, the office record card for employees registered for old age benefits. Both of these had been requested by the Conference of State Administrators. The board turned this problem over to the lawyers, because the information had been obtained under the sanctions of the Bureau of Internal Revenue for which the board had acted as agent. Not satisfied with its general counsel's favorable opinion, it wrote to the Secretary of the Treasury asking permission to make this information available to the states. Acting Secretary Magill replied in February 1937 agreeing that there was no legal reason why the information could not be given the states, but suggested that the board ask the Attorney General's opinion. So the board wrote the President requesting the Attorney General's opinion and on March 8 a favorable opinion was given the President. The principal legal question had been whether the disclosure of information on form SS-5 violated section 3167 of the Revised Statutes because the tax for which the form had been an instrument was technically an income tax, and the disclosure of income tax returns was prohibited.

Still somewhat fearful of objections that might be made by trade-union leaders to the disclosure of information about employees, the board agreed in March 1937, at the Conference of State Unemployment Compensation Administrators, to let the states have copies of SS-4 (the employer form) and the stubs of SS-5 forms (the account name and number of the employee) within two weeks. It also agreed to make available, soon after June 30, the other half of the office record card (form OA-702) which gave more detailed information for identifying the employee. Some further delay was encountered, however, because Remington Rand, Incorporated, with which the board had contracted for the reproductions of copies of SS-4, defied the rulings of the National Labor Relations Board in connection with a decision involving a dispute with a machinists union. While the board felt it could not break its own contract, it advised the states which were planning to employ the same company to make copies of SS-4 not to do so. The board, therefore, had to help the states find other methods of obtaining the information on the forms. At the close of this study it was considering two ways of doing this: (1) to have its sixty-four field offices which corresponded to the Internal Revenue district offices make photographic copies which the states might inspect; (2)

to furnish duplicates of the master punch cards from the Baltimore office to the states desiring to use them.

Chairman Winant believed that one of the major tasks of the Bureau of Research and Statistics would be the study of administrative problems, but he was not very clear how this would dovetail with the administrative planning functions he envisaged for the coordinator. Perhaps he expected it to concentrate on foreign experience and federal-state relations, but the justification sheets submitted with the April 1936 budget estimates gave a narrower purpose, listing (in paragraph E) as one service to be rendered to state unemployment compensation administrations "Standards of administration will have to be developed for the guidance of the States, and these standards will constantly need to be evaluated in the light of experience." Accordingly, a Division of Legislation and Administration was established, but it had a very small staff which did a variety of jobs for the operating bureaus. Its most important function was the preparation of a set of proposals on budgetary control of state agencies administering unemployment compensation and public assistance for the Committee on Control of State Expenditures.[51]

Late in June 1936, this function came in for discussion and some clarification as a result of a request from Miss Hoey for the employment of staff for her Special Studies Division in the Bureau of Public Assistance. That division was to be responsible for making administrative studies in the states. The board wanted the jurisdictions of this division and Hamilton's clarified, so the two bureau chiefs prepared a joint memorandum for the board in which they stated:

(1) The Special Studies Division of the Bureau of Public Assistance will make current investigations of the organization and administration practices and procedure of the States and Counties charged with administration of the several categories of public assistance. These investigations will be made to keep the Bureau of Public Assistance continually informed of the actual, localized operations of state plans in order that the Board may know that the states are following the standards laid down by the Social Security Act, conformance with which is a prerequisite for obtaining federal grants-in-aid.

It is expected that the Bureau of Research and Statistics will assist the Bureau of Public Assistance in planning these studies and drawing conclusions from the material collected. However, the recommendations for action in relation to the state plan or in relation to suggested changes in organization or administration will of course be made by the Bureau of Public Assistance.

(2) The Legislation and Administration Division in the Bureau of Research and Statistics will conduct long-time research regarding policies and practices in the administration of Federal and State social security laws; will study and

[51] For additional information about this committee's work see "The Process of Making Administrative grants to the states," chap. 5.

critically review (in the light of European experience) administration policies and procedures and legislative proposals developed by the Bureau of Public Assistance and the Bureau of Unemployment Compensation for suggestions to the states or for federal enactment; will conduct research in the field of comparative legislation regarding social security; and in general will carry on comparative studies involving not so much current operations as the bearing of past experiences and social and economic factors upon policies, plans and administration of social security laws. The conclusions of such studies will be utilized by the operating bureaus as a basis for suggesting changes in state laws and practices.

When this report was submitted, the board suggested that "European experience" be struck out in the fourth sentence in Hamilton's section 2 and "developing experience here and elsewhere" be substituted.

It should be noted, parenthetically, that the bureau was not equipped with personnel to make comparative studies of foreign administrative experience. Except for two foreigners occupying limited and rather obscure positions, no senior member was well enough equipped with thorough training in European legislation and administrative practice to be available for comments and recommendations when important administrative proposals were made by the bureaus of Old Age Benefits and Unemployment Compensation. With the above two exceptions, not a single member of the research staff had a sufficient mastery of French or German to be regularly used for such a purpose. Apparently the mastery of foreign languages was not considered important when the staff was selected. Thus, the administrative research functions of the Bureau of Research were restricted to advising the operating bureaus on their research enterprises and to "long-time" administrative research questions. Actually it did almost nothing of a long-time character, and such slight administrative research work as it did undertake was hardly distinguishable in kind from the operating bureau research. Whether the Bureau of Research was too remote from the stream of administrative experience or whether it lacked the personnel to become interested and effective in administrative studies is difficult to say. Some critics affirmed that both explanations were true. But it should be noticed that so far as the administrative problems growing out of unemployment insurance, placement, and public assistance are concerned, the Bureau of Research and Statistics was at least two and sometimes three removes. These problems were dealt with by state and local organizations, and therefore the contact of a separate research unit in the board's structure with the stream of administrative experience was bound to be a very loose and spasmodic one.

One thing is certain about administrative research activities, and that is that the bureau did not develop or use any staff person thoroughly conversant with European legislation and administrative practice in the field of social insurance for systematic critical scrutiny of proposals emanating from the bureaus of Old Age Benefits and Unemployment Compensation. Despite the chairman's interest in European experience, and despite the fact that the board financed a brief European trip in the late summer of 1936 for certain of its operating bureau heads, including an associate director of research, there seems to have been no pronounced feeling that it was important to employ full-time consultant specialists in European administrative experience.[52] Comparative administrative experience filtered into the board spasmodically and from outside consultants, most of whom were interested in matters other than administration.

If the Bureau of Research and Statistics was to perform the central planning function for the board, it would be expected that its chief opportunity to fulfill that role would be in the preparation of amendments to the Social Security Act. But in actual practice during this period its role was inconsequential. There were two active periods of amendment study and decision, one in the late spring of 1936 and the other in the fall and early winter of 1936. Because the character of the amendments in which the board was interested during the first period was limited largely to relatively small changes for administrative conveniences, and because the Bureau of Research and Statistics was then securing its initial staff, it was perhaps natural that it was not used.[53]

Late in September 1936 Bane revived the question of amendments, and a committee was appointed to prepare the board's annual report and to sift amendments suggested by the bureau heads. The committee actually confined its attention to the report, while Altmeyer became the motive force in the consideration of amendments and in the initiation of proposals involving new policy. In performing the studies required, Altmeyer's personal assistant, Wilbur J. Cohen, was as important as any member of the research staff. Clague was also used for this purpose, but the director of the bureau seems not to have figured either in the preparatory studies or in the many board and staff discussions that were held from early November 1936 into the middle of March 1937. The principal contribution of the bureau appears to have been made in connection with discussions to liberalize the provisions for paying old

[52] This hesitation may be partly explained by a feeling that Europeans do not understand American conditions, and by a reluctance to incite criticism by employing foreigners. Late in the spring of 1936, however, Arnold Steinbach, for ten years head of the Viennese Industrial Commission, was employed by the Bureau of Research and detailed to the Bureau of Unemployment Compensation. In the fall of 1936, Karl Pribram, author of the Austrian unemployment insurance law of 1920, was given a post of minor importance.

[53] The amendments were not acted upon by Congress largely because the board was so late in submitting them. The subcommittee of the Ways and Means Committee, to which they were referred after holding two hearings, refused to meet again because the end of the session was so near.

age benefits (Title II), but the staff members of the operating bureaus were just as important as sources of suggestion and were used freely in board discussions. The lawyers of the General Counsel's Office were probably more important, perhaps because of the issue of constitutionality which still hung like a cloud over the board's future. Statisticians from other agencies and university specialists in social insurance were also called in for advice. Thus, in the short run, high policy seems not to have been the special province of the Bureau of Research any more than (or in some respects as much as) it was of the operating bureaus or of the personal aides or friends of board members.[54]

[54] Because the second list of amendments also came to naught, there seems little point in telling the detailed story of their formulation, the negotiations with the Treasury over the differences between tips and wages, and the last-minute changes required when the President decided, late in the spring of 1937, to press for a balanced budget and thus threw out all amendments calling for increased expenditures. The defeat of all proposals was due to an unintended offense to the House Ways and Means Committee, when during hearings before the Senate Finance Committee, and Vandenburg's proposals relating to the elimination of the reserve for old age benefits and other phases of that part of the act, the board had agreed to the selection of an advisory council to be jointly appointed by the Senate committee and the board, to study these questions. Chairman Doughten was affronted that his committee had no part in selecting this advisory council; he put all the board's amendments in his desk and never showed them to the members of the House Ways and Means Committee during the session.

.8.

A FEW CONCLUSIONS

When McKinley finished his original summary of the first eight months of the board's history, he felt that the period had been too short to justify definitive conclusions about most of the larger questions of organization and administrative policy. The period had been largely one of planning rather than of operating activity. When Frase came to the end of March 1937, however, he too felt that not enough had been precipitated in the way of administrative results to allow more than tentative conclusions about most issues. Many of the actions taken and policies decided could be judged only in terms of their ultimate consequences, and these would not be forthcoming for a considerable period of time. Thus, it would have been sheer guesswork to state whether or not old age benefits would be paid promptly and economically through the system of wage records, Treasury collection of taxes and information, and field offices where claims would be filed. It would have been equally hazardous to assert that state unemployment compensation agencies would effectively handle their responsibilities since, except for one state, the payment of benefits would not begin until 1938. Were the public assistance staff, Bane, and the board correct in dealing with the states through a policy of persuasion, teaching, and friendly leadership, or were their critics in the FERA right when

Authors' note. This summary of observations was written in August 1941, four and one-half years after the end of our detailed observation. Because knowledge of subsequent developments within the board's organization and experience since the summer of 1937 was fragmentary and partial, an effort has been made to rule out of consciousness these wisps of information and to record judgments as of the end of the first year and one-half of the board's history. This is done with full consciousness that already some of these judgments might be wholly or partly invalidated by subsequent experience. But without reentering the board's situation and rechecking these conclusions upon the basis of a careful scrutiny of the current situation, we feel intellectually obligated to set down what we thought the facts warranted early in 1937.

they wanted to rely on federal standards vigorously enforced by sanctions, to supervise public assistance grants-in-aid? The amount of headway made in obtaining adequate state and local administration during this period was impossible to measure. It was clear that there was a long distance to go in eliminating politics and plain inefficiency, but whether any other policy offered a better highway with speedier transit to the goal could not be known.

Assured conclusions about most of the issues raised in the foregoing story must wait upon time. Therefore, most of the conclusions offered are either about secondary problems or are tentative in character.

By the end of March 1937, only one major administrative conclusion appeared clearly warranted: namely, that the board structure was inadequate for operating the social security program. Winant, Miles, and Bane were emphatic in their judgment that a board was unsuited to this task, and even Altmeyer joined in a formal board conclusion to that effect.[1] The authors had reached the same conclusion.

As we have already shown, the intention of the board to limit itself to policy and leave administrative direction to the executive director was not realized in practice. This plan was never instrumented either by a definition of the content of policy and administration or by a listing of the major tasks for which each would assume primary responsibility.

During the first eight months, it seemed possible that the board might find a good deal of its time occupied with the job of approving and rejecting state laws for unemployment compensation and public assistance grants. But that activity would come to an end once the states had constructed the statutory foundation for these functions. The approval of state administrative plans involved in the renewal of quarterly grants was, of course, basic to the state and local administrative process, and was undoubtedly a task that the bureaus of Public Assistance and Unemployment Compensation would primarily determine. It went to the heart of their administrative responsibilities and could not be separated from them.

There were, for the board, the possible quasi-judicial functions of holding hearings to determine whether or not state agencies had failed to administer their grants in accordance with the stipulations of the Social Security Act, and the consideration of evidence justifying such hearings. But that function of withdrawing approval of a state plan would only occur spasmodically, and indeed only one such case, that of North Carolina aid to the blind, took place during the first year and a half.

---

[1] Winant, in his post-election assignment, recommended to the President the board's elimination and a reallocation of its tasks. We are emphasizing this judgment because Altmeyer now in 1941 appears to believe that the board is a satisfactory organizational device, and that the difficulties of the earlier period have been exaggerated or were the result of either newness or unsuited personalities.

Nor did the board possess those quasi-judicial functions involving private interests which are characteristic of the multimembered regulatory agencies. Its relation with the states was, in the true sense of the term, a political one in which it served as the agent of the federal government to see that the state policies harmonized with the stipulations of the act. Nearly all the other federal grant-in-aid activities, including public roads, vocational education, employment offices, and public health services were vested either in the heads of operating bureaus or in the secretaries of the departments. While the administration of old age benefits involved the rights of individual citizens those rights consisted of claims for payments from the United States Treasury, provided the individuals had fulfilled certain requirements of the act. There were two other agencies with similar functions: the Veterans Bureau, headed by a single administrator, and the Railroad Retirement Board, which was regarded as a semigovernmental organization carrying out the policies of railroad employers and railway labor unions through a board dominated by representatives of these two interests. This does not deny the need of making provision for a tribunal to decide contested claims for old age benefits, but for that purpose the board had contemplated the erection of a tribunal within the bureau and would not itself have served that function.

If members of a board are employed on a full-time basis and they cannot find enough to do to keep reasonably occupied while considering policy problems, they will be inclined to look for something else. Decisions on policy matters did not and would not require the full-time services of the board. Because they were not lazy or uninterested or willing to submerge themselves in the work of speaking, writing, and studying long-range problems, they quite naturally became concerned with detailed administrative questions which, under the organizational format they had adopted, belonged to the executive director and the heads of the bureaus.

Even if the chairman and Altmeyer had been temperamentally able to live up to the self-denying ordinance the board had set for itself, it is probable that their sense of legal responsibility for the actions of the whole organization which the Social Security Act generated would not have permitted them or any other group of three full-time board members to keep consistently within the sphere of policy determination, granted the possibility of determining just what that sphere included. According to the statute, the board was liable for the expenditure of funds appropriated by Congress and would have to answer for the mistakes of its staff. A latent but pervasive awareness of this legal responsibility for administration would doubtless rest in the minds of most men placed on such a board, particularly if they were in earnest about the success of the act. To that force compelling them toward intervention in administrative details was added the pressure of politics. When the ordinary congressman asked for a favor or protested some real or alleged offensive act by a staff member, he was not likely to be satisfied when told that the board had restricted its sphere to policy-making, and that the executive director was responsibile for administration. It may be doubted if any board would dare fulfill this theory of administration by such an open declaration. Yet, unless free acknowledgment of the curtailment of its sphere of activity was made, congressmen would be bound to assume that the board was running the show and to bring pressure for their customary privileges. That is what happened, and thus it was that against the wishes of the bureau chiefs and the executive director, the board appointed a number of placemen even though it was difficult to find jobs which most of them could do.

As an administrative device for making policy decisions and directing operations during this period, the board system led to indecision, delay, and guerrilla warfare among certain of the top staff and their followers within the bureaus. The frequent and interminable board meetings during the first eight months particularly reflect the difficulty of three men reaching conclusions, even though those conclusions were often about small matters. A single administrator may carry within his own breast many conflicting desires and vacillating impulses; but he resolves these without the necessity of revealing the full extent of his uncertainty or confusion. But a three-man board undertaking such a function cannot escape the exhibition of conflict or vacillation in long discussions which threaten to become endless if the men are, as these men were, particularly sincere in their desire to launch successfully the administration of an agency charged with duties they regarded as of the highest public importance. Their concern to do the right thing, whether in deciding an issue fraught with potential political consequences or in picking the best man even for a subordinate but important job, was bound to prolong discussion. The more sensitive they were to the nuances of each situation, the more they felt the need to be certain of the judgment made, even if it meant postponement or reconsideration. The more each member knew about the people of the staff, or the technical jobs to be done, the more time required to make decisions on small points because each board member had an inner urge to match his knowledge of detail or technique against that of his administrators and technicians. This was partly the result also of the fact that there was no American experience, outside of private company systems, with the administration of old age benefits, and only slight experience in one state with unemployment compensation. Because Altmeyer had helped launch that pioneer state undertaking and had spent his mature life as a student and administrator of labor legislation, and because there were few people on the board's staff better informed than he, he was prone to match his judgment of details with that of the bureau chiefs and their technicians. These often had to be canvassed and recanvassed, in board meetings and out, before he was satisfied.

There were two other possibilities of board organization that might have avoided existing and potential difficulties. Both involved the abandonment of the distinction between policy and administration. The first would have been to parcel out the duties among the three members, making each responsible for the administration of one segment of the board's functions. Something like this had been done in the Railroad Retirement Board, and Latimer thought it worked very well. It had also been followed in the case of the TVA which was, however, experiencing widely publicized difficulty on that account during 1936–37. It is not clear what kind of tripartite division the board might have attempted with best hope of administrative success, and this system requires a great deal of mutual trust if action is to be expedited. Otherwise, nearly every question would have to be taken to the board as a whole, where discussion would greatly slow up decision. But if such trust is mutually accorded there arise difficulties that have dogged the path of the commission form of city government—a tacit conspiracy to refrain from scrutinizing the acts of each other resulting in no central responsibility for administrative behavior.

The second possibility presented more likelihood of success. That would have been an arrangement by which the chairman became the recognized administrative head of the organization, with the other members content to play minor roles. But that plan would need a peculiar combination of personalities which the original board did not have. None of the three, even though Winant was accorded first place, would have been content to submerge his views or sink his personality into the obscure busywork or handshaking or quiet observation implicit in such an arrangement. Each member was too able and determined a personality to allow that scheme to be tried. Moreover, for the chairman to integrate the administration in his own hands, that officer would require such clear superiority in administrative talents for the job that he could carry his board with him when he needed its support. Such obvious superiority of capacity did not, in the eyes of his fellows, cling to any single member of the first board.

One other observation about the board as an administrative device may be made here. During the closing weeks of this study Winant's resignation left the board with only two members. This gap was unfilled for some months because Latimer, whom the president had nominated, was not confirmed by the Senate. During this time, differences between the two remaining members threatened the board with stalemate on important questions. This check-and-balance system, with its concomitant delay or horse-trading agreement, was implicit in an incomplete board structure, as was the carrying of tales to the Hill by Miles when he became sufficiently vexed or disappointed to want to indulge in that form of pressure.

Our account of the executive director has shown there was an accretion of power in that office not only because of his position of command over the regional office organization but also because of the gravitation of functions from various bureaus into his hands. This last development seemed to be an indication of the faulty division of duties promulgated by the board in its last organization chart of December 4, 1935. Perhaps the mere designation of some of the service units as bureaus hampered a development which ought to have gone further in making the executive director a genuine general manager. Thus, it was difficult for Bane's office to take over some of the activities integrally related to his function as manager. For example, the personnel director was head of a subdivision within the Bureau of Business Management, the other duties of which related to furnishing supplies, equipment, and space. Yet, as the story of personnel has shown, it was perhaps the most important control tool of the board. It could have been exercised with more insight, and without the wear and tear of bureau opposition to a subordinate unit of a sister bureau, had it been under the immediate direction of Bane's office.

There are good grounds for doubting the organizational validity of the Bureau of Accounts and Audits. It might have been better had field auditing and constructive accounting been assigned to the bureaus of Public Assistance and Unemployment Compensation. These activities were so integrally related to the work of the last two bureaus that a very close tie was indicated. So far as concerns the preservation of the independence of the auditors from the spending of grant funds, it must be remembered that neither of these two bureaus spent the money in which the auditors were interested. Both bureaus were supervisory, checking agencies whose duties were quite compatible with the financial check inherent in the auditing function. The constructive accounting task was clearly of primary value as an aid to effective state administration of subsidized activities.[2]

Even publicity could have been handled more satisfactorily had the group in charge of publicity not been given the status of a bureau, thus causing it to compete with the other bureaus for attention from the board. It, too, might have performed the educational-publicity job better if it had been made a division of the Executive Director's Office, sharing the director's prestige with the other bureaus, and his access to the board. Some of its extraneous functions, added to obtain high salary classification, might have been given to other units.

In every large organization it is difficult to achieve a successful working relationship between operating administrative units and research activities. The board's experience was also not wholly satisfactory. Whether this was

[2] The needs for accounting service for the Washington staff could have been taken care of by an administrative services unit in the office of the executive director.

due primarily to faulty structure or to personality difficulties it is impossible to say. The fact that the director of the Bureau of Research and Statistics was the choice of the chairman and that the two other members increasingly distrusted his competence may be simply another unhappy manifestation of the board form of organization. Or the unsuccessful effort of the director to shift the active direction of the bureau to his associate, with the result that there was no continuous and informed supervision of much of the staff work, may have been an important factor in the relative ineffectiveness of this research agency.

But there were some basic organizational obstacles growing out of the separation of the bureau from many of the operating problems it was expected to help solve. The problem was all the more difficult because the bureaus of Public Assistance and Unemployment Compensation were themselves one full remove from the operating job, and in the case of the former, two removes from the counties and towns where much of the actual administrative work was taking place. The research unit was thus so physically remote from the scene of administrative activity that there was, as expressed by the assistant director, a continual fight with the operating bureaus to keep sufficiently informed on problems to be useful in helping solve them.

These questions were subject to a good deal of discussion among members of the staff. The most frequent suggestion for improvement was that the operating bureaus should incorporate the research function.[3] The stock argument against that proposal was that it would subordinate research on basic long-term needs to evanescent service jobs. Still, it might have prevented a situation in which the bureau assigned one of its staff to a study of the concept of social security in American history while neglecting to give anyone the job of analyzing the character of American unemployment, knowledge of which was so limited that the state unemployment compensation laws were all based on actuarial data assembled in a single state a number of years before.

Because organization and personality factors were peculiarly intertwined in the problems of research and planning, it is impossible, on the basis of the short period studied, to make definitive suggestions for better arrangements. We can conclude that the board did not make very effective use of the staff of its research agency, and that the fruits of basic or long-term research did not develop appreciably or ripen by the end of March 1937. The board itself

---

[3] It is interesting that in Germany and England there were no separate research units in the departments administering social insurance. These departments did have units for compiling statistics needed for operating and policy purposes, but other problems involving research were handled by administrators and technicians responsible to them.

pursued a defensive attitude toward questions of "high" social policy, keeping silent about the larger economic problems in which its functions were enmeshed. Such an attitude was not a favorable environment within which to pursue long-term research questions.

We put forth these alternative suggestions about bureau organization quite tentatively, because the length of our observation was not sufficient to permit the sifting of personality from organizational factors. Winant belonged to that school which believes that if an agency can employ capable staff, organizational arrangements are of small importance. He thought in terms of particular personalities. When personal conflicts developed he attributed them not to organizational, but to personal causes, for which the remedy was to hire "really good men." Had the suggestions listed above been tried, undoubtedly there would have been great difficulty in obtaining the salaries Winant and the other members felt were necessary to attract the people they wanted. The proliferation of bureaus was essential to provide the desired top salary classifications. The fiasco of the coordinator experiment still leaves uncertain the validity of such a position. Is there any place in a large administrative organization for a critic of administrative processes who is divorced from administrative responsibility and, at the same time, not accountable to the chief administrative officer? This hypothesis is too simply put to describe all that Seidemann advocated and Winant supported, until disillusioned, under the coordinator concept. For Seidemann made the coordinator a participant as well as critic. Acting as a czar ruling over procedures and forms thrust the coordinator into the mainstream of administrative responsibility. So did Seidemann's expectation of a special advisory status on the choice of personnel for second- and third-string positions. Even though the latter activity was temporary because peculiarly attached to Seidemann's personality, the other duties would have left the coordinator as both initiator and check on essential methods and devices for doing administrative work all over the organization. How hold him accountable unless he was to be made a member, as the board at last decided, of the executive director's office? Even had the position of coordinator been deliberately launched rather than generated as a way of getting out of a personnel jam, it is our feeling that the odds were heavily against its successful operation.

One other organization form may be questioned: the regional and field pattern which the board adopted. It was a combination designed to serve three operating programs, and it was not ideal for any one of them. Probably the operation of old age benefits, a federal program, would have profited by division into regions on an industrial basis grouped around central cities and without regard to state lines. But the other two programs worked through official state entities, and thus needed regions based on groups of states, though each may have profited from a different cluster. New York State, for example, was a region unto itself. Suitable as this may have been for old age benefits, it seemed highly questionable that a regional and managerial staff could be kept sufficiently busy working with a single state. There can be little doubt that the hurry to get regional executives chosen and offices opened up was wasteful, because there was almost nothing for the high-priced directors and their assistants to do for four or five months. The difficulties that developed between the directors and the field representatives of the bureaus may have been the inescapable consequences of a new enterprise for which there were no people sufficiently equipped to make an easy, clear demarcation of administrative relationships. While the growth of smooth-working organizational relationships was beginning to show in some of the regions as the study closed, there were still a number of uncertainties and a good deal of confusion and conflict in other regions, which promised to linger for some time. The board's regulations for the regional establishment were still subject to varying interpretations by bureaus and regional directors.

The personnel policy of the two dominant members of the board was, from the beginning, on a very high level. There can be no doubt that Winant and Altmeyer were eager to get the best possible men for as many positions as was feasible. This enlightened policy was extended to the establishment of an in-service training course for new employees in the spring of 1936 and a liberal attitude on promotions. In addition, a rather strong, if not completely consistent, resistance was offered to patronage pressure.

Yet a judgment on the board's personnel policy on June 30, 1937, when the total number of employees was over six thousand, would be less than frank if it did not point out that these good intentions and practices did not automatically produce superior results. There were many reasons for this, but among the most important was an excessive reliance upon the expert provision in the act. The board was not solely responsible for this; many of the bureau directors as well showed a marked preference for this channel of recruitment. But the board must be held responsible for the appointment of so many bureau directors and their chief assistants according to this provision. Plainly put, the board considered its judgment superior to the competitive civil service process, and it preferred to appoint people of whom it had personal knowledge and acquaintance, either directly or indirectly. Insecurity of tenure for experts did not bother the board—in fact, it seemed to prefer insecurity for bureau directors lest they become too contented and lethargic.

Morale is difficult to judge, but in our opinion it was definitely weakened in those bureaus having a large number of experts. During the summer of 1936, when Landon seemed to be a serious threat for the presidency, many of the experts were clearly apprehensive that they might be left out in the cold after November 3. It seemed to Frase that there was a definite slowing down of activity and postponement of positive action until the results of the election were known. Much more serious was the disagreement with Senator Glass which led to the rider in the 1938 appropriation act requiring Senate confirmation of lawyers and experts receiving more than five thousand dollars a year. It is impossible to judge the direct and indirect effects of this incident, which would never have arisen had the board appointed its chief officers through regular civil service channels. Certainly a great deal of time was lost by board members, the executive director, and the bureau directors in being "nice" to members of Congress. The board's amendments to the act were not pushed forward vigorously for fear of arousing antagonism on the Hill, and they were not even reported on by the House Ways and Means Committee. A number of additional patronage appointments were made to conciliate senators, and throughout the organization there was the feeling that it was being dragged into politics.

Two corollaries of this resort to the expert clause were the relatively minor use of transfer from other government agencies and the tardiness in setting up competitive examinations. Minor personnel were selected through transfer, but only the bureaus of Accounts and Audits and Business Management were headed by persons with civil service status transferred from other government departments.

Were the key people in the various bureaus who were selected primarily through the expert clause superior to those who might have been recruited by holding national civil service examinations? Such a question is rendered impossible of categorical answer because of the large number of undetermined variables in the situation. Most of the unassembled examinations for higher positions given by the Civil Service Commission had not been satisfactory, and it may have been that the board secured better personnel than could have been recruited in that manner. Aronson, the personnel officer of the board, inclined to that opinion. On the other hand, had the board determined to cooperate with the commission and to recruit its major personnel through civil service examinations, it is possible that the commission might have been willing to modify its policies on examinations to make them more adequate for the selection of high-level executive and technical employees. The board always gave the slowness of the examinations procedure as the reason for using the expert clause, but this does not explain why examinations were not announced in the spring of 1936 to supplement the employment of experts from the fall of 1936 onwards. The real reason for no examinations was the fear that once registers were set up, the board would no longer be able to secure commission approval of experts. Only one conclusion seems to stand out clearly: neither the customary recruitment methods of the commission nor the expert clause provided an adequate method for the recruitment of executive and technical personnel for a large agency undertaking a new and permanent governmental function.

For failure to use more fully the possibilities of recruiting personnel through transfer, the board alone must be held responsible. For the majority of its key positions the board selected people not in the federal service or with relatively little experience in government. In the first year no persons were transferred, for example, from the Bureau of Labor Statistics, the Central Statistical Board, the United States Employment Service, or the Children's Bureau—all reservoirs of experienced personnel. The result was that board action was delayed because the newcomers simply did not know elementary facts about government procedures and traditions, nor did they have the advantage of a large circle of acquaintances in official Washington.

It is clear that the administrative process operated within a political context that continually influenced it at many points. The relations between board administration and politics had at least four phases. First was the relation with Congress and particular congressmen. We make this distinction because the relation to Congress as a collective whole was less constant than that with congressmen acting in their own political interest. Perhaps a clear-cut distinction cannot be made; nevertheless, the constant bombardment of the board by individual congressmen asking for favors in appointments and location of field offices was not a collective activity reflecting the congress's interest. It was in no sense a politically responsible function, when a Democratic member of the House or Senate insisted on getting a job for a friend, or when he demanded that a field office be located in his home town. Even when a member of the Appropriations Committee made such demands, he did it not on behalf of a Democratic party program, but as a part of his own effort to maintain his personal strength in his district. Yet the board, like every other federal department, was subject to this particular pressure and, because it might need the friendly aid of some of the more important committee members, it was obliged to yield to this kind of political importunity. The centrifugal character of party politics as practiced in Congress required the board, as it has other agencies, to occasionally yield its administrative virtue lest it lose, at a critical juncture, its support for funds or essential statutory changes. Congressional procedure on such substantive matters is so intricate that lethal blows can often be dealt by a small group of ill-willed congressmen or, on occasion, by a single hostile solon. The board had no strong outside pressure group behind its work, nor did it have the close personal tie with the President that would guarantee his special guardianship in case of difficulties with Congress. We cannot, therefore, criticize the board because it conceded some of these demands for patronage and special favor. The principal criticism which we have felt warranted in making is that it weakened its defences by clinging too tenaciously and too long to the use of the expert clause. As a result, the snarl with Senator Glass which grew out of this situation created a further tangle in the location of the board's field offices. It is notorious that congressmen are particularly interested and influential in determining the location and staffing of federal field establishments. Scores of them came in person to urge the claims of their districts or their home towns, and some of them were allowed to argue their cases before the whole board. We have no statistical count of the number of deflections from original field location plans which these demands caused. Nor is there any way of qualitatively appraising the administrative disadvantages which may have resulted from such politically induced location and staff selections. But if time should demonstrate continuing administrative handicaps because of the locations accepted, it will be very difficult to remedy them because of the vested interests in their continuance which will develop in each locality.

Where the board dealt with Congress on legislative matters—in which congressmen had much less interest—it took a much firmer stand. With the support of the Bureau of the Budget which, in accordance with the procedure inaugurated by the Roosevelt administration, cleared each letter sent to the House Ways and Means Committee and the Senate Finance Committee, every bill introduced to amend the act which did not conform to the policies of the board was commented upon adversely, no matter whose bill it was. In most cases these amendments proposed the limitation or extension of coverage in ways which seemed clearly unwise. Senator Hayden, on the other hand, was given the fullest cooperation in working out an amendment to provide for the assumption of the entire burden of old age assistance toward Indians by the federal government, because the board felt that only this solution would eliminate discrimination against Indians by the western states. The board's cold shoulder to Senator Vandenburg's proposal to drastically reduce the size of the old age reserve account is of less significance, because this was a Republican proposal. On the whole, the board conducted itself well in opposing inadvisable amendments proposed in Congress, but it failed to push strongly enough for changes which it knew full well were desirable. Although there were extenuating circumstances in both years, the board cannot be entirely absolved from the responsibility for taking no action on proposed amendments in either the 1936 or the 1937 sessions of Congress. As indicated above, relations between Congress and an administrative agency are all of one piece, and action on amendments and appropriations cannot be divorced from patronage. Toward the end of the 1937 session it seemed that the board was beginning to feel that perhaps it had played the game too "straight"; that it should have made use of state officials in both public assistance and unemployment compensation to bring pressure on Congress for action on the amendments which it thought desirable.

The second phase of the board's political relationships was its contacts with the President. About them it is much more difficult to generalize because, for the most part, they were conducted in a way which kept them out of range of observation. There is very little documentary evidence of any kind because the results of such contacts were not put into memoranda or letters, and even indirect references to them in other documents are rare. While Winant (and later Altmeyer) occasionally saw the President they were, on the whole, very reluctant to discuss what had taken place in their meetings. Neither were such matters reported in the minutes of board meetings in anything but the briefest and most cryptic form.

Nevertheless, it can be said that the board was always eager to carry out the President's wishes, but was subject to relatively little control by him. The board was also very reluctant to go to the White House for favors. The request for an executive order to secure noncompetitive examinations for the board's original group of non-civil-service employees was debated for many months, and then submitted through the Budget Bureau without a direct appeal to the President. Space negotiations were carried out with the Interior Department through Undersecretary West and Secretary Ickes, with no direct appeal to the President, although Seidemann and others on the staff felt that this was the only way to secure adequate consideration of the board's needs. As far as the authors know, Winant's request that the President order the Post Office Department to cooperate in registration, his earlier request that the President urge O'Neil to accept the job as czar of registration, and Altmeyer's request in the spring of 1937 that a third member be appointed to the board, were the only occasions on which the board asked directly for anything from the White House. Except in the case of the Post Office Department, the board did not appeal to the President to resolve its conflicts with other departments and federal agencies.

On the other hand, the board did try to ascertain the President's views on important matters of policy. There were probably more instances of this than we discovered. Of course, routine matters like comments upon bills referred by the House and Senate committees were cleared through the budget bureau. But in the spring of 1936, Winant asked the President if he would agree to increase the federal share of aid to dependent children to one-half, and received an affirmative answer. During the last month of the presidential campaign of 1936, the President's views on the dates for starting the assignment of account numbers were asked and accepted. Positive action on the part of the White House was more rare. The one case known to the author was a notation by the President on a letter to him from the solicitor general in November 1936, suggesting quick action in amending the old age benefits and unemployment compensation provisions of the act in order to make them better able to stand a test of constitutionality. The President agreed to the solicitor general's suggestion and asked the board to work out and submit amendments shortly thereafter. As far as the Social Security Board was concerned, the President was "the Administration."

Relations with the Democratic party were much more amorphous. Miles did keep in touch with Farley's office and the Hill, but the extent and effect of these relationships were largely unknown to the authors. In connection with the approval of the Kentucky plan for old age assistance in July and August 1936, Farley called Miles, at the request of Governor Chandler, but asked the board to do whatever it saw fit. In that case the board postponed action until after the primary election, and Chandler's actions were neither approved nor censured.

The pre-election period was a special case. The board and the Social Security Act were attacked by the Republicans, and the board joined forces with both the Administration and the Democratic National Committee. But even in this case, the cooperation was not as active as that undertaken by other independent agencies. Joseph P. Kennedy, chairman of the Maritime Commission, for example, took the stump for the President. Winant resigned rather than become a partisan defender of the act, on the grounds that members of independent administrative boards should keep out of politics. If the testimony of one of his followers on the staff can be accepted, even Miles shared this point of view to some extent. Frase was told that Miles had promised Farley that he would make several political speeches in the last month of the campaign, but he declined to give them after Winant resigned, because he wanted to "keep the board out of politics." Nevertheless, the board and its staff did assist the Democratic National Committee and groups aligned with it—like the American Federation of Labor—to fight the Republicans.

These are the facts in so far as we know them; the conclusions can be stated very briefly. The board followed the President's direction as much as did any cabinet officer in matters of policy and administration. The President did not ask the same kind of political loyalty and active support from the board as he did from cabinet officers; neither did the Democratic party through the Democratic National Committee and its chairman. The board succeeded pretty well in keeping out of partisan politics and in convincing the public that it was nonpartisan. It was not commonly regarded in Washington as just another New Deal Agency.

The political aspects of the board's relations with the states in connection with unemployment compensation and public assistance could not be observed with any completeness. It was possible to follow the board's action in many cases, but the negotiations of the field staff, Frank Bane's ambassadorial visits to governors, and the configurations of the political terrain in each of the states were impossible to follow in detail, because of the lack of time. To get at the background in each case—particularly in old age assistance—would have required extensive field trips and interviews with governors and state officials. It is perhaps unfortunate that this aspect of social security administration was not captured and recorded in more detail, because any realistic appraisal of the system of grants-in-aid must be based on a wealth of information about the actual working out of the programs in each state.

Certainly, politics played a much more important role in the field of public assistance than in unemployment compensation. Perhaps the explanation for this difference is as follows. Public assistance, particularly old age assistance, is a relief function which involves cash grants to individuals at the discretion of state officials. The aggregate amounts granted total very large sums of money, of which the federal government supplies one-half or one-third. In most states there had been no permanent state department of public welfare before the depression of 1930–35, these functions being handled by each locality under general poor relief statutes. With the building up of large, temporary state relief organizations under the stimulus of federal grants from the Federal Emergency Relief Administration, governors and the dominant state political organizations naturally proceeded to fill the new jobs with political appointees. Although the great bulk of the money for their salaries came from the federal government, this was local rather than federal patronage. Such patronage greatly increased the power of governors sometimes at the expense of senators and congressmen. A large proportion of the public assistance plans approved by the board during its first year were temporary, based on emergency relief legislation. Naturally, the governors and state politicians hoped that their patronage would continue under the social security system. Was there not a parenthetical clause in each of the public assistance titles of the Social Security Act which removed "the selection, compensation, and tenure of office of personnel" from the board's control?

But they did not reckon with other provisions of the act which called for efficient administration or with the personnel of the board and its staff. During the entire period studied, the Bureau of Public Assistance, Frank Bane, and the board were engaged in a continuous process of persuading and coercing states to improve their administrative practices and raise their personnel standards. In some cases persuasion was relied upon entirely; in others the threat or implied threat of withholding grants was used. After its decision of July 30, 1936, the board was formally committed to the policy of insisting on minimum personnel standards. Other grants were made on the oral or written promise of governors and other officials that specific changes and improvements in administrative practices would be made, or objective personnel standards set up. Nevertheless, although a great deal was accomplished in the way of improved administration in some states by this mild coercion, the real "bad boys," such as the governors of Missouri, Ohio, Illinois, Kentucky, and Oklahoma, were not much impressed and continued their unregenerate ways. They were perfectly willing to make unlimited promises to get their quarterly grants, but they did not keep them.

It was not until after this study was terminated that the board began to crack down. Missouri was the first state of which the board intended to make an example, but the governor avoided the hearing demanded by the board through successive pleas for postponement, and finally through the passage of new legislation in June which embodied an administrative organization satisfactory to the board. To Illinois, then, fell the honor of being the first state hauled before the board for a hearing, on July 27, 1937. Its old age assistance grant was terminated until the board's demands for certain enumerated improvements in administrative practices were met. The attitude of Governor Horner and his administration toward this hearing was typical of that of other governors. He appeared to think the board had not the courage to suspend the grant—and was mightily surprised when it did.

It would, however, be unjustifiable to assume that there will be freedom from state politics in the future. The old age pension movement in the states may be expected to continue to be a political hot potato so long as many of the aged are insecure. The board and its staff will, therefore, be compelled to carry on their work with the states in an atmosphere of clashing political aspirations. To keep from becoming enmeshed in some of these conflicts will be impossible. The field staff and the board must have knowledge of the political topography of the states if they expect to steer a successful course. Undoubtedly negotiation, compromise, aversion of the eyes, and occasional cracking down will all be necessary administrative methods under certain circumstances, and a good administrator will have to be prepared to accept and apply them when the situation indicates. In this sense, politics and administration will have to march hand in hand.

In unemployment compensation there had not been enough experience to justify conclusions on the question of the board's relation to state politics. Future developments may throw this area into politics to an extent equal or greater than has happened with public assistance. The main features of unemployment insurance legislation have been political issues of the first magnitude in both England and Germany. But during 1936 there were only a few states with unemployment compensation laws, and of these a considerable number like Wisconsin, California, New York, and Massachusetts had state civil service laws and a background of effective administration of labor laws. In some of the other states, such as New Hampshire and Oregon, administration was in the hands of capable officials who apparently kept their offices free of serious political entanglements. The Bureau of Unemployment Compensation—and in one or two cases the board itself—had its wrangles with the states, but for the most part they were disputes about the amount of quarterly grants. In fact, during 1936, the Bureau of Unemployment Compensation set up practically no standards and requirements for administration aside from the control it exercised in making quarterly grants. Although the bureau secured the names of all persons employed by the state agencies, no direct pressure was brought to insure minimum personnel standards. Some states were given assistance in preparing examinations to be used for recruiting personnel for the unemployment compensation agencies on a merit basis.

With the passage of unemployment compensation laws in practically all the remaining states late in 1936 and early in 1937, the situation changed. Among these new states were many in which the tradition of political administration was strong. Having decided that the Social Security Act gave it the authority to prescribe personnel standards in order to insure proper administration of the state laws, the board went ahead with a rather ambitious scheme of assisting the states in setting up personnel systems, despite the opposition to this move expressed by several states at the conference of unemployment compensation administrators in Washington in March 1937. By the time this study closed, the work had not progressed far enough to indicate whether any considerable resistance would be encountered from state officials and politicians, but things seemed to be going surprisingly well.

It may be that for the first few years, at least, no serious conflicts will develop between the board and state officials and politicians over the administration of unemployment compensation. There are indications that a recognition exists in the states that unemployment compensation is a difficult and technical subject which requires capable personnel. Then too, the federal subsidies involved are confined to administrative expenses and are not grants to individuals. At any rate, this chapter in the board's history cannot be written for several years to come.

The board's administrative responsibilities did not interest pressure groups very greatly. When unemployment and old age benefits begin to be paid, it may be that labor unions and other groups will take a more active interest in social security administration. In European countries, trade unions and their affiliated political parties have been actively concerned with the administration of the social insurances. They have aided their members in dealing with public authorities and have made critical suggestions to the ranking officials in the headquarters of the social insurance institutions. It would seem probable that similar practices would grow up in the United States, but the social security program has not yet progressed to that stage. There is no doubt that this first board was sympathetic to labor and would have responded to any show of interest on the part of organized labor. Likewise, their leading staff members, including most of the regional directors, except perhaps those in the Bureau of Old Age Benefits, generally shared the board's orientation. Evidence of this disposition was indicated in the board's handling of the Remington Rand affair (described in the section on the employer account numbers) and on a number of other occasions. Thus, the board sought labor's opinion on the use of duplicate SS-5 forms by state unemployment compensation agencies and on the suggested use of an age code in the old age benefit account number, which it dropped when labor disfavor was manifested. It joined with the AFL and the CIO in combatting the payroll-stuffing attack on the Social Security Act during the 1936 campaign.

Employers' organizations, while given considerate attention and courteous treatment by the board, were not thought of as "one of the family." The United States Chamber of Commerce and the National Association of Manufacturers never approached the board directly to request changes or modifications in administrative policy or practice. In the spring of 1936, the board attempted to sound out employer opinion on registration through a questionnaire to trade association executives, but this resulted only in guarded and equivocal replies. Only through the subcommittee on social security of the Business Advisory Council of the Department of Commerce was the board able to get the advice and opinion of business on such problems as payroll reporting, industrial classification, and other technical matters of so much concern to employers. The Business Advisory Council served a very useful function in this regard, but the board could have profited by other such contacts with employers and employer groups had the latter shown friendly interest in the act. The Business Advisory Council members represented the point of view of the large employer with a large office and payroll staff and mechanized equipment, and the needs of the small employers were not presented to the board so adequately.

Employer groups probably were reluctant to have any dealings with the board because of the political feud then raging between them, the President, and the New Deal agencies. The only trade association which had direct dealings with the board in connection with the assignment of account numbers was the National Retail Dry Goods Association composed, in part, of the employers who made up the National Retail Federation, which had supported and defended the Social Security Act and other Administration measures designed to increase and stabilize the purchasing power of the lower income groups. This association requested the board to postpone the assignment of account numbers in department stores and other retail dry goods shops until after the Christmas season. The board, after hearing the case presented in person by their representatives, decided that it could not open the door to further requests for exceptional treatment by granting this request.

The American Bankers Association dealt with the board on a proposed amendment to the Social Security Act. The Bureau of Internal Revenue had ruled that national banks and all member banks of the Federal Reserve System were government instrumentalities and therefore exempt from taxation under Titles VIII and IX. The association, knowing that the board would ask for an amendment to the act covering all banks, offered its cooperation in drafting the amendment in order to get one of which it approved.

In all its relations with interest groups, the action of the board was determined more by its own judgment of what these groups might think or do than by actual pressure brought by the groups themselves. Since this is true of any administrative body, there would seem to be a distinct advantage in actually conferring with the groups, because the administrator's guess at their reactions may not be accurate, and conferences between the parties may lead to more satisfactory solutions of detailed technical points. Besides, the knowledge which the representatives of these groups can bring to the discussion of any problem is often valuable.[4]

The record of the board's relationships with lobbyists and interest groups reveals no sinister influences of any kind, nor any undue pressure. The relationship was in the nature of the best kind of cooperation in the public interest.

An outsider watching the administrative process of a great national agency like the Social Security Board must beware of lightly criticizing the men in administrative positions who must find and live with the administrative solutions they adopt for their tasks. It is relatively easy, after the fact, to note an error here and a missed opportunity there. But it must be clearly acknowledged that what looked like a mistake to an observer seeing only a part of the total situation was perhaps, in reality, the only choice which circumstances allowed. The administrator in our society is caught in a web of personal, organizational, and political relationships which limit what can actually be done. He is, moreover, burdened with a mass of daily detail that often obscures his vision even when he is disposed to take a long look ahead. Like Lemuel Gulliver, he finds himself held by a multitude of invisible Lilliputian bonds that often deprive him of much freedom of choice and action. The road to administrative righteousness may seem perfectly clear to the outsider, but the responsible administrative official may know that it is effectively blocked and that the only way around is by a long detour. These are the considerations that make us hesitate to reach any general appraisal of the board's work during its first eighteen months. Undoubtedly it made mistakes, but just as surely it avoided many which it might easily have made. It selected very

---

[4] This point may be illustrated by the example of Altmeyer's insistence upon employers issuing receipts to employees showing the amount of social security tax deducted from their wages each time they were paid. The Treasury Department very reluctantly agreed to make this mandatory (sec. 206 of Regulations 91). Altmeyer was under the impression that this receipt would be stamped onto the payroll envelopes or be noted on a special tear-off stub when payment was made by check. It developed later that the actual payment methods of employers were not as Altmeyer had thought, and this reqirement would force employers to revise their whole payroll procedure. (The Treasury later relaxed the rule and accepted ordinary checks as fulfilling this requirement.) Conferences with, say, the Comptrollers' Association of America, would have made this information available to the board and permitted the establishment of a procedure more adapted to current business practices.

able and sincere people for its leading staff posts, and it appointed a few of more modest talents or less earnest purpose. What in view of all the surrounding circumstances should the score have been? We do not know.

Certain unmistakable achievements of the period can be recorded: unemployment compensation laws were passed by all the states largely with the board's advice; public assistance plans were adopted by a majority of the states and services were inaugurated for multitudes of disadvantaged citizens; twenty-five million people were assigned account numbers for the beginning of a national system of old age annuities. How workable the state laws on unemployment compensation would prove to be, how adequate the systems of state administration of aid to the aged, the blind, and dependent children, and how complete and accurate the records for the payment of old age benefit claims, only the future would tell. Into that realm the authors had no friendly administrator offering them a confidential look.

LIST OF NAMES

1936 ORGANIZATIONAL CHART

INDEX

LIST OF NAMES

Ahern, Leonard W.   Staff member, Estimates Division, Bureau of the Budget.

Altmeyer, Arthur J.   Member, Social Security Board; Chairman after resignation of Winant. Former Second Assistant Secretary of Labor; Chairman Technical Advisory Board, Committee on Economic Security; Secretary, Wisconsin Industrial Commission.

Aronson, Albert.   Director of Personnel, Social Security Board. Former Assistant Director of Personnel, Farm Credit Administration.

Ashe, B. F.   Regional Director, Social Security Board, Birmingham. Former President, University of Miami.

Austin, Miss Mary.   Chief of Division of Field Service, Bureau of Public Assistance, Social Security Board. Came to board from NYC Welfare Council.

Bakke, E. Wight.   Consultant to Social Security Board on labor and educational matters; Professor, Economics Department, Yale University.

Bane, Frank.   Executive Director, Social Security Board. Former Director, American Public Welfare Association; Chief of Welfare Department, Knoxville, Tenn.; Public Administration Service specialist for state and local survey work; consultant on welfare administration to Brookings Institute of Public Administration.

Banning, Paul D.   Second Director of Social Security Board's Bureau of Accounts and Audits. Transferred from U.S. Treasury, where he headed Accounting Control Division.

Baruch, Ismar.   Chief of Classification Division, U.S. Civil Service Commission.

Bary, Miss Helen V.   Senior Technical Adviser in charge of Social Security Boards, Bureau of Public Assistance, until Miss Hoey was appointed early in January 1936. At first on loan to Board from NRA. Transferred to Field Division at San Francisco.

Batzell, Paul E.   Chief Constructive Accountant and Assistant Director, Bureau of Unemployment Compensation, Social Security Board.

Beach, Charles F.   Assistant Chief of Records of Division; later Chief of non-

mechanical section of Bureau of Old Age Benefits, Social Security
   Board.

Bell, Daniel W.   Acting Director, Bureau of the Budget. A long career in U.S.
   Treasury Department, including service as Commissioner of Accounts
   and Deposits and Assistant to the Secretary.

Bennett, James V.   Acting Business Manager, Social Security Board, during
   the first year serving in same capacity for Bureau of Prisons.

Blakeslee, Miss Ruth.   Specialist for problems of the blind, Bureau of Public
   Assistance, Social Security Board; Chief of Standards and Procedures
   Division. Came to Social Security Board from Federal Emergency
   Relief Administration and Works Progress Administration.

Bowers, Glenn. Administrator, New York State Unemployment Compensation
   Program.

Brown, Douglas.   Consultant to Social Security Board on labor questions; Professor of Economics, Princeton University.

Brown, M. L.   Representative of Governor Davey of Ohio, for Public Assistance
   Administration.

Buhler, Ernest O.   Assistant to Roger Evans in supervising registration job
   and establishing field offices for Bureau of Old Age Benefits. Came
   from Aetna Life Insurance Co.

Calhoun, Leonard J.   Assistant General Council, Social Security Board. Former
   member of legal staff, Department of Labor. Detailed during most
   of 1935 to Senate Finance Committee.

Cheek, Dr. Roma.   Executive Secretary, North Carolina Commission for the
   Blind.

Clague, Ewan.   Assistant Director, Bureau of Research and Statistics, Social
   Security Board; leader of staff study of Ohio public assistance diffi-
   culties. Former member of economics faculties at University of
   Washington and University of Wisconsin; on research staff of Yale
   Institute of Human Relations; Professor of Social Research at Uni-
   versity of Pennsylvania.

Clearman, Wilfred J.   Assistant Coordinator, on budget matters, Social Security
   Board. Former administrative officer, Export-Import bank.

Cliff, Frank B.   Accountant, General Electric Co. Lobbyist for unemployment
   compensation bills before state legislatures.

Cohen, Wilbur J.   Staff member, Committee on Economic Security; aided congressional committee and Thomas Eliot in drafting Social Security
   Act. An early employee of the Social Security Board, assigned to
   Bureau of Unemployment Compensation. Moved to Altmeyer's office
   when Altmeyer became chairman of the Board. Graduate training
   at the University of Wisconsin.

Collins, Maurice.   Assistant Commissioner of Accounts and Deposits, U.S.
   Treasury Department.

Copeland, Morris A.   Staff member, Central Statistical Board. Served on subcommittee on registration.

Corson, John.   Assistant to and later Assistant Executive Director of Social

Security Board; replaced Hodges as Chief of the Bureau of Old Age Benefits. Former member of economics faculty, University of Richmond; Director of National Recovery Administration for Virginia; Assistant Director, National Youth Administration.

Couper, Walter J. Technical staff member (Senior Industrial Economist), Bureau of Unemployment Compensation, Social Security Board. Transferred from Department of Labor.

Coy, Wayne. Collaborator with Donald Stone in special survey of the Board's organizational problems. State welfare administrator, Indiana, 1936–37; Assistant Federal Security Administrator, 1939–41; Special Assistant to the President, 1941.

Crowell, Benedict. Regional Director, Social Security Board, Cleveland. Distinguished military career during and after World War I.

Culp, C. A. Staff member, Committee on Social Security of the Social Science Research Council; Professor, specialist in unemployment compensation.

Davidson, Ronald. Retired official of British Ministry of Labor serving in administration of social insurances, especially for unemployment compensation. Part-time consultant to Social Security Board.

Dedrick, Calvert L. Assistant Chief Statistician, Bureau of Census. Served on interdepartmental committee concerned with statistical matters in the Social Security Board's work.

Deiken, Dr. Lobbyist for American Optometrists Society.

Dill, William L. Regional Director, Social Security Board, Philadelphia. Formerly a New Jersey state judge.

Douglas, James. Political aide to Vincent Miles; later Chief of Motion Picture Division of the Bureau of Informational Service. CCC camp official in Louisiana, 1934–35.

Dunne, T. Morris. Chairman, Industrial Accident Commission of Oregon. The Commission administered Oregon's Unemployment Compensation program.

Ehringhous, John C. B. Governor of North Carolina.

Eilenberger, Clinton B. Third Assistant Postmaster General; involved in registration job.

Eliot, Dr. Martha. Assistant Director, U.S. Children's Bureau, Department of Labor.

Eliot, Thomas W. General Counsel, Social Security Board. Chief draftsman of Social Security Act. Former Associate Solicitor, Department of Labor.

Ellis, Frank H. Assistant Superintendent, Division of Post Office Service, U.S. Post Office. Member joint committee concerned with registration.

Emerson, Thomas. Principal attorney, General Counsel's Office, Social Security Board. Formerly in similar position with National Labor Relations Board.

Evans, Roger. Temporary special supervisor of registration, Bureau of Old Age Benefits, 1936–37. Former Director of Industrial Bureau, Philadelphia Chamber of Commerce.

Fenn, Miss Kathryn D.   Technical Adviser and Associate Attorney, Bureau of
        Unemployment Compensation, Social Security Board. Formerly with
        Resettlement Administration.

Foster, Miss Ethel.   Retired British Civil Servant, Ministry of Labor. Expert
        in some aspects of health insurance and other social insurances.

Galvin, William.   Chairman, Social Security Board's field organization subcom-
        mittee on forms and procedures; Assistant Executive Director, attend-
        ing chiefly to field office methods.

Gellhorn, Walter.   Regional Attorney, Social Security Board, New York; Pro-
        fessor of Administrative Law, Columbia University Law School.

Gibbons, Stephen B.   Assistant Secretary of the Treasury.

Givens, Meredith B.   Part-time staff member of Social Security Board during
        late 1935, working on personnel matters; later, Research Director of
        New York's Division of Placement and Unemployment Insurance.
        Formerly on staff of National Recovery Administration and Social
        Science Research Council.

Glass, Carter.   U.S. Senator from Virginia; Chairman of Senate Appropriations
        Committee.

Gross, John E.   Regional representative, Bureau of Unemployment Compensa-
        tion, Denver. Former Secretary-Treasurer, Colorado State Federation
        of Labor.

Hamilton, Walton H.   Director of Bureau of Research and Statistics, Social
        Security Board. Former Professor of Economics, Amherst College;
        Director of the Graduate School of the Brookings Institution; mem-
        ber of the Yale Law School faculty.

Harper, Heber.   Regional Director, Social Security Board, Denver. University
        of Denver faculty in social science. Distinguished career as minister,
        teacher, civic worker in Denver; war service during World War I.

Harris, Ralph B.   Member of Social Security Board Field Organization Com-
        mittee. Became Associate Director of Bureau of Old Age Benefits
        under Seidemann. The Board's Supervisor of Training, 1936.

Harrison, Miss Gladys A.   Social Security Board Regional Attorney, Minne-
        apolis. Former attorney in the Department of Agriculture.

Hays, Will.   Acting Chief of Claims Division, Bureau of Old Age Benefits.

Hodges, LeRoy.   Succeeded Seidemann as Director of the Bureau of Old Age
        Benefits. An economist with career in Virginia government, federal
        service, and consulting work.

Hoey, Miss Jane M.   Director of Social Security Board's Bureau of Public
        Assistance. Came to Board from New York Welfare Council. Profes-
        sional social worker of long city and state experience in New York.

Hoff, Harry.   Consulting engineer employed by the Social Security Board for
        limited period to design methods for keeping records, and structures
        to house them.

Hohman, Miss Helen F.   Social Economist on staff of Bureau of Research and
        Statistics, Social Security Board.

Hopkins, Harry. Special Assistant to President Roosevelt; Administrator, Federal Emergency Relief Administration, Civil Works Administration, Works Progress Administration, etc. Member of Committee on Economic Security.

Howes, William W. First Assistant Postmaster General and from time to time Acting Postmaster General.

Hughes, Avon J. Director, Bureau of Accounts and Audits, Social Security Board; later, Associate Director. Formerly an investigator for the General Accounting Office.

Huse, Robert E. Associate Director, Bureau of Informational Service, Social Security Board. Former special adviser on industrial relations to Department of Labor.

Hutchinson, Mrs. Mary. Technical staff member, Bureau of Unemployment Compensation, Social Security Board. Formerly with San Francisco relief organization.

Jackson, Clarence A. Director, Indiana Unemployment Compensation Commission.

Jeter, Miss Helen. Chief of Public Assistance Statistics, Bureau of Research and Statistics, Social Security Board. Formerly with American Public Welfare Association.

Kimball, Arthur A. Grants Adviser in Division of Liaison on Compensation and Placement, Bureau of Unemployment Compensation, Social Security Board. Came to Board from National Recovery Administration.

LaDame, Miss Mary. Director of Federal-State Relations, U.S. Employment Service; special Employment Service representative of Department of Labor.

Latimer, Murray W. Director of Old Age Benefits until September 1937, Social Security Board, serving also as Chairman of the Railroad Retirement Board. Former economist and old age insurance expert for Industrial Relations Counselors, Inc., staff of Federal Coordinator of Transportation; member Technical Advisory Board, Committee on Economic Security.

Lenroot, Katherine L. Director, Children's Bureau, Department of Labor. Social worker with distinguished career in Wisconsin before going to Washington.

Lowrie, Kathleen J. Field Representative, Public Assistance Bureau, Social Security Board. A longtime social worker on staff of the American Association of Social Workers, New York City, before joining Social Security Board.

Lubin, Isidor. Director, Bureau of Labor Statistics.

Magill, Roswell. Under Secretary, U.S. Department of the Treasury.

Marshall, John. Unemployment Compensation Commissioner, Washington D.C.

May, Geoffrey. Associate Director, Bureau of Public Assistance, Social Security Board. Came to Board from the Family Service Society of Richmond, Virginia.

McCallister, Lambert. Attorney, Office of General Counsel, Social Security Board. Came to Social Security Board from NRA.

McCarthy, H. L. Regional Director, Social Security Board, Chicago. Former Dean of College of Commerce, De Paul University.

McChord, Miss Beth. Field Representative, Bureau of Public Assistance.

McCormack, Col. E. J. Special Assistant to the Social Security Board; member of field committee on organization planning, became chairman on resignation of Dr. Stead; transferred to Bureau of Old Age Benefits when Seidemann became Director, and became Associate Director.

McDonald, Francis J. Chief of Claims Division, Bureau of Old Age Benefits, Social Security Board.

McDonald, Edward. Regional Director, Social Security Board, Kansas City, Mo. Formerly worked for insurance and bond sales company in Oklahoma City; before that, head of State of Oklahoma Highway Department.

McReynolds, William Henry. Administrative Assistant to Secretary of the Treasury. Long career in federal government, first with the Bureau of Efficiency, where he became Assistant Chief, then as Director of Classification Board, as Assistant to Director of the Bureau of the Budget, and as Administrative Assistant to the Governor of the Farm Credit Administration.

Miles, Vincent. Member of Social Security Board, and lawyer in private practice. Political background in Arkansas. Former member of Democratic National Committee.

Mires, Frank. U.S. Treasury Department; Coordinator with Social Security Board.

Mitchell, William L. Succeeded Bennett as Director of Bureau of Business Management, Social Security Board. Former State of Georgia Director of the National Emergency Council.

Montgomery, Newton. U.S. Treasury, Bureau of Internal Revenue, Office of Chief Counsel. Chairman of Secretary's Committee on Social Security and contact man between the Treasury and the Social Security Board.

Mulliner, Miss Maurine. Secretary of the Social Security Board. Detailed from the Department of Labor as Assistant Technical Adviser. Detailed from Labor Department to Senator Wagner, 1933–36.

Murray, Merrill G. Associate Director, Bureau of Unemployment Compensation, Social Security Board. Former Acting Director, Federal-State Relations, Department of Labor; detailed to the Social Security Board.

Neustadt, Richard. Senior Technical Adviser to Social Security Board; later named Regional Director, Social Security Board, San Francisco. Former Managing Director of National Retail Code Authority.

Parker, Glowacki R. Regional Director, Social Security Board, Washington, D.C. Former Regional Director for NRA at Washington.

Pearson, John. Regional Director, Social Security Board, Boston. Former Managing Director of New Hampshire Foundation, Concord, N.H.

Peebles, James. Constructive Accountant, Bureau of Accounts and Audits, Social Security Board.

Persons, Frank W. Director of U.S. Employment Service, Department of Labor. Formerly Director of Enrollment of the Civilian Conservation Corps.

Powell, Oscar. Regional Director, Social Security Board, San Antonio, Texas. Attorney with many civic interests. Chairman, Central Relief Committee of San Antonio; Chairman, Texas Regional Labor Board.

Prettyman, E. Barrett. District of Columbia Corporation Counsel; Adviser to D.C. Unemployment Compensation Insurance Commissioner; Professor of Taxation, George Washington University; General Counsel, Bureau of Internal Revenue.

Pribram, Karl. Austrian expert on that country's social insurance system; Senior Statistician, Bureau of Research and Statistics.

Raushenbush, Paul A. Director, Wisconsin Unemployment Compensation Division of Wisconsin Industrial Commission.

Rector, Stanley. Technical staff member of Wisconsin Unemployment Compensation Division; on loan to Social Security Board as senior technical adviser.

Resnick, Louis. Director, Bureau of Informational Service, Social Security Board. Resigned as Director of Department of Public Information, Welfare Council, New York City, to accept Board post. Newspaper background.

Reticker, Miss Ruth. Industrial Economist, Bureau of Unemployment Compensation, Social Security Board.

Rice, Dr. Carl. Ophthalmologist, U.S. Public Health Service. Adviser to Social Security Board on medical problems of the blind.

Rice, Stuart A. Chairman, Central Statistical Board. Former Assistant Director, Bureau of the Census.

Roseman, Alvin. Technical Adviser, Bureau of Public Assistance, Social Security Board. Formerly Employment Technician, FERA.

Rosenberg, Anna. Regional Director, Social Security Board, New York. Former State of New York Director of NRA.

Saunders, Richardson. Department of Labor representative, Coordinating Committee of Social Security Board and Labor Department for the Employment Service and the Bureau of Unemployment Compensation.

Schoeneman, George J. Supervisor of Accounts and Collection, Bureau of Internal Revenue Service; member of subcommittee on registration.

Seidemann, Henry P. Coordinator, Social Security Board. Later Chief of Bureau of Old Age Benefits. Longtime member of Brookings Institute staff.

Sorrells, William C. Staff member of U.S. Civil Service Commission assigned to aid the Social Security Board in appointments and classification; general consultant in personnel procedures.

Stead, Dr. W. T. Associate Director and Executive Officer of U.S. Employment Service. For a time, Chairman of Social Security Board Committee on Field Organization.

Steinbach, Arnold. Staff member, Bureau of Research and Statistics, assigned to Bureau of Unemployment Compensation, Social Security Board. Former head of Industrial Commission, Vienna.

Stone, Donald. Director of Research, Public Administration Service; employed by Social Security Board (with Wayne Coy) to survey Board's organizational problems. Adviser on organization and accounting for CWA, WPA, TVA, and FERA, 1934–36.

Stutz, John G. Director, Kansas State Emergency Relief Committee.

Sweet, Lennig. Instructor in basic training course for new professional and administrative personnel of the Board, 1935–37. Former YMCA Director of Training in various U.S. cities and in China.

Tapping, Miss Amy P. Regional Representative, Bureau of Public Assistance, Social Security Board.

Tate, Jack B. Assistant General Counsel, Social Security Board. Former attorney for NRA.

Tindale, Keith T. Administrative Assistant to Executive Director Bane, Social Security Board. Former member of staff, American Public Welfare Association.

Tixier, Pierre. Expert in European social insurance programs. Loaned from staff of International Labor Office for consulting services to the Social Security Board.

Tucker, Leonard L. Senior Auditing Clerk, Bureau of Accounts and Audits, Social Security Board.

Utley, Clinton H. Superintendent, Division of Post Office Services; Post Office representative on joint committee working on Bureau of Old Age Benefits registration.

Wagenet, R. Gordon. Director, Bureau of Unemployment Compensation, Social Security Board. Formerly with U.S. Department of Labor.

Watt, Robert. Labor representative on Massachusetts Unemployment Compensation Commission.

Way, Elwood. Assistant Director, Bureau of Old Age Benefits, Social Security Board; Chief, Division of Records; Assistant Chief, Mechanical Section. Formerly with U.S. Treasury.

White, Carl C. Constructive Accountant, Bureau of Accounts and Audits, Social Security Board.

White, Leonard. Member U.S. Civil Service Commission, on leave from the University of Chicago Department of Political Science.

Wilcox, Fred M. Regional Director, Social Security Board, Minneapolis.

Wilder, R. U. Staff member, Bureau of Old Age Benefits, Social Security Board; member, Committee on Field Organization.

Williams, Edward B. Senior and principal attorney, General Counsel, Social Security Board. Formerly with NRA.

Williamson, William R. Chief Actuary, Bureau of Old Age Benefits, Social Security Board. Formerly with Travelers Insurance Co.

Winant, John G. Chairman, Social Security Board. Former member, Advisory Committee to Committee on Economic Security; Director of International Labor Office; twice, Republican Governor New Hampshire.

Witte, Edwin E. Part-time consultant to Social Security Board. Director of Committee on Economic Security; Chairman, Department of Economics, University of Wisconsin. Long career in public service for Wisconsin and as researcher for studies in state and federal industrial-economic problems.

Witte, Ernest F. Field representative, Bureau of Public Assistance, Social Security Board. Came to Board from directorship of Federal Emergency Relief Administration in Nebraska.

Woodrum, Clifton A. Congressman from Virginia, sixth district. Chairman of subcommittee of House Committee on Appropriations, which reviewed Social Security Board estimates.

Wyatt, Birchard D. Technical Adviser, instructor in charge of training in Old Age Benefits portion of original in-service training program. Came from Equitable Life Assurance Society, where he was group annuity specialist.

Young, Edgar B. Assistant to Director Persons of the U.S. Employment Service, 1933–34.

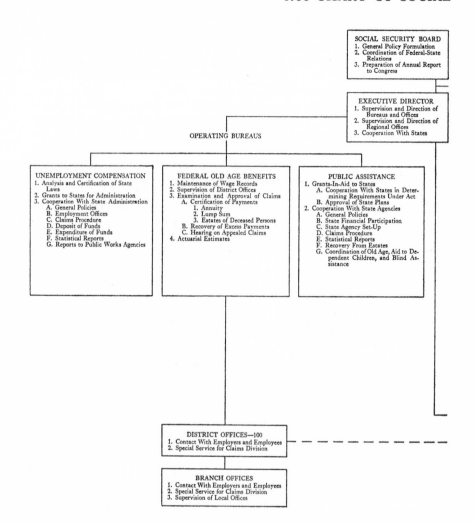

SOCIAL SECURITY BOARD
1. General Policy Formulation
2. Coordination of Federal-State Relations
3. Preparation of Annual Report to Congress

EXECUTIVE DIRECTOR
1. Supervision and Direction of Bureaus and Offices
2. Supervision and Direction of Regional Offices
3. Cooperation With States

OPERATING BUREAUS

UNEMPLOYMENT COMPENSATION
1. Analysis and Certification of State Laws
2. Grants to States for Administration
3. Cooperation With State Administration
   A. General Policies
   B. Employment Offices
   C. Claims Procedure
   D. Deposit of Funds
   E. Expenditure of Funds
   F. Statistical Reports
   G. Reports to Public Works Agencies

FEDERAL OLD AGE BENEFITS
1. Maintenance of Wage Records
2. Supervision of District Offices
3. Examination and Approval of Claims
   A. Certification of Payments
      1. Annuity
      2. Lump Sum
      3. Estates of Deceased Persons
   B. Recovery of Excess Payments
   C. Hearing on Appealed Claims
4. Actuarial Estimates

PUBLIC ASSISTANCE
1. Grants-In-Aid to States
   A. Cooperation With States in Determining Requirements Under Act
   B. Approval of State Plans
2. Cooperation With State Agencies
   A. General Policies
   B. State Financial Participation
   C. State Agency Set-Up
   D. Claims Procedure
   E. Statistical Reports
   F. Recovery From Estates
   G. Coordination of Old Age, Aid to Dependent Children, and Blind Assistance

DISTRICT OFFICES—100
1. Contact With Employers and Employees
2. Special Service for Claims Division

BRANCH OFFICES
1. Contact With Employers and Employees
2. Special Service for Claims Division
3. Supervision of Local Offices

504

SECURITY BOARD ORGANIZATION

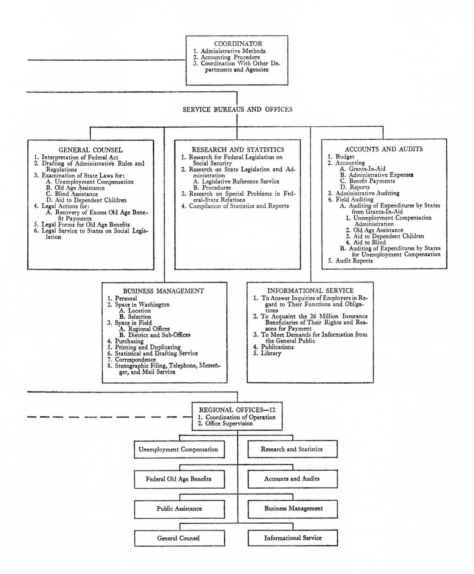

COORDINATOR
1. Administrative Methods
2. Accounting Procedure
3. Coordination With Other Departments and Agencies

SERVICE BUREAUS AND OFFICES

GENERAL COUNSEL
1. Interpretation of Federal Act
2. Drafting of Administrative Rules and Regulations
3. Examination of State Laws for:
   A. Unemployment Compensation
   B. Old Age Assistance
   C. Blind Assistance
   D. Aid to Dependent Children
4. Legal Actions for:
   A. Recovery of Excess Old Age Benefit Payments
5. Legal Forms for Old Age Benefits
6. Legal Service to States on Social Legislation

RESEARCH AND STATISTICS
1. Research for Federal Legislation on Social Security
2. Research on State Legislation and Administration
   A. Legislative Reference Service
   B. Procedures
3. Research on Special Problems in Federal-State Relations
4. Compilation of Statistics and Reports

ACCOUNTS AND AUDITS
1. Budget
2. Accounting
   A. Grants-In-Aid
   B. Administrative Expenses
   C. Benefit Payments
   D. Reports
3. Administrative Auditing
4. Field Auditing
   A. Auditing of Expenditures by States from Grants-In-Aid
      1. Unemployment Compensation Administration
      2. Old Age Assistance
      3. Aid to Dependent Children
      4. Aid to Blind
   B. Auditing of Expenditures by States for Unemployment Compensation
5. Audit Reports

BUSINESS MANAGEMENT
1. Personal
2. Space in Washington
   A. Location
   B. Selection
3. Space in Field
   A. Regional Offices
   B. District and Sub-Offices
4. Purchasing
5. Printing and Duplicating
6. Statistical and Drafting Service
7. Correspondence
8. Stenographic Filing, Telephone, Messenger, and Mail Service

INFORMATIONAL SERVICE
1. To Answer Inquiries of Employers in Regard to Their Functions and Obligations
2. To Acquaint the 26 Million Insurance Beneficiaries of Their Rights and Reasons for Payment
3. To Meet Demands for Information from the General Public
4. Publications
5. Library

REGIONAL OFFICES—12
1. Coordination of Operation
2. Office Supervision

Unemployment Compensation	Research and Statistics
Federal Old Age Benefits	Accounts and Audits
Public Assistance	Business Management
General Counsel	Informational Service

INDEX

Accounts and Audits, Bureau of: with Bureau of Public Assistance, 26–27, 216; shake up of, 31, 134; organization of, 40, 478; budget of, 51, 65, 70, 72; and personnel, 70, 387, 389, 442, 482; and field trips, 156; on withholding of payments, 162; and auditing, 193–94, 197, 272, 273, 275; and grants, 198, 199–200, 201–2, 208; and state budgets, 260, 265, 268; and interest on funds, 276; on constructive accounting, 289, 290, 292; with Seidemann as director, 393, 394; and classification, 413, 414; and political appointments, 426, 427; mentioned, 41, 197n, 202n, 254, 285, 402, 405, 430

Administrative Order No. 8: on coordinator's duties, 395

Administrative Order No. 11: on duties and organization of regional offices, 110–111; on power of regional directors, 117, 118; proposed revision of, 119–120, 121, 121n, 122, 122n; on regional representation, 363; mentioned, 126, 130n

Administrative Order No. 12, 121n, 123

Administrative Order No. 23: on quarterly grants, 288–89

Administrative Order No. 24: on claims policy, 378

Advisory Committee on Social Security of the Business Advisory Council: cooperated with registration, 340, 345

Agricultural Adjustment Act, 6, 107, 392

Ahern, Leonard W.: discusses budget, 74–76

Altmeyer, Arthur J: and technical board, COEC, 9–18; named chairman, Social Security Board, 30; at Public Assistance meeting, 143; on aid to the blind, 189, 190; and unemployment compensation, 226, 228, 231-32, 235, 245, 256, 291, 292, 294; on USES, 297–98; and letter to Attorney General, 357–58; on publicity, 358, 448, 453; background, 384–85; and Chart No. 1, 392; and planning function, 459; on industrial classification, 467; on amendments, 471; on inadequacy of board structure, 474; on relations with the President, 485; mentioned, 21, 49, 161n, 307, 406, 407, 475, 476, 491n

—on budget: and appropriation estimate, 37; and hearings, 48–49, 59, 60–61; organization of, 51, 57; appropriation revision, 56; for Bureau of Unemployment Compensation, 66; for Old Age Benefits and use of Treasury, 68; for Office of the General Counsel, 69; for Bureau of Accounts and Audits, 70; and Bureau of Budget recommendations, 75–76; and deficiency appropriation consideration, 91–92; on legality of use of other federal aid funds, 201, 204; and travel grants, 241

—and federal-state organization: and

regional offices, 100, 102; on selection of regional officers, 105, 106, 107, 112; on functions of the regional manager, 107; attitude toward regional plan, 116–18; on powers of the regional director, 118–22; on decentralization, 125; on regional organization, 129–30; on "fair hearing," 148; and Arkansas problem, 152; and North Carolina plan, 154, 223–24; and Wisconsin problem, 158; and state noncompliance, 163; and Kansas plan, 167; and Ohio plan, 169; and Kentucky plan, 180; and Illinois plan, 184, 187; and Utah problem, 222; and passage of state laws, 251; and control over state, 261n; and conflict over supervision of field office, 362

—and personnel: and hiring of Evans, 349; on appointment of, 387–90; on coordinator, 396; and confidence in Corson, 402; on Civil Service Commission, 411, 416, 418; on political appointments, 425, 428; on recruitment of, 433; on in-service training, 441; on personnel director conflict, 444, 446; on importance of capable staff, 481; mentioned, 393

—on registration: and stamp tax system, 314, 315, 317; on meaning of remuneration, 319; on numbers system, 323, 324; on identification, 328, 343; on date, 333; on account number, 334; organization of, 338, 343; on information to employees, 344; on Post Office help, 346, 360, 372; mentioned, 341, 350, 351, 355

American Federation of Government Employees, 440

American Federation of Labor: and registration, 345; on distribution of circular, 358; mentioned, 447, 486, 490

American Legion, 425, 426, 455

American Public Welfare Association: and model bills for states, 196; mentioned, 144, 189, 193

Appropriation Act of 1937: summary and itemization, 63–64; and match grants, 208, 211

Aronson, Albert: as personnel director of board, 58, 408, 444, 445, 446; before Senate Appropriations Committee, 85, 87, 88; on recruitment, 106, 433, 434,

436, 438; and Civil Service Commission, 417, 437, 482; on political appointments, 427, 429, 430, 431; campaign against, 431, 431n; personal qualities of, 446n; mentioned, 284n

Asay, Ivan: with Public Assistance, 140, 142; on Committee on the Control of State Expenditures, 262

Ashe, B. F., 102n, 112n

Association of the State Unemployment Insurance Commissioners: and work with Unemployment Compensation, 33

Attorney General: and order for expert exemption, 109; proposed letter to, regarding employer resistance, 357; opinion on disclosing information to states, 468

Austin, Miss Mary: and Illinois plan, 187

Bachmann: and unemployment compensation, 220–21, 235, 241, 258; and constructive accounting, 290–94 *passim*

Bakke, E. Wight, 328, 441, 442

Bane, Frank: as executive director, 19, 382–91 *passim;* settles Buchanan-Winant proposition, 63; at Public Assistance meeting, 143, 144; his diplomatic skill, 181; on number system, 320; on organization of office, 401–2; and publicity, 447; on amendments, 471; on inadequacy of the board structure, 474; mentioned, 25, 31, 57, 102, 119–22 *passim*, 155, 157, 307, 315, 337, 340, 379, 389n, 434n, 446n, 465, 473, 478

—on budget: distribution of public relief moneys, 9; on estimates, 38; and location of function, 51–52; and hearings, 59, 60, 62, 78, 80, 80n, 81, 87, 88; on organization of, 65; for old age benefits, 68, 90, 204; for regional offices, 71; feud with Senator Glass, 85; back-dating of estimates, 199–200; on retroactive grants, 209; and constructive accounting, 291; on adjudication of claims, 377

—and federal-state organization: on regional officers, 105–6, 108, 136; on regional organization, 105, 113n, 129–31; on federal-state relations, 145; and Kansas plan, 167; and Ohio plan, 170, 171, 173; and Kentucky problem, 177,

179, 180; and Indiana and personnel, 182; and Illinois plan, 183–88 *passim;* and Utah act, 222; and North Carolina, 223; and his trips to governors, 486; and personnel level of states, 487
—and personnel: on coordinator, 396; and Civil Service Commission, 412, 415, 416; and number of staff, 417*n*; and political appointments, 428; on nonstatus employees, 439; on personnel director, 444, 445; on Resnick's duties, 452, 453

Banning, Paul D.: replaces Hughes, 216; on auditing, 274–75; on interest earned on funds, 276; on constructive accounting, 294

Baruch, Ismar: on expert clause, 409, 411*n*, 412, 413, 423

Bary, Miss Helen V.: as social worker, 19; and Public Assistance Bureau, 104, 140, 142; and success of Public Assistance meeting, 144; and federal-state relationships, 145, 146, 181; as field representative, 150, 156, 160, 176; discovers reimbursements, 202

Batzell, Paul E.: at budget review of Bureau of Unemployment Compensation, 65–66; and Division of Grants and Procedures, 257; on scrutiny of state budgets, 258–59, 261*n*, 268, 271, 273; on state personnel, 277; on regional organization, 285

Beach, Charles F., 68

Beard, Charles and Mary: on mood of 1933, 5

Bell, Daniel W.: interview with F. D. R., 48; and discussions on board's budget, 55, 75–77, 81; and appropriations for old age, 90, 93; on organization of railroad retirement registration, 370

Bennett, James V.: and duties, 21, 51–52; at budget hearing, 59, 61; and Civil Service Commission, 106, 108–9, 412, 415, 415*n*; and administrative manual, 407; on political appointments, 428, 429

Bigge, George E.: as board member, 30; on industrial classification, 465

Blakeslee, Miss Ruth: on aid to blind, 189, 191–92, 193

Bowers, Glenn: on unemployment compensation law problems, 225, 228, 232, 236,

240; complains of board control, 261; on USES and board, 302–3; mentioned, 236*n*, 239

Brown, Douglas, 328

Brown, M. L., 169–74

Brownlow, Louis, 112, 393, 393*n*

Buchanan (Chairman of House Appropriations Committee): and Townsend movement, 11*n*; and hearings, 61, 62, 78; "propositions" Winant, 62–63, 102

Budget: estimates of, 39, 41; itemizations of, 42, 44, 53–54, 75–76, 83; summaries of, 72, 89; and grants-in-aid to states, 73–74; and administrative control, 94–95. *See also* Budget, Bureau of the; House Appropriations Committee

Budget, Bureau of the: and budget of the board, 39, 43, 53, 58, 65, 74; and cuts, 45, 74–77; and hearings, 46, 48, 55, 61, 83; and unexpended balances, 76*n*; and itemization of public assistance requests, 90; and old age assistance appropriations, 90, 91–93; and order for exemption, 109; and funds to USES, 297; on duties of coordinator, 394; mentioned, 25–26, 42, 52, 57–58, 69, 416*n*, 440, 484, 485

Buhler, Ernest O., 362, 363

Business Advisory Council of the Department of Commerce, 349, 490

Business Management, Bureau of: Administrative Division, 50; functions of, 51–52, 407; budget estimates of, 71–72, 135; and personnel, 71–72, 387, 388, 410, 413, 432, 439, 442, 485; and Lynchburg problem, 86–87; and regional organization, 103–4, 113; personnel director within, 478; mentioned, 347, 402, 444, 446

Calhoun, Leonard J.: and amendments, 50; at budget hearings, 59, 60; on retroactive grants, 212, 213; on administration of estates, 310-11; on date for registration, 335; on Civil Service Commission, 419; mentioned, 377

Census, Bureau of the: and registration, 61, 331*n*, 338, 338*n*, 339, 344; and number system, 320, 321, 322; mentioned, 342

Central Statistical Board: and number system, 320, 321; and examinations, 435; mentioned, 62, 88n, 483

Chandler, A. B. (Governor of Kentucky), 177–79 passim, 486

Cheek, Dr. Roma, 154–55

Children's Bureau: and field organization, 23, 134, 146, 155; and public assistance, 141, 143; Seidemann's interest in, 394; mentioned, 13, 13n, 483

Civil Service Commission: and expert clause, 22, 25, 30, 34, 40, 56, 60, 324, 407–24 passim, 424n, 431–32; and Bureau of Accounts and Audits, 70; and Miss Snead affair, 86; on status of regional directors, 108–9, 109n; and Miss Hoey, 165; and unemployment compensation administration, 237; and field offices, 361; and Bane, 383; and powers, 388; and patronage pressure, 424, 426; and attorneys, 427; on recruitment, 432–39 passim; and nonstatus employees, 439–40; and a publicity man, 448, 449; and examinations, 482; mentioned, 194, 395n, 443, 447

Clague, Ewan: selected assistant chief, Research and Statistics, 22; on Ohio investigation, 169, 170–72; on Committee on Control of State Expenditures, 263; on registration, 342; in charge of statistical work, 463–67 passim; and studies, 471

Classification Act of 1923, 56, 407–21 passim

Clearman, Wilfred J.: and budget, 52, 54, 57, 59, 61; on interviewing candidates, 106; and his draft bill, 246, 248; mentioned, 45n

Cliff, Frank B., 246, 248

Cohen, Wilbur J.: and budget, 50; and the unemployment compensation administration, 232, 239–40, 244, 254–55; on New York budget cuts, 261n; help in 1936 campaign, 359; and annual report, 406; on amendments, 471; mentioned, 234n, 389

Collins, Maurice, 231

Committee on Economic Security, 9, 10

Comptroller General: and decision on Civil Service Commission, 30, 419; and opinion on function of board, 56; and Title II opinion, 58; on field personnel, 124, 361; on reimbursement from old age assistance, 149, 204–7 passim; on matching board's funds, 200–201; on retroactive public assistance grants, 208–14; on duties of Claims Division, 310; on registration, 355; on reimbursement to Post Office, 359–60; on forms for claims, 377, 378; mentioned, 27, 200, 201, 291, 292, 347, 378n. See also McCarl

Congress (United States): and passage of Social Security Act, 10–11; and board's budget, 49, 77–93, 475; and grants-in-aid, 149; and exemptions from Civil Service Commission, 414, 423–24; and political appointments, 427–28; on personnel director, 446; and no action on amendments, 471n; and relation of board with, 483–84; mentioned, 4–5, 6, 7, 19, 370, 380, 425

Control of State Expenditures, Committee on: 262–67, 272, 469

Coordinator, Office of, 391–400

Copeland, Morris A., 344

Corson, John: and budget, 65, 70, 75–77, 76n, 77, 83, 200; and hearings, 78, 79, 80, 81, 85, 87; and duties, 94, 216, 401–6; on regional organization, 119–26 passim; and Washington director, 136; on identification, 328; and annual report, 406; investigates training programs, 442–43; and publicity, 452; mentioned, 36, 196, 377, 386, 388

Couper, Walter: and states' laws, 244, 248, 251; and use of business machines, 293n; mentioned, 234n, 389

Coy, Wayne, 122n, 126–29

Crowell, Benedict, 112, 178

Culp, C. A., 233–34

Davey, Martin L. (Governor of Ohio), 26, 26n, 169–70, 173–74, 194

Davidson, Ronald, 21, 237–38, 311

Dedrick, Calvert L., 335, 339

Deficiency Bill, First, 41, 65

Deficiency Bill, Third, 37, 42, 43, 45, 46, 48, 50, 145

Deiken, Dr., 193

Democratic National Committee, 358–59, 486

Dill, William L., 112, 124

Douglas, James: criticizes Field Organization Committee, 101; as chief of motion picture division, Informational Service, 358; on political appointments, 428–29; writes on social security, 441; plans films, 458; mentioned, 455

Dunne, T. Morris: seeks advice, 234; on personnel system, 284; mentioned, 249

Eagles, 26, 26n, 170, 171, 173

Economic Security, Committee on: organization of, 9; and recommendations to the President, 9, 10; and Jan. 1935 report, 12; inherited personnel, 18, 22, 439; draws up model bill, 23, 236, 243–44, 247; reports on grants to aged, 138–39; reports on unemployment, 139–40; mentioned, 17, 302, 313, 454

Eilenberger, Clinton B., 360

Eliot, Dr. Martha, 141

Eliot, Thomas H.: drafts Social Security Bill, 18; at budget hearings, 59; appoints regional attorneys, 113, 412–13; and his work, 142; on public assistance grants, 143, 209, 211, 212, 213–24; on specific state problems, 152–53, 167, 222, 223–25; on payments to states, 162; and personnel standards, 184n, 282–83; on reimbursement problems, 206; on meaning of benefits, 219, 220; on employer contributions in trust, 227–28, 227n; begins redraft of model bill, 244; on interest earned on funds, 276–277; on administration of estates, 311; on remuneration, 319

Ellis, Frank H., 361

Emerson, Thomas, 497

Ehringhaus, John C. B., 223–25

Evans, Roger: on registration, 34, 348–49, 360–61, 367–68, 371, 372–73; on conflict over supervision of field offices, 362, 363; on collection of taxes, 367–68; and his appointment, 387–88; mentioned, 447

Executive Director, Office of: itemization of personnel, 70; support of regional director, 122–26; budgets of, 122n, 265; organization and power of, 126–27, 382–91, 400–407; and conflict with Bureau of Old Age Benefits, 362, 363; and personnel director, 446–47; and publicity, 452; mentioned, 70, 426, 478

"Fair hearing," interpretation of, 148

Farley, James A.: asks for investigation of Kentucky, 177; and Miles, 486; mentioned, 428, 429

Federal Emergency Relief Administration (FERA), 7, 8, 12, 18, 19, 142, 161, 189, 200–201, 473, 487

Fenn, Miss Kathryn D., 290

Field Organization Committee: organization of, 96–105 passim; and offices for Bureau of Old Age Benefits, 122; and plans for registration, 333–34; and letter to employers, 337; and training program, 440

Foreign and Domestic Commerce, Bureau of, 107, 363, 401, 440

Foster, Miss Ethel, 21, 449

Galvin, William: on regional directors and bureau field staff relations, 107; summarizes regional organization, 113; and his duties, 122, 401

Gellhorn, Walter, 282

General Accounting Office: and claims, 130; on reimbursement, 206; on retroactive grants, 214; and field auditing, 215, 437; and expert clause, 419; mentioned, 20, 198, 291, 377, 378, 381, 393

General Counsel, Office of the: and budget, 69, 72, 260; and Arkansas, 152; and North Carolina, 154; on noncompliance, 162; on withholding payments, 162; and Kentucky, 179, 180; on aid to the blind, 191; on back-dating of estimates, 199–200; on reimbursement, 202, 203; and grants, 208, 209, 268; on definition of benefits, 219; on bill-drafting, 252; opinion on state law libraries, 275; interpretation of Claims Division duties, 310–11; on political appointments, 427; mentioned, 198, 202, 254, 285, 472

Gibbons, Stephen B., 498

Givens, Meredith B.: as personnel officer, 19; complaint to unemployment compensation administration, 232; on number system, 323; on hiring, 408; on employer number, 464, 465

Glass, Carter: holds up appropriations, 30–31; disputes with board, 80, 85–88, 431, 482; on expert clause, 423–24; on hiring of former FBI men, 445; mentioned, 92, 483

Gross, John E., 251–52

Hamilton, Walton H.: selected chief of Research and Statistics, 21; and budget, 42, 71, 75; on stamp tax, 314; and Civil Service Commission, 416, 435; on training program, 440, 441; and functions of bureau, 460–62, 469–70; on statistics, 463

Harper, Heber, 112

Harris, Ralph B., 96

Harrison, Miss Gladys A., 252

Hayes, Will, 377, 388

Hodges, LeRoy, 36, 377, 388

Hoey, Miss Jane M.: as director, 21, 147; on amendment, 80; and Senator Glass and Miss Snead, 85; on regional headquarters, 113; on state staff, 115, 133, 155, 162–63, 194, 195; on specific state problems, 136, 153–87 *passim;* on state laws, 148; on definition of a public agency, 150; and organization in Public Assistance headquarters, 164–65, 165n; on her diplomatic skill, 181; and aid to the blind, 190; memorandum on reimbursement, 202; on accounting advice to states, 292; on state contact work, 386; mentioned, 31, 163, 417n, 469

Hoff, Harry, 376n

Hohman, Miss Helen F., 406

Hopkins, Harry, 8, 8n, 9, 10, 17, 146

Horner, Henry (Governor of Illinois), 184–88, 488

House Appropriations Committee: and board hearings, 46–49, 58–62, 77; and understanding with board, 53; on board's budget, 77–82; cuts budget, 83–84; on retroactive appropriations, 149; and the Census Bureau, 331n, 338n; dis-

cusses expert clause, 416–17; mentioned, 52, 309, 318, 330, 460

Howes, William W., 349, 351

Hughes, Avon J.: and budget organization, 65, 70, 74, 75, 402; on regional offices, 115, 117, 125; and Arkansas problem, 153; on public assistance grants, 198–204 *passim,* 209, 214; and Comptroller General, 209n; on auditing, 215, 216, 273–74, 390, 393; his demotion, 216; on constructive accounting, 291, 292, 294; on registration, 335

Hurwitz (New York Unemployment Compensation Administration): and Treasury, 231; wants help, 233; on executive committee, 240; questions board control, 261; on registration, 323, 324, 326

Huse, Robert E.: as associate director, Informational Service, 21; and memo on replies of businessmen, 340–41; on civil service exams, 437; on publicity, 452; and duties, 454; mentioned, 380

Hutchinson, Mrs. Mary: and state personnel standards, 278–80, 283; heads coordinating committee, 299; and memo on money and administration of placement, 301–2; gives up, 303

Independent Offices Appropriation Act of 1938, 81, 92, 93

Industrial Classification, Committee on, 464, 468

Informational Service, Bureau of: and publicity, 30, 358, 447–59; on registration, 34; organization and function of, 40, 50–51, 131–32; budget of, 42, 54, 69, 75, 77, 135; itemization of personnel, 69; salaries for, 95, 411n; relations with regional manager, 103; on claims procedure, 380; on staff appointments, 387; and classification, 410, 413, 437; and political appointments, 426; Resnick's organization of, 454–56; mentioned, 29, 41, 221n

Internal Revenue, Bureau of: and use by Old Age Benefits, 68, 248, 312; and location of collection offices, 99; on stamp tax, 317; and registration, 344, 355, 374; and Social Security taxes, 366–

68, 456, 457; on record keeping, 375*n*; and account number, 464; and statistics, 468; mentioned, 54, 335, 361, 490

Interstate Conference on Unemployment Compensation

—Crawford Notch, New Hampshire (July 1936), 279–80, 465, 467, 468

—Madison, Wisconsin (October 1936), 279, 280–81

—Washington, D.C. (March, 1937), 283–84

Jackson, Clarence A., 499

Jeter, Miss Helen: appoints field staff, 115; at Public Assistance meeting, 143; investigates Ohio, 170; and identification, 328; on public assistance statistics, 463

Johnson (Governor of Colorado), 174–75

Kimball, Arthur A., 262–63

Labor, Department of: friction with USES, 298; coordination, 299, 306; mentioned, 12, 62, 413, 447

Labor Statistics, Bureau of, 60, 62, 320, 321, 483

La Dame, Miss Mary, 295–96, 299, 307

Landon, Alf M. (Governor of Kansas and presidential candidate): attacks Social Security Act, 29, 357; on public assistance problems, 166–68; mentioned, 389, 481

Langer, William (Governor of North Dakota), 252

Lansdale, Robert, 197

Latimer, Murray W.: as director and his resignation, 21, 28, 30, 34, 67, 308, 348, 400, 477; and budget for Bureau of Old Age Benefits, 61, 68, 309–11; on regional organization, 104–5, 115, 117, 118–122, 118*n*, 125; on location of actuarial work, 318–19; on registration, 324–37 *passim;* on Census Bureau, 338*n*; helps in 1936 election, 359; duties with Railroad Retirement Board, 387; on political appointments, 431; on publicity, 453; on classification, 467; mentioned, 42, 113, 341, 388, 477

Lehman, Herbert H. (Governor of New York), 261

Lenroot, Katherine L., 143

Long, Huey (Senator from Louisiana): and "share the wealth," 11; and his filibuster, 18, 139; mentioned, 247

Lowrie, Kathleen J., 156, 159

Lubin, Isidor: and board cooperation, 62; on identification, 328; mentioned, 240

McCallister, Lambert, 499

McCarl (Comptroller General): ruling on unemployment compensation, 50, 64, 231; mentioned, 257, 257*n*, 447

McCarthy, H. L.: as regional representative, 112, 116*n*, 286; on no need for attorneys, 115; on Illinois plan, 187; works on passage of Iowa law, 251–52

McChord, Miss Beth: field trips, 156–57; on state relations, 181

McCormack, Col. E. J.: on regional organization, 38, 106, 362; on the Field Organization Committee, 96, 103*n*; and plans for registration, 333–44 *passim;* and use of the Post Office, 346–51 *passim;* and his selection, 388, 389; on recruitment of personnel, 433; on in-service training, 441; on the personnel director conflict, 444; mentioned, 104, 122, 338, 377, 394

McDonald, Francis J., 308, 341, 377, 379

McDonald, Edward, 112

MacReynolds, William Henry, 312–13

Magill, Roswell, 468

Marshall, John, 233, 240

May, Geoffrey: defends budget, 66–67; and the Kentucky problem, 179; on aid to the blind, 191; on field staff, 195–96; on Comptroller General's decision on reimbursement, 206; on retroactive grants, 208; on duties of the field auditors, 216

Miles, Vincent: as a member of the board, 18; on the budget, 59, 65, 66, 69; and regional organization, 100–102, 105, 106, 117–18, 282; at Public Assistance meeting, 143; on problems of specific states, 157, 167, 169–73 *passim,* 177, 187, 222, 225; on the use of other federal funds, 201; on reimbursement from old age benefits, 204; on registration, 332, 333, 343; on letter to Attorney General, 357; and his background, 385; on personnel, 388, 389, 408, 416–17; on the coordinator, 396; and political patronage, 425–30 passim, 477, 486; on personnel director conflict, 444, 445; on publicity, 453; on inadequacy of board structure, 474; mentioned, 72, 97, 192, 291

Mires, Frank: on cooperation of Treasury, 312; on stamp tax system, 316–17; on registration, 334; mentioned, 344

Mitchell, William L., 71–72

Montgomery, Newton: and registration, 335, 355, 356; on letter to Attorney General, 357; mentioned, 367–68

Morgenthau, Henry A. (Secretary of the Treasury): member COEC, 9; on payment of unemployment compensation to treasury, 229, 230; on cooperation with registration, 355; mentioned, 6, 227n

Mulliner, Miss Maurine: and annual report, 406; and Informational Service, 452

Murray, Merrill G.: and budget, 37, 65–66, 74; and Utah act, 222; on contributions in trust, 228; on unemployment compensation administration, 232, 238–39; on problem of interstate coverage, 234–35; on state laws, 243–44, 251; and revision of draft bills, 247–49; on auditing, 272; on regional organization, 285, 286; on constructive accounting, 289; on meaning of remuneration, 319; mentioned, 234n, 242, 245, 389

Nance, A. Steve, 102n, 112, 112n

National Recovery Act (NRA): staff to social security, 18, 19, 22, 105–6, 107, 439, 445; mentioned, 388, 401, 413, 440

National Reemployment Service, 12, 55, 295, 327

Neustadt, Richard: as regional representative, 111, 286; on no need for attorneys, 115; on California unemployment compensation, 267n; works with coordination, 299; and memorandum on placement, 301–2

New York Division of Placement and Un-

employment Insurance, 136, 250, 261, 283, 286, 302, 344, 464

Old Age Benefits, Bureau of: coordination with Treasury, 312–13; and stamp tax system, 314; and letter to Attorney General, 357; and the civil service, 361, 467; conflict with Office of the Executive Director, 362, 363; staff problems, 376–77, 387–89; and Seidemann's interest in, 393; bulletin, 405; and political appointments, 425, 426, 431; in-service training, 442; publicity, 453; mentioned, 114, 115, 137, 293, 296, 336, 349, 378, 381, 386, 417n, 439n, 444–46, 470–71, 489

—budget: and salary of director, 41; consideration of, 42, 54, 67–69, 73, 309–11; and itemization of personnel, 67; and cuts, 72; discussed in Bureau of Budget meeting, 75, 76; explanation to House subcommittee, 78; discussed at hearings, 79–80; and deficiency appropriations, 90–93

—general organization: explained, 24–25, 28–29, 33–36, 38, 308–11; and estimate of staff, 39; on Organization Chart No. 2, 41; and Seidemann's appointment, 399–400, 400n; Corson takes over, 407

—regional organization: explained, 97, 113; and duties and powers of regional directors, 104, 117, 118, 119–20, 122n; and relationship of Bureau with field offices, 126–32 passim, 135

—and registration: discussion of number system, 24; field offices set up for, 129; organization of, 330, 339; plans for, 342, 343, 346; report on process of, 370; recruitment of personnel for, 417–18, 433, 436, 438–39

Organization Chart No. 1, 37, 50, 96, 382, 392

Organization Chart No. 2, 40–41

Parker, Glowacki R., 112

Pearson, John, 108, 111, 112, 233n, 286

Peebles, James, 294

Perkins, Miss Frances (Secretary of Labor), 9, 306–7, 341, 371, 390

Persons, Frank W.: on organization of

U.S. Employment Service, 295–96; on registration, 297, 330; on refusal to register, 297n, 339; and draft bills, 298; and financing of state placement, 299; and number system, 325; and use of account number, 371; mentioned, 252, 298, 307

Postmaster General, 347, 348, 361, 368–72 passim

Post Office Department, U.S.: and registration, 34–35, 68, 129n, 333, 375; and account number, 130; agreement to handle registration, 346–56; on question of postage, 359–60; and forms, 366; and report on process of registration, 370; on assignment of numbers to railroad employees, 370–71; on extension of registration, 371–72; on cost, 372; and evaluation of registration, 372–74; and personnel, 417–18; involved in appeal to President, 485; mentioned, 314, 361, 362, 377

Powell, Oscar, 63, 102, 108, 111, 115

President. See Roosevelt, Franklin Delano

Prettyman, E. Barrett, 233

Pribram, Karl, 328

Public Administration Service: organizational advisers to board, 278, 400

Public Assistance, Bureau of: organization of, 23, 26–27, 31–32, 163–66; budget, 56–57, 66–67, 72, 92; and grants, 73–74, 208, 209, 214; and auditing function, 134; and volume of early work, 142; on interpretation of "fair hearing," 148; on withholding of payments, 162; on aid to the blind, 189–94 passim; and conflict with auditors, 197, 442; on back-dating of estimates, 199–200; on use of other federal money, 200–201; and clash over reimbursement from old age assistance, 202; and field auditing, 215, 216; and civil service examinations, 436–37; and "Public Assistance Statistics" (bulletin), 463; work with Bureau of Research and Statistics, 463; and Special Studies Division, 469; and administrative responsibilities, 474, 478, 479; mentioned, 114, 195, 196, 202n, 292, 383, 400, 454

—and personnel: itemization of, 66–67; field staff, 118; field organization, 132–33; and staff appointments, 387; and political appointments, 426; and raising level of states, 487

—state organization: and administration of grants, 140; and acceptance of state plans, 147; and problems of specific states, 149–86 passim; and noncompliance with state plan, 162–63; and standards of administration, 180–81; and new public assistance legislation, 196–97; and state contact, 386

Public Health Service: and field organization, 134, 155; and aid to the blind, 191, 193; mentioned, 13, 13n, 189, 190

Railroad Retirement Board: registration done by Post Office and Social Security Board, 35, 370–71, 475, 477

Raushenbush, Paul A., 229, 230, 243, 250

Records Office, Baltimore, 364, 372, 374–76, 374n

Rector, Stanley: on administration of unemployment compensation, 235; and state plans and Title III, 254, 255; and letter to states on granting of laws, 256, 257; works with coordination, 299; on administration of grants for placement, 300–301

Regional directors: and budget requests for offices, 71, 135; functions of, 104; selection of, 105–10; and itemization of salaries, 109–10; open offices, 110–13; and slowness of hiring staff, 114; duties of, 128

Research and Statistics, Bureau of: organization of, 40, 40n; budget, 41–42, 60, 61–62, 71, 75–77, 263; itemization of personnel of, 71; and auditing, 272; and statistics and business machines, 293n; and stamp tax system, 314; and staff appointments, 387, 389; and Civil Service Commission, 416, 435; and in-service training, 440, 442, 443; functions of, 459–72; competence of director, 479; mentioned, 54, 242, 407

Resnick, Louis: as director of Informational Service, 21, 447–56 passim; and duties, 51; budget, 59, 60, 75; and regional organization, 113; appoints regional staff, 115; and distribution of circulars, 358–59; summarizes publicity campaign, 364–66; and claims forms, 380; and political appointments, 429–30; mentioned, 378, 451*n*

Reticker, Miss Ruth, 256

Rice, Dr. Carl, 190, 191, 193

Rice, Stuart A., 322, 323

Roosevelt, Franklin Delano: and beginnings of the New Deal, 4–10 *passim;* given advice, 30, 468; persuades Post Office to conduct registration, 34; and budget, 45, 55, 149; and exemptions from civil service, 106, 109, 409, 414, 433; statement to Congress, 140; and the Colorado problem, 175; and the Kentucky problem, 177; and a timetable, 357; and relations of board with, 390–91, 484–85, 486; and political appointments, 427; mentioned, 3, 43, 297, 339, 340, 342, 348, 457, 490

Roseman, Alvin: and budget for Public Assistance, 66–67; and staff of Public Assistance, 140; goes to Ohio to investigate, 170, 172; and the Texas plan, 182; and aid to the blind, 191

Rosenberg, Anna: as regional director for New York, 108; and staff, 115; on board control, 261; on use of regional offices, 286; mentioned, 108*n*, 112, 379

Saunders, Richardson, 307

Schoeneman, George J., 344

Security in Your Old Age (pamphlet), 358

Seidemann, Henry P.: as coordinator, 19, 20, 391–400 *passim;* appointment as director of Bureau of Old Age Benefits, 67, 348; support of Coy's alternative, 127; at Public Assistance meeting, 143; organizes Association of State Unemployment Insurance Officers, 240; and meaning of remuneration, 319; his technique, 334*n*; and letter to Attorney General, 357; resignation from Bureau of Old Age Benefits, 376–77; on claims, 377, 381; on executive director and board, 386; on staff, 388, 389, 395*n*; on organization of bureau, 400*n*; on personnel director conflict, 444, 445; and

functions as coordinator, 480; on appeal to the President, 485; mentioned, 21, 339, 387, 414*n*

—and budget: considerations of, 38, 44, 52, 54, 57, 58, 68, 76*n*; hearings, 46, 59–62 *passim,* 79–80, 80*n*; on location of function, 51–52; defends it before Bureau of Budget, 75; distribution of money, 149; on field auditing, 197; on uniform payroll forms, 241; on constructive accounting, 290

—and regional organization: discussed, 96; on staff, 115; on offices, 118; on offices and control, 129–30; on forms for states, 141; on conflict over supervision, 362, 363; gets tax information out, 367

—and registration: and the number system, 320–24; and identification, 327, 328, 329; on information on identification cards, 327*n*; plans for, 329, 332, 333, 334, 341; and budget for, 330; on Post Office cooperation, 355, 356; and estimate of cost, 372

Senate Appropriations Committee, 85–89, 445

Sherrill, Colonel: investigates and reports on Ohio plan, 169–72

Social Security Act of 1935: introduction to, 3; recommended by Committee on Economic Security, 10; legislative history of, 11; basic features of, 12–17; limitations of, 16–17; and proposed amendments, 23*n*, 91, 406*n*, 471; and grants, 77, 161, 199, 219; attacks on, 131, 356–59, 486, 490; interpretations of, 141, 141*n*, 282, 441; as related to Children's Bureau, 143; and personnel, 161, 179, 184, 258, 280, 407, 428, 487, 489; and specific state plans, 167–68, 175, 185, 221, 223–25; and old age benefits, 308; and publicity, 359, 447–59 *passim;* mentioned *passim*

—Title I (old age assistance, grants to states): 13, 81, 90, 140, 153, 201, 204, 205, 210, 213, 382, 461

—Title II (old age benefits, federal): 13, 15–16, 23*n*, 30, 33, 35, 54, 56, 58, 309–10, 313, 347, 351, 357, 377, 453, 461, 472

—Title III (unemployment compensation): 13, 23*n*, 33, 42, 43, 49, 74, 79, 82,

225, 227, 254, 255, 264, 265–66, 267, 271, 273, 275, 276, 281, 382, 453, 461
—Title IV (aid to dependent children): 13, 73, 81, 140, 201, 204, 205, 210, 213, 382, 461
—Title V (maternal and child welfare): 461
—Title VI (public health): 13
—Title VII (Social Security Board): 13
—Title VIII (taxes with respect to employment): 16, 20, 23n, 28, 32, 34, 49, 124, 248, 312, 315, 317, 319–20, 332, 344, 345n, 350, 352, 353, 357, 360, 367, 370, 374, 375n, 382, 453, 456, 457, 466, 490
—Title IX (taxes on employers): 13, 20, 23n, 32, 48, 79, 124, 222, 225, 226, 227, 229, 246, 249, 250, 252, 253–54, 267, 319–20, 366, 394, 449, 453, 456, 464n, 490
—Title X (aid to the blind): 13, 73–74, 81, 140, 201, 204, 205, 210, 213
Social Security Board, mentioned *passim*
Sorrells, William C.: and staff, 19; works with board, 408; and political appointments, 428, 430, 431
Stark, Louis: and publicity, 448, 454n
Stead, Dr. William T.: as chairman of Field Organization Committee, 96, 99; resigns, 103n; on organization of U.S. Employment Service, 104, 296; recommendations for coordinating committee, 298; on number system, 320, 321, 323, 325; and plan for registration, 329–30; views on organization of registration, 338–39; mentioned, 240, 302
Steinbach, Arnold, 471
Stern, Max: and publicity, 448, 454n
Stone, Donald: and study of field establishment, 126–29; reports on organization of Executive Director's office, 400–405 *passim;* mentioned, 122n
Stutz, John G., 166–68
Sweet, Lennig, 442
Supreme Court of the United States: declares Agriculture Adjustment Act unconstitutional, 22–23, 24, 453; validates a New York unemployment compensation law, 30, 250, 253; and the Alabama cases and Titles VIII and IX, 32

Tapping, Miss Amy P., 159–60, 164
Tate, Jack B.: decision on Maryland Workshop, 150; on Oregon legal problem, 150; on Arkansas problem, 152; on hearings for noncompliance, 163; on aid to the blind, 190, 191, 192; on the back-dating of estimates, 200; on the use of other federal aid money, 200–201; on reimbursement from old age assistance, 203, 204, 206; on state law libraries, 275; on personnel, 282; mentioned, 196
Tindale, Keith T.: investigates Ohio, 170; and administrative manual, 407
Tixier, Pierre: as adviser to board, 20–21; on administrative organization, 233; on Old Age Benefits and Treasury cooperation, 311–12; on stamp tax system, 314; on Pitney Bowes proposal, 314–15; on registration, 329, 331; on need for educating the public, 449; gives advice on planning function, 462–63
Townsend Plan: influence of, 11, 11n; author of, 11, 19; publicity against, 454; mentioned, 139, 145, 149, 195, 448
Treasury, U.S. Department of the: duties under Titles VIII and IX, 13, 13n; and old age benefits, 13–14, 28, 34, 68; and unemployment compensation, 14–15, 74, 226–31 *passim,* 254; and benefit payments, 16; and grants to states, 23; and registration, 54–55, 314–70 *passim;* on actuarial duties, 61; and use of its lawyers, 69; on the transfer of funds, 90; and getting money out, 149; and payments, 162; and prosecution on 1929 income tax returns, 166; and North Carolina unemployment compensation, 224–25; and New York unemployment compensation law, 225–26; and certification of state budgets, 260; and coordination of auditing, 274; and legal status of grants-in-aid, 277; on coordination with Social Security Board, 312–13; and death payments, 378; on claims, 381; and Seidemann's work with, 394; on publicity, 456, 457; and statistics, 464; mentioned, 49, 152, 203, 204, 210, 242, 468, 473, 475, 491n
Tucker, Leonard L., 294

Unemployment Compensation, Bureau of:
organization of, 23–24, 27–28, 32–33;
budget of, 65–66, 72, 74; itemization
of personnel, 66; auditing function,
134; on Indiana and personnel, 182;
legal problems with specific state laws,
218–226; on New Hampshire certification, 228; on model unemployment
compensation bill, 236, 245, 247–50; on
Association of State Unemployment Insurance Officers, 240; and need for
surveillance of state laws, 247; on raising of labor standards, 267n; and its
booklet, 269–71; on constructive accounts, 293; on stamp tax system, 314;
on staff appointments, 387; and study
of, 400; on civil service, 435, 436; and
statistics, 463; on administrative responsibilities, 474, 478, 479; mentioned,
32, 114, 161n, 236, 276, 303, 383, 454,
470, 471
—regional organization: and field assignments, 29; and passage of state laws,
30, 251–53; and lack of, 113, 133; and
delay of board, 254; and state budgets,
260–62, 263–64, 265, 267; and state
agencies on placement, 304, 305; and
problem of personnel, 488–89
Unemployment Trust Fund, federal, 14–
15, 82n, 223, 226, 229–30, 231, 247, 254,
274, 275
United States Employment Service
(USES): aid to board, 22; coordination
with unemployment compensation, 27;
and registration, 29, 55, 297, 326, 327,
329–30, 333, 338–39, 346, 350; and location with board field organization,
99; and state laws, 251, 252; and use of
regional offices, 285–89; background
and organization of, 295–96; and tensions with the board, 295–307; and
coordination, 299; and problem of
identification numbers, 296–97; and
draft bills, 298; and the number system,
320, 321, 325, 374n; and the use of
account numbers, 371; mentioned, 12,
20, 32, 40, 237, 241, 261n, 483
Utley, Clinton H., 347, 361

Wagenet, R. Gordon: chosen to head

Unemployment Compensation, 21; at
budget hearings, 64; on state organization, 105, 110, 114, 125, 133, 251–62
passim, 275, 282–83, 285–88; on problems of specific states, 222, 261n, 267n,
290–91; on employer contributions in
trust, 227–28; on administration of the
bureau, 236–39, 249; on auditing, 273–
75; on interest earned on funds, 276; on
coordination, 298, 299, 301; recommends
grants, 302; on agreement with U.S.
Employment Service, 305–6; on the
meaning of remuneration, 319; on the
registration problem, 343; on civil
service examinations, 435–36; on statistics, 463; on industrial classification,
467; mentioned, 239, 245, 389
Wagner-Peyser Act, 12, 28, 251, 252, 295,
297–305 passim
Watt, Robert, 324
Way, Elwood: assistant director, Old Age
Benefits, 38, 308; at budget hearings,
59; on administration of unemployment
compensation, 233, 241; on number system, 239, 320–24, 343; on board control,
262; on constructive accounting, 292; on
registration, 326, 328–29, 332, 333, 341;
and plan for identification, 327n, 342
We the People and Social Security (motion picture trailer), 358, 458
White, Carl C., 294
White, Leonard, 411n, 416
Wilcox, Fred M., 112, 251, 252
Wilder, R. U.: on use of the Post Office,
346–49 passim; and conflict over supervision of field offices, 362, 363
Williams, Edward B., 152, 153
Williamson, William R., 341
Winant, John G.: chairman of board, 18,
29, 477; resignation, 29, 357; return,
30, 377; on aid to the blind, 192; on
the trusteeing of employer contributions,
226, 227, 228; on problems of unemployment compensation administration, 232–
33, 236; appoints Committee on the
Control of State Expenditures, 262; on
accord with Treasury, 313; on stamp
tax system, 314; on registration, 333,
339, 348; trip to Geneva, 341; thanks
to Post Office, 371–72; and claims form,

379; background, 384–85; and politics, 390n; and Stone's study, 402; and political appointments, 425, 428; and Informational Service, 447–56 *passim;* on tasks of Research and Statistics, 469; on inadequacy of board structure, 474, 474n; and relations with the President, 485; mentioned, 49, 201, 245, 406, 451n
—and the budget: considered, 44, 57, 58, 65; interview with F. D. R., 45; hearings, 48, 59, 60, 78, 80; location of the budget function, 51; and Chairman Buchanan's proposition, 62–63; of Unemployment Compensation, 66; of Accounts and Audits, 70; and cuts by Bureau of the Budget, 76; and letter to Senator Glass, 85
—on personnel: on type of people for regional directors, 108; on appointment of, 386–90; on coordinator, 393; on confidence in Corson, 402; and Civil Service Commission, 411, 415, 418; and in-service training, 441, 442; and personnel director conflict, 444, 446; and Hamilton, 462; and importance of capable staff, 480, 487
—and regional organization: offices of, 100–102; and selection of officers of, 105–6; and attitude toward, 116–18;

and Arkansas problem, 152; and Pennsylvania problem, 159; and state administrations, 162; and state noncompliance, 163; and the Kansas plan, 166–68; and the Ohio plan, 170; and the Colorado problem, 175; and the Kentucky problem, 178; and the North Carolina plan, 223, 225; and New York's law, 225; and conflict over supervision of field offices, 362

Witte, Edwin E.: background, 10; on the Townsend Plan, 11n; on amendments, 23n; recommendations on state organization, 164; mentioned, 302, 454

Witte, Ernest F.: as field representative, 156; on field trips, 157–58, 187–88

Woodrum, Clifton A.: attacks budget requests, 61; and hearings, 78, 80, 81; and cuts, 83, 84; solves deficiency appropriations, 93; discusses expert clause, 416; mentioned, 92, 318–19

Works Progress Administration (WPA): allotment to Social Security Board, 18, 19, 22, 24, 160; and registration, 340, 371, 373; and a grant, 439; mentioned, 8, 142, 321, 327, 447, 464

Wyatt, Birchard D., 503

Young, Edgar B., 304